PHILOSOPHIES OF EXISTENCE

PHILOSOPHIES OF EXISTENCE
ANCIENT AND MEDIEVAL

Edited by

PARVIZ MOREWEDGE

1907

New York

FORDHAM UNIVERSITY PRESS

1982

LC 81–66643

ISBN 0–8232–1059–6 (*clothbound*)

ISBN 0–8232–1060–X (*paperback*)

Printed in the United States of America

CONTENTS

Introduction 1

Parviz Morewedge

Ancient

1. Why Existence Does Not Emerge as a Distinct Concept in Greek Philosophy 7

Charles H. Kahn

2. Being and Forms in Plato 18

Paul Seligman

3. The Doctrine of Being in the Aristotelian *Metaphysics*—Revisited 33

Joseph Owens, C.Ss.R.

4. Aspects of Ancient Ontologies 60

John P. Anton

Medieval

5. The Ontological Relation Between Evil and Existents in Manichaean Texts and in Augustine's Interpretation of Manichaeism 78

Christopher J. Brunner

6. Ontological Problems in Nyāya, Buddhism, and Jainism: A Comparative Analysis 96

Bimal Krishna Matilal

7. A Scotistic Approach to the Ultimate Why-Question

Allan B. Wolter 109

8. The Relationship Between Essence and Existence in Late–Thirteenth-Century Thought: Giles of Rome, Henry of Ghent, Godfrey of Fontaines, and James of Viterbo 131
John F. Wippel

9. Metaphysical Foundations of the Hierarchy of Being According to Some Late-Medieval and Renaissance Philosophers 165
Edward P. Mahoney

10. Attribute, Attribution, and Being: Three Islamic Views 258
Richard M. Frank

11. Al-Suhrawardī's Critique of the Muslim Peripatetics (*al-Mashshāʿūn*) 279
Majid Fakhry

12. Greek Sources of Some Near Eastern Philosophies of Being and Existence 285
Parviz Morewedge

13. Post-Avicennan Islamic Philosophy and the Study of Being 337
Seyyed Hossein Nasr

PHILOSOPHIES OF EXISTENCE

Introduction

PARVIZ MOREWEDGE
Baruch College
The City University of New York

THE ESSAYS IN THIS COLLECTION have been written by specialists on various dimensions of ancient and medieval ontology. In this introduction I shall (*a*) clarify three criteria used for the selection of the various articles; and (*b*) single out three problems which provide some thematic unity for the different studies in this volume on Greek, Islamic, Christian, Indic, and Manichaean systems of ontology.

The following guidelines were adopted in the selection of the articles:

I · THE NEED FOR A COMPREHENSIVE STUDY OF THE GREEK GENESIS OF ONTOLOGY AND OF THE GROWTH OF A RICH NATIVE TRADITION OF ISLAMIC ONTOLOGY

Because of its Greek genesis and the dearth of studies covering all stages of the development of ontology — but particularly the later phase of its Islamic development — the salient ontological contributions of these two traditions are covered in this volume. The Greek phase is explored in four comprehensive essays: those by Kahn (on "existence" from Parmenides to Aristotle), Seligman (on form and participation in Plato), Owens (on the meaning of "being" as subject matter of Aristotelian metaphysics as treated by commentators up to the present time), and Anton (on predication, the categories, and the genera of being in Aristotle, the Stoics, and Plotinus). Devoted to the Islamic tradition are the studies by Frank (on the ontology of early Islamic theology), Morewedge (on the development of Greek ontological issues in three types of Islamic philosophical schools in both the classical and the later phases of Islamic philosophy), Fakhry (on rejections of the Islamic Aristotelianism by the master of the illuminationist school of thought), and Nasr (on the ontology of the post–ibn Sīnian schools). Taken together the studies render this volume a unique collection of essays on major aspects of both Western and Islamic ontology, covering even key figures who did not play a role in the "Arabic to Latin" dimension of Muslim culture.

II · The Wish to Present In-depth Treatments of Selected Key Issues in Ontology Focusing on the Rich Tradition of Christian Medieval Thought, Including the Lesser Known Figures Within that Tradition

The articles of Mahoney and Wippel undertake detailed analyses of two key issues in ontology as they were addressed by both major and lesser figures in the medieval Christian tradition. Mahoney's extensive and comprehensive essay depicts the theme of being in an eschatological hierarchical structure from Proclus to the less well-known scholars of the Italian Renaissance; his study brings to light the ontological structure of a number of Western thinkers who have usually been mentioned only in passing in previous studies. In a similar vein Wippel points out fine but significant differences in the theories of four late–thirteenth-century thinkers who concerned themselves with the essence–existence distinction. Wolter confronts the perennial question of existence from the medieval Christian perspective of Scotus in a manner which allows the peculiar philosophical contribution of this medieval thinker to emerge in a modern version of the controversy which surrounds this question.

III · The Importance of Broadening the Contemporary Vision of Ontology by Including in its Scope Non-Western Cases

It is well known that the subject matter of the Graeco-Islamic–Christian medieval tradition is well integrated because of the all-pervasive influence of Plato and Aristotle. Even today an Arabic version of Aristotle's categories is usually the required introductory text in Muslim theology in Middle Eastern curricula. The interplay and flow of philosophical ideas from Aristotle to ibn Sīnā and from ibn Sīnā to Aquinas is also well known. In addition to comparative studies of the Graeco-Islamic–Christian trialogue, there are two essays on other "non-Western" traditions dealing with thematically closely related subject matter. The first essay, by Brunner, probes into the Manichaean ontology of Good and Evil through the lens of the Augustinian criticism of Manichaean doctrine. The second by Matilal examines from a fresh perspective major controversies in metaphysics in the "substance–event" language of Aristotle as well as in the "Whiteheadian" process language in an Indic metaphysical context.

In spite of the fact that each contributor treats "existence" (or "being" and its other semantic cognates) from the perspective of his own field, three focal points emerge as topics which inform these studies with a thematic unity — at least in the treatment of what may be considered the central problems of ancient and medieval ontology.

A. *Existence and Modality: The Necessary Existent*

Much discussion has centered on a clarification of how modalities (necessity, contingency, and impossibility) may be applied to being. Perhaps the emphasis on this topic is partly due to the fact that, from the Islamic tradition on, the God of monotheism has often been defined as "That whose essence is no other than existence." It should be noted that even among contemporary metaphysicians and logicians modalities play a central part in ontology independent of references to their theological origin. It is especially noteworthy that Kahn, in his essay on why "existence" does not emerge as a distinct concept in Greek philosophy, remarks,

> My general view of the historical development [of the concept of existence] is that existence in the modern sense becomes a central concept in philosophy only in the period when Greek ontology is radically revised in the light of a metaphysics of creation. . . . The new metaphysics seems to have taken shape in Islamic philosophy, in the form of a *radical* distinction between necessary and contingent existence. . . .

Father Owens, in "The Doctrine of Being in the Aristotelian *Metaphysics* — Revisited," traces the history of the interpretation of what is held to be the subject matter of metaphysics in Aristotle from the Greeks to the present. He is of the opinion that Aristotle's concept of being is the most determinable and empty concept of being in theology possessing "a fullness of actuality, the most complete perfection." This object of primary philosophy or theology is said to be "the richest of all in content." Another extreme contrast between two notions of being and existence arises in Brunner's study of "The Ontological Relation Between Evil and Existents in Manichaean Texts and in Augustine's Interpretation of Manichaeism." The dualism in the Manichaean system between God as Light, on the one hand, and Hyle as Darkness and Evil, on the other, as well as the treatment of the normal dimensions of the controversy between the Augustinian and the Manichaean systems, adds the normative dimension to the concepts of existence and necessity in late-ancient and early-medieval philosophy and gnosticism. Wolter, in "A Scotistic Approach to the Ultimate Why-Question," places the ultimate philosophical question of the problem of existence in the Scholastic context of medieval theology, relying, however, on a modern perspective by using, among other concepts, that of "Necessary Being or Existence." He proffers a clarification and a solution for a version of the problem which includes the notion of God as an entity whose essence is existence.

B. *A Contest Between the Categorical Scheme of Aristotle and the Hierarchical, Eschatological System of Neoplatonism*

In a typical medieval text on metaphysics, one encounters, after the specification of metaphysics and being as primary subject matter, a delineation of the Aristotelian categories as the first division of being into substance and the nine accidents. Competing with the Aristotelian categories among ancient philosophies of existence is the emanationistic doctrine of Plotinus, in which categories are rejected as the basis of metaphysics. Although Aristotle's categorical scheme was a convenient philosophical basis for medieval physical sciences and subject–predicate forms of logic, the Neoplatonic language was better suited to depictions of the mystical aspects of medieval thought for topics such as the mystical union and the process of self-realization. Anton, in "Aspects of Ancient Ontologies," examines the theory of predication in light of the theory of categories and the theory of genera of beings in Aristotle, the Stoics, and Plotinus. Concerning the last, Anton remarks,

> His [Plotinus'] entire program to recast the role of predication in the logic of reality and to replace the Aristotelian genera of being with the new hierarchical orders in ontology makes him the precursor of medieval Arabic, Jewish, and Christian efforts to integrate the world of faith and the universe of reason.

Matilal, in "Ontological Problems in Nyāya, Buddhism, and Jainism: A Comparative Analysis," examines the theory of categories as well as the riddle of existence and non-existence in these systems. He shows that at least in one school "the Jaina conception of reality . . . comes very close to that of Whitehead, for whom the chief aim of philosophy is the 'elucidation of our integral experience' of both the flux and the permanence of things." This conception was opposed by another school, "the Vaiśeṣikas" which belonged to the Aristotelian school of substance–attribute depictions of reality. As can easily be imagined, the battle between those upholding a categorical–Aristotelian perspective and those supporting a process type of Neoplatonism (which is more analogous to Whitehead's ontology of actual entities) engrained itself in the Indic tradition. The same controversy appears in Islamic philosophy, as Fakhry affirms in his essay, "Al-Suhrawardī's Critique of the Muslim Peripatetics (*al-Mashshāʿūn*)," when he remarks that al-Suhrawardī attacks the Aristotelians in their theories of categories, of definition, and of substance; he states that al-Suhrawardī explicitly adopts a Neoplatonic type of metaphysics, according to which the entire world is depicted in terms of a hierarchy of lights.

In an extensive and comprehensive essay Mahoney studies "Metaphysical Foundations of the Hierarchy of Being According to Some Late-Medieval and Renaissance Philosophers." Beginning with Proclus, Pseudo-Dionysius, and the *Liber de causis*, Mahoney traces the eschatological depiction of a hierarchy of being in every major school, including Western medieval and Renaissance philosophy. In concluding his essay he makes six observations which have bearing on the entire hierarchical scheme, including the recurrent Neoplatonism in medieval and Renaissance philosophies affecting levels of entities and their relationships. Mahoney ends his essay with an analysis of spatial metaphor in depicting this hierarchy of being, and with a reflection on the value of metaphor for metaphysical systems.

C. *An Isomorphism Between the Problem of Universals and the Essence–Existence Distinction*

The third and last problem singled out in this collection deals with the ontology of forms which took its origin from Plato's metaphysics. It appears that this ontological problem has been transformed isomorphically into two problems: (*a*) the problem of universals and (*b*) the essence–existence distinction. Though the expression of the problem in the language of the essence–existence distinction became dominant in the Islamic tradition, schools of realism, nominalism, and conceptualism centered in the problem of universals in the Western tradition. Because of the close contact in the medieval period between Islamic philosophy and Latin interpreters and the convenience of the use of the concept of the Necessary Existent for the realm of theology, there exists a rich "Western literature" on the essence–existence controversy. The same obviously holds for the Muslims who philosophized explicitly about the nature of universals yet waged most of their ontological battles over the essence–existence controversy.

Paul Seligman, in "Being and Forms in Plato," achieves a synthesis of the original expression of the Platonic depiction of Forms by pointing out factors, such as the dual function of Forms in the world of being and becoming, and the use of the language of analogy to depict some special features of the theory of participation. Wippel, in "The Relationship between Essence and Existence in Late-Thirteenth-Century Thought: Giles of Rome, Henry of Ghent, Godfrey of Fontaines, and James of Viterbo," traces the relationship between essence and existence in entities other than God in thirteenth-century Western philosophy. Wippel points out variations among the distinctions held by the thinkers in question; he sees Giles of Rome as defending real distinctions between essence and existence and between thing and thing; Henry of Ghent as the representative of intentional distinctions between them; Godfrey of Fontaines as rejecting both of the above and admitting nothing more than logical distinctions. Morewedge, in "Greek Sources of Some Near Eastern Philosophies of Being and Existence," examines three problems of ontology which were transmitted from the Greeks to the Muslims: namely, the subject matter of ontology, Porphyry's version of predicables, and the nature of the Aristotelian categories. Finally, alternative positions to these problems are formulated, and in light of the general essence–existence distinction three schools of thought are presented: the analytical school of ibn Sīnā, which took an intermediate position, Nasafī's version of "essence philosophy," and the Mullā Ṣadrā school of "existent philosophy." Nasr, in "Post-Avicennan Islamic Philosophy and the Study of Being," traces the development of the concept of "being" in later Islamic philosophy. Nasr's survey brings to light different positions of ontology among major philosophical thinkers in the Islamic world about whom little is known in the West. Ibn ʿArabī, al-Suhrawardī, Ṭūsī, Mīr Dāmād, and Mullā Ṣadrā are included among these thinkers.

In sum, the modality of existence, the categorical or the eschatological depiction of existence, and the problem of essence–existence / universal–particular dimensions of existence emerge as the three salient problems of ancient and medieval ontology.

I

Why Existence Does Not Emerge as a Distinct Concept in Greek Philosophy

CHARLES H. KAHN
University of Pennsylvania

IN THE EXTENDED DISCUSSION of the concept (or concepts) of Being in Greek philosophy from Parmenides to Aristotle, the theme of existence does not figure as a distinct topic for philosophical reflection. My aim here is to defend and illustrate this claim, and at the same time to suggest some of the reasons why it is that the concept of existence does not get singled out as a topic in its own right. Finally, I shall raise in a tentative way the question whether or not the neglect of this topic was necessarily a philosophical disadvantage.

Let me make clear that my thesis is limited to the classical period of Greek philosophy, down to Aristotle. The situation is more complicated in Hellenistic and Neoplatonic thought, for here we find two technical terms corresponding more or less to the notion of existence: the verb *ὑπάρχειν*, with its noun *ὕπαρξις*, which renders "existence" in Modern Greek, and the verb *ὑποστῆναι*, with its noun *ὑπόστασις*, which corresponds to the Latin verb *subsistere*, and is thus a rather close cognate of *exsistere*. I suspect that a careful study of these Greek terms would reveal that even in their usage we find no real equivalent of our concept of existence. In any case, this later terminology of *ὕπαρξις* and *ὑπόστασις* plays no part in the formulation of Plato's and Aristotle's ontology, and I shall ignore it here. My general view of the historical development is that existence in the modern sense becomes a central concept in philosophy only in the period when Greek ontology is radically revised in the light of a metaphysics of creation: that is to say, under the influence of Biblical religion. As far as I can see, this development did not take place with Augustine or with the Greek Church Fathers, who remained under the sway of classical ontology. The new metaphysics seems to have taken shape in Islamic philosophy, in the form of a *radical* distinction between necessary and contingent existence: between the existence of God, on the one hand,

and that of the created world, on the other. The old Platonic contrast between Being and Becoming, between the eternal and the perishable (or, in Aristotelian terms, between the necessary and the contingent), now gets reformulated in such a way that for the contingent being of the created world (which was originally present only as a "possibility" in the divine mind) the property of "real existence" emerges as a new attribute or "accident," a kind of added benefit bestowed by God upon possible beings in the act of creation. What is new here is the notion of *radical* contingency, not simply the old Aristotelian idea that many things might be other than they in fact are — that many events might turn out otherwise — but that the whole world of nature might not have been created at all: that it might not have *existed.*[1]

I leave it to the historians of Islamic and medieval philosophy to decide how far my hypothesis is correct and to determine just when, or in what stages, the new concept of existence was formulated. But, as far as I can see, it is against the background of Scholastic discussion of the themes just mentioned that the modern concept of existence gets separated out as a distinct topic for debate. By the modern concept I mean the notion articulated in Descartes' doubts about existence and in his proofs of his own existence, the existence of God, and the existence of the external world, and further developed after Descartes in the arguments about the existence of "other minds." The modern concept of existence took a new, contemporary turn as a result of the development of quantification theory in logic. And it was applied to a new set of problems as a consequence of Russell's puzzles about denoting in the case of non-existent subjects such as "the present king of France," as well as in the more directly puzzling case of negative existentials such as "Santa Claus does not exist." (It is interesting to note that although sentences of this form occur in classical Greek philosophy — "Zeus does not exist" or "centaurs do not exist" — their structure is never recognized as problematic. There seems to be little or no concern for the problem of reference as such.[2]) We might summarize the modern concept of existence as the notion for which one analysis is suggested by Quine's dictum "to be is to be the value of a variable."

This brief survey of discussions of existence from Descartes to Russell and Quine is intended merely to identify what I mean by the concept of existence which does *not* emerge as a theme in Greek philosophy. It might be supposed that this non-emergence could be explained quite simply by the fact that classical Greek has no distinct verb meaning "to exist" and hence must make do with the more general verb "to be" (*εἰμί–εἶναι*). But this explanation will not take us very far. On the one hand, it is perfectly possible to discuss questions of existence without relying on a special verb "to exist," as Quine emphasizes in his essay "On What *There Is*," and as Descartes showed in his phrase "Je pense, donc je *suis*." And it seems clear that Aquinas has a theory of the existence of created things, although the verb which he regularly uses to describe their existence is simply the verb "to be" (*esse*). (Similarly, in Anselm's formulation of the ontological argument the expression for "existence" is *esse in re*.) On the other hand, the Greek verb "to be" has (from Homer on) a number of quite characteristic, idiomatic uses which we unhesitatingly recognize as "existential."[3] That is, ancient Greek has a set of idioms corresponding to our use of "there is" in such sentences as "There is life on other planets" or "There are no flying saucers." Such idioms are used by Plato in arguing for the existence of the gods (in *Laws* X) and by Aristotle in discussing whether or not there is an infinite or a void (in *Physics* III and IV). So although the presence of a special verb "to exist" may encourage or facilitate the emergence of existence as a distinct philosophical topic, it is neither necessary nor sufficient for that development: not necessary for the reasons just given, and not sufficient because the Latin verb *exsistere* was in continual philosophical use (alongside *esse*) from the time of Lucretius and Cicero until the end of classical antiquity without giving rise to this notion of existence: I mean, the notion which we find in Anselm and Aquinas *without* the use of a special verb. Here, as elsewhere, the thesis of linguistic relativism, or linguistic determinism, tends to obscure more than it reveals.

Since I have just mentioned Plato's argument for the existence of the gods and Aristotle's discussion of the existence of the infinite and the void, I must make clear that my thesis about the non-emergence of existence as a distinct topic is not intended as a denial of the obvious fact that the Greek philosophers occasionally *discuss* questions of existence. My thesis is rather that the concept of existence is never "thematized": it itself does not become a subject for philosophical reflection. We might say: the notion of existence is used, but never mentioned. Even this statement has to be qualified, since there are several passages in Aristotle where he shows that he is on the verge of isolating existence as a distinct topic. For example, he distinguishes in passing between the use of "to be" in "Homer is a poet" and the "absolute" use of the verb in the sentence "Homer is" (in *De interpretatione* 11); and he repeatedly distinguishes in *Posterior Analytics* II between the questions "What is x?" (*τί ἐστι;*) and "Whether x is or not?" (*εἰ ἔστιν ἢ μή;*). Since his initial examples of this second question are "whether there is a centaur or not" and "whether there is [a] god" (89B32), the point of the *εἰ ἔστι* question seems clearly existential in our sense. But such passages are almost the exception which proves the rule. In the first case the sentence "Homer is" (*Ὅμηρός ἐστιν*) is apparently taken to mean

"Homer is alive [now]," so that the existential sense is at the best very limited and specific. And in the more systematic distinction between types of questions in *Posterior Analytics* II, it is not at all clear that the question of existence as such (εἰ ἔστι) — "whether X is or not" — is carefully kept separate from the question of propositional fact (ὅτι ἐστί) — "whether or not X is Y" or "whether XY is the case." As Ross says (in commenting on II.1), "the distinctions become blurred in the next chapter."[4] Aristotle's interest seems to shift, inevitably and almost imperceptibly, from the existence of individual substances such as centaurs or gods to the "existence" of states of affairs such as the moon's being eclipsed. Now, interpreting these chapters in the *Analytics* is extremely difficult, and I am not at all sure that I know just what Aristotle has in mind. But what does seem clear is that our difficulties in interpreting are in part due to the fact that Aristotle does not consistently regard the "whether-X-is-or-not" question as a question about the existence or non-existence of individual entities of a specified kind, such as centaurs or gods. Even in this passage, then, which seems to be the nearest thing to an explicit distinction of the topic of existence in Aristotle, the distinction does not quite come off.

The upshot is that, although we can recognize at least three different kinds of existential questions discussed by Aristotle, Aristotle himself neither distinguishes these questions from one another nor brings them together under any common head or topic which might be set in contrast to other themes in his general discussion of Being. The three kinds of questions (which have been carefully catalogued by G. E. L. Owen[5]) are (*a*) questions of individual existence over time, in the sense in which we say that a man or a block of ice comes into existence and goes out of existence (i.e., that the man dies or the ice melts); (*b*) questions of sortal existence, timelessly understood: whether there are such things as centaurs (which Owen identifies with the modern use of the existential quantifier); and (*c*) more abstract or conceptual questions of existence in connection with items like the infinite, the void, and the subject matter of geometry: in what sense we want to say that such things do or do not exist. What is important to note for our purposes is that, although these three topics may quite reasonably be grouped together from the point of view of the modern notion of existence, there is nothing in Aristotle's own conceptual scheme which serves to bring them together. The closest correlate to the notion of existence within Aristotle's own scheme is the concept of potency and act. And that, I suggest, is not very close.

What is true for Aristotle is true *a fortiori* for Parmenides and Plato. And here I will turn from documenting the absence of existence as such to the more constructive task of identifying the decisive concept which in fact dominates the view of Being in classical Greek ontology. More precisely, I want to point to the concept which determines the meaning or sense of "Being" (τὸ ὄν) when the term is first introduced into philosophic discussion, in the poem of Parmenides and the early statement of Plato's theory of Forms.

My claim, then, is that the concept of Being in Parmenides and Plato — and to some extent in the later tradition as well — is understood primarily by reference to the notion of truth and the corresponding notion of reality. The question of Being is first of all the question of the nature of reality or the structure of the world, in the very general sense of "the world" which includes whatever we can know or investigate and whatever we can describe in true or false statements. The question of Being, then, for the Greek philosophers is: How must the world be structured in order for inquiry, knowledge, science, and true discourse (or, for that matter, false discourse) to be possible? In linguistic terms, this means that the decisive use of the verb in the creation of Greek ontology is what I call the veridical use, in which the verb ἔστι means "is true" or "is the case."

Before pursuing this thesis I must pause for a few linguistic remarks. Plato and (even more) Parmenides have often been accused of confusing or conflating the copula and the existential uses of "to be," and hence of producing the pseudo-concept of Being by the mistaken assumption that the verb had a single meaning when used for predication and for statements of existence. I do not wish to deny that such confusions sometimes arise in Greek philosophy; I insist only that they play no essential role in the creation and articulation of the concept of Being by Parmenides and Plato. They play no essential role because both predication (with a copula use of "to be") and statements of existence (with an existential use of the verb) may be regarded as special cases of the more general and more fundamental use of "to be" to express the content of a truth claim as such: the so-called veridical use to affirm a propositional content or an objective state of affairs. Since I have illustrated this use in detail elsewhere,[6] and have pointed to its archaic origins in the prehistoric use of the Indo-European participle **sant-* (corresponding to Greek ὄν, ὄντος), a usage reflected both in the old English word "sooth" and in the Sanskrit forms *sat* and *satya*, I need only recall here that this prehistoric idiom is alive and well in colloquial American English today, in the locution "Tell it like it *is*." The "is" here is a pure veridical. The peculiar grammatical features of the veridical use are (*a*) that its understood subject is propositional in form — a fact or a state of affairs asserted to obtain, and not an object or concept whose existence is affirmed; and (*b*) that it is typically construed (without any predicate) in a clause of comparison with verbs of saying or knowing (*verba sentiendi et dicendi*): "*Tell* it *like* it is." Thus the canonical form of the veridical construction of "to be" in Greek, from Homer on, is as follows: "Things are [in fact] as you say [or think or know] them to be" (*ἔστι ταῦτα οὕτω ὥσπερ σὺ λέγεις*). As this locution shows, the prephilosophic conception of truth in Greek (and in Indo-European generally, if not in all languages) involves some kind of correlation or "fit" between what is said or thought, on one side, and *what is* or *what is the case* or *the way things are*, on the other. Let us call this the correlation between assertion and reality, where "assertion" is used neutrally both for *saying that it is so* and *thinking that it is so*, and "reality" is used simply as a convenient abbreviation for *the fact that it is so* or *what happens to be the case.*

My claim, then, is that in the formation of the Greek concept of Being, the key notion is that of truth — the goal of science and the proper aim of declarative speech. If we bear in mind the structure of the veridical use of the verb, we shall easily see how the philosophers' interest in knowledge and truth, taken together with this use of "to be," immediately leads to the concept of Being as reality. I repeat, I am using "reality" here not in any large metaphysical sense but simply as a convenient term for the facts which make true statements true and false statements false, or for whatever it is "in the world," for whatever "is the case," which makes some assertions and some judgments correct and others mistaken. If I assert — either in thought or in speech — that the sun is shining, and if what I assert is true, then the corresponding "reality" is simply the fact that the sun is shining.

So far I have said nothing about *be* as verb of existence or as copula. I have shown only that, starting from the veridical locutions and the notion of Being as truth we immediately get to the related notion of Being as reality, in a suitably loose and generalized sense of "reality." Of course, we can easily see how the existential and copula uses of *be* will also turn up if we think of the reality in question as expressed by a subject–predicate sentence — for instance, by the sentence "The sun is shining." For if this sentence is true, then its subject (the sun) must exist. And the sentence uses the copula verb *is* to predicate something of this subject: namely, *that it is shining*, or *that its light reaches us.* So when we are talking about truth and reality, the existential and copulative uses of *be* are never far away. But I insist that if we *begin* to interpret the concept of Being by looking for existential or copula uses of the verb, not only shall we make unnecessary trouble for ourselves, we may miss the real point. We shall fail to grasp the essential features of the Greek concept of Being.

Consider now what Parmenides says about Being or *what is* (*τὸ ἐόν*). He introduces it (in fragment II) as the object for knowledge and the territory or homeland of truth. "These are the only ways of inquiry there are for knowing [or "for understanding" (νοῆσαι)]: the one, *that it is* . . .; the other, *that it is not.*" The former he calls "the path of Persuasion, for she follows upon Truth"; in other words, Being, or *what is,* is what we can and should believe (be persuaded by) because it leads to (or is identical with) truth. The other path (*that it is not*) he rejects as "unheard of" or "uninformative" (παναπευθής), a way which cannot be trusted, "for you cannot know *what is not* . . .; nor can you point it out." Parmenides' explicit reason here for rejecting *what is not* (τὸ μὴ ἐόν) is that it cannot be an object of knowledge (γνῶναι), a path for understanding (νοῆσαι), or a topic of information discourse (φράζειν). Since in Greek the expressions τὸ μὴ ὄν and τὰ μὴ ὄντα would normally designate the content of lies and false belief, it is obvious why these labels will not signify an object of knowledge or reliable information. The peculiarly Parmenidean touch is to identify "the thing which is not," as the content of falsehood and error, with *nothing* or non-entity (μηδέν in frag. VIII.10; cf. VI.2).

I submit: The guiding thought at the outset of Parmenides' poem, the thought which motivates his articulation of the concept of Being, is the idea of Truth as the goal of knowledge and inquiry. But of course the "being"which is known and truly asserted must be a "reality" in the very general sense indicated earlier. So for Parmenides the veridical notion of Being leads directly to the concept of Reality as opposed to Appearance or false Seeming: Being and Truth — τὸ ἐόν and ἀλήθεια — are explicitly contrasted with the erroneous Opinions (or Seemings, δόξαι) of mortals. By setting this contrast between true Reality and false or mistaken Appearance at the center of his doctrine, Parmenides passes beyond the commonsense, pretheoretical notion of "reality" implied by the ancient locutions for truth, and articulates for the first time a metaphysical concept of Being.

Parmenides' theory of Being has many other aspects which are not directly accounted for by the veridical sense of the verb: its contrast with Becoming, for example — that is to say, its eternal and perfectly static character as an entity which cannot change or move — and its spatial extension and indivisible bodily mass. My aim here is not to offer a complete account, or even a general sketch, of Parmenides' ontology, but simply to identify the concept which gives meaning to his quest: the concept which can permit us to understand what the Greek project of ontology was all about. Now, aside from the properties of spatial location and bodily mass, all the Eleatic attributes of Being are preserved in the ontology which Plato develops for the Forms in the middle dialogues. A brief look at the *Phaedo* (65–66), where the general doctrine of Forms is introduced for the first time by a systematic use of the terminology of Being (ὄν, οὐσία),[7] or a glance at the even more Parmenidean passage in *Republic* V (478–480), where *το ὄν* as the stable object of knowledge is contrasted with the many sensible particulars which are the object of *δόξα*, would suffice to show that here too the initial clue, the key to the concept of Being in Plato as in Parmenides, is provided by the notions of truth and knowledge, and by the very general concept of reality or what is so which is required by these two notions.

In the first instance, then, Being for Plato is characterized as the reality which is sought after in intellectual inquiry, apprehended in noetic cognition, and described or defined in true discourse. But when we pass from these general "veridical" contours to a more detailed analysis, the copula construction emerges as the primary formula for the articulation of the concept of truth and its grounding in the reality of the Forms. Every truth for Plato can properly be expressed in the copula form "X is Y." Even the existential proposition can be so expressed; "Justice exists" is expressed as "Justice is something [*τι*] ." Now, the copula proposition in turn is to be interpreted ontologically in terms of participation: "X is Y" is true only if and because X participates in Y-ness or in the Y. In the last analysis, I suggest, Plato's concept of Being is the being-of-a-Form, or the being-related-to-a-Form by way of participation. The concepts of truth and predication, which concern statement and knowledge, are grounded upon these more fundamental notions of Being which concern the nature of things: Forms and participation.

Summarizing our positive results so far, we can say: in Greek ontology, from Parmenides on, the question of Being is a question as to what reality must be like — or what the world must be like — in order for knowledge and true (or false) discourse to be possible. It is, in effect, the first question which Wittgenstein set out to answer in the *Tractatus*: How must the world be structured if logic and scientific language are to be possible? Since for Plato knowledge is assimilated to discourse, and discourse is analyzed in the predicative form "X is Y," the problem of knowledge and true discourse becomes, in part at least, the problem of predication: What must reality be like if predications such as "X is Y" are to be possible, and sometimes true? What will X be like? What will Y be like? And how can the two be related to one another?

In Aristotle the concept of Being becomes more complex — too complex for summary statement here. We would have to begin by analyzing the doctrine of the categories, and go on to consider the concepts of potency and act. Let me remark only that the scheme of the categories, which is formulated as a device for distinguishing types of predication, serves in effect for analyzing types of existence as well. To the various forms of predication recognized by the division into categories correspond so many different modes of existence. The most fundamental mode is, of course, that of the primary category, the being of substances, that is to say, the existence of individual entities of a definite kind — which in the paradigm case means the existence of a living organism belonging to a definite species: a human being, or a horse, or a pine tree. For Socrates *to exist* is for him *to be a (living) man*, to live a human life; for a particular tree to exist is for it to be a living oak or a chestnut. For white *to exist* is *to be a color*, that is, a quality, belonging to some particular substance. For walking *to exist* is *to be an action* performed by some man or animal. Thus the general tendency of this Aristotelian method in ontology is for the existential idea to be absorbed into the theory of predication and to be expressed linguistically by copula uses of the verb. So we find that the key ontological formula of Aristotle's metaphysics, the *τὸ τί ἦν εἶναι*, defines the mode of existence for any subject whatsoever, but it does so without any existential use of the verb. The concrete being of Socrates is a compound of matter and form, body and psyche; but the matter itself is determined by the essence, the *τὸ τί ἦν εἶναι* for man, the being-what-it-is. Socrates' being or existence is his being-human, his being-what-a-man-is, that is to say, his being that particular kind of thing which is specified in the definition which answers to the question: What is X? What is a human being (*τί ἐστιν ἄνθρωπος*)? Thus for Aristotle as for Plato, existence is always *εἶναί τι*, being something or other, being something definite. There is no concept of existence as such for subjects of an indeterminate nature.

To return now to the question with which we began: Why does existence not emerge as a distinct concept in Greek philosophy? In principle the answer is clear. My explanation is that in Greek ontology in its early stages, in Plato and Parmenides, the veridical concept was primary, and the question of Being was the question of "reality" as determined by the concept of truth. Since this conception of reality is articulated in Plato by copula sentences of the form "X is Y," it turns out that even the concept of existence gets expressed in this predicative form: as we have seen, Platonic Greek for "X exists" is "X is something" (*εἶναί τι*). In the scheme of categories which Aristotle takes as the starting point for his own investigation of being, this same predicative pattern serves as the primary device for analyzing *τὰ ὄντα*, *what there is*, and for showing how the various kinds of being are related to one another. So it is naturally the theory of predication, and not the concept of existence, which becomes the central and explicit theme of Aristotle's metaphysics, as it was the implicit theme of Plato's discussion of Being in the *Sophist*.

If we conclude, now, by raising the question whether it was a philosophical disadvantage for Greek ontology to begin with the concept of truth and reality (as the object of knowledge and the content of true statement), and whether it was a mistake to proceed by developing a theory of predication and neglecting the concept of existence as such, we cannot hope to answer such a question with any brief statement. I will simply hint at the line which a defense of Greek ontology might pursue. Let us imagine Parmenides, Plato, and Aristotle responding as follows.

"Granted: our starting point in ontology does not provide a theory of reference or denotation, and hence does not confront the problems of negative existentials or statements about non-existent subjects. After all, a discipline in its initial stages cannot hope to deal with *all* the problems. But by articulating our own doctrines of being around the topics of truth and predication, we pointed to the notions of propositional analysis and truth for sentences or statements [*λόγος*] which provide the conceptual framework within which a theory of reference and a clear account of existence become possible. It is scarcely necessary to defend our achievements by pointing to the contemporary relevance of a Platonizing ontology for the discussion of universals and the theory of mathematical objects (numbers, sets, etc.) or to the obvious role which Aristotelian ideas about individuals, predication, and natural kinds continue to play in modern work in ontology, logic, and the theory of language. We should perhaps emphasize what is less obvious: that the veridical starting point for Greek theories of Being or reality anticipates in a rather striking way the contemporary standpoint which (following and developing certain ideas of Tarski) takes the notion of truth for sentences as basic in any theory of meaning and knowledge. (Consider the view of Donald Davidson in his presidential address "On the Very Idea of a Conceptual Scheme,"[8] or the parallel doctrine which Henry Hiz calls "aletheism.") Above all, we would insist that the articulation of Greek theories of reality around the topics of truth and predication or *λόγος* guarantees that philosophical speculation — as long as it is faithful to this starting point — will remain in close contact with genuine problems of knowledge in the sciences and with careful work in logic.

"Now, we must admit" (these philosophers will conclude) "that our neglect of the topic of existence as such does leave us without any ready means of formulating Cartesian doubts about the existence of the external world, just as it also leaves us without the concept of existence which provides the nerve of Anselm's ontological argument. From the standpoint of our ontologies, no one could ever have formulated either Anselm's argument or Descartes' radical doubts about existence. But, depending upon one's view of the value of the ontological argument and the philosophical importance of skepticism concerning the external world, these deficiencies in our standpoint could perhaps be counted as assets rather than as liabilities."

NOTES

1 This is the conceptual basis for the intellectual pathos of contemporary "existentialism," as expressed, for example, by Jean-Paul Sartre in a famous passage of *La Nausée*: "Aucun être nécessaire ne peut expliquer l'existence: la contingence n'est pas un faux-semblant, une apparence qu'on peut dissiper; c'est l'absolu, par conséquent, la gratuité parfaite. Tout est gratuit, ce jardin, cette ville et moi-même. Personne n'a le droit; ils sont entièrement gratuits, . . . ils n'arrivent pas à ne pas se sentir de trop" (Paris, 1938; p. 185).

2 There is an interesting approach to the problem of reference in Aristotle's discussion of the difference between contraries and contradictories in *Categories* X, where he considers the different consequences for the truth value of sentences about Socrates in the case where "Socrates is not at all" (*μὴ ὄντος ὅλως τοῦ Σωκράτους*, 13B15–35). In this case it is only contradictories, and not contraries, of which one must be true and the other false. Aristotle's example is: "Socrates is sick" will be false in this case, but "Socrates is not sick" will be true (13B32). It is worth noting that he does not distinguish this from the parallel assertion "Socrates is dead," which I believe he would regard as true. For I assume that what Aristotle has in mind here is the temporal existence or duration of individual living things and not existence in general, timelessly understood. See the distinction, p. 10.

3 I have documented these uses in some detail in *The Verb "Be" in Ancient Greek* (The Verb "Be" and Its Synonyms, VI, ed. J. W. M. Verhaar; Amsterdam 1973), chap. 6.

4 See W. D. Ross, *Aristotle's Prior and Posterior Analytics* (Oxford, 1949), pp. 610–12.

5 "Aristotle on the Snares of Ontology," in *New Essays on Plato and Aristotle*, ed. Renford Bambrough (New York, 1965), pp. 69–95.

6 See "The Veridical Use," in *The Verb "Be" in Ancient Greek*, ed. Verhaar, chap. 7.

7 See, for example, John Burnet's comments on *Phaedo* 65c3 and 65c9 (in his edition [Oxford, 1911] of the dialogue), and my own fuller statement of these remarks about Parmenides and Plato in "Linguistic Relativism and the Greek Project of Ontology," in *The Question of Being*, ed. G. M. C. Sprung (University Park, Pa., 1978), pp. 31–44.

8 *Proceedings and Addresses of the American Philosophical Association*, 47 (1973–74), 5–20, esp. 16ff.

2

Being and Forms in Plato

PAUL SELIGMAN
University of Waterloo

I

IN A FAMOUS PASSAGE Aristotle tells us that the question "What is being?" (*τί τὸ ὄν;*) was raised of old, is raised now and always, and is always the subject of doubt (*Met. Z* 1). From this we may conclude that he took the nature of being as a fundamental problem of Greek philosophy which he was going to solve. As to Plato, he did not raise the question of being in so many words until in the *Sophist* he confesses (through the mouth of the Eleatic Stranger) that when he was younger he was at ease even about not-being but now experiences puzzlement concerning both being and not-being (243Bf.). And in his brief survey of his predecessors he seems to anticipate Aristotle's view that "being" was their prime concern. His own concern had emerged with the theory of forms in the *Phaedo/Republic* period where the *εἶδος*, as then conceived, represents Plato's first answer to the question "What is being?" "Real being," *ὄντως εἶναι* — i.e., being in a paradigmatic sense — is ascribed to the forms, and to them alone, so that the entities which they name constitute the nature of being. In the survey in the *Sophist* just mentioned, the "friends of the forms" claim that *ἀληθινὴ οὐσία* consists of certain intelligible and bodiless *εἴδη* (246B), a statement which I take to have autobiographical significance.

In rendering *οὐσία* we here require a richer term than "being," for which the empty extensional sense predominates. Since the Platonic forms are natures — the just, the beautiful, etc. — they cannot be said to constitute existence as signified in modern logic by $\exists$. They supply its intension. For this reason I shall render *οὐσία* by the German word "Wesen," which can mean essence, or nature, but also entity, i.e., a characterized being.[1] We may say then (again in German) that the forms are the "Wesensbestimmungen des Seins"; they define the essence of *εἶναι*, which thus appears in Plato's middle period as intrinsically plural. Not only are they possessed of being, as is suggested when they are spoken of as *ὄντως ὄντα* (this refers to their existence); but the world of forms constitutes the whatness of being — its wealth, if we like.

As "Wesensbestimmungen des Seins," the forms are unmixed and unchanging, transcendent, eternal,[2] and unique, i.e., they are *καθ' ἕκαστον*, not *καθόλου*. They are intelligible, i.e., known by, but not constituents of, the intellect (*Parm.* 132Bff.) — they are "Wesen," not ideas in the mind.

The "Wesenbestimmungen des Seins," the Platonic *οὐσίαι*, are imitated by, or reflected in, sensible things which come to be, are subject to change, and pass away — in short, make up our empirical world, the world of becoming. The temporal things obtain their "Wesensbestimmungen" from the forms, after which they are named,[3] "striving to be like them but only deficiently succeeding" (*Phaed.* 74Ef.). *Qua* temporal and changing and often qualified by their very opposites (*Rep.* 479A–B), they cannot enduringly possess them. And it is only in virtue of coming to have a borrowed and tenuous share in *ἀληθιναὶ οὐσίαι* that the things in the world come into being (*Phaed.* 101C), and may be said to exist. Being and essence are but two sides of one coin, as far as both the forms and the things in the world are concerned. Neither forms nor things can be considered as existents *tout court*, and the "Wesensbestimmungen" of the latter are as precarious as their existence; they come and go. Put in later terminology: the world of becoming is contingent, both in that it is and in what it is.

The forms, then, have a dual function in the world of being and in the world of becoming. I therefore consider form *qua* "Wesensbestimmung" a homonym as applied to "Sein" (being) and as applied to sensible things, and I shall speak of "$\text{Wesensbestimmung}_b$," in the one case, and of "$\text{Wesensbestimmung}_t$," in the other ($W_b$ and W_t for short).[4] Can this homonymity, we may ask, be adequately accounted for in terms of "individual" (for W_b) and "universal" (for W_t) respectively? Do the unique Platonic forms *qua* reflected in the world of becoming function as universals?[5]

II

I shall approach this question by way of an analogy, suggested by the language of the Divided Line. If we look at a painting such as Monet's *River* or Cézanne's *Lac d'Annecy* and compare the landscape on the shore with its reflection in the water, we shall notice that the latter is wavering if not blurred; its outline is not clearly *defined*. Still, the images are sufficiently recognizable to be named after the objects on the shore.

Next, suppose we take a walk along the bank of a river or lake; we shall notice that, as we go along, there are many variations in the reflections on the water surface of any one object, depending on our position, changes in the illumination, etc. If on our way we should make continuous use of a ciné camera and then compare the shots of the reflections with one another, their differences would become apparent; yet they may be sufficiently similar to be recognized as many reflections of the same object, allowing us to designate them by its name — say, tree. Still, the reflected image of the tree (not to speak of its prototype on the shore) is not a universal identical element in all these occurrences. It is not in any of them present without qualification, and therefore not amenable to univocal description. It would follow that forms *qua* W_t cannot function as Aristotelian universals, are not *καθόλου* — a term which, incidentally, does not occur in the Dialogues.[6] Plato's procedure is to posit a form whenever a common name is used (cf. *Rep.* 507B). In our analogy the observed similarity of the reflections has enabled us to "recollect" the tree itself — the one over the many — and to pass from uncertain W_t's to paradigmatic W_b.[7] On this route the common name by which we have designated the reflections may be held to function as a universal term in our sentences. But this does not imply that the form functions as a universal. The name is but another reflection — a verbal image — of the form, another signpost, then, on the Platonist's way of truth (see *Crat.* 438D–439B).

It was one of Aristotle's complaints that Plato's forms *qua* universals cannot be *οὐσίαι*, only individuals can. But the Platonic transcendent forms are individuals — individuals, moreover, which will not universalize, keeping aloof from their many reflections in things. Against Aristotle, on the other hand, the corresponding complaint has been raised — viz., that his immanent forms which *qua* objects of definition and discursive knowledge are universals do not individualize, and hence, on his own showing, could not be *οὐσίαι*, the "what-it-is" of perceptible individuals. But does not Plato himself, one may argue on Aristotle's behalf, in making forms objects of knowledge, and the only legitimate objects of knowledge, by that very fact make them universals, quite regardless of their many instances? Is it not the case that our *λόγοι* about the forms can be stated universally just because they steer clear of the variety of their precarious reflections?

Plato's and Aristotle's apparent *ἀπορίαι* alike are concerned with the relation between individual and universal, and we may compare their answers. Aristotle apprehends the immanent intelligible form of his perceptible *οὐσίαι* by intuitive reason (cf. *Eth. Nic.* 1143A35ff.) prior to its definition in a universal formula. Form in Aristotle is individual but is spoken of universally. Plato through sensible contact with its many reflections "recollects" and, aided by reasoning, intuitively apprehends the individual form (*νοήσει*, *Tim.* 28A). The reasoning, i.e., the universal *λόγοι*, is a necessary condition of coming to know the transcendent forms (*Ep.* 7, 342Bf.).[8] But this does not entail that they are universals — the *λόγοι* do not catch them in their meshes, as it were — just as Aristotle's definitions do not allow us to draw a similar conclusion concerning his immanent forms.

But again it may be argued that Plato's most important terms for the relation between things and forms imply a particular/universal relation, e.g., things partake of, or participate or have a share in, forms; and again: howsoever a thing may have gained its characterization, it is through the presence (*παρουσία*) or communion (*κοινωνία*) of the form.[9] Critics have held that these terms are but metaphors for the predication of an attribute of a subject. But *οὐσία*, according to Aristotle (*Cat.* 2A11), is neither predicable of (as a universal of a particular), nor present in, a subject (as an attribute in its possessor).[10] Now, we do attribute beauty, justice, and the rest to things in the world (. . . is beautiful, . . . is just, etc.), and it would again follow that Platonic forms are not *οὐσίαι*.

I think this argument can be met in terms of our previous W_b/W_t distinction, between "Wesensbestimmungen des Seins" and their reflections in things. When the Platonist reads the statement "This statue is beautiful" as "This statue participates in beauty" or similar locutions, he does not claim that the form of beauty is its attribute. He claims that the statue is beautiful (W_t) for the sole reason that it participates in the form of beauty (W_b). The sensuous beauty which he ascribes to the statue is a reflection of that transcendent beauty which can be apprehended only by the mind, the apprehension of which may be engendered by the contemplation of the visible statue but is not equivalent to it. The form is present in, or has communion with, the statue as a third thing, as the *raison d'être* of the attributed quality, but can be neither deduced from, nor reduced to, the latter. The attribute has been named after the form on which it depends and towards which it aspires. The form is individual, the paradigmatic *οὐσία* which is fully realized, neither in any of its participants nor in all of them collectively, but only in separation from them. Its nature is conveyed, not in terms of, but in contrast to, its manifestations in the sensible realm (see, e.g., *Rep.* 476D, 479A).

Participation and kindred words do not stand for, or mask, a logical relation; they are not metaphors for the "is" of predication. Their ontological signification is prior to their semantic function. They express, with the conceptual means at Plato's disposal, the dependence of the temporal on the eternal, trying to establish a link between becoming and being. There is one proviso, though: the link needs to be understood as intensional, not in the spatial mode of part and whole suggested by the very terminology which Plato employed, and which at one point became a trap from which he seemed unable to extricate himself (*Parm.* 130E–131E).[11]

W_t, then, is neither part of, nor identical with, W_b, but an imperfect reflection (image, copy) of it. The form itself is not immanent in particulars. W_t is (formally) like W_b in that both exclude opposites, as Socrates states at *Phaed.* 102Df. and similarly at 103B: "An opposite *itself* can never become its own opposite whether the opposite in question be in us [W_t] or in the world of true being [φύσει] [W_b]." The epithet "itself" (*αὐτό*), which elsewhere is Plato's standard designation of forms, here merely stresses the contrast to the concrete thing, mentioned in the preceding sentence, in which opposites are generated from opposites, referring to earlier argument at 70E. So also the following sentence (103B):

> There we were speaking of things which *have* opposites and calling them by the names of those opposites which they possessed [ἐχόντων] but now [we are speaking] of those opposites themselves from whose being in them [ὧν ἐνόντων] the things named after them have their name [trans. after Hackforth].

Interpreters who hold that Platonic forms in their own nature (W_b) are identical with their reflections in things (W_t) may draw support from this passage, insofar as it is suggested here that things receive their names from the latter (the opposite which they possess, the opposites in them), whereas at 102B we are told that they have their names in virtue of participating in the former. Must the two not be the same? This does not follow. As pointed out (n. 3 above) things are named after W_t immediately, hence mediately after W_b, and therefore may be spoken of as named after either without surrendering the distinction between them.[12]

I would not claim, however, that a separate ontological status[13] can be ascribed to W_t, with the implication that the ontology of the middle period is a three-tier one: forms, particulars which participate in forms, and their immanent characters derived from the forms. This would make the particular a bare particular analogous to the receptacle of the *Timaeus*. Although this may be the logical outcome of Plato's metaphysical structure, I see no evidence for it in the earlier texts which do not separate the particular thing from its characterizations. (What are separated are characterization and transcendent form.) At this point Plato can still significantly speak of Simmias and the tallness in him without showing awareness that the form/copy analysis could legitimately be extended to his other qualities as well, which would ultimately make him bereft of any characteristics whatsoever, a mere locus of participations with nothing left to do the participating.

III

We are still concerned with the forms as the vehicles and plural essence of being as met with in the middle dialogues. I shall now turn to some of the roots of the doctrine. The theory of ideas has been linked with Socrates' search for definitions of notions of excellence, such as justice, beauty, etc., of that one abiding element in their many instances which makes these just, beautiful, and so on. In Plato's earlier Socratic dialogues these notions are sometimes spoken of as εἴδη but there is no indication that the historical Socrates made ontological claims for them. As Aristotle points out, he did not separate them from their occurrences. Indeed in the *Phaedo* Socrates professes lack of interest in cosmological speculation (96Aff.), such as Aristotle in *Met. Z* 1 and Plato in his survey in the *Sophist* (242cff.) link with enquiries into the nature of being. Socrates' concern was man and his soul. In vindicating Socrates' quest, Plato undertook to make secure the objectivity and stability of the values for which his master had lived and died. He conceived them as of the very essence of reality (ἀληθιναὶ οὐσίαι) inviolate and apart from the pretensions and imperfections of mortal life — apart, yet connected and intrinsically relevant to human conduct and effort. The theory of ideas anchors the Socratic quest in the nature of being, and as it first emerges comprehends being in terms of Socrates' ideals, the moral forms. They are given "elated" (*pace* Crombie) if not divine status, and whatever the condition of the human soul in this world, it can strive after their realization.

Reminiscent of the Pythagoreans who extrapolated from the nature of musical harmony to the constitution of the cosmos, Plato began to build the intelligible world of forms on the foundation of his Socratic legacy. But the edifice itself owes much more to Parmenides' "Way of Truth."

The Platonic form was modelled on the Eleatic notion of one being, unbegotten and imperishable, self-same, single and changeless, untouched by sensible appearances. The forms were Parmenidoid in character, the worthy heirs to Eleatic being. Moreover, like Parmenidean being, they were the only legitimate objects of knowledge and rational discourse. Again Plato followed Parmenides in identifying being and truth; in fact, he did not know otherwise.

But there are also three significant departures:

(*a*) Like the post-Eleatic cosmologists, Plato pluralizes being. There are many forms, many vehicles of being, not one. But, as against Empedocles,

Plato's many forms are not sensible constituents of the cosmos; they have neither colour nor shape and cannot be touched (*Phdr.* 247c).

(*b*) Eleatic being was not empty, not entirely built on the Is/Is-not dichotomy.[14] It had intension, "Wesen," e.g., indivisible, homogenous, cohesive, like a sphere, equally poised in every direction, staying uniformly within its limits, etc. But these are spatial properties, so that the intension of Parmenidean being turns out to be the intension of extended being, a blueprint for a cosmos, as it were.[15] Plato, on the other hand, in the first place conceived the intension of being qualitatively. *Οὐσία* is what the many forms name: that is, justice, courage, temperance, etc.

(*c*) In contrast to Parmenides, Plato attempted to account for the sensible world of becoming under the aspect of, and in relation to, being. Parmenides had put it in a separate part of his poem "The Way of Seeming," and seeming was cut off from being, related to it as deceit is related to truth.[16] In Plato seeming is related to being as opinion is to knowledge, and opinion may be true and may lead to knowledge. The sensible realm reflects *ἀληθινὴ οὐσία*, is causally dependent on it. The *ἀρχή*-function of the Presocratic tradition, relinquished by Parmenidean being, has thus been restored to the Platonic *εἴδη*.

IV

The symbiosis of being and forms which characterized Plato's middle period will eventually break up. The first step in this direction is already taken in the *Republic* with his conception of the form of the Good. It is from the Good that the objects of knowledge (the forms) not only receive their power of being known, but also derive their very being (*εἶναι*) and essence (*οὐσία*) (509b). But the Good, though spoken of as a form, is itself not an *οὐσία*, and that means it cannot be accounted for within the realm of being. Rather, it is the ultimate principle of being and essence, as though answering to the Leibnizian question "Why should there be anything at all [and hence anything knowable] rather than nothing?" As Plato puts it, the Good surpasses *οὐσία* in dignity and power. Here, then, a form has been received which is not constitutive of being as proposed by "the friends of the forms."

The decisive step in the differentiation of being and forms is taken in the *Sophist*, with the recognition that being itself is a form, albeit a special type of form.[17] Unlike the forms at large it has no descriptive content; its nature cannot be stated in terms of the other forms, which therefore cease to function as "Wesensbestimmungen des Seins." They exist *qua* participating in the form of being, not *qua* essence of being. Though still conceived as unchanging[18] and eternal, they lose their privileged position as the only vehicles of being. Anything which is, which has come to be (*Soph.* 219B, 245D), whether changeless or changeable (249D), participates in being and has real existence as what it is. Even "an image, though not having the true being of the original from which it is copied, somehow [πῶς] is . . . it really is a likeness [εἰκὼν ὄντως] (240Af.).[19] Although the categorical distinction between forms and things in the world is maintained, and the latter continue to receive their "Wesensbestimmungen" from the forms, they no longer receive their being from them. Forms as well as things in the world receive their being by participating in the form of being, and therefore Plato no longer recognizes a difference in degree of being between them.[20] Consequently being — the form of being— cannot be defined in terms of the being/becoming contrast.

The position which concerns us now — that being itself is a form or kind[21] — is bound up with Plato's increasing interest in forms which, while they themselves have no specific content, apply to all things, whatever their natures. Examples of these "common notions" are likeness and unlikeness, unity and plurality (*Parm.* 129Df.), and sameness and difference (otherness — τὸ ἕτερον) (*Theaet.* 185C). These are purely formal determinants, not substantive determinations, and I have therefore termed them "metaforms." Significantly, in the *Theaetetus* Plato adds being and not-being to his list.[22] Finally, in the *Sophist* he speaks of such forms as μέγιστα γένη, "very great kinds," possibly with their all-pervasiveness in mind, and he distinguishes five of these: being, sameness, difference, motion (change), and rest.[23]

Plato's growing concern with metaforms is paralleled by the development of the science of dialectic, culminating in the *Sophist* doctrine of the communion of forms. Here in particular two of the μέγιστα γένη, being and difference, play a pivotal role. They pervade all the forms, respectively holding them together so that they can intermingle,[24] and traversing them so as to make their separation possible (253C). They are thus ultimately responsible (αἴτια) for the structure of reality which the dialectician retraces in his collections and divisions.[25]

I shall say more presently about the combining and differentiating functions of the two metaforms. In the meantime we should note that the forms at large have now shed their Parmenidoid insularity. By participating in other forms they no longer are conceived as undifferentiated unities but have become complex.[26] Together they constitute "wholes," articulated systems of participations and differentiations, within which they can be defined.

Given these developments in Plato's ontological thinking, what might be his answer to the question "What is being?" One thing should be obvious: the form of being cannot be defined in terms of the system of forms plus the things in the world which severally *are* because they participate in being. They constitute the extension, not the intension, of being. Plato clearly distinguishes *τὸ ὂν κατὰ τὴν αὑτοῦ φύσιν*, being in its own nature (250C), from *τὸ ὄν τε καὶ τὸ πᾶν*, the sum total of things (249D). Put in terms of participation, this means that although all forms (whether generic or specific) and all things participate in being, being does not participate in them. This extends even to motion and rest, which Plato has included among his *μέγιστα γένη*. Being in its own nature neither moves nor is at rest but lies outside these alternatives (250D).[27] Its intension cannot be designated qualitatively but must be *purely* formal.

I shall set it out in two stages:

In the first place it consists in the symmetrical pattern of participation of the three metaforms being, sameness, and difference. By participating in sameness and difference, being remains its single self, howsoever many things may participate in it, and is different from all the other forms, including the forms of sameness and difference themselves. This formal structure of being determines the formal structure of all existents which *qua* participating in being are self-identical and different from all other existents.

But, secondly, existents also participate in other existents,[28] and this means that the combining function of being must be an essential character of its nature. At *Soph.* 255cf. the Eleatic Stranger distinguishes the two metaforms being and difference[29] by pointing out that though difference is always other-referring, and is difference *from* something, being partakes of both the "in-itself" (*καθ' αὑτό*) and "referring to others" (*πρὸς ἄλλα*) — and these characteristics too are here spoken of as forms — metaforms, I would gloss. Just as difference[30] would be incomplete if not other-referring — difference from what, we need to know — so "being in itself" in an important sense is incomplete; it bestows existence which *qua se* is empty (Ǝ). But being too is other-referring, so that for anything to exist, i.e., to participate in being, involves participation in many other existents.[31] It is in this sense that Plato will say that "in the case of every one of the forms being is many" (256E), where being is to be understood as referring to the many other forms in which a form participates.[32] Thus the *πρὸς ἄλλο* character of being is the formal basis of the *συμπλοκὴ τῶν εἰδῶν*. It takes its place together with identity and difference as essential aspects of the nature of being at this stage of Plato's thinking. Taking a synoptic view, we may see these three aspects as elements of rational order, and this seems to be the gist of Plato's answer to the question of being. It may be contrasted with the isolated luminosities of the "friends of the forms."

V

Does Plato in the *Timaeus* restore the symbiosis of being and forms which predominated in the *Phaedo/Republic* period? I refer to the well-known distinction at the beginning of Timaeus' discourse (27DF.) between that which always is (ὂν ἀεί) and has no becoming, and that which is always becoming (γιγνόμενον ἀεί) and never is (ὂν οὐδέποτε). The distinction between being and becoming was never abandoned by Plato,[33] but with the conception of a form of being (in the *Sophist*) in which changeable things participate no less than that which always is (the forms), the essence of being could no longer be defined in terms of the latter, and in contrast to the former. The present passage, however, sharpens the distinction into a dichotomy and outright denies being to generated things. It seems as though the forms have slipped back into their privileged position as the only vehicles of being and constituents of its essence. In the context of the *Timaeus* this would apply in particular to the Demiurge's eternal model, and we may wonder whether it is the intelligible living creature, in whose likeness the cosmos was fashioned (30C), which is now to give us the intension of being.

I shall first suggest some reasons why Plato may have felt the need to preface his cosmology the way he did. I shall then point to some diverging passages in the dialogue which show that the *Phaedo/Republic* position has not been revived here, and lastly I shall consider whether the *Timaeus* offers any contribution of its own to the question of being.

(1) The immediate use to which Plato puts his disjunction is to affirm that the universe has come to be (28B), thereby implying that being cannot be identified with the visible cosmos. He seems intent on breaking up a symbiosis rather than re-creating one. As he is here for the first time going to give a systematic account of the physical world — in itself a radical departure from the example of Socrates (*Phaed.* 96Aff.) — he may at the very outset have felt the need to differentiate his own approach from the cosmologies of his predecessors — the "giants" of the *Sophist.* On the basis of his distinction, he can deny that fire, air, water, and earth, as the elements of physical bodies, constitute *οὐσία*. More trenchantly he might have claimed that the atoms of Leucippes and Democritus,[34] moving aimlessly and at random, could not even constitute the order of the physical world, as evinced by the regular circuits of the heavenly bodies.

Next Plato uses his distinction to show that the universe, being always in a state of becoming, can have been framed, not after a model which itself had come to be, but only after the eternal (29A).[35] The universe, Plato tells us, is the best thing which has come to be, implying that although becoming in itself is not a good (since it is impervious to knowledge), well-ordered becoming is. Becoming is contrasted with being, but the order of becoming approximates being.

(2) (a) In contradistinction to the position of Plato's middle period that many visible things may imitate (or partake of) the same form, the generated cosmos is like its prototype in being one and unique (31B; cf. 92C). It possesses an essential characteristic appertaining to forms, and it appears that as the discourse progresses, the initial dichotomy is not maintained.

(b) Thus at 35A Plato distinguishes between *οὐσία* which is indivisible and always in the same state, and divisible *οὐσία* which becomes (*γιγνομένης*) in bodies. These too, then, like the forms have *οὐσία*.[36] Moreover the demiurge compounds an intermediate type of *οὐσία* composed of the indivisible and the divisible kind. Proceeding similarly regarding sameness and difference, he blends the three mixtures into unity — the world-soul. This passage, too, cuts across the initial disjunction, but may also give us an additional reason why it was put forward at all. The sharpened contrast between being and becoming is to be bridged, and it seems to be a function of soul as compounded of both eternal and generated *οὐσία*, and partaking of reason and harmony (36Ef.), to mediate between them.

(c) In the *Timaeus* the forms are no longer the sole causes (*Phaed.* 100Cff.). They are the models of the images transiently reflected in space, thus giving content to the generated cosmos, but are not responsible for the imaging itself. The forms cannot account for the fact that they should be reflected at all. This is the work of the divine artificer, "the best of causes" (29A), conceived as soul, possessed of mind and reason, and hence the mediating agent *κατ' ἐξοχήν*. As he created the soul of the world in his own likeness,[37] so he refashions chaotic becoming to be as far as possible like the eternal prototype.

(d) There are three crucial aspects of his work. He persuades the blind necessity, which prevailed in the disorderly precosmic welter of genesis, "to guide the greatest part of the things which become towards what is best" (48A).[38] He gives a distinct configuration to the aimless fiery, watery, air- and earthlike whirl[39] by geometrical shapes and numbers (53B), imposing a limit by (in later language) primary qualities on diffuse secondary ones. Thus they receive their permanent identity and become true elements, the interchange of which is orderly and has been rendered intelligible.[40] The third and most significant aspect is the creation, together with the cosmos, of "a moving likeness of eternity . . . everlasting and moving according to number" (37D). This is time, the measure of the uniform motions of the heavenly bodies, the ordering framework of becoming. To the eternity of the model "which abides in unity" (37D) there corresponds the existence through all time of the one perpetually becoming universe which "has been and is and shall be" (38C).

(3) If we look to the *Timaeus* for a contribution to the question of being, we cannot leave out the activity of the divine mind. The *Timaeus* takes up the question, raised by the Eleatic Stranger in the *Sophist* (248Eff.), whether "we are really so easily to be convinced that change [motion], life, soul, and understanding are not present to absolute being . . ., whether being stands immutable in solemn aloofness, devoid of mind." In the *Sophist* Plato goes as far as to allow for change (motion) and changing things (and hence becoming and living things) to have being (cf. p. 22). But the form of being itself is changeless. While change (motion) participates in being, being does not participate in it (cf. p. 26). And this is equally true of the intelligible living creature, the eternal prototype of the universe; it itself is not *ἔμψυχον*, not living but "always in the same state." Yet it is not purely formal in the sense of the metaforms of the *Sophist*. It is a generic form comprising in itself the models of all the kinds which were to become in the created cosmos. Although a static principle, it is the principle, not of a static, but of an organic, order. And mind is present to it, so as to redeem it, as it were, from its "solemn aloofness," refashioning the living order of becoming in its likeness. In this way the *Timaeus* bridges the gulf which separates being from becoming.*

NOTES

1 In its use as the stem of the perfect participle of "sein," "to be," "Wesen" has as close an affinity with that verb as *οὐσία* has with *εἶναι*, as *essentia* with *esse*. "Wesen" also means property ("Anwesen" = real estate), and thus covers pretty much the connotative range of *οὐσία*.

2 The question whether Plato conceived of the forms as durationless or as eternally enduring can remain outside our consideration.

3 *Phaed.* 78E, 102B; Aristotle, *Met.* 987B8. In the first place it is the characteristics which particular things possess and in terms of which they are described that are named after the forms. Particular things in turn are named after those characteristics and hence derivatively after the forms which their characteristics reflect. The beauty which we

attribute to statues is named after the form of beauty, and it is *qua* beautiful that statues are named after the form and are spoken of as τὰ καλά (e.g., 100D). Of the terms which Plato uses to characterize the controversial thing/form relation, I concentrate at the moment on "reflect" ("image," "imitate") (see *Rep.* 510f.); others will be referred to as I go along.

4 This corresponds to Plato's distinction at *Phaed.* 102Df. between "tallness itself" and "tallness in us," etc. — "the tallness Simmias happens to possess" (102C); cf. *Parm.* 130B.

5 I locate the nerve of Plato's ontology in the contrast between W_b and W_t, between the forms *qua* intelligible essence of being and their reflections in sensible things. Rather than considering forms and things simply as two classes of existents, I concentrate on the similarity *cum* difference in their characterization. My question may also be put thusly: Do the "Wesensbestimmungen" of being when dispersed among the indefinite multitude of ὄντα appear as self-identical common properties? Do Plato's παραδείγματα universalize, or are they reflected in ever-varying gradations?

6 As W. D. Ross points out, in *Plato's Theory of Ideas* (Oxford, 1951), p. 18: "There is one phrase [at *Meno* 77A] which may be the origin of Aristotle's term καθόλου and of our term 'universal'— 'saying about virtue, as about a whole (κατὰ ὅλου) what it is.'"

7 In the language of the *Phaedo*: we pass from "tallness in us" to tallness itself. In his middle period Plato's ontological thinking was not directed towards an understanding of the world of becoming. W_t's were signposts to the world of being, not to physical science.

8 Conversely, once a man knows them, he will be able to give an account of them (*Phaed.* 76B).

9 *Ibid.* 100Df. Note that Socrates, though hesitant concerning his terminology, is quite definite that "the many beautiful things are beautiful through [= in virtue of participating in] beauty."

10 With the exception of secondary οὐσία (species, genus) which is predicated of primary οὐσία (*Cat.* 3A10).

11 One wonders, though, what made Socrates trade off his "day" simile against Parmenides' "sail" (*ibid.* 131B); cf. J. M. Rist, "The Immanence and Transcendence of the Platonic Form," *Philologus*, 108 (1964), 217–32, esp. 218–19.

12 On the confusion by interpreters of μετέχειν with ἔχειν and ἐνεῖναι and the diminishing occurrence of ἔχειν and ἐνεῖναι in the Dialogues, see Norio Fujisawa, "Ἔχειν, *Μετέχειν*, and Idioms of 'Paradeigmatism' in Plato's Theory of Forms," *Phronesis*, 19 (1974), 30–58. Another source of the view that forms are immanent in particulars may be traced in their interpretation as universals which are *instantiated* in particulars, substituting instantiation for Plato's image/copy/reflection terminology (and hence for his "Urbild–Abbild" conception; cf. Olof Alfred Gigon, *Platon: Lexikon der Namen und Begriffe* [Zürich, 1975]).

13 See Gregory Vlastos, "Reason and Causes in the *Phaedo*," in *Platonic Studies* (Princeton, N.J., 1973), pp. 76–110, at pp. 83ff.; also available in *Plato: A Collection of Critical Essays*, ed. Gregory Vlastos, 2 vols. (Garden City, N.Y., 1971), pp. 132–66, at pp. 139ff. The original version of this article appeared in *The Philosophical Review*, 78 (1969), 291–325.

14 As against Leonardo Tarán's position (*Parmenides* [Princeton, N.J. 1965]) and my own earlier view (see, e.g., *Being and Not-Being: An Introduction to Plato's Sophist* [The Hague, 1974], p. 69*n*9).

15 Not, however, a description of our cosmos. Parmenides parted company with the cosmological speculations of his predecessors: τὸ ἐόν is not to be identified with the universe — that is taken care of in the δόξα.

16 Cf. frag. VIII, 50ff.

17 At *Rep.* 478E Plato speaks of the objects of opinion as partaking of being and not-being (cf. 477A); they are and are not. "Partaking" here is not used in the technical sense applying to forms. Plato did not discover a "form" of not-being (= being other) prior to the *Sophist*, and since not-being is conjoined with being here, I conclude that neither is conceived as a form in this passage.

18 See my *Being and Not-Being*, § 10 and Appendix.

19 In the *Sophist* Plato sets out to prove that false judgments are possible with the implication that the images or semblances which the Sophist creates in discourse have real being (cf. *ibid.* § 7).

20 On my interpretation that being and essence are "but two sides of one coin" in Plato's ontology, I would not — as against W. K. C. Guthrie, *A History of Greek Philosophy*, 5 vols. (Cambridge, 1975), IV 493ff. — ascribe to him a doctrine of degrees of existence in abstraction from the nature of the existents concerned. Cf. Gregory Vlastos, "A Metaphysical Paradox," *Proceedings and Addresses of the American Philosophical Association*, 39 (1966), 5–19; and "Degrees of Reality in Plato," in *New Essays in Plato and Aristotle*, ed. Renford Bambrough (London, 1965), pp. 1–19. Both these essays have been reprinted in Vlastos, *Platonic Studies*, pp. 43–57, and 58–75, respectively.

21 Plato uses the terms interchangeably.

22 185C. In the words of Socrates, τὸ ἔστιν and τὸ οὐκ ἔστι, followed up by Theaetetus with οὐσία and τὸ μὴ εἶναι. I suggest that οὐσία be read here as being (εἶναι), not as essence or "Wesen."

23 Plato has included motion and rest (already mentioned at *Parm.* 129D) among his μέγιστα γένη. Although they are needed for the build-up of his argument, they are not at the same level as the other three. Their inclusion is justified in so far as between them they extend over the entire field of existence; anything which is either moves or is at rest.

24 Cf. R. S. Bluck, *Plato's Sophist*, ed. G. C. Neal (Manchester, 1975), pp. 119, 121.

25 They function like the vowels in the alphabet, which are responsible for the possibility of combining letters into syllables (253A). But vowels themselves are constituents of the syllables which result from their combining (and separating!) functions. Plato's use of the vowel analogy as well as his choice of the epithet "very great" for his metaforms tend to blur the difference in type towards which he works his way.

26 Though the inner complexity of the forms means that they no longer are Parmenidoid absolutes, it does not entail that they cease to be self-identical individuals. In contradistinction to the conception of Plato's middle period, forms now partake of both unity and plurality, a point not explicitly made in the *Sophist*, where unity and plurality have not been included among the μέγιστα γένη.

27 With the consequence that being is neither Heraclitean nor Parmenidean in essence. Cf. n. 23.

28 The reference is to the doctrine of the communion of forms; see p. 25 above.

29 The interpretation of not-being in terms of difference from other need not be considered here.

30 The form of difference is other-referring and, hence, anything which is different — i.e., participates in difference — necessarily participates in the form of "other-referring."

31 Existents here = forms. The entire section of the *Sophist* (251A–259D) is concerned with the structure of the world of forms.

32 It seems that Plato has now made his forms relatives, which may be hard to accept. Plato's range of relatives, however, is wide, from fractions and comparatives at one end of the scale to knowledge at the other: knowledge *καθ' αὑτό* is incomplete because knowledge is always knowledge of something. I feel that this is precisely how the newly discovered complexity of his erstwhile absolutes must have presented itself to Plato. As against *Crat.* 388Bf., forms as named are not completely understood and need to be defined in terms of their relations to other forms.

33 See H. F. Cherniss, "The Relation of the *Timaeus* to Plato's Later *Dialogues*," in *Studies in Plato's Metaphysics*, ed. R. E. Allen (New York & London, 1965), pp. 339–78 at pp. 350ff.

34 Plato never mentions them by name.

35 If the model itself had come to be, Plato would have been involved in an infinite regress. See R. E. Allen, "Participation and Predication in Plato's Middle Dialogues," *The Philosophical Review*, 69 (1960), 147–64; repr. in *Studies in Plato's Metaphysics*, ed. Allen, pp. 43–60, and in *Plato*, ed. Vlastos, I 167–83.

36 Cf. Cherniss, "Relation of the *Timaeus*," p. 354. I do not follow Cherniss in invoking 52D2–4 in this connection: "being, space and becoming, all three *exist* (*εἶναι*)." I read *εἶναι* = "there are" (Cornford), i.e., without ontological commitment. Becoming is one of the three factors but *qua* becoming.

37 I do not follow Cornford and others in identifying the demiurge with the world-soul. His is a task which alone a god can perform. (The rationalists of the seventeenth and eighteenth centuries invoked God for similar reasons.)

38 And thereby make them like himself (29E), we must add. Goodness appertains equally to the maker and to the model. The chaos of the *Timaeus* recalls Anaxagoras' *ὁμοῦ πάντα*, and mind here accomplishes what, according to Socrates' complaint (*Phaed.* 97f.), mind in Anaxagoras failed to achieve.

39 Since Plato in the *Timaeus* (see 37A) still considers soul as *ἀρχὴ κινήσεως* (the doctrine of *Phdr.* 245cf.), scholars have wondered how the discordant motion of precosmic soulless becoming could be explained. But since there has always been becoming, there must always have been motion. Chaos could not conceivably have been in a state of rest, for this would have assimilated it to being ("always in the same state"). The difference between chaotic and soul-engendered motion must be accounted for in terms of absence from the former, and presence to the latter, of mind and reason, and, hence, of order.

40 How far short of being, one wonders, does this transformed genesis fall? Have we not penetrated to a formal structure which can no longer be apprehended by the senses?

* I should like to express my gratitude to Professor M. Husain for her valuable comments on an earlier version of this paper.

3

The Doctrine of Being in the Aristotelian *Metaphysics* — Revisited

JOSEPH OWENS, C.Ss.R.
Pontifical Institute of Mediaeval Studies

I

WITHOUT CLOSE ATTENTION to the way this territory was originally mapped by Paul Natorp in 1888, the obstacles encountered by those who since have trodden its intricate paths prove difficult to understand. Nor will the really live issue at stake be appreciated. I have noted elsewhere how two distinct series of texts had been marked off by Natorp in Aristotle.[1] One set, as he sketched the terrain, made the primary philosophy (later called metaphysics) deal with the most universal and most abstract of objects, that is, with being in general. The other set of texts made it bear on the highest and most excellent type of being, that is, on divine being. In the philosophical perspective from which Natorp viewed these two objects, they appeared as "mutually exclusive opposites." One was general; the other, particular. Any attempt to make them coincide would usher in an "intolerable contradiction." In this Wolffian framework of general and special metaphysics, the difference between the two objects came to lie between the one which was most empty of content and the one which was the richest and most perfect of all. Natorp's map made the line of demarcation between them a barrier which rendered unicultural melding impossible.

That was the original map of the terrain upon which a now almost century-old conflict of views has been carried on. It is, accordingly, a modern conflict, sustained by the modern concern about content or lack of content in the notion of being. Actually, the long tradition of Greek commentators had failed to notice the drastically divisive cleft which stood out in the late–nineteenth-century cartography. The landscape had presented a relatively serene picture for centuries, offering a unitary conception of metaphysics. It was the science of the divine, the science of the primary instance of being, thereby treating universally of all beings. Furthermore, the medieval writers, in spite of deep divergencies in their own respective viewpoints, continued to regard the Aristotelian metaphysics as a unitary science. Was the double object, then, an optical illusion on the part of Natorp? Or was it there from the start as the result of a natural upheaval in the primordial crust, a fault which had gone unnoticed and unmapped by his predecessors, yet which kept cutting off their entry into the genuine pastures of Aristotelian thought? How was it to be dealt with? Left as it was sketched by Natorp, its two mutually contradictory phases barred effectively any entrance into what should be a fertile and habitable terrain.

Five main lines of explanation became prominent in the seventy-five years (1888–1963) which followed Natorp's original visit. His own solution was sweeping: Excise all the theological passages as later additions by Platonically inclined editors. The theological obstruction is thereby totally removed, and the way opened completely to what subsequent writers have correctly labeled, from Natorp's Wolffian background, the "ontological" view. The terrain is thereby made safe for full ontological exploitation.[2]

The second line of explanation was sketched vividly by Eduard Zeller in immediate (1889) reply to Natorp's critique. The two phases are indeed mutually contradictory, but have to be left there. The ontological and the theological aspects lie at the very root of Aristotle's metaphysical object. They both pertain to his notion of *οὐσία*. Excision of certain texts, therefore, cannot remove the theology.[3] Zeller's acceptance of Natorp's map leaves both the ontology and the theology intact, and clashing with each other in mutual contradiction. That situation, apparently, is something not to be worried about on Aristotelian terrain, from the viewpoint of this conception of Aristotle's thought. It leaves his metaphysics radically hopeless.

The third and perhaps most widely known explanation is the chronological theory developed so brilliantly by Werner Jaeger. As with Zeller, the two contradictory accounts remain in the *Metaphysics*. Both belong authentically to Aristotle, but to different stages of his philosophical development. According to this reading of the map, then, the two openly contradictory phases present no hindrance to intellectual entry into the Aristotelian territory. Their chronological separation prevents any clash. Rather, the map at last opens the way to genuine understanding of the Stagirite.

The fourth main line of interpretation lies in the view of Aristotle's philosophy as essentially aporematic. The two contradictory phases are found in the problematic faced by Aristotle, and never rise in his thought above the dialectical level. Neither can function as science. As a result, the *Metaphysics* "seems to oscillate unceasingly between an inaccessible theology and an ontology incapable of saving itself from dispersion."[4] The *Metaphysics*, accordingly, is but the detailed account of a failure, and is to be valued only for its humanizing influence. This view of the terrain, sketched in attractive fashion by Pierre Aubenque (1962), accepts the dichotomy of Natorp's approach. Rated as sciences, one conception would exclude the other. But, in point of fact, neither is present in Aristotle as a science. Both the one and the other are effectively eliminated from the level on which Aristotelian thought has traditionally been prized.

These four approaches all remain within the contours sketched by Natorp. As outlined by him, the problem gives both ontological and theological passages to be accounted for in the Aristotelian text. Natorp excised the theological; Zeller retained both in admitted reciprocal contradiction; Jaeger defended the authenticity of both but assigned them to different chronological stages; and Aubenque eliminated both as sciences but accounted for their presence in the text as dialectical problems. A fifth main line of explanation bypassed the framework in Natorp and vindicated the traditional interpretation of the Greek commentators. It maintained that there never had been an ontology in the Aristotelian texts,[5] but only a theology which dealt universally with all beings *qua* beings. Both sets of passages signalized by Natorp describe one and the same science, a theology. Not only is the primary philosophy a unitary science, but it is unitary in the sense of a theology only, and not as a unified combination of ontology and theology. The meaning is that there is no ontology there to enter into the structure of the science. Its object, the nature of being, being *qua* being, is a definite nature — namely, substance. The object is ultimately the primary instance of substance — namely, separate substance. The nature of being is not an object which can be abstracted from any random instance, as the nature "man" may be abstracted from Plato or Aristotle or any other singular of the species. Rather, the nature of being is the nature of its primary instance, which is seen by reference in every other instance. There is, accordingly, no ontological phase to be excised or to be retained or to be located chronologically or to be reduced from scientific to dialectical status. There is only the theology from start to finish. Its object is a definite nature, not an abstraction from random instances. But because only it is the science which has the nature of being as its object, it alone is the one which is equipped to treat universally of all beings.

This defense of the traditional Greek cartography needs, of course, to offer an explanation of the way the notion of ontology forced its way into Aristotelian discussions. Historically the task is not difficult. Wolff's distinction of ontology from natural theology had conditioned the teaching of philosophy in the schools during the eighteenth and nineteenth centuries.[6] It had become the only way in which pre-Kantian metaphysics was viewed. It had been taken for granted by Kant in the Copernican revolution meant to overthrow traditional metaphysics.[7] No other approach to Aristotle at the time of Natorp could be expected. From this perspective the optical illusion of an ontology in Aristotle was practically unavoidable. In Aristotle there was explicitly a science of being *qua* being which dealt universally with all beings. The only science which fitted this description at the time was ontology. Hence the mirage of an ontology in his writings.

From these considerations the radical distinction of the traditional Greek interpretation from the other four should become sharp. There is no question here of accepting Zeller's basic position that both an ontology and a theology are present in Aristotle, with an effort to show that they are compatible. On the contrary, it means there never was in reality an ontology in Aristotle. The ontology reported there turns out to be only an optical illusion on the part of those who accept Natorp's mapping of the territory. Nor is it a question of words or labels. Whether "ontology" or *metaphysica generalis* or any other term is used, as long as it designates a science the object of which is in some way other than the object of theology, the rejection is the same. The study of being *qua* being, as commenced in sensible things, has to be a theology from start to finish. It is this conception, not the designation, which is at stake.

These five positions, each in its own way an extreme, circumscribe quite adequately the available options. They form a recognizable and comprehensive circumference in relation to which the views expressed during the last three decades may be investigated and assessed.

II

The lively discussions during the 1950s and '60s remained in one way or another within this pentagonal ambit.[8] There were sharp critiques of different views, ecumenically minded efforts to soften the barriers between various conceptions, and defenses of one or the other under appropriate conditions or restrictions. First, a look at the '50s. In Spain Salvador Gómez Nogales, in a comprehensive coverage of the area (1955), saw three parts or sides in the Aristotelian metaphysics. One, the etiological, was the means for reaching the supersensible. The second, the exclusively theological, dealt with the properties of supersensible being. The third, the ontological, used a procedure of analogy to study the principles and properties of being wherever it is found. This "theological–ontological fusion" assures for Gómez a unitary metaphysics, but is compromised in

Aristotle by the reliance solely on final causality to link the sensible with the supersensible order, a task for which the efficient causality of creation is required.[9] Like Zeller's, this interpretation recognizes the presence of both an "ontological" and an "exclusively theological" procedure in the Aristotelian metaphysics; but unlike Zeller's, it regards them as compatible and not as mutually contradictory. Basically, it finds the two philosophical procedures in Aristotle, but seeks to conform the duality with the unitary conception of metaphysics established in the tradition. It is, accordingly, a compromise rather than a basically new interpretation, and in this way remains within the contours of the pentagonal territory just sketched. But it manifests a tactic which continued to be used extensively in earnest and penetrating efforts towards a unitary interpretation during the ensuing fifteen years.

In Italy Ambrogio Manno found (1957) similarly that Aristotle had identified ontology ("general metaphysics") with theology ("an entirely particular science"), raising but not solving the problem of their identity, though he had the theory of the causes and principles in a mediating position between the two.[10] In France Louis-Bertrand Geiger endeavored (1957) to smooth out the sharp contrast between the ontology and the theology by applying the overall Scholastic doctrine of abstraction in a natural procedure from being *qua* being through mobile substance to immobile substance, and from the study of substance to theology.[11] His attitude shows sensitivity to the restrictions involved in Natorp's outline of the problem, but at the same time accepts being *qua* being as an object which is not completely identified with the object of theology. It serves rather as the initial steppingstone to it. In Belgium Augustin Mansion saw (1958) against the background of the Scholastic three degrees of abstraction the science of the immaterial taken up in some way under the metaphysics of being *qua* being, allowing Aristotle (through a desire for unity but at the sacrifice of absolutely rigorous exactitude) to affirm that the primary philosophy is also the universal science.[12] In Germany Simon Moser regarded (1958) theology and ontology as necessarily belonging together in Aristotle, with the ontology depending on the theology, but with the problems both of the necessary union and of the dependence left in a rather aporematic state.[13] In a different way Willy Theiler looked upon (1958) Aristotle's *Metaphysics* as left incomplete after six stages of development, with a general metaphysics born of dialectic, and with a universally extensive theology based on natural philosophy. The theology reached a peak allowing the inference that God contained all the natural forms, but Aristotle himself shied away from drawing the ultimate conclusions.[14] In a still different fashion Hans Wagner saw (1959) specifically Aristotelian thought joined with characteristically Academic views in the concept of the primary philosophy, and though he found the situation badly mixed up and almost discouraging, he regarded Merlan's return to the traditional Greek interpretation the best course which had yet been offered.[15]

This brief survey of the new writers on the topic during the last half of the '50s shows an all-pervasive tendency towards a unitary view of the Aristotelian metaphysical doctrine. Yet there is hesitancy or express uncertainty in regard to the success of a viable union between ontology and theology in Aristotle, with a couple of attempts to go outside Aristotle for the means to make the union satisfactory. Chronological stages were called upon to render the divergencies more palatable; ontology was made dependent in different ways on the theology; less rigorous canons for the union were allowed; the nature of both the union and the dependence was regarded as left in an aporematic state; or Academic infiltration was invoked to account for the difficulties experienced when preference was given to the traditional Greek understanding of the topic. In one or more of these ways all five basic interpretations, except for Natorp's violent excision of texts, continued to exercise their influence during this period. Natorp's dichotomy into ontology and theology in the texts, of course, remained, and caused the trouble and uncertainties and hesitations. Even before Aubenque's articles and books the technique of leaving the crucial questions in a state of aporia was employed. Apart from the rejection of Book *K* on the part of some, the integrity of the generally received Aristotelian writings was respected, and the overall desire for a unitary interpretation prevailed. But the conviction that this unity could be satisfactorily shown within the Aristotelian context itself was none too strong.

III

The 1960s, in contrast, witnessed a succession of convinced, carefully meditated, finely detailed, and deeply penetrating defenses of the thoroughgoing union of ontology with theology in the Aristotelian *Metaphysics*. There were, as may be expected, deviators here and there. First, then, a quick look at two dissidents. Leo Lugarini, approaching (1961) the theme under certain Heideggerian and phenomenological influences, found that Aristotle did not identify ontological with theological science, since theology is a *particular* science which neither eliminates nor absorbs but presupposes and helps to articulate the *universal* science of being *qua* being.[16] The two sciences accordingly remain separate but cooperative. Much more drastic is Ingemar Düring's estimate (1966) of the situation. After a survey of the controversy he still finds the contradiction in the Aristotelian text as clear as it had appeared to Natorp and Jaeger. He asks why any attempt should be made to explain it away. It is far better to admit that Aristotle is trying to fuse together two different conceptions of the primary philosophy, and then to account for the conflicting conceptions by the Stagirite's change of view in different chronological stages of his development. Düring does not see in the Aristotelian text any statement to the effect that theology deals with the universal.[17] This is obviously an intensification of the situation as Jaeger saw it, and of developmental stages as its solution. The ontology and the theology remain different pursuits, separated from each other in concept as well as in time.

But the overwhelmingly dominant motivation among new writers on the topic during this decade was the search for a unitary understanding of the *Metaphysics*. Günther Patzig in an important article on the question at the beginning of the period (1960) showed that the Aristotelian theology *precisely as a theology* is able to be a universal ontology, and that, conversely, the Aristotelian ontology *precisely as an ontology* must be essentially and principally theology. The reason is the one given by Aristotle himself: namely, that the divine substances are the primary instance of being. Patzig calls this notion of ontology a paronymical ontology, because the instances are paronyms. In the later stage of Aristotle's development, Patzig finds that this type of ontology passed over into an analogical ontology, in which the identity of the object in the procedure is guaranteed, not by an identical primary instance, but by the identity of the relation to it in the instantiations.[18]

This approach has the merit of seeking a thoroughgoing solution within the Aristotelian context itself. No appeal is made to outside philosophical conceptions. Patzig deftly touches the sensitive nerve of the difficulty. The Aristotelian text, taken at its face value and without any watering down, requires that theology precisely *qua* theology must treat universally of being *qua* being. But with Patzig the double aspect plotted out by Natorp still remains. One can say, conversely, that the Aristotelian ontology *qua* ontology is a theology. How has this situation come about? A little reflection, Patzig maintains, shows that two distinct conceptions of ontology have been introduced into the discussion. Neither of them is identical with the original Wolffian ontology the object of which had been shown by Natorp to exclude effectively the object of theology. For Patzig the object of the ontology is completely identical with the object of the theology.

Quite obviously, the term "ontology" is now designating a type of science radically different from the type whose object could not be identified with the object of theology, apart from open contradiction. Patzig's paronymical ontology deals, in fact, with an object of maximum content, with the definite type of being which Aristotle calls *οὐσία* and in which he locates the nature of being. It clearly is not an object of minimum content ranged in like fashion over all the particular types of being, in the way the object opposed to the object of theology had been understood in Natorp's original mapping of the terrain. Make the two objects identical from the start, and the problem disappears. But may the term "ontology" be conveniently used in this perspective? Is it not deceptive? Does it not continue to create an illusion as long as it remains? It insinuates that there is in Aristotle a universal science of being which can initially be regarded as in some significant way different from theology. But it is the acceptance of this initial presupposition, even for the sake of discussion, which generates open contradiction in the Aristotelian procedure. Only by refusing completely to acknowledge any ontological cast in the Aristotelian being *qua* being from the start can the genuine unity of that procedure be successfully upheld. Even a toe allowed inside the door will continue to prevent the closing of a case against duality in the Stagirite's metaphysical thought.

This seems the appropriate place to discuss the feasibility of retaining the term "ontology" in the context while radically changing its meaning. Patzig's discussion offers a clear use of the term in different senses. One sense would be that in which ontology is, *qua* itself, theology. May it not legitimately be given that sense? May it not be allowed a use in which it becomes an entirely interchangeable term for philosophical theology?

Words are of arbitrary imposition. If general acceptance should be given to a sense of "ontology" as "philosophical theology," the question would be settled. But that does not seem to be the case at present. No matter how much the various ontologies may eventually become concerned with problems about God, not Paul Edwards' *Encyclopedia of Philosophy* (s.v.), not the *Enciclopedia Filosofica* (s.v. *Ontologia*), not *The Oxford English Dictionary*, seems aware of a use in which "ontology" is synonymous with "philosophical theology." Rather, "being *qua* being" is regularly considered a different object from divine being. In the Wolffian schematizing, the distinction is clear-cut, and in recent conceptions of ontology the term bears on being which is not *a* being, that is, on a notion of being which does not coincide with any one of its instances. The notion of ontology therefore can hardly be regarded as a general concept which has theology as one of its species. At most the term would have to be an umbrella device covering any science which purports to treat universally of all beings. But at present that use to cover a theology does not seem to be established. To introduce it without further ado or explanation in this particular area can hardly help but carry with it the implication of an object which differs in some relevant way from the divine being. It is hard to see how this does not render the Aristotelian problem insoluble from the start.

As it is, Patzig's "paronymical ontology" is, in fact, a "universal theology" in Aristotle, because of the way things are called beings through reference to a primary instance. The designation "paronymical" holds in its Aristotelian sense for the models of "healthy" and "medical," and perhaps, with some reservations, for *οὐσία* as a paronym (from *ὄν*) of the Greek "being." But it is more difficult to regard "primary *οὐσία*" as a paronym of *οὐσία* itself. However, these are merely technical considerations. With Patzig's "analogical ontology," though, greater difficulties arise. If the identity is placed in the relation of the various secondary instances to the primary instance, it can hardly escape having a univocal character. It would make being (*ὄν*) as neat an object for ontology as the visible world (*κόσμος*) is for cosmology, soul (*ψυχή*) for rational psychology, and God (*θεός*) for natural theology. In a word, the philosophical universe would again be safe for exploitation in the Wolffian framework. Rather, the Aristotelian model for focal reference, "healthy," calls for significant difference of relation in the various kinds of secondary instances. In food, it means cause of health; in exercise, preservative of health; in good color, sign of health. The relation is far from identical in these different occurrences. Patzig's "analogical ontology" can scarcely be regarded as a later development growing out of the "paronymical ontology." It requires an entirely new approach. It abandons the focal reference framework, and finds the aspect of being in an identical proportionality which all beings without exception are somehow supposed to exhibit. It is disappointing that Patzig's article lacks a more detailed explanation of the way this analogy functions, in contrast to mathematical proportion. But a similar attempt may be seen in detail later in the decade.[19] Patzig's motive seems to be the wish to keep the problem within "the realm of possible experience" (p. 204).

In Italy Giovanni Reale in a comprehensive study (1961) of the *Metaphysics*[20] upheld the basic unity of thought ("omogeneità speculativa," p. 1) throughout the treatises, in a primary philosophy which has four different aspects. These are "aitiologia" or "archeologia" (science of the first causes or principles), theology, ontology, and ousiology (the science of substance). It is in the last of these that the other three perspectives are opened up, and their applications included (p. 314). But how is the notion of ontology understood in this context? It is carefully distinguished from both the seventeenth-century and the phenomenological conceptions (pp. 312–14). It is basically an ousiology (p. 33), for the *ὄν* rests squarely on the *οὐσία* ("si reduci esattamente all'altra," p. 312). Again, the ontology envisaged is not the study originally introduced into the controversy, the study of an object with minimum content. Rather, the object exhibits all the richness of *οὐσία* in its various definite and complex significations. The object is divine, the universal cause of all things, the object of a universal theological science.

Similarly, Enrico Berti at first (1965) maintained the strictly unitary character of the Aristotelian wisdom. The science has its ontological and its theological aspects.[21] Its unity is brought about by the Aristotelian reference of being, first to substance in general, and then to the primary or immobile substance, God (p. 147). Later (1970) Berti expressed dissatisfaction with his own earlier interpretation, on the ground that for Aristotle the relation between God and other beings is different from the relation between sensible substance and the other categories, insofar as God as transcendent cannot provide an object for human science. To this allegation, however, may one not reply that separate substance seems regarded as a demonstrated conclusion in Book *Λ*, and is not left as a problem? In the Aristotelian context, accordingly, Berti's hesitation does not seem sufficiently grounded.

In Germany Hans Joachim Krämer was, in general, in accord (1967) with a unitary interpretation, but sought to tone down the seemingly harsh-sounding statement that being *qua* being means the divine being.[22] He proposed as a middle way the stand that being *qua* being appears in its purest form "in der ersten Sphäre" (p. 350*n*126), but is also present in the others. If "in the first sphere" should mean the whole order of the separate substances, this view would coincide in its general lines with the interpretation that being *qua* being is found in separate substance as in its primary instance, and in sensible substance and in all the categories of real being as in secondary instances. It must be insisted that the correct interpretation of being *qua* being is essential to the solution of the whole problem, for the solution ultimately depends on whether being *qua* being is understood as possessing maximum or minimum content. On this point Krämer's view is developed against the background of the Academy's "derivation system" (pp. 350–51). The Aristotelian doctrine here is according to him to be understood *only* in the way the elements-metaphysics provides.[23] Accordingly, separate substance would be first in rank, but not necessarily the nature to which all other instances are oriented as the accidents are to sensible substance. Hence Krämer can hold that this problem is not necessarily involved in the question of the unitary character of the primary philosophy. On that stand, of course, there is disagreement with the view that separate substance specifies the Aristotelian primary philosophy and thereby gives it its unity. Rather, with Klaus Oehler, the content of the primary οὐσία is to be regarded as somehow replete with the content of all being whatsoever.[24]

The tendency to make philosophical theology identical with ontology was pursued (1969) in an exceptionally interesting way by the Finnish scholar Lauri Routila.[25] His instructive monograph, replete with penetrating insights into the relevant issues, unites comprehensive coverage of the problem with close study in detail. In its conclusion (pp. 142–43) it agrees that for Aristotle the general science of all being always led back to the science of form. But it interprets this to mean that while the theological superstructure remained the same throughout, the ontological substructure changed from categories *logically* independent of one another (p. 138) to something new: namely, the πρὸς ἕν conception (pp. 124, 143). The new ontology is identical with the theological pursuit (p. 142). It is an onto-theology. Accordingly, in it the two different ways of presenting the science — namely, as ontological and as theological — are not at all contradictory. But the ontological cast remains intact in the final version of the primary philosophy. In this way Routila's interpretation is meant as a *Gegenthese* (pp. 10, 103) to the understanding of the expression "being *qua* being" in a way which excludes all ontology from the *Metaphysics*.[26]

Routila wishes to avoid the Wolffian *metaphysica generalis*, which ceases to function in Aristotle (p. 120). He finds in him two preliminary conceptions of the study of being in general. One is the science of the first principles as under discussion in Book *A* of the *Metaphysics*. The other, found in the *Organon* without clear outlines, is dialectic (p. 97). Dialectic is not a science in the strict Aristotelian sense, because it does not deal with a single genus and because it does not proceed from established principles (p. 98). Yet it is open to metamorphosis ("Umbildung," pp. 100–101; cf. p. 143) into a general science which bears upon a single genus. The transformation takes place through an application of the πρὸς ἕν notion of being, made possible by the *qua* approach. In this approach the "all things" which formed the object of the preceding pursuits were regarded under just one aspect — namely, "being" — to the exclusion of all other viewpoints (pp. 116–20). The development involved was from a cosmological ("meta-physical,"[27] p. 143) to an ontological ("meta-dialectical") science. Dealing in this way with a genus (οὐσία, pp. 125–26) and proceeding from first principles (pp. 129–36; cf. p. 140) the primary philosophy as an onto-theology is indeed a universal science of being (pp. 125–26).

This carefully thought-out development theory on Aristotle's changing interests makes the final stage meta-dialectical, offering an attractive explanation for Aristotle's lack of interest in existential questions about being. But by the same token does it not make being *qua* being an abstract object, open to the objections against the Wolffian *metaphysica generalis*? In failing to identify that object with a definite type of being, does it really leave enough content to serve as the object of a science? Does it not continue to regard the universal notion of being as distinct from the notion of any one of its instances?

Routila (p. 120; cf. pp. 103–104), in fact, alleges that the stand which he opposes denies the understanding of the primary philosophy as a universal science of being in Book *Γ*. But is not the alleged denial rather a conclusion drawn by Routila himself through his requirement of an ontology for this universal science?

What is to be thought of this allegation? Surely nobody would seriously think of denying the universal character of the primary philosophy as presented in Book *Γ*, and as explicitly reaffirmed in the crucial passages at *E* 1, 1026A30–32 and *K* 7, 1064B6–14. Routila's named opposition here would certainly be at the contrary pole of any desire to claim ("behaupten," p. 120) that the Aristotelian theology is not a universal science of being. A universal science of being does not have to be an ontology. Conversely, to reject an ontology is not to reject the existence of a universal science of being. Even though an ontology is never proposed in the Aristotelian text, the way is wide open there for a philosophical theology which treats universally of all things, under their aspect of being. In this Aristotelian context an ontology would be a science which has as its object a notion of being in some way other than the divine being. The presence of that type of science in the *Metaphysics* is what the late Philip Merlan denied in the passage quoted by Routila (p. 103). The question is about its actual presence there. Does the notion of an ontology in fact form part of the "unitary problematic" (p. 120) faced by Aristotle? Is the notion at all implied by his use of the formula "being *qua* being"? Further, is it even compatible with the problematic which actually confronted him?

Routila (pp. 104–20) gives an excellent analysis of the formula "being *qua* being" in conjunction with the adverbial bearing of the Aristotelian term *καθόλου* and with the notion of the phrase *per se*. He shows convincingly that the first element in the formula — namely, "being" (or, in the plural, "beings" — 1003B15–16, 1005A27, 1005B10; cf. *K* 4, 1061B6, 1061B9) — means "whatever has being" ("ein jedes *ὄν*," p. 109). The second element — namely, "*qua* being" or "*qua* beings" — focuses on the notion under which the being or beings are here considered. But after this painstaking and exact analysis, Routila concludes that being *qua* being in its Aristotelian sense cannot be regarded as identical with *οὐσία*. His reason (pp. 120–21) is that this would be understanding being *qua* being as a thing (cf. "ein Ding," p. 110) instead as of a formal structure.[28]

Can this reason be sustained in a close examination of the Aristotelian text? Is not the basic question at issue here whether the nature (*φύσις* — 1003A34, 1003B14, 1003B23; cf. 1003A27) *by which* (*qua*) things are called beings is a universal notion with minimum and perhaps no content, or a real nature with maximum content? *Τὸ ὄν*, as is clear from *Γ* 2, 1003A33, means the multiplicity of things which constitute the realm of being. It signifies the things which are called beings. *Οὐσία* is one of those definite things. But that same *οὐσία* is the nature by which all are called beings. In the phrase, the *qua* bears upon a real definite nature, not a notion taken immediately from any haphazard individual instance of being. It is not obtained in the way "man" is taken from Socrates and Coriscus. Rather, something is a being insofar as it expresses the definite nature of *οὐσία*, a genus (1004A4–5; cf. Routila, p. 125) of beings. Each of the two elements in the phrase "being *qua* being" accordingly denotes a thing, contrary to Routila's explanation.

Routila acknowledges that the background furnished by the *Categories* does not offer Aristotle without further ado ("nicht ohne weiteres," p. 120) the possibility of an object for the science of being. One can readily agree. In *Met.*, *Γ* 2, 1004B20, the predicate "a being" is accepted as common to all things, yet not as "universally and identical over all" (1005A9) but through reference to a primary instance. In the actual problematic the universal notion of "a being" does not confront the mind immediately in the manner of a generic object from the categories, as would "man," "animal," "soul," or "body." That possibility had in point of fact been excluded by Book *B* (3, 998B22–27; cf. *APo.* II, 7 [92B12–14]) in the demonstration that being is not a genus. Book *Γ* makes no attempt to counter or weaken the demonstration when it faces the problem. Instead it shows in its second chapter that the requirement for the object of a science (*γένος* — 1003B19, 1003B22, 1005A26) can be satisfied by a nature to which other instances have reference in various ways. The object here is indeed a genus, the first of the categories, even though the other instances of being do not come under it in strictly generic fashion.

What is the "nature" in the case of being? It is shown to be *οὐσία*, in the sense in which *οὐσία* is the first of the categories in contrast to the accidents, and accordingly a *γένος* in this context. So, while being is not a genus, the nature which constitutes it the object of a science is in fact a genus. Further, however, and still in Book *Γ* (3, 1005A35), the object of the primary philosophy is located in the primary substance, that is, the substance prior to the kind dealt with by the philosopher of nature. This can mean only separate substance. The philosopher who deals with it is thinking in universal scope (his "inquiry is universal and deals with primary substance"[29]).

Does not this mean clearly enough that the "nature" by which a thing is called a being is substance and ultimately supersensible substance? It is not a "one-over-many" aspect but a definite nature to which all other beings have reference. Something is a being insofar as it expresses that nature, at least by reference. *Qua* being, the thing either is substance or has reference to substance. The *qua* signifies this bearing on substance. The whole phrase "a being insofar as it is a being" means in this setting a being insofar as it exhibits the "nature" of substance. Since *οὐσία* is what constitutes being the object of the science, may not Aristotle without hesitation use the terms *οὐσία* and "being *qua* being" interchangeably (compare 1003A31–32 with 1003B18–19) to designate that object? May he not on occasion use "being *qua* being" (*K* 3, 1061A8–10) instead of *οὐσία* for the subject of the accidents, or for all the categories insofar as they make possible both truth and accidental predication (*E* 4, 1028A3–4)? And since the primary instance is separate substance, may he not all the more use "being *qua* being" (*K* 7, 1064A29) to characterize it, and state (*E* 1, 1026A29–31) that the philosophy treating of it proceeds in universal fashion? On all three levels is not "being *qua* being" used quite as *οὐσία* would be used?[30] No difficulty whatever seems felt by Aristotle in regarding the two as interchangeable, even though the occasions are few in number. The possibility is there, because in the *Formalstruktur* of the phrase both the elements denote things.

The "unitary problematic" of Books *Γ* and *E* as well as of the central books of the *Metaphysics* is in this way fully respected by the identification of *οὐσία* and being *qua* being. The unitary problematic actually confronted is the status of being as an object which is, not univocal, but expressed in various ways of reference to a single nature. That is the problematic traced back by Aristotle (*N* 2, 1089A2–15) as far as Parmenides.[31] So approached, the science of being *qua* being is inevitably seen as the science of the primary instance of being. If the highest science is about separate substance, the science is accordingly a philosophical theology. That follows from an examination of a unitary problematic. In finally locating the science as a theology, the examination gives rise spontaneously to a concluding aporia. How can the science of a definite nature treat universally of all beings? In both *Γ* and *E* the answer, as is to be expected in the light of preceding development, is given very briefly. The science proceeds universally because of its primary status.[32]

No extraneous element, then, has been introduced into the problematic to give it a direction different from its intrinsic tendencies. From Routila's viewpoint, the alien insertion of the meaning *οὐσία* into being *qua* being comes from current translations of the opening sentence of Book *Γ* in which one has "simply presupposed" ("schlicht vorausgesetzt," p. 109) that being *qua* being means a thing to which something else can belong. Rather, as has just been seen, this notion of being *qua* being follows naturally from the one problematic. Routila (p. 36; cf. pp. 12–14) has shown convincingly that the thesis of two *contradictory* conceptions of the primary philosophy is a postulate and does away with the real problem. But does not his own insertion of an ontology, whether contradictory to or compatible with the theology, break the factual and verifiable unity of the Aristotelian problematic? The problematic as actually faced left no room for conceiving being as a genus. It could not allow entrance for being as the object of an ontology. It is a unitary problematic which accepts being as a single object through focal reference to a definite nature, *οὐσία*, and not as an object located immediately in the nature of each and every one of its instances.

In the actual problematic it seems impossible to accept Routila's claim that the *qua* formula as such has no reference to the theme of *οὐσία* ("keinen Hinweis auf die *οὐσία*-Thematik," p. 121), or that being *qua* being has in its interpretation as *οὐσία* no rational bearing on *all* things ("in keiner vernünftigen Beziehung auf das *πάντα* steht," p. 109). Rather, the primary status of *οὐσία* in this context makes it bear on *all* other beings in a way which fully satisfies Routila's further requirement that "diese Wissenschaft *allgemein* von solchem handeln soll, was allem gemeinsam ist" (p. 107).

These considerations, in fact, allow full agreement with the conclusions expressed by Routila (p. 121) in the last paragraph of his seventh chapter, even though those conclusions are understood in so different a way. "Being *qua* being" does express a *Formalstruktur.* It can be used by Aristotle in place of *οὐσία.* Beings which are not substances are being only because of their bearing on substances. A First Philosophy of being is possible for Aristotle only through a consideration of being in the *qua* fashion. One can fully agree with all these conclusions of Routila's and at the same time maintain both that the notion of an ontology is nowhere to be found in the actual Aristotelian problematic, and that the unity of the problematic is broken by the insertion of that historically (cf. above, n. 2) much later notion. It is also interesting to note contrast between analogical stage in Routila and in Patzig. For Patzig (see above, n. 18) the "analogical ontology" is the last stage in Aristotle's development, while for Routila the analogy phase belongs to the earlier dialectic, anteceding the science of being.[33]

The question whether being *qua* being is restricted to substances or also includes being in the other categories was faced the following year (1970) by Eckard König.[34] His view (pp. 232–33*n*9) was that the question seems quite idle when the other categories are regarded as bearing upon substance and every science as occupied with the necessary properties of its genus. Yet is not the whole problem just to explain that point?

IV

The 1960s, accordingly, maintained a dominant theological tendency. But with the '70s, views again became dispersed. In 1971 Heinz Happ[35] discussed the many views in the controversy at considerable length, insisting (p. 311*n*2) that "ontology" in this Aristotelian context has nothing to do with "'Ontologie' à la Christian Wolff usw." With this in mind, he was able to say that the theological approach is correct, but because of its one-sidedness does not do justice to the "Komplexität des Textbefundes" (p. 394; cf. p. 480 *nn* 83–84). Against this background he required (pp. 395–99) the presence of an ontology in the *Metaphysics*. But since the theological interpretation by no means requires that being *qua* being be restricted ("ausschliesslich," p. 395) to separate substance, but on the contrary in the Aristotelian setting of focal reference that it extend to all being, thereby having content (p. 399), Happ's explanation seems to be divergent only in its use of the term "ontology" to describe the aspect of universal extent inherent in the Aristotelian primary philosophy.[36]

A corresponding agreement, though from a different approach, was renewed[37] by Salvador Gómez Nogales in 1972.[38] Having shown "the profound meaning of Aristotelian metaphysics with its theory of universal teleology" (p. 333), the author concluded that "primary substance is universal since it contains the perfection of the rest. The main argument, therefore, for intrinsicality is not dependence on efficient causality but the prior containing of a universal exemplarity" (p. 338).

Two other studies published the same year (1972) tended, however, to be noncommittal on the topic while allowing a theology to develop from an ontology. Leo Elders[39] was content to remark:

> There is every reason to assume that Aristotle at first tried to establish a general science of being along the lines of Academic thought. This first philosophy dealt with the essence of things. . . . It is possible, or perhaps even likely, that in this general science of being, that part of it which was devoted to the study of these first principles was somewhat singled off and was on the way of becoming a theology [p. 72].

In this way the theology was regarded as developing within the general study of being, or of a "Platonic ontology" (p. 73), showing through a text which had been retouched. Likewise Werner Marx,[40] after surveying the discussions (pp. 69–80), concludes that "die letzte Erfüllung der Ousiologie die Theologie ist" (p. 81), after having shown that "die aristotelische Ontologie ihrem Sinne nach eine Ousiologie ist" (ibid.). Although the Aristotelian philosophy is regarded as aporematic rather than systematic, there appears a necessary connexion of thought between the ontology and the theology (p. 82). Again, an ontology is seen as developing into a theology.

Different, however, was the attitude of still another study published the same year (1972). Karl Bärthlein[41] reviewed the state of the controversy (pp. 111–53) but under the presupposition (p. 113) that the answer is already determined on systematic philosophical grounds before the question is even approached in the Aristotelian texts. The only problem is whether or not Aristotle correctly conformed to that predetermined framework. What is to be thought of Bärthlein's approach? Implicitly this attitude may be detected, of course, in commentators who approach the Aristotelian problem from Scholastic or Kantian or Hegelian or Heideggerian backgrounds. But here it is, in Bärthlein, explicitly asserted. The objection to it is that Aristotle is forced into a philosophical framework which is not his own, and is judged by philosophical principles which he cannot be expected to accept. With Bärthlein being *qua* being "can be established only as the correlate of a primitive knowing" (p. 203). Accordingly, it is of minimal content and cannot be identified with the divine. It can be the object only of an ontology, not of a theology. Elaborate textual critique of *E* 1 and *K* 7 rejects the passages which describe theology as the science of being *qua* being (pp. 114–47). The case that in Aristotle himself the science of being *qua* being is only an ontology and not a theology is thereby completed.[42]

The following year (1973) Eugene E. Ryan, concluding that "we cannot foist the paradoxical doctrine of pure form on Aristotle," found that the refusal to see an "'ontological' conception" of the primary philosophy in Aristotle stems in great part from "attributing the pure form doctrine" to him.[43] The reasoning, of course, rules out any theology which would have the requisite meaning to function as a science of being *qua* being. It implies that there can be no theology in Aristotle, since there are no separate forms to be its objects.

Finally, Walter Leszl in 1975 made an all-out effort in a long book[44] to establish an autonomous ontology in Aristotle. He described ontology as "a universal science of being" (p. 21), autonomous in the sense that it is not "subordinated to theology" (p. 22), and meant by it "a clarification of certain conceptual structures of our intellectual apparatus (esp. of language)" (p. 2; cf. p. 402). It turned out to be "a sort of logic, taking this word in a rather wide sense" (p. 540). It neither required nor excluded "a theological principle of the whole" (p. 22). He laid special stress (pp. 22,

176–90, 550) on the objection[45] that the theological interpretation makes ontology consequential upon theology, and excised (pp. 550–52) the passages in Book *K* which run counter to his thesis. The meaning of the text at the end of *E* 1 is watered down to fit the conception of an autonomous ontology.

Leszl's position, unlike the one just noted in Ryan, does not imply the exclusion of theology from Aristotle. It merely makes theology irrelevant to the problem. There is no need to bother about it, since its presence or absence in Aristotle has no bearing upon the problem of the object of metaphysics. This is not an outright return to the stand of Natorp, though it does resemble Natorp's method in excising the texts in *Metaphysics K* which are in opposition. Likewise it is not a reversion to a fully Wolffian ontology for interpreting the Aristotelian text. Rather, it is a deliberate move towards a logic in the fashion of mid-twentieth–century analysis as the means of understanding the Stagirite's metaphysical thought. So it does not exactly mean the return of a circle to its starting point in Natorp's excision of the theological texts, after having swung through the high points of theological dominance during the '60s. But it does represent a further step in attempting to interpret the Aristotelian metaphysics in the light of a philosophy which happens to enjoy popularity at the moment, as the Wolffian ontology did in the mid-nineteenth century.

Leszl's understanding of "focal meaning" is discussed at considerable length in his *Logic and Metaphysics in Aristotle*.[46] But he cannot see it providing the universality required for metaphysics as the science which treats of all beings: "What would be erroneous is to suppose that there is a recourse to focal meaning, in *Metaph. Γ*, to establish the universality of the science of substance with which metaphysics should be identified" (p. 532). This stands in rather sharp contrast with Routila's stand that even in regard to separate being the universality of the separate substances, from the thematic viewpoint, is something which explains itself ("eine Selbstverständlichkeit," pp. 123, 124) according to Aristotle's conception. Once the separate substances have been established as the primary instance of being, Aristotle, in the light of the already mentioned notion of predication through reference to a primary instance, can state so briefly that the science treating of it treats universally of all beings. The universality in this sense comes only last, after the separate substance has been established. Hence, one can work out "die eigenen Betonungen und Antriebe der aristotelischen Problemstellung" (Routila, p. 104) without presupposing that the science of separate substance is the science which treats of being universally. Different scholars keep reading the texts carefully, yet continue to disagree radically about their meaning.

V

This rapid survey shows that the troubles occasioned by Natorp's map have not yet come to an end. The territory is still being explored vigorously. There is still lively struggle with its problems. The only adverse symptom noticeable is a touch of battle fatigue, in a tendency to dull the basic issue at stake. Does the situation correspond to the mentality of casual opera-goers who sit through *Tristan und Isolde* with mild interest but without realization of the depth of meaning back of the lines and notes?

That query brings to the fore the motive of the inquiry. What real importance has the whole question? Why wear out so many typewriter ribbons about it? What is actually involved?

The modern problem began when Natorp set the contrast between a science which ranged in equal fashion (" . . . gleichermassen übergeordnet")[47] over all the other sciences of beings. The science of the highest being was not at all excepted. This can mean only that the universal science has for its object a notion of being which abstracts from all its instances. It envisages an ontology in the full sense of the term as used in Wolff and Kant. It makes the Aristotelian primary philosophy bear upon "the most abstract of whatever can be the object of scientific investigation."[48]

But what happens if one tries to obtain that type of concept when the object is being? You can abstract the common nature "man" or "humanity" from Socrates and Plato just as readily as you can abstract the notion "politician" from Liberal and Conservative, Democrat and Republican, hawk and dove. You have then the abstract nature "man" as an object for study, with everything human as its content. You can go further and abstract the nature "animal" from man and horse, obtaining a concept with all the plenitude of sense life as the object of study. Similarly, you can abstract the notion "living thing" from animal and plants, and the notion "body" from the animate and the inanimate. In each of these cases there is an object with ample content for philosophical investigation. But, at each stage, the content of the object lessens as its extent increases. Yet the process does leave content in each. But what happens when you finally try to extend the object without restriction to all beings?

Actually, a surprising situation arises. In the previous abstractions you have always left something out which serves as the subject of which the notion is predicated. The individuating differences of Socrates and Plato were left out of the object "man." The specific differences of man and animals were left out of the object "animal," and so on. In each case the differences characterized a subject of which the abstracted object could be immediately predicated. But what happens when you come to the all-embracing notion "being" which leaves nothing out? As Aristotle (*Met.*, *B* 3, 998B22–27) insisted, being is predicated of all its differences. If the differences did not have being, they would be nothing. They would not be able to function as differences. As differences, they cannot be immediately conceived apart from being.

Since being already contains its differences, it has to be predicated of them, and it is thereby barred from strictly generic status. A genus in the strict sense cannot be predicated precisely of its differences. Plato and Socrates are men, but the individuating differences which distinguish the one from the other are not men. A man and a horse are animals, but their specific differences are not animals. Yet every difference is a being of some kind. The result is that being not only has the widest extent, but *for that very reason* somehow has the richest content. By extending to everything without exception, it includes the subject of which it is predicated. Perhaps that may be what is meant by "toppling the Porphyrian tree"[49] or by "the intension of extension" in the unique logical type found in "being."[50] Aristotle expresses the tenet by saying that being, unlike a genus, is predicated of its differences. But whether expressed that way, or in the dictum that the Porphyrian tree on reaching its summit is overturned to the fullness of its base, or in the notion that the fullness of extension necessarily involves the fullness of intension, the meaning is that being contains in some way all its differences and is accordingly the richest of all objects.

But can this happen when you try to regard being as abstracted from its differences in the way "man" or "animal" or any generic object is abstracted? A close scrutiny, like that of Hegel,[51] shows that it lacks all determination and therefore coincides with the concept "nothing." For Kant,[52] ontology could have no given objects. In consequence the notion of being has been regarded as an empty concept, an utter blank, a surd, a non-predicate, with the demand that the very term "being" be banished from the vocabulary of philosophy.

The really important issue at stake, then, is the understanding of being in such a way that it can function as the object of the science of metaphysics. For this task the nature of being needs content — in fact, maximum content. To regard it as abstracted from random instances, in the way the nature of man or the nature of animal is abstracted, is to view it as an object without any content whatsoever. By locating the nature of being in its primary instance, *οὐσία*, Aristotle has made metaphysics bear upon a definite genus, the first of the categories. By further regarding the primary philosophy as a theology, he is seeing in its object the fullness of actuality, the most complete perfection. The object is the richest of all in content.

For those who do not care overmuch about metaphysics, or who consider it a phantom pursuit, blacking out its object may not seem anything like a disaster. But for those who strive to continue in the long Western tradition which has come down from Parmenides, Plato, Aristotle, and Plotinus, the question is really important. Moreover, for those who are interested in seeing metaphysics serve as the handmaid (Philo's simile) of revealed doctrine and wish to *understand* as far as possible the God who gave his proper name as *I am who am* (Ex 3:14), a fully developed and meaningful science of being is of the highest moment.

Objections to regarding metaphysics in this way have become standard. The oldest in the context of Natorp's map is that the science of one definite type of being, the divine, has an object which is particular, not general, and therefore *excludes* the other particular types of being. This has been answered sufficiently in the course of the present essay. The science which treats of the nature of being, found identified with its primary instance, is the science which deals universally with everything in which the aspect of being is found, that is, with all things whatsoever. This objection is comparable to the stand in ethics that Aristotle's intellectual contemplation cannot be complete *εὐδαιμονία* because it does not include the other types of goods.[53] As it is, both richest context and widest extent characterize the object of Aristotelian metaphysics. It enjoys the best of both worlds.

Another objection is that for Aristotle being is studied in sensible things before it can be studied in its highest instance, separate substance. This procedure should mean that the first object which the science studies is sensible being, and only derivatively and subsequently does it extend its knowledge to the immaterial beings. The answer which should emerge from the foregoing investigation is that wherever you encounter being, you encounter an object which is found in its own nature only in separate substance. In the sharp contrast of being with becoming, as seen in the Greek background from Parmenides through Plato, being was what did not become or change. The qualities, quantity, relations, and activities keep changing, yet they have being. The being is the substance of which they are accidents, for the substance endures while changing in those accidental ways. But sensible substances come into being and perish. The being which is seen in them is found to the full extent of its nature in separate and eternal substance. In that way the being which is studied from the start in sensible things is the nature of separate substance.

Again, it has been asked how Aristotle can be seeking the "principles of being *qua* being" (*Met.*, *Γ* 1, 1003A27–32) or "of beings *qua* beings" (3, 1005B10–11). The same difficulty has to be faced when he says that if *οὐσία* is the primary instance, "the principles and causes of *οὐσίαι*" (2,

1003B18) have to be had. The one principle actually pursued in the context is the first principle of demonstration, the principle that a thing cannot be and not be in the same respect at the same time. Insofar as a thing is a being, to that extent does it manifest this aspect of necessity found in the primary instance of being. The procedure is from the sensible composites to their substance as cause and principle, and then to the primary substance (3, 1005A35) in its universal scope. In this setting it seems quite compatible to regard the object of metaphysics as substance or being *qua* being, and yet say that one is seeking the principles of substance or of beings *qua* beings. In a word, the primary instance is the object of the science and serves as principle and cause to whatever comes under the science.

Finally, there is the objection that this interpretation makes ontology dependent on theology. But in this interpretation, as the preceding analysis has insisted, there is no ontology in Aristotle to be dependent on the theology or on anything else. The interpretation allows no room for the nature of being as an abstract object, as would be required by an ontology. To take "ontology" in a special sense here in which it would coincide with philosophical theology would be to destroy the terms of reference as outlined on Natorp's map.

In conclusion, then, this revisit strengthens the stand that the science of being *qua* being in Aristotle is a theology only. The survey of the '50s has shown the commentators branching off in various directions, hesitant and indecisive. In the '60s the tendency was strong towards a unitary interpretation of the Aristotelian primary philosophy, in spite of a subtrend towards leaving it in an aporematic and divided setting. With the advent of the '70s, there was a return to the view of an ontology independent of theology. It may be hoped that this relapse will be but temporary. In maintaining that being was predicated of all its differences and therefore could not function in the generic manner required for the object of a science, and that the object of the universal science of being is a definite genus, substance, Aristotle set the tone for an abiding tradition in Western metaphysics. He did not pursue the topic as far as it demands. He has left lots of scope for future work on it. But in giving it the direction which he did, was he not definitely on the right track?

NOTES

1 *The Doctrine of Being in the Aristotelian Metaphysics*, 2nd ed. (Toronto, 1963).

2 About the meaning of the term "ontology" in its original setting, see José Farrater Mora, "On the Early History of 'Ontology,'" *Philosophy and Phenomenological Research*,

24 (1963), 36–47. See also the editor's introduction to Wolff's *Philosophia prima sive ontologia*, ed. J. Ecole (Hildesheim, 1962), pp. vii–xviii. On the Wolffian divisions of metaphysics, see Christian Wolff, *Preliminary Discourse on Philosopny in General*, trans. Richard J. Blackwell (Indianapolis & New York, 1963), pp. 39–46, nos. 73–79.

3 "Bericht," *Archiv für Geschichte der Philosophie*, 2 (1889), 270–71.

4 ". . . la science sans nom . . . semble osciller sans fin entre une théologie inaccessible et une ontologie incapable de s'arracher à dispersion" (Pierre Aubenque, *Le problème de l'être chez Aristote* [Paris, 1962], p. 487). See my review of the book in *Gnomon*, 35 (1963), 459–62.

5 "There never was any *metaphysica generalis* in Aristotle" (Philip Merlan, *From Platonism to Neoplatonism*, 2nd ed. [The Hague, 1960], p. 208). This remark remains unchanged from p. 180 of the first edition, published in 1953. Merlan (p. 209; first ed. p. 181) expresses in a footnote general agreement with my interpretation of the object of Aristotelian metaphysics, in spite of some disagreement in regard to the causality of the supreme sphere. Merlan acknowledges a "rift" (p. 210; first ed., p. 182) in Aristotle's description of the subject matter of metaphysics, noting four possibilities of explaining it and concluding that it was immaterial "in the present context" (p. 212; first ed., p. 184) which of the four was accepted. The context was the development to Neoplatonism. For Merlan's views on the objects of Aristotelian metaphysics, see also his "Metaphysik: Name und Gegenstand," *Journal of the History of Ideas*, 77 (1957), 87–92, and "*Ὂν ᾗ ὄν* und *πρώτη οὐσία*: Postskript zu einer Besprechung," *Philosophische Rundschau*, 7 (1959), 148–53.

6 On the implications of the Wolffian conceptions for the direction of Western metaphysics, see Etienne Gilson, *Being and Some Philosophers*, 2nd ed. (Toronto, 1961), pp. 108–21.

7 See *Kritik der reinen Vernunft*, B 16–17, B 36–37.

8 See the survey in Giovanni Reale, *Il concetto di filosofia prima e l'unità della metafisica di Aristotele*, 3rd ed. (Milan, 1967), pp. 322–76, and my discussion in *Doctrine of Being*, pp. 13–26.

9 *Horizonte de la metafísica aristotelica* (Madrid, 1955), p. 239. "Relaciones puramente teleológicas" (ibid.) join the material to the immaterial order.

10 *Valore e limiti della metafisica aristotelica* (Naples, 1957). For "metafisica generale" and theology as "una scienza tutto particolare," see p. 8. Cf. "Aristotele, benchè lo abbia posto, non riesce a risolvere il problema, e identifica l'uno con l'altra" (p. 10), and "mediatrice tra i due è la theoria delle quattro cause con tutti i rimanenti principi trascendentali riguardanti l'essere sensibile" (p. 11).

11 "De la question de l'être en tant que tel à la substance, de la substance mobile aux substances immobiles, de l'ousiologie à la théologie le passage est naturel. Le problème serait tout différent dans la perspective d'une ontologie générale, ou d'une science des êtres parfaits" ("Saint Thomas et la métaphysique d'Aristote," in *Aristote et saint Thomas d'Aquin* [Louvain & Paris, 1957], p. 200).

12 "Philosophie première, philosophie seconde et métaphysique chez Aristote," *Revue Philosophique de Louvain*, 56 (1958), 209.

13 "Nach unserer Interpretation könnte es doch so sein, dass einerseits die Frage nach dem Ganzen des Seienden und seiner Ursache und andererseits die Frage nach dem Seienden als Seienden notwendig ursprünglich Frageansätze sind und beide notwendig zusammengehören. . . . Aristoteles ist im ganzen weniger Systematiker, als man weithin glaubt, und mehr Aporetiker. . . . Auf die Frage der notwendigen Einigung beider, das heisst der Abhängigkeit der Ontologie von der Theologie . . ." (*Metaphysik einst und

jetzt [Berlin, 1958], p. 11*n*12; cf. pp. 10, 40–42). This tends rather strongly in the direction later preconized by Aubenque.

14 The final stage allowed by the sequence of thought but not developed by Aristotle is a metaphysics based not so much on mobile nature as on immaterial form: "Entsprechend umfasst Gott alle natürliche *εἴδη*, und sich selber denkend . . . denkt er diese *εἴδη* und ist als Summe aller zweckvollen Formen das höchste Gut" ("Die Entstehung der Metaphysik des Aristoteles mit einem Anhang über Theophrasts Metaphysik," *Museum Helveticum*, 15 [1958], 100). This would place the whole knowable content of sensible being in separate substance, at least if taken at its face meaning. But for Theiler the *Metaphysics* as it stands contains "eine Metaphysica specialis et generalis, eine *πρώτη φιλοσοφία* die zugleich *καθόλου* ist" (p. 89). Even though dialectic itself is not a science, it is able in his interpretation to serve as mother to the *Metaphysica generalis* (p. 91).

15 "Zum Problem des aristotelischen Metaphysikbegriffs," *Philosophische Rundschau*, 7 (1959), 129–48, esp. 145, 147.

16 *Aristotele e l'idea della filosofia*, 2nd ed. (Florence, 1972), p. 266. The first edition appeared in 1961 (see p. 252).

17 "Wozu dient ein Versuch, diesen klaren Widerspruch wegzudisputieren? Ist es nicht besser einzuräumen, dass Aristoteles hier zwei Auffassungen vom Gegenstand der Ersten Philosophie zu verschmelzen versucht?" (*Aristoteles* [Heidelberg, 1966], p. 599). For a survey of the controversy, see pp. 594–96.

18 ". . . Ontologie gerade *als* Ontologie wesentlich und vornehmlich *Theologie* sein muss" ("Theologie und Ontologie in der 'Metaphysik' des Aristoteles," *Kant-Studien*, 52 [1960–1961], 197). Also: "nicht wie bei der paronymischen garantiert durch die Identität eines Beziehungspols, sondern durch die Identität der Beziehung selbst" and "wir können sie als den Übergang von einer paronymischen Ontologie zur analogischen Ontologie characterisieren" (p. 205). On Aristotle's requirement of difference in word ending for paronyms, see *Cat.* 1, 1A12–15).

19 See below, nn. 30 and 33. On Klaus Kremer's explanation (1961) in the setting of the Greek commentators, see below, n. 53.

20 "In conclusione, la teologia è scienza universale, perchè ha come oggetto la causa universale o la causa di tutte le cose" (*Il concetto di filosofia prima e l'unità della metafisica di Aristotele* [Milan, 1961], p. 314). There was a second edition in 1965, a third in 1967 (see above, n. 8).

21 ". . . la distinzione che abbiamo fatto in precedenza tra aspetto ontologico e aspetto teologico della sapienza, ovvero tra ricerca e possesso pieno" (*L'unità del sapere in Aristotele* [Padua, 1965], p. 111. A survey of the various views is given in Berti, *La filosofia del primo Aristotele* (Padua, 1962), pp. 51–56. In "La Nouvelle Métaphysique d'Aristote," *Akten des XIV. internationalen Kongresses für Philosophie* (Vienna, 1970), v 453–55, Berti announced the change in his tenets. The influence of Aubenque was noticeable: "la métaphysique n'aboutit pas à un échec, à un naufrage; mais, puisque cette solution dépasse le cadre de l'expérience, donc celui même du discours sur l'être, elle n'est jamais objet de science et, par conséquent, la métaphysique reste problématique" (p. 454).

22 "Zur geschichtlichen Stellung der aristotelischen Metaphysik," *Kant-Studien*, 58 (1967), 313–54.

23 "Diese 'Erstheit,' aus der die Allgemeinheit zwingend folgt, ist nur von der spezifischen Reihenbildung der Elementen-Metaphysik her zu verstehen" (p. 350). From this viewpoint "Owens' und Merlans darüber hinausgehende und heftig discutierte These . . . ist mit der Frage der Einheit der 'ersten Philosophie' nicht notwendig verbunden"

(p. 350*n*126). Krämer finds the *καί* at *Met.*, *K* 7, 1064A29, as "nicht explikativ, sondern spezialisierend gebraucht" (ibid.). This, though quite possible grammatically, is not necessarily required by the context. The "identifizierend" meaning is preferred by Heinz Happ, *Hyle* (see below, n. 36), in dealing with Krämer's suggested interpretation, though maintaining that the latter does not affect his own position that the ontological component should not be reduced to the "theologische" (p. 410*n*491).

24 "Der Terminus *πρώτη οὐσία* als Bezeichnung der Transzendenz hat aber noch eine zweite Bedeutung. Er bezeichnet daneben in singularischer Weise Gott, den Ersten Beweger, und zwar als den Inbegriff der Transzendenz — und im begründend umfassenden Sinne als den Inbegriff alles Seienden überhaupt" ("Die systematische Integration der aristotelischen *Metaphysik*," in *Naturphilosophie bei Aristoteles und Theophrast*, ed. Ingemar Düring [Heidelberg, 1969], p. 173).

25 *Die aristotelische Idee der ersten Philosophie: Untersuchungen zur onto-theologischen Verfassung der Metaphysik des Aristoteles*, Acta Philosophica Fennica 23 (Amsterdam, 1969).

26 I.e., it opposes "die im Anschluss daran angestrebte Ausscheidung einer ontologischen Interpretation" (p. 103). Routila seems to take for granted as an unquestioned presupposition that a science treating universally of beings has to be an ontology.

27 Routila (pp. 18–20) regards the designation "metaphysical" as prejudicial in the direction towards a Platonic tendency. He himself uses "First Philosophy" for the Aristotelian science, with "theology" ("Theologik") and "ontology" denoting its respective sides. Under the umbrella designation "First Philosophy," however, it does not seem possible to find any term which would be absolutely neutral to "ontology" and "theology." If the notion "First" in it is meant to bear upon the most abstract of notions, it can hardly bear at the same time on the object which is richest of all in content.

28 Yet because it signifies a *Formalstruktur* "kann Aristoteles es auch so verwenden, dass es anstelle von *οὐσία* tritt" (Routila, p. 121; cf. p. 109). From this standpoint the problem is what being *qua* being meant *at first* for Aristotle. Routila uses the Husserlian notion "bracketing" ("Einklammerung," p. 118) for what is excluded by the *qua*. But here the "bracketing" of other *viewpoints* does not necessarily imply the "bracketing" of anything in the *object* which sets up the viewpoint in question. *Qua* being (or in "Form als solcher," in the sense of the object of the primary philosophy, mentioned by Routila, p. 98), no intelligible aspect should be excluded from the object. *Qua* mobile, there is addition — namely, of unintelligible matter — to the form. But again no category is excluded, even though the object now does not extend to supersensible substance. Only in mathematics, where sensible matter is excluded, is there question of "bracketing." The *qua* indicates the thing to which reference is made — e.g., mobile nature, quantity, or being — but of itself does not imply either adding to or subtracting from. Against the deep Parmenidean background, is not what was hovering (cf. Routila, p. 107) before Aristotle's vision as he wrote the opening chapters of Book *Γ* rather the specter of a being which absorbed all its differences and determinations, and in this way included them all? That was what being meant in the Parmenidean setting, and what should be expected to enter into the Aristotelian problematic under the caption "*qua* being."

29 *Met.* 1005A35, in *The Works of Aristotle.* VIII. *Metaphysica*, trans. W. D. Ross (Oxford, 1928).

30 *Οὐσία* is used at times by Aristotle for accidents; see, e.g., *Met.*, *H* 2, 1043A24 and *De Anima*, II 1, 412B13. Routila (p. 139; cf. pp. 83–84) gives a good explanation of this in terms of analogy — an analogy, however, which is not sufficient to ground a science of being.

31 The more immediate background is to be sought in the doctrines of the Academy. See Hans Joachim Krämer, *Der Ursprung der Geistmetaphysik* (Amsterdam, 1964), pp. 140–91; Routila, pp. 127–30. Against this total background the question of how the science of being *qua* being is the science which treats universally of all being is far from a *Scheinproblem* (Routila, p. 103); nor is the proof for the tenet superfluous (ibid., p. 121). To grasp the first principles of being *qua* being (*Met.*, *Γ* 2, 1003A31–32), may be expressed as having the principles and causes of *οὐσίαι* (1003B18–19), and the reason is that all other beings (1003B15–17) depend upon *οὐσία* as the primary instance of being and through it are designated as beings. Proof has to be given that all other beings in fact depend upon immaterial substance as upon a primary instance, and that they can be called beings only through their reference to it. This proof is far from easy or obvious.

32 *Γ* 3, 1005A35–1005B1; *E* 1, 1026A29–32 (*K* 7, 1064A11–14). As may be seen from this order, there is no reversal ("Umkehrung" — Routila, p. 104) of the traditional sequence of Books *Γ* and *E* in the appearance of the tenet that the primary type of substance, with which the primary philosophy deals, is beyond the type dealt with by the natural philosopher.

33 Routila, p. 143; cf. pp. 83–84, 139.

34 "Aristoteles' erste Philosophie als universale Wissenschaft von den *ἈΡΧΑΙ*," *Archiv für Geschichte der Philosophie*, 52 (1970), 225–46.

35 *Hyle* (Berlin, 1971), pp. 310–460.

36 "Die zutreffende Deutung liegt gleichsam in der Mitte: ein 'erfüllter' Seinsbegriff, dessen Massstab und 'Inbegriff' die göttliche Substanz ist" (ibid., p. 399).

37 See above, n. 9. In the article cited in the following note, Gómez maintained that his book proved the "survival of a teleological metaphysics à la Plato in every stage of the evolution of Aristotle's thinking" (p. 339).

38 "The Meaning of 'Being' in Aristotle," *International Philosophical Quarterly*, 12 (1972), 317–39.

39 *Aristotle's Theology* (Assen, 1972).

40 *Einführung in Aristoteles' Theorie vom Seienden* (Freiburg i. Breisgau, 1972).

41 *Die Transzendentalienlehre der alten Ontologie* (Berlin, 1972).

42 See my review of Bärthlein's book in *Archiv für Geschichte der Philosophie*, 57 (1975), 217–22.

43 "Pure Form in Aristotle," *Phronesis*, 18 (1973), 222–23.

44 *Aristotle's Conception of Ontology* (Padua, 1975).

45 The position may be seen in Moser; see above, n. 13.

46 (Padua, 1970), pp. 83–450.

47 "Thema und Disposition der aristotelischen Metaphysik," *Philosophische Monatshefte*, 24 (1888), 49.

48 Ibid., 39.

49 This apt expression came to me from a colleague in conversation. As I could not ascertain his own understanding of it, I am repeating it in the sense that being, which is placed at the top of the Porphyrian tree, belongs with equal truth at the bottom.

50 Martha Husain, "The Question 'What is Being?' and Its Aristotelian Answer," *The New Scholasticism*, 50 (1976), 293.

51 *Logik*, no. 87.

52 *Kritik der reinen Vernunft*, B 873.

53 This stand has recently been defended by John M. Cooper, *Reason and Human Good in Aristotle* (Cambridge, Mass., 1975), pp. 90–177. The two types of universality as expressly distinguished in the Greek commentators need to be kept before one's mind

in these questions. Klaus Kremer noted this clearly in regard to the problem of being: "dass die Theologik, in dieser Weise als allgemeine Wissenschaft verstanden, sich nicht mit der ersten Bedeutung von 'allgemein' (= allgemeine Seinslehre) deckt" (*Der Metaphysikbegriff in den Aristoteles-Kommentaren der Ammonius-Schule* [Münster, 1961], p. 207). The alleged contradiction, Kremer maintains, arises only from a modern approach (p. 206), for the tradition of the Greek commentators saw no opposition between the two sides (pp. 209–16). Rather telling against the background of Natorp's map is Kremer's assertion that Aristotle's query (whether theology treats universally of being *qua* being) is meant to *set aside* rather than to bring out a contradiction: "Die Aporie . . . macht den Widerspruch nicht noch sichbarer, sondern beseitigt ihn" (p. 204).

4

Aspects of Ancient Ontologies

JOHN P. ANTON
Emory University

INTRODUCTION

A PHILOSOPHICAL ACCOUNT of theories of predication must regard it necessary to go beyond the examination of the logical issues related to problems of the form or structure of propositions. To be complete, such an account must exhibit the deeper connections between the theory itself and the conceptual framework within which true and false statements function as ontic disclosures. But more importantly, the account must include an accurate delineation of the ontology on which a given theory of predication rests.

For the limited purposes of this essay, I shall assume that types of ontology and predication are intimately related in systems of categorial thought. Therefore, it would seem that in order to offer a philosophical account of a categorial system one must also inquire into its corresponding theory of being. In this essay I plan to discuss certain basic aspects of ancient ontologies by way of emphasizing what genera of being each ontology considers ultimate and irreducible. Furthermore, I shall try to explain the significance which such genera have and the place which they occupy in the logic of predication.

Before proceeding with the main theme of the discussion, it is important to introduce at this point what I think is a much needed distinction between a theory of categories and a theory of genera of being. The basic function of a theory of categories is to establish and defend modes and canons of correct attribution in elemental sentential forms. In contrast, a theory of genera of being seeks to identify the fundamental types of things which are said to be and to make explicit the ways in which instances of such types are connected either as distinct individuals to their classes or as structural and functional wholes in which integral parts inhere in determinate patterns. The conflating of these two distinct philosophical enterprises, as many interpreters of ancient thought have done, especially in the case of Aristotle's logic and ontology, is simply the result of a reductionist thesis, and as such stems from a serious misunderstanding of Aristotle's doctrines. If my proposed distinction has theoretical merit, it may prove rewarding to undertake a fresh examination of the relationship between ontology and categorial thought, between being and discourse as we would say today, or if one prefers another comparable distinction, between reality and language.

The scope and breadth of the topic are such that I am compelled to exclude from my account any discussion of Plato's views on the highest genera or a treatment of the problem of being in Presocratic cosmologies. There will be occasion to refer to the Presocratic thinkers and also to Plato, but only insofar as the argument requires. The general plan is to inquire into certain fundamental aspects of the relationship of being and predication in the philosophies of Aristotle, the Stoics, and Plotinus. More specifically, I intend to show that their distinct ontologies require correspondingly distinct categorial theories. Because of the complexity of the problems, the present essay is primarily meant to serve as a statement of position accompanied by the bare essentials of a supporting argument.

The Aristotelian Account

In this essay I am taking the position that Aristotle has drawn a clear distinction, in the treatise which has come down to us under the title *Categories*,[1] between a theory of being and a theory of categories. It is a distinction which almost every major interpreter of his thought has either overlooked or opted not to consider beyond the point of mere notice. The theory of categories seems to have been designed in response to the need to correlate predication and existence. The central problem which Aristotle had to solve was how to formulate the canons which language must observe to reflect accurately the complex ways in which the existential exemplars of the ultimate genera of being are disclosed in experience.

Κατηγορεῖν, I shall argue, is the verb Aristotle uses as a technical term to indicate acts of predication. It is one of a number of expressions which he uses to cover specific operations in the process of constructing well-formed and significant statements.[2]

It is generally agreed that the verb *κατηγορεῖν* originally referred to the legal act of accusing. Aristotle has preserved this use of the verb in the *Rhetoric*.[3] But he was also the first to use the derivative noun *κατηγορία* in a technical sense in his logical works and theoretical writings, especially the *Metaphysics*. Yet the *Metaphysics* contains no special essay devoted to an investigation of the foundations of categorial theory; nor is there in the *λεξικόν*, i.e., Book *Δ*, a chapter or an entry for "category," although there are chapters discussing particular genera of being. But to return to the verb itself, its technical meaning is "to predicate" or "to assert something of something."

The thesis which I am defending here claims that for a proper analysis of Aristotle's categorial theory we must be as careful as possible not to use interchangeably the Greek words we consider to be equivalent to our expressions "predication" and "predicate": *κατηγορία* and *κατηγόρημα*.[4]

"Category" is also used to cover the extended meaning of the term which Aristotle did not include in his account in the *Categories*: modes or figures of predication, *σχήματα τῆς κατηγορίας*.[5] These modes or figures presuppose the sorting of well-formed statements of attribution and in accordance with criteria derived from the inquiry into the ultimate genera of being. The genera, ten in all, are given in the list in the *Categories*, 1B25–27, but the detailed discussion of the grounds on which the distinctive types of being rest was evidently reserved for the science which he was to call First Philosophy. Thus although only the typology of basic forms of predication is presented in a general and preliminary way in the *Categories*, the more theoretical aspects were not discussed until the investigations in ontology were well under way. Still, the *Categories*, although an early work, provides the reader with a useful set of terms and distinctions which on the whole will be preserved with slight modifications and used in the extended explorations which Aristotle undertook into the relationship between discourse and being. With this in mind, we may proceed with some observations on how Aristotle builds his theory in the *Categories*.

By way of ontology, his principal concepts in this work are that (*a*) the meaning of the term "being" is equivocal, and we can talk only about the genera of being, not of being as such, in the sense that it can mean an all-encompassing genus of all genera; (*b*) the genera of being are divided into two basic groups, *οὐσίαι*, substances, and *συμβεβηκότα*, co-incidentals, whereby the latter can *be* only in the sense that they inhere in and are properties of the former; and (*c*) the genus of substance presents a problematic side to it and hence demands that we distinguish its primary sense, which denotes whole and unified individuals, from its secondary meaning, which stands for the species and genera of individual substances.

Κατηγορεῖται, "to be attributed as a predicate," is a key verb which Aristotle introduces as a technical expression in the *Categories* only after he has made a number of important distinctions so that we may be clear about the functional limits of our signifying words and expressions. The signified beings, depending on what they are and how we name them by virtue of our acts of naming, form three distinct groups and are called (*a*) homonymous, (*b*) synonymous, and (*c*) heteronymous. These identifications are needed in order to avoid errors in reference and in correlating the entities signified. Furthermore, before we can proceed to perform correctly in cases of attribution we must note how our words and expressions can issue signification either in combination as complex meaningful units or without combination: κατὰ συμπλοκήν, ἄνευ συμπλοκῆς.

As it turns out, statements can only be cases of the former; the latter type covers all simple expressions which denote instances of single predicates as well as nouns which signify substances. The remainder of chapter 2, 1A20–1B9, is given to a presentation of the four fundamental ways in which significant terms referring to beings can or cannot belong to the beings of which the former are predicated and in what manner. Reference and attribution are thus tied to the ultimate modes in which experience declares things can be:

1. Some things *are said* of a subject but *are not* to be found in any one in particular.
2. Some things *are in* a subject but *are not said* of any subject.
3. Some things *are said* of a subject and *are in* a subject.
4. Some things *neither are in* a subject *nor are said* of a subject.

Καθ' ὑποκειμένου λέγεται and ἐν ὑποκειμένῳ ἐστί are the two basic referential types of signifying beings in relation to the limits of attribution. Together they provide the requisite criteria for determining the ontological and the logical contexts of the subjects, the ways in which they can be distinct and the conditions under which they converge. They are the guideposts we must obey, first to identify the referents of our uncombined expressions, and, even more importantly, to recognize them as the source of the rules according to which simple referential units can combine properly to yield attributive assertions.

With chapter 3, we have a clear-cut canon of veridical attribution, anticipating the special case of why and how secondary substances are predicated of primary ones (chapter 5). The canon obtains on the condition that the uncombined expressions denote things which are synonymously related, i.e., share in the name and the definition of substance. In its sweeping application, the canon will include the area of definitive attribution. It reads: "When one thing is predicated [κατηγορεῖται] of another, all that is predicated of the predicate will be predicable also of the subject" (*Cat.* 1B10–12).[6]

The canon itself does not say which uncombined expressions can or cannot appear in the predicate position. First, we need to be presented with a complete list of the ultimate genera of being under which all uncombined expressions with referential force are classifiable. The objective of chapter 4 is thus (*a*) to present such a list; (*b*) to stipulate the conditions which must be met for significant utterances to serve as carriers of truth or falsehood; and (*c*) to prepare the ground for identifying the significant uncombined expressions which can never function as predicates. The last item is of decisive importance since it leads to the determination of the genus of being which alone can serve as the ultimate subject in all meaningful discourse. After the list of significant uncombined expressions is presented — viz., substance, quantity, quality, relatives, place, time, position, possession, acting, and undergoing — the section ends on the following note:

> Each of the aforesaid cannot be spoken of as an affirmation; it is only by way of combining one with another that an affirmation is made. For it seems that every affirmation is either true or false, whereas none of the uncombined expressions by itself can be either true or false, as, for instance, "human being," "white," "runs," "wins" [*Cat.* 2A7–10].

Aristotle's general position in the *Categories* is quite clear. Once the genera of being are shown as constituting two groups, the genus denoting substance and the genera comprising the entire domain of co-incidentals, we have what elementary discriminations are needed to guide us in making systematically correct statements. Having the power to speak is one thing; making correct statements which accurately reflect the order which prevails in the domain of being is quite another.

Κατάφασις is Aristotle's term for "affirmation."[7] In order to qualify as a correct affirmation, an assertion must comply with the order of things and satisfy the rules of syntax. On the whole, the logical function of a categorial theory is to identify the norms of syntax and to formulate the canons of correct attribution. To meet the demands of this task, the theory must exhibit the logical range of predicates with the aid of a complete inventory of the ultimate genera of being. The end result of Aristotle's inquiries in this area was a set of categorial schemata or figures, i.e., a finite set of types of attributive statements conforming to canons which regulate the corrigibility of each predication.

All predicates, whether they signify co-incidentals as inhering features of primary substances or the species and genera predicable of such substances, ultimately refer back to substance in the primary sense: the primary and ultimate subject of predication. In the absence of explicit canons, neither the truth nor the falsity of attributive statements can be decided with certainty.

Λέγειν, "to speak meaningfully," once it reaches the complex level of *κατάφασις*, "affirmation," needs further control, which can be achieved only with the aid of predicational rules, the rules attended to in *κατηγορεῖσθαι.* These requirements are introduced since referential precision is often compromised not only because of the great variety of possible affirmations, but mainly because of the syntactical properties of certain uncombined expressions. Insofar as they are nouns and signify any of the diverse kinds of being other than primary substance, they too can occupy the subject position. Affirmations as such are not self-clarifying. This is what precipitates the transition from *κατάφασις* to *κατηγορία.*

The canons of correct predication derive their validity from the ontology which underlies the referential claims of the uncombined signifiers. A category therefore is not merely an affirmation. To be more exact, it is a predicative statement which has met all the requirements of correctness by reflecting the existential conditions of inherence and non-inherence. This, I take it, is the hitherto neglected part of the technical meaning of *κατηγορία.*

In light of this wider and technical use of *κατηγορία,* Aristotle wrote the treatise *Categories* not for the purpose of offering an elementary inventory of the ten ultimate genera of being, together with a simplified account of signifiers or predicates corresponding to the denotative range of generic terms. Reservations such as the above have led me to the conclusion that it is a serious mistake to conflate the ten categories and the ten genera of being. Such a conflation makes no sense at all — to say nothing about being a conspicuous redundancy.

The *Categories* states explicitly well-attested Aristotelian doctrines, chief among them (*a*) that the types of being are signified by a variety of uncombined expressions, and (*b*) that *τὸ ὄν,* being, cannot be regarded a supreme genus encompassing all the other genera. Aristotle has made it plain enough that there can be no more than ten genera of being: one is substance, and the other nine kinds signify co-incidentals. However, when one turns to his *Metaphysics* for further information on the question "What is being?" one cannot help but wonder whether Aristotle did not mean to introduce more types of being.

Metaphysics, Book *A,* 982B9, states that wisdom is the study of first principles, and Book *Γ,* 1003A26, refers to causes of something in respect of its own nature. This something is *τὸ ὄν* itself. Hence, the inquiry which he called First Philosophy may be understood to presuppose being in this new sense, though it concentrates on the whole on the study of principles and causes. Yet the four causes neither are beings nor stand for any of the genera of being. The same holds true for the essential attributes of being *qua* being:

> There is a science which investigates being as being and the attributes which belong to this in virtue of its own nature. Now this is not the same as any of the so-called special sciences; for none of these others treats universally of being as being [*ἐπισκοπεῖ καθόλου*]. They cut off a part of being and investigate the attribute [*συμβεβηκός*] of this part; this is what the mathematical sciences for instance do. Now since we are seeking the first principles [*τὰς ἀρχάς*] and the highest causes [*τάς ἀκροτάτας αἰτίας*], clearly there must be something to which these belong in virtue of its own nature. If then those who sought the elements of existing things [*τὰ στοιχεῖα τῶν ὄντων*] were seeking these same principles, it is necessary that the elements must be elements of being not by accident but just because it *is* being. Therefore it is of being qua being that we must also grasp the first causes [*Met.* 1003A21–32].

The essential attributes intimated in this passage are: sameness, contrariety, otherness, genus, species, whole and part, perfection and unity. This additional list, regardless of the relationship which it bears to Plato's *Parmenides* and *Sophist* (principal Forms and highest Kinds), adds nothing new to the scope of genera of being any more than does the lexical chapter of Book *Δ*.

Book *E*, due to a different formulation of the division of knowledge into practical, productive, and theoretical, refers to objects existing as both non-moving and separate; as such they are studied by the science of theology. Such a science is possible only if there is a being which is at once unchanging and self-existing. This is, of course, a particular kind of being, evidently *sui generis*, and hence not covered by what was said in the *Categories*. Book *E* prepares us for the division of the study of substance into three departments as stated in Book *Λ*, where substance is classified as (*a*) eternal sensible (the heavenly bodies), (*b*) perishable sensible (the particulars), and (*c*) the insensible and unmovable (the Divine and the Intelligences).

One is now left with a perplexing question: Has Aristotle introduced new genera of being with the writing of his *Metaphysics*? The answer seems to be no. The opening sentences of Book *Λ* give the needed clue to the solution:

> The subject of our inquiry is substance [*οὐσία*]; for the principles and the causes we are seeking are those of substances. For if the universe [*τὸ πᾶν*] is of the nature of a whole [*εἰ ὥς ὅλον τι*], substance is its first part; and if it coheres merely by virtue of serial succession, on this view also substance is first, and is succeeded by quality and then by quantity. At the same time these latter are not even being in the full sense [*ὄντα ὡς εἰπεῖν ἁπλῶς ταῦτα*], but are qualities and movements . . . [*Met.* 1069A18–22].

Strange as this statement may sound, the inquiry is about *οὐσία* not *ὄντα*. If so, we are dealing here with one of the senses of *τὸ ὄν*, not all of them. Only that of *οὐσία* is broadened. Hence, to the initial two theses — that (*a*) being has many senses, and (*b*) there are 10 genera of being — a new one is added: (*c*) *οὐσία* is now a *πολλαχῶς λεγόμενον*.

It may be objected that Aristotle is in fact dealing with all *ὄντα*, as evidenced in his reference to the universe as a whole. Since the inquiry is about principles and causes of substances, it seems reasonable to consider briefly the implications of a holistic conception of the universe. Now, if we grant this hypothetical case "the universe is a whole," what place would *οὐσία* occupy in it? The answer is obvious: it would be its first part. Clearly, *οὐσία* as a genus of being takes precedence in this sort of conceptual model, while the other genera fall in line: *qualium*, *quantum*, etc. The remaining genera receive no mention. The unsuitability of the model is evident not only from the fact that the holistic approach is not at the heart of Aristotle's own interests, but also because it requires the introduction of a principle of ontological hierarchy to justify a serial arrangement of the genera of being in a scheme of first–last accidental beings. Now, why Aristotle would even want to consider substance in the context of a holistic conceptualization, is something else again. The reader is free to speculate in whichever direction he wishes.[8] A likely explanation is that Aristotle was writing these lines at a time when he was struggling to free himself from dominant Platonic elements and perhaps in response to alternative views held by other contemporary Platonists, such as Speusippus (cf. 1075B37). Holistic models were not only favored by members of the Academy but also adopted later on by leading Stoics. This interesting development figured largely in the non-Aristotelian views on the genera of being. But as such it is a separate issue in the history of ancient ontologies.

We must now proceed to see whether Aristotle modified his basic position on the genera of being as he proceeded with his metaphysical investigations.

Book *E* makes it clear that Aristotle's inquiries into the nature of *συμβεβηκότα*, or co-incidentals, yet ontic, properties are not meant to be part of the *Metaphysics*. By excluding them from the subject matter of the *Metaphysics*, he did not thereby cease to regard them as genera of being.[9] Each *συμβεβηκός*, since it belongs to objective contingency, cannot be the object of scientific knowledge. Should a certain accidental property prove capable of exhibiting a definite regularity, which may be called a law of its own, once this law is discovered, the property would have to be elevated to the level of an essential attribute. Be that as it may, it makes no difference to Aristotle's general doctrine of being whether the *Metaphysics* excludes the study of co-incidentals on the ground that they do not yield scientific knowledge; the important thing here is the admission of their genuine ontic status. In this respect the *Metaphysics* in no way contravenes the doctrines put forth in the *Categories*. The former work is a systematic analysis of *οὐσία*; the latter, a preliminary investigation of the *γένη τοῦ ὄντος* and the canons which govern the fundamental types of correct attribution. This is essentially the position which I developed in my article "Some Observations on Aristotle's Theory of Categories."[10]

The Stoic Account

In my treatment of Aristotle I began with his theory of predication and showed its connection with his ontology. In discussing the Stoics and Plotinus I shall start with their ontologies and show that the function of categorial thought must be reinterpreted in the light of their respective theories of being. Before proceeding with my analysis, I think it will be helpful to bear in mind the following pertinent aspects of Stoicism: (*a*) the revival of interest in Presocratic cosmology; (*b*) the placing of ontological theory within the framework of a genetic view of the world; and (*c*) the transformation of the Aristotelian conception of *ὄντα*, especially that of *οὐσία*.

A few remarks on the cosmology of the Stoics are needed at this point. It is generally agreed that the Stoics adopted a materialistic position and made every effort to maintain it with as much consistency as their presuppositions permitted. Diogenes Laertius (VII, 150) reports that "The Stoics mean by *οὐσία* the primary matter of all beings" (*τῶν ὄντων ἁπάντων*); and that "Matter is that out of which anything whatsoever is produced."

All that is necessary at this particular point to appreciate these remarks on the use of terms is to remember that the Stoics reverted to a model of cosmology closely resembling that of the Presocratics. A formless *οὐσία*, primitive and primordial matter, acts upon itself and is acted upon by itself. Substance is at once the agent of action and the passive recipient; *qua* activity, it is *πνεῦμα*, and it acts to provide the otherwise formless and motionless matter, itself, with qualities. This *πνεῦμα*, *λόγος*, or god, although separable in thought, does not exist independently from unqualified matter or substance. This matter–quality relationship is found in primal substance as well as in particular substances, for *πνεῦμα* is present in both.

Let us leave aside the cosmology of the Stoics to concentrate for a moment on the special vocabulary. The expression *οὐσία τῶν ὄντων* (substance of beings or beingness of beings) is totally un-Aristotelian. The same holds for the other related Stoic expression *οὐσία ἄποιος*, substance without quality; for to speak of substance in this manner is to render it unintelligible. Clearly, the difference between Stoic and Aristotelian conceptions of substance is irreconcilable. We are dealing with two different ontologies, or, rather, rival ontologies. Therefore, it is misleading to suggest that the Stoics improved upon the Aristotelian ten genera of being by proposing four instead. This Stoic doctrine, generally referred to as the "Stoic doctrine of categories," was not meant to solve problems in Aristotle's or Plato's or in any one of the Presocratic ontologies. There is an element of incommensurability here, the importance of which should not be ignored. What I mean to emphasize is that (*a*) the differences go far deeper than any similarities; and (*b*) the cosmology of the Stoics, with its attendant ontology, is far more original than many scholars are prepared to admit. Hence, it is a serious mistake to regard Stoicism merely as a revival of a particular Presocratic cosmology.

If the task of ontological theory is to investigate the problems pertaining to the genera of being, then it should be distinguished from that of categorial theory as well as that of cosmology. Let us consider, for instance, the issue of the "production" of the genera of being. As such it belongs to cosmology, not ontology. The logical aspects of their serial arrangement may be explored by both ontology and categorial theory but need not invoke the employment of a cosmology unless the system presupposes the necessity for such consideration. In the case of Aristotle, evidently no such problem emerges, but the same cannot be said of the Stoics. This difference is too fundamental to ignore. Whereas Aristotle nowhere offers a "deduction" of the genera of being or proposes a cosmic overview of their "production" from a single primordial source — the unmoved mover is not a productive or creative principle — the Stoics have a cosmology which accounts for the serial arrangement of the genera of beings. According to the Stoic "productive" account, the most general types of being, the inclusive genera, evolve from a primordial single source, *οὐσία ἄποιος*; and the return of all things to this source, the reverse of the productive process, is *ἐκπύρωσις*, translated as "conflagration."[11]

Although this is not the place to debate the celebrated problem of the "Stoic categories," I have serious reservations about the interpretations which identify the Stoic types of being with four basic categories. Since this issue still awaits its definitive answer, I shall adopt for purposes of terminological consistency the expression "types" or "genera" of being and avoid any reference to "categories."[12]

The types or genera of being form a sequence with first matter at the head as substance without qualities, capable of differentiating itself into qualities, dispositions, and relative dispositions. The ensued cosmos is a system of increasingly complex genetic developments, just as the process which marks its undoing is a relapse into the undifferentiated original *οὐσία*. From the standpoint of cosmogony, the Stoics had, understandably, emphasized an approach to ontology which we today would not hesitate to call "process philosophy." But their epistemology demanded that the fourth and last genus in the series of being, relative disposition, be given its due not only because inquiry shows that certainty is based on appearances which are most concrete and determinate, but also because material things cannot really be known unless they are things requisitely differentiated to be the individuals which *καταληπτικὴ φαντασία* grasps. The answer to the question "What is a thing?" can be given only after we are able to answer the basic question "What is its relative disposition?"

The above remarks suffice to make clear how the Stoics formulated their ontological and epistemological doctrines in radically non-Aristotelian ways. In both fields they appear to be critics of Aristotle's system, and, in particular, of his "horizontal" conception of the genera of being. The Stoic ontology, when considered as a "process philosophy," renders Aristotle's view of *πρώτη οὐσία* inapplicable to a theoretical inquiry into the origin and end of the cosmos. Comparably their epistemology leads to a denial of the Aristotelian claim that the individual is a "surd," but more importantly it elevates the genera of accidental being to a superior cognitive level. For the Stoics, the completion of the physical existent *qua* individual is a consequence of the features which emerge with relative disposition. In contrast to Aristotle's insistence on the fundamental role of the formal aspects of the individual in ontology and epistemology, the Stoics introduced a novel note in philosophy when they sought to found the intelligibility of the individual on what Aristotle declared to be genera of accidental being. Unless evidence can show otherwise, I am inclined to conclude that the philosophical trend in Hellenistic practice to blur the difference between definition and description as it pertains to the logic of individuals originates with the innovations which the Stoics introduced in the theory of genera of being. Beginning with Stoicism we have a clear-cut ontological defense of individuality *in extremis*.[13]

What counts, according to the Stoics, is not "man" the species as defined with the aid of such concepts as *οὐσία, γένος, εἶδος, διαφορά*, which are required by the procedures of Aristotelian logic, but the individual human being as determined in a variety of ways by the particularities of relative disposition. The "productive" model of the Stoic genera of being supported a logic well suited to a conception of a "process universe," a cosmos subject to continuous qualifications, from the amorphous unity of matter to minutely differentiated individuals. The logic which the Stoics developed proved capable of handling problems of inference in a world of individuals without essences.

Plotinus' Account

I now turn to the ontology of Plotinus and its relation to his theory of predication. In approaching this subject one must keep in mind that all aspects of Plotinus' philosophy constantly refer to an ultimate unity, the One. Since nothing can be predicated of the One, predication is automatically limited to inferior kinds of reality. It must also be remembered that for Plotinus, unlike Aristotle, the ultimate objects of predication are, not sensible objects, but intelligible ones: *νοῦς* and the ideas of *νοῦς*. Since the One is beyond categorial attributions, it follows that the genera of being are subordinate philosophical principles; therefore, any ontology which attaches ultimate significance to them must be a defective one. If one grants Plotinus these points, his critique of the Aristotelian and Stoic ontologies appears justified.

The opaqueness of the sensible object in Plotinus' system is as puzzling as its value is low. It never comes near to having the respectable place which we find it occupying in either the investigations of Aristotle or the speculations of the Stoics. This peculiarity is mainly due to the primacy of the ethical progress of the soul. The way we understand our place in the world of sensible objects, according to Plotinus, remains riddled with questions and ambiguities, unless we view it as a prelude to the voyage of the Great Return. Even so, it still depends on whether the direction in which we see ourselves moving is that of the downward or the upward path. If the former, the body cannot be other than the soul's prison, and hence no place in this sensible world is good enough for us. But if the latter, then we see with increasing transparence that the soul's destiny lies in the ideal world and has its terminus in the original source of all, the One. The concluding sentences of the *Enneads* read:

> If one rises beyond oneself, an image rising to its model, one has reached the goal of one's journey. When one falls from this vision, one will, by arousing the virtue that is within oneself, and by remembering the perfections that one possesses, regain one's lightness and through virtue rise to Intelligence, and through wisdom to the One. Such is the life of gods and of divine and blessed men, detachment from all things here below, scorn of all earthly pleasures, and flight of the alone to the alone [VI.ix.11].

Since only the One is the supreme, even the world of intelligible objects, Plato's world of the Forms, appears marred with the blemishes of plurality and dependence.[14] Beyond all levels of being radiates eternally the source of perfect unity and all reality. At the other extreme we encounter, not

Non-Being, but the accidental composites which have no corresponding models in the world of the intelligibles.

> It may further be asked whether the intelligible world contains Ideas of objects which are derived from decay or are otherwise repugnant, such as Ideas of mud or excreta. . . . The accidental composites which are formed not by Intelligence but by the conjunctions of sense objects have no Ideas corresponding to them in the intelligible world. Things that proceed from decay are produced only because the soul is unable to produce anything better [V.ix.14].

In sharp contrast and at the other end of the spectrum is the One: "This principle is none of the things of which it is the principle. It is such that nothing can be predicated [κατηγορεῖσθαι] of it, neither being, substance, nor life, because it is superior to all these things" (III.viii.10).

Yet, the place from which one normally starts on the ascending path is the world of the senses, and when properly seen it discloses before the soul a vast panorama, one which helps us to "admire the magnitude and beauty of the sense world, the eternal regularity of its movement, the visible and invisible divinities it contains, its demons, animals, and plants" (V.i.4). The model of this world is the superior reality of the intelligibles, contained in Intelligence itself. However engaging the panorama of the sensible world may be, its objects remain imperfect realizations of the Forms. Generated by the perfect world above, the sensible world depends on the higher one for its existence and for its intelligibility. Hence, to give accounts of events in this world by appealing to the natural origins of such events is to give insufficient causal explanations. All reasoned explanations must comply with the chain of being by discerning causes in the realm of the higher realities. The archetypes of all things and of all events are located in the intelligible world, including archetypes of quantities and qualities (V.ix.10). The world of Forms contains exemplars of everything in the sensible world, except accidental composites, and these in turn are the true objects of thought. When the mind fails to view the sensible objects through their Forms, they become opaque, aimless, and worthless. Before the mind can seek ecstatic union with the One, it must illumine the sensible world by rising to the world of the Ideas. The path of the philosopher is the road of dialectic.

> The philosopher is naturally disposed to rise to the intelligible world. Being, as it were, endowed with wings, he rushes to it without still needing to disengage himself from sense objects, as do the preceding kinds of men. His only uncertainty will concern the road to be followed and all he will need is a guide. He must therefore be shown the road, possessing as he does the desire by his nature and being already detached from sense objects [I.iii.3].

He turns to dialectic because:

> It enables us to say into how many kinds Being falls and to distinguish Being from that which is not Being. . . . It sets an end to the error attendant upon dealing with sense objects, and it establishes itself in the intelligible world. It concentrates its whole attention there; and after having left deception behind, it lets the soul, in the words of Plato, feed in the meadow of truth. It uses the Platonic method of division to discern the Ideas, to define each object, to distinguish the supreme genera of being [I.III.4].
>
> Dialectic, however, does not care for the theories that deal with propositions which to it are as letters to words. Nevertheless, because it knows the truth, dialectic also knows the nature of propositions and in general the operations of the soul [I.III.5].

Plotinus' view of the sensible object is that of a moralist who adopts a Platonizing ontology but shuns commitment to the practical objectives of the political life. With the ideals of the classical *πόλις* gone, he appears reluctant to assign to the sensible world anything but a low place in the hierarchy of ontic levels. What is left of the sensible object is but membership in the unstable realm of flux, a temporary abode, where things can make no claims to anything but fleeting truths. The sensible objects exist by virtue of a borrowed unity and possess but a finite number of immanent properties to which only their corresponding Forms can bestow value and being. Whatever there is to be said of the sensible objects, the predicates turn out to be equivocal assignations since the authentic meanings on which theirs depend have an eternal home in the higher world. Even as whole substances, the sensible objects are nothing but imitations, just as their essences collapse in verbal emptiness but for their dependence on the ideal models in the realm of the Intellectual principle.

Given this ontological view and the place which the sensible objects occupy on the ladder of cosmic values and orders, it is small wonder that the Plotinian and the Aristotelian accounts of the genera of being differ as widely as do the methodological principles which each philosopher employs to understand this world. Once Plotinus has assigned to the sensibles the status of pseudo-substances, he must find Aristotle's first substances, so central to the doctrines we see in the *Categories*, wanting in both primacy and significance. All the reader has to do to ascertain Plotinus' condescending treatment of Aristotle's sensible objects, as well as their properties, is to read through the first Treatise of the Sixth *Ennead*. If the critique is destructive and reconstructive, this is because none of the Aristotelian genera of being, as Aristotle understands what these are, can have a counterpart in the intelligible world. Given Plotinus' own view on the nature of the sensible realm, Aristotle's theory on what the genera of being are, what the uncombined expressions signify, and how predication functions is but a clumsy and inadequate tool for the disclosure and description of the grade of being which the sensibles can have.

Plotinus did not have to go far to find the methodological and ontological principles he needed to attack Aristotle's conception of the genera of being and its attendant theory of predication. As a "Platonist" he had already extended the doctrines which he found in Plato's *Sophist* beyond the limits within which the master had intended the higher dialectic to function, just as he redefined the status of the higher genera in the world of the Forms.[15] Hence the first three Treatises in the Sixth *Ennead* contain no surprises to the reader already familiar with the doctrines of the "Three Principal Hypostases," discussed in *Enneads* V.I. There he had stated that:

> The leading terms therefore are Intelligence, Being, Identity, Difference; and we must add Movement and Rest to them. Movement is implied in the thinking activity of the intelligible realm; Rest, in its sameness. Difference is required for the distinction between the thinking subject and the object thought; for without Difference they are reduced to unity and hence silence. . . . The proper character of each of them constitutes quality. From these terms taken as originating principles everything else proceeds [V.I.4].

What is noteworthy in a comparative context about this part of Plotinus' doctrine is that his conception of the genera of being bears little if any resemblance to Aristotle's own. Even more noteworthy is the fact that he has gone beyond Plato on three fundamental points: he (*a*) modifies the Platonic list of the highest genera; (*b*) posits the One as the source of all unity and plurality; and (*c*) interprets motion to be both real and supra-sensible by making νοῦς dynamic and the efficient cause of motion. Given this extended and modified list of Plato's highest genera as "primals" in the intelligible realm, the ineptness of what has become traditionally known as "Aristotle's theory of Categories" — a characterization which owes more to Plotinus than we suspect — follows with strict necessity. When we come to the critical discussion and systematic refutation of each Aristotelian thesis in *Enn.*VI.I, we see Plotinus reshaping the entire string of concepts which Aristotle had used to cope with the problems of predication in a world conceived as being intelligible without the benefit of Plato's theory of Forms, only to re-introduce the same terminological devices by asking them to do far more than what Aristotle had in mind, viz., to rise to the level of the superior tasks of the Neoplatonic dialectic. Along with this new dialectic came a radical redefinition of the ultimate purpose of philosophy.

> If the object of contemplation and of thought is to be alive, it must not have the life of plants, animals, or any other animate existence. Those beings too are various kinds of thought, the vegetative, sensuous, and psychic ways of thought. They are thoughts because they are rational forms. All life is some sort of thought which, like life itself, shows various degrees of strength. The clearest thought is also the highest life, and the highest life is identical with the highest intelligence. The supreme life is also the supreme thought . . . [III.viii.8].

When Plotinus declared that the One is "beyond being" and that it transcends activity just as it transcends mind and thought, he struck a note which carried his voice beyond the reaches of classical ontology. The Greek text is far more suggestive of Plotinus' formulation of the radical transcendence of the One than our translations can intimate. We read in *Enn.* I.vii.1 that the Primal Good is *ἐπέκεινα τῆς οὐσίας, ἐπέκεινα καὶ ἐνεργείας καὶ ἐπέκεινα νοῦ καὶ νοήσεως.* Although this is not the place to discuss whatever parallel meanings these expressions could have for Plato, Aristotle, and the early Stoics, it is evident that Plotinus' way of phrasing the transcendence of the One, by using three distinct proposed *ultima* and conjoining them serially, conveys an ontological vision which could not be framed within any of the classical conceptions of Being. However, while the break with the Platonic and Aristotelian ontologies served Plotinus well in his effort to introduce his own departure from the old ways, he had to make sure that the knower's ascent to the One would follow, as far as this was possible, the path of reason. If his purpose was to ensure the ontological union with the source of Being (*Enn.* IV.viii.1), part of the means for preparing the disciples to understand the new *νόστος* was his critique of categorial theories and established approaches to the genera of being.

Plotinus' rejection of Aristotle's views on these two branches of theoretical knowledge appears to have been part of an attack which was meant to carry the argument beyond the demands of traditional Platonism, the revival of which called at least for restoring the highest genera at the center of the intelligible realm. The general direction of Plotinus' concerns indicates that he was determined to grant the highest genera a conceptual status above and beyond what was suggested in the *Sophist.* In effect, Plotinus assigned them new axiological functions.

The new elements which Plotinus introduced were of his own making and in accord with the needs of his times. His extension of the quest of ontology, combined with the expanding interest in religious concerns, was decisive in shifting the center of gravity in the ancient world from the classical emphasis on the excellences of the citizens in the *πόλις* to the quest of philosophical salvation and away from the tribulations of the cosmopolis. With Plotinus, the philosophical pursuits became those of the transphysical flight of the alone to the alone. The sensible world, together with the requisite excellences for understanding and achieving the human fulfillment, became secondary and subsidiary to the new Platonists of Plotinus' generation. They sought new religions and new regions in the universe. They were determined to trace the source and the goodness of the universe, and in the process they found there things which Plato and Aristotle would have never encompassed in their own visions of the cosmos. The record shows that the new Platonists found the traditional ontologies too restrictive.

Next to the Stoics, Plotinus is one of the major critics of Aristotle's conception of substance and of the genera of being. In another sense, he is more than the leading Neoplatonist who challenged the efficacy of Aristotle's categorial theory. His entire program to recast the role of predication in the logic of reality and to replace the Aristotelian genera of being with new hierarchical orders in ontology makes him the precursor of medieval Arabic, Jewish, and Christian efforts to integrate the world of faith and the universe of reason. Considered in the light of his own philosophical innovations, Plotinus is the author of a radically different ontology of the sensible object. If anything, this doctrine contains basic components and presuppositions which are non-Hellenic in character.[15] In its novelty and complexity it is also the foundation for a new tradition. As a leading "post-classical" ontologist, Plotinus proved to be a new force in the transformation of the classical world as well as a creative response to the demands of the emerging religious culture.

NOTES

1 The following variants have been recorded:

'Αριστοτέλους Κατηγορίαι,
Liber Aristotelis De decem predicamentis,
Πρὸ τῶν τοπικῶν,
Περὶ τῶν γενῶν τοῦ ὄντος,
Περὶ τῶν δέκα γενῶν,
Κατηγορίαι δέκα

(*Aristotelis Categoriae et Liber de interpretatione*, ed. L. Minio-Paluello [Oxford, 1949], 3).

2 *De interpretatione*, 4–5, esp. 17A8–9: *῎Εστι δὲ εἷς πρῶτος λόγος ἀποφαντικὸς κατάφασις, εἶτα ἀπόφασις.*

3 *Rhetoric* I, 1358B11, where accusation is opposed to apology: *δίκης δὲ τὸ μὲν κατηγορία τὸ δὲ ἀπολογία.*

4 Simplicius' formulation belongs to the early phase of the tradition which established the generally accepted view that category and genus of being are interchangeable; thus his *In Cat.* 36: *ἡ μὲν λέξις κατηγορία λέγεται, ὡς κατὰ τοῦ πράγματος ἀγορευομένη, τὸ δὲ πράγμα κατηγόρημα.*

5 Cf. *Met.*, *E*, 1026A36; *Physics* 227B4. See also, for parallel formulations, *Met.*, *Θ*, 1051A35; *Δ* 1024B13, *I*, 1154B35–1155A1, 1158A13–14.

6 The translations of passages from Aristotle's *Categories* are my own; those from the *Metaphysics* are taken from *The Works of Aristotle*. VIII. *Metaphysica*, trans. W. D. Ross (Oxford, 1928). The translations of passages from Plotinus' *Enneads* are from J. Katz, *The Philosophy of Plotinus : Representative Books from the Enneads* (New York, 1950).

7 *Κατάφασις* occurs first in *Cat.* 2A6f. Its meaning is given here as "affirmation," leaving its opposite *ἀπόφασις*, "negation," out of the discussion. The elements which need to be brought together to form an affirmation are uncombined expressions consisting of nouns and verbs. These elements, insofar as they designate beings, are basically nouns and verbs. Thus every affirmation is made in one of two ways: either by combining definite nouns and verbs or by means of indefinite nouns and verbs. See *De Int.* 4–9 for a fuller treatment of affirmation; on the above, cf. 19B10f.

8 W. Jaeger and others have argued in favor of an early date for *Metaphysics*, Book *Λ*. It would not be unreasonable to hold that the views which Aristotle expresses in this essay were probably crystallized prior to the formulation of the ontological doctrines stated in the *Categories*. The opening chapter of Book *Λ* shows inferior handling of the theory of the genera of being as stated in the *Categories*. The terminology is certainly inadequate and even non-technical.

9 Alexander of Aphrodisias remarks that the divisions of being worked out in the *Categories* are outcomes of investigations Aristotle did in his First Philosophy; see *In Met.* 245, 33–35.

10 *Diotima*, 3 (1975), 67–81.

11 With *ἐκπύρωσις* comes the dissolution of the cosmos at the end of a particular cycle. See Diogenes Laertius, VII, 157 (in *Stoicorum veterum fragmenta*, ed. Hans von Arnim, 4 vols. [Leipzig, 1905–1924], II 22, no. 811; Alexander of Aphrodisias, *In Meteor.* 90A (ibid., A II 594).

12 Compare Phillip De Lacy, "The Stoic Categories as Methodological Principles," *Transactions and Proceedings of the American Philological Association*, 76 (1945), 246–63; Margaret E. Reesor, "The Stoic Categories," *American Journal of Philology*, 78 (1957), 63–82; John M. Rist, *Stoic Philosophy* (London, 1969), chap. 9, "Categories and Their Uses," 152–72; J. Christensen, *An Essay on the Unity of Stoic Philosophy* (Copenhagen, 1962); A. C. Lloyd, "Grammar and Metaphysics in the Stoa," in *Problems in Stoicism*, ed. A. A. Long (London, 1971), pp. 58–74; and A. A. Long, "Language and Thought in Stoicism," ibid., pp. 75–113.

13 In his important study on the Stoic "categories" as methodological principles, De Lacy points out the radical implications which this position had for theological inquiry. He states: "It is also clear that, as in the case of logic, the final steps in the theological inquiry, providence and the relative disposition of God to man, are the most important for the understanding of the nature of the universe and man's place in it" ("Stoic Categories," 225). Probably it would be more to the point to say instead "each individual's place in it."

14 "All beings, both the supreme beings as well as those who are called beings on any pretext whatsoever, are beings only because of the unity. . . . Deprived of their unity, they would cease to be what they are" (*Enn.* VI.IX.1).

15 For further remarks on this, see my "Plotinus' Approach to Categorial Theory" in *The Significance of Neoplatonism*, ed. R. Baine Harris, Studies in Neoplatonism: Ancient and Modern I (Albany, N.Y., 1976), pp. 83–99.

5

The Ontological Relation Between Evil and Existents in Manichaean Texts and in Augustine's Interpretation of Manichaeism

CHRISTOPHER J. BRUNNER
Encyclopaedia Iranica
Columbia University

THE PHENOMENOLOGY OF THE MANICHAEAN GNOSIS is established from a wide range of primary source material, as well as with the aid of Muslim commentary and Christian polemical literature.[1] These confirm the unique status held by the corpus of St. Augustine's anti-Manichaean writings, which were for so long a principal source for knowledge of the religion. Augustine's methodical, rhetorician's attacks on Mani indicate the fundamental and pervasive role of myth in the apostle's religion and the literalistic mentality of the Manichaean teachers. His accuracy is supported not only by Archelaus, Ephraem, Severus of Antioch, and the abjuration formulas, but also by the preserved or imputed words of his opponents. Faustus is the most vigorous and resourceful of these Manichaeans; but Felix and Fortunatus also make useful contributions. The primary sources, to which Augustine himself provides some reference, furnish the ultimate confirmation.

St. Augustine's polemics remain all the more interesting with the knowledge that doctrines and themes closely associated with Manichaeism remained prominent in his thought. His concept of the "two cities" echoes the Manichaean perception of the metaphysical disparity of being. The prominence given to *concupiscentia* as the primary manifestation of human downfall and the explanation for the individual's moral enervation compares with the status of Greed and Lust in Manichaean cosmogony; functional equivalence is also close. Correspondingly, the decisive role of grace in Augustine's theology closely resembles the activity of the Light Nous. These continuing affinities in Augustine's thought and feeling with the spirit of the rejected religion may have inspired some of the vehemence in his attacks upon it.[2]

Being and Myth in Manichaeism

The only truly ontological principle articulated in Manichaean doctrine is the fundamental one of *duo principia* (Middle Persian: *dō bun*). Any further generalizations are those of the modern student of the religion, not the explicit concepts of the apostle which were then clothed in mythic dress. Manichaeism enunciated a history rather than an ontology (reflecting the discipline of philosophy) or a science of symbols (by which metaphysical concepts were systematically translated into imagery). This grand historical narration explained the processes of being according to three stages — before, during, and after the mingling of the two eternal metaphysical essences.[3] Although, in the third stage, equilibrium will be restored, the universe will forever remain modified from its primal state; cosmic history will have eternal consequences. St. Augustine, in reaction, carefully confined the notion of history to the human sphere. His stages are: God made man through his goodness, punished him through his justice, and redeemed him through his mercy (*De libero arbitrio* 3.4.15); thus any concept of a primeval, divine history is excluded.

The centrality of the world-historical, i.e., mythical, narrative within Manichaeism is evident from the religion's literature. Particularly important in this regard are the fragments of the apostle's writings — the *Šābūragān*, the *Kawān*, the beginning of the *Epistula fundamenti* analyzed by Augustine — and the discourses compiled in the *Kephalaia.* That the myth is the content of doctrine, not symbolic or aesthetic dress, is further demonstrated by the Manichaean polemicists; and Augustine could attack Faustus on the point that the apostle spoke only *veritatem nudam et propriam*, that Mani came to interpret Scriptural metaphors and veiled sayings, not to use such devices himself.[4] Severus of Antioch, in portraying Manichaeism as a mythology, was seizing on its essential characteristic,[5] and pointing to its archaism. For Manichaeism is archaic precisely in its mythological perception, thought, and feeling regarding existence. It is thus intellectually parallel to contemporary Zoroastrianism in Sasanian Iran, from which Mani borrowed the outline of his mythology. The apostle did not codify his understanding in a rational philosophy which could bear analysis and criticism (whether or not such a procedure, in his cultural milieu, was open to him). Rather he embodied it in the myth narrations, the archetypal events of which provide illustrations and patterns which render coherent the function and goal of human existence. The precepts and rituals enjoined on the believers likewise found their explanation in the mythology and served to render the faithful part of the history of the travail of Light.[6]

Mythology as factual history helped to foster the intellectual literalism of the Manichaeans. In considering Augustine's accusation that Faustus failed to understand the difference between moral and symbolic (e.g., ritual) precepts in the Old Testament, one might argue that Faustus deliberately refrained from such discrimination, since his purpose was to discredit the Jewish Scriptures, as a whole, by ridicule (*Contra Faustum* 6.2). But it is equally possible that a true Manichaean would be oblivious to Augustine's distinction as applied to divine commands. For him each authentic religious rule should relate directly (and therefore with comparable weight) to the cosmic drama and the problem of its resolution. It may be noted that a process of explicit symbolizing was used in Manichaeism, but on a quite different level from that of mythic perception. Literary allegory was practiced with didactic intent; important doctrines could be impressed on the Hearers by means of easily remembered parables.[7]

The Zoroastrian parallel in literalism is instructive. Within the Sasanian church, doctrine comprised a well-interwoven body of moral teachings, mythic narrative, and traditional folklore. The relationship between men and the gods was expressed in ritual action, the efficaciousness of which hinged on accurate performance (as communicated by the priestly tradition) and right-mindedness. Not until late Sasanian times, at the earliest, are there any indications of any Zoroastrian rationalism or attempts to abstract systematic dogma. Zoroastrianism readily assimilated (as did Manichaeism and Mandeism as well), not rational philosophy, but Hellenistic astrology. The latter science could build on traditional lore regarding the luminaries, and it strongly reinforced the theology of myth.

Manichaeism, as a mythology, could exert a powerful appeal to Mesopotamian gnostics and Iranian Zoroastrians, using their own intellectual terms. It gave dramatic immediacy to cosmic history by teaching the role of the world and of humanity in it.[8] It also had the advantage of total certainty about existence, from its origin to the mechanics of the universe. Felix pointedly indicates this to St. Augustine.[9] Augustine, once separated from the Manichaean church, formulated a formidable series of questions on the problem of evil and existence (*De ordine* 46) which would have been excluded from the purview of the firm believer.

In spreading the prophet's religion westward from its original culture area, the Manichaeans necessarily adapted to the pressures of orthodox Christianity. The mythology must have been advanced, from the beginning, together with some Christian imagery and Pauline terminology, plus Mani's claim to be the "apostle of Jesus Christ."[10] But greater appearance of harmony with the Christian Scriptures had to be fashioned, and Mani's mission fitted into Christian history. Hence, the arbitrary exegesis of Scripture, of which Faustus could be accused; hence, as well, the presentation of Mani as the promised Paraclete.[11] This more exalted title would have rendered his word still more authoritative to the believer. For argument from authority was the Manichaean's primary tool; and faith, the prime requisite of the convert to the foreign mythology.[12] The function of reason, in the context of Western Manichaeism, was to guard the faith.[13] Reason was apparently applied primarily in dialectic (e.g., Faustus in *Con. Faustum* 21.1), where devices of logic might cover the bare reiteration of doctrines — which seems to have been the Manichaean apologists' ordinary defense. Augustine attacked the Manichaean teachers for having promised to demonstrate "the entire, open truth" by means of "pure and simple reason."[14] They offered, in fact, the mythology (the *aniles fabulas* of the same passage) and commanded faith (*De utilitate credendi* 14.31; cf. *Letter of Secundinus* 6).[15] Ultimately they lacked any real means of defense against Augustine's methodical and minute examination of the logical inconsistencies in Manichaeism. Thus Secundinus resorts to the principle *Excedit enim divina ratio mortalium pectora* (ibid.).

The validity of Mani's mythology was supported, within his culture area, by a certain inherent probability; but it depended, ultimately, on the authenticity of his apostolic mission. Contemporary Iran offers a partial analogy. Zoroastrianism, in Mani's lifetime, was being organized into a state church with a hierarchy of offices and embracing certain civil functions. Problems of doctrinal and ritual correctness must have become more acute with the centralization of the church; and the priest Kirdēr, Mani's archenemy at the Sasanian court, aimed to resolve these by appeal to authority. His inscriptions relate his soul-journey to the spiritual (*mēnōg*) world and the confirmation of religious truths by the spiritual beings.[16] Kirdēr thus places himself in the prophetic tradition of Zarathushtra and his conversations with Ahura Mazdā. Mani, with his visions of his twin Light-being, assumes authority in similar fashion but is not bounded by the conventions of Zoroastrian priestly tradition. It is true that Kirdēr may represent only a passing, organizational phase of the church. In the fourth century, in any case, Ādurbād Mahraspandān validated his line of Avestan tradition by the ordeal of molten metal, not by claims based on visions. The revelational principle survived in literature, however — not only in scripture and myth, but also in the story of Ardā Wirāz.[17]

Although the world-views inherent in the Zoroastrian and Manichaean mythologies are strongly opposed, both systems employ the same dynamics; for it is the force of necessity which governs the origin and unfolding of mythic history. It was inevitable that Evil eventually become aware of good, and the necessary consequence was conflict. With this conflict began the middle epoch, that of measured time. Measured time, in contrast to eternity (i.e., duration not bounded in one extension), is a compressed embodiment of necessity. In implying its own end, it sets a limit to the cosmic conflict. While in Zoroastrianism Ohrmazd is made to set the limit and to govern measured time, he nevertheless exists within it, as does the Manichaean Light-Father.[18] Augustine asserted, against the Manichaeans, God's eternity and his creation of time.[19] But to the Manichaean, as to the Zoroastrian, the inevitability of the entire world-historical process, including its outcome (e.g., *Kephalaia*, p. 104.25–26), was a source of ultimate reassurance. God's subjection to necessity — to Augustine an attribution of evil[20] — was regarded as simply an aspect of his finiteness. (This point of contention underlines the contrast between a mythic understanding of God and a rational definition of him.) The governance of necessity in Manichaeism and Zoroastrianism may be summarized as follows: (*a*) The eternal beings act in accord with their natures, which express the diverse primal essences. (*b*) This diverseness implies a tension, the realization of which in conflict proceeds from potential to actual, and will ultimately be resolved. This implied supremacy of necessity, so well reinforced by astrology, is based partly in the exigencies of myth. But it also lay rooted in Iranian religion, as a principle of the effectiveness of ritual observance.

Evil and Primal Being

Unoriginated being, according to Manichaeism, exists in plural (i.e., two) and incommensurable essences. This doctrine of the two principles was the cornerstone of the religion and is therefore referred to at or near the head of all summaries and discussions of the faith.[21] The doctrine was given the status of an empirical statement, since the pervasive presence of evil in the world was evident (see *Contra Fortunatum* 21ff.). Augustine understandably gave primary attention to this principle in his polemics. His arguments that God is the source of all being *qua* being and that evil consists of the deprivation of being may have reassured Christians; but to a believing Manichaean they contradicted the evidence of common sense.[22]

The two self-existent (from eternity) sources of being were God and Hyle, who by their existence rendered one another finite.[23] The complex worlds which each created and ordered delimited each other along a common border within absolute space. The Manichaeans stressed, however, the incommensurability of God and Hyle. The two differ in origin (*principium*; Middle Persian: *bun*), *essentia* (or *οὐσία*), *substantia* (Middle Persian: *gōhr*), *natura* (or *φύσις*), and *species*; their creations, accordingly, differ in genus.[24] They are opposites in the sense that their substances, natures, and manifest actions are antithetical. God is Light, characterized as truth, goodness, and soul; Hyle is Darkness, characterized as falsehood, evil, and body.[25] But the substances of Light and Darkness are not on the same metaphysical level and are not simply mutual negations. Such a conceptual symmetry could imply a possible relationship; and the very object of Manichaeism was to avoid the "pagan error" (from Faustus' viewpoint) which made good and evil ultimately derivable from one and the same principle. Therefore the two essences are termed alien to one another. Faustus strenuously denies the possibility of subsuming God and Hyle under a common term (*Con. Faustum* 21.1); but metaphors establish the point more vividly. God is called the living air, Hyle the dregs (of matter); and Severus says the two were compared to a king and a hog.[26]

The two essences contrast notably in their state of existence. God is perfect being, complete in himself; and this perfection is manifest in his omniscience and prescience. The finiteness of his power is a simple fact, conditioned by the power of existent evil (cf. *Con. Faustum* 25.1). Hyle is incomplete, deficient being; and, accordingly, his knowledge is experiential. This deficiency motivated Hyle's drive to possess God's Light, once he became aware of the latter's existence. Hyle sought to equalize being by possessing Light or at least by depriving God of part of his substance. It was assumed by the Manichaeans that Hyle, although alien, would feel an attraction to Light's perfection. Himself poor, he wished to be like Light, to acquire it with its fragrance and peace (*Psalm-Book*, pp. 203.27–33, 205. 15–21). Thus his creations immediately worshipped the Light-envoy and invited him to their land (ibid., pp. 214–15). This attraction itself, as well as the war which it inspired, was evil in the Manichaean view, since Light could be impaired only by mingling with Darkness. But Christian polemicists could find the ambition of Hyle for fulfillment natural and praiseworthy. It furnishes Augustine with part of his argument that God and Hyle, as depicted in the mythology, are both mixed good and evil and not pure substances.[27] To Ephraem this attraction was contradictory to the primordial natures; while to Severus it implies their sharing a common basis of being after all.[28] A certain amount of ambiguity lay in the myth itself; for the result of Hyle's absorbing light by swallowing the members of Primal Man is depicted as both beneficial to Hyle and harmful, depriving him of strength.[29] Both effects are necessary to the myth, but the Manichaeans would have stressed how Evil was subverted, not enhanced, by the capture of Primal Man.

If Manichaean doctrine elevates the metaphysical status of evil by recognizing it as existent and primordial (see, e.g., *Retractationes* 1.9.2), its intent is only to discover the truth of the cosmic drama. It is felt to be more important to establish the clear innocence of God from any responsibility for, or consent to, the evil and suffering present in the world. The notions of God's infinity and omnipotence, vital in Christian thought, were unacceptable to Mani as necessarily destroying God's innocence.[30] In principle the Manichaeans denied that God was vulnerable to the attack of Hyle;[31] but the middle world-epoch is initiated in a manner which emphasizes the initiative and strength of Hyle. Thus Augustine dwells attentively on the real vulnerability of the Manichaean God, an aspect which is necessary to the myth but foreign to Augustine's rational conception of God (in, e.g., *Con. Faustum* 14.11). The Manichaean God is described as fearing Hyle, grieving at the prospective loss of his Light-substance, and undergoing a humiliating pollution and corruption which is temporizing and not entirely successful, and which gives Hyle scope for greater evil through the eventual spawning of fleshly creatures.[32] Augustine's aim is to discredit the Manichaean explanation of each stage of the cosmic struggle. In the *initium*, why did God, if invulnerable, consent to fight at all; in the *medium*, the present state of mixture, what has become of his vaunted incorruptibility; and in the end, how can he be unable to redeem all his substance from Darkness (*Con. Faustum* 13.6)? By raising such questions against the mythology, he might disrupt its flow and cumulative effect in the Hearer's mind.

Augustine frequently attacked the Manichaeans for their "materialism" — i.e., for depicting the Light-world and God's Light-nature in physical terms.[33] This aspect of the religion is genuine, despite Secundinus' description of the state of being of Light as *inennarabile . . . atque ineffabile* (*Letter* 6). For dependence on the bodily senses for definition of a metaphysical scheme is part of the archaism of Manichaean mythology. Thus the universe has absolute direction; God exists in it, has dimensions and a subtle body, and moves; and his Light-kingdom is similarly material.[34] Physical light, which the senses even of animals perceive, is part of God's substance.[35] In short, the overall cosmic struggle and the present earthly one are rendered closely analogous in the mythology. Augustine may ridicule the frank physicality of the process by which the Elect assist the liberation of Light from matter.[36] The believer, however, would feel in this, as in the other articles of faith, a reinforcement of his own close relationship to the divine world. As to Hyle, matter is his substance and his offspring; and so it is necessarily described physically. Since Hyle is manifest in subtle bodies, as well as in gross, an unavoidable parallel with Light's state of existence is approached.[37]

Mani's "materialism," like his basic notion of two metaphysical principles, is in harmony with Zoroastrian tradition. Zoroastrianism distinguished two states of existence. The *gētīg* state is that of visible, tangible matter; the *mēnōg* state, that of invisible, subtle form.[38] A *mēnōg* being does, however, possess extension and other physical properties. The two states differ more in degree than in nature, thus allowing in Zoroastrianism a perception of the unified, hierarchical order of being, which is comprehended throughout in material terms. The *mēnōg* world is attainable by the soul in dreams or visions (cf. Kirdēr and Ardā Wirāz); and the *mēnōg* divinities are closely involved in the maintenance of the *gētīg* world.

The primal essences of Zoroastrianism, the god Ohrmazd and the demon Ahreman, exist in the *mēnōg* state;[39] and a certain parallelism of being is acknowledged between these two antithetical natures. Moreover, the religion may have contained, from its early days, a faction prone to reductionist thought, which would derive the two opposed beings from a single pre-existent principle. Such speculation would have found some basis in Zarathushtra's own words; since he calls the "two *mēnōg*" twins (*Yasna* 30.3; cf. *Yasna* 45). He apparently derives both Beneficent Mēnōg (Spənta Mainyu) and Evil Mēnōg (Aŋra Mainyu) from Ahura Mazdā; and their differentiation into good and evil is attributed to their free choice to be beneficial or destructive. In Sasanian Zoroastrianism Ohrmazd and Ahreman simply follow their innate inclinations and are eternally opposed. But the strong influence of astrology must have encouraged the speculation (perhaps largely confined to Iranians of Mesopotamia) which made the god Zurwān into a unifying, ultimate principle. A remote deity of both eternity and measured time, Zurwān embodied the force intrinsic to the measuring of time and the necessity which rules mythic history.[40] His engendering of evil, besides good, was attributed to a defect in his state of mind while performing ritual action.

Iranian Manichaeans obviously could not have used the terms *mēnōg* and *gētīg* to designate the primal essences without ambiguity; their mutually alien character and the evil of Hyle would have been poorly indicated by these words. Therefore the Manichaeans used either the terms "light" and "darkness" (*rōšn*: *tār* or *tam*) or "soul" and "body" or "corpse" (*gyān*: *tan* or *nasāh*).[41] The latter set anticipates the essential manifestations of the primal essences in the process of their combat.

Evil and Derived Being

God and Hyle alike produce dependent, animate beings, both before and after the mixture of the two essences. God creates by evocation, i.e., he "utters" new forms with which he individuates his own substance. This process is intrinsically good. Hyle produces evilly by procreation. Thus each existent creature is genetically linked with one of the two self-existent beings and shares its nature.[42] The central problem of existence, subsequent to the capture of Primal Man, is the complex mingling of the two essences within the genus of hylic creatures. Each being which manifests this mixing of Light with Darkness is thereby an integral part of the cosmic struggle and an object of God's (and the believer's) concern in his efforts to reclaim his lost substance.

As the combat developed, its field shifted, and was dramatically narrowed, to the material world; for the Living Spirit had fashioned it from corpse-matter of Hyle specifically to catch the Light which the hylic Archons were forced to emit. Mani's geocentrism compares in function with that of Zoroastrian myth, although in the latter the world stands as a thoroughly good creation; and the infestation of evil creatures is due to the world's position as first line of defense against the invasion of Evil.[43] The Manichaean world is a makeshift device which retains the same nature as the hylic beings who make it their lair. In order to keep possession of the remaining captured Light, Hyle spawned life in the world, causing it to multiply by the degrading means of sexual intercourse.[44] All these life forms, with their gross bodies, are of one with Hyle and the world, thus with Darkness and death.[45]

The final outcome of the evolution of hylic life is mankind. But, although human nature is evil, each person contains a high concentration of Light and is therefore a desirable prize, for which God and the Archons do battle.[46] The chain of procreation which eventually generated man was initiated and directed by the demoness Lust (Middle Persian: Áz), and the human being may be described as her handiwork *par excellence*.[47] He is a sophisticated hylic device for the retention of Light; for, dominated by the passion of his ancestress, he practices sexual intercourse and thereby perpetuates Light's imprisonment within his offspring.[48] The various other evil acts which he commits ensure his own metempsychosis.[49]

The Manichaeans obviously could not assent to the Zoroastrian view, according to which human nature is a harmonious combination of *mēnōg* constituents with a *gētīg* body. Iranian Manichaean texts thus ignore the scheme of perceptual faculty (*bōy*), psychic soul (*ruwān*), pneumatic soul (*gyān*), and pre-existent guardian spirit (*frawahr*). For these are substituted new *mēnōg* elements, which are said to be of the same substance as the body, i.e., hylic: rage (*xēšm*), greed, and lust (*āz*, *āwarzōg*).[50] The term *gyān* is retained to designate the trapped Light-soul. This analysis of human nature as *gyān* vs. the *mēnōg* components and the body is paralleled by the Coptic Manichaean distinction between the πνευματικὸν εἰκών vs. the *ψυχικὸν εἰκών* and the *σωματικὸν εἰκών* (*Keph.*, pp. 269.19–25, 270.13–20). St. Augustine summarizes roughly by saying: *Duas animas esse in uno corpore existimant* (*De vera religione* 9.16). Thus the cosmic antagonism between the two essences is reproduced within the human being, but with inversion of the relative power of God and Hyle.

The ultimate dilemma of mankind, as the highest of the creatures in the mixed state, is how to help to achieve the separation of the divine substance from Hyle. Only that nullifying of metaphysical evil can restore peace and joy to the entire realm of being. It may be noted that Mani taught a microcosmic doctrine (analogous to that of Zoroastrianism), in which he compared the structure of man to that of the material universe.[51] The Manichaean believer could, further, comprehend the human existential situation by analogy between himself and the earth. For within that greater hylic body are enclosed a mass of Light particles. Striving to concentrate within trees and fruits, they are the "suffering Jesus" whose agony and salvation parallel man's own.[52] The pneumatic soul of each human being, similarly, is a portion of God's substance yearning (when it is conscious) for liberation from the hylic flesh.[53] When this liberation is attained, the person will yet retain his individuality in reunion with God and the Light-emanations; while his body, which defined his human nature, will, within the mass of Hyle, await the final, consuming fire.

The immediate dilemma of man is his moral impotence, a state due to the domination of human nature by necessity. This necessity is chiefly manifest in the compulsions of lust — the "teaching" which the Archons have instilled in the body (*Keph.*, p. 79.4ff.). The Light-soul itself is blameless for this moral powerlessness, since it is checked by the hosts of Archons which drive the body to action (*Keph.*, pp. 169–70). At the same time, of itself, it is helpless to overcome the Archons. The condition of natural man, in short, is that *carnis enim commixtione ducitur, non propria voluntate* (*Letter of Secundinus* 2).

St. Augustine, although as pessimistic as Mani regarding the present condition of man, denied that it was natural. Just as he rejected the concept of existent metaphysical evil as inconsistent with his understanding of the nature of divinity, so he denied the Manichaean teaching of created evil. He asserted, in contradiction, that the idea of evil pertains to the moral sphere alone. It is, essentially, sin: *origo et caput mali peccatum* (*Con. Fortunatum* 21). There exist no evil natures (ibid., 15). But man, possessing a free will, may decline to seek the greater good, in accord with the natural order of the universe, as God established it. This desertion from the unchangeable good by the will of the changeable good is unjust, negatory action.[54] It is the prior form of evil; and the just punishment which the sinner suffers for it is the consequent evil. Augustine often repeated this twofold distinction of evil.[55] He thus asserted against Mani that (*a*) evil lies in a negative departure, toward non-being, from the natural order of being; (*b*) creatures alone are affected by it; God remains unsullied (*Contra Felicem* 2.18–20); (*c*) will is the source of evil. The last point, like the first, is frequently reiterated.[56]

Even if Augustine chose to stress the concept of free will against the Manichaeans and to deny that human evil exists by cosmic necessity (*De lib. arb.* 3.2.4), his affinity with them emerges from his view of humanity after the Fall. The punishment of Adam and Eve (and of the entire human family for which they were responsible) was a natural consequence of the disordering of their wills. Those wills became weakened; and passion rose to harass human nature (*Retrac.* 1.15.2) and to disrupt the soul's control of its actions (*De lib. arb.* 1.11.22). Only after the Fall did the practice of sexual intercourse begin (*De Genesi contra Manichaeos* 1.19.30), which would, from generation to generation, express the domination of concupiscence over mankind.[57] The predisposition to sin inherited from the human parents did not, however, remove individual responsibility: "Even the sin by which one consents to the concupiscence for sin is not committed except by the will."[58]

It is evident that both Mani and Augustine required the concept of an external agent in order to offer mankind any hope of overcoming evil. In Augustine's doctrine, God dispenses grace freely and mysteriously to whomever he chooses, in accord with the overall divine plan (*Retrac.* 1.9.4). Grace rightly orders the soul's will and thereby accomplishes good thoughts and actions through the individual (*De diversis quaestionibus ad Simplicianum* 1.2.10-13, 20–21). Against the Manichaeans Augustine did not elaborate on the mystery of grace;[59] for it lay close to their own view; whereas his extreme defense of free will created the sharp opposition of doctrines which he wished.

The overwhelming reality, to the Manichaean believer's perception and understanding, was the presence, the immanence, of metaphysical evil. All the world's ills are seen as precisely natural to it. Man, in his gross, natural state, does not fully comprehend evil. But, by his "embodiment" of God, he has the potential for an awareness of reality. The alien element in human nature, Light, must be brought to recall its true nature and origin. The subsequent overcoming of moral evil, leading to the dissolution of the human being, becomes a step toward the conquest of cosmic evil. Although this achieving of true knowledge implied emphatic alienation from the world, the believer could derive support both from the Church and from the presence of the divine around him. He was now aware of his solidarity with the Suffering Jesus, of the Holy Spirit in the atmosphere (*Con. Faustum* 20.2), of the significance of the sun and moon — the divine, Light-giving (φωστήρ) ships which bear witness to Mani and are a "dovecot" for the oppressed soul.[60]

Just as the Holy Spirit is God's agent in the world to aid the striving of the Suffering Jesus, so the Light-Mind (νοῦς; Middle Persian: *Manuhmēd*) is his emissary to man, aiding souls to overcome hylic necessity. By the indwelling of Light-Mind, the soul achieves *scientia rerum* (*Con. Fortunatum* 20) — i.e., knowledge of the dichotomy of being and its manifestation in existents, of its own nature and condition, and of the way to the release of Light (cf. *Keph.* p. 79.6–7). With the continuing support of Light-Mind, the soul is empowered actually to carry out its new will and resolve.[61] The enlightened person is literally reborn. The Old Man, the tool of the Archons, is fettered; and the New Man is fashioned in his stead. Faustus quotes, with literal application, Col. 3:10 regarding "the new [man] who is renewed in the knowledge of God according to the image of Him who made him in you."[62] This renewal of the individual begins the repetition of Primal Man's redemption and points toward the final subjugation of Hyle.

A consequence of the soul's renewal was its responsibility for its acts of will. For it then possessed the capacity deliberately to consent to evil-doing (*Keph.*, p. 215.1–12). The soul could thus put the Light-Mind into confusion and force it to leave (*Keph.*, p. 99.13–14).[63] By making itself again an ally of the Archons, the soul incurred damnation with Hyle within the "clod" (βῶλος) — the burnt remains of the material universe.[64]

This difficult doctrine regarding the eternal loss of part of God's substance (whether or not universally accepted in the Church or maintained without modification) underscores the permanent impact of evil on the realm of perfect being. Hyle, even when reduced to helplessness within its prison and forgotten, will have modified the pattern of existence of the Light–substance forever.

NOTES

1 For an extensive listing of primary and secondary literature, see Jens P. Asmussen, *X^uāstvānīft: Studies in Manichaeism* (Copenhagen, 1965), pp. 265–86. Major modern surveys of the sources on Manichaeism (but prior to extensive publication of the Iranian materials) are Gustav Flügel, *Mani: Seine Lehre und seine Schriften* (Leipzig, 1862); Konrad Kessler, *Mani: Forschungen über die manichäische Religion* I (Berlin, 1889);

Prosper Alfaric, *Les Ecritures manichéennes*, 2 vols. (Paris, 1918). An important collection of references is gathered in the notes to Henri-Charles Puech, *Le Manichéisme: Son fondateur — sa doctrine* (Paris, 1949). Still a major source is I. de Beausobre, *Histoire critique de Manichée et du manichéisme*, 2 vols. (Amsterdam, 1734–1739; repr. 1970). The following interpretation of the place of evil in the Manichaeans' history of being aims, as much as possible, to supplement rather than to repeat these works. It assumes familiarity with the mythic narrative.

2 For Augustine as a Manichaean, and for extensive commentary on his polemics, see P. Alfaric, *L'Évolution intellectuelle de saint Augustin* (Paris, 1918); P. J. de Menasce, "Augustin manichéen," *Freundesgabe für Ernst Robert Curtius* (Bern, 1956), pp. 79–93. Extensive citations from Augustine's works are used in F. C. Baur, *Das manichäische Religionssystem* (Tübingen, 1831; repr. Göttingen, 1928). Quotations from Augustine's texts follow the Maurist (Benedictine) edition. Manichaean texts frequently cited include: *Kephalaia* I, edd. H. J. Polotsky and A. Böhlig, Parts 1 and 2 (Stuttgart, 1940, 1966); and *A Manichaean Psalm-Book, Part II*, ed. C. R. C. Allberry (Stuttgart, 1938).

3 "Manichaeus . . . per suam praedicationem docuit nos initium, medium et finem" (*Contra Felicem* 1.9; cf. 2.1). Zoroastrian mythic history contains the same division, implicit in the alternation between unbounded time (*zamān ī akanārag*), bounded time (*zamān ī kanāragōmand*) — "time of the long dominion" (*zamān ī dagrand-xwadāy*) — and back to unbounded time. In both traditions the middle stage is further subdivided. See *Keph.*, p. 55.20. For Zoroastrianism, see particularly the first chapters of the *Bundahišn* and *Wizīdagīhā ī Zātspram*: *The Bûndahishn*, ed. T. D. Anklesaria (Bombay, 1908), pp. 2–10; trans. B. T. Anklesaria, *Zand-Ākāsīh: Iranian or Greater Bundahišn* (Bombay, 1956), pp. 4–15; idem, *Vichitakiha-i Zatsparam* 1.1–9 (Bombay, 1964), pp. lxvi–lxix. Cf. R. C. Zaehner, *Zurvan: A Zoroastrian Dilemma* (Oxford, 1955), pp. 278ff., 339ff.

4 "Cum tibi praecipue laudari Manichaeus non ob aliud soleat, nisi quod remotis figurarum integumentis, ipse tibi veritatem nudam et propriam loqueretur" (*Contra Faustum* 15.5). "Tu vero praecipue Manichaeum ob hoc praedicas, quod non ad talia dicenda, sed potius ad solvenda ultimus venerit: ut et figuris antiquorum apertis, et suis narrationibus ac disputationibus evidenti luce prolatis, nullo se occultaret aenigmate. . . . iste autem, qui sciret post se neminem adfuturum, sententias suas nullis allegoricis ambagibus texteret" (15.6).

5 Franz Cumont, *Recherches sur manichéisme* (Brussels, 1908), p. 121.

6 See particularly the hymn literature. In the cultic context the believer experienced continuity with the divine substance; he passed through the full range of emotions associated with the sufferings and triumphs of Light.

7 The parable device (Middle Persian: *āzind*) is well illustrated by the text M 47 II, re-edited in Werner Sundermann, *Mittelpersische und parthische kosmogonische und Parabeltexte der Manichäer* (Berlin, 1973), pp. 86–89. Besides the other fragments published there, see W. B. Henning, "Sogdian Tales," *Bulletin of the School of Oriental and African Studies*, 11 (1945), 465–87.

8 Zoroastrianism, in theory, provided an equally dramatic world-view. It seems that, in practice, however, the repercussions of the cosmic conflict within the world were minimized in favor of the stability of ritual routine.

9 "Manichaeus . . . docuit nos de fabrica mundi, quare facta est, et unde facta est, et qui fecerunt, docuit nos quare dies et quare nox; docuit nos de cursu solis et lunae" (*Con. Fel.* 1.9). For the last point, cf. *Con. Faustum* 20.6; Mani's doctrine incorporated a primitive world-mechanics similar to that preserved in the *Bundahišn* (for which see

D. N. MacKenzie, "Zoroastrian Astrology in the *Bundahišn*," *Bulletin of the School of Oriental and African Studies*, 27 [1964], 511–29). Augustine, in contrast to Felix, had to argue the unknowability of God's ultimate design for creation; see, e.g., *De diversis quaestionibus ad Simplicianum* 1.2.6; *Con. Faustum* 21.3; *De utilitate credendi* 10.14, 11.25, 12.26.

10 See *Acta Archelai* 5.22, ed. C. H. Beeson (Leipzig, 1906), *Con. Faustum* 13.4, *Contra epistulam quam vocant fundamenti* 5.6.

11 The former point appears frequently in the *Contra Faustum*; see, e.g., 11.2, 13.17, 18.3, 22.15. For Mani as the Paraclete, see *Keph.*, pp. 14.4ff., 16.29–31; *Psalm-Book*, pp. 3.21, 9.2, 14.14–15, 16.23, 20.6, 24.14–15, 32.10; *De haeresibus* 16.16; *Con. Fel.* 1.9; *De utilitate credendi* 3.7; *De agono christiano* 28.30.

12 I.e., to the *fabula Persica* (*De util. cred.*, 18.36) recorded in *Persicis libris* (*Con. Faustum* 13.17), which was taught by the *falso Christo Persarum* (ibid., 11.5).

13 *Psalm-Book*, p. 200.21.

14 "Non aliam ob causam nos in tales homines incidisse, nisi quod se dicebant, terribili auctoritate separata, mera et simplici ratione eos qui se audire vellent introducturos ad Deum, et errore omni liberaturos . . . qualem me tunc illi invenerunt, spernentem scilicet quasi aniles fabulas, et ab eis promissum, apertum et sincerum verum tenere atque haurire cupientem" (*De util. cred.* 1.2). Augustine thus implies that he expected to find an esoteric philosophy behind the myths. Cf. *Confessions* 3.6–7 for the Manichaeans' approach in winning Augustine over.

15 Augustine himself, of course, would come to stress the primacy of faith (*De moribus ecclesiae catholicae* 2.3, 10.17) and of *canonica auctoritas* as the guide to *certa ratio* (*Con. Faustum* 11.5; cf. *De vera religione* 24.45).

16 See, in particular, P. Gignoux, "L'Inscription de Kartir à Sar Mašhad," *Journal Asiatique*, 256 (1968), 387–418 (see too the reference to the previous publications) and C. J. Brunner, "The Middle Persian Inscription of the Priest Kirdēr at Naqš-i Rustam," *Near Eastern . . . Studies in Honor of George C. Miles* (Beirut, 1974), pp. 97–113 (also with regard to n. 17). Quite significant is the condensed formulation in the Naqš-i Rajab inscription; see *Corpus inscriptionum Iranicarum* III/II Plates, Portfolio III, *Minor Inscriptions of Kartīr* [London, 1963], pls. 81–84.

17 For Ādurbād, see the texts and references in H. S. Nyberg, *A Manual of Pahlavi* I (Wiesbaden, 1964), pp. xx–xxi, 107–12; and in *The Book of Arda Viraf*, edd. M. Haug and E. W. West (Bombay & London, 1872).

18 Although "time of the long dominion" was the first of Ohrmazd's creations, it was fashioned from the pre-existent unbounded time: "For it [i.e., time] was unbounded before the mixture of Ohrmazd's eternity. It was fashioned as bounded, out of that unbounded [time], so that there might be a 12,000-year compact from the original creation, when creatures were created, until the end, when Evil Mēnōg will become powerless, so that bounded [time] will merge [and] turn back into limitlessness, when indeed the creatures of Ohrmazd will exist forever in purity with Ohrmazd. As it says in the Religion: 'Time is mightier than both creations' — the creation of Ohrmazd and that of Evil Mēnōg" (*Bundahišn*, p. 10.2–9).

19 "Deus enim fecit et tempora: et ideo antequam faceret tempora, non erant tempora. Non ergo possumus dicere fuisse aliquod tempus quando Deus nondum aliquid fecerat. Quomodo enim erat tempus quod Deus non fecerat, cum omnium temporum ipse sit fabricator?" (*De Genesi contra Manichaeos* 1.2.3).

20 He states: "affirmant omnipotentem Deum necessitate oppressum esse" (*De agono chr.* 4.4); "Deus ante bellum sine commixtione mali habebat necessitatis malum" (*Con.

Faustum 21.16); cf. *Con. Secundinum* 20 and *De natura boni* 42. He also comments: "Causas enim voluntatis Dei scire quaerunt, cum voluntas Dei omnium quae sunt, ipsa sit causa" (*De Gen. con. Man.* 1.4.2).

21 See, e.g., *Acta Arch.*, p. 9.11ff.; Theodore Bar Khonai and Severus of Antioch in Cumont, *Recherches*, pp. 7, 89–90; *De haer.* 16.2; and the beginning of the *Epistula . . . fundamenti* in *Con. ep. . . . fund.* 13.16.

22 Augustine frequently formulates his diametrical opposition to the two principles: "omne quidquid esset, quoniam esset, in quantumcumque esset, ex uno Deo esse" (*De duabus animabus* 6.9); "omnem naturam, in quantum natura est, bonam esse" (*Con. ep. . . . fund.* 33.36); "non ergo mala est, in quantum natura est, ulla natura" (*De nat. boni* 17.17); "malum nihil esse quam corruptionem" (*Con. ep. . . . fund.* 35.39). See also *Con. Sec.* 12, 15; *Enchiridion* 4.12–14; *De moribus Manichaeorum* 1.1–2.2; *De Gen. con. Man.* 2.29.43; *De diversis quaestionibus 83* 6.

23 *δύο σέβει θεοὺς ἀγεννήτους, αὐτοφυεῖς, ἀΐδιους* (*Acta Arch.*, p. 9.12–13). Hyle was identified with the devil of Christianity, and with the Zoroastrians' Ahreman. Augustine points out the great contrast between this Hyle, an active, organizing, evil principle, and the prime matter of the pagan philosophers, which was good in its capacity for form (*Con. Faustum* 20.3; *De nat. boni* 18.18). Faustus argues God's finiteness thus: "Quoniam quidem si non est malum, profecto infinitus est Deus; habet autem finem, si malum est: constat autem esse malum: non igitur infinitus est Deus: illinc enim esse mala accipiunt, ubi bonorum est finis" (*Con. Faustum* 25.1).

24 In the Manichaean context, these terms tend to be interchangeable. See *Keph.*, p. 4.1–2; *Con. Fort.* 14; *Con. Faustum* 6.6; *De mor. Man.* 2.2. On the latter point, see *De du. anim.* 1.1.

25 Thus *Acta Arch.*, p. 9.13–14 continues: *ἕνα τῷ ἑνὶ ἀντικείμενον · καὶ τὸν μὲν ἀγαθόν, τὸν δὲ πονηρὸν εἰσηγεῖται, φῶς τῷ ἑνὶ ὄνομα θέμενος και τῷ ἑτέρῳ σκότος.* Note Severus' problem as to which terms define and which are descriptive of evil, darkness, and Hyle (Cumont, *Recherches*, pp. 89–90). Cf. the Zoroastrian terms in n. 39.

26 *Keph.*, p. 265.17–19; Cumont, *Recherches*, p. 97. Cf. *Acta Arch.*, p. 39.2–4: "Manes dixit: Bonus deus et nihil habens commune cum malo, firmamentum posuit in medio, quo alienum a se et separatum faceret malignum."

27 See *Con. Faustum* 21; *De mor. Man.* 9.14–17. *Con. Faustum* 19.24 likewise points out Hyle's laudable ambition.

28 *S. Ephraim's Prose Refutation of Mani, Marcion and Bardaisan* I, ed. and trans. C. W. Mitchell (London, 1912), pp. xxix–xxx; Cumont, *Recherches*, p. 113.

29 See *Psalm-Book*, pp. 54.30, 172.13; and *Keph.*, p. 130.23–24.

30 See Faustus' argument in *Con. Faustum* 25.1; *Keph.*, p. 267.10–18; *Letter of Secundinus* 6.

31 Ibid.; *Con. Sec.* 20; *Con. Fel.* 2.4. Hence Augustine's insistent question: "Nihil nocere poterat gens tenebrarum Deo, quare huc misit partem suam miscendam et polluendam a natura daemonorum?" (*Con. Fel.* 2.11).

32 Thus, e.g., *Con. Faustum* 5.4, 6.3, 6.8–9, 11.3, 18.7, 21.15–16, 22.98; *De mor. Man.* 11.21–22, 15.36–37; *De Gen. con. Man.* 2.8.11.

33 He addresses them: "Crassas omnino mentes et corporeorum simulacrorum pestifero pastu morbidas ad divina iudicanda defertis" (*De mor. eccl. cath.* 17.30). "Vos, qui cum carnem destestamini, nihil aliud quam vestram regulam detestamini, qua bona et mala metimini. Neque enim potest in vobis esse cogitatio vel malorum, nisi qualibus carnalis sensus offenditur, vel bonorum, nisi qualibus carnalis acies oblectatur" (*Con. Faustum* 21.4).

34 See, e.g., *Con. Faustum* 25.2, 32.20; *Con. ep. . . . fund.* 15.19–20; *De mor. eccl. cath.* 10.17; *De du. anim.* 2.2, 8.10; *Quaes. 83,* 29.

35 "Lucemque istam corpoream animantium mortalium oculis adiacentem . . . dei dicunt esse naturam" (*De haer.* 16.7). "Non enim norunt isti lucem, nisi quam carneis oculis vident" (*De Gen. con. Man.* 1.3.5).

36 E.g., *Con. Faustum* 2.5, 6.4, 20 passim; *Conf.* 3.10; *De haer.* 16.5–6, 11. Augustine's description of the ritual consumption of human semen (*De. haer.* 16.9), apparently by sectarian extremists, is plausible; for such a eucharist would have represented a logical application of Manichaean doctrine.

37 Severus in Cumont, *Recherches*, pp. 125–26.

38 "*Gētīg* is existence in visible and tangible corporeality" (*hād gētīg ast stī ī pad tanōmandīh wēnišnīg ud girišnōmand* (*Dēnkard*, ed. D. M. Madan [Bombay, 1911], p. 120.15–16; see J. de Menasce, *Le Troisième Livre du Dēnkart* [Paris, 1973], pp. 125–28). Cf. H. W. Bailey, *Zoroastrian Problems in the Ninth-Century Books* (Oxford, 1943), pp. 98ff.

39 The two essences (*xwadīh*) are: one of "the good substance" (*gōhr ī nēk*), one of "the evil substance" (*gōhr ī wad*); see F. C. Andreas, *The Book of the Mainyō-i Khard* (Kiel, 1882), p. 9.7–10. The two substances consist, respectively, of light (*rōšn*) and darkness (*tārīgīh*) (*Dādistān ī Dēnīg*, ed. T. D. Anklesaria [Bombay, 1911], 36.37), although darkness is also referred to as identical with evil (ibid., 36.70). The two essences are also termed "the Light-existence" (*stī rōšnīh*) and "the Darkness-existence" (*stī tārīgīh*) (*Bundahišn*, p. 11.2, 10), within which Ohrmazd and Ahreman dwelt primordially (*Zātspram* 1.1–2). See Bailey, *Zoroastrian Problems*, pp. 89–90.

40 See the texts collected in *Zurvan*, ed. Zaehner.

41 "Body" conveyed the sense "*gētīg*"; cf. "the body [is] that [which is] *gētīg*" (*tan ān gētīg, Bundahišn*, p. 34.6) "Corpse" established clearly the desired connotation.

42 I.e., the two trees of being (*Keph.*, pp. 17.5–9, 22.32) bear appropriate fruit (*Con. Fortunatum* 22).

43 See *Bundahišn*, chaps. 1ff.

44 See *Keph.*, pp. 122–23, 136–37.

45 This motif is frequent in the *Psalm-Book*; see pp. 50.11, 53.2, 55.19–20, 57.17, 70.30, 75.16–17, 79.20, 82.15, 87.1, 89.25, 99.4, etc. The creatures may also be viewed as in bondage: "Ego duas naturas esso dico, . . . malam vero esse tam mundum hunc quam omnia quae in eo sunt, quae quasi ergastula in parte maligni posita sunt" (*Acta Arch.*, p. 26.5–9).

46 On the one hand, "Manes dixit: Sed homo a mala natura plasmatus manifestum est" (ibid., p. 31.7–8); "per naturam gentis tenebrarum . . . esse hominem malum" (*Con. Faustum* 19.24; cf. 20.15 and *De mor. Man.* 15.37). The presence of Light, on the other, has modified this evil: "Deus autem miscendo bonitatem suam huius fabricae malitiam temperavit" (*Con. Faustum* 21.9). See *Keph.*, pp. 157–58 on the battle for possession of man.

47 "And all humankind, male and female, who are born in the whole world are the handiwork of Āz" (*ud mardōhm nar ud māyag čē hāmšahr zāyēnd hān harw āz dēsišn hēnd*), M 7983 II R II, 16–19 in F. C. Andreas and W. B. Henning, *Mitteliranische Manichaica aus Chinesisch-Turkestan* I, *Sitzungsberichte der Preussischen Akademie der Wissenschaften*, Abh. 10 (1932), 202. Lust, in effect, is the agency of sin by which mankind was created (*Keph.*, p. 138.17–18). Eve is the proximate representative of Āz: *τὴν δὲ Ἔυαν ὁμοίως ἔκτισαν, δόντης αὐτῇ ἐκ τῆς ἐπιθυμίας αὐτῶν πρὸς τὸ ἐξαπατῆσαι τὸν Ἀδάμ* (*Acta Arch.*, p. 20.5–6).

48 "Et si utuntur coniugibus, conceptum tamen generationemque desistent ne divina substantia, quae in eos per alimenta ingreditur, vinculis carneis ligetur in prole . . . cum pater eorum [i.e., Adam and Eve] nomine Saclas . . . quidquid inde commixtum divinae substantiae coeperat, cum uxore concumbens in carne prolis tanquam tenacissimo vinculo colligasset" (*De haer.* 16.13–14; cf. *Con. Faustum* 6.3).

49 E.g., "Manes dixit: Radix quidem mala, arbor autem pessima, incrementum vero non ex deo, fructus autem fornicationes, adulteria, homicidia, avaritia et omnes mali actus malae illius radicis" (*Acta Arch.*, p. 30.7–10); see pp. 15–16 on metempsychosis, as well as the texts in A. V. M. Jackson, "The Doctrine of Metempsychosis in Manichaeism," *Journal of the American Oriental Society*, 45 (1925), 246–68.

50 See M 9 II R in F. C. Andreas and W. B. Henning, *Mitteliranische Manichaica aus Chinesisch-Turkestan* II, *Sitzungsberichte der Preussischen Akademie der Wissenschaften*, Abh. 7 (1933), 299–300. On the Zoroastrian doctrine in the *Bundahišn* and *Dēnkard*, see Bailey, *Zoroastrian Problems*, pp. 98–100.

51 *Keph.*, pp. 169.31–170. Cf. *Bundahišn* 28, which begins: "It says in the Religion that the body of people [is] analogous to the world" (*pad dēn gōwēd kū tan mardōhmān handāzag ī gētīg*, p. 189.3–4).

52 "Patibilem Jesum . . . omni suspensus ex ligno" (*Con. Faustum* 20.2). See *Psalm-Book*, pp. 121.22–23, 134.19–20; and cf. the teaching on the "cross of Light" in *Keph.*, pp. 208–10, 220.25, 224.4.

53 "Sed Manichaei corpora humana opificium dicunt esse gentis tenebrarum et carceres quibus victus inclusus est Deus" (*Con. Faustum* 20.22); "putando se esse naturam et substantiam Dei" (ibid. 12.13).

54 "Peccatum vel iniquitas non est appetitio naturarum malarum sed desertio meliorum" (*De nat. boni* 34.34). "Nequaquam dubitare debemus, rerum quae ad nos pertinent . . . causam . . . malarum vero ab immutabile bono deficientem boni mutabilis voluntatem prius angeli, hominis postea" (*Enchiridion* 8.23).

55 E.g., "unum [sc. *malum*] quod homo facit, alterum quod patitur: quod facit, peccatum est; quod patitur poena . . . . ita homo male facit quod vult, ut male patiatur quod non vult" (*Contra Adminatum* 26). Cf. *Con. Sec.* 19; *Con. Fort.* 15; *De lib. arb.* 1.1.1.

56 Thus: "Improba voluntas malorum omnium causa est" (*De lib. arb.* 3.17.48). "Est ergo vitium voluntatis quo est homo deterior" (*Quaes. 83* 3). "Nullo modo sit peccatum si non sit voluntarium" (*De vera rel.* 13.17).

57 See *De div. quaes. ad Simp.* 1.1.3 and 10, *Con. Fort.* 22, *De lib. arb.* 3.52–53.

58 "Quamquam et hoc peccatum quo consentitur peccati concupiscentiae, nonnisi voluntate committitur" (*Retractiones* 1.15.2). See also *Enchir.* 9.31.

59 Regarding *De lib. arb.* he says: "In his atque huius modi verbis meis, quia gratia Dei commemorata non est, de qua tunc non agebatur" (*Retrac.* 1.9.4).

60 *Psalm-Book*, pp. 19.19, 86.19, 95.23, 134.19. Cf. *De haer.* 16.6, 18; *De vera rel.* 37.68; *De mor. eccl. cath.* 20.37.

61 *Psalm-Book*, p. 200.27. Light-Mind is the Noah who carries the soul in the ark of the Commandments over the flood of lust to the harbor of peace (ibid., pp. 157.20, 171.20–22, 176.30, and 177).

62 "Novum [sc. *hominem*] qui renovatur in agnitione Dei, secundum imaginem eius qui creavit eum in vobis" (*Con. Faustum* 24.1, where Eph. 4:22–24 is similarly applied). Cf. *Keph.*, pp. 89.22–24, 215.1–5, 256.20–21.

63 "Et id esse peccatum animae, si post commonitionem Salvatoris nostri et sanam doctrinam eius a contraria et inimica sui stirpe se segregaverit anima, et purioribus se

adornans anima" (*Con. Fort.* 21). Cf. *Letter of Secundinus* 2; *Keph.*, pp. 144.4–7, 222.25–223.9, 287.22–23. See also *Con. Fel.* 2.5. and *De du. anim.* 12.18.

64 *εἶτα πάλιν ἀφίησι τὸν βῶλον μετὰ τοῦ νέου αἰῶνος, ὅπως πᾶσαι αἱ ψυχαὶ τῶν ἁμαρτωλῶν δεθῶσιν εἰς τὸν αἰῶνα* (*Acta Arch.*, p. 21.7–8). Cf. *De haer.* 16.19, *Con. Sec.* 20, *Con. Fel.* 2.8. A. V. W. Jackson's belief ("The Doctrine of the Bolos in Manichaean Eschatology," *Journal of the American Oriental Society*, 58 [1938], 225–34) that the loss of some Light was not part of Mani's original doctrine is against the evidence. For the continuing influence of the Bolos concept and other Manichean doctrines on Augustine, see E. Buonaiuti, "Manichaeism and Augustine's Idea of 'Massa Perditionis,'" *Harvard Theological Review*, 20 (1927), 117–27; A. Adam, "Das Fortwirken des Manichäismus bei Augustin," *Zeitschrift für Kirchengeschichte*, 69 (1958), 1–25.

6

Ontological Problems in Nyāya, Buddhism, and Jainism: A Comparative Analysis

Bimal Krishna Matilal
All Souls College
and
The Oriental Institute
Oxford

The term "ontology" came to be used to indicate the most general part of metaphysics in seventeenth-century Europe, although for the origin of ontology as a general theory of real entities, or as a theory of being *as* being, one has to go back to Aristotle and to the Presocratic philosophers of ancient Greece. Aristotle did not use either the term "ontology" or the term "logic," yet the history of both logic and ontology in the Western tradition seems to start with him. Aristotle talks about a "first philosophy," which, he says, is about being as being, and this is taken in later Western tradition to be the nearest analogue of "ontology." For the present discussion, I shall assume ontology to mean a general theory of "what there is" and try to apply it to the Indian tradition. There are many other problems usually discussed in connection with ontology in the West, such as the doctrine of the distinction of essence and existence, or the theory of the transcendental properties of all entities, but these topics will not directly concern us in this essay.

The Nyāya-Vaiśeṣika ontological problem is connected with the Vaiśeṣika doctrine of categories (*padārtha*), and the category of substance is at the focal point of this doctrine. The system of Vaiśeṣika categories is generally regarded as a classification of real and fundamental entities. It is also possible to view it as an analysis of the "concrete" objects of our experience into their various parts in order to form a theoretical basis for philosophical discussion. But the Nyāya-Vaiśeṣika philosophers believe that if we can analyse and classify the concrete object of our experience in this manner into substance, quality, and action, we shall achieve a satisfactory explanation of "what there is," i.e., an explanation of what is meant when we say "that object exists."

The Buddhists, on the other hand, think that the so-called concrete object of our experience is at best a synthetic object and hence is analysable into a number of fundamental properties or elements called *dharmas.* The Buddhist conception of a *dharma* is that it is by nature a non-substance (cf. *anātman*).[1] The question "What is there?" can be answered, according to the Buddhists, if we can prepare a satisfactory list of such non-substances or *dharmas* which we can refer to while we are accounting for and analysing the objects of our experience. The *dharmas* are also in perpetual flux, "in a beginningless state of commotion," and *nirvāṇa* is posited as the ultimate cessation of this "commotion" for a person. *Nirvāṇa* is also said to be the ultimate reality, the ultimate nature of things, to be contrasted with the phenomenal existence of *dharmas*, but, as I have already indicated, this problem will not be our concern in this context.

Our prephilosophical common sense tells that there are things around us which somehow undergo change. Our philosophical worries start with our recognition of the phenomenon of change vis-à-vis our feeling for the continuity and sameness which underlie it. In India this problem was reflected in the old dispute of *Sat*-cosmology vs. *Asat*-cosmology (found in the Ṛgveda as well as in the Upanishads). The philosophic resolution of this dispute is to be found in the two rival theories about causation and creation in ancient India: (1) *sat-kārya-vāda*, "the theory of the pre-existence of the effect in the cause"; and (2) *asat-kārya-vāda*, "the theory of the new creation of the effect which was non-existent before." For those who prefer a comparative approach, it is significant to note that the so-called paradox of change and permanence, of being and becoming, was as much a live issue for the early Indian philosophers as it was for the Greeks, i.e., the Presocratics. Those who were inclined towards permanence not only posited the notion of an enduring substance but also argued that change was only the superficial transformation of the existent (the substantial) from one state into another. The Sāṃkhya and the early Vedānta belonged to this group in so far as they gave prominence to *Sat*, "the existent." The Vaiśeṣikas belonged to the group of *Asat* cosmologists inasmuch as they admitted change to be real and the function of the cause to be the creation of new things, effects. But they also posited the doctrine of substance — in fact, of the plurality of substance — and their substantial elements were said to be persistent through changing states. The Buddhist variety of *Asat* cosmologists were very radical, for they argued that change alone was real; the notion of continuity or persistence, illusory; and the notion of soul-substance, a myth. The Jaina school, as we shall see, was a compromise between the Buddhists and the Nyāya-Vaiśeṣikas.

The ontological positions of Nyāya-Vaiśeṣikas, Buddhists, and Jainas were of necessity influenced by their respective stands on the problem of change and continuity. The Buddhists, for example, were pre-eminently anti-substantialists in the Indian tradition. This anti-substantialism culminates in their "flux" doctrine, according to which the components of every object, all *dharmas*, change completely from moment to moment. A comparativist might be reminded here of the anti-substantialism of Heraclitus of Ephesus, who held, in contrast to Parmenides' denial of change, that change was incessantly occurring. But it is not certain that the Heraclitean acceptance of change as reality amounted to the "flux" doctrine, as it was understood by both Plato[2] and Aristotle.[3] The "flux" doctrine may be due to an interpretation of the Heraclitean position by the philosopher Cratylus. This would at least give credence to the anecdote related by Aristotle about the "river" example of Heraclitus. Aristotle says that Cratylus "criticized Heraclitus for saying that it is impossible to step twice into the same river; *he* [Cratylus] thought one could not do it even once" (*Met.* 1010A13–14). Thus, Cratylus was probably much closer to the Buddhists in this regard.

The Nyāya-Vaiśeṣikas, on the other hand, were substantialists, though they also accepted change much in the same manner as Aristotle did. But we need not proceed in this comparative vein any longer. It is important to understand now the Nyāya-Vaiśeṣika doctrine of existence as well as their notion of substance. *Vaiśeṣika-sūtra* 8.14 asserts that what exists can be analysed into three categories: substance, quality, and action.[4] Existence in this system is regarded as a generic property common to the members of the three classes. Each of these classes has a class property or generic property, viz., substance-ness, quality-ness, and action-ness; but these generic properties are to be distinguished from "existence" as a generic property.[5] Candramati, in fact, regarded existence as a completely separate category (*padārtha*), while class-properties such as substance-ness were included under the category of "generality" (cf. *sāmānya* or *sāmāya-viśesa*). But Praśastapāda interpreted "existence" as the highest generic property and thus brought both existence and other class-properties such as substance-ness and quality-ness under one category (*padārtha*) called generality.[6] But still a special place was accorded to existence as the all-inclusive generic property, which should be distinct from the included (*vyāpya*) generic properties such as substance-ness and quality-ness. A particular substance is characterized by the *being* of substance or substance-ness much as it is also characterized by many qualities and probably by some actions. But it is also characterized by "existence" (inasmuch as it exists), which is not to be identified with its substance-ness or with any of its qualities.

The best way to explain the notion of existence in this system is to contrast it with the notion of "real" and with that of the non-existent. Existence and other included generic properties are themselves real but not existent. For, otherwise, we should have to indulge in talking about the existence of existence and so on *ad infinitum*. Similarly, the important relation called *samavāya*, which combines the generic property existence with the particular existents, such as a substance or a quality or an action, is also regarded as real but not existent.[7] Thus, the generic properties and their inseparable relation with the particulars are posited as real, as means of explicating the notion of existence. Hence, to avoid the problem of self-dependence and regress, they themselves should not be construed as "existents." Nonetheless, these notions — existence, generalities, and *samavāya* — are claimed in this system to be real in the sense of their being independent of our thoughts or minds and thus distinct from a non-entity. A non-entity is non-existent and hence unreal — the sky-flower, the son of a barren woman, the rabbit's horn, and the unicorn, for example.

Briefly stated, the "existents" in this system (early Vaiśeṣika) are equivalent to the particulars, such as a chair, a particular colour, a particular action. The class of existents is a sub-class of the class of reals. Universals (including relations) are thus not existents but reals. Praśastapāda used two significant notions in order to separate the class of existents from that of universals: *sattā-sambandha* and *svātmasattva*. The first notion characterizes each existent, for it means that existence resides in the particular entity by *samavāya* relation. The second notion became a bit puzzling for later commentators. Udayana explains it as "lacking existence" (*sattā-viraha*). Śrīdhara gives almost the same interpretation but points out that "existence" could be ascribed to the universals only by mistake. Vyomaśiva says that, although the first notion means that existence is correctly applied to the class of particulars, the second notion means that existence is only metaphorically applied to the class of universals.[8]

The riddle of existence and non-existence is further complicated in the later Nyāya-Vaiśeṣika by the acceptance of negative properties as real. Our negative statements, according to the later Nyāya-Vaiśeṣika, are expressions of something, some negative facts. The affirmative–negative dichotomy among judgments is interpreted differently in this system. Thus, just as a positive judgment attributes a positive property to a thing, so a negative judgment attributes another property, a negative one, to the thing denoted by the subject term. Just as a positive property predicated by a judgment can be construed as a real property, so a negative property, the absence of some positive property, predicated by a judgment can be construed as a real property. Thus, "the room is dark" can be interpreted as expressing the room which is characterized by the property of the absence of light. Now, this property, the absence of light, and the like are regarded by the Nyāya-Vaiśeṣika as real inasmuch as they are to be distinguished from the unreal such as the round square and unicornhood. But, again, care should be taken to note that the absence of light is not existent in this system in the sense in which a substance or a quality or an action is existent. It may also be noted that, although the negation of an entity is construed in this system as expressing absence of that entity, a so-called negative property, no non-entity such as the sky-flower or the unicorn can be negated (in other words, absence of such non-entities will not be an acceptable negative property in this system[9]).

Leaving aside the riddle of existence and non-existence, let us concentrate on the Nyāya-Vaiśeṣika doctrine of substance and quality, which was at the focal point of their ontology. Several notions of substance have been emphasized in the Vaiśeṣika at one time or another: (*a*) substance as the locus of qualities and actions;[10] (*b*) substance as the substratum of change;[11] and (*c*) substance as capable of independent existence.[12] It is difficult to say whether the concept of substance as the logical subject was at all implied in early Nyāya-Vaiśeṣika doctrine, for it was never thoroughly worked out. Later Nyāya and Buddhist logicians (notably Diṅnāga) developed the concept of *dharmin*, "property-possessor," which was the nearest Indian analogue for "logical subject." But this concept was regarded as neutral to the ontological beliefs of the logicians. The concept of substance as the unchanging "essence" was prevalent in the Sāmkhya school as well as in the early Vedānta (cf. the spiritual substance), but the concept was not treated seriously in the Vaiśeṣika school. It is also to be noted that the Mādhyamika Buddhists were uncompromising critics of the doctrine of *svabhāva*, "own-nature," which was analogous to the notion of essence or inner immutable core of things.

The doctrine of substance as the substatrum of change needs further elaboration in the present context, for this will throw much light on the Vaiśeṣika theory of causation and change. For any effect, the Nyāya-Vaiśeṣika will identify a particular substratum cause (*samavāyi-kāraṇa*) in which that particular effect is supposed to inhere. If the physical conjunction of two material bodies is taken to be the effect in question, its substratum cause will be the two bodies themselves. If the taste of a fruit is regarded as the effect, its substratum cause will be the fruit-stuff itself. But when the effect is nothing but a concrete individual such as a pot, its substratum cause will be the pot-parts or, in final analysis, the atomic constituents of the pot material. Thus, the substratum cause of an effect need not be an ever-unchanging substratum. We do not have to posit an unchanging substantial core as the locus of change. What is needed is only the temporal stability, persistence through a period of time, of the substance which acts as the locus of the effect.

Substances, according to the Nyāya-Vaiśeṣika, are either impermanent (having origin, stability, and decay) or permanent (without origin or decay).[13] Material bodies of intermediate size (called *avayavin*, "whole," in this system) such as a pot or a table are of the first type. They have temporal stability and can be the loci of qualitative change. These substances are divisible into parts and those parts into further parts. But the atomic constituents of these substances, along with other non-material substances — such as soul, sky, time, and space — are of the second type, i.e., permanent. An important part of this doctrine of substance is the ontology of the "whole" as distinct from the assemblage of parts. A material body, e.g., a piece of chalk, is a whole which is a distinctly existent entity, to be distinguished from the integration of its parts or the combination of its atomic constituents. It is a new entity which is created as soon as the parts or atoms are put together. Moreover, if one should draw a line on the board with this piece of chalk, one would create a new piece, for some parts of the old piece are lost. The seeming identity of the new one with the old piece works for all our practical purposes, but ontologically the two are distinguishable.

The Buddhist anti-substantialism finds its extreme expression in the Sautrāntika doctrine of momentariness. According to this doctrine, a seemingly stable object such as a chair is dissolved into a cluster of continuously fluctuating chair-moments or chair-stages. The real entity is a point-instant, an exclusive particular, an essentially unqualifiable, ineffable "here-now" subject. Everything else in this system is only a conceptual construction — an interplay of the commonly shared imagination. In what sense does a moment exist? A moment exists insofar as it functions in some way or other. Thus, Dharmakīrti has argued that *to be* means to be capable of functioning in some way or other.[14] If a thing does not have causal efficacy, it does not exist. Starting from this initial position Dharmakīrti and his followers formulated a proof of their "flux" doctrine.[15]

1. To be is to do something, i.e., to function or to have causal potency.
2. To have causal potency means to be actually doing what is supposed to be done.
3. If something has causal potency at a particular moment, it must do its work at that moment. (This is a rephrasing of 2.)
4. If something does not do its work at a given moment, it must be causally impotent to do that work. (This is a contraposition of 3.)

5. The same thing cannot be both causally potent at one moment and causally impotent at another (next) moment, for potency and impotency are contradictory properties, mutually incompatible.
6. Therefore, the thing at the moment of its potency must be held to be ontologically different from the thing at the moment of its impotency. A difference in qualities implies a difference in the thing itself!
7. Everything, in this manner, can be shown to be in perpetual flux. We cannot step twice into the same river!

The Buddhist takes his most crucial step here when he identifies causal potency with actuality or actual doing. In other words, the notion of potentiality is completely rejected; if a thing exists and is capable, it must function without lying in wait for anything to come to help. If we posit two different functionings at two different moments, we must construe them as belonging to two different things or objects. In each moment a new object (*bhāva*) emerges when a new functioning sets in and the old functioning perishes. Thus, what exists is the ever-fluctuating here-and-now. Even the ontology of stages or moments is not quite satisfactory to the Buddhists. For moments or stages are also hypothetical abstractions in the face of the continuum. Thus, we have to say that there is only process, only flux, without there being something to fluctuate. There is only transmigration without there being any transmigrating soul (cf. the "non-soul" doctrine).

Udayana, setting forth a defence for the Nyāya-Vaiśeṣika doctrine of substance, has criticized this Buddhist argument by pointing out that it is essentially dependent upon the total rejection of the notion of potentiality. Why, asks Udayana, is it to be assumed that the causally potent cannot (and should not) "wait" for its accessories? Causality operates with two mutually compatible notions: *svarūpayogyatā*, "potentiality," and *phalopadhāyakatā*, "actuality." The former relates to the general; the latter, to the particular. If the Buddhist equates potentiality with actuality, then, Udayana argues, part of the Buddhist argument is reduced to tautology; for he would have to say that X is actually functioning because it actually functions. And tautology is not a good philosophic argument. In fact, potentiality is explained by Udayana, not as an essential constituent of the thing, but as the mere presence of the thing coupled with the absence of some accessory or other and the consequent absence (or non-arising) of the effect.[16] Thus, Udayana argues, if X does not cause Y when and only when Z is absent, then it follows that when Z is present X produces Y. This is only another way of saying that Z is an accessory to X in bringing about Y. Besides, the properties of causing Y and of not causing Y are not two mutually incompatible characters as cow-ness and horse-ness are. A cow, of course, can never be a horse. But a thing, if it is not just a flux, can cause Y at time t_1 and may not cause Y at time t_2.[17] In fact, what Udayana says is reminiscent of Aristotle's rejection of potentiality: "There are some who say, as the Megaric school does, that a thing 'can' act only when it is acting, and when it is not acting it 'cannot' act, e.g. that he who is not building cannot build, but only he who is building, when he is building; and so in all other cases. It is not hard to see the absurdities that attend this view" (*Met.* 1046B28–32). It is rather significant that the arguments and counter-arguments of Dharmakīrti and Udayana were presupposed much earlier in the Megaric school and in Aristotle.

Dharmakīrti's argument to prove his "flux" doctrine was not entirely an innovation in Buddhist tradition. He must have derived his idea from Nāgārjuna's dialectic; for Nāgārjuna argued, for example, that if something exists it should always exist, and if it does not exist at one time it cannot exist at any time.[18] This is how Nāgārjuna criticized the concept of existence and "own-nature." Dharmakīrti first assumes that to be means to have causal potency. Then he argues that if something has causal potency, it must be functioning all the time, and if something does not have the causal potency at one time, it would never have it at any other time. But Nāgārjuna's philosophic conclusion is rather different from Dharmakīrti's. With the above argument Nāgārjuna wishes to avoid the extremes of eternalism and annihilationism and to follow the Middle Way. Dharmakīrti, on the other hand, intends to conclude that since functioning is instantaneous, existence is also instantaneous. And when we think of Udayana's counter-argument, we are again reminded of Aristotle:

> Again, if that which is deprived of potency is incapable, that which is not happening will be incapable of happening; but he who says of that which is incapable of happening either that it is or that it will be will say what is untrue. . . . But we cannot say this, so that evidently potency and actuality are different (but these views make potency and actuality the same, and so it is no small thing they are seeking to annihilate) . . . [*Met.* 1047A10–20].

The Jaina ontological position is influenced by both the Buddhists and the Nyāya-Vaiśeṣika. The Jainas were also substantialist, but in a very qualified sense of the term. Their conception of existence (*sat*) is intimately related to their doctrine of substance. The *Tattvārthasūtra* 5.29 asserts: "What there is has the nature of substance."[19] And the next sūtra (5.30 in the Digambara tradition) adds: "what there is [the existent] is endowed with the triple character: origin, decay, and stability [persistence]."[20] The *Tattvārthabhāṣya* explains that whatever originates, perishes, and continues to be is called the existent; anything different is called the non-existent.[21] The next sūtra asserts that the existent is constant for it never gives up its being (essence?).

In sūtra 5.37, substance is again characterized as the possessor of qualities (*guṇa*) and modes (*paryāya*). Here the broad category "attribute" is apparently divided into two sub-categories, qualities and modes, but the distinction between the two is not found in the sūtra. Umāsvāti points out that qualities are permanent attributes of the substance, while the modes are only temporary attributes which are subject to origin and decay.[22]

In the above analysis of the *Tattvārthasūtra*, two compatible notions of substance are emphasized: (1) substance as the core of change or flux; and (2) substance as the substratum of attributes. Kundakunda combines these two notions as he defines substance in his *Pravacanasāra*:

> They call it a substance, which is characterized by origin, persistence, and decay, without changing its "own-nature," and which is endowed with qualities and accompanied by modifications. For the "own-nature" of the substance is its existence [*sad-bhāva*] which is always accompanied by qualities and variegated modes, and, at the same time, by origin, decay, and continuity.[23]

The Vaiśeṣika school, as we have already seen, emphasized both these aspects of substance, but did not equate the "own-nature" of the substance with existence. Aristotle, who in fact suggested several notions of substance either implicitly or explicitly, remarked in *Categories* 4A10–14 that "The most distinctive mark of substance appears to be that, while remaining numerically one and the same, it is capable of admitting contrary qualities." Aristotle also implied, in *Metaphysics* 1028A29–30, that the substance is what is independently existent; for existence, in the proper sense of the term, applies to substances only, and qualities and relation have a secondary existence, a parasitic mode of being: "Therefore that which is primarily, i.e. not in a qualified sense but without qualification, must be substance." The Jainas too identify the notion of "it is" or "it exists" with the notion of substance, and then they explain that "it is" means that it is endowed with the triple character of origin, decay, and stability.

In fact, the Jainas explain the notion of substance in such a way as to avoid falling between the two stools of being and becoming. It was a grand compromise of flux and permanence. The Jainas inherited from Mahāvirā and his later followers the well-known doctrine of "many-natured" reality (cf. *anekānta-vāda*), and thus a "compromise" position was an important trait of their creed. Substance, in their analysis, is being; it is also becoming. Kundakunda observes that a substance has both natures: from the point of view of one "own-nature," it is being (*sat*, unchanging); from another point of view, it has triple character, origin, decay, and continuity, i.e., fluctuations.[24] Siddhasena Divākara made the point more forcefully: "There is no substance which is devoid of modification; nor is there any modification without an abiding something, a substance. For origin, decay, and continuance are the three constituents of a substance."[25] It should be noted that the notion of continuity involved in the triple character of the substance is not identical with the notion of the permanence of the substance. The former notion means persistence or continuance (cf. *pravāha-nityatā*); the latter, immutability. It is the notion on the background of which the triple character of origination, destruction, and continuity becomes understandable. The notion of continuity, on the other hand, is essentially dependent upon origin and decay. Thus, Kundakunda observes: "There is neither origin without destruction nor destruction without origin; and neither destruction nor origination is possible without what continues to be."[26]

The Jainas were well aware of the Mādhyamika critique of the "own-nature" concept and of the problem involved in the doctrine of the permanent substance. It is true that the immutability of "own-nature" invites a host of problems. But the notion of flux, the Jainas point out, is not sacrosanct. Thus, just as the Buddhists argue that there is only fluctuation, there being no permanent being, so the Jainas maintain that if there is no permanence, there can be no change, no fluctuation, for only the permanent can change. Only the persisting soul can transmigrate.

When the *Tattvārthasūtra* defines substance as the substratum of qualities and modes, it was probably influenced by the Vaiśeṣika school. Thus, Siddhasena points out that the rigid Vaiśeṣika concepts of substance and quality were not compatible with the Jaina ontological principle of *anekāntatā*, "many-naturedness" or "non–one-sidedness." In fact, it would be as good as a heresy in Jainism if one should maintain a rigid distinction between substance and quality. The notion of triple character, origin, decay, and continuity, embodying the principle of (conditioned) reality, was derived from the Buddhist source. The Buddha, for example, predicated this triple character of all the conditioned (*saṃskṛta*) entities. Thus, in the *Aṅguttara* I, the Buddha said: "Of the conditioned entities, monks, the origin is conceived, even so their decay and their stability [persistence]."[27] Nāgārjuna directed his dialectical attack against the notion of the conditioned (*saṃskṛta*), however, and concluded that "Since the notion of origin, persistence, and decay cannot be established, the conditioned does not exist. And if the conditioned is not established, how will the unconditioned be established?" But why then did the Buddha speak of the triple character of the conditioned entities? Nāgārjuna replied: "Just as magic, dream, and the cloud-castle are unreal (but, nevertheless, are spoken about) so also origin, stability, and decay have been described."[28] The Jainas postulate the triple character in the case of each event, each happening or change of state. Each fluctuation embodies origin, continuity, and decay. Samantabhadra illustrates the point as follows: if a golden pot is destroyed and a golden crown is made out of it, destruction, origination, and continuity — all three — happen simultaneously and give rise to sorrow, joy, and indifferent attitude in the minds of three different kinds of people, those in favour of the pot, those in favour of the crown, and those in favour of the gold stuff.[29]

Siddhasena has shown great philosophic insight in expounding the Jaina ontological problem. According to him, reality can be viewed from two important standpoints, being and becoming, permanence and change. That is why Lord Mahāvīra acknowledged only two *nayas* or standpoints: "substance exists" and "modification exists." If X is an element of reality, then, according to Siddhasena, X can be viewed as a substance from the standpoint of being, and as a property from the standpoint of becoming. The standpoint of "becoming" (modification) reveals that everything originates, stays, and perishes; the standpoint of "being" ("it is") reveals everything as existent eternally without birth or decay. And, Siddhasena asserts, there cannot be being without becoming, or becoming without being; therefore, a substance (= reality) is defined as the combination of being (the existent) with becoming (origin, stability, and decay).[30]

The "being" aspect, according to Siddhasena, is the result of generalization; the "becoming" aspect, of particularization. In our ordinary description of things, we necessarily combine the general with the particular. From the point of view of the highest generalization, a thing is described as "it is," which reveals the permanent being, the substance. But when, in ordinary descriptions, a thing is called a piece of wood, or a chair, or a red chair, we have an intermixture of "being" and "becoming" aspects. In so far as the thing is identified as a non-fluctuating substance, it is the "being" standpoint. And in so far as the attributes of the thing, such as being a piece of wood, being a chair, or redness, are revealed by the description, it is the "becoming" standpoint. Qualities are nothing but modes or states of the substance. In any characterization or description of the thing, there is thus an overlap of "being" and "becoming" standpoints, until we reach the ultimate particularity, pure becoming, i.e., the point-instants (*kṣaṇas*) of the Buddhists.[31]

Thus, the Jaina conception of reality, in bringing together the opposing viewpoints of the Buddhists and the Nyāya-Vaiśeṣika, comes very close to that of Whitehead, for whom the chief aim of philosophy is the "elucidation of our integral experience" of both the flux and the permanence of things. Whitehead has said that philosophers who started with "being" have given us the metaphysics of "substance" and those who started with "becoming" have developed the metaphysics of flux. But Whitehead also points out the inseparability of the two:

> But, in truth, the two lines cannot be torn apart in this way; and we find that a wavering balance between the two is a characteristic of the greater number of philosophers. Plato found his permanences in a static, spiritual heaven, and his flux in the entanglement of his forms amid the fluent imperfections of the physical world. . . . Aristotle corrected his Platonism into a somewhat different balance. He was the apostle of "substance and attribute," and of the classificatory logic which this notion suggests.[32]

In the Indian context, one may observe that the Buddha's search for *nirvāṇa*, the unconditioned state, freedom from suffering or *duḥkha*, spelled out a philosophy for the later Buddhists, according to which the flux of things, impermanences, "the fluent imperfections of the physical world" are identical with suffering (*duḥkha*; cf. whatever is impermanent is suffering). And *nirvāṇa*, the unconditioned state, is actualized with the cessation of this *duḥkha*. The Vaiśeṣikas, on the other hand, were, much like Aristotle, the apostles of substance-and-attribute duality.

NOTES

1 T. Stcherbatsky, *The Central Conception of Buddhism* (repr. Delhi, 1974), pp. 24–25.

2 "Socrates: Heraclitus is supposed to say that all things are in motion and nothing at rest; he compares them to the stream of a river, and says that you cannot go into the same river twice" (*Cratylus* 402A, in *The Collected Dialogues of Plato*, edd. E. Hamilton and H. Cairns [New York, 1963]).

3 "It was this belief that blossomed into the most extreme of the views above mentioned, that of the professed Heracliteans, such as was held by Cratylus . . ." (*Metaphysics* 1010A10; this and all subsequent translations of Aristotle are taken from *The Works of Aristotle*, ed. W. D. Ross, 12 vols. [Oxford, 1908–1952]).

4 "*Artha iti dravya-guṇa-karmasu*" (*Vaiśeṣika-sūtras* of Kaṇāda, ed. Muni Sri Jambuvijayaji [Baroda, 1961]).

5 See ibid. 1.2.7–18.

6 Thus it is that Praśastapāda explains *sāmānya* as being of two types: *para* and *apara*. *Parasāmānya* is existence. Substance-ness, etc., are *aparasāmānya*. See Praśastapada, *Padārthadharmasaṃgraha* with *Kiraṇāvali*, ed. J. S. Jetly (Baroda, 1971), p. 15. For contrast, see Candramati: *The Vaiśeṣika Philosophy*, ed. H. Ui (London, 1917), pp. 99–101.

7 I am using the term "real" for the Vaiśeṣika term *padārtha*, "existence" for the Vaiśeṣika term *sattā*.

8 Praśastapāda, *Padārthadharmasaṃgraha*, pp. 20–21; Udayana, *Kiraṇāvālī*, ibid., p. 21; Śrīdhara, *Nyāyakandalī*, ed. D. Jha (Benares, 1963), pp. 49–50; Vyomaśiva, *Vyomavatī*, comm. on Praśastapadā, edd. G. Kaviraj and D. Shastri (Benares, 1930), p. 118.

9 See my "Reference and Existence in Nyāya and Buddhism," *Journal of Indian Philosophy*, 1, No. 1 (1970), 83–103.

10 *Vaiśeṣika-sūtra* 1.1.7: "*kriyā-vad guṇa-vat samavāyi-kāraṇam iti dravyal akṣaṇām.*"

11 Ibid. 1.1.17; "*dravya-guṇa-karmaṇām dravyaṃ kāraṇaṃ sāmānyam.*"

12 This is implied by the Navya-nyāya doctrine that a substance can exist by itself at the moment it is produced, without being joined by qualities and action (cf. *utpattikṣaṇāvacchinno ghaṭo nirguṇo niskriyaś ca.*

13 See Praśastapāda, *Padārthadharmasaṃgraha*, p. 22. Udayana comments: *anityadravyatvaṃ cānyatra nir-avayava-dravyebhya iti.*"

14 *Pramāṇavārttika* 2.3: "*arthakriyāsamarthaṃ yat tad atra paramārthasat*" (ed. Swami Dwarikadas Shastri [Benares, 1968], p. 100).

15 For the most elaborate presentation of the "flux" doctrine, see Jñānaśrīmitra: *Jñānaśrīmitranibandhāvali*, ed. A. Thakur (Patna, 1959), pp. 1–159.

16 See the first chapter of *Ātmatattvaviveka*, ed. Dhundhirāja Śāstri (Benares, 1940), esp. pp. 16–25: "*yad yad-abhāva eva yan na karoti tat tat-sadbhāve tat karoty eveti.*"

17 Ibid., p. 24.

18 *Mādhyamika-śāstra* 7.30–31 (ed. P. L. Vaidya [Darbhanga, 1960]).

19 "*Sat dravya-lakṣaṇam*" (Umāsvāti: *Tattvārthasūtra-bhāṣya*, ed. K. Siddhantasastri [Bombay, 1932]).

20 "*Utpādavyayadhrauvyayuktaṃ sat*" (ibid.).

21 Ibid., sūtra 5.29.

22 Ibid., sūtra 5.40.

23 *Pravacanasāra* 2.3–4 (ed. A. N. Upadhye [Agas, 1964]).

24 Ibid. 2.7.

25 *Sanmati* 1.12 (edd. Sukhlal Sanghavi and Bechardas Doshi, 5 vols. [Ahmedabad, 1924–1931]).

26 *Pravacansāra*, 2.8.

27 Quoted by Candrakīrti; see Nāgārjuna, *Mādhyamika-śāstra*, ed. Vaidya, p. 73.

28 See *Mādhyamika-śāstra*, 7.34.

29 *Āptamīmāṃsā* 3.57 (ed. Gajadharlal Jain [Benares, 1914]).

30 *Sanmati* 1.11–12.

31 Ibid. 1.9.

32 Alfred North Whitehead, *Process and Reality* (New York, 1929; repr. New York, 1969), pp. 240–42.

7

A Scotistic Approach to the Ultimate Why-Question

ALLAN B. WOLTER
The Catholic University of America

THIS TITLE AND SUBJECT warrant a word of explanation. On reading Paul Edwards' article "Why"[1] and Milton K. Munitz' earlier work on the why of the world's existence,[2] I wondered how a medieval philosopher might approach their problem. At the time I was lecturing on Aquinas, Scotus, and Ockham, so my speculation began with them.

Edwards is concerned to defend an empirical position which he puts in the mouth of Wittgenstein. If a question can be framed at all, "it can be answered.... doubt can exist only where there is a question, and a question only where there is an answer, and then only when something can be said."[3]

He distinguishes, among other meanings of why-questions, two which he calls cosmic. The first is the "theological why," which would be satisfied with a theistic answer as to why the world of becoming exists. This could be meaningful, given certain semantic qualifications. The second, and more important, question, however, is the one which he calls the "super-ultimate why-question." It is the sort of query which goes beyond God or transcendent being, and asks — as Heidegger asks at the beginning of his *Einführung in die Metaphysik*[4] — "Why is there anything at all?" "In the beginning God created heaven and earth is not an answer to . . . and cannot even be brought into relation with our question," says Heidegger. The believer who stops with God is not pushing his question "to the very end."

Edwards aims to prove that in this form the question is simply meaningless, not just unanswerable, and for the reasons which Wittgenstein speaks of in his *Philosophical Investigations*. "The super-ultimate question 'why' has lost . . . its ordinary meanings without having been given a new one."[5]

As Edwards notes in his bibliography, Munitz's *The Mystery of Existence* is "the only detailed attempt to reply to arguments such as those urged in the present article and to show that the super-ultimate why-question is meaningful, although it is in principle unanswerable."[6]

In point of fact, however, Munitz admits that the question as formulated by Heidegger, Leibniz, and others before him is linguistically faulty and malformed because of the indefiniteness of words like "everything" or "anything." "Would 'anything,' for example, include the number 'three,' or the possibility that my chair might collapse in the next five minutes, or the smile of the Cheshire cat?"[7]

Hence, he reformulates the super-ultimate why-question as "Why does the world exist?" or, as a later transformation, "Is there a reason-for-the-world's-existence?" and sets out to prove that these are indeed well-formed formulas, since the terms "world," "exists," and "why," etc., can all be given appropriate and straightforward meanings according to accepted linguistic usage. The remaining portion of his interesting book is devoted to showing that, although well-formed, the question is in principle unanswerable — not, however, in the sense that there must be an answer which our human condition prevents us from knowing (as a subscriber to Leibniz's "Principle of Sufficient Reason" would claim), but in the disjunctive sense that we do not know one way or the other whether there is any reason. If such a "reason" exists, it is no ordinary reason, since it is peculiar or proper to the existence of the world alone. (That is why he hyphenates the expression "reason-for-the-world's-existence" in his second formulation of the question above.)

It is this philosophical agnosticism which creates the "mystery of existence" and prompted Aristotle's comment that philosophy begins with wonder. "At first men wondered about the more obvious problems that demanded an explanation; gradually their inquiries spread further afield, and they asked questions on such larger topics as changes in the sun and moon and stars, and the origin of the world."[8]

So much for Edwards and Munitz. What of my three medievals, Aquinas, Scotus, and Ockham?

Aquinas, it must be admitted, attempts some kind of answer or sort of explanation in his *Summa contra gentiles* (I, 75) — at least to the question as formulated by Munitz — when he writes:

> Everyone desires the perfection of that which for its own sake he wills and loves: for the things which we love for their own sakes we wish to be excellent, and ever better and better, and to be multiplied as much as possible. But God wills and loves His essence for its own sake. Now that essence is not augmentable and multipliable in itself, but can be multiplied only in its likeness, which is shared by many. God therefore wills the multitude of things, inasmuch as He wills and loves His own perfection.[9]

In his classic *The Great Chain of Being*,[10] Arthur Lovejoy takes St. Thomas as a paradigmatic medieval example of the theistic confusion of Platonic origin, the history of which he is tracing: namely, the idea that God is a transcendent, all-perfect, immutable good, and yet is the real explanation why a world of becoming and change exists and why it contains precisely what it does.

Since Lovejoy's interpretation of Aquinas was subsequently challenged by Henry Veatch and Anton Pegis, with rejoinders by Lovejoy,[11] I had no wish to pursue a possible Thomistic answer to the super-ultimate why-question, where specialists might disagree.

Scotus, Lovejoy thought, escaped the dilemma by choosing one horn only— as Bruno and Spinoza were to do later in selecting the other.[12] And since Ockham, on this issue at least, is in substantial agreement with, and could be called a follower of, Duns Scotus, I decided to explore a Scotistic approach to the ultimate why-question.

Both Munitz and Edwards admit that some form of the cosmic why-question could be meaningfully asked, even if perhaps it could never be answered. Munitz, for instance, concedes that theism could provide an answer if one were to accept the "Principle of Sufficient Reason" and with it the cosmological argument for the existence of God — neither of which he is prepared to grant, however — at least on philosophical or rational grounds.[13] Agnosticism, not atheism, is the only tenable philosophical position, because it still leaves open the possibility that some "reason" might exist.[14]

Edwards, while arguing that the super-ultimate why-question is simply meaningless, is willing to admit that every theological why-question may not be so. Nevertheless, he finds the typical theist's answer bristling with difficulties, among which are not only the justifying arguments which the theist gives for a transcendent deity — which Munitz also questions — but also the very intelligibility of theological discourse as such.[15] How can one speak of a "disembodied mind, be it finite or infinite" or of "creation," to say nothing of the expression "necessary being" or "existence" in the sense of a predicate or perfection? And why should our quest for the reason for existence suddenly cease with God? Is this not treating the causal principle like a "hired cab" — to use Schopenhauer's metaphor — to be dismissed when we reach our destination? Or, as Nagel puts it: those who refuse to inquire into the reasons for the existence of the alleged absolute are "dogmatically cutting short a discussion when the intellectual current runs against them."[16]

These contemporary concerns, then, suggest some specific problems which a medievalist might want to look into. Two "semantic problems" — to use Edwards' phraseology — which stand out are these: (*a*) How to render theological utterances intelligible? Or, negatively, How to prove that the theist's notions or descriptions of God are not self-contradictory at worst, or very muddled at best? (The same would seem to apply to Munitz's hyphenated version of "reason-for-the-existence-of-the-world.") How to show that such a notion makes sense at all when the only "reason for the existence of the world" which we can imagine would be of the unhyphenated variety? (*b*) How to establish the plausibility of any specific description of God? What reason, in short, have we that any kind of God exists, or that there just might be a hyphenated "reason-for-the-existence-of-the-world"?

Scotus, I think, addressed himself in his own way to both these problems, as I should like to show in this essay. I should like, too, by way of a corollary, to sum up what he might have said about the super-ultimate why-question itself.

On the Intelligibility of Philosophico-theological Discourse

Some General Observations

Scotus, of course, like Aquinas and Ockham, was a professional theologian rather than a philosopher, but he had an extensive background in both the logic and the philosophy of the day. The *Sentences* of Peter Lombard — the accepted "theological textbook" of their time — determined the topical framework and sequential order in which subjects of their own choosing might be raised. Since the "Master" treats the existence and unity of God (together with the Trinity or plurality of persons) in distinction two of the first book, and the questions of God's knowability from the *vestigia* or reflected images which he leaves behind in creatures in distinction three, we find Scotus reversing the order of our two questions in his *Commentary on the Sentences* (the *Ordinatio*). Thus his philosophical proof for God's existence and uniqueness precedes his discussion of the logical structure of our theistic concepts.

His question relevant to the latter reads "Utrum Deus sit naturaliter cognoscibilis ab intellectu viatoris"[17] — which I translate somewhat freely, in view of the way in which Scotus frames his answer, as "Is the intellect of a person in this life able naturally to form a concept of God?" Believing that he has demonstrated that among beings one and only one exists which is infinitely perfect, Scotus now inquires into the logical structure of this and other theistic conceptions.

After mentioning some current opinions, notably that of Henry of Ghent, he presents his own analysis in the form of five theses. (1) Our concepts are meant to be descriptions of God's essence or quiddity, i.e., they are answers to the question "What is he [*Quid est*]?" (2) The descriptions are not all analogous to our everyday notions of creatures, but contain at least one affirmative core concept or predicate which can be univocally affirmed of either God or a creature: namely, *ens* (which can be translated as "a being" or "a thing," where "thing" escapes the indefiniteness alluded to by Munitz by being carefully restricted to something which actually exists or can exist extramentally).[18] (3) Since we know God only through such imperfect descriptions as can be pieced together from elements and bits derived from creatures, the intellect of a person in this life cannot know God "properly in his unique individuality" — or, to use a well-known distinction of Russell's: we know God, not by acquaintance, but by description. An acquaintance-encounter, Scotus explains, is never something natural; it depends on God's will.[19] (4) How a "descriptive phrase" can be formed which zeroes in on what we mean by God, as distinct from creatures, is explained in theses four and five. Four reads:

> I say that we can form many concepts proper to God which are not applicable to creatures. Such are the concepts of the pure perfections [*perfectiones simpliciter*] understood in their maximal sense. And there is a still more perfect concept, in which as it were we have a kind of description in which God is known most perfectly, viz., when we conceive all pure perfections globally and each in a maximal sense. . . .[20]

This global attribution to God of what is simply perfect can be achieved by the use of a simpler concept which Scotus regards as logically equivalent to the other, viz., "infinite being." I shall have occasion to analyze the practical import of this notion later, so I shall say no more of it here and move on to thesis five.

> I say that those things which are known of God are known from their likenesses [*species*] in creatures. . . . That which can impress a less universal *species* in the intellect can also cause a *species* of anything more general, and thus creatures, which impress the likenesses [*species*] proper to themselves, can also impress the *species* of the transcendentals, which are applicable commonly to themselves and to God.[21]

If we abstract from the Aristotelian theory of concept formation which Scotus is working with, and substitute a more contemporary equivalent, what he is saying substantially is this. In our encounter with the world of experience we are able to conceive of, or to classify, things according to various degrees of generality. To use Munitz' example: "reason" as used in the unhyphenated version of "reason for the existence of the world" comprises the set of such reasons as we have occasion to use in speaking of the everyday objects we work with; specifically, it may have the meaning of "purpose," "evidence," or "causal action." "Reason" in the sense employed in the hyphenated version is only equivocal (or analogous at best) to the meaning of "reason" in the unhyphenated version, since the latter is radically different from any of the three aforementioned meanings, being applicable, if it is not vacuous, to "existence of the world" and to no other "existence." Nevertheless, Scotus would insist, since we have no experience of such, no direct knowledge of the other analogate or term, we must construct some notion of what it would be if it did or does exist. And for this we need at least some univocal affirmative notion with which to begin the construction. This will be a more general meaning of "reason" of which both the hyphenated and unhyphenated versions are more specific instances. Now, the same set of everyday objects, so to speak, can spark man's creative intellect to form a more general, refined notion of "reason" which, though applicable to the original set of things (purpose, evidence, and causal action), no longer is proper to any of them, but could be applied to some theoretical entity, which, besides this common feature, had others which are antithetical to any of these everyday common meanings.

Philosophers of science have analyzed in detail the moves which the mind makes in such concept construction. We begin by refining such everyday notions as "speed" or "change in speed" in order to form more precise notions such as "velocity" or "acceleration." And when we move from the macrocosmic world to the microcosmic realm, we find the need to introduce theoretical entities, such as electrons, mesons, fields, and so on, each with a peculiar set of properties unknown in combination at the macrocosmic level, yet each component of which is an affirmation, negation, or modification of what characterizes other objects of experience. In their finished state, these complex theoretical concepts are only analogous to any concepts directly applicable, more or less, to the world in which we move. Yet as Mary Hesse has pointed out,[22] in using models and analogies, we must distinguish an affirmative, a negative, and a neutral element. The affirmative indicates those features of the model which are found in the familiar things about us (Scotus would say that this is the univocal component or concept); the negative element represents the denial of certain features which are usually associated with the former (Scotus speaks of this in connection with theistic discourse as the removal of such imperfections or express limitations or inconsistencies as are usually found to be joined with common univocal notions insofar as they are proper to creatures); and finally there is the neutral area in which one can neither affirm or deny categorically, nor specify clearly, what further to expect. And in the field of science, at least, it is this neutral area which suggests new insights which account for the growth or "fruitfulness" of a theory. This neutral sphere, upon exploration, reveals new interrelations, arising from the unusual combinations of affirmative and negative elements, which suggest experimental tests which "confirm" or "falsify" the theory in question.

Here I am not concerned with the "corroboration" or "falsification" of any specific construct which we may use to describe what we believe God to be, for this is a special aspect of problem two. The only point I wish to make is that, for Scotus at least, the method of forming concepts of God, and hence of understanding "theistic discourse," is not essentially different, as I see it, from the way in which a physicist deals with theoretical entities which he regards not as simply fictitious, but in a very important sense as "real," since he sees what he believes to be their "calling cards" in the ionization tracks in a Wilson cloud-chamber, Gasser bubble-chamber, or stack of photographic-emulsion plates.

This interpretation gains plausibility in the exact parallel between the way Scotus constructs his concepts of God and the way Ockham forms his notion of what to him was not just a conceptual abstraction, but a real theoretical entity which could, by the power of God at least, exist in the extramental world apart from any form, substantial or accidental: namely, "primary matter."[23] Ockham does not consider this, like substantial form, to be something known directly or immediately. It does not belong to the class of simple concepts used to categorize our perceptual experience. Nor does it refer to the more abstract or refined conceptions which still have some measure of more or less direct verification at the observational level. The notion of primary matter is actually a complex concept built up by combining more elementary notions. Some of the latter, taken in themselves, designate something common to primary matter and to other things as well. But others refer only to things other than such matter. By affirming some and denying others, Ockham believes it possible to get a proper combination which applies to primary matter and to nothing else. To say that such "composed concepts" are constructs is not to say that they have no reference to anything in the extramental world, or that the properties described are not possessed in a simple, holistic fashion by the referent.[24] Whenever such theoretical entities are needed to account plausibly for the existence or behavior of the world, as we know it, we have rational grounds for believing in the existence or reality of such entities. Scotus elsewhere refers to such constructs which have been corroborated in this way as "inferred concepts which have the form of a conclusion."[25]

What I wish to emphasize, if it is not already obvious, is that the crude caricature of God as a "disembodied mind" does not do justice to the careful way in which Scotus at least moves from concepts characteristic of the experiential world and those he believes to be descriptive of God. Nor are the resulting concepts at which he arrives any more anomalous, for instance, than a popular science writer's use of "wavicles" to indicate that microcosmic "particles" have a de Broglie wave function, where the wave length is inversely proportionate to their velocity and mass.

I might note further that, like the physicist, the philosopher–theologian, at least, does not usually begin his theistic theory construction in a vacuum. He also believes that God has left his "calling cards" with mankind.

The God of Abraham, Isaac, and Jacob "visited his people"; the "Son of God" performed signs and wonders in Galilee, etc. All great religious movements seem to have their origin in some kind of "theophany." And despite the question of how such intervention of the divine in human affairs is possible or how it is to be verbally transmitted to the followers of a given sect in a reasonably convincing fashion, the phenomenon is too widespread to be ignored.

Philosophical discussion of "God" in connection with such phenomena has been concerned largely with ironing out the anomalies which stem from the metaphorical and anthropomorphic language associated with such revelation accounts. The aim of the philosopher–theologian is to come up with a theoretic construct of God which is not internally inconsistent or self-contradictory. Often this gets identified, or, better, integrated, with the Weltanschauung, or even — as was the case with Aristotle or the *falasifa* — with the astrophysical theories of the time, and comes to be regarded as an independent rational "proof" for the existence of a God of this sort. But when such "cosmic" theories or philosophies change, the proof, as an independent argument, runs into difficulty, Still this, again, is no different from the fate of scientific theories in times of what Thomas Kuhn has called "scientific revolutions."[26]

Some Specific Theistic Concepts

Two specific instances illustrating Scotus' use of this construction technique are his remarks about how we conceive God as infinite and as the highest good. What he would say about God as a necessary being can also be construed from what is implicit in his writings.

(*a*) "The Highest Good." After his observation in the fifth thesis that whatever can imprint or cause a *species* of what is less universal can also impress the *species* of what is more universal, and in particular the transcendental notions common to, or univocally predicable of, God and creatures, he goes on to say:

> Then the intellect in virtue of its own power can make use of many such *species* simultaneously, in order to conceive at one time those things of

which these are the *species*. For instance, it can use the *species* of "good," the *species* of "highest," the *species* of "act," to conceive "the highest good that is pure act." This is clear from the dialectical rule *a minori*,[27] for the imagination is able to use the *species* of different things perceptible to the senses and thus imagine a composite of these different elements, as is apparent, for instance, when we imagine a gold mountain.[28]

(*b*) "Infinite Being." In thesis four Scotus mentions that "infinite being" is a simpler concept which is logically equivalent to the global notion or "quasi-description" of God as the locus of "all pure perfections, each present to the maximal degree," a point I shall return to later in connection with problem two. In question five of his *Quodlibetal Questions*, he indicates specifically what he believes to be the conceptual moves which enable us to form such a notion. He begins with the purely mathematical description of quantity given by Aristotle, moving from strict arithmetical "addition" to the way in which non-additive or intensive properties could be arranged serially, and arriving at the theoretical construct "defined popularly" (*vulgariter*) as "An infinite being is that which exceeds any finite being whatsoever not in some limited degree, but in a measure beyond what is either defined or can be defined."[29]

(*c*) "Necessary Being or Existence." To clarify the exact meaning of these terms, which linguistic philosophers claim are unclear, muddled, or malformed, let me begin by stating what Scotus understands by "a being or thing" (*ens* or *res*) and by "existence" (*esse*) in this connection. In question three of his *Quodlibetal Questions*, Scotus has an extended discussion of the various meanings which these equivocal terms may have.[30] In its narrowest and strictest sense, as used by Aristotle in Book VII of the *Metaphysics*, a being or thing refers to a real substance and excludes accidents, which "are called beings, because they belong to a being."[31] Boethius uses it in a somewhat broader sense as common to the first three Aristotelian categories (viz., substance, quantity, and quality), whereas "relation" and the other five categories are not "things" but modes or "circumstances of a thing." It can be given a more extended meaning, however, as Scotus points out, which "is sufficiently justified by linguistic usage."

> Understood very broadly, it covers anything that is not nothing, and this can be given two interpretations. Nothing, in its truest sense, is what includes a contradiction and only that, for such excludes any form of existence, either within or without the intellect. Just as what includes a contradiction cannot exist outside the soul, so neither can it be an intelligible something as a being in the soul [i.e., a concept]. Two contradictory notions cannot constitute one intelligible thing, either as a union of two objects or of an object and its mode. In another sense, nothing refers to what neither is nor can be some being outside the soul [i.e.

> extramental]. . . . Avicenna seems to have this sense in mind when he says that "thing" and "being" are common to all genera.[32] And that this does not refer to the words in one language, for in every language there is one undifferentiated concept that applies to everything that exists outside the soul. For concepts [according to Aristotle[33]] are the same in all.

Since Avicenna seems to be the proximate source of the medieval usage of "necessary existence" (*necesse esse*) as a description of God, and of "contingency" (*possibile esse*) in the sense of something which *can* but *need not* be, so far as what it is is concerned, we may safely say that "existence" refers to real, or extramental, existence. Since this need not be restricted to what is sense perceptible, it could include such theoretical entities as we have reason to believe are real or actual and in some sense responsible for the world open to observation (in regard to either what it is or how it behaves).

Although *necesse esse* and *contingens esse* seem to be primarily existential modalities, they do represent in some sense a partial answer to the question *Quid est?* ("What is it?" or "What is its nature or essence or quiddity?") rather than an answer to the question *An sit?* ("Does it exist?"). As I have pointed out elsewhere, "It seems intuitively clear that what *must be* the case, *is* the case, and what *is* the case, *can be* the case. In other words, 'necesse esse' entails facticity or *esse*, and facticity entails possibility or self-consistency. The reverse order of entailment is of course not valid."[34]

And though facticity does not tell us anything about the essence or nature of what exists, and hence questions about the essence or nature of a thing are basically different from questions about its existence, the two modal expressions "necessary being" and "possible being" are indications as to the nature of their respective subject. "That is why [Scotus] insists that *ens*, defined as 'cui non repugnat esse,' is an essential or quidditative term. It indicates that the individual subject is capable of existing in the extramental world and hence differentiates it from the whole realm of the mythical or fanciful entities such as chimaeras, gremlins or leprechauns"[35] — or, I might add, Munitz' "the smile of [Alice's] Cheshire cat." "Facticity, however, is not an essential attribute of any subject other than God, and here only because 'to exist necessarily' entails 'to exist now.'"[36]

"Contingent being" or "contingent existence," however, though also expressing something of the quiddity of its respective subject, goes beyond the idea of mere "possibility." For it is a complex notion, implying two logically distinct or separable notions: viz., "possibility" (in the sense of self-consistency, and hence a characteristic of what exists either necessarily or contingently), and "the possibility of non-existence" — either in a temporal or atemporal sense I shall return to later. The theoretical entity "necessary being" is constructed from the notion of "contingent being" by affirming one of its characteristics (viz., "possibility" or "able to be") and denying the other (viz., "it is not the case that it is able not to be" or "it is not possible that it should not exist"). Since "able to be" and "able not to be" may refer to different times, contingency may be given a temporal sense, and it would follow that if something non-eternal exists, it is contingent according to this definition. Necessary being, as involving the denial of "able not to be," would entail that it is "eternal" as well.

Scotus assumes with Richard of St. Victor that, of the four possible logical combinations of the two disjunctions "to be of another (or 'caused')" and "not to be from another," on the one hand, and "to be eternal" and "not to be eternal," on the other, only the combination "to be non-eternal and not to be from another," which is equivalent to asserting that something pops into existence without any originative connection with anything else in the universe, seems repugnant to "higher reason." If, then, one assumes as a reasonable metaphysical axiom that whatever begins to be has some originative connection — let us call it "cause" in the broad sense in which Scotus uses this term — with something else in the universe, then to assert simultaneously of some subject that it is both possible and uncaused is to imply not only that the subject in question is actual but that it is a necessary being as well. (Both these implications figure in Scotus' proof for the existence of God as a necessary being.) Hence, as I have pointed out elsewhere, "I think Scotus would regard 'necesse esse' as being logically equivalent to the conjunction of three other predicates: viz, able to be, unable to be produced, and eternal, i.e. always was and always will be."[37]

However, Scotus uses "contingency" in a narrower or atemporal sense, where it becomes equivalent to a counterfactual assertion about an existing subject — namely, that although the subject in question actually exists at time T, it could have been non-existent at time T. Contingency in this sense cannot be derived from any consistent set of necessary propositions, and in that sense is both a positive and a primitive notion. Its ultimate source, he insists, must be traced to some self-determining agent or "cause" — namely, one endowed with free will.[38]

Let us turn now to our second problem. How would Scotus or a Scotist attempt to justify the assertion that some being does exist which possesses such properties?

Justification of Some Theistic Concepts

On the Contingency of the World

Munitz makes much of the fact that we cannot prove that the world as a whole is contingent. Though observable portions of it may be, it is a fallacy of composition to argue that the whole is contingent. Scotus would not go along with this. He insists that just as a contingent proposition cannot be deduced rigorously from any set of necessary ones, so also if the ultimate "cause" which effects the world and continues to conserve it were to cause necessarily, then any contingency in the world would be impossible, as would change, imperfection, and so on. A world ruled inexorably by reason, stemming necessarily from the immutable perfection of God, as Lovejoy pointed out, also leads to what William James called a "block world" in which everything is fixed and, presumably, immutable.[39]

Even if God as a free, creative cause did not act in cooperation with created causes, as Scotus — like most theologians of his time — believed, it is still difficult to see how human freedom, or genuine free will, would be possible in a universe governed by blind, impersonal determinism. And then the personal experience of one's own inner freedom to choose this rather than that or vice versa, or ethical responsibility, and so on, become meaningless.

Contingency, either in a temporal sense of change or in the more radical counterfactual sense that with respect to a given moment two possibilities are open before the choice is made, cannot be proved; nor need it be. Recall Aristotle's observation that in regard to some things argument is out of place. What a skeptic requires is either senses or punishment. Avicenna comments that one who denies the principle of contradiction should be beaten or burned until he admits that this is not the same as not to be beaten or burned. And so, too, says Scotus: "those who deny that some being is contingent should be exposed to torments until they concede it is possible for them not to be tormented."[40]

It is also in this particular question that Scotus attempts to show that contingency, inasmuch as it is a primitive, irreducible notion which cannot be deduced from anything non-contingent or necessary, requires some positive source which in the last analysis can only be a free will.

Ockham challenges this inference, suggesting that contingency could enter a world, the outer framework of which at least is rigorously deterministic or fixed, by reason of the extreme complexity of the celestial machinery.[41] This seems not unlike the way in which Sir James Jeans was wont to speak popularly of the indeterminacy governed by Planck's constant $\frac{h}{2\pi}$ as "the loose-jointedness" of the universe.

This whole argument, however, seems faulty. Genuine chance or random behavior makes little sense as ultimate causal explanations. Given the fact that all macrocosmic physical instances of such seem to be secondary phenomena, resulting from the complex interplay of more fundamental entities, each of which behaves in a rigorously fixed and deterministic fashion, we can appreciate the dissatisfaction of Einstein, de Broglie, and, more recently, David Bohm with what has come to be called the Copenhagen interpretation of quantum mechanics by Bohr and Heisenberg.

However, it would seem that a non-theist would be forced to locate the source of indeterminacy or contingency in the ultimate material elements. And this appears to me to imply some sort of monadology, in which the individual elements or monads turn themselves off and on at will, as it were. Nor does the more recent field-theory approach seem to fare much better.

The Scotus–Ockham Version of the Cosmological Argument

The Scotist version of the cosmological argument, I might note, can hardly be dealt with in the cavalier fashion of Schopenhauer's hired-cab analogy.

It can be argued persuasively that things do not exist for an instant only, but have some degree of duration. The same seems to be true of various states of change. We seem to be committed to what I have called a "quantum theory of becoming" rather than to a smooth continuous process of change.[42] The point which Avicenna, and Scotus and Ockham after him, insist upon is that a true productive cause cannot be dismissed after the first moment of a new state of existence; some explanation must be given for the continued duration. As Ockham puts it, the productive cause must also be a conserving cause.[43]

Against David Hume, I might note that the artisan who makes an artifact is not the only, or perhaps even the most important, efficient cause operative. He can build obsolescence or relative permanency into the object, depending on the materials used; and in such cases it is the properties of these materials which account for the conservation of the effect in question. Actually, the materials do not seem to function as a strict material cause would in an Aristotelian sense, for they are not merely passive; the very cohesiveness of materials employed is due to the same electrostatic or electrodynamic forces holding the atoms together.

But if this be so, we are dealing with a conserving efficient cause which operates for a time period only. And this, I think, creates the difficulty. Why do the ultimate material constituents act, as it were, intermittently; why do they attract or repel one another at one time and not another; what accounts for their varied, yet limited, powers? Even the field-theory approach to matter requires some measure of distinction or difference between various portions of space. All this seems to be going back to an old philosophical insight that something extrinsic in the way of an efficient–conserving cause is needed. As Scotus puts it, where a change of form becomes cyclic or uniform, something is required to account for the regularity. Though there are many places where he appeals to this principle,[44] which he ascribes in one passage to Aristotle, perhaps the most concise is the *De primo principio* version:

> If we assume an infinity of accidentally ordered causes [i.e., a series such as Hume envisaged], it is clear they are not concurrent, but one succeeds another so that the second, although it is in some way from the preceding, does not depend upon it for the exercise of its causality. For it is equally effective whether the preceding cause exists or not. A son in turn may beget a child just as well if his father be dead or alive. But an infinite succession of such causes is impossible unless it exists in virtue of some nature of infinite duration from which the whole succession and every part thereof depends. For no change of form is perpetuated save in virtue of something permanent which is not part of that succession, since everything of this succession which is in flux is of the same nature. Something essentially prior to the series [i.e., a conserving efficient cause] then exists, for everything that is part of the succession depends upon it, and this dependence is of a different order from that by which it depends upon the immediately preceding cause where the latter is part of the succession.[45]

The advantage of using what Scotus calls essentially ordered causes, or what Ockham calls conserving efficient causes, is that the cause must co-exist with the contingent effect as long as it is conserved in existence. In such a series of concatenated causes, if more than one exists, what is ruled out is the possibility of infinite regress, since each higher cause (in the case of an efficient or productive agent) or lower (in the case of a material cause or underlying support) must "bear the weight," as it were, of all that precedes it in the series. In such a case, it seems intuitively clear that one will never achieve independence in a given order simply by increasing the number of dependent elements. Hence, to claim that an infinitely long chain of conserving causes might by reason of its infinity be independent as a whole seems to be a case of the fallacy of the false question.

It is interesting that Scotus points out that even if the series of dependent causes should be infinite, and all exercise their respective degree of conservation, one would still need something which is qualitatively "outside" the infinite sequence in much the same way as a limit of an infinite sequence or segment is outside the progression itself — a kind of a hook on which to hang an infinitely heavy chain.[46] Note that in such a case the same question cannot be asked of the limit as could be meaningfully asked of the elements which approach ever closer to the limit. The basic conclusion which both Scotus and Ockham wish to make is that some self-sufficient or necessary being exists in the sense in which this term was defined earlier.

At this point I should like to say something about the traditional concept of God as "infinite being" or being all-perfect, since the modern mathematical way of dealing with infinity seems to have muddled the meaning of the term as used in theological discourse.

A Quasi-Parmenidean Model of Infinity

Infinity, as used by the Scholastics in speaking of God, seems to be of rather late origin. For the Greeks, ἀπείρων (endless, boundless, countless) indicated indefiniteness or lack of specific form, and hence imperfection. I have no wish to trace the history of the way in which an idea, originally associated with imperfection, became transformed into Damascene's "infinite sea of substance" to which Scotus and other Scholastics alluded when attempting to define the endless perfection of God.[47]

Mathematicians such as Georg Cantor have reintroduced something of the indeterminateness of the Greek conception, inasmuch as they no longer consider that there is a greatest cardinal number in the hierarchy of transfinite or infinite numbers — viz., one which cannot be exceeded — since for any infinite cardinal, say $\aleph_n$, there is always a greater, viz., $\aleph_{n+1}$.

Hence, I should like to substitute another conception, philosophically simpler, for Scotus' notion of infinite being, and show that it is logically equivalent to what he had in mind in defining "infinite" in what he calls a "popular definition" as "that which exceeds the finite, not exactly by reason of any finite measure, but in excess of any measure which could be assigned."[48] His definition in the *Quodlibetal Questions* is similar.[49]

Infinite perfection, or, better, the fullness of perfection, is obviously not understood to exclude the existence of other beings of a finite or limited degree of perfection. Hence, some clarification is needed to indicate why an additional number of such beings does not add to the perfection of the universe as a whole in such a way that one could argue that God, no matter how perfect in himself, is still finite in perfection and in some sense in need of the created world which stems from him as its productive source. One way of putting the matter is that the presence of creatures adds quantitatively, not qualitatively, to the perfection of the universe. Still, this is not wholly clear, since creatures can be said to be qualitatively different from the all-perfect God and hence, for all their limited perfection, they do add something qualitatively other than what would have existed had God alone been actual.

Scotus' approach to the problem was in the tradition of Anselm of Canterbury, who distinguished those which were purely and simply perfection (let us call them "pure perfections") from those which were only perfection *secundum quid* (let us called them "mixed perfections" or "perfections in a qualified sense").[50] The characteristic difference is this. Pure perfections do not exclude one another in virtue of their formal definitions. Neither are they by definition limited to a specific degree.[51] Knowledge, power, wisdom, and the like would be examples of pure perfections. Scotus believes that it is possible to define the fullness of the perfection which is God in terms of something lacking nothing which is a pure perfection, nor any degree to which it would be possible to have it. Recall in this connection what he said in thesis four.

If one concedes this definition of pure perfection, or something akin to it, the following plausible conclusions could be drawn:

(1) A being of which anything conceivable as a pure perfection could be predicated could be called by stipulation "all-perfect" or "fully perfect" in the sense that no being with only some perfections of this kind or with such perfections in less than a maximal degree could not be designated as "all-perfect."

(2) Such a being would not be caused in any way, since "caused" — in any of the four ways envisaged by Aristotle — would introduce some limitation.

(3) Such a being would be eternal; that is to say, there never would have been a time when it did not exist, nor be one in which it would cease to exist.

(4) Since "distinct individuality" in the sense of Russell's "bare individual" does not seem to imply added perfection in the straightforward way in which descriptive predicates expressing pure perfections appear to do, a problem arises whether there is one "all-perfect being" or many. Apart from the fact that a plurality of anything has about it an unintelligibility which the "one" does not, and that the factual existence of a definite number of any specific thing is normally explained in terms of external causes, such as the lack of additional material, or the intent of the person to make just so many, both Scotus and Ockham use the following argument to exclude plurality in the case of the all-perfect being. Whatever can be multiplied can in principle be multiplied *ad infinitum*. If the all-perfect could be so multiplied, it would actually be multiplied *ad infinitum*, since it is uncaused, and hence if possible, would be actual. Thus the only plausible or intrinsically intelligible alternative would be that there can be but one such being.

If fullness of perfection in this sense is possible, and if possible, is actual, a question arises in cases of things which fall short of such fullness: "Why the limitation?" or "Why do limited beings exist?" — a question inapplicable or meaningless as regards the all-perfect. If this be coupled with the fact that limited beings also exist only for a time period, and if it be admitted that they require not just a producing cause to bring them into existence, but also a conserving cause to keep them existing (a cause which cannot be just inert matter, but must involve a measure of efficient causality — to use Aristotelian categories), and conceded that material entities which shut themselves off and on at will hardly seem to be the ultimate satisfactory answer, then it seems plausible to ascribe the contingency of the visible world in some way to the all-perfect being, which is copresent to the entire flux of change and relatively permanent existence of limited beings. If we call this influence of the all-perfect on the limited being a "causal action," then we must note several features which are distinctive or peculiar to it. If it is to account for the contingency in the world, though its essence may be necessarily existing, its causal activity must be "free" — analogous to our own freedom to act or not to act. If it is truly free, then it is not governed by any "Principle of Sufficient Reason" of the Leibnizian variety. Hence, the existence of the all-perfect would be at most a necessary condition for the existence and characteristics of the finite realm of beings. And if one should find the ultimate material constituents of the universe — even if eternal — to be also discrete and finite in their essence or nature, as well as variable in their action or interactions, it would seem plausible to assume that they are not the ultimate answer or explanation for their limitations, and that this too is the result of the way in which they depend upon the all-perfect. They could, then, by definition be called "created" in the second meaning of that term — viz., of themselves they are only "possible being" (which is a form of *non-esse*) — and their existence (*esse*) as stemming from an extrinsic source is ontologically or by nature posterior (*post*) to what they are in themselves.

Returning to the nature of the all-perfect being's relationship to finite beings, we could say that this creative activity of the former with respect to the latter has the following characteristic.

(5) What is created is less perfect than that which creates. It seems obvious that it is less perfect, in the sense that caused existence is less perfect than uncaused existence. But it also seems plausible to assume that what it contains in a limited degree is also present in an unlimited or eminent degree in the all-perfect.

Using more traditional terms, we can speak of the finite being as a "participation" in the perfection of the all-perfect — not in any pantheistic sense, but in the sense that the same formal perfection as one possesses in a limited degree is also characteristic of the all-perfect, where it not only is present in a maximal degree, but co-exists in holistic fashion with other pure perfections.

(6) Though there may be an indefinite number (or even an infinitude) of ways in which the all-perfect might be "participated" or imitated, if you will, even if all these should be taken together, their total perfection would not equal that of the all-perfect, if for no other reason than that the latter possesses its perfection in an holistic fashion, and from this aspect, one can say that "the whole is more than the sum of the parts." The perfection of the all-perfect, in a word, would differ from the perfection of any or all finite beings combined "by a non-finite degree." In short, it would seem to have all the properties which Scotus ascribes to God in speaking of him as "an infinite being."

If one asks whether such a quasi-Parmenidean being would be finite or infinite,[52] one could point out that it is certainly not finite in the sense of lacking any given pure perfection or lacking the maximal degree to which it is possible to have such. In that sense it is non-finite, or the fullness of what is simply perfect intensively. The only possible perfection existing beyond it would be in the order of extension — viz., other individual beings whose perfection is less than its own — and is present in itself in a more eminent way.

One might, of course, imagine a process whereby the all-perfect is divided mentally into so many parts, and then go on to think of adding one more perfection (even though one could not conceive of what sort of thing that addition would be). But such mental gymnastics would yield no more self-consistent notion or concept than "a stone greater than the all-perfect." In short, it would be correct to say there is nothing in the way of intensive perfection beyond the all-perfect.

Such a conception of the most perfect or self-sufficient being, I submit, has all the logical properties ascribed to "infinite being" as applied by the Scholastics to God, without the attendant ambiguities which stem from the customary way in which infinity or transfinitude is dealt with in mathematics.

Conclusion

As for the super-ultimate why-question, Scotus (or Ockham) would say: If it is a univocal sort of answer you are looking for, forget it! The question is meaningless. But if one is content with something short of that, the question may not necessarily be without meaning and can in some sense be answered. To explain: "Universe" itself can be an ambivalent term if it is taken to be logically equivalent to "everything." That is to say, "universe" is not a class-concept term, where "thing" (or, better, "constituent") is applied univocally to all that falls under it, as one could do, for example, to the parts of a watch spread out on a jeweler's workbench. As an integrated whole, its "constituents" are interrelated, and the relationships themselves must be considered among its primitive or irreducible elements. Now, if one uses the Aristotelian categorial scheme as Scotus did, then one could raise the question whether "thing" (or *ens*) can be predicated univocally of the proper concepts of what the ten categories cover. Scotus, we know, gave a negative answer.

Specifically in regard to God, who transcends all categories, Scotus would point out that an infinite or necessarily existing being differs radically from a contingent, finite being. The way in which "is" or "exists" applies to the two beings is also radically different. Hence, if one asks "Why the existence of anything?" no simple answer can be given. If you specify "Why does God exist?" Scotus would reply "Because 'to be' is of his essence." Existence is predicated of deity in the first mode of *per se* predication. On the other hand, if you ask "Why does any creature exist?" one meaningful answer could be: "Because God willed it so!" Assuming the answer to be correct, the "super-ultimate why-ist" is tempted to ask in the same vein: "But why did God will this and not that?" But this question becomes meaningless unless further modifications of the meaning of "Why?" are taken into account. Consider some of the following points.

(*a*) God's existence is not a sufficient condition of itself for the existence of any creature. It is only a necessary condition. Hence, in no ordinary sense of the word is the existence of God, in the assumption that it is true, an adequate explanation of or answer to the why of finite or created beings. For it is not just the existence of God, but the fact that he freely wills them, which "explains" their existence, if you will. And to put "God exists" and "God's will (in their regard) exists" as parallel, or univocal, instances of "exists" is to commit, to Scotus' mind, the grossest of category mistakes.

(*b*) Furthermore, if one is seeking a "reason" which will necessarily account for God's willing anything other than himself, then "Why?" again becomes a meaningless question. Of the two conflicting views of God developed by Lovejoy in *The Great Chain of Being,* Scotus would opt for the second: that the fact of any creation, or of this specific creation, cannot be "explained" as a rigorous and inevitable consequence of "reason." There is running through the actually existing realm of reality an element of arbitrariness. God's will is not determined necessarily by anything either in his nature or in the nature of the creature which requires him to create it. His actually doing so represents an artistically free, creative decision.

(*c*) Note, however, that if reason cannot explain God's choice, "that something be reasonable" is a necessary, but not sufficient, condition for God to be able to will it.[53] Arbitrariness is not whimsicality, and certainly not irrationality. For Scotus puts certain restrictions, as it were, on God's freedom in regard to creation, since God is *ordinatissime volens*. These restrictions stem largely from the fact that God is what he is, an all-perfect being. But because Scotus does not believe that "the best of all possible worlds" is a meaningful expression, the infinite perfection of God does not provide even an elliptical answer as to why *this* world exists. Put another way: God, like any artist, must be free to produce what he likes. But the fact that he is what he is will ensure that the result is a masterpiece, and the order which relates the individual elements to the end which he had in mind will itself be "reasonable."

(*d*) Another point to keep in mind is that God's choice of a specific end (and a specific type of creation) does not itself fall under the causality of that end. As a self-determining agent, his will, as it were, creates its own end as well as the way in which the means are ordered to that end. Given a freely chosen end, call it Y, and given X as a necessary means to that end, then "Why does X exist?" can be given a meaningful answer in terms of Y; yet the same question cannot always be meaningfully extended to Y itself — and here lies the Scotistic reason for the mystery of existence.

(*e*) Apart from the question "Why does God will what he does?" — which is meaningful only with respect to the relationship of means to end — what must one say of the question "Why does God exist?" Here I would want to push the answer beyond that which Scotus himself would give, perhaps.

If fullness of perfection in the quasi-Parmenidean sense explained above is possible, and if possible, is also actual, then a question arises only in cases of something short of that fullness: viz., "Why the limitation?" or "Why do limited beings exist?" What I want to suggest is that the question "Why does God exist?" — where "God" is the name given to this theoretically simply perfect being — is often logically equivalent to the question "Why is God limited?" and then it is obviously meaningless.

To conclude: I think there is a sense in which Edwards is right. If one is looking for a single univocal answer applicable to everything, then the super-ultimate why-question becomes meaningless.

Like Wittgenstein, one must distinguish the various ways in which "Why?" is used in conjunction with "exists" with respect to the constituents of the universe. But if one considers disjunctively the various meanings covered by the umbrella phrase "Why does such and such (or X) exist?" it may be possible to say that "Why?" can be meaningfully asked (in some sense) of everything, and this may account for the widespread tendency among philosophers as well as non-philosophers to raise the super-ultimate why-question.

NOTES

1 *Encyclopedia of Philosophy* (New York & London, 1967), VIII 296–302.

2 *The Mystery of Existence: An Essay in Philosophical Cosmology* (New York, 1968).

3 *Tractatus Logico-Philosophicus*, 6.5, 6.51.

4 Heidegger, *Einführung in die Metaphysik* (Tübingen, 1953), trans. R. Manheim as *An Introduction to Metaphysics* (New Haven, 1959), pp. 6–7.

5 "Why?" 301.

6 Ibid., 301.

7 *Mystery of Existence*, p. 45.

8 *Metaphysics* I, 2 (982B12ff.).

9 *Of God and His Creatures*, trans. J. Rickaby (Westminster, Md., 1950), p. 57.

10 (Cambridge, Mass., 1936; repr. New York, 1960), pp. 73–81.

11 Veatch, "A Note on the Metaphysical Grounds for Freedom, with Special Reference to Professor Lovejoy's Thesis in 'The Great Chain of Being,'" *Philosophy and Phenomenological Research*, 7, No. 3 (March 1947), 391–412; Lovejoy, "The Duality of the Thomistic Theology: A Reply to Mr. Veatch," ibid., 413–38; Veatch, "A Rejoinder to Professor Lovejoy," ibid., No. 4 (June 1947), 622–25; Lovejoy, "Analogy and Contradiction: A Surrejoinder," ibid., 626–34; Pegis, "*Principale Volitum*: Some Notes on a Supposed Thomistic Contradiction," ibid., 9, No. 2 (August 1948), 51–70; Lovejoy, "Necessity and Self-Sufficiency in the Thomistic Theology: A Reply to President Pegis," ibid., 71–88; Pegis, "Autonomy and Necessity: A Rejoinder to Professor Lovejoy," ibid., 89–97; Lovejoy, "Comment on Mr. Pegis's Rejoinder," ibid., No. 2 (December 1948), 284–90; Pegis, "Postscript," ibid., 291–93.

12 *Great Chain of Being*, p. 81.

13 *Mystery of Existence*, pp. 105ff.

14 Ibid., pp. 220ff.

15 "Why?" 299.

16 E. Nagel, *Sovereign Reason* (Glencoe, Ill., 1954), p. 30.

17 *Ordinatio* I, d. 3, q. 1, in *Opera omnia*, 6 vols. to date (Vatican City, 1950—), III 1ff.

18 Cf. John Duns Scotus, *God and Creatures: The Quodlibetal Questions*, trans. F. Alluntis and A. B. Wolter (Princeton, N.J., 1975), nn. 3.6–3.14, pp. 61–63.

19 Ibid., n. 14.63, p. 332. See also *Ordinatio* IV, d. 49, q. 11, n. 9 (ed. Vivès, XXI 417–18). For a more detailed explanation of God as a "voluntary object," see my "Duns Scotus on the Natural Desire for the Supernatural," *The New Scholasticism*, 23 (1949), 297–99.

20 *Ordinatio* I, d. 3, n. 58, in *Opera omnia*, III 40.

21 Ibid., n. 61, p. 42.

22 "Models and Analogies in Science," *Encyclopedia of Philosophy*, V 354–59.

23 *Summulae in libros Physicorum* (Venice, 1506); cf. my "The Ockhamist Critique," in *The Concept of Matter*, ed. E. McMullin (Notre Dame, Ind., 1963), pp. 148–49.

24 Cf. Scotus' discussion in *Ordinatio* I, d. 8, nn. 137–50, in *Opera omnia*, IV 221–27. See also *Collatio* 13, n. 5, in *Collationes seu disputationes subtillissimae* (ed. Vivès, V 202): "Licet in altissimo conceptu nihil concipimus, nisi modo composito, tamen intendimus conceptum simpliciter simplicem."

25 *Collationes*, ibid., n. 4, p. 202: "Dico quod conceptus conclusi per modum complexionis conveniunt Deo, nec conveniunt creaturae; hujusmodi sunt conceptus compositi, non autem simplices conceptus, cujusmodi sunt conceptus entis, boni, etc. nam tales conceptus dicuntur univoce de Deo et creatura."

26 *The Structure of Scientific Revolutions* (Chicago, 1962; 2nd. enl. ed., 1970).

27 The medieval logicians listed a number of *loci* from which a dialectician might draw his arguments. The *locus a minori* (argument from the inferior) assumes that what is within the power of the less perfect is also within the power of the more perfect. Cf., for example, William of Sherwood's *Introduction to Logic*, trans. Norman Kretzmann (Minneapolis, 1966), p. 96; *Petri Hispani Summulae logicales*, ed. I. M. Bochenski (Rome & Turin, 1947), tr. 5, p. 54. The argument here is that the intellect, a purely spiritual faculty, is more perfect than the imagination, an organic faculty.

28 *Ordinatio* I, d. 3, n. 61, in *Opera omnia*, III 42.

29 *God and Creatures: The Quodlibetal Questions*, n. 5.9, p. 111.

30 Ibid., nn. 3.6–3.14, pp. 61–63.

31 Ibid., n. 3.13, p. 63.

32 *Metaphysics* I, 6 in *Opera latina* II (Venice, 1508), fol. 72^{r}.

33 *De interpretatione* I, 16A5–10.

34 "Is Existence for Scotus a Perfection, Predicate or What?" in *De doctrina Iohannis Duns Scoti* II, Studia Scholastico-Scotistica 2 (Rome, 1968), p. 177.

35 Ibid., p. 178.

36 Ibid.

37 Ibid., p. 176.

38 Cf. the following section, "On the Contingency of the World."

39 Lovejoy, *Great Chain of Being*, p. 328.

40 *Ordinatio* I, d. 39, suppl., in *Opera omnia*, IV 414.

41 *Ordinatio* I, d. 43 q. 1, in *Guillelmi de Ockham opera theologica* IV (St. Bonaventure, N.Y., 1979), pp. 631–33.

42 "Chemical Substance," *St. John's University Studies*, Philosophy Studies 1 (Jamaica, N.Y., 1960), pp. 101–103.

43 *Ordinatio* I, d. 2, q. 10, in *Guillelmi de Ockham opera theologica* II (St. Bonaventure, N.Y., 1970), pp. 354–57.

44 *Lectura* I, d. 2, n. 55, in *Opera omnia*, XVI 130–31; *Ordinatio* I, d. 2, n. 54, in ibid., II 160; *Ordinatio* IV, d. 12, q. 3, n. 14 (ed. Vivès, XVII 560b).

45 *A Treatise on God as First Principle*, trans. A. B. Wolter (Chicago, 1966), n. 3.14, pp. 48–50.

46 *Ordinatio* I, d. 2, n. 53, in *Opera omnia*, II 158.

47 See, for example, E. Gilson, "L'Infinité divine chez saint Augustin," *Augustinus Magister* I (Paris, 1954), pp. 569–74; idem, *History of Christian Philosophy in the Middle Ages*, trans. L. Shook (New York, 1955), 571; L. Sweeney, "Divine Infinity: 1150–1250," *The Modern Schoolman*, 35 (1955–1956), 38–51; idem, "Damascene and Divine Infinity," *The New Scholasticism*, 35 (1961), 76–106; Meldon C. Wass, *The Infinite God and the Summa Fratris Alexandri* (Chicago, 1964), pp. 1–13.

48 *Ordinatio* I, d. 2, n. 133, in *Opera omnia*, II 207.

49 See text at n. 29.

50 *Monologium* 15, in *S. Anselmi opera omnia* I, ed. F. S. Schmitt (Edinburgh, 1946), pp. 28–29.

51 Cf. my *The Transcendentals and Their Function in the Metaphysics of Duns Scotus* (St. Bonaventure, N.Y., 1946), chap. 7, pp. 162–75.

52 Parmenides, of course, in the interest of definitiveness held that the totality of being — which is the "model" I am adapting — was finite.

53 Cf. my "Native Freedom of the Will as a Key to the Ethics of Scotus," in *Deus et homo ad mentem I. Duns Scoti*, Studia Scholastico-Scotistica 5 (Rome, 1972), pp. 359ff.

8

The Relationship Between Essence and Existence in Late–Thirteenth-Century Thought: Giles of Rome, Henry of Ghent, Godfrey of Fontaines, and James of Viterbo

John F. Wippel
The Catholic University of America

Introduction

One of the more controverted points in late–thirteenth-century Western metaphysical thinking had to do with the relationship between essence and existence in all beings other than God. This issue is also sometimes used as a basis of comparison and contrast between Thomas Aquinas and Duns Scotus. The more generally held interpretation of Aquinas today maintains that for him essence and existence really differ, or — phrased more precisely — enter into real composition in all finite beings.[1] Whatever may have been his own view as to their exact relationship, Duns Scotus surely denied any real distinction and/or real composition of essence and existence in creatures.[2] Rather than discuss the positions of Thomas and Scotus on this matter here, however, I propose to concentrate on some lesser-known figures who were quite prominent at the University of Paris in the final decades of the thirteenth century. Henry of Ghent, a secular, held forth as *magister regens* in the theology faculty from 1276 until 1292.[3] Giles of Rome, an Augustinian, suffered some interruption in his career in theology at Paris shortly after the Condemnation of 1277, but after his return from "exile" from that faculty in 1285, served as regent master until 1291.[4] Godfrey of Fontaines, another secular, lectured as *magister regens* there from 1285 until 1303 with an apparent interruption after 1297.[5] And another Augustinian, James of Viterbo, replaced Giles in the Augustinian chair of theology in 1292 or 1293 and remained there until 1296.[6] This being so, I have selected these four figures in order to illustrate different positions on the essence–existence question which were developed during the period between the death of Thomas Aquinas in 1274 and that of Duns Scotus in 1308.

Because at least three clearly distinguishable theories had been defended by the time James considered the issue in his first quodlibetal debate in 1293, I shall begin with his reconstruction of the controversy. I shall then identify each of the other three masters with one of the positions which James outlined and study them in greater detail. Finally, I shall conclude by returning to James's discussion in the 1290s in order to determine his personal view.

In Quodlibet I, q. 4, James addresses himself to the issue: Can creation be maintained if existence (*esse*) and essence do not really differ in creatures?[7] In normal Scholastic fashion he begins by offering an argument for and an argument against the need for such diversity if one is to defend creation. The argument in favor of real diversity is based on an analogy between creation and generation. Just as matter must really differ from form if generation is to occur, so too there can be no creation unless essence and existence really differ. The argument against the need for such diversity distinguishes the kind of production involved in creation from that involved in generation. When an entire whole is produced, real diversity of factors therein is not required. But through creation everything found in the creature is produced. Therefore such diversity (of essence and existence) is not required to allow for creation.[8]

James now introduces some precisions with respect to terminology, that is to say, with respect to his understanding of essence and existence (*esse*).[9] The term "essence" can be applied to any predicamental reality, whether substance or accident. For essence is as general and as applicable to the predicaments as being is. But since substance alone is described as being without qualification (*simpliciter*) and accident as being only in a qualified sense (*secundum quid*), when the term "essence" is employed without further ado it should be understood as referring to substance. And when the term "essence" is applied to substances composed of matter and form, taken most strictly it includes both matter and form in its meaning. In short, for the purposes of this discussion, James will identify essence with substantial essence or nature.[10]

As regards the term *esse*, James observes that it may be used in three different ways. First of all, one may take *esse* as a noun. When it is so used, it means the same as essence.[11] Secondly, it may be used as a verb to signify the act of existing (*actus essendi*). So used, therefore, it means the same as "to exist" (*existere*), as illustrated by statements such as "God is" or "a man is."[12] Finally, it may be used as a verb in another way, not to express the act of existing or existence, but to indicate that a predicate inheres in a subject. So employed it is the copula, as in the statement "Man is an animal."[13] In the present discussion James proposes to apply the term *esse* in the second way, as signifying the act of existing. In sum, therefore, he will understand by essence a thing's substantial nature and by *esse* its act of existing. (I shall often translate the latter as existence.[14])

James now turns to the different views on this question developed by various "modern" doctors. He suggests that just as the philosophers had differed in their treatment of being (*ens*), so the moderns do in their understanding of existence (*esse*). He wonders whether the earlier disagreement among the philosophers might not have been responsible, or at least the occasion, for the current disagreement with respect to existence. He surmises that such seems likely since being (*ens*) and existence (*esse*) seem to imply the same thing, just as reading (*legens*) and to read (*legere*) do.[15]

As regards the philosophers, he finds Aristotle and Averroës in agreement in maintaining that being signifies the essence of that of which it is affirmed. Thus each and every thing is and is described as being by reason of its essence.[16] But, James continues, Avicenna held that being signifies something superadded to that of which it is affirmed. According to him, therefore, things are named being not by reason of their essence but by reason of something else, just as a white or black object is so named not by reason of its essence but by reason of something else which is accidental to the thing in question. Hence, Avicenna described being as an accident or accidental disposition in that of which it is affirmed.[17]

Among the moderns, James distinguishes three positions with respect to existence (*esse*). According to one view, existence does not indicate a thing which differs from essence. If, therefore, existence seems to differ in any way from essence, it can only be in the logical order (*secundum rationem*).[18] Godfrey was well known as a defender of this opinion.

According to the second position, existence is indeed a thing or *res* which differs from essence. In accounting for this interpretation, James notes that although it concedes some actuality to essence, it denies that essence as such can account for the fact that a given entity actually exists. In order to explain this — the fact that something actually exists — another distinct actuality must be superadded to essence. This is described as *esse actuale*, or actual existence. But existence is not an accident. It belongs more to the predicament of substance. But it is neither form or matter, nor their composite, but a superadded act by reason of which the composite and all found therein actually exist.[19] Some have suggested that James has in mind here both Thomas Aquinas and Giles of Rome, but his usage of the term *res* to describe *esse* as well as his reference to the *Theoremata* further on in the discussion suggest rather that he is referring to Giles and to Giles alone.[20]

According to a third theory, *esse* does not bespeak a thing (*res*) which is different from essence. Nonetheless, they are said to be intentionally distinct. As James briefly indicates, this view holds that to differ intentionally is less than to differ really and more than to differ logically. As he also notes, this theory maintains that existence signifies essence together with a relationship to its efficient cause. Though essence viewed with this relationship to its cause is not really distinct from essence viewed without such a relationship, it does involve an added *intentio.* Here James is obviously referring to Henry of Ghent's well-known theory of intentional distinction between essence and existence (even though he finds some possible foreshadowings of this in Robert Grosseteste).[21]

In sum, then, James has identified three distinctive positions on the essence–existence question. I shall now consider each of these individually, but in the following order: (*a*) Giles of Rome, as defending real distinction between essence and existence and as between thing and thing; (*b*) Henry of Ghent as the representative of intentional distinction between them; and (*c*) Godfrey of Fontaines as rejecting both of the above and admitting nothing more than logical distinction.

Giles of Rome

In his first quodlibetal debate of 1276 Henry of Ghent had reacted sharply against a theory of real distinction between essence and existence. Although it is difficult to determine with certainty precisely what written source or sources Henry then had in mind, it seems most likely that Giles of Rome was his primary target. Some have suggested that the series of arguments offered for the real distinction and then refuted by Henry in this discussion reflects not only Giles's thinking but possibly his personal oral intervention in that original discussion.[22] Be that as it may, there is no doubt that Henry and Giles would be involved in open controversy on this issue after Giles's return to the theology faculty in 1285.[23] Considerable work remains to be done with respect to the presence or absence of this distinctive doctrine in Giles's earliest works (prior to 1275). But certain references in his *Commentary* on Book I of the *Sentences* as well as in his *Theoremata de corpore Christi* suggest that by 1275 or 1276 — hence by the time of Henry's first Quodlibet of Christmas 1276 — Giles had already begun to develop his personal solution.[24]

Thus in his *Commentary on I Sentences* Giles addresses himself to this question: Is there composition of essence and existence (*esse*) in God?

Needless to say, his answer is in the negative. But in developing this response he already seems to imply that a creature's existence differs from its essence and enters into composition with it, at least in some way.[25] Shortly thereafter in this same *Commentary* Giles raises our very question: Is every creature composite? Already in the *In contrarium* of this discussion Giles presents an argument for composition in creatures based on the fact that every such being has only limited existence. Limited existence must be received in something else. Therefore, in every creature there is composition of that which receives and of that which is received.[26] In his reply Giles defends composition of "that which is" (*quod est*) and existence (*esse*) in every creature which exists in itself, that is, not merely as a part or constituent of something else. If an entity is created, then it receives its existence from another. But that which receives existence from another is in potency to such existence, and hence cannot be identified with it. Were one to deny this conclusion, Giles continues, and to identify the creature with its existence, one would then imply that such an entity is pure act and completely devoid of potentiality. This would amount to denying that it needed to be brought into being or to be caused. In brief, to reject such composition of essence and existence in created entities is really to deny that they are created.[27]

In his *Theoremata de corpore Christi*, which dates from roughly the same period (ca. 1275–1276), Giles again touches on the problem. Interestingly enough, in this text Giles seems to imply that separability is practically the only criterion sufficient for one to establish real distinction.[28] He then draws an interesting parallel between quantity and its extension, on the one hand, and the divine essence and its existence (*esse*), on the other. Just as quantity is extended by its very nature and not by something else which is superadded, so too the divine essence and the divine essence alone is its very existence. But in all other entities, entities which receive their *existence* from God, this existence is something added to their nature or essence. Hence it is "accidental to" every creature, is received by the created nature, and really differs from it.[29] ("Accidental" as used here by Giles need only imply that existence is not essential to the creaturely essence, hence that it "happens to it." As will be seen below, Giles will not admit that existence is to be identified with a predicamental accident.)

Finally, Giles adds an important precision. If there is real diversity between a creature's essence and its existence, this must not be equated with the kind of difference or distinction which obtains between two essences. I stress this point because of Giles's later and fairly frequent reference to this as the kind of difference which obtains between thing and thing (*res* and *res*), even though he refuses to commit himself on that score in the present passage. He is well aware that more remains to be said about the exact kind of distinction intended here and promises to devote himself to fuller discussion of this on another occasion.[30] But at least two items can be taken as established from this reading of his *Theoremata de corpore Christi*: (*a*) some kind of real diversity or distinction between essence and existence is already implied; and (*b*) whatever Giles may understand by that diversity in this discussion, he does not wish to liken it to or identify it with that which obtains between two essences.

In his *Theoremata de esse et essentia*, probably written between 1278 and 1280,[31] Giles presented the fuller treatment he had promised. And shortly after his return to the theology faculty at Paris he again addressed himself to this matter in great detail, this time in his *Quaestiones disputatae de esse et essentia* (1285–1287). These are really his two most thorough discussions of the issue. But since they along with Giles's other treatments have been studied in considerable detail by others,[32] I shall restrict myself here to a few selected themes in order to set the stage for my subsequent considerations of Henry, Godfrey, and James.

First of all, in these more mature treatments Giles continues to be most concerned with accounting for the truly created character of all beings save God. (This theme was already present in his *Commentary on I Sentences.*) Without the real distinction, he frequently argues, one cannot safeguard the possibility of created being or account for the fact that it is truly contingent.[33] Closely connected with this contention is the parallel which he draws between creation, on the one hand, and generation, on the other. Thus in Theorem 5 of the *Theoremata* he reasons that if one will philosophize in accord with man's way of knowing, one must move from a knowledge of sensible things to an understanding of intelligibles such as separate substances: "Let us say, therefore, that just as generation made us know that matter differs from form, so creation makes us understand that essence differs from existence."[34] Strictly speaking, it is neither matter nor form which is generated but the composite consisting of these two. So, too, it is neither essence nor existence (*esse*) which is created, but the composite of essence and existence.[35]

Again, just as form is a certain actuality and perfection of matter, so existence is a certain actuality and perfection of essence. Just as matter really differs from form, so essence really differs from *esse*.[36] Finally, just as form is impressed on matter by the generating agent, so existence is impressed on essence by the creating agent.[37] (For certain differences between the matter–form composition and that of essence and existence, see Theorem 6.[38]) To suggest that essence could exist without the addition of existence would be to make of it a necessary being and thus to deny its created and contingent character.[39]

Giles also offers other arguments for the real distinction in this same treatise. For instance, in Theorem 5, a first argument is grounded on the fact that a created nature can exist or not exist. Therefore, Giles reasons, it is in potency to existence. Given the distinction between potency and act, the essence which receives existence in creation is as distinct from its existence as potency is from act.[40] Another argument is based on limitation. If a separate intelligence were not really distinct from its existence, its existence would not be received in something else but would exist of itself. It would then be pure and unlimited. But to be unlimited or infinite existence is repugnant to the nature of any creature.[41] Again, without real distinction of essence and existence there would be no composition in pure intelligences. Thus, if they are pure *esse*, they would be completely simple and immutable.[42]

In *Disputed Questions* 9 and 11 Giles clearly argues against Henry's rejection of the real distinction in his Quodlibet 1 of 1276.[43] He repeats some arguments presented by Henry against his (Henry's) position, that is to say, arguments in favor of the real distinction: (*a*) If a creature is identical with its existence, then, since the creature subsists, its existence will also subsist. But subsistent existence is pure existence, and pertains to God alone. (*b*) Since existence as such is not self-limiting, if a creature were identical with its existence, it would not be limited. (*c*) If there is no real diversity between the creature and its existence, then, since existence cannot be separated from itself, the existence of the creature could not be separated from that creature. In brief, it would be impossible for the creature not to be.[44] Further on in this same discussion, Giles presents some other arguments for his position, that is to say, for real diversity of essence and existence in creatures. The first is the most interesting and most fully developed, and is again based on the analogy between generation as implying matter–form composition, on the one hand, and creation as implying essence–existence composition, on the other. Giles finds this argument especially forceful with respect to the case of pure spirits.[45]

In these same *Disputed Questions* he also presents an argument based on participation. Already in Question 9, in the course of refuting Henry, he observes that without real composition of essence and existence, one cannot account for the fact that the creature merely participates in existence without being subsistent *esse*.[46] And in *Disputed Question* 11 this same theme is developed in depth. There Giles lists six truths which cannot be maintained without admission of his real distinction. The second of these is precisely this: that every created essence participates in existence, and that existence as found in creatures is participated.[47] Giles observes that the term "participate" derives from *partem capere* (to take, as it were, a part rather than the whole). That which possesses a perfection in its fullness does not participate in it. Precisely because potency falls short of act, it does not receive act in its fullness or totality. Therefore, insofar as potency receives act, it merely "participates" in it. But one cannot account for the limited presence of the participated act or perfection without postulating that it is received by a distinct and potential principle. Therefore, if one finds limited and participated beings, this can only be because in each of these act or existence (*esse*) is received and limited by something which is really distinct from that existence. In fact, if such an act, existence, were not received by a distinct and limiting potency, it would be infinite. Again the assumption is that act as such, here existence as such, is not self-limiting. Finally, this distinction between the receiving and limiting potency (essence) and the received and limited act (existence) must be real. Otherwise, the act (existence) would not really be limited and participated.[48]

Another of Giles's arguments for the real distinction is reminiscent of a discussion in Thomas Aquinas' *De ente et essentia*,[49] but in fact goes considerably further. The first truth which cannot be maintained without the real distinction according to Giles in *Disputed Question* 11 is this: that the essence of a creature can be understood as not-existing. As he briefly rephrases the argument here, nothing can be understood with the opposite of itself, that is, as opposed to or excluding itself. Therefore, if something is understood with that which is opposed to itself, the former must really differ from the latter. But since essence can be understood with that which is opposed to itself, its non-existence, then essence must really differ from existence.[50] Or, as he reasons while refuting another of Henry's criticisms in *Disputed Question* 9, if essence and existence were identical in a creature, perhaps one could understand such an essence without thinking of its existence. But one could not understand that essence as not-existing. In fact, adds Giles, it would be impossible for such an essence not to exist.[51]

In the light of these and other arguments, therefore, Giles insists that essence and existence are not merely logically distinct, or intentionally distinct (as Henry would have it), but really distinct, and distinct as thing and thing (*res et res*). Thus he writes in Theorem 16: "That existence [*esse*] which is caused by the form of the whole, as will be evident in Theorem 19, is a thing [*res*] which differs from that form itself."[52] In Theorem 19 he comments that he has shown in Theorem 5 and again in Theorem 12 by many arguments, and will do so here again, that "existence and essence are two things [*res*]." From this it follows that existence is a kind of actuality which is superadded to essence and that every creature is really composed of such existence and essence.[53] In this same theorem he also writes: "And just as matter and quantity are two things [*res*], so essence and existence are two things [*res*] which really differ."[54] Similar terminology reappears in the *Disputed Questions*. Thus in *Disputed Question* 9 he writes: "That very thing [*res*] which is existence [*esse*] is in the genus of substance. But existence has a kind of accidental mode insofar as it is superadded to substance."[55] In *Disputed Question* 11, while briefly restating the argument based on the analogy between creation and generation and the "changeable" character of creatures, Giles maintains that by reason of the fact that essence can lose and acquire existence, in itself it is undetermined (*informe*) or neutral with respect to existence and non-existence. Therefore, existence is the perfection of essence and a different thing (*res*) from essence.[56]

Expressions such as these have led to considerable disagreement on the part of recent and contemporary interpreters of Giles. As we have already seen, there is close association in his mind between separability and real distinction. For him, separability is the clearest proof of real distinction.[57] Were one to assign separate existence either to essence or to finite existence, one would reduce Giles's theory to the absurd. In all fairness to him, however, it must be noted that he himself would never admit that one can have an existing essence without its existence, or a finite existence without its corresponding essence.[58] Still, just as matter and form can be separated in order to allow for corruption of a material entity, so, too, essence and existence are separable in order to allow for the contingent character of created being. But this does not imply that essence can ever exist in separation from its existence (*esse*).[59]

Closely connected with this difficulty in fairly interpreting him is his usage of the terms *res* and *res* or thing and thing to signify essence and existence. On the one hand, it would be absurd to appeal to composition of two independent entities, an essence-being and an existence-being, in order to account for the limited, contingent, and participated character of creatures. One would then have to account for the limited, contingent, and participated character of these constituting sub-beings by postulating similar composition of each of them, *ad infinitum*. Hence the danger in his employment of terms such as *res* and *res* to express essence and existence. At the very least, he was bound to be misunderstood by less than sympathetic critics, and his theory would be interpreted as leading to absurd consequences.[60]

On the other hand, Giles himself was not so naïve. As we have already seen, he makes it quite clear that in describing essence and existence as *res* or things he does not wish to reduce existence to the level of an essence or to suggest that the two unite as two essences.[61] Moreover, while defending his theory against the objection that existence can be neither substance nor accident and must, therefore, be nothing, he suggests that existence pertains in some way to the category or predicament of substance, but only by reduction. Both in *Disputed Question* 9 and in the *Theoremata de esse et essentia* he illustrates his meaning by drawing an analogy with a point and its relationship to the predicament of quantity. Suppose, for the sake of discussion, that there were only two predicaments, substance and quantity. To which would a point belong? Strictly speaking, Giles replies, a point is neither substance nor quantity. Even so, the point will pertain to the predicament of quantity, not in the sense that it itself is quantity, but insofar as it is the terminus of quantity. Therefore, without belonging to that predicament directly, it will pertain to it as the terminus of a line. So too, continues Giles, it must be denied that existence is either substance or accident. Nonetheless, existence pertains to the predicament of substance by reduction, insofar as it is the act of substance or the act of essence. But just as a point itself is not to be described as quantity, existence as such is not to be described as substance.[62]

Well and good, one might reply, but just what does Giles mean by distinguishing between essence and existence as between thing and thing? This continues to be disputed by his interpreters. There are those who emphasize the points which I have isolated above: separability and the terminology of *res* and *res* or thing and thing. They trace these back to Giles's undue reliance on the imagination, together with a heavy Neoplatonic influence. Such would have led him to "reify" or to treat as things principles of being — in this case, essence and existence. By so doing he would have prepared the way for that "monster" which so shocked subsequent critics such as Scotus and Suárez.[63] Nash would go even further, assigning to Giles a "fundamentally essentialist" position, due in large measure to the influence of Boethius, Proclus, and Avicenna.[64]

Others have risen to Giles's defense. They point out that for him separability of essence and existence does not imply that either can exist without the other. Granted: his choice of terminology may have been unfortunate; yet he refused to equate his distinction between essence and existence, even when described as between *res* and *res*, with that which obtains between two essences. We are reminded that he was attempting to contrast his theory of real diversity of essence and existence with the merely intentional distinction defended by Henry of Ghent, and that he steadfastly refused to permit existence to be identified with a relationship which runs from the creature to God as its efficient cause. His defenders maintain that Giles never conceived of the real distinction between essense and existence as the kind which obtains between two more or less absolute entities, and that one need not conclude that his distinction is opposed to that which holds between principles of being or *entia quibus*.[65]

Granted, therefore, that Giles continues to find his critics and defenders today; I would here restrict myself to the following comment: whatever his original understanding of the terms *res* and *res* may have been when applied to the essence–existence relationship, his choice of terminology was surely unfortunate. It left him open to charges and interpretations (or misinterpretations) similar to those indicated above. But one thing is surely clear: his terminology and his way of defending the theory of real diversity between essence and existence became standard in his own day and for quite some time thereafter.

Henry of Ghent

In his first Quodlibet, of Christmas 1276, Henry addresses himself to the problem: Is a creature its own existence (*esse*)?[66] After presenting and then sharply criticizing what I have taken to be Giles's theory of real distinction between essence and existence, Henry presents his own solution. On the one hand, it cannot be said that the essence of a creature is pure and subsisting existence. Such is true of God alone. On the other hand, it is not to be denied without some qualification that a creature is its *esse* since, Henry has just maintained, a creature's existence is not really distinct from its essence. He then resolves the question by distinguishing between *esse essentiae* (essential being) and *esse existentiae* (actual existence). *Esse essentiae* is said to pertain to the creature essentially, but still by way of participation insofar as it depends on God as its formal exemplary cause.[67] *Esse actualis existentiae* (actual existence) belongs to a creature only insofar as it is efficiently caused by God and thus results from divine volition. It is by reason of the first, essential being, that a creature falls into one of the predicaments and can be an object of knowledge even prior to its actual existence. But it is by reason of the second that it actually exists.[68]

Henry then comments that if one takes *esse* in the first sense, as *esse essentiae*, since such differs only logically from the essence itself, one may indeed say that the created essence is its *esse*. But if one takes *esse* in the second way, as actual existence, then one should not say that the creaturely essence is its *esse* (existence). This is so because although such *esse* (existence) does not really differ from the creature's essence, neither does it differ in a purely or merely logical way (by a mere distinction of reason). It also differs intentionally. Of God alone then can it be said that his essence is his existence.[69] To illustrate this he cites other examples, such as the terms *currens* (one who runs), *cursus* (race), and *currere* (to run). Though they signify one and the same thing in reality, one cannot say without qualification that *cursus* (race) is *currere* (to run). So, too, one cannot say that being (*ens*) is its *esse*, even though they are one and the same in reality.[70]

In Quodlibet 10, q. 7 (Christmas 1286), Henry replied to Giles's *Disputed Questions* 9 and 11.[71] Against Giles, Henry stresses the point that *esse* is not something absolute added to the essence of the creature. This is not only true of *esse essentiae*, but also of *esse existentiae* (actual existence). Actual existence adds nothing but a relationship to God as creative and efficient cause, or indicates the created essence insofar as it is actually so related.[72]

Once more Henry observes that the creaturely essence is not to be identified with its existence without some qualification. Though he emphatically rejects real distinction between them, he again appeals to his intentional distinction. Obviously nettled by Giles's complaint that he had been unable to understand this intentional distinction, Henry now illustrates. Man and rational animal are only logically distinct. Such is the distinction which obtains between a definition and that which is defined. Substance and accident are really distinct, and enter into real composition. But what of the distinction between a genus and a difference, such as between animal and rational? According to Henry this distinction is more than purely logical and less than real. Therefore one must admit his intermediary or intentional distinction. It is in this way, then, that essence and *esse existentiae* (actual existence) differ. Against Giles he also contends here that his intentional distinction is sufficient to allow for creation.[73]

In Quodlibet 11, q. 3, he again returns to this discussion. There he notes that although actual existence (*esse existentiae*) does not add anything real to essence, it does not follow from this that the creature's essence is its existence. For existence does add a relationship involving a distinct *intentio* to essence. Because existence adds this as an intentional accident rather than as a real one, it follows that essence is not its existence.[74] Without pausing here to belabor the point, let it suffice for me to note in passing that both Henry's theory of intentional distinction and his peculiar understanding of *esse essentiae* were sharply controverted by others — by Giles, to be sure, but especially by Godfrey.

Godfrey of Fontaines

Because much of Godfrey's positive teaching on essence and existence is developed in confrontation with the theories of real and intentional distinction considered above, a few remarks are now in order with respect to his knowledge of and reaction to each of them. Godfrey enters into detailed discussion of the theory of real distinction between essence and existence in Quodlibet 3, q. 1 (Christmas 1286). Here he is seeking to determine whether a creature may be called a being by reason of its essence when it is not such by reason of its existence.[75] He comments that one's reply will depend on one's understanding of the essence–existence relationship. If essence and existence differ in some way, one might at least hesitate in denying that a non-existing creature can be styled a being by reason of its essence. But if they differ in no way, the denial automatically follows.[76]

Godfrey then turns to the theory of real distinction. Although he does not name its defender here, both his terminology and his choice of arguments in its favor strongly suggest that he, too, has Giles of Rome in mind. Thus terms such as *aliquid* (something) and *res* (thing) are applied to existence. As Godfrey presents the theory, existence is the act of essence just as form is the act of matter. Just as matter is in potency to form and its privation, so essence is in potency to existence and its privation.[77] He then presents a series of arguments which have been offered in support of this theory: (*a*) an argument based on the possibility of knowing essence without existence and even as non-existent; (*b*) another grounded on the distinction between that which participates and that in which it participates; (*c*) another based on the need for real distinction to account for limited presence of *esse* in simple beings (angels).[78]

He then presents a series of arguments against this theory. Being involves less addition than does unity to that of which it is affirmed. But unity adds nothing real to the essence of that of which it is predicated. Consequently, neither does being (*ens*) and, therefore, neither does existence (*esse*). Again, one must admit that each and every thing is a being (*ens*) by reason of itself and not by reason of something which is superadded, that is, not by reason of a really distinct *esse* or existence. Otherwise one will have to account for the being of this superadded factor in the same way (by adding another *esse*), *ad infinitum*.[79] These arguments are interesting in that they seem to take existence as though it were another *res*.

Another argument tells us much about Godfrey's own position on essence and existence. The concrete noun, the abstract noun, and the verb do not signify really distinct things, granted a difference in their mode of signification. Just as this is true, for instance, of *currens* (one who runs), *cursus* (race), and *currere* (to run), so, too, Godfrey contends, is it true of *ens* (being), *essentia* (essence), and *esse* (existence). Nor will it do to reply that *ens* taken as a noun (a being) means the same thing as *essentia* (essence) but not when it is taken as a participle (*ens*: be-ing). Godfrey counters that *legens* whether taken as a noun (one who reads) or as a participle (reading) really signifies the same thing as *legere* (to read), granted again a difference in the mode of signification. The same applies, therefore, to *ens, essentia, entitas,* and *esse.* All signify the same thing, granted that they differ in mode of signification.[80]

Godfrey returns to this theme many years later in Quodlibet 13, q. 3 (1296 or thereafter).[81] Some had argued in favor of real distinction for this reason. That which essence signifies is taken as something fixed and permanent, somewhat like a habit. But that which existence signifies is taken as something in a state of process or becoming, like an act continuously exercised. Hence the two must differ. In reply Godfrey suggests that the relation between essence and existence is similar to that between "heat" and "to heat," "light" and "to give light," etc. In these more particular instances that which is signified by the noun is not really distinct from that which is signified by the verb. Therefore, the same should hold for more general terms such as essence and *esse.*[82]

A final argument is drawn from the implication of real distinction of essence and existence with respect to the structure of finite beings, especially material beings. As Godfrey presents the argument, in such beings either essence and existence will unite as pure potency and unqualified act so as to constitute a being which enjoys *per se* unity, or they will unite as potency in a qualified sense and act in a qualified sense (*secundem quid*) resulting in an accidental kind of unity (*unum per accidens*). According to Godfrey, neither proposal is acceptable. If one chooses the first alternative, then essence will be to existence as pure potency is to act *simpliciter.* But, Godfrey continues, pure potency is simply prime matter. Therefore, in a material being its essence will be pure potency or prime matter (according to the hypothesis), which in turn will be composed of prime matter and substantial form. Moreover, its existence will be act *simpliciter* which, contends Godfrey, is the same as substantial form. If one adopts the second alternative, equally unacceptable consequences follow. Now, essence and existence will unite as potency *secundum quid* and act *secundum quid.* But to consider existence as act *secundum quid* is to reduce it to the level of an accidental form. Moreover, if an essence is to receive existence as its accidental form, then, at least by priority of nature, that essence must already actually exist. For Godfrey, therefore, the theory of real distinction of essence and existence is indefensible under either hypothesis.[83]

Space will not permit me to follow Godfrey in his detailed refutation of Giles's arguments for the real distinction. Let it suffice to note that for Godfrey the overriding principle is this: whatever is true of essence is true of existence; and whatever is known of essence is known of existence. Therefore, essence can neither be nor be known with the opposite of its existence. Therefore, against Giles's argument that one can know an essence as non-existent, he replies: essence in act cannot be known as such without actual existence; essence in potency can be known only with potential existence. When an essence is understood as not actually existing, this is because neither the essence nor its existence is actual. Both are only potential. Rather than leading to any real distinction between essence and existence, such argumentation entails distinction between being and being, being in act and being in potency.[84]

His reply to the argument that real identity of essence and existence will eliminate composition in non-material entities is interesting. Here he argues that because the finite essence is less perfect than God, its source, it is potential. Insofar as it exists, it is actual. Therefore, there is some kind of potency and act found therein, enough to distinguish such being from God.[85] His theory of the real identity of essence and existence controls his answer to the question originally raised in Quodlibet 3, q. 1. When something is not being in terms of its existence, it is not being in terms of its essence. Whatever is true of one is true of the other.[86]

Godfrey is also quite familiar with Henry's theory of intentional distinction and his view that *esse essentiae* is to be assigned to a creature by reason of its dependence on God as formal exemplar, while actual existence is to be assigned to it by reason of its dependence on him as efficient cause.[87] He refutes this theory on a number of levels. First of all, he challenges Henry's theory of *esse essentiae*.[88] Secondly, he rejects his notion of intentional distinction as a viable intermediary kind between the purely logical and the real.[89] Thirdly, he raises a host of objections against Henry's efforts to treat of existence (*esse existentiae*) as the relationship of essence to God as efficient cause.[90] He realizes that Henry has been partly motivated in developing his theory of *esse essentiae* by a desire to account for the possibility of true knowledge of non-existent possibles. Godfrey finds it easy to account for this by application of his own understanding of potential and actual being. Controlling Godfrey's position again is his conviction that essence and existence are really identical. If an essence is realized in act, then the existence with which it is identical is also given in act. If the essence is realized only in potency, the same is true of its existence.[91] For Godfrey, then, it remains that essence and existence are entirely the same in reality and differ only in the way we understand and signify them. They no more enter into composition than do *currere* (to run) and *cursus* (race). They are neither really nor intentionally distinct.[92]

James's Solution

After his review of the other three theories on essence and existence, James advances a position which he describes as probable, but which appears to be his own.[93] He takes as his point of departure a passage from Anselm's *Monologium*: As light (*lux*), to give light (*lucere*), and that which gives light (*lucens*) are to one another, so are essence, *esse*, and *ens* (being).[94] James interprets this to mean that light and to give light are related to one another as the abstract and the concrete. Because it is a verb, the infinitive *lucere* (to give light) signifies light itself, but by way of action. Wherefore, suggests James, *esse* and essence are to one another as the concrete and the abstract. Hence, just as the concrete differs from the abstract, so existence (*esse*) differs from essence.[95]

It remains to determine whether a concrete term and its corresponding abstract term signify the same thing or different things. James's reply is that the concrete expression always signifies more than the abstract does. The abstract term signifies the form alone, but the concrete term signifies the form together with its subject. In the case of creatures, the form and the subject of that form are not identical. In creatures, therefore, the concrete term signifies something more in reality than the abstract does. But in the case of God there is no distinction between form and the subject of that form. When applied to God, therefore, a concrete expression signifies more than an abstract one only in the logical order, not in the real order.[96]

James now introduces an important precision. With respect to creatures, granted that a concrete term signifies both the form and its subject, it does not do so with equal immediacy. It signifies the form, first and foremost (*primo et principaliter*), and the subject only in a secondary way. Therefore, as regards their primary meaning, the concrete and the abstract signify one and the same thing. But with respect to that which is signified in this secondary sense, that which is signified concretely differs from that which is signified abstractly, and really so in creatures.[97]

Given these preliminaries, James is now in position to apply the above to essence and existence. Since these are related as abstract and concrete, they are one and the same in their primary meaning. But as regards their secondary meaning they differ, logically in the case of God, but really (*secundum rem*) when applied to creatures. By this James means that that which they signify really differs in creatures. Thus the term "existence" (*esse*) signifies essence first and foremost. But in a secondary way it also signifies all that is conjoined with essence and without which essence cannot be realized in actuality. A created essence cannot actually exist without being united with certain other factors with which it enters into real composition. Therefore, in this secondary meaning, existence (*esse*) signifies something in addition to essence, something which really differs from it.[98] (Presumably James has in mind things such as proper accidents, individuating notes, etc., without which a given essence cannot exist in fact.[99])

In accord with Boethian terminology, one may refer to *ens* (concrete being) as "that which is." And since "that which is" is identified with the *suppositum*, James now equates his distinction between essence and existence with that which obtains between essence, on the one hand, and the *suppositum* (concrete substantial being), on the other. Although the term "supposit" signifies essence in its primary meaning, in a secondary way it signifies the other factors which unite with essence in the concrete existent. For, as Damascene says, the supposit is the substance plus its accidents.[100] To the extent that one finds factors included in the supposit which are not signified by essence, therefore, and identifies existence (*esse*) with the supposit, one may conclude to a real distinction between essence and existence, that is to say, between essence and supposit. This James does. As he puts it, *esse* signifies essence insofar as it is realized in and constitutes the supposit, that is to say, insofar as it implies something in addition to essence.[101]

Before I compare James's theory with the other three positions, I should make one final clarification. His solution implies that in one way essence and existence are really identical, that is, in terms of that which they signify in their primary meaning. In another way, however, they really differ, since existence includes in a secondary way something not signified by the term essence, that is, the accidents, etc., with which essence must be united if it is to exist in actuality. James now comments that identity and diversity should be most properly assigned in terms of primary signification. Therefore, essence and *esse*, taken in their primary meaning, signify the same thing. That which they signify is one and the same. Essence and existence are the same. But when existence is taken in terms of its secondary meaning as well, it implies something more than essence does. So understood, they are not the same. But to say that this difference arises only from a secondary consideration is not to say that it is unimportant. On the contrary, James remarks, it is necessary since it follows from a composition which must be present in every creature.[102]

James and the Other Theories

James finally passes judgment on the other three positions. He tries to find something good in each of them. Nonetheless, his view clearly differs from the others. As regards Giles and his theory of real diversity of essence and existence, James must have found himself in an embarrassing position. He, an Augustinian, had just succeeded Giles in the Augustinian chair of theology at the University of Paris. His treatment of Giles's position is indeed a masterpiece of tact and diplomacy.[103] He finds the theory reasonable, but experiences difficulty with the way in which it is expressed, especially, in its description of *esse* (existence) as a superadded actuality which is not matter, nor form, nor the composite, nor an accident. As James evaluates the situation, neither cogent demonstration nor the voice of authority forces one to adopt such a view. He then concludes with the general words of praise for Giles to which I have referred above.[104]

As regards Henry's intentional distinction between essence and existence James again attempts to be accommodating. He agrees with Henry that a creature is related to God both as to its exemplar and as to its efficient cause. But, James contends, such relationship is not expressed by every term which is applied to the creature. Although relative expressions such as "to be created" or "to be made" do signify such a relationship, terms such as essence and *esse* (existence) do not appear to do so.[105] One might counter that in its secondary and consequent meaning *esse* does imply such dependency upon God, just as it implies those other "accidents" without which the essence is never realized in fact. After considering this possibility James finally acknowledges that this attempted reconciliation between his own theory and Henry's also fails. According to Henry both essence and existence bespeak relationships to God: one to him as exemplar, the other to him as efficient cause. James thinks it more likely that essence as such simply signifies the thing or nature in itself without any such relationship. If existence (*esse*) does imply such a relationship, it does so only in a consequent and secondary way, not in its primary meaning. James declines here to comment further on Henry's application of intentional distinction to essence and existence or on the disputed issue as to how a relationship differs from its foundation.[106]

At first sight, at least, James seems to be much closer to Godfrey on this question. Nonetheless, their views are not identical. For Godfrey essence and existence are one and the same. Existence is not to be construed as implying accidents in addition to essence in its secondary meaning and by way of consequence. Hence Godfrey firmly refuses to admit that one may say that essence and existence really differ. In brief, therefore, James does not stress identity of essence and existence so forcefully as Godfrey does.[107]*

NOTES

1 For some general discussions by those who find this view in Aquinas, see N. del Prado, *De veritate fundamentali philosophiae christianae* (Fribourg, 1911), pp. 23–79; J. de Finance, *Etre et agir*, 2nd ed. (Rome, 1960), pp. 94–111; C. Fabro, *La nozione metafisica di partecipazione secondo s. Tommaso d'Aquino*, 2nd ed. (Turin, 1950), pp. 212–44; E. Gilson, *History of Christian Philosophy in the Middle Ages* (New York, 1955), pp. 420–27; idem, *Being and Some Philosophers*, 2nd ed. (Toronto, 1952), pp. 171–78; M. Grabmann, "Doctrina s. Thomae de distinctione reali inter essentiam et esse ex documentis ineditis saeculi XIII illustratur," *Acta hebdomadae thomisticae Romae celebratae 19–25 Novembris 1923 in laudem s. Thomae Aquinatis* (Rome, 1924), pp. 131–90; J. Owens, "Quiddity and Real Distinction in St. Thomas Aquinas," *Mediaeval Studies*, 27 (1965), 19–22; L. Sweeney, "Existence / Essence in Thomas Aquinas's Early Writings," *Proceedings of the American Catholic Philosophical Association*, 37 (1963), 97–131. For the negative view, see M. Chossat, "Dieu," *Dictionnaire de Théologie Catholique* IV, col. 1180; idem, "L'Averroïsme de saint Thomas: Note sur la distinction d'essence et d'existence à la fin du XIIIe siècle," *Archives de Philosophie*, 9 (1932), 129 [465]–177 [513]; F. Cunningham, "Distinction According to St. Thomas," *The New Scholasticism*, 36 (1962), 279–312; idem, "Textos de santo Tómas sobre el esse y esencia," *Pensamiento*, 20 (1964), 283–306; idem, "The 'Real Distinction' in John Quidort," *Journal of the History of Philosophy*, 8 (1970), 9–28.

2 See A. Wolter, "The Formal Distinction," *Studies in Philosophy and the History of Philosophy*. III. *John Duns Scotus, 1265–1965* (Washington, D.C., 1965), pp. 54–59; A. J. O'Brien, "Duns Scotus' Teaching on the Distinction Between Essence and Existence," *The New Scholasticism*, 38 (1964), 61–77; W. Hoeres, "Wesen und Dasein bei Heinrich von Gent und Duns Scotus," *Franziskanische Studien*, 47 (1965), 170–71.

3 For further details with respect to Henry's life and career, see F. Ehrle, "Beiträge zur den Biographien berühmter Scholastiker. I. Heinrich von Gent," *Archiv für Literatur und Kirchengeschichte*, 1 (1885), 365–401, 507–508; J. Paulus, *Henri de Gand: Essai sur les tendances de sa métaphysique* (Paris, 1938), pp. XIII–XIX; idem, "Henry of Ghent," *New Catholic Encyclopedia* (1967), VI 1035–36; F. Cunningham, "Some Presuppositions in Henry of Ghent," *Pensamiento*, 25 (1969), 104–106.

4 For Giles's life and career, see P. Nash, "Giles of Rome," *New Catholic Encyclopedia*, VI 484–85; idem, "Giles of Rome: Auditor and Critic of St. Thomas," *The Modern Schoolman*, 28 (1950–1951), 1–2. For discussion as to why he was "exiled" from the theology faculty at Paris, see P. Mandonnet, "La Carrière scolaire de Gilles de Rome," *Revue des Sciences Philosophiques et Théologiques*, 4 (1910), 484–91; and, especially, E. Hocedez, "La Condamnation de Gilles de Rome," *Recherches de Théologie Ancienne et Médiévale*, 4 (1932), 34–58. See also R. Zavalloni, *Richard de Mediavilla et la controverse sur la pluralité des formes* (Louvain, 1951), pp. 489–91.

5 On Godfrey's life and career, see M. de Wulf, *Un Théologien-Philosophe du XIIIe siècle: Étude sur la vie, les œuvres et l'influence de Godefroid de Fontaines* (Brussels, 1904); R. J. Arway, "A Half Century of Research on Godfrey of Fontaines," *The New Scholasticism*, 36 (1962), 192–202; J. F. Wippel, "Godfrey of Fontaines," *New Catholic Encyclopedia*, VI 577–78. For fuller discussion of some problems relating to the chronology of some of his Quodlibets, see Wippel, "Godfrey of Fontaines: The Date of Quodlibet 15," *Franciscan Studies*, 31 (1971), 300–69; idem, "The Dating of James of Viterbo's Quodlibet I and Godfrey of Fontaines' Quodlibet VIII," *Augustiniana*, 24 (1974), 348–86.

6 For James's life and career, see D. Gutiérrez, *De b. Iacobi Viterbiensis O.E.S.A. vita, operibus et doctrina theologica* (Rome, 1939); E. Ypma, "Recherches sur la carrière scolaire et la bibliothèque de Jacques de Viterbe † 1308," *Augustiniana*, 24 (1974), 247–82; idem, "Recherches sur la productivité littéraire de Jacques de Viterbe jusqu'à 1300," ibid., 25 (1975), 223–82. For my reservations about the 1293 date proposed by Ypma for James's promotion as *magister* and my defense of late 1292 as a possibility, see my "The Dating of James of Viterbo's Quodlibet I," cited in n. 5. In his study of 1975 (just cited) Ypma remains unconvinced (see p. 249*n*55; but see also p. 274*n*147), yet he offers no further evidence for his case nor any refutation of mine. Even if James was promoted late in 1292, his first Quodlibet would still more than likely date from Lent 1293.

7 "Quarto quaeritur: Utrum salvari posset creatio si non differrent realiter esse et essentia in creaturis," in *Jacobi de Viterbio O.E.S.A. Disputatio prima de quolibet*, ed. E. Ypma (Würzburg, 1968), p. 43. On James and the relationship between essence and *esse*, see Grabmann, "Doctrina s. Thomae de distinctione reali," pp. 162–76; F. Casado, "El pensamiento filosófico del beato Santiago de Viterbo," *La Ciudad de Dios*, 164 (1952), 314–31; H. Rüssmann, *Zur Ideenlehre der Hochscholastik unter besonderer Berücksichtigung des Heinrich von Gent, Gottfried von Fontaines, und Jakob von Viterbo* (Freiburg im Breisgau, 1938), pp. 114–23.

8 *Disputatio prima de quolibet*, p. 43:1–12.

9 Even before doing so, James makes the following remark which merits quotation in that it gives some clue as to what his final solution will be: "Ad istam quaestionem sine praeiudicio, immo cum debita reverentia cuiuscumque opinionis, videtur mihi esse dicendum quod, si nullo modo differrent realiter essentia et esse in creaturis, non posset salvari creatio. Si tamen non differrent realiter illo modo quo doctores quidam ponunt ea differre, posset nihilominus salvari creatio" (ibid., 14–18).

10 James acknowledges that less properly either matter or form, viewed in themselves and separately, may be described as essence, and form more so than matter. But such will not be his usage in this discussion (ibid., p. 44:28–47).

11 "Esse autem sic acceptum est illud quod dicitur esse essentiae id est quod est ipsa essentia" (ibid., 56–58). In support of this usage James appeals to the authority of the grammarians, according to whom infinitives can be taken as nouns: "Et hoc modo esse idem est quod essentia, sicut legere nominaliter sumptum idem est quod lectio" (ibid., 49–51). He also appeals to the famed Boethian axiom ("Diversum est esse, et id quod est"), Gilbert of Poitiers' commentary on the same, and Aristotle's frequent practice. For Boethius, see his *De hebdomadibus* in *Boethius, The Theological Tractates*, edd. and trans. H. F. Stewart and E. K. Rand (Cambridge, Massachusetts, 1968), p. 40. For Gilbert, see *The Commentaries on Boethius by Gilbert of Poitiers*, ed. N. Häring (Toronto, 1966), pp. 193ff. See p. 194 where Gilbert seems to equate *esse* with *subsistentia*, and which James obviously identifies with *essentia*. James refers to no particular Aristotelian text. For all this, see James, *Disputatio prima de quolibet*, p. 44:51–56.

12 "Alio modo sumiter esse verbaliter, secundum quod significat actum essendi. Nam verba significant per modum actionis vel passionis; et hoc modo esse idem significat quod existere. Et hoc est esse quod dicitur actualis existentiae et significat idem quod hoc verbum est quando praedicatur secundo adiacens, ut cum dicitur: homo est vel Deus est" (ibid., pp. 44:59–45:63).

13 Ibid., p. 45:64–68.

14 Ibid., 75–85. James observes that one might discuss the question of the *esse* or "act of existing" of accidents and of its relation to accidental essence. But just as accidents possess essence only in a qualified sense (*secundum quid*), so, too, their acts of existing

(*existere*). In the present discussion he proposes to restrict the term *esse* to substantial existence.

15 Ibid., p. 46:92–96.

16 Ibid., 97–101. For Aristotle see *Metaphysics* IV, 2 (1003B25–30). For Averroës see *In IV Met.* (Venice, 1562), vol. 8, fols. 66vb–67ra; see also fol. 68va.

17 *Disputatio prima de quolibet*, p. 46:102–107: "Avicenna vero dixit quod ens significat intentionem seu dispositionem superadditam illi de quo dicitur, ita quod unumquodque dicitur ens non per essentiam suam, sed per aliquid superadditum, sicut res aliqua dicitur alba vel nigra per aliquid superadditum, quod est accidens illi rei. Unde posuit quod ens dicit accidens sive accidentalem dispositionem in eo de quo praedicatur." Though it is not my intention here to discuss the accuracy of James's reading of Avicenna, let it suffice to note that this was a widely accepted interpretation of his position in the Latin West at this time, an interpretation undoubtedly influenced by Averroës' criticism: "Avicenna autem peccavit multum in hoc, quod existimavit quod unum et ens significant dispositiones additas essentiae rei" (*In IV Met.*, fol. 67ra). For similar interpretations of Avicenna, see Thomas Aquinas, *In IV Met.* (Turin, 1950), n. 556. Note Thomas' comment shortly thereafter: "Sed in primo quidem non videtur dixisse recte. Esse enim rei quamvis sit aliud ab eius essentia, non tamen est intelligendum quod sit aliquod superadditum ad modum accidentis, sed quasi constituitur per principia essentiae" (n. 558). Siger of Brabant also seems to share this view of Avicenna. See *Siger de Brabant, Questions sur la Métaphysique*, ed. C. Graiff (Louvain, 1948), pp. 12 ("Item, auctoritate Avicennae . . . res imponitur a quidditate in communi, et intentio rei et entis imaginantur ab hominibus duae intentiones; ergo ratio essendi est alterius rationis quam ratio rei"); and 18, where he explicitly follows Averroës in his criticism of Avicenna. Thus Avicenna is chided for having failed to distinguish between dispositions added to a thing's essence, such as white or black, and essential dispositions which pertain to the essence itself. For more on these points and on this question in Siger, together with an edition of the text itself, see A. Maurer, "*Esse* and *Essentia* in the Metaphysics of Siger of Brabant," *Mediaeval Studies*, 8 (1946), 68–86. On Siger and Averroës vs. Avicenna, see pp. 78ff. For recent defenses of Avicenna's doctrine based on his Arabic text rather than on the medieval Latin translation, see F. Rahman, "Essence and Existence in Avicenna," *Mediaeval and Renaissance Studies*, 4 (1958), 1–16; "Ibn Sīnā," in M. M. Sharif, *A History of Muslim Philosophy* I (Wiesbaden, 1963), pp. 483–86; P. Morewedge, "Philosophical Analysis and Ibn Sīnā's 'Essence–Existence' Distinction," *Journal of the American Oriental Society*, 92 (1972), 425–35.

18 *Disputatio prima de quolibet*, p. 46:108–11: "Similiter autem et de esse est varius modus dicendi apud doctores. Quidam enim dicunt quod esse non dicit aliam rem quam essentia. Si autem aliquo modo ab essentia differre videatur, hoc erit solum secundum rationem."

19 Ibid., 112–20. Note the final comment: "Et ita est res alia ab essentia."

20 For the view that James has in mind here both Thomas and Giles, see Grabmann, "Doctrina s. Thomae de distinctione reali," pp. 174, 176. For James's later reference to the *Theoremata* (hence to Giles), see *Disputatio prima de quolibet*, p. 54:379–84: "Et licet non videatur esse aliquid cogens ad ponendum huiusmodi esse, negari tamen aut improbari non debet tamquam aliquid falsum aut impossibile, praecipue cum excellentes doctores hoc posuerint, qui nobis multorum bonorum causa fuerunt et ad quorum altissimum intellectum, quem de hoc et de multis aliis pulchris theorematibus habuerunt, ego et mihi similes ascendere ac pervenire non sumus idonei." This is surely a reference to Giles's *Theoremata de esse et essentia*, perhaps also to his *Theoremata de corpore Christi*.

The plural (*excellentes doctores*) need not signify more than one individual, that is, Giles, according to the accepted practice of that time.

21 *Disputatio prima de quolibet*, pp. 46:121–47:132. For the reference to Grosseteste, see: "Hunc autem modum dicendi videtur aliqualiter tangere Lincolniensis circa principium, *II Posteriorum*, ubi dicit quod 'esse dictum de causa prima indicat ipsam essentiam ipsam omnino simplicem causae primae. Dictum vero de aliis non praedicat nisi ordinationem et dependentiam eorum ab ente primo quod per se est. Et haec ordinatio et dependentia nihil multiplicat in essentia dependente.'" For Grosseteste himself, see *In Aristotelis Posteriorum Analyticorum libros* (Venice, 1514; repr. 1966), fol. 26rb. James acknowledges that the theory owes its present form to "others," that is, to Henry of Ghent: "Sed alii posteriores hunc modum dicendi magis expresserunt et declaraverunt, et ad ipsum aliqua addiderunt" (*Disputatio prima de quolibet*, p. 47:131–32).

22 See E. Hocedez, "Le Premier Quodlibet d'Henri de Gand," *Gregorianum*, 9 (1928), 92–117 (see 100–101, 104); Paulus, *Henri de Gand*, pp. 280–82.

23 On the controversy between Giles and Henry, see, in addition to the references cited in n. 22, Hocedez, "Gilles de Rome et Henri de Gand sur la distinction réelle (1276–1287)," *Gregorianum*, 8 (1927), 358–84; idem, "Deux questions touchant la distinction réelle entre l'essence et l'existence," ibid., 10 (1929), 365–86; idem, *Aegidii Romani Theoremata de esse et essentia: Texte précédé d'une introduction historique et critique* (Louvain, 1930), pp. (82)–(84); Paulus, "Les Disputes d'Henri de Gand et de Gilles de Rome sur la distinction de l'essence et de l'existence," *Archives d'Histoire Doctrinale et Littéraire du Moyen Age*, 13 (1940–1942), 323–58.

24 In addition to the studies by Hocedez cited in the two preceding notes, for treatments of Giles's teaching on the essence–existence relationship, see A. Pattin, "Gilles de Rome, O.E.S.A. (ca. 1243–1316) et la distinction réelle de l'essence et de l'existence," *Revue de l'Université d'Ottawa*, 23 (1953), 80*–116*; G. Suárez, "El pensamiento de Egidio Romano en torno a la distinción de esencia y existencia," *La Ciencia Tomista*, 75 (1948), 66–99, 230–72; P. Nash, "Giles of Rome on Boethius' 'Diversum est esse et id quod est,'" *Mediaeval Studies*, 12 (1950), 57–91; idem, "The Accidentality of Esse According to Giles of Rome," *Gregorianum*, 38 (1957), 103–15; and, finally, a series of articles by G. Trapé, bearing either directly on the essence–existence distinction in Giles or on related themes in his metaphysics: "Il Platonismo di Egidio Romano," *Aquinas*, 7 (1964), 309–44; "L''esse' partecipato e distinzione reale in Egidio Romano," ibid., 12 (1969), 443–68; "Il Neoplatonismo di Egidio Romano nel Commento al 'De causis,'" ibid., 9 (1966), 49–86; "La dottrina della partecipazione in Egidio Romano," ibid., 10 (1967), 170–93; "Caratteristiche dell' 'esse' partecipato in Egidio Romano," *Lateranum*, 34 (1968), 351–68; "Causalità e partecipazione in Egidio Romano," *Augustinianum*, 9 (1969), 91–117. On the chronology of Giles's development of this doctrine and his debates with Henry of Ghent, see Paulus, *Henri de Gand*, p. 281; Trapé, "L' 'esse' partecipato e distinzione reale in Egidio Romano," 455. Note that Paulus and Trapé place Giles's *Commentary on I Sentences* and his *Theoremata de corpore Christi* in 1276 and prior to Henry's Quodlibet 1 of Christmas 1276. Pattin follows Suárez in placing the *Commentary on I Sentences* ca. 1275 ("Gilles de Rome," 82*). He places the *Theoremata de corpore Christi* ca. 1275–1276 (85*). On the presence or absence of this theory in Giles's earlier works, see the doctoral dissertation on essence and existence in Giles being prepared by M. Quaresma at The Catholic University of America.

25 "Utrum in deo sit compositio essentiae et esse" (*In I Sent.*, d. 8, p. 2, pr. 1, q. 2 [Venice, 1521], fol. 52^{v}). Here Giles lists three ways in which the divine existence (*esse*) may be said to differ from that of creatures. According to the third of these, the divine

existence does not differ from the divine quiddity. For this and the other two reasons which he has just cited, Giles concludes that existence in God does not enter into composition with the divine substance or essence ("Tertio, esse divinum non differt a quidditate. ... Propter haec tria, esse in deo non facit compositionem cum substantia sive cum essentia"). Presumably, therefore, a creature's existence does differ from its essence and does enter into composition with it in some way.

26 "Primo, utrum omnis creatura sit composita" (ibid., pr. 2, q. 1, fol. 53[vb]). For the second argument of the *In contrarium*, see fol. 54[ra]: "Omne creatum habet esse finitum. Sed esse finitum est esse receptum in alio. Ergo in omni creato est compositio ex recepto et recipiente."

27 Ibid. "Respondeo dicendum quod in omni creato quod habet per se esse, oportet nos concedere esse compositionem ex quod est et esse. Et est ratio: quia si creatum est, ab alio habet esse. Omne quod ab alio habet esse est in potentia ad esse et non est ipsum esse. Quia si ipsum esse esset, tunc esset actus purus sine aliqua potentialitate. Non igitur indigeret aliqua essentialiter differente ab eo quod ipsum ad esse produceret. Ponere igitur creatum sic esse est ponere creatum non esse creatum." On this text as well as for a second argument offered by Giles in the same immediate context, see Nash, "Giles of Rome on Boethius' 'Diversum est esse et id quod est,'" 66–67. Later in this same discussion Giles draws on a theory of totalities derived from Proclus in order to show that in a created subject or supposit even its constituting parts, including its existence (*esse*), may be said to be "composite." See *In I Sent.*, d. 8, p. 2, pr. 2, q. 1, fol. 54[ra–b]; see also Nash, "Giles of Rome on Boethius' 'Diversum est esse et id quod est,'" 67–68. On this, see also idem, "Giles of Rome: Auditor and Critic of St. Thomas," 15–18. Giles realizes that existence itself cannot be said to be composed of essence and existence. Nonetheless, by reason of the fact that it is received in something else, it is not received according to its totality, but only *secundum partem*. This he describes as a whole (*totum*) *in parte*. Insofar as *esse* is received in differing ways or degrees in different beings, it falls short of perfect unity, immutability, and simplicity. Hence it may be said to be "composite" in this rather unusual sense (*In I Sent.*, d. 8, p. 2, pr. 2, q. 1, fol. 54[ra–b]). On the essence–existence relationship in this same work, see Suárez, "El pensamiento de Egidio Romano," 94, 96; Pattin, "Gilles de Rome," 84*; Trapé, "Il platonismo di Egidio Romano," 330–37; idem, "L' 'esse' partecipato e distinzione reale in Egidio Romano," 450–52.

28 "Licet res unius praedicamenti prout induit modum alterius praedicamenti non diversificet essentiam nec mutat [Venice: mutet] praedicamentum, tamen si competeret ei actualis existentia sine illo [Venice: modo], et cum illo [Venice: modo], ut haberet talem modum et ut careret eo, sortiretur realem differentiam" (*Theoremata de corpore Christi* [Bologna, 1481], fol. 119[rb]). On this see also Pattin, "Gilles de Rome," 85*–88*. There Pattin is following and citing at considerable length the Venice edition of 1502, an edition not directly available to me. Hence I have indicated the variants between his citation of that edition and the Bologna text. As we shall see below and as Pattin also indicates (p. 85*n21), Giles even more explicitly states this point that separability is the best proof of real distinction in his *Theoremata de esse et essentia*, pp. 67–68.

29 For more on the context leading up to this passage, see Pattin, "Gilles de Rome," 85*–87*. The passage itself reads: "Ex hiis autem iuvamur ad intelligendum esse et essentiam creatorum. Videmus enim quod sola quantitas est sua extensio, quia [Venice: et quod] extensio in quantitate non est aliquid superadditum quantitati. Non enim quantitas est extensa per aliud sed seipsa est quid extensum. Propter quod non competit ei extensio participatione, sed essentialiter est ipsa extensio. . . . cetera autem praeter

quantitatem sunt extensa per participationem et extensio dicit quiddam [Venice reading] additum naturae eorum. . . . Nam sola essentia divina est suum esse, quia esse in essentia dei non dicit aliquid superadditum naturae eius. . . . cetera autem entia quia [Venice: quae] habent esse per divinam essentiam esse dicit aliquid additum naturae, propter quod esse non pertinet ad naturam alicuius entis creati. Ex his clare patet quod esse accidit cuilibet creaturae et dicit aliquid receptum in natura cuiuslibet creati [et dicit additum cuiuslibet entis creati: omitted in Venice ed.] et facit realem differentiam in rebus creatis" (*Theoremata de corpore Christi*, fol. 119[vb]).

30 "Utrum tamen esse dicat aliquam essentiam additam essentiae creaturae (videtur enim absurdum quod essentia et esse dicantur duae essentiae). Quomodo autem [Venice: ergo] habeat esse ista realis differentia, et utrum essentia et esse possint dici duae res, et quomodo esse fluit ab essentia et est actus eius, ostendere non est praesentis speculationis. Tamen quia ut plurimum circa esse creaturarum fatigantur addiscentes, et multi cum loquuntur de esse et essentia in solis verbis sustentantur, cum locus occurrerit, domino concedente, intendimus hoc diffusius pertractare" (ibid., fols. 119vb–120ra). On this same discussion in Giles, see also Suárez, "El pensamiento de Egidio Romano," 96–97; Trapé, "L' 'esse' partecipato e distinzione reale," 452–53.

31 Paulus simply places this work between 1278 and 1286, that is to say, during Giles's period of exile from Paris ("Les Disputes d'Henri de Gand et de Gilles de Rome," 328). In this he follows Hocedez; see the latter's edition of the *Theoremata de esse et essentia*, (12). For the 1278–1280 dating, see Suárez, "El pensamiento de Egidio Romano," 80; Pattin, "Gilles de Rome," 91*. Trapé simply places it in 1278 ("L' 'esse' partecipato e distinzione reale," 453). Z. K. Siemiatkowska would place it somewhat earlier, that is to say, before Giles's exile, and therefore sees it as directly envisioned by Henry in his attack on the real distinction in 1276. See "Avant l'exil de Gilles de Rome: Au sujet d'une dispute sur les 'Theoremata de esse et essentia' de Gilles de Rome," *Mediaevalia philosophica Polonorum*, 7 (1960), 4–5, 31, 48.

32 See Hocedez' comments in "Gilles de Rome et Henri de Gand sur la distinction réelle (1276–1287)," passim; and in his edition of the *Theoremata de esse et essentia*, pp. [33]–[43]. See, too, Paulus, "Les disputes d'Henri de Gand et de Gilles de Rome," 328–33, 342–45; Pattin, "Gilles de Rome," 92*–102*; Trapé, "La dottrina della partecipazione in Egidio Romano," 170–93; idem, "Caratteristiche dell''esse' partecipato in Egidio Romano," passim.

33 *Theoremata de esse et essentia*, th. 19: "Quia tota causa quare nos investigamus quod esse sit res differens ab essentia ex hoc sumitur ut possimus salvare res creatas esse compositas et posse creari et posse esse et non esse . . . " (p. 129). See also his *Quaestiones disputatae de esse et essentia*, q. 9 (Venice, 1503): "sic creatio facit scire quod essentia esset [read: est] aliud ab esse quia ex hoc est creatio inquantum essentia acquirit esse" (fol. 21[ra–b]). For citation and analysis of many other texts bearing on this, see Suárez, "El pensamiento de Egidio Romano," 240–47.

34 "Dicamus ergo quod, sicut generatio fecit nos scire materiam esse differentem a forma, sic creatio facit nos cognoscere essentiam esse differentem ab esse" (*Theoremata de esse et essentia*, p. 19). See his *Quaestiones disputatae de esse et essentia*, q. 9: "Dicemus ergo sicut generatio facit scire materiam aliud esse a forma, sic creatio facit nos scire essentiam esse aliud ab esse" (fols. 20[vb]–21[ra]).

35 *Theoremata de esse et essentia*, th. 5, pp. 19–20.

36 Here Giles is attempting to explain his understanding of existence (*esse*): "Nam esse est quaedam actualitas et quaedam perfectio essentiae, sicut forma est quaedam

actualitas et perfectio materiae, et sicut realiter differt materia a forma, sic realiter differt essentia ab esse" (ibid., p. 20).

37 Ibid., pp. 20–21. Note in particular: "sicut fit generatio prout a generante imprimitur forma materiae, sic fit creatio prout a creante ipsi essentiae imprimitur esse." See p. 21 for more on the parallelism between generation as enabling us to reason to matter–form differentiation and creation as leading us to recognize the essence–existence diversity in creatures.

38 Already here in th. 5 Giles points out certain differences between matter–form composition and that of essence and existence. In the case of generation, matter pre-exists before receiving a given form, while in creation essence does not pre-exist before receiving its existence (ibid., p. 21). As he indicates in th. 6, matter pre-exists in this sense: that it is subject to one form at one time, and subject to another at another time. But numerically the same essence is never subject to one existence at one time and then subject to another at another time. As a second point of differentiation, he observes that although matter is pure potency, essence is not. Thirdly, material things composed of matter and form can be brought into being by purely natural and material agents. Separate entities in which there is essence–existence composition can be produced only by a separate entity. From these he argues that three further differences also follow: (*a*) the essence–existence composition is more general than is that of matter–form; (*b*) from matter–form composition a third nature results, but not so from that of essence–existence; and (*c*) the form inhering in matter can be the immediate terminus of motion or change, but such is not true of existence (ibid., pp. 26–27; see pp. 27–30 for fuller discussion of these three last-mentioned points).

39 "Nam si essentia de se diceret tantam actualitatem et tantum complementum quod sine additione alterius posset existere et esse in rerum natura, tunc talis essentia non posset non esse, nec haberet ab alio esse. . . . Ideo nec natura sine esse, nec esse sine natura, creari potest" (ibid., pp. 21–22). Passages such as these should be used to counterbalance the attempt to assign a theory of pre existence or "quasi-eternity" of essence to Giles (at least by implication) on the part of at least one recent commentator. See William Carlo, *The Ultimate Reducibility of Essence to Existence in Existential Metaphysics* (The Hague, 1966), pp. 14–17, 19, 31, 66, 67, 83. On this point Carlo supports a charge raised against Giles by Henry of Ghent (pp. 14, 83). For this in Henry, see also Paulus, "Les Disputes d'Henri de Gand et de Gilles de Rome," 347–48. Carlo is aware of Giles's protest that essence "does not pre-exist *esse*, even though he can present no alternative" (p. 88). Although fuller discussion of Giles's treatment of essence, especially as found in his *Commentary on the Liber de causis* (Carlo's principal source for his interpretation), must be reserved for another occasion, it does appear to me that a somewhat more nuanced and sympathetic account can be given. See, for instance, Trapé, "Il Neoplatonismo di Egidio Romano nel Commento al 'De causis,'" esp. 78–81. This *Commentary* dates from 1290 (ibid., 50).

40 *Theoremata de esse et essentia*, th. 5, pp. 23–24. Note the remark with which he introduces these three arguments: "His itaque praelibatis, possumus triplici via incedere ostendentes quod nulla natura creata, quantumcumque sit forma immaterialis et abstracta, est suum esse sed a suo esse est realiter differens et distincta" (p. 23). Giles sums up the heart of this argument in the following lines: "Et quia actus et potentia habent quandam oppositionem, et unum non est aliud, ideo in creatione esse quod imprimitur essentiae habet rationem actus et essentia quae suscipit esse habet rationem potentiae, et unum non est aliud sed ad invicem realiter differunt" (p. 24). Also see th. 12, pp. 71–72, 74–75.

41 Ibid., th. 5, pp. 24–25. Although Giles has developed this argument with respect to separate substances, he then concludes that this same composition of essence and existence obtains in the corporeal realm as well: "Et quia quaecumque compositio habet esse in substantiis separatis, habet esse in corporalibus rebus, oportet haec corporalia et per consequens omnia creata habere naturam differentem ab esse" (p. 25). As will be evident below in my consideration of argumentation taken from Giles's *Disputed Questions*, this particular line of reasoning assumes that act as such, and hence existence as such, is not self-limiting. For the same see th. 1: "Nam omne esse quod non est receptum in alio, sed est per se existens, oportet quod sit purum et infinitum" (p. 1). See also pp. 2–4. For similar reasoning see th. 20, pp. 141–42.

42 Ibid., th. 5, pp. 25–26. "Tertia via sumitur ex naturae creatae compositione. Nam si natura creata esset suum esse, esset omnino simplex. . . . Quare si natura aliqua creata esset ipsum esse, nullo alio participare posset, esset ergo omnino simplex et per consequens omnino immutabilis etiam per naturam, quod creaturae convenire non potest." Cf. also th. 20, pp. 140–41.

43 For details of this controversy, see the articles cited in n. 32. Let it suffice for me to note that in *Disputed Questions* 9 and 11 (1285/1286) Giles responded to Henry's Quodlibet 1 of 1276. Henry replied at considerable length in his Quodlibet 10, q. 7 (Christmas 1286). Giles responded to this new intervention on Henry's part in *Disputed Questions* 12 and 13 (1287). In his Quodlibet 11, q. 3 of Christmas 1287, Henry replied to the last-mentioned *Disputed Questions*.

44 *Quaestiones disputatae de esse et essentia*, fol. 18ra: "Prima talis. Si creatura esset suum esse, cum creatura sit quid subsistens, ergo esse creaturae esset esse subsistens. Sed tale esse est esse purum quod non competit nisi soli deo. Ergo etc. Secunda talis. Cum esse secundum quod huiusmodi non sit quid limitatum, si creatura esset suum esse, creatura non esset quid limitatum, et ita non esset quid finitum, quod est inconveniens. Tertia talis. Si creatura non est aliud re a suo esse, cum esse non possit separari a seipso, esse creaturae non posset separari a creatura. Ergo sicut impossibile est ipsum esse non esse, ita impossibile esset non esse creaturam."

45 Ibid., fols. 20vb–21va. Note his final comment: "Sufficit autem ad praesens scire quod sicut nos non possumus salvare generationem et corruptionem in entibus nisi ponamus in eis compositionem ex materia et forma, sic nec possumus in istis entibus salvare creationem nisi ponamus in eis compositionem ex essentia et esse" (fol. 21va).

46 Ibid., fol. 19ra. See his introductory remark: "Sed si consideratur quid importatur nomine participationis salvare non possumus quod esse creaturae sit esse per participationem nisi essentia substernatur ipsi esse et nisi sit ibi realis compositio ex essentia et esse. Nam quicquid participat aliquo est aliquid aliud praeter illud."

47 "Secundum est quia quaelibet essentia creaturae participat esse et omne esse in creaturis est quid participatum" (ibid., fol. 24vb).

48 Ibid., fols. 24vb–25ra. Note the following in particular: "Sed si esse creaturae non esset esse receptum non esset esse diminutum. Actus enim non dicitur esse quid diminutum nec quid participatum nisi ratione potentiae in qua recipitur. . . . Nisi ergo intelligamus quod esse sit aliquid in essentia receptum, tollimus quod non sit quid participatum nec in se nec respectu alterius. Actui enim non competit limitatio nisi ratione potentiae in qua recipitur. Nec dici potest quod ista differentia non sit secundum rem. Quia si ex hoc ponimus quod esse creaturae est quidam diminutus actus quia non recipitur in potentia secundum suam plenitudinem, oportet quod recipiens sit re differens a recepto. Aliter enim non reciperet ipsum diminute" (fol. 25ra).

49 For Thomas, see *Le ' De ente et essentia' de s. Thomas d'Aquin*, ed. M.-D. Roland Gosselin (Paris, 1948), p. 34: "Omnis autem essentia vel quidditas potest intelligi sine hoc quod aliquid intelligatur de esse suo. . . ."

50 "Primum est quod omnis essentia cuiuslibet creaturae potest intelligi cum opposito ipsius esse. . . . Nam nihil potest intelligi cum opposito sui ipsius. Quicquid ergo potest intelligi cum opposito alicuius [text: aliter] est realiter differens ab ipso. Erit ergo essentia realiter differens ab esse" (*Quaestiones disputatae de esse et essentia*, fol. 24vb).

51 "Sic si idem esset in aliqua creatura essentia cum suo existere, possemus forte intelligere essentiam illam non intellecto eius existere, sed non possemus intelligere ipsam essentiam quod non existeret. Et impossibile esset talem essentiam non existere" (ibid., fol. 20va). Note that in th. 12 of the *Theoremata de esse et essentia* he develops this argument more fully in order to show that it entails a real distinction rather than a mere distinction of reason. In order to make this point, he argues that things which are really separated are really distinct. But since sensible natures are capable of not existing, they are in potency to existence and must have an essence which really differs from it. Therefore, because one can understand a created essence without understanding it to exist, such an essence is not identical with its existence (pp. 67–70).

52 "Esse autem quod causatur a forma totius ut in decima nona propositione patebit, est res differens ab ipsa forma" (ibid., p. 101).

53 "Verum quia in propositione quinta et etiam in duodecima multis rationibus probabatur et etiam hic ostendetur quod esse et essentia sunt duae res, ita quod esse nihil est aliud quam quaedam actualitas realiter superaddita essentiae ex quo esse et essentia realiter componitur omne creatum . . ." (ibid., p. 127).

54 "Et, sicut materia et quantitas sunt duae res, sic essentia et esse sunt duae res realiter differentes" (ibid., p. 134).

55 "Res ergo ipsa quae est esse est in genere substantiae. Habet tamen ipsum esse quemdam modum accidentalem actualem inquantum est superadditum substantiae" (*Quaestiones disputatae de esse et essentia*, fol. 20vb).

56 See ibid., fol. 24vb. Note in particular: "et per consequens intelligitur quod esse sit alia res ab essentia."

57 See the text from the *Theoremata de corpore Christi*, cited in n. 28. See also n. 51 for the text from the *Theoremata de esse et essentia*. Note especially the following: "Et si dubium est utrum aliqua realiter diversa possunt realiter separari, tamen dubium esse non potest quod realiter separantur, realiter differunt" (pp. 67–68).

58 See n. 39. See also *Theoremata de esse et essentia*, th. 5: "Dicebatur enim supra quod ipsa essentia aliquam actualitatem importat, licet illa actualitas non sit tanta quod sine esse possit existere. . . . Sed essentia non praeexistit ipsi esse . . ." (p. 29). Also, th. 7: "Ipsa enim forma, ut in praecedentibus dicebatur, licet de se dicat quandam actualitatem, non tamen dicit tantam actualitatem quod possit esse actu sine esse. Ipsum ergo esse dat quandam actualitatem formae" (p. 37). See too th. 10: "Non tamen dicit quidditas actualitatem tantam quod per se possit existere sine esse . . ." (p. 57). For other passages see Pattin, "Gilles de Rome," 102*–105*. See, in particular, *Disputed Question* 11, ad 10 (*Quaestiones disputatae de esse et essentia*, fol. 26va), also cited by Pattin, but from another edition (see "Gilles de Rome," 104*–105*).

59 It is one thing to suggest that essence and existence are *separable* and therefore that any created being is contingent. It is another to hold that either could ever exist *in separation* from the other. Though Giles does admit the first, he consistently rejects the second. In addition to the reference to Pattin cited in n. 58, see Suárez, "El pensamiento de Egidio Romano," 252–54, 270, and the texts cited there.

60 See, for instance, two arguments against Giles as presented by Henry of Ghent in his Quodlibet 1, q. 9 (*Quodlibeta* [Paris, 1518; repr. Louvain, 1961]), fol. 7r: "Primo, si nihil in creaturis haberet esse per suam essentiam sed per rem additam suae essentiae, nihil in creaturis esset ens per se. Secundo, quoniam si illud esse sit res aliqua super essentiam creaturae, cum non sit dare quod sit Deus et res increata, erit ergo res creata. Res autem quaelibet creata de se habet non esse, et si habet esse, hoc est participatum et acquisitum. Si ergo esse acquisitum et participatum semper aliud est in re ab eo cui acquiritur et a quo participatur, de illo esse illius rei additae essentiae . . . quaero utrum sit aliud re ab essentia illius rei cui acquiritur. Et tunc aut erit procedere in infinitum, aut status erit in aliqua essentia cui acquiritur esse quod nullo modo est aliud re ab illa essentia cui acquiritur. Et qua ratione statur in una essentia et natura creata, eadem ratione et in qualibet." Similar argumentation is presented by Godfrey of Fontaines against Giles (see below).

61 See the passage from the *Theoremata de corpore Christi* as cited in n. 30.

62 See *Disputed Question* 9 (*Quaestiones disputatae de esse et essentia*, fol. 20vb). Note especially: "Res ergo ipsa quae est esse est in genere substantiae. Habet tamen ipsum esse quemdam modum accidentalem actualem inquantum est superadditum substantiae. . . . Sed punctus sic est quid additum lineae quod non est in genere per se, sed reducitur ad idem genus in quo est linea; sic esse ita est superadditum substantiae quod non est in genere per se, sed reducitur ad idem genus cum ipsa substantia in qua recipitur. Bene igitur dictum est quod res ipsa quae est esse [est] in genere substantiae, sicut res ipsa quae est punctus est in genere quantitatis." See his reply to Objection 8 (fol. 22rb). See also the *Theoremata de esse et essentia*, th. 22, pp. 155–59.

63 See *Theoremata de esse et essentia*, pp. [62]–[65], as well as p. [117] where the editor comments: "Gilles est l'inventeur du monstre qui a effarouché Scot et Suarez." See also Paulus, *Henri de Gand*, pp. 283–84. Needless to say, these authors stress the difference between Giles's theory and that of Thomas Aquinas.

64 See his "Giles of Rome on Boethius' 'Diversum est esse et id quod est'" and "The Accidentality of Esse According to Giles of Rome," cited in n. 24, and "Giles of Rome," in the *New Catholic Encyclopedia*, cited in n. 4. In the first of these articles, Nash finds the divergence between Giles and Thomas even greater than Hocedez and Paulus had. For him this divergence is not merely due to Giles's "Platonically inspired 'imagination.'" Rather, Giles's "world was a Boethian world in which the creature is distinguished from the Creator by being a plurality of parts . . . ," that is to say, of essence and existence (see p. 58; see also pp. 90–91). In the second, he comments that he had previously overemphasized Giles's view that *esse actuale* is "accidental." There he continues to stress the priority of essence and the posteriority of existence in Giles's theory (see pp. 104–105, 108, 109–15), although he also clearly acknowledges that essence can never exist by itself without its corresponding existence. For an even stronger stress on this priority of essence, see Carlo, *Ultimate Reducibility of Essence to Existence*, as cited in n. 39.

65 See Suárez, "El pensamiento de Egidio Romano," 66–99, 230–72. See, in particular, 251–54 and 270–71 (separability of essence and existence does not imply that either can exist without the other); 262–63 and 266–68 (*res* and *res* terminology does not imply "reification" in the proper sense). See also Pattin, "Gilles de Rome," esp. 90* (Giles's real distinction is not to be viewed as opposed to real distinction between principles of being or *entia quibus*); 102*–106* (granted Giles's Platonism or extreme realism, this must not be exaggerated). See as well Trapé, "L' 'esse' partecipato e distinzione reale," esp. 445ff., 467–68; and "Il Platonismo di Egidio Romano," 309–44.

66 See Henry's Quodl. 1, q. 9, fol. 6v: "Utrum creatura ipsa sit suum esse." On the dates of Henry's Quodlibets, see P. Glorieux, *La Littérature quodlibétique de 1260 à 1320* I (Le Saulchoir, 1925), pp. 87–93, 177–99; J. Gómez Caffarena, "Cronología de la 'Suma' de Enrique de Gante por relación a sus 'Quodlibetos,'" *Gregorianum*, 38 (1957), 116–33 (also for the correlation of the dates of Henry's Quodlibets with those of his *Ordinary Questions*). On this particular text in Henry, see Hocedez, "Le Premier Quodlibet d'Henri de Gand (1276)," ibid., 9 (1928), 92–117; Paulus, "Les Disputes d'Henri de Gand et de Gilles de Rome," 324–27; Cunningham, "Some Presuppositions in Henry of Ghent," 107–13; Gómez Caffarena, *Ser participado y ser subsistente en la metafísica de Enrique de Gante* (Rome, 1958), pp. 72–73.

67 See Quodl. 1, q. 9, fols. 6v–7r (for his distinction between two ways of accounting for participated being and his rejection of one of these, and for his arguments against the theory of real distinction between essence and existence). Then he begins to expound his own theory: "Est hic distinguendum de esse secundum quod distinguit Avicenna in quinto in fine Metaphysicae suae, quod quoddam est esse rei quod habet essentialiter de se, quod appellatur esse essentiae, quoddam vero quod recipit ab alio, quod appellatur esse actualis existentiae. Primum esse habet essentia creaturae essentialiter, secundum tamen participationem [text: participative], inquantum habet formale exemplar in deo" (fol. 7r). I have followed Paulus in changing the *participative* of the printed text to *participationem* (see his "Les Disputes d'Henri de Gand et de Gilles de Rome," 325). The text continues: "Et per hoc cadit sub ente quod est commune essentiale ad decem praedicamenta, quod a tali esse in communi accepto imponitur. Et est illud esse rei definitivum quod de ipsa ante esse actuale solum habet existere in mentis conceptu, de quo dicitur quod definitio est oratio indicans quid est esse" (fol. 7r).

68 "Secundum esse non habet creatura ex sua essentia sed a deo inquantum est effectus voluntatis divinae iuxta exemplar eius in mente divina. Unde quia istud esse non habet ex sua essentia sed quadam extrinseca participatione . . . " (ibid.). See Quodl. 3, q. 9 fols. 60v–61r) where Henry connects his understanding of *esse essentiae* with Avicenna's discussion of the threefold way in which an essence or nature can be considered, especially with the possibility of viewing it in itself without adverting to its existence in the intellect or in the singular existent. For some of the texts in Avicenna to which Henry refers there, see Avicenna's *Metaphysica* I, 6 and V, 1 and 2 (Venice, 1508), fols. 72va, 86vb–87rb, and 87va. Henry then goes on to correlate these three modes of consideration which he has borrowed from Avicenna with three modes of being which such an essence may enjoy: "Triplicem quidem habet intellectum verum sicut et tres modos habet in esse. Unum enim habet esse naturae extra in rebus; alterum vero habet esse rationis; tertium vero habet esse essentiae. Animal enim, acceptum cum accidentibus suis in singularibus, est res naturalis; acceptum vero cum accidentibus suis in anima, est res rationis; acceptum vero secundum se, est res essentiae de qua dicitur quod esse eius est prius quam esse eius naturae, vel rationis . . ." (fol. 61r). Godfrey of Fontaines will sharply criticize Henry for having so interpreted Avicenna (see his Quodlibet 2, q. 2 [*Les Philosophes Belges* II (Louvain, 1904), p. 59]). For more on this, see my "Godfrey of Fontaines and Henry of Ghent's Theory of Intentional Distinction between Essence and Existence," in *Sapientiae procerum amore: Mélanges médiévistes offerts à Dom Jean-Pierre Müller O.S.B.*, ed. Theodor Wolfram Köhler, Studia Anselmiana 63 (Rome, 1974), pp. 298–304. To return to Henry's Quodl. 3, q. 9: he then comments: "Quid intelligo: quia tale esse [esse essentiae] non convenit alicui nisi cuius ratio exemplaris est in intellectu divino, per quam natum est fieri in rebus extra, ita quod sicut ex relatione et respectu ad ipsam ut ad causam efficientem habet quod sit ens in effectu, sic ex relatione quadam et respectu ad ipsam ut

ad formam extra rem habet quod sit ens aliquod per essentiam . . ." (fol. 61r). See also Henry's Quodl. 9, q. 2, fol. 345v.

69 See Quodl. 1, q. 9, fol. 7r–v, and especially: "Si loquamur de primo esse creaturae, illud sola ratione differt ab essentia creaturae, nec potest ei abesse quia non habet illud ab alio effective sed solum formaliter. Unde . . . potest dici de essentia creaturae quod ipsa est suum esse participatum formaliter licet non effective. . . . Si vero loquamur de secundo esse creaturae, illud, licet non differt re ab essentia creaturae, non tamen differt ab illa sola ratione . . . sed etiam differt ab illa intentione . . . et ideo de tali esse non potest concedi quod essentia creaturae est esse suum; quia esse essentiae nunc existens in actu potest esse non ens, sicut prius fuit ens. In solo autem deo verum est quod de tali esse loquendo ipse est suum esse." In this passage Henry admits of nothing more than logical distinction between essence and *esse essentiae.* He later seems to have changed on this point so as to admit of intentional distinction even between them, but ended by returning to his original position, allowing for only logical distinction. See Paulus, *Henri de Gand*, pp. 311–14; Hoeres, "Wesen und Dasein," 146*n*77.

70 Quodl. 1, q. 9, fol. 7v: "Idem enim sunt omnino re et idem significant currens, cursus, et currere, lux, lucens, lucere, vivens, vita, et vivere, sicut ens, essentia et esse, et tamen non possum dicere cursus est currere, vel lux est lucere. Similiter etiam non possum dicere ens est suum esse, licet idem sint in re." Henry later finds it necessary to reject the analogy between some of these examples and the relationship of *ens*, *essentia*, and *esse.* See Paulus, *Henri de Gand*, p. 308*n*2.

71 On the general chronology of the debate between Giles and Henry, see Paulus, *Henri de Gand*, pp. 280–81, and "Les Disputes d'Henri de Gand et de Gilles de Rome," passim.

72 Fols. 417r–418r. See in particular: "Sic ergo sentiendum est quod esse non sit aliquid absolutum additum essentiae creaturae et inhaerens ei per creationem ut forma inhaeret materiae per generationem, et hoc non solum esse essentiae ut ille [Giles] confitetur, sed etiam esse existentiae, quod negare contendit. . . . Ut secundum hoc esse existentiae non addat super essentiam nisi respectum ad efficientem" (fol. 417r).

73 Fols. 417v–418r. For more on this particular question, see Paulus, *Henri de Gand*, p. 250*n*2, and "Les Disputes d'Henri de Gand et de Gilles de Rome," 334–43; Hocedez, "Gilles de Rome et Henri de Gand sur la distinction réelle (1276–1287)," 365*n*69. On Henry's theory of intentional distinction, see Paulus, *Henri de Gand*, pp. 220*n*36; Hoeres, "Wesen und Dasein," 129–40. On his application of the theory to the essence–existence relationship, see Paulus, *Henri de Gand*, chap. 5 (esp. pp. 284–91); Hoeres, "Wesen und Dasein," 144–50; and Gómez Caffarena, *Ser participado*, pp. 65–92. Note that Cunningham has presented in English translation a. 28, q. 4, of Henry's *Summae quaestionum ordinariarum.* As Cunningham indicates, in this treatment dating from 1280 one finds a relatively succinct résumé of Henry's general position. See "Some Presuppositions in Henry of Ghent," 138–43.

74 Fol. 441r–v: "Unde ex eo quod dicimus quod esse existentiae nihil reale addit super essentiam, non sequitur quod essentia creaturae sit ipsum esse suum, quod soli deo competit. Sed tunc illud sequeretur si nec respectum alterius intentionis adderet essentiae, quem quia addit ut aliquid accidentale illi et ut accidens non reale sed intentionale, sequitur quod essentia non sit suum esse sed quod ut accidente quodam intentionali participat ipsum esse. . . ." For some interesting reflections on Henry's theory of intentional distinction (as well as his distinction between *potentia subjectiva* and *potentia objectiva*), see L. Hödl, "Neue Begriffe und neue Wege der Seinserkenntnis im Schul- und Einflussbereich des Heinrich von Gent," *Miscellanea mediaevalia*, 2 (1963), 607–15.

75 See *Les Philosophes Belges* II, p. 156: "Utrum creatura possit dici ens ratione suae essentiae, cum ipsa est non ens quantum ad esse existentiae." Godfrey's major work appeared in the form of fifteen quodlibetal debates, dating from 1285 to 1303/1304, which have been published in Louvain in the series *Les Philosophes Belges* in volumes 2 (1904), 3 (1914), 4 (1914, 1918, 1931), 5 (1932, 1935), and 14 (1937); hereafter cited as PB. On the dating of the debates, see Glorieux, *La Littérature quodlibétique* I, pp. 151–66, as well as the studies cited in n. 5. On Godfrey's knowledge of and reaction to the theory of the real distinction between essence and existence, see my "Godfrey of Fontaines and the Real Distinction Between Essence and Existence," *Traditio*, 20 (1964), 385–410.

76 PB 2.158.

77 ". . . quod esse existentiae est aliquid differens realiter ab essentia sive etiam ab esse essentiae, et est actualitas ipsius essentiae, sicut forma est actualitas materiae. Sicut enim materia de se est in potentia ad formam et ad privationem eius, sic essentia quantum est de se est in potentia ad esse et ad privationem eius" (ibid.). For a shorter redaction of this same question, see PB 2.302: "dicunt quidam quod esse et essentia sunt diversae res in creaturis. . . ." According to O. Lottin, these shorter redactions of Quodlibets 3 and 4 also stem from Godfrey. See his "Une Question quodlibétique inconnue de Godefroid de Fontaines," *Revue d'Histoire Ecclésiastique*, 30 (1934), 852–59, esp. 857*n*1. If this is the case, special weight should be assigned to them since the longer versions of Quodlibets 1 through 4 appear to be *reportationes* (see de Wulf, *Un Théologien-Philosophe du XIIIe siècle*, p. 64; see also PB 2.xv–xvi). But P. Stella has more recently proposed Hervé of Nedellec as the party responsible for "abbreviating" these Quodlibets of Godfrey's. See his "Teologi e teologia nelle 'Reprobationes' di Bernardo d'Auvergne ai Quodlibeti di Goffredo di Fontaines," *Salesianum*, 19 (1957), 185–86. For another text in which Godfrey presents the theory of real distinction in Giles's terms, see Quodl. 2, q. 2: "aut esse dicit *rem aliam* ab ipsa essentia. Si autem esse dicat *rem aliam* quae sit actualitas essentiae realiter alia ab ipsa essentia . . ." (PB 2.60; emphasis added).

78 See Quodl. 3, q. 1. For the first of these arguments, see PB 2.158 and PB 2.302 (short version); for the second, see pp. 158–59 and p. 302 (short version); for the third, see p. 159. In the longer version of argument two, the parallel between matter and form, on the one hand, and essence and existence, on the other, is also stressed. The third argument appears only in the longer version. The similarity between these arguments and several of those presented above in the discussion of Giles of Rome is evident.

79 See PB 2.163–64 for the long version and p. 303 for the shorter redaction. Both versions explicitly connect this argumentation with Aristotle's discussion of being and unity in *Met.* IV, 2 (1003B26–35) and with Averroës' commentary on the same (*In IV Met.*, fol. 67^{ra-va}). In the short version this reasoning is presented in the form of three distinct arguments, but all three are joined to form one more or less continuous chain of reasoning in the longer text. For earlier applications of this argumentation to the essence–existence question see *Siger de Brabant, Questions sur la Métaphysique*, ed. Graiff, pp. 13–14, 18; and Henry of Ghent, Quodl. 1, q. 9, fols. 6^{v}–7^{r}. Henry repeats this in Quodl. 10, q. 7, fol. 416^{v}, which dates from the same period as Godfrey's Quodl. 3.

80 PB 2.164–65 (long version) and pp. 303–304 (short version). For similar analogies in Henry of Ghent see n. 70. However, although in agreement with Godfrey in rejecting the real distinction between essence and existence, Henry defends intentional distinction between them. Hence, perhaps, his later reservations about the appropriateness of some of these analogies. See also the reference to Paulus in n. 70.

81 On the possibility of dating Quodl. 13 in the academic year 1297–1298 rather than in 1296 (as proposed by Glorieux), see my "The Dating of James of Viterbo's Quodlibet I and Godfrey of Fontaines' Quodlibet VIII," 375–78.

82 PB 5.207–208. See in particular his remark on p. 208: "Sed non videtur posse dici quod talia quae per huiusmodi terminos speciales importantur, sint aliqua realiter differentia. Ergo similiter dicendum est hoc in terminis quantumcumque generalibus. Quod enim una et eadem res non possit significari per tales terminos sic diversos non debet dici. Idem enim significant lectio, legere, lector, legens, et sic de aliis, quantum ad id quod per tales terminos primo et per se ut principale significatum importatur. Inconveniens ergo est dicere quod esse et essentia differant realiter." This final remark well may refer to the qualified way in which James of Viterbo defends real distinction of essence and existence. For more on this, see below.

83 PB 2.167–69 (long version) and p. 304 (shorter version). In the long version this argument is introduced by Godfrey's refutation of the contention that one must appeal to essence–existence composition in order to account for the caused or produced character of contingent being (see pp. 166–67).

84 PB 2.171 and p. 305.

85 PB 2.306. Also see Quodl. 4, q. 3 (PB 2.245), and Quodl. 7, q. 7 (PB 3.359–60).

86 PB 2.174–75, 177.

87 See Quodl. 4, q. 2 (PB 2.235); Quodl. 8, q. 3 (PB 4.34–36); and esp. Quodl. 2, q. 2 (PB 2.53–56).

88 In Quodl. 2, q. 2, Godfrey acknowledges Henry's effort to find some support for his views on *esse essentiae* in Avicenna (PB 2.57–59), although he also contests the accuracy of this interpretation (see PB 2.61–63 and Quodl. 14, q. 5, PB 5.429–30). For his criticisms of Henry's theory on philosophical grounds, see PB 2.61, 67ff.; and Quodl. 4, q. 2 (PB 2.235).

89 "Nec potest dici quod virtus illa sit res intentionis ita quod differat a substantia rei non secundum rem neque secundum rationem sed secundum intentionem quia non est aliud differre ratione et intentione. Cuius ratio est quia ens sufficienter dividitur tanquam per differentias primas et immediatas per ens diminutum et incompletum quod est ens rationis et per ens completum et perfectum quod est ens reale habens esse ratum in natura. Unde non est ibi medium ens intentionis" (*Disputed Question* 12). For this text see my "Godfrey of Fontaines: Disputed Questions 9, 10, and 12," *Franciscan Studies*, 33 (1973), 368.

90 For criticisms of Henry's theory of intentional distinction of essence and existence and his view that actual existence is the real relation of essence to God as its efficient cause, see Quodl. 3, q. 1 (PB 2.175–77).

91 For this and for different ways in which a being may be said to be in potency — e.g., by reason of proximate intrinsic causes, by reason of remote intrinsic causes, or only by reason of an extrinsic cause — see Quodl. 2, q. 2 (PB 2.63–65), Quodl. 4, q. 2 (PB 2.237–38), Quodl. 8, q. 3 (PB 4.38).

92 Quodl. 4, q. 2 (PB 2.235): "Sed mihi videtur quod esse existentiae et essentia omnino sint idem secundum rem et differunt solum secundum rationem et modum intelligendi et significandi, nullam omnino compositionem facientia, sicut nec currere et cursus vel huiusmodi. Et ideo, in quantum manet res secundum esse essentiae manet etiam secundum esse existentiae et e converso. . . ." For more on Godfrey's understanding of and reaction to Henry's theory of intentional distinction between essence and existence, see my "Godfrey of Fontaines and Henry of Ghent's Theory of Intentional Distinction Between Essence and Existence," 289–321.

93 "Diversis igitur opinionibus de differentia essentiae et esse utcumque decursis, quid mihi de hoc probabiliter tenendum videatur, consequenter exponam" (*Disputatio prima de quolibet*, p. 47:136–38).

94 "'Sicut se habent ad invicem lux, lucere et lucens, sic sunt ad se invicem essentia, esse et ens, hoc est existens sive subsistens.' Per quam expositionem apparet quod loquitur de esse existentiae actualis" (ibid., 139–41). Note that James interprets Anselm's usage of *esse*, *ens*, *existens*, and *subsistens* to refer to actual existence. For Anselm see *Monologium* 6, ed. F. S. Schmitt (Edinburgh, 1946), I 20.

95 ". . . et ideo, sicut differt concretum a suo abstracto, sic differt esse ab essentia" (*Disputatio prima de quolibet*, p. 47:147–48).

96 Ibid., pp. 47:149–48:158.

97 Ibid., p. 48:158–72. See also 166–70: "Et secundum hoc dicendum quod abstractum et concretum, quantum ad principale significatum, idem significant et idem sunt; quantum vero ad id quod concretum significat secundario, differt ab abstracto." In support he appeals to Averroës and to Anselm. "Unde dicit Commentator, in *V Metaphysicae*, quod nomen denominativum, quod idem est quod concretum, significat subiectum et accidens, sed accidens primo, subiectum autem secundario. Et Anselmus dicit, in libro *De Grammatico*, quod nomen denominativum significat accidens per se et subiectum per aliud." For Averroës see *In V Met.*, fol. 117ra; for Anselm see his *De grammatico* 12–13, ed. Schmitt, I 156–57. Here James is interpreting Anselm rather than literally citing him.

98 *Disputatio prima de quolibet*, p. 48:173–79.

99 Ibid., 180–82.

100 Ibid., pp. 48:182–49:198. For the reference to Damascene, see *Dialectica* 42, 43 (PG 94:611–14), cited in ibid., p. 49.

101 "Unde secundum hoc posset dici quod esse et ens dicunt ipsam essentiam ut est in supposito, et ut constituit suppositum; quia dicunt essentiam ut coniunctam aliis quae per suppositum ex consequenti importantur" (*Disputatio prima de quolibet*, p. 49: 211–14). At times, James suggests that if the concrete term, e.g., *esse*, signifies substantial essence in its primary meaning, in its secondary meaning it signifies the subject (see p. 48:158–66). At other times he maintains that in its secondary meaning *esse* signifies those things, accidents presumably, with which the essence unites in the supposit (p. 49: 193–95, 203–207). James avoids inconsistency by distinguishing two ways in which the term "subject" may be understood: (*a*) as the whole aggregate or supposit including its accidents; and (*b*) as that which is found in the supposit only insofar as it "stands under" or is subject to accidents, hence substance viewed as subject to accidents. If one understands subject in the first way, then while the concrete term *esse* primarily signifies the substantial essence, in a secondary way it signifies it as united with accidents. Thus *esse* signifies subject so understood by way of consequence. But if one takes subject in the second way as substantial essence standing under accidents, then the concrete term *esse* signifies by way of consequence not essence but the accidents themselves, presumably because it signifies substantial essence directly and in its primary meaning. Hence his conclusion: "ens et esse uno modo possunt dici significare subiectum ex consequenti, alio modo non, sed ea quae sunt essentiae coniuncta" (p. 51:266–68).

102 "Et quia identitas et diversitas magis debent considerari secundum principale significatum, ideo potest dici quod essentia et esse principaliter et simpliciter sunt idem, ex consequenti autem et secundum aliquid non idem. Quantumcumque autem haec differentia sit ex consequenti, est tamen necessaria, quia provenit ex compositione quae necessario invenitur in qualibet creatura; et ideo non est abicienda, sed consideratione

digna" (ibid., pp. 53:353–54:359). James also appeals to his theory as a possible way of reconciling Aristotle and Averroës with Avicenna (see nn. 16 and 17 above and the corresponding text). In holding that each and every thing is a being (*ens*) by its very essence, Aristotle and Averroës were viewing being (*ens* and *esse*) concretely and in terms of its primary meaning, therefore, as signifying essence. In suggesting that *ens* signifies something added and something accidental in creatures, Avicenna may have been taking *ens* concretely but in its secondary or consequent meaning, as implying the accidents with which essence unites in fact. See pp. 52:320–53:350.

103 This point has already been made by Hocedez and others. See *Theoremata de esse et essentia*, pp. [29]–[30].

104 See *Disputatio prima de quolibet*, p. 54:368–84. For his words of praise for Giles, see n. 20 above.

105 Ibid., pp. 54:385–55:392.

106 Ibid., pp. 55:393–56:434. Note James's final comment: "Et quamvis dicta opinio dubitabilis aliquibus videatur, quia tamen viri non parvae auctoritatis ipsam posuerunt, ideo non est sicut inconveniens improbanda."

107 James is aware that his position differs from that which defends no more than logical distinction between essence and existence: "Si vero intendat excludere omnimodam differentiam dubitabilis est, quia, ut iam patet ex dictis, saltem secundario diversum aliquid dicit esse ab essentia" (ibid., p. 54:365–67). Godfrey appears to have James's position in mind in the following comment: "Idem enim significant lectio, legere, lector, legens, et sic de aliis, quantum ad id quod per tales terminos primo et per se ut principale significatum importatur." (So far James would agree.) "Inconveniens ergo est dicere quod esse et essentia differant realiter." (Here James would not fully agree.) See Quodl. 13, q. 3 (PB 5.208). Finally, for James's effort to show that his theory on essence and existence does suffice to allow for defending the created character of beings other than God (n. 7 above), see *Disputatio prima de quolibet*, pp. 56:452–61:623. Without following his detailed development of this here, let it suffice for me to note: (*a*) that without some kind of real distinction (presumably such as he has defended) James maintains that creation cannot be defended; (*b*) that he also contends that one need not adopt the theory (of Giles) according to which *esse* is a superadded actuality of essence in order to account for creation. If some act–potency diversity is required to allow for it, that of substance and accident will suffice.

* For a more extensive treatment of the relationship of essence and existence in the thought of Godfrey of Fontaines, see my *The Metaphysical Thought of Godfrey of Fontaines: A Study in Late Thirteenth-Century Philosophy* (Washington, D.C., 1981) chap. 2, which appeared while the current volume was in press.

9

Metaphysical Foundations of the Hierarchy of Being According to Some Late–Medieval and Renaissance Philosophers

EDWARD P. MAHONEY
Duke University

SINCE NEARLY HALF A CENTURY HAS PASSED since the publication of Arthur Lovejoy's *The Great Chain of Being*,[1] it seems appropriate that a volume on metaphysics include some discussion of the concept of the hierarchy or order of being in Western medieval and Renaissance philosophy. Obviously, I cannot hope to cover all the concepts and doctrines developed under the rubric of the hierarchy of being during the period which extended from the late-thirteenth century to the end of the sixteenth century. My purpose is more modest. I shall attempt to trace in rough outline the development of a conceptual framework which was used by a variety of thinkers who often differed on the crucial question of the relationship of essence to existence. What I have in mind is that various medieval and Renaissance accounts of the hierarchy of being at some point or other invoke God in some way as the measure of the scale and explain that a thing has its place or grade in the scale according as it approaches to God and recedes from non-being and matter, or, to put it the other way around, as it falls away from God and approaches matter or non-being. This conceptual scheme, which was developed by Thomas Aquinas from passages in the pseudo-Dionysius and the *Liber de causis*, has its immediate origins in Proclus.[2] Thomas was no doubt inspired in part by Albert the Great's lectures on the *De divinis nominibus* which he was fortunate enough to have heard while he was Albert's student at Cologne.[3] I shall therefore begin with a brief discussion of Proclus, the *Liber de causis*, and the Pseudo-Dionysius, examine quickly the manner in which their key ideas appear in Albert, and then sketch out the way in which these ideas found more systematic form in the works of St. Thomas. I shall also trace the use of these same ideas in his famed contemporary Ṣiger of Brabant. In the following section, I shall take note of the persistence of some of these same ideas in Giles of Rome, Godfrey of Fontaines, and Henry of Ghent. Immediately thereafter, I shall examine John Duns Scotus and John of Jandun to indicate how and why they did not accept the scheme, and add some brief remarks on other developments in fourteenth-century philosophy. I shall then take up the further history of the conceptual framework of God as measure and ascent to and retreat from him and non-being as it reappears in a variety of Renaissance philosophers, including such thinkers as Marsilio Ficino, Paul of Venice, and Pietro Pomponazzi. Limitations of space have prevented me from examining here the positions of Augustine, Bonaventure, Nicholas of Cusa, and others regarding the scheme. The highly critical examinations of the scheme during the Renaissance and the heated interchanges which ensued are particularly noteworthy. In the conclusion, I shall make some tentative remarks about the historical fate of the scheme and pass some judgment on the difficulties which seem implicit in doctrines presupposed by that scheme. My final and necessarily brief remarks will be directed toward the major question of using spatial metaphors in metaphysical analysis.

The Background of the Scheme: Proclus, the Pseudo-Dionysius, and the 'Liber de causis'

The God of the Pseudo-Dionysius, unlike the One of earlier Neoplatonism, is a single creator God, who alone creates, and creates according to an order which he wills.[4] But, just as with Proclus, the scheme of *πρόοδος* and *ἐπιστροφή* still explains in some way the hierarchy of things. For Proclus and Neoplatonism in general, the procession from the One operates according to a progressive degradation proportionate to the distance of each of the terms engendered from the principle which engendered it. However, in Dionysius' thought the intermediary beings cease to play the causal role which they enjoyed in the scheme of Proclus. Moreover, Dionysius breaks with earlier Neoplatonism both by relating being, life, and intelligence directly to God and by maintaining that other beings have being, life, and intelligence only by participating in God himself. Divine transcendence is protected, however, by the infinite gap between the God who is One and Three and the highest being in the celestial hierarchy.[5]

According to the second and fourth chapters of the *De divinis nominibus*, the transcendent God alone serves as the common measure (*μέτρον*) and number (ἀριθμός) of all other things, whether they be in the celestial or the ecclesiastical hierarchy. From one point of view, the inequality among the Intelligences depends on their degree of participation, which is in accord with the Divine Ideas and Wishes.[6] And it is according to the degree or rank which an Intelligence has by reason of its falling away from God that it receives more or less purification, illumination, and perfection from him. By a general law of "mediation" implicit in the concept of πρόοδος and ἐπιστροφή, as we descend or ascend the hierarchical scale these three divine operations will be more or less intense: namely, according as the capacity to receive these operations is greater or less.[7] By a kind of law of continuity, Dionysius sees the lowest in a higher rank touching the highest in a lower rank.[8]

The *Liber de causis*, originally composed in Arabic and translated into Latin before 1187, presents theses formulated from ideas in Proclus' *Elements of Theology*.[9] However, since the *Liber* presents its positions in accord with a monotheistic conception of God, it is not wholly Proclean in doctrine. Its dependence on Proclus was, of course, recognized by St. Thomas, though he does not seem to have realized the striking differences in its doctrines.[10] The *Liber* speaks of God as the One, pure Goodness, and the Infinite, but also as pure Being. However, it is Unity which seems to have primacy.[11] Everything other than God participates in unity, and the power which a thing has will be more intense and its operations higher as it itself is more united and approaches more closely to the true and pure Unity — namely, God.[12] The diversity of things and the grade which they occupy in the scale of being thus depend on the mode according to which they are able to receive perfections from above. It is precisely the mode of closeness (*propinquitas*) to the First Cause which determines the mode of a thing's being (*modus esse sui*); it receives according to its "quantity" (*quantitas*).[13] The goodness and the gifts received from God are thus proportionate to the receiver. That is to say, the beings receiving his goodnesses do not receive them equally; some of them receive more than others. Each thing receives according to the mode of its potency.[14] The Intelligences closer to the One have less quantity and more power, while those farther from the One have more quantity and less power. As a result, the intelligible forms received in the higher Intelligences are more universal than those in the lower Intelligences.[15]

St. Albert the Great, St. Thomas Aquinas, and Siger of Brabant

Albert the Great's (ca. 1200–1280) commentary on the Pseudo-Dionysius' *De divinis nominibus* was probably composed around 1250. As early as the first chapter, Albert explains that God is said to be the extrinsic measure (*mensura*) of being since he is a simple essence (*simplex essentia*), and everything participates more or less in being according as it approaches to his likeness (*unumquodque magis et minus participat de esse, secundum quod accedit ad similitudinem eius*).[16] The greater the falling away from the simplicity of the First Being, the greater the diversity and composition.[17] Only God lacks all composition and all admixture of potency, and only in him are the *quod est* and the *quo est* identical, for he does not have his existence (*habet esse*) from another — that is, he does not participate in existence.[18] Participation and approaching God are interrelated. The more things participate in God, the closer (*propinquiora*) they are to him; and they are said to exist more truly (*verius esse*). Their being (*entitas*) is a certain image (*imago*) of the First Being, and though they do not have the truth of the First Being, they have a second or third truth according to the grade of their nature (*secundum gradum suae naturae*). Although things cannot properly be said to exist more or less in the sense of intension and remission (*intensio et remissio*), since the principles of existing are not increased or decreased (*non intenduntur neque remittuntur*), they can be called more or less in the sense of the priority and posteriority in participating.[19] From the First Being there flows a form which is the similitude (*similitudo*) of his essence and through which all things which exist participate. The existence of creatures is particularized;[20] that is, it is limited or terminated by the termini of their essences.[21] The degree of universality of an Intelligence's cognition depends, of course, on how close it comes to the One and recedes from matter.[22]

Similar views are to be found in Albert's *Liber de causis et processu universitatis*. The First Infinite Being is not subject to any comparison by way of increase and decrease (*intensio et remissio*), but serves rather as the principle, cause, and measure (*mensura*) of every existing, living, and thinking thing. There is difference or grade (*gradus*) in all such things since there is in them an admixture of potency; their *esse* and *quod est* are different.[23] The more an Intelligence approaches (*accedit*) to the Simple and the One — namely, God — the more it is vivified and made simple.[24] That is to say, the closer something is to the First and Simple Being, the more vehement is its unity. This will also mean that the farther away from the First Being an Intelligence is, the less universal are its intelligible forms, the more contracted and determined its composition, and the more inclined it is to matter. Consequently, the closer Intelligences approach to the First Being, the less is their quantity of composition and the greater their simplicity and power.[25]

In his early *Scriptum super libros Sententiarum*, dated around 1256, Thomas Aquinas (1225–1274) sets forth the key notions of God as the measure and of the ascent and descent in the scale of being. God is the uncomposed First Principle from whom being descends to the creature.[26] A measure (*mensura*) in the proper sense of the word is that by which the quantity of a thing (*quantitas rei*) becomes known. In the genus of quantity, it is the minimum in the genus — namely, the unit — which provides the measure. However, the term "measure" (*mensura*) has been transferred (*transumptum*) to all genera, so that what is first, simplest, and most perfect in each genus is said to be the measure of everything else in that genus. Each thing is thus recognized to have more or less (*plus et minus*) of the truth of that genus according as it approaches to or moves away from the measure (*magis accedit ad ipsum vel recedit*) — as, far example, white in the genus of colors. In the case of the genus of substance, it is God who has the most perfect and the simplest being and who is therefore called the measure. Indeed, just as unity is the measure in numbers, so God is the measure of all things in all genera and not simply the perfection of one determinate genus.[27] All things other than God which are complete substances — a man, for instance — have some sort of composition inasmuch as they fall away from the divine simplicity (*talis creatura ita deficit a simplicitate quod incidit in compositionem*).[28] There is an essential division in composite beings of matter and form, or *esse* and the *quod est*.[29] The essence or quiddity of an angel has more and more possibility and less and less actuality as it recedes (*recedit*) from likeness (*similitudo*) to the divine nature, just as it has less potency and more actuality and is closer to God in the degree to which it is closer through likeness to the divine being (*propinquior per similitudinem ad divinum esse*). There will be for Thomas different grades (*diversi gradus*) of natures among the angels.[30]

All these ideas reappear in Thomas' other works. In another early work, the *De ente et essentia* (Eschmann and Weisheipl: pre-March 1256), Thomas says that the forms closest to the First Principle, which is pure act, subsist without matter, whereas those which are distant are material. This is because there is more potency and less actuality in things as they are more distant from God and closer to matter.[31] The grade of perfection (*gradus perfectionis*) is determined precisely by retreat (*recessus*) from potentiality and approach (*accessus*) to pure act.[32] Thomas also appeals to *Metaphysics* II, 1 (993B24–31) to argue that whatever is the greatest and truest in any genus is the cause of all in that genus.[33]

The key doctrines of God as measure, the ascent and descent, the grades, and participation are found in various of Thomas' *Quaestiones disputatae*. In the *De veritate* (Eschmann and Weisheipl: 1256–1259), Thomas explains that the more a creature approaches (*accedit*) to God, the measure of all beings, the more it has of being (*habet de esse*), while the more it recedes (*recedit*) from him, the more it has of non-being. But Thomas is careful to add that although there is a similitude between God and the creature, there always remains an infinite distance (*infinita distantia*) between them.[34] Since creatures exist only by participation, their being is contracted or determined — their *modus essendi* is determined by their essences.[35] In the *De potentia dei* (Eschmann: 1259–1268; Weisheipl: 1265–1266), when speaking of something participated in diversely, Thomas states axiomatically that things have more or less of a perfection according to their closer or more distant approach (*accessus*) to something which is one. Consequently, all things less perfect receive their being from the most perfect and the truest being.[36] And while Thomas insists that God cannot be in a genus as if contained by that genus, since he is uncomposed and not determined to the limits of one genus, he will allow that God can be said to be in the genus of substances by reduction, since he is the principle or measure of all substances (*mensura substantiarum omnium*), just as unity is the measure in the genus of numbers.[37] And in the *De spiritualibus creaturis* (Weisheipl: 1267–1268), Thomas again cites Dionysius and relates the order of greater and lesser perfection of created things to their being closer (*propinquior*) to God, who is infinite act (*actus infinitus*), and thus not contracted (*contractum*) to any genus or species. Even the spiritual beings, which especially approach (*maxime appropinquant*) to God's perfection, contain some potency: namely, their essence, which receives and contracts being, participated being (*esse participatum*). Their *quod est* (their form) is different from their *quo est* (their participated being).[38] Finally, in the disputed questions *De anima* (Weisheipl: 1269), Thomas explains that all difference of grades (*diversitas graduum*) of perfection must be through an ordering (*ordo*) to some one principle. In material substances, the different grades causing different species are ordered to matter as their first principle, while in immaterial substances the order of grades of different species (*ordo graduum diversarum specierum*) is according to a comparison (*comparatio*) to God, the most perfect being. Matter is the lowest grade among the material substances, while the human soul, since it is in potency to the intelligibles, just as prime matter is to sensible forms, holds the lowest grade (*ultimus gradus*) among the immaterial substances. Thomas cites both Dionysius and the *Liber de causis* when he adds that the closer an intellectual substance or angel is to God, the more elevated and universal are its innate intelligible forms. He also uses Aristotle, *Metaphysics*, VIII, 3 (1043B36–1044A2) as an authority for his own position that the species of things in the physical world are like species of numbers in which the addition or subtraction of unity causes a change of species. Thomas sees such specific variety not only among the animals (the highest of which is man), but also among the elements, minerals, and plants.[39]

The Great Return theme of Neoplatonism as found in the Pseudo-Dionysius has been seen by more than one modern scholar as the perspective which St. Thomas adopted to study the rhythm of the universe. He appears to have adopted it even in his early work on the *Sentences*, where he considers the first part to be about divine things according to their *exitus* from God as First Principle and the second and third parts to be concerned with them according to their *reditus* to God as End.[40] This rhythm served to provide the plan of his great systematic works, the *Summa theologiae* (Weisheipl: 1266–1273) and the first three books of the earlier *Summa contra Gentiles* (Eschmann: 1261–1264). The doctrines of God as measure and of approaching to and receding from him also reappear. In the *Summa contra Gentiles*, Thomas again announces that the most perfect in every genus serves as the measure according as things in the genus approach more or less to it. God, who contains all perfections, serves as the measure of all things — Dionysius is quoted from the *De divinis nominibus*.[41] All things fall short of God and yet retain some resemblance (*similitudo*) to him according to a diminished participation (*deficiens participatio*) — Dionysius is again quoted.[42]

The *Prima pars* of the *Summa theologiae* reveals the strong influence of the Pseudo-Dionysius: the doctrines which we have been examining reappear once again.[43] We are told that God is not in a genus, but now it is added that he cannot be reduced to a genus as its principle. That is to say, though he is the principle and measure of all things, he is not a measure proportioned to anything else (*mensura proportionata alicui*). He is thus unlike the principles of continuous and discrete quantity — namely, the point and unity — which are reduced as principles to those particular genera and do not extend outside their respective genera. God is called the measure of all things simply from the fact that as much as each thing has of being, so much does it approach to him. But Thomas also gives some kind of warning that he does not understand "distance" from God in any sort of imaginative or spatial fashion, especially since God is always intimately present in all things as the creating and conserving cause of their existence. Things are said to be "distant" from him through an unlikeness of nature or grace (*per dissimilitudinem naturae vel gratiae*). Since God is above all things by reason of the eminence of his nature, all his creatures will in this sense be "distant" from him.[44]

When discussing the perfection of God, Thomas relies heavily on Dionysius in arguing that God possesses pre-eminently all the perfections of creatures as their cause. Creatures are assimilated to God insofar as they are beings; but since he is a being by essence and they are beings only by participation, they have only an imperfect likeness (*similitudo imperfecta*) to him: namely, according to some sort of analogy (*analogia*).[45] Dionysius is also cited to the effect that spiritual substances have proceeded from God in a certain grade (*gradus*) and order (*ordo*).[46] Each created being is placed in a species according as it is established in a determinate or special grade among things.[47] Taking remarks of Dionysius as his starting point, Thomas explains that there are various participations in the diffusion of the processions from God, who alone is Pure and Infinite Being. That is to say, participated being is limited by the capacity (*capacitas*) of the receiver.[48] The nearer an angel is to God the less multiplicity there will be in its composition.[49] Thomas also cites Dionysius to argue that neither in the angel nor in any other creature are power and substance identical; that the angels must receive intelligible species from God, since they cannot know through their essences; and that the angels closer and more like the First One — namely, God — know through fewer and more universal intelligible species.[50]

Many of the above ideas are, of course, to be found in Thomas' commentary on the *De divinis nominibus* (E.: pre-1268; W.: 1265–67).[51] In his *Expositio super Librum de causis* (E.: post 1270; W.: after beginning of 1271; Saffrey: 1272), Thomas shows knowledge of Moerbeke's translation of Proclus' *Elements of Theology* (1268). He makes frequent reference to the Pseudo-Dionysius. The entire set of doctrines which we have been tracing reappears: namely, that a creature participates more in being and has more unity as it approaches the First Being; that the first in a genus is the measure (*mensura*) according to more–less and approach–receding; and that there are different *gradus* according to the closeness of things to God. Thomas clearly states that there is a twofold diversity among the Intelligences: one according to their metaphysical composition and the degree of perfection resulting from their closeness to or distance from God; the other according to the universality of their intelligible species.[52]

No doubt, Siger of Brabant (ca. 1240–1281/1284) is the best known of St. Thomas' philosophical adversaries. The evolution of his psychology from rigid Averroism to a stance resembling that of Aquinas has recently been established. Moreover, his use of Thomas' works on other issues has been noted by historians of medieval philosophy.[53] In the *Quaestiones* on the *Metaphysics*, Siger takes up the question whether *esse* in caused things pertains to their essence. We cannot tarry with Siger's critique of Thomas and the presentation of his own position — namely, that *esse* and essence do not really differ in creatures, though the one has the mode of act and the other has the mode of a potency. But what must surely be noted is that Siger boldly takes both Thomas' doctrine of participation and the notion that God is the measure of all things and incorporates them into his own position.[54]

Siger presents Thomas' position in his commentary on the *Sentences* as that everything other than the First Being must recede from its simplicity, and he adds that he does not know whence Thomas derived it. He agrees with Thomas that things other than the First Being recede from it and are multiplied by the fact that they approach matter. They will participate more in being according as they approach more to the First Being (*magis accedunt ad Primum*). And just as numbers differ in relation to unity, the principle of number, so different substances cannot approach (*appropinquent*) the First Being, the measure of all beings (*mensura omnium entium*), in a wholly equal way. Consequently, they will have different natures. Siger denies that this imports any composition of essence and existence, however, since the receding may be through the kind of knowledge which things below God enjoy — that is, they know through intelligible species which are other than their existence.[55] God exists by essence as the most perfect being, whose being is his very existence. But his existence is not the being or formal substance of other things, for he is, rather, their exemplar and principle.[56] There can be only one such all-perfect being, and all other things imitate him by way of an exemplar, since he is their measure (*mensura*). The more something approaches (*magis accedit*) him the more perfect it is; the less it approaches (*minus accedit*) him the less perfect it is.[57] Each being other than God moves toward potency as it recedes from him. Since it exists only by participation, it cannot have the whole perfection of existence but must necessarily have a defective or lessened existence.[58]

In his late *Quaestiones super Librum de causis*, which were probably written between 1274 and 1276, Siger makes use of Thomas' *Summa theologiae*, the commentary on the *Physics*, the *De unitate intellectus*, and the *Expositio super Librum de causis*. Indeed, some of Siger's questions are simply résumés of articles from the *Summa*.[59] There is an order in things which differ according as some are more perfect and others are less perfect — as, for instance, among the separate substances.[60] The Intelligences differ only specifically, and there is an order of higher and lower among them according as they know through more universal and less universal intelligible forms or species.[61] Whereas God as First Cause knows simply through his very essence taken as an intelligible species, the Intelligence knows through something added to its essence by God at creation — namely, intelligible species — and the human intellect must gain intelligible species during this life by the agent intellect's abstracting them from phantasms.[62]

In these discussions Siger invokes the "ascent" and "descent" thesis. He explains that things hold a lower grade (*inferior gradus*) in the order of the universe (*ordo universi*) the more divided and less united they are in their perfections. Matter and the bodily senses will thus be more divided in their forms than the human intellect, while God, the First Cause, is in the highest degree simple and one (*summe simplex et una*). Siger therefore takes it as probable (*verisimile*) that the Intelligences ranged between God and the human intellect will hold an order of natures according as those which approach closer to the nature of God (*magis accedunt ad naturam causae primae*) are more united and less divided in their intelligible forms; that is, the higher will know by more universal forms and the lower by less universal forms.[63] When explaining why the human intellect holds the lowest grade (*inferior gradus*) in the genus of intellectual natures, Siger explicitly invokes the axiom that each thing holds a lower grade in the order of the universe according as it approaches closer (*magis accedit*) to corporeal, bodily nature and the nature of potency and as it draws away (*recedit*) from actuality.[64] The *esse* in Intelligences is contracted by the nature receiving it, while God's *esse* is pure.[65]

Henry of Ghent, Giles of Rome, and Godfrey of Fontaines

Although they disagreed among themselves regarding the relation of essence and existence and were also divided on the value of Stephen Tempier's famed Condemnation issued in 1277,[66] Henry of Ghent, Giles of Rome, and Godfrey of Fontaines all made use of the scheme which we are studying. We shall see, however, that Godfrey's use of the scheme is more tentative and cautious than that of his two contemporaries.

If we begin with Henry of Ghent (d. 1293), we again find frequent allusions to the conceptual scheme of God as measure and to the descent–ascent theme. Not surprisingly, the doctrine of participation is also much in evidence. Henry cites the Pseudo-Dionysius' *De divinis nominibus* when he explains that there must be some sort of identity and unity between God and the creature: namely, an analogy of imitation. Henry goes on to point out that although the minimum is the measure (*mensura*) in material things — that is, the principle of knowledge by which the determinate quantity of a thing is known — God is the minimum and measure of substances (*minimum et mensura substantiarum*). In every genus, that in which the nature of the genus most truly and perfectly shines forth is called the first and simplest minimum and measure of all other things in the genus. Since all things other than God have existence by participation, they will approach him through a certain imitation and assimilation. According as they approach more or less, their being will be more or less determinate and their essences will have more or less composition and simplicity. Henry is quick to add that when Aristotle says that in each genus there must be some first minimum (*primum minimum*), "genus" should be taken broadly.[67] Henry cites Augustine and both Aristotle and Averroës from the *Metaphysics* II, 2 to argue that there is an order (*ordo*) from the First Being among things which participate according as they are closer to or farther from him and closer to pure matter.[68] The more they approach him the closer they are to him in grade and in the order of the universe (*in gradu et ordine universi*). Dionysius is cited to make the point that a multitude of things participating in one thing is necessarily reduced to something existing by essence.[69] When discussing the question whether God is perfect by the perfection of any creature, Henry makes repeated use of the Pseudo-Dionysius and reiterates the themes which we have just sketched out: a created thing is more perfect in its nature as it approaches to God in the nature of its existing, so that all created things are ordered in their grade of perfection according to a below and an above (*secundum sub et supra*). Since God alone exists by essence and they exist by participation, he is the measure (*mensura*) of every creature. Each of them will have being of a higher grade the more it approaches the First Being (*appropinquans esse primo*). While the creatures' essence can receive only a finite being, one which is limited to a determinate grade, all the existence and perfection which they have are to be found in a united way (*ut unite*) in the essence and being of God — that is, without any limitation, grade, or distinction.[70]

In spite of the fact that Henry and Giles of Rome (d. 1316) engaged in a bitter dispute regarding the distinction of essence and existence — the former maintaining his somewhat puzzling intentional distinction; the latter, the troublesome real distinction[71] — they are united in the acceptance of the conceptual scheme which we have been tracing: the explanation for this unnoticed agreement may lie in their common attraction to Neoplatonic ideas. In his *Quaestiones metaphysicales super libros Metaphysicae Aristotelis*, Giles explains, citing Averroës, that the concept of measure (*mensura*) has been transferred from discrete quantity to other things. Measure according to Aristotle is that by which we learn the quantity of something. And since all things in a genus have being according to an order of grades — namely, according to a greater or lesser approach or retreat (*appropinquatio et remotio*) in regard to that by which the nature of that genus is measured — we can say that the First Being is the measure of all beings, since from knowledge of it we have knowledge of other beings. But this takes place by analogy in such fashion that God as measure is not, as is the case with numbers, within the genus itself.[72] It should perhaps be noted that Giles also argues that although, from the perspective of human knowledge, the concept of measure (*mensura*) is transferred from discrete quantity, in fact it is God who properly and principally has the *ratio* of measure: namely, uniformity, simplicity, and indivisibility.[73]

Giles emphasizes that the First Cause, which is the measure in the genus of substances, is not *per se* in that genus, directly or by any sort of reduction, since its causality is universal and not limited to any particular genus. God, who is the simplest act and infinitely distant from whatever form is received in matter, has the *ratio* of an infinite number since he has not only the perfections of all existing things, but also the many more perfections which could exist.[74] Consequently, since God is infinite, there can never be a rest in the approach of creatures toward him (*unde in creatura non est status in appropinquando ad primum*), though there can be a rest in their receding toward prime matter (*sed in distando est status ut ad primam materiam*). There can indeed be an infinite number of things between God and prime matter or nothingness.[75]

In his questions on Book I of the *Sentences*, Giles again defends the thesis that God is the measure (*mensura*) of all things, citing as authorities Averroës, Dionysius, and Proclus.[76] God should be called their measure properly and not in a transferred sense (*transumptive*) since everything of the *ratio* of measure is to be found in him. Indeed, every creature is a number in respect of God's indivisibility.[77] The conceptual scheme of God as measure, ascent–descent, grades, and participation is even more in evidence in Giles' questions on Book II of the *Sentences*. God is characterized as an *unitas simplicissima* to whom creatures are related by an order (*ordo*) comparable to that of number to unity, that is, by a lineal distance. This means that things in the same species are at the same distance from God. Since all creatures are beings by participation, that is, they have as it were a part imperfectly (*quasi partem habere imperfecte*), there will be as many modes of falling away from God as there are modes of participating (*tot ergo sunt modi participandi quot sunt modi deficiendi*). Creatures thus proceed from God in an order of more or less (*magis et minus*) falling away from him. Consequently, no two creatures which are essentially different fall away from God equally (*equaliter deficientes a deo*), just as two numbers specifically different cannot be equally distant from unity. Creatures are simply beings which are lacking in regard to God (*creaturae sunt quaedam entia deficientia a deo*). And just as there would not be a diversity of species among things if there were not this falling short of God, so too, Giles argues, there would not be a plurality of individuals in the same species if individuals did not fall short of the species. There can be multiplicity in created things only because they are deficient beings (*potest et est multitudo in entibus creatis, quia sunt entia defectiva*).[78] As the being which exists by essence, God is the measure of all beings which exist by participation — Dionysius' *De divinis nominibus* is cited.[79]

Giles sees two termini among all things, God as pure act and matter as pure potency. Since things nearer to God are more united and simpler, there are grades (*gradus*) which compose an order (*ordo*) among all things — Giles cites Dionysius as an authority for the position that there are grades in all things. By approaching nearer to God, who is Pure Act, a thing will have less and less potency, though in all things other than God there must be some admixture of potency. Giles compares the resulting order (*ordo*) to species of number. But he is careful now to point out that although God can always create yet another species of angels, there will never actually be an infinite number. The angels differ in their more or less noble being, intelligence, essence, and form.[80] Citing the Pseudo-Dionysius and the *Liber de causis*, Giles also points to the isomorphism between the number and degree of universality of the intelligible species which an angel has and the degree or grade of being which it has as it falls away from God.[81] The closer an angel is to the unity of God, the fewer are the species which it needs for its cognition, and in this, of course, it more closely resembles the mode of knowing in the divine essence itself. The scale of cognition descends downward from God to angels and then to human beings.[82]

Godfrey of Fontaines (d. 1306/1309), who may have studied with Henry of Ghent and also with Siger, opposed both the real distinction and the intentional distinction between essence and existence. His position, which is similar to Siger's, is that there is an identity of essence and existence and that any distinction between them is merely logical.[83] In a quodlibetal question concerning whether there is an advance to infinity in the essential perfections of things or in perfections having an essential order, Godfrey makes a tentative, cautious use of the scheme. He carefully warns his reader that he is not determining or resolving the issue in a definitive way, but only conjecturing about it in a probable fashion, that is, proposing a possible position for which arguments can be offered (*Sed nihil circa hoc determinando sed probabiliter coniecturando, videtur posse poni contrarium . . .*). The position which is then advanced contains the key elements of the conceptual scheme the history of which we have been tracing. Godfrey allows that the species of things can be compared to numbers, but he does not want to admit that there could be infinite and indeterminate grades of things, since God alone is infinite. In each genus there is an ultimate or first which is the maximum and the measure of all other things in that genus. And yet, though God is outside every genus, he is in some ways to be called the first in the genus of substance. Just as the essential order of numbers (*ordo essentialis numerorum*) demands that there be a halt in some first number, which is as it were immediately produced by unity and than which no other can be closer to unity, so the order of beings (*ordo entium*) demands that there be some creatures proximate to God and than which there can be no creature more perfect or closer to God — that creature will have the first and the least composition. In like fashion, just as numbers are in an essential order according to their approach to (*accessus*) or retreat from (*recessus*) unity, so things exist in their essential order in regard to the first unity, that is, according to a certain receding (*recessus*) from God's unity and simplicity and a certain approach (*accessus*) to composition and multitude. Godfrey concludes that the order of things is to be taken from a greater or lesser distancing (*elongatio*) from the First Being and only *per accidens* through distance to or from the last or lowest being. It is surely noteworthy that Godfrey cites both Dionysius' *De divinis nominibus* and Proclus' *Elements of Theology* in this discussion, but it is even more important to note that he is emphatic that the whole of creation remains infinitely distant from God. In a word, he appears to be concerned about certain possible implications of the scheme which would compromise God's infinity. In like fashion, he is careful to point out that the distinction of grades (*gradus*) in creatures does not bespeak distinct grades of perfection in God, since each creature imitates the whole of the divine essence. Indeed, it is the very simplicity and unity of the divine essence which enables it to serve as the foundation (*ratio*) and measure (*mensura*) of each creature according to that creature's retreat (*recessus*) from the divine unity and its approach (*accessus*) to multiplicity.[84]

The emphasis on divine unity and the use of the hierarchical scheme are notable in Godfrey's seventh Quodlibet. He follows the *De divinis nominibus* of the Pseudo-Dionysius closely in underscoring the complete simplicity and utter unity of God, whose attributes are identical with his very essence —there is no distinction between them. All things are contained in a united and unmeasured way in him, just as all numbers are contained unitedly in the *monas*.[85] Godfrey later quotes the second proposition of Proclus' *Elements of Theology* — that all that participates in unity is both one and not-one — explaining that God, who is primarily one, is First and Pure Act, while everything else recedes from the First One through an approach to the not-one. Things other than God only participate in the One and are therefore only secondarily one through some falling away and retreat (*defectus et recessus*) from it. They fall away from the First One and approach those things which have multiplicity according to a more and less (*plus et minus*). However, perfect beings such as the angels do so in such fashion that there is no real multiplicity in the various principles which compose their essence and give them actuality and potentiality. In a manner reminiscent of Siger's questions on the *Metaphysics*, Godfrey uses the scheme of ascent to and descent from God in order to explain the composition of angels. He does so in such a way that he avoids positing any sort of real distinction of essence and existence in them. By receding from the actuality of the First Being and approaching potentiality *simpliciter*, the angel has in some way a composition of potency and act, not in reality but according to reason (*habet quodammodo compositionem, non rei, sed rationis ex potentia et actu*). Godfrey is careful to add that this composition is not the result of an invention of reason (*non quidem fictae rationis*) but is in agreement with reality (*rei convenientem*) according as the angel is compared to what is above and below it.[86] A somewhat similar approach to the question of the composition of the Intelligences will be adopted, as we shall see, by Agostino Nifo and Marcantonio Zimara in the late-fifteenth and early-sixteenth centuries. But before turning to the Italian Renaissance and such thinkers as Nifo and Zimara, both of whom do in fact make use of the scheme in their writings, let us examine first the attitudes exhibited toward the scheme by various fourteenth-century philosophers.

Duns Scotus, John of Jandun, Developments in Fourteenth-Century Philosophy

Two of the most important and influential philosophers of the fourteenth century show evidence of acquaintance with the conceptual scheme of God as measure at one extreme and non-being or matter as a sort of measure at the other extreme and all things achieving their grade or species as they approach or recede from these two extremes. But neither of these philosophers wholly accepts the scheme, though each will speak of God as in some way the measure of all existing things. The two philosophers are John Duns Scotus and John of Jandun. Needless to say, I in no way mean to suggest that these two thinkers were of one mind. Indeed, I shall show that their own positions vis-à-vis the conceptual scheme are quite different. But what might be argued is that the adoption of the scheme by the late–thirteenth-century philosophers already discussed forced Scotus and Jandun to take a stand in regard to the scheme and the issues which it raised.[87]

John Duns Scotus (ca. 1266–1308) is one of the most celebrated and original thinkers of the late-medieval period. The positions which he adopts on the topic of metaphysical hierarchy underscore both his individuality and the critical attitude which characterize his philosophy. Although he will use some of the language and the concepts which we have already met, Scotus presents an account of metaphysical hierarchy which is so adapted to his own metaphysical doctrines that the result is in some ways at odds with the conceptual scheme of his predecessors.

Like the six medieval philosophers studied above, Duns Scotus adopts a doctrine of metaphysical participation. Each thing other than the infinite being, God, is to be called a being by participation since it has part of that entity which is in him completely and perfectly — finiteness means "partialness" of being (*partialitas entitatis*). Nevertheless, unlike Thomas, Scotus does not see the composition in finite or participated beings to be a composition of potentiality and actuality, a composition which Scotus takes to be that of positive "things" (*res*). On the contrary, he considers the composition to be that of something positive and a privation, that is, of some entity which the individual has, along with the lack of some grade of perfection (*gradus perfectionis*) of that entity. Scotus' example is the mole and its lack of sight.[88] Presumably the special privation of entity defines the species in the case of each kind of finite thing, though it cannot, as a privation, belong to that thing's positive essence. In a sense, the composition of finite beings can be understood only in relation to the infinite being in whom there is no privation.[89]

Scotus is as insistent as his predecessors that God is not a member of any genus, but unlike them he is equally insistent that the concept of being is predicated equally of creatures and God since it is univocal.[90] He also accepts the metaphysical axiom that whatever is first in any genus is the measure of all in that genus, adding that this is also true of the "genus" of being.[91] However, Scotus rejects Averroës' position that the First Mover, that is, God, is a measure within the genus of substance, maintaining instead that God is the extrinsic measure (*mensura extrinseca*) of all genera, though more immediately of substance than of accidents, since they are farther (*remotiora*) from him.[92] In one text, Scotus suggests that for Aristotle the first species in the genus of substance — whatever it might be — serves as the "one" which measures all else in the genus. God is, properly speaking (*proprie*), not the measure of any species, but only the extrinsic measure of all species, though he measures substance more closely (*propinquius*) since substance participates in him more perfectly (*perfectius participat*).[93] When speaking in his own name and not simply explicating Aristotle, Scotus asks us to imagine a being which is actually infinite in all ways and having nothing outside it, a being which is intensively infinite (*infinitum intensive*) in perfection or power. Such an infinite being exceeds every finite being beyond all possible determinate proportion (*determinata proportio*). And yet Scotus envisages the infinite and the finite as composing an essential order (*ordo essentialis*) in which ascent necessarily comes to a halt (*status*) in a single and wholly highest being. The doctrines of participation and measure here prove to be interrelated for Scotus. The infinite being is a whole (*totalitas*) in comparison with finite or participated being since the fullness of its quantity of power (*plenitudo quantitatis virtualis*) enables it to measure everything else as greater or less according as it approaches or recedes from it (*mensurans omne aliud ut maius per accessum ad ipsum et minus per recessum*).[94] Though it might seem at first glance that we have returned again to the conceptual scheme of Albert, Thomas, and the others, there are some fundamental differences. But before I delineate how Scotus is unlike his predecessors, let me note first the significance of the doctrine of "essential order" presumed in this discussion of measure.

One basic meaning of "order" (*ordo*) for Scotus is that it is the relationship of things ordered to one another — he claims to find this meaning in Augustine and Aristotle.[95] Such an order exists because all other members of the order are related to one thing which is eminent over them; there is a prior and a posterior. In the case of God and creatures, it is God, of course, who is the prior and more perfect which exceeds (*excedens*) all else, just as it is the creature which is posterior and exceeded (*excessum*).[96] This order is called an "essential order" (*ordo essentialis*) because it exists among essences — Scotus, following Aristotle, considers the forms or essences of things to be related like a series of numbers. And just as all species within a genus have an essential ordering to the first of that genus in such fashion that there is univocity among the species, so univocity must hold even more regarding the nature of being since all comparing of measured to measure or of exceeding to exceeded demands something univocal.[97] Scotus is insistent that every being must fall into an essential order, as either exceeding or exceeded, and he considers the entire universe to involve an essential order to the First Being. The things in the world will be more or less perfect as they approach more or less (*magis et minus appropinquantes*) to that being. Indeed, there could be no order of the universe if there were not the various ordered natures which differ in their quantity of perfection (*quantitas perfectionalis*). But while Scotus is insistent that God must fall into an essential order and that we must come to a halt when ascending in an essential order, he is also careful to say, as we have already noted, that inasmuch as God is infinite, he does not excel all other things according to a merely finite proportion.[98]

Despite the language of measuring all things other than God according to their approaching to or receding away from him, Scotus' conception of metaphysical hierarchy contrasts noticeably with the conceptual scheme the history of which we have been tracing. First of all, he assigns basic meanings to the terms "grade" (*gradus*), "mode" (*modus*), and "contracting" (*contrahere*) which are different from those found in the philosophers examined above. Unlike them, Scotus deliberately distinguishes the mode or grade of a thing from its specific difference and essence. Being of itself is indifferent to whether it is found in an infinite thing or a finite thing. It is contracted to be one or the other through the intrinsic grade (*gradus intrinsecus*) or mode (*modus intrinsecus*) of infinity or finitude, neither of which should be confused with specific difference. Being is thus divided first into the infinite and the finite, and then into the ten categories — namely, the highest genera, since being as infinite or finite is transcendent and outside all genera. Scotus carefully explains that while the expressions "finite" and "infinite" are said properly only of quantity of mass (*quantitas molis*), they are predicated in a transferred sense (*transumptive dicta*) of quantity of power (*quantitas virtutis*).[99] The finiteness of each created thing means precisely the grade and quantity of power (*quantitas virtualis*) of its essence; infinity is the proper grade of each of the attributes of God.[100]

It is difficult to understand precisely how for Scotus the species of things are set up in an essential order by approaching toward and receding from God, especially since "contraction" seems reserved for the "grades" or "modes" of the infinite and the finite.[101] Moreover, modern scholars have pointed out that Scotus provides no explanation to account for the hierarchical structure among the angels, even though he does appear to maintain that there are sub-species of angels.[102] He also allows that there is a finite distance between any creature and nothingness, just as he maintains that there is an infinite distance between each creature and God; but nowhere does he speak of creatures as being placed in the hierarchy of things according as they approach to or recede from non-being.[103] Indeed, it has been argued by one scholar that for Scotus the creature is no less a being (*res*) than God and that the creature is not an admixture of non-being.[104] The central point in the conceptual scheme of the philosophers studied above — that things take their grade and essence as they recede from God to non-being — is absent from the thought of Scotus. Perhaps this can be taken as an indication that he was wary of the metaphysical scheme to be found in the Pseudo-Dionysius, a scheme which much influenced his age.[105]

John of Jandun (d. 1328) was one of the most famous exponents of the Averroist interpretation of Aristotle at Paris during the Middle Ages.[106] Although there are clear traces of the language of the conceptual scheme in his writings, it will become obvious that Jandun does not accept key aspects of the scheme. Like the philosophers studied above, Jandun states that in every genus there is some first thing which is that sort of thing to the greatest degree (*maxime tale*) and which serves as the cause and measure of all else in that genus.[107] The concept of measure (*ratio mensurae*) belongs primarily and essentially to the unity which is the principle of numbering: namely, the indivisible minimum which enables us to measure the quantity of things, both the discrete and the continuous. The concept of measure has been transferred (*translata est*) from the unity in numbering to all other contexts in which something simply indivisible is used as a unity to measure other things. All that is required for such an extension of the concept of measure to other genera is that there be something in these other genera which is proportionate to the concept of indivision.[108]

But while there must be a measure or first in each genus, that measure can be either extrinsic or intrinsic to its genus. Examples of an intrinsic measure (*intrinseca mensura*) are the matter and form which are principles enabling us to know something, just as the efficient and final causes provide examples of the extrinsic measure (*extrinseca mensura*) of something. Although God is not *per se* a member of the genus of substance, Jandun argues that he is a member by reduction and that this suffices to consider him the extrinsic measure of all things, as their efficient and final cause.[109] Jandun explicates Averroës to have held in Book XII of the *Metaphysics* that God is the principle of all substances, and indeed of all things, as their efficient, formal, and final cause, for he is that actuality in which there is no admixture whatever of potentiality.[110] However, it should be underscored that while Jandun does call God the efficient cause of all things, he does not mean this in the literal sense.

Jandun argues that for Aristotle and Averroës there are two kinds of agents or efficient causes: namely, an agent simply and properly and what is called an agent according to a certain likeness (*secundum similitudinem*). Since the former kind of efficient cause is found only where there is motion and a subject in potency to being and non-being, and eternal substances such as the Intelligences cannot not be, such substances are not caused by an efficient cause in the proper sense. Jandun will grant that according to the Christian faith and truth everything other than God, the Intelligences included, have been created by God from nothing and *de novo*. As a result, God is the true efficient cause of all things and he alone is eternal. However, since creation is a supernatural production which cannot be demonstrated, Jandun bids his reader remain within the compass of philosophy. He interprets Averroës to have held that God can be called an efficient cause by similitude inasmuch as all the eternal substances depend on God, their final cause, for their existence and conservation. In a word, Jandun considers the final cause somehow to give and conserve existence and thus to be by a certain likeness an efficient cause.[111]

Some refinements on these ideas can be culled from Jandun's other works. In his questions on the *De substantia orbis,* he tells us that the Intelligences are the immediate movers of the heavens both as efficient and as final causes, while God is their mediate mover only as a final cause. The First Intelligence, which is to be distinguished from God, moves the first orb as an efficient cause, but in turn it itself moves by reason of desiring and knowing God.[112] And in a disputed question on whether eternal beings have an efficient cause, Jandun again takes Averroës to hold that God is the cause of the existence of all things; but he adds once again that God is an efficient cause only in an improper sense (*improprie*), or according to a certain likeness (*secundum similitudinem*), since he is in fact a final cause for whose sake all else exists and comes into being. On the other hand, the First Intelligence is the efficient cause (*causa efficiens*) of the motion of the first orb and is without composition. In a word, the orb not only needs an Intelligence as the efficient cause of its motion, but also requires God as the cause of its continuity (*causa continuationis*), to which its existence is ordered and by which it is rendered eternal. By serving as the eternal final cause of the orb's Intelligence, God can be considered by metaphor or transfer of meaning (*secundum metaphoram*) to be an efficient cause, just as he can be considered in this improper sense to be the efficient cause of the universe since he is its final cause.[113]

The problem which remains is to determine at least in summary form Jandun's outlook regarding the hierarchic ordering of things. First of all, it should be carefully noted that in contrast to the philosophers already discussed Jandun does not accept the doctrine of participation.[114] Jandun nowhere uses the axiom that whatever is such by participation is reduced to what is such by essence in order to show any creature's direct dependence on God for its existence.[115] Consequently, when he speaks of God's serving as the measure of all things so that they can be said to be more or less perfect according to their closeness to or remoteness from (*secundum appropinquationem vel remotionem*) God; or when he says that things depend on God in an order (*ordinate*) such that some depend on him immediately and are simple, while others are more remotely distant from him and approach more to matter (*magis remote distant et plus accedunt ad materiam*), adding that that distance is the cause of composition (*illa distantia est causa compositionis*), we must be careful not to understand this in the context of a participation metaphysics. In the latter text he accounts for the descending order (*sic descendendo secundum ordinem*) of the Intelligences by explaining that the First Intelligence depends directly on God as its final cause, whereas the Second Intelligence does so only indirectly by means of the First Intelligence and so on for all the other Intelligences.[116]

In one passage of his questions on the *Metaphysics*, Jandun sets up an ordering of the Intelligences which is based on wholly physical considerations. He reads Aristotle and Averroës as maintaining that the order in dignity and nobility (*dignitas et nobilitas*) of the movers of the heavenly bodies, that is, the Intelligences, follows the order in magnitude and location of the heavenly bodies themselves (*secundum ordinem mobilium in magnitudine et loco*). That is to say, the higher and greater the orb, the nobler and more dignified (*nobilior et dignior*) the Intelligence, so that the First Intelligence, the mover of the first or outermost sphere, will be nobler than all others. Jandun adds, however, that Averroës appears to vacillate on the precision of this ordering. He therefore suggests that there is a definite ordering of the movers of the orbs — the Intelligences — if they are compared to God the first mover, no matter how they be viewed, since he is always wholly prior to them. On the other hand, if they are compared to one another, there is an imprecise ordering since they can be prior and posterior to one another, and thus of more or less dignity, depending on the perspective from which they are treated. For example, the sun and Saturn are more and less noble than one another when viewed from the different perspectives of life and fixity. Jandun pointedly observes that comparisons between a man and an ass which are made from different points of view lead to a similar ambiguity, since from one perspective the man has more dignity while from the other the ass does. There is no trace here of any hierarchy of species in the natural realm and the skeptical tendency which Jandun exhibits regarding the ordering of such species would appear to undercut the conceptual scheme being traced in this essay.[117]

It is not surprising that those in the fourteenth century who opposed anything which hinted at an emanationist metaphysics carefully avoided the scheme. Such would appear to include William of Ockham (d. 1349/1350), John Buridan (d. ca. 1358), and Albert of Saxony (d. 1390).[118] Moreover, the conceptual scheme which we have been tracing did not always survive when scrutinized by thinkers like John Dumbleton. When he discusses the question whether substances considered abstractly can be compared in terms of more and less, he answers that they cannot. Since he holds that each specific essence is indivisible in its nature, substances as a series can form neither a continuum nor any sort of latitude.[119]

Perhaps the most interesting developments in the fourteenth century are found in discussions concerning the latitude of forms and the perfection of species. Both topics demanded the development of mathematical conceptions — especially the mathematics of infinity — to be used to determine how to measure the approach to the highest being, God, or to the highest and most perfect species, and how to measure the distance from the zero grade (*recessus a non gradu*) or from prime matter. John of Ripa attempted to compare the "intensity" of species relative to particular perfections by ranging the zero grade of separate perfections along a single scale beginning with "absolute zero." By comparing the zero grade (*non gradus*) of *vivere simpliciter* or that of *vivere intellectualiter* to that of "absolute zero," he attempted to formulate rules governing the ratio of species to one another. More ingenious attempts to express the chain of specific perfections mathematically can be found in Jacob of Naples and Peter Ceffons of Clairvaux, though Ripa denounces the use of *exempla mathematica*, much like Peter's, in treating species.[120] In any case, various aspects of the doctrine of the intension and remission of forms were to have striking influence on discussions concerning the scale of being throughout the fifteenth and the sixteenth centuries.[121]

The Italian Renaissance: Cardinal Bessarion, Marsilio Ficino, Paul of Venice, Gabriele Zerbo, Cardinal Grimani, Pietro Pomponazzi, Antonio Trombetta, Thomas de Vio, Agostino Nifo, Marcantonio Zimara, Alessandro Achillini, and Others

The scheme of God and matter or non-being serving as two termini measuring the scale or hierarchy of being received constant and frequently highly critical attention from a variety of Renaissance thinkers. One of the problems which intrigued many of them was how God could serve as a measure if he was infinitely distant from each and every creature, since it would then seem to be without purpose to speak of creatures varying in species according as they are closer to or more distant from him. Ingenious attempts were made to overcome this problem: among the solutions offered were that when God is taken as the measure of creatures he is not to be considered as infinite, and that the measuring of creatures should be determined only from the zero grade of being and not in any way from the highest grade, that is, God. The latter solution appears to have been inspired in great part by applying to the question of the hierarchy of being Richard Swineshead's view that the intension and remission of forms can be measured only from the zero grade and not from the highest grade. But this move was vigorously opposed by other philosophers, some of whom maintained that only God should serve as a measure. One counter-attack which they adopted was to argue that non-being or matter itself cannot serve as a measure since it is completely indeterminate. The critical approach evidenced by several of the thinkers whom we shall now survey should surely give lie to the prejudice that the philosophers of the Renaissance period lacked analytical talent. We shall take up first two of the most celebrated figures of the tradition of Renaissance Platonism, Bessarion and Ficino, before turning to the Aristotelian tradition proper.

In his *Comparatio philosophorum Aristotelis et Platonis,* written in late 1457 and published in 1458, George of Trebizond (1395–ca. 1472) accuses Plato of having postulated a series of intermediate gods, and he suggests that Plato thus agrees with those who worship snakes and cattle, since every creature is equally distant by infinity from God (*equaliter in infinitum distat a primo*). On the other hand, when contrasting this view with that of Aristotle, George distinguishes things closer (*propinquiora*) to God from those farther away (*longius absunt*), such as those things which enjoy sempiternity and those things which are subject to generation and corruption.[122] Cardinal Bessarion (ca. 1403–1472) takes note of this discussion in his own *In calumniatorem Platonis,* which was written in Greek in the first few months of 1459 but revised thereafter and published only in a Latin version in 1469.[123] As to Trebizond's remark that all creatures are equally distant from God insofar as they are infinitely distant from him, Bessarion suggests somewhat contemptuously that George is merely using a sophism common to disputations among students and given to them for the sake of dialectical exercise. Bessarion's own escape is to explain that the relation of creatures to the creator can be understood either as to an infinite being or as to a being which is both more perfect than all other beings and the highest being. If the relationship be taken in the latter sense, then, since the perfect does not signify the infinite, some creatures can be more like and closer to God than others. It is according to the nature of each individual that it will stand more or less distant from the First Being, God. Bessarion seeks to justify his stand by considering further the proportion (ἀναλογία) of the creator to the creature. He argues that God does not create according as he is simply infinite, since he would then create something infinite and not finite. On the contrary, God creates only according as his power is commensurate to the nature of what is being created. Consequently, if we compare one creature to another by referring both to God taken as their creator, then we must not refer them to him by reason of his being simply infinite. Moreover, it is, not by reason of God's being simply infinite, but by the limits of each of the creatures themselves, that one creature is more or less distant than another from their infinite creator.[124]

To strengthen his case, Bessarion presents a long quotation from St. Thomas' commentary on the *Sentences* which states that since the power of God as creator is proportioned, not to the infinite distance between being and non-being, but only to a finite distance, there need be assumed only an infinite power *secundum quid*, one measured in regard to some determinate matter. Moreover, only God, not creatures, should be considered to be at an infinite distance from non-being. Thomas appears to hold that these distinctions are necessary if creatures are to be called closer to or more distant from non-being. Bessarion comments that if things are related to one another such that one is of more value (τιμιώτερον) than another, then the former must approach closer to the creator and depart farther from non-being. The added authority of Augustine's remark in *Confessions* 12.7, that God has created something near himself and something near non-being — namely, angels and matter — is borrowed from Thomas, "the greatest theologian and the wisest man."[125] Bessarion has thus defended the scheme by using the authority of one of its most distinguished medieval proponents.

The reaction to Bessarion's work on the part of Marsilio Ficino (1433–1499), perhaps the most celebrated philosopher of the *Quattrocento*, can only be described as enthusiastic.[126] It should not be suprising that Ficino, who translated and studied Plotinus, Proclus, and the Pseudo-Dionysius, and whose favorite medieval Christian philosopher (other than Augustine) seems to have been Thomas Aquinas, accepted and utilized the conceptual scheme of God as measure and grades of being determined by approach to and receding from him. But the constant use which he makes of the scheme is striking.[127] We shall see that the concern with how God can measure all other beings if he is infinitely distant from them much vexed Ficino.

In his commentary on the *Philebus*, Ficino seems eager to show that there cannot be an infinite number of species in the hierarchy of being. Because of the unequal and unlike effects and species in the world, he conjectures that there is a distinct series (*series*) of things with higher and lower grades (*gradus*). However, this progression of species (*progressio specierum*) can neither ascend (*ascendere*) nor descend (*descendere*) to infinity. If it ascended to infinity, there would be no first species, which is the cause of the other species, and thus no middle species. There is a variation among species such that one species is more one, true, and good than another because of a greater or lesser distance and nearness (*propter minorem vel maiorem distantiam et propinquitatem*) in regard to that which is primarily and principally such. That is to say, since species are unequal, one species will be closer (*propinquior*) to, and another more distant (*remotior*) from, the First Being. As a consequence, the First Principle, which is primarily and principally one, true, and good, cannot be infinitely distant from the species, since then none of them would be any closer to him than any other.

Nor can there be an infinite descent of species away from the First Principle if there is to be any correspondence between the beginning and the end, ascent and descent, and the maximum and the minimum. And just as Ficino demands that the extremes be at a finite distancef rom one another, so he also demands that there be a middle between the extremes, lest they collapse into one another.[128] Ficino cites the celebrated passage in Plato's *Laws* 715E–F when explaining how God must be taken as the measure (*mensura*) of all things, since he measures the ascent (*ascensus*) and the descent (*descensus*) of them all. Things are thus called better (*meliora*) or worse (*deteriora*) according as they are nearer (*propinquiora*) to or more distant (*remotiora*) from him, since he is the First Good to which we compare and measure all other goods. As a *monas* which is wholly simple, he serves as the measure of the composite by the replication of his own being (*replicatio sui esse*), just as the point and the moment serve respectively as the measures of physical bodies and time. But God is also a measure for Ficino in a more active manner. Unmeasured by anything else, God is the measure of all things by bestowing on each thing a certain and definite nature (*certa, propria, determinataque natura et vis*) and by arranging all things in distinct grades (*distincti gradus*) and in an ordered series (*ordinata series*).[129]

The same worries about infinity are to be found in Ficino's *Theologia platonica*, but here the tensions in his position become more obvious. Ficino adopts the axiom that in every genus of things there is a highest (*summum*) of that genus which is one in number. God is that highest of all things: as the highest unity to which the finite number of species is referred, he brings about the order of all things.[130] Were there many gods, they would be infinite causes of things, and their effects would then be infinite in number. Ficino insists that we cannot descend without stop through species or there would be unlimited effects, just as we cannot ascend without end, since it is obvious that at some time we must come to that which is highest (*summum*). If there were no highest good (*bonitas summa*), but we ascended toward it to infinity, then Soul and Body would both be at an infinite distance (*infinitum intervallum*) from it. And since one infinity is no greater and no less than another, there would be no way to rank as better than one another the levels in Ficino's metaphysical hierarchy: namely, Angel, Soul, and Body. In like fashion, since there would be no measure, there would then be no order among things. If there is no first grade (*gradus primus*), then there will be no middle or last grade, and each middle grade will depend on an infinite number of higher grades and each higher grade will produce an infinite number of inferior grades. In fact, all things will be equally infinite. Worse yet, all science would be rendered impossible and our appetites would remain unmoved, since they would lack a final end.[131]

Despite these strong statements, which give every appearance of placing God within a genus as its highest or first grade and of describing him as at a finite distance from his creatures, Ficino is equally adamant that God is in no way to be considered finite in power. On the contrary, his power is infinite (*summa infinita potestas*). The human mind is ordered to an infinite progression (*infinita progressio*) in always thinking of some further grade of perfection which God could have. All these innumerable grades must be found in God, who serves as the infinite terminus (*terminus infinitus*) of the human mind. Ficino takes the effortless and infinite activity of God over the ages as a sign of his infinite power, citing with approval Orpheus for calling the divine nature an infinite end.[132] The modern reader, however, may be less than satisfied with the consistency of Ficino's saying that there must be a highest in the hierarchy of being, thereby seeming to say that God is finite and within the "genus" of being, and his likewise insisting that we can conceive without cease of higher and higher grades of perfection of the infinite God. On the other hand, the modern may be led to realize that Ficino is pointing to the basic antinomy of a mode of thinking which attempts to transcend the limits of the finite and yet can never reach the infinite limit which is God himself.[133]

Ficino clearly accepts the conceptual scheme of God and prime matter as the two poles setting bounds to the hierarchy of being. Matter holds that position because it is farthest away from the First Being and closest to non-being.[134] The gradation in being (*in essendo gradatio*) is brought about through an approach (*accessus*) to and a receding (*recessus*) from the Supreme Being (*esse summum*), who is God.[135] No two species can be equally perfect, that is, be on the same grade of perfection (*gradus perfectionis*). The more in act a species is, the farther (*longius*) it will be removed from matter — that is, by so many more grades — and the closer (*propinquior*) it will be to divine actuality.[136] While Ficino maps out main "orders" or "spheres" such as Mind, Soul, and Body, the true elements of his hierarchy of being are the natural species of things. The species itself does not admit of more and less (*species magis minusve non suscipit*), but consists in a certain grade of nature (*certus gradus naturae*) to which nothing can be added or taken away if the species is not to be altered. Ficino makes his point by comparing species to the "species" of numbers (*species numerorum*), noting that if one is added to the "seventh species" of number a new species is created, the "eighth species." However, it must be observed that he nowhere attempts to assign numbers to natural species in the world about us and to set them in any sort of serial ordering.[137]

Although Ficino does assert that there are two poles measuring the hierarchy of being, he appears to put special emphasis on God as a measure. No doubt this is due to his making a central theme in his metaphysical system the axiom that the first in any genus is the principle and cause of all else in that genus.[138] His allegiance to the axiom and his scorn for those who would reject it is especially underscored in one passage of the *Theologia platonica.* After citing various of Plato's dialogues, Ficino carefully differentiates goodness and beauty themselves, which Plato calls Ideas, from the things which are good and beautiful by reason of their participation in the former. He then invokes as an explanation that the first and highest in every genus of things is only one in number and is simply that perfection without admixture of its opposite. For Ficino, all the Ideas are, of course, to be identified with God, who is unity, goodness, and beauty itself. Each of these eternally existent Ideas measures all the temporal things which belong to the relevant class and participate in the respective Idea. Consequently, beauty itself is the measure of all beautiful things, since things are judged to be more or less beautiful (*magis minusve pulchrae existimantur*) according to their approach (*accessus*) to or receding (*recessus*) from the First Beauty (*prima pulchritudo*). What is at issue here is not simply Ficino's doctrine of beauty but his entire theory of metaphysical hierarchy and the creature's participation in God, since he explicitly states that the First Beauty is identical with the First Essence (*prima essentia*) — that is, with God himself. Whatever falls away (*cadit*) from all beauty falls away from all essence, and whatever possesses (*possidet*) all beauty will have all essence (*totam habet essentiam*). In a word, there is the same participation in beauty itself and ranking in regard to it as there is participation in essence or being itself and ranking in regard to it. Ficino therefore attacks "certain barbarians" (*Barbari quidam*) — Paul of Venice is probably one of his targets — who deny that beautiful things can be measured by their approach (*accessus*) to beauty itself, that is, God. Their argument is that since God is infinite, it is not possible for one thing to approach him any more closely (*propius ad ipsum accedere*) than another. The position which these "barbarians" adopt instead is that the measure of beautiful things is to be determined through the receding (*recessus*) from the complete privation of beauty (*pura pulchritudinis privatio*). Ficino attempts to turn their objection back upon them by arguing that if the pure act which is God is a positive infinity (*infinita affirmatione*), so a pure privation is a negative infinity (*infinita negatione*). He therefore questions what could be more foolish than to want to discern by means of a privation the positive aspect (*habitus*) of beauty, which comes into being with nature itself. Nor will Ficino allow of any attempted compromise — one such as Bessarion's — which would claim that the comparison of beautiful things is not to the divine essence itself, which is completely infinite, but only to an Idea of beauty, which is somehow finite as regards the creature. He simply points out that an Idea is a certain determination of divine perfection, leaving his reader to add the necessary observation that that perfection is essentially infinite. Ficino is adamant that the beautiful things which have received a similitude of the divine essence in a purer fashion do in fact approach more closely (*accedunt propius*) to it, while those which have received it less purely recede (*recedunt*) from it. It is God himself who remains for Ficino the first measure (*prima mensura*) which is not measured, the unmeasurable measure (*mensura immensurabilis*).[139] The conceptual scheme is thus reaffirmed, but it is God who serves as the more important of the two measures.

The scheme had already been discussed in detail by Paul of Venice (d. 1429). In his commentary on the *De anima*, after stating that for Averroës all Intelligences besides the first — namely, God — are composed of act and potency, he adds that act and potency are not essential differences. On the contrary, they are modal differences (*differentiae modales*) in the manner in which the "intense" (*intensum*) and the "remiss" (*remissum*) divide each grade (*gradus*). That is to say, a grade is called intense because it is distant from the zero grade (*distat a non gradu*), just as it is called remiss because it is nearer (*propinquius*) to the zero grade. Indeed, distance and nearness (*distantia et propinquitas*) themselves are said to be modes of things (*modi rerum*). Something is thus in act because it is distant from prime matter, while something is in potency because it is distant from the First Being (*distat a primo ente*).[140] Elsewhere in the same commentary Paul carefully notes that not all species which are diversified within a genus according to an above and a below (*sub et supra*) and are set out in grades (*gradualiter*) will diversify or change the genus itself. Such would be, for example, the degrees of whiteness within the genus of whiteness. Paul distinguishes this sense of grades and species from that in the scale or latitude of being (*latitudo entis*), which begins with the zero grade of being (*non gradus entis*) and ends with the First Cause (*causa prima*). He goes on to admit that species are like numbers in the sense that just as no numbers are equal so no species are of equal perfection, since no two species are equally distant (*equaliter distant*) from the zero grade of being.[141]

Further nuances of Paul's view of the scheme can be culled from his commentary on the *Physics*. He mentions in passing Albert the Great's statement that intension and remission (*intensio et remissio*) sometimes occur, not through the admixture or separation of a contrary, but through an approach (*accessus*) to or a receding (*recessus*) from the best (*optimum*), as in the case of the good, which has no true contrary but only a privation. Paul comments that it would be better to say that intension and remission take place through a receding from and an approach to the zero grade.

He points out that if heat itself were assumed to be infinite, then heat at the eighth grade would be more intense than heat at the fourth grade, and yet it would be no closer than heat at the fourth grade, since both would be at an infinite distance (*distantia infinita*) from infinite heat itself. Arguing by analogy, Paul then observes that although God's infinite goodness is greater than the goodness of a man, and a man's goodness and perfection are greater than those of a horse, the goodness of a man is still no closer to the highest goodness (*bonitas summa*) — namely, God — than is the goodness of the horse, since in each case there will be an infinite distance from the finite grade of goodness to the infinite grade (*ad gradum infinitum*). The man is, on the contrary, better and more perfect than the horse because he is farther distant from the zero grade of goodness and perfection *simpliciter*.[142]

In the *Liber coeli et mundi* of his *Summa naturalium*, Paul also discusses grades of perfection and defends the view that the perfection of a thing is measured, not according to an approach (*appropinquatio*) to the highest being (*summum*), but rather according to the distance from the zero grade (*distantia a non gradu*). Indeed, if the opposite were the case, then God could have no perfection whatever: already the highest grade in the entire latitude of beings (*gradus summus in tota latitudine entium*), God could hardly be said to "approach" that grade. Paul goes on to say that the closer something is to the zero grade the less is its perfection, and the more distant it is from that grade the greater is its perfection. He also carefully emphasizes that God can be called "greater than" or "more perfect than" creatures only in an improper sense, since the proper sense of these terms demands a determinate or finite proportion (*determinata proportio*) between the terms of the comparison.[143] There is a more extensive discussion in the *Liber metaphysicae* of Paul's *Summa naturalium*, but the limits of the present essay preclude a detailed analysis of it. What must surely be noted is that Paul objects to determining the perfection of created things not only by their approach or nearness to the highest being but also by the replication of divine unity in the manner of a mathematical unity. However, Paul finally faces the problem of how, if the created thing's perfection is determined solely by its distance from the zero grade, God can be said to be a measure. He argues that the perfection of the created being can in a sense be said to be determined by its imitation of the first grade of perfection (*imitatio primi gradus*), since the more distant something is from the zero grade the more it imitates the nature of that first grade. Since God is the purest act, containing no imperfection, he is the measure of all things in the latitude of beings. By this rather tortured line of reasoning, Paul can finally apply to God the axiom of Aristotle which we have noted in so many of the other thinkers: namely, that in every genus there is one thing which is the standard and measure (*metrum et mensura*) of all the other things belonging to that genus; and yet he will still not admit that the grade of perfection of creatures is measured or determined by their approach to God.[144]

Despite these long discussions in Paul's writings, his student Gaetano da Thiene (1387–1465) shows little interest in the scheme and certainly does not adopt Paul's position that grades in the hierarchy of being are determined by a receding from a zero grade. In his commentary on the *Physics* (1439), Thiene merely alludes to the fact that some maintain a *latitudo entium* extending from prime matter, which holds the zero grade of perfection, to God, who holds the highest grade, with the Intelligences, celestial bodies, men, animate and inanimate bodies, elements, and accidents ranked between.[145] Likewise, in his later commentary on the *De anima* (1443), reference to the scheme appears only in an argument which Thiene himself does not seem to accept.[146] Nicoletto Vernia (d. 1499), Thiene's student, alludes to the scheme in an argument, but he does not otherwise appear to make it the object of direct concern.[147] On the other hand, it is adopted by another philosopher who, like Paul of Venice, Gaetano da Thiene, and Nicoletto Vernia, taught for a time at Padua: namely, Gabriele Zerbo (ca. 1435–1505). In his metaphysical questions, Zerbo relates that for Scotus everything is measured by its approach (*accessus*) to or receding (*recessus*) from that which is infinite in quantity of power (*quantitas virtutis*) and in which all things participate. He then goes on to use both Augustine and Albert the Great as authorities for the precise scheme which we are tracing: that is, that the grade of a thing and its place in the latitude of the perfection of things (*latitudo perfectionalis entium*) is determined by its distance from the highest grade of perfection or from the zero grade of being (*non gradus entis*). Thomas too is cited regarding spiritual magnitude (*magnitudo spiritualis*) and the doctrine of participation and also as maintaining that that which is most perfect in each genus measures all else in the genus and is the cause of everything else in the genus.[148] Both Albert and Averroës are presented as holding that the perfection of things is measured by their approach to or receding from the most perfect being. But Zerbo remarks that he will not settle here whether it is the nearness (*approximatio*) to or the receding (*remotio*) from the most perfect being which determines the perfection of everything else, since either account is sufficiently probable (*satis probabile*), whatever the "Calculator" — that is, Richard Swineshead — may have said on the matter. In Zerbo's judgment, the arguments which Swineshead presents in his treatise on the intension and remission of forms are not demonstrative.[149] What Zerbo is referring to is that in the first treatise of his *Calculationes*, which is entitled *De intensione et remissione qualitatis*,

Swineshead rejects two opinions regarding intension and remission of qualities: (*a*) that intension of a quality is measured according to nearness (*appropinquatio*) to the most intense grade of its latitude, while remission is measured according to the distance (*distantia*) from that grade; and (*b*) that intension is measured according to the distance from the zero grade (*penes distantiam a non gradu*), while remission is measured according to the distance from the most intense grade of that latitude. Swineshead himself defends a third position — namely, that intension and remission are measured respectively according to the distance (*distantia*) from and the approach (*accessus*) to the zero grade — and he gives arguments, dismissed by Zerbo, against any use of the highest or most intense grade to measure the other grades in a latitude.[150]

In a critical commentary on Swineshead's treatise, Cardinal Domenico Grimani (1461–1523), who received his *laurea* from the University of Padua in 1487, interrelates the question of intension and remission with the problem of metaphysical hierarchy. He announces that he holds the first of the three positions analyzed by Swineshead to be the true one, and adds that by establishing its truth he will undercut the other two positions. He claims, first of all, that the manner in which people speak about the intension and remission of qualities corresponds to the manner in which they discuss the perfection and imperfection of things. He therefore argues that if it can be proved that the perfection of things is measured according to their nearness (*propinquitas*) to the most perfect being (*perfectissimum*) and their imperfection according to their distance (*distantia*) from it, then it will follow that the intension of a quality will be determined according to its nearness to the highest grade and its remission according to its distance from the same grade, just as the first position wants. To prove that the perfection and imperfection of things are in fact determined by their nearness to or distance from the most perfect being, Grimani immediately appeals to the authority of Aristotle in *Metaphysics* II, 1 (993B24–993B27) which he interprets with the help of citations from the commentaries of Averroës, Albert the Great, and Thomas Aquinas.[151] God is the measure of all things, and a substance is said to be more or less perfect according to its nearness to or distance from God. On the basis of these authorities, Grimani claims victory for the first position regarding intension and remission, and he judges the other two positions to be erroneous in whole (the third position) or in part (the second position). However, it is to Grimani's credit as a philosopher that he takes up a puzzle regarding the position which he has defended. An opponent could object that since Aristotle says that in each genus there should be some first "one" (*unum*) or indivisible which is the measure of all else in that genus, then that measure should be, like the principle of number, the minimum measure in that genus. But this would appear to take us away from the first position and back to the third position, that of Swineshead, which measures intension and remission by nearness to or distance from the zero grade (*non gradus*) — the latter Grimani identifies with non-being or nothingness (*non ens et nihil*). He is quick to deny that this objection, constructed from remarks of Aristotle, does in fact prove that either the second or the third position is true. Grimani begins his reply by pointing out that although Aristotle spoke of the measure as a minimum and as indivisible, he meant it to be a real thing (*ens reale*). He then observes that the "first" (*primum*) in each genus, which Aristotle said was the measure of all else in that genus, must be either the zero grade (*non gradus*) or the most perfect grade (*gradus perfectissimus*) in that genus. The first position, of course, takes the measure to be the highest grade alone; the second position appeals to both the highest grade and the zero grade; the third position accepts only the zero grade. But the proponents of the second and third positions cannot really even know the zero grade (*non gradus*) since it is non-being (*non ens*), and they therefore must accept as the "first" (*primum*) which measures all else in a genus something which is a being and real (*ens et reale*): namely, the most perfect and the highest in each genus (*perfectissimum et summum in quoquoque genere*).[152]

Later in the work Grimani tries to explain what is meant by "nearness" (*propinquitas*) and "distance" (*distantia*) in the context of the present discussion. When taken materially, nearness and distance are nothing but the distant or near quality (*qualitas distans vel propinqua*); when taken formally, they are the relation of the distant quality (*qualitas distans*) to that from which it is distant (*distat*) and the relation of the near quality (*propinqua qualitas*) to that to which it approaches (*appropinquatur*). All three positions sketched above take nearness and distance formally, that is, as relations, but they differ as to whether these are real relations or relations of reason (*relationes vel reales vel rationis*). Turning to the second and third positions, he argues that inasmuch as the zero grade (*non gradus*) is in fact nothing — or is at best a product of the intellect — there can be no real relation of nearness and distance between it and the quality which is more or less intense and remiss. Those two positions are seen to fail again. Nonetheless, even on the basis of the first position, which involves only real relations, Grimani denies that the real relation is the efficient, the final, or the formal cause of the intension of a quality. On the contrary, distance and nearness are posterior to the intension and remission of qualities. Grimani goes on to claim yet another advantage of the first position over the other two: since knowledge of relations is a necessary condition for knowledge of intension and remission, and relations of reason are far less knowable than real relations, the first position is preferable insofar as it bases itself on the real relations of nearness to and distance from the highest grade; the other two postulate the relations of reason of nearness to and distance from the zero grade. Presumably Grimani would consider all these considerations to count against measuring the grade of something in the hierarchy of being not only by its distance from or nearness to God but also by its distance from or nearness to the zero grade.[153]

Strong opposition to Swineshead's position as an account of the hierarchy of reality is also expressed by Pietro Pomponazzi (1462–1525) in his commentary on Averroës' *De substantia orbis*, which was completed at Padua in 1508. He remarks that that matter — namely, the matter of the heavens — is nobler and more perfect which approaches the First Being (*appropinquat primo enti*); and he adds that the more something is distant (*distat*) from potency the more it approaches to perfection and to the purest act, which is God in his glory (*tanto magis appropinquat ad perfectionem et ad purissimum actum qui est Deus gloriosus*). He therefore denounces the error of the "Calculator" in his treatise on intension and remission for thinking that intension is measured according to the zero grade (*non gradus*) and for damning (*damnat*) the first position, which is Aristotelian (*aristotelica*). Since Aristotle himself says, in *Metaphysics* X, 1 (1052B19–1052B20), that there is a one in each genus which is the measure of all others in that genus, Pomponazzi feels free to insist that Aristotelians measure all things according to the highest grade (*gradus summus*).[154] Although Pomponazzi seems to leave open the possibility that potency plays some role in measuring the perfection of things, such is not the case with the Franciscan theologian Antonio Trombetta (1436–1517). In his metaphysical questions, Trombetta states that God, who is the simplest and most actual being (*actus simplicissimus et actualissimus*), places each thing in its proper existence or grade of perfection (*in suo esse aut in gradu suae perfectionis*). In a word, all things are measured in their being according to the approach to or receding (*accessus vel recessus*) from God.[155] But if Trombetta is loyal to Duns Scotus in omitting non-being as a measure of the hierarchy of being, his Dominican concurrent Thomas de Vio (1469–1534) is just as loyal to St. Thomas in his commentary on the *De ente et essentia*, completed at Padua in 1495. He presents both God and prime matter as the two extremes which determine the grades of all other things as they approach to or recede from these two extremes.[156] The same conceptual scheme can also be found in the contemporary lay Thomist Jacobus Brutus, who cites Thomas' *De ente* in his discussion.[157] On the other hand, the Jewish thinker Elia del Medigo (d. ca. 1493) reveals no interest in the scheme in his Latin writings, though he does speak of God as the First in the genus of unity. The existence of the Intelligences depends on the First, since it is he who gives them their unity: every composed thing needs an extrinsic cause which makes it to be one. However, Elia explains the hierarchy of Intelligences, not through participation and the scheme, but rather according to the mode of their knowledge of God.[158] While he will refer to the nearness and removal (*propinquitas et remotio*) which the heavenly bodies have in relation to God, he is speaking about the number of motions which they require, not any sort of metaphysical distance in a hierarchy of perfection.[159]

Toward the end of the fifteenth century, that is, in 1497, a young professor of philosophy at Padua published a work in which the conceptual scheme of God as measure and the ascent to and the receding from God and matter as determining the grades of perfection of things is given a central role. The philosopher was Agostino Nifo (ca. 1470–1538); the work, his commentary on the *Incoherence of the Incoherence* of Averroës in the medieval Latin translation, the *Destructio destructionum*. Nifo seems fascinated with the scheme and the ways in which it can be introduced to solve the various problems raised by the text of al-Ghazzali and Averroës. Nifo's commentary will have some impact, and the views which he ascribes to Averroës will be taken up and debated by other Renaissance philosophers.[160]

Various passages in the *Destructio* which seem of Neoplatonic origin enable Nifo to present in his exegesis of Averroës the conceptual scheme, the history of which we have been tracing. It seems highly likely that his reading and study of such medieval philosophers as Albert and Aquinas strongly influenced his interpretation of Averroës.[161] Moreover, the *Liber de causis* is cited on several occasions.[162] God is taken to be the absolutely simple one (*unus simplex summe*). All other things exist by participating (*participando*) in God, who is the cause of the existence which is diffused (*diffusum*) through the species and natures of things, even to matter. Although God acts by his very essence (*per essentiam*), all other things act by participation, since they exist by participation (*secundum participationem*).[163] The Intelligences as caused beings fall short of the perfection of God (*deficiunt a perfectione primi*), but they do not recede (*recedentes*) equally, since some recede more than others. That which is closer to the complete simplicity of God will be less composed. Nifo takes Averroës to mean by composition in the Intelligences a composition of a grade of perfection and a grade of imperfection: this is what makes a latitude (*latitudo*) among them possible.[164] In everything other than God there are two grades: the grade of perfection (*gradus perfectionis*), by which the thing approaches (*appropinquat*) the best and most perfect and recedes from the most imperfect; and the grade of imperfection (*gradus imperfectionis*), by which the thing approaches the zero grade of perfection — perhaps matter (*non gradus perfectionis qui forte est materia*) — and recedes from the best. The true reason why such grades are found in everything except God is that they all are caused by God and fall short (*deficit*) of their cause. God is the *extremum perfectissimum*, which is a cause only and is in no way caused; matter or the zero grade of perfection is the *extremum imperfectissimum*.[165] Nifo calls the composition in Intelligences one of essence and *esse*, by which he means simply some sort of composition between potency and act.[166] In the case of the lowest Intelligence, which for Averroës is the single intellect for all men, the grade of imperfection is called the potential intellect and the grade of perfection is called the agent intellect.[167] Not surprisingly, Nifo cites Aristotle and Averroës as holding that there must be a standard and measure (*metrum et mensura*) in every genus which measures all else in the genus. He then says that God is in the highest grade of being (*summus gradus entis*) and by essence embraces the perfection of being, and he goes on to argue that God cannot share that being with others in a univocal fashion. He does not state here, however, whether he considers God to be infinite for Aristotle and Averroës and whether God is somehow within the genus of being which he measures.[168] Nonetheless, he is helpful in distinguishing two causes for the latitude (*latitudo*) among the Intelligences: the unity of essence (*unitas essentiae*) which they receive according to a more and less (*magis et minus*), and the variation which occurs in their knowledge of God.[169] Finally, Nifo's own special view on the kind of distinction involved in the two grades in all things other than God should be signaled. He holds that in the Intelligences these grades are identical in their subject, differing not in reality but only in mode (*modus*), that is, according to the mode of our understanding. On the other hand, the grades of matter and form in a physical thing, such as a fly, differ both in mode and in reality. Needless to say, all these striking explications of Averroës would not be accepted by others who valued the Commentator, but it is clear that Nifo's edition and commentary marked a turning point in Renaissance Averroism.[170]

In a work finished and published only a few years later, in 1505, another professor of philosophy at Padua, Marcantonio Zimara (1460–1532), takes up the doctrine of composition in the Intelligences according to a falling away from God. The heavy use which he makes of the *Destructio destructionum* reveals the strong influence of Nifo's work. Zimara attributes to Averroës the doctrine that God exists by essence (*per essentiam*) and all other things exist by participation (*per participationem*). In all the latter, there is some potentiality and privation (*potentialitas et privatio*) in relation to the perfection *simpliciter* which it lacks. Consequently, though the First Intelligence, who is God, is beingness and unity itself (*ipsa entitas et ipsa unitas*), even the second Intelligence, since it falls short of the perfection of the First (*deficiat a perfectione primae*), is a being and one only with some composition and multiplicity — namely, of something which is positive and something which is a privation (*ex positivo et privativo*). Moreover, even the second Intelligence does not have the mode of knowledge enjoyed by the First. The Intelligences are produced by God according to a certain order (*ordo*), and they differ among themselves in their essential perfection (*perfectio essentialis*) according as each approaches more or less to the First Intelligence (*magis et minus appropinquat primae*), which is the principle and perfection of them all and *summe simplex*.[171] In the lowest of the Intelligences — namely, the intellective soul (*anima intellectiva*) or rational soul (*anima rationalis*), which is one for all men — there is a real composition (*realis compositio*) of two substances which are essentially distinct (*ex duabus substantiis essentialiter distinctis*), the agent and potential intellects. In the Intelligences other than the First Intelligence, and with the exception of the lowest Intelligence, there really is no potential intellect, since the Intelligences in question do not depend on any object of knowledge other than themselves. Nonetheless, if we consider them in relation to God, the First Intelligence, we must say that in them there is a certain imperfection and dependence. Accordingly, if we take "possible intellect" to mean a certain imperfection and privation, then we can say that even the other Intelligences are composed of a possible and an agent intellect, not as of two parts essentially distinct, but rather as of something positive and something negative (*tanquam ex positivo et privativo*). Such a composition exists only according to a judgment of the mind (*secundum existimationem tantum*), since there is something potential in them only by a mental precision or a metaphorical way of speaking (*secundum existimationem et metaphoram quamdam*).[172]

All the major themes of the conceptual scheme reappear in Zimara's major philosophical work, the *Theoremata*, which consists of commentaries on 129 propositions. Zimara attributes to both Aristotle and Averroës the axiom that in every genus there is a standard and measure (*metrum et mensura*) of all the other things in the genus. Things will participate in the perfection and actuality of God, and their being and perfection will be measured according to their approach (*approximatio*) or receding (*recessus*) in regard to him.[173] Consequently, the Intelligences do not proceed equally from God, the First Intelligence, since one Intelligence will approach God more than another according as it participates more in his perfections, just as one number will approach unity more than another. And just as the approach and receding in regard to the number one (*accessus et recessus ad unum*) generates the order of priority and posteriority among numbers, so the variation in the Intelligences' knowledge of and participation in God, the First Intelligence, generates the very different distances (*distantiae*) and the order of priority and posteriority among them.[174] Zimara goes on to cite the Pseudo-Dionysius in his *De coelesti hierarchia*, *Letters*, and *De divinis nominibus* as an authority for the scheme, but he also uses him to emphasize that the "distance" in question is not local distance but rather that involved in a comparison to God. He dismisses as far from the truth the *sophistae* and *calculatores* who think that intension and remission of forms is determined according to the retreat from the zero grade (*recessus a non gradu*), but he does admit that a problem arises for the scheme on the supposition of God's infinity. Granting that God is infinite, Zimara insists that he can still serve as the standard and measure of all things. To the argument that all creatures would be equally distant from an infinite God, since there is no proportion between the finite and the infinite, he replies that the perfection of God is formally infinite when it is considered in itself, but not infinite when it is taken as imitable and participable by creatures (*imitabilis et participabilis a creaturis*). No creature can participate in infinite perfection since it is infinite, but all creatures can participate in and imitate that perfection in different grades (*gradus*) and thereby be measured according to their approach and receding (*accessus et recessus*) in reference to God.[175]

Zimara's statement of the nature of the composition of the Intelligences is almost identical to that in his earlier work. Those things which stand between the two extremes of the latitude of beings (*latitudo entium*) — namely, God, who is the First Form (*prima forma*) which holds the highest grade in the genus of actuality, and prime matter, which holds the highest grade in the genus of potentiality — must participate (*participant*) in the nature of each extreme. All things will therefore be composed of potency and act, but in different ways since the distances of things (*distantiae entium*) are quite different. He explains that in the case of the Intelligences it is a composition, not of two positive things, but of that which is positive and that which is privative (*tanquam ex positivo et privativo*), claiming the authority of both Henry of Ghent and Duns Scotus for this view. He rejects any real composition (*realis compositio*) in the Intelligences, with the possible exception of the lowest, and characterizes their composition as one according to reason (*secundum rationem*). Zimara admits a real composition of the agent and potential intellects as two essential parts only in the intellective soul (*anima intellectiva*) — that is, the lowest Intelligence — and a true composition (*vera compositio*) of matter and form in generable and corruptible things. He thus once again rejects the position of Nifo, whom he does not cite by name, that there is no real composition in the intellective soul or lowest Intelligence.[176] The only variation to be found in the *Theoremata* is that in one passage Zimara adopts the language of the intension and remission of forms. He speaks of the two extremes of the latitude of forms (*latitudo formarum*) as the more remiss extreme (*extremum remissior*), prime matter, and the more intense extreme (*extremum intensior*), God, who is the first mover of all things. What is fascinating is that Zimara then arranges all forms in a ranking from the forms of the elements to inanimate mixed bodies, such as minerals and stones, to vegetables, plants, sponges, and the animals. Man, of course, serves as the terminus here in the lower world (*mundus inferior*). There is a similar order (*ordo*) in the higher world (*superior mundus*), ascending by grades (*gradatim ascendendo*) from the human soul, which is the lowest of the forms in the other world, to the Intelligence of the moon, to that of Mercury, which is in a nobler grade of being (*in nobiliori gradu essendi*) than that of the moon, until the first mover is reached. In this passage, Zimara has interrelated the order of Intelligences with the order of the orbs, and he has sketched out the entire chain of being from the lowest physical level up to God himself. What should be noted is that he does not attempt a settled ranking of the species in the living world. That would be the project of later thinkers.[177]

Another philosopher of the Italian Renaissance who faced the questions discussed by Paul of Venice, Nifo, and Zimara was Alessandro Achillini (1463–1512). The basic problem raised in his *De intelligentiis*, first published in 1494, is whether the latitude of intellects is uniformly varying (*Utrum latitudo intellectuum sit uniformiter difformis*). Borrowing the language of the intension and remission of forms tradition, he speaks of the possible intellect, which is one for all men, as the most intense of material beings and the most remiss of separate beings (*intensissimum materialium et remississimum abstractorum*) and of God, the "agent intellect," as the most intense extreme (*extremum intensissimum*) of the latitude of intellects. He considers a latitude to be infinite if any of its parts is infinite. God is the internal terminus (*terminus intrinsecus*) of the most intense extreme of the latitude, since he is the intellect above (*supra*) whom there is nothing and below (*infra*) whom is everything else. If God is infinite, then the latitude of Intelligences will be infinitely intense (*infinite intensa*). Aristotle's position, however, is that God is of finite force (*finitus vigor*).[178] Nonetheless, Achillini himself holds as the truth that the middle Intelligences (*intelligentiae mediae*) in the latitude are created by God and are infinitely distant from him (*in infinitum distant*). Although other Intelligences of higher species can always be created by God, they will never reach him, since he cannot produce one equal to himself.[179] Since there is thus an infinitely great receding (*recessus*) and distance (*distantia*) between the First Intelligence, who is

God, and the middle Intelligences, there can be no nearness (*propinquitas*) among them and therefore no order in receding or approaching (*ordo in recedendo aut appropinquando*). But an order by grade (*ordo secundum gradum*) is possible among them if one is speaking of their essential or accidental perfections.[180] Achillini denies that the perfection of the Intelligences is extended according to their approach to the highest being (*penes appropinquationem summo*). Nevertheless, granted the view of philosophers like Aristotle, who hold that God is finite, one can ask whether perfections are proportioned between God and the lower Intelligences in a geometrical or an arithmetical fashion. Achillini would thus appear to consider it plausible, but only on the assumption that God is finite, to speak of a composition in the Intelligences resulting from approaching to him. However, he himself seems to prefer to speak of two perfections of each thing, neither of which is determined by its distance from God. The one is the perfection which is measured according to the zero grade of the perfection of being (*penes non gradum perfectionis entis*); the other, the perfection which is measured according to the distance from the zero grade of its proper species (*penes distantiam a non gradu propriae speciei*). Achillini again reveals his interests in the *calculatores* tradition by then comparing the variation of such perfections to the intension and remission of the quality of heat through its various grades (*gradus*). Yet he insists that even God himself could not increase or decrease (*intendere aut remittere*) the essence of something as regards the grade of its essential perfection (*gradus perfectionis essentialis*) without turning it into another species. Achillini will admit that the theologians concede it to be possible to go to infinity in the number of middle Intelligences, but this view is, of course, not that of Aristotle. Following traditional doctrine, he also cautions that there is not, properly speaking, a proportion (*proportio*) among the Intelligences, since proportion really is a relationship of quantities (*habitudo quantitatum*) to one another. But he will allow that proportions in the manner of quantity can be imagined (*imaginantur*) to exist between them. Not surprisingly, he accepts Aristotle's remark that species are related as numbers, which he takes to mean that as no two species of number are equally distant (*equaliter distantes*) from unity, so no two species are equally distant from the zero grade of being (*non gradus entis*). But he gives the remark a further meaning, one which would suggest that he took the comparison of species to numbers rather literally and not simply as a suggestive analogy: namely, that as the addition or subtraction of unity varies a number, so the addition or subtraction of an essential difference varies a species. Finally, Achillini sees another likeness: that is, that one can ascend to infinity (*in infinitum ascenditur*) both in numbers and in species.[181]

Although there are other instances of discussion and even adoption of the scheme during the sixteenth century, the already extended limits of this essay prevent my presenting them here.[182] Especially interesting are the views on hierarchy and the scheme to be found in the writings of Francesco Buonamici (ca. 1540–1603) and his one-time student Galileo Galilei (1564–1642), as well as in those of two of Galileo's close acquaintances who were academic philosophers, Jacopo Mazzoni (1548–1598) and Cesare Cremonini (ca. 1550–1631).[183] The great diversity of views in hierarchy among the medieval and Renaissance philosophers whom we have surveyed and the highly critical examinations given to the three rival schemes — namely, God alone as the measure, non-being or the zero grade alone as the measure, and both God and non-being as measures — testify to the philosophical vitality of the period. The growing concern throughout the fourteenth, fifteenth, and sixteenth centuries with a scheme which postulated an infinite God as the measure of varying grades of finite things is surely one of the most noteworthy aspects of philosophical discussions regarding hierarchy during these centuries. It is simply a lack of historical accuracy to believe that such criticisms of the concept of metaphysical hierarchy arose only during the modern period.[184] On the contrary, I shall note in the conclusion that some of the early modern figures who treat of a hierarchy topped off by an infinite God seem somewhat naïve in comparison to those whom we have already studied.

Conclusion

In the preceding sections, we have examined the use of a conceptual scheme in the metaphysical thought of a variety of medieval and Renaissance thinkers. This scheme, the origins of which were traced to Proclus, the Pseudo-Dionysius, and the *Liber de causis,* involves two termini which measure all other things. According as things "approach" God and "recede" from matter or non-being, they are established at a particular level or grade in the metaphysical hierarchy. The scheme is also found in some of the writings of St. Augustine, but limitations of space prevented my discussing him here.[185] Although elements of the scheme appear in some of the figures studied by Lovejoy in his famed book, philosophers as a group paid far less attention to it after the sixteenth century.[186] Indeed, the mechanism adopted by René Descartes (1596–1650) would appear to undercut the very notion of grades of perfection in the non-human physical realm, and his apparent lack of interest in the metaphysical arrangement of the angels completes his negative attitude toward hierarchical conceptions.[187] Spinoza's (1632–1677) metaphysical system is decidedly anti-hierarchical, but on occasion he uses the language of an order of grades extending from the highest to the lowest.[188] On the other hand, Leibniz (1646–1716) unashamedly adopts a metaphysical hierarchy and at times uses language similar to that of the scheme which we have been studying: namely, chain or series, grades or degrees of perfection, "quantity" of essence, descent by degrees from the infinite being of God, and approaching closest to nothingness. What does not seem to concern him at all is the question of how a God infinitely distant could be the measure of anything else. Apparently God is not such a measure.[189]

Not surprisingly, Richard Hooker (1553–1600) sets forth some general hierarchical notions, but he in no way adopts anything like the refined metaphysical scheme of the medieval and Renaissance thinkers who interested us above. Hooker simply tells us that the angels are in order or degree one above another and that they look up toward God and down toward man. He appears to underline the difficulty of setting out a gradation in the physical realm when he notes that the brutes have a more refined sense capacity than man, that stones are inferior to plants in the "dignity" of their nature and yet exceed them in strength and durability, that plants exceed animals in their power of vegetation or fertility, and that man is capable of greater perfection than any of them. The scheme of God and non-being as the two extremes which measure all other beings according as they approach toward or recede from them is not to be found here.[190] Although John Locke (1632–1704) limits our knowledge to nominal essences, he does not preclude our mind's setting up some sort of ranking or hierarchy. He suggests that when it comes to our ideas of "spirits" and God, we take the simple ideas which our mind forms by reflecting on its own operations and attribute them to God in an unlimited degree and to the spirits in a higher or lower degree. For Locke, God is "infinitely more remote" from the most perfect creature than is the "greatest man, nay, purest seraph" from the "most contemptible part of matter." Locke argues at one point that it is "probable" that since we see no "chasms or gaps" in the sensible world there must be more species of intelligent beings above us than exist below us in the sensible and material realm. There is a "descent" from us by "easy steps" in a "continued series of things"; the species differ "but in almost insensible degree."[191] Indeed, what Locke is claiming is that he is arguing by analogy from the observable to the unobservable. We see such a "gradual connexion" in the observable order that we cannot easily discover the bounds between the "ranks of beings." However, this enables us to argue that "by such gentle steps, things ascend upwards in degrees of perfection." That is to say, the "gradual and gentle descents downwards" below man enable us to argue with probability by the rule of analogy that there are ranks of intelligent beings which excel man "in several degrees of perfection, ascending upwards towards the infinite perfection of the Creator, by gentle steps and differences."[192] Here too there is no sense of God as measure of the grades of things, but we do have much of the spatial language of the scheme. Moreover, Locke seems to accept almost innocently and uncritically the possibility of ascending toward an infinite being which presumably will never be reached. When we turn to George Berkeley (1685–1753), we find him appealing to Iamblichus when setting forth what he calls "a received notion of the Pythagoreans and Platonics": namely, the chain or scale of beings which rise from the lowest to the highest by "gentle uninterrupted gradations."[193] But there is no affirmation of God and non-being as measuring these grades or gradations according as they go up to God or down to non-being. On the contrary, the use of the phrase "up" and "down" is applied rather to the moral ascent and descent of the soul.[194] Despite Berkeley's acquaintance with the writings of the Pseudo-Dionysius, there seems no inclination on his part to adopt the scheme.[195] We may thus conclude that although Hooker, Locke, and Berkeley have some conception of hierarchy, none of them adopts the scheme which we have been studying, and the most we find in Locke and Berkeley is adoption of some of the language used by the scheme. Of the three, Locke retains the greatest number of conceptual elements implicit in the scheme.

There was in fact a decline of allegiance to a hierarchical scheme regarding the angels on the part of various Renaissance thinkers, due no doubt in great part to the discrediting of the authenticity of the Dionysian corpus.[196] But explicit and strong rejection of any hierarchic scheme such as that which we have examined is especially noteworthy in Martin Luther (1483–1546)[197] and Giordano Bruno (1548–1600).[198] And while Nicholas of Cusa (1401–1464) adopts the major themes of the scheme in his early *De concordantia catholica* (1433), he appears to overturn the scheme in his later *De docta ignorantia* (1440), though he still makes use of the language of "up" and "down," ascending and descending, and grades.[199] On the other hand, basic elements of the scheme much interested various literary figures during the early modern period.[200] The concept of grades was also applied rather literally to species in the physical world by some natural scientists.[201] Indeed, some recent scholars have even seen the concept of the hierarchy of being as having played a role in the intellectual background of the theory of evolution.[202]

Whatever be the final judgment on the place of the concept of the hierarchy of being in the development of Western thought, there are certain issues and problems raised by the scheme studied above which merit at least brief mention. First of all, it is noteworthy that the various thinkers who made use of the scheme in their metaphysical systems held opposing views on the famed issue of the distinction of essence and existence. The scheme thus appears to be indifferent to this question. However, it must also be noted that the thinkers studied above who adopted the scheme were agreed that everything other than God owed its existence to him and somehow participated in his existence. They also agreed in accepting the hierarchy of being in their metaphysics. On the other hand, although St. Bonaventure (1221–1274) maintained participation, hierarchy, and the basic elements of the scheme, he adapts the scheme to his own exemplaristic metaphysics and Christology. Consequently, though he knows the works of the Pseudo-Dionysius, he is interested less in using the theme of *πρόοδος* and *ἐπιστροφή* to structure a metaphysics than in adapting it to show God's *descensus* to man, the soul's *ascensus* to God by knowing him through his creatures, and finally the soul's *regressus* to God through grace. Bonaventure is evidently determined to make Christ central and all Neoplatonic themes secondary and instrumental.[203]

The second point to be made, one which arises from the Neoplatonic background, concerns the ambiguity engendered by the language of "receding" and "approaching." Besides the "falling away" from the One involved in the Neoplatonic Great Return theme of the *πρόοδος* and *ἐπιστροφή* of all things, there is also the "fall" of the soul from and its eventual return to its primeval source. The former "falling away" or "receding" explains the metaphysical scheme of different levels, while the latter "fall" is used to provide an account of the soul's present psychological and moral state. The obvious puzzle is how one connects the metaphysical hierarchy with the return of a soul, which, though presumably occupying a rank in the hierarchy, can cut across levels and ascend to union with the highest level of all. One finds Augustine using the "approaching" and "receding" language both when alluding to the metaphysical hierarchy and when speaking of the soul's "fall" from and "return" to God.[204] Using the same language to describe both a metaphysical hierarchy and the moral fate of the human soul would appear to create a needless ambiguity.[205]

Related to this is a third issue, one which also has its roots in Neoplatonic discussions. How indeed can one speak of "approaching" toward and "receding" from a God who is supposedly omnipresent? The medieval and Renaissance philosophers whom we have surveyed agreed that God created from nothing and maintains all things in existence by his constant causal presence. Granted that these same thinkers had a conception of the physical universe according to which the earth was the center of reference and "up" and "down" had evaluative overtones, it remains that they also held that God is not really to be located in space but is omnipresent. How then can one speak of things "approaching" toward God or "receding" from him? Or why can one say that things are "up" or "down" in relation to him? This tension in the scheme, which appears as early as the writings of Plotinus and Augustine,[206] would seem at first glance to result from its imaginative, "spatial" outlook and therefore its inability to do justice to the concept of an omnipresent, creator God. However, I shall return to this question in my closing remarks about the problem of the role of metaphorical language in metaphysics.

The fourth point involves a problem which also results from the spatial language used by those who adopted the scheme. How can one speak meaningfully about things differing according as they approach "nearer" to God and then make the qualification that they all always remain at an infinite "distance" from him? It was reasonable for the philosophers to argue that if all creatures are infinitely distant from God, then they are all at an equal distance from him and thus on the same grade. A fifth point related to this one is the problem of seeing how God can be the measure of a "genus" when he is taken to stand outside that genus. It is not surprising that Aquinas, at least in the judgment of some,[207] therefore tends at times to speak of God as if he were a member of the "genus" of being, while Ficino appears to describe him that way in some texts.

A sixth point which is noteworthy about the scheme is its comparison of God and the hierarchy of being to the generating of the series of natural numbers from the number one. This comparison, which came down from Proclus, fascinated various of the thinkers whom we have studied. However, if the comparison is taken *literally* so that the series of all conceivable species in the physical world is mappable on or isomorphic to the series of natural numbers and if we then add the notion or principle of continuity, there should be no "jumps" or "gaps" in the series. As a result, it would appear that God would have had to create all possible species or types without exception lest there be such a jump or "missing link," as it were, in the hierarchy of things.

With these six points laid out — and they are not the only problems which could be mentioned — we are in a position to make some final comments about the problems raised by the scheme and to show what philosophical issues remain for further discussions.[208] Perhaps it would be easiest to begin with the sixth point just mentioned: namely, the comparison of God as the measure of the hierarchy of being to the way in which the prime number, one, generates the series of natural numbers. Some of the medievals whom we studied emphasized that this manner of speaking about God and the species in the hierarchy is analogical. Giles of Rome, for example, was especially careful to call the comparison an analogy. He and the other medieval and Renaissance philosophers did not think of searching for all the species in the plant and animal kingdom lest there be any "gaps" in the hierarchy, since they did not believe that there was a strict correspondence between the "series" of species and natural numbers.[209] The hunt for the missing "links" in the chain of being was a modern development, one which resulted, I would suggest, from a literal reading of the comparison.[210] Whatever its importance in the history of ideas, this literal approach should not be attributed to the medieval and Renaissance proponents of the scheme studied above. Nor could they have allowed that all possible species had in fact been created by God. For example, Aquinas himself explicitly teaches that there are species or kinds of things of which God has knowledge but which he has not made and never will make. This being the case, it is difficult to see how Thomas could have taken literally the comparison of the hierarchy of actually existing species to the series of natural numbers.[211] Besides, the very notion of one species following another in a quasi-numerical series would suggest that the "higher" species included all in the just previous "lower" species except for the addition of one more defining note or specific difference. Of all the thinkers we surveyed, only Ficino and Achillini appeared to say anything like that. Perhaps it would be plausible to think of the Intelligences or angels in this fashion, since they differ primarily by a "more" or "less" in regard to the universality of their intelligible species, but it seems quite another thing to attempt to arrange the species of living and sentient things in such a quasi-numerical series. None of the medieval and Renaissance philosophers mentioned above seems to have attempted such an enterprise.

Finally, we must face the underlying presupposition of the conceptual scheme which we have traced from the late-thirteenth to the sixteenth century. It is, of course, the assumed validity of using what is essentially a spatial metaphor to explicate the concept of hierarchy. Although even a cursory examination of the vast literature on metaphor is out of place in this study, perhaps we can take as a working minimal definition that metaphor involves the transferring or transposing of language or terminology appropriate to one universe of discourse and the applying of it to another.[212] The use of imagery, analogy, similes, and metaphors to communicate or to evoke in some manner a conception of beings which are immaterial and therefore by definition beyond the sensible was hardly invented by medieval and Renaissance philosophers. Such techniques are already to be found in the works of Plato and Plotinus, both of whom are well aware that the images and metaphors which they use always fall short of the realities which they are trying to present.[213] The great danger in using metaphors, especially spatial metaphors, is, of course, that one all too easily forgets that they are metaphors and begins to treat them as literal "pictures" of that for which they stand.[214] In the case of the scheme, God would then be imagined as spatially located somewhere "up there" above the earth.[215] This negative point will allow us to introduce what I believe explains the power and the attraction of the scheme for so many thinkers from late antiquity down through the sixteenth century and even into the early modern period.

It is clear that "up" and "down" and "higher" and "lower" are terms not only for spatial location or direction but also for rankings in value or "dignity."[216] Though it may be too much to claim that the merging of the experience of spatial location and direction with evaluative judgment is something basic to human nature and to be found universally among mankind, European languages and Western culture do make such an identification.[217] Perhaps this is best brought out by the pair of terms "superior" and "inferior" which one finds not only in English but also in French, Italian, and so forth. Although it seems an exaggeration to claim that all language is metaphorical, surely it is in order to emphasize that such spatial language, which plays such an important role in our evaluative language, is metaphorical.[218] So too is it metaphorical to speak of God as infinitely "distant" from us, when the God under discussion is neither an anthropomorphic god sitting somewhere among the celestial spheres nor even Aristotle's Unmoved Mover, whose causality and "presence" are as it were limited to the outermost sphere. The power of the metaphor comes from its enabling us to picture the hierarchy, that is, to map it on a spatial background which rises from the lowest (both in place and in value) to the highest (again both in place and in value).[219] The great danger, as I have mentioned, is that the "picture" will be taken literally, a danger which many of the medieval and Renaissance philosophers studied above appeared eager to avoid. Such diverse thinkers as Aquinas, Scotus, and Pomponazzi, to name but three, were careful to indicate that the spatial or physical language which they were adopting was being transferred or transposed from another universe of discourse in order to be applied to beings which were neither in space nor physical. Since St. Thomas himself correctly spoke of such a transferral from spatial language as metaphorical, it is surprising that so few of his philosophical followers (apparently only Penido and Montagnes among recent writers) have clearly brought out the metaphorical use of such language as "infinite distance" or "approaching" to and "receding" from God.[220] After all, since the God of Thomas and Pomponazzi was an omnipresent God, they could hardly (at least if they kept their philosophical wits about them) take this language about "approaching" or "receding" literally. It is when we turn to someone like Achillini that we appear to have a thinker who let his imaginative picturing of the scheme get the better of his philosophical good sense.

The obvious question which remains is whether it is valid to use metaphors, let alone spatial metaphors, in metaphysics. One rejoinder to those rejecting all metaphors in metaphysics has been the attempt to work out a comparison between the use of such metaphors in philosophy (and in theology) and the use of models in science.[221] The drawback to this reply is that although models in science may contribute at least indirectly to some sort of experimental verification of a theory, metaphors in metaphysics are being used about entities which are not verifiable in any ordinary sense. The leading answer to this criticism seems to be that metaphors in philosophy and theology enable one to gain an insight or understanding not otherwise available, one comparable to that provided by the models of the scientist. The claim is also made that criteria are available to judge the metaphor or metaphysical "model" and the understanding which it evokes.[222] However, at this point I believe that the antagonists have neither proved nor disproved their rival outlooks, though I admittedly have little patience with hard-liners who dismiss out of hand the use of metaphor and even analogy in metaphysics.[223]

My own tentative position is that while the spatial metaphors which we have studied carry with them the intrinsic danger that they are so easily "pictured" or "imagined" that they are read literally and the metaphor is thus misunderstood, they do bring with them advantages discerned by some theories of metaphor. First of all, they encapsulate economically much which would have to be spelled out in tedious detail; secondly, they arrest attention by reason of the evaluative overtones of "height" and "depth"; and, thirdly, they communicate a structural analogy between spatial and mathematical relationships and the relational structure of a series of graded perfections. In regard to the last point, I might say that through the comparison of this structural similarity the metaphysician and the theologian are able to illuminate in vivid fashion their subject matters.[224] As to the second point, the introduction of evaluative overtones in a metaphysical scheme by reason of the language which it employs is hardly unique to medieval and Renaissance philosophy. What better way to underscore the ranking of matter than to put it "below" us or what better way to point to the infinity of God than to evoke the awe and respect which we have for great heights, or even for parents towering above us in childhood.[225] Metaphysical systems do in fact often appear to be built on root metaphors.[226] Since the experiences of height and depth or of approaching to and going away from a valued object are so very basic to human experience, it seems as plausible and defensible to construct a conceptual scheme on the basis of these experiences as it is to adopt either mechanism or process as the keys to the universe of being.[227] Nevertheless, certain disadvantages of the scheme must also be admitted. One might wonder, for instance, whether the scheme is in fact adequate to provide the conceptual framework for an omnipresent God. Does not the very notion of grades between the "lower" and the "higher" of the hierarchical series involve the concept of intermediary beings? That is to say, although the medieval and Renaissance proponents of the scheme whom we studied above insisted on a direct causal connection between God and each of his creatures, does not the very conceptual scheme which they borrowed from Neoplatonism make sense only if there are indeed intermediary causal beings between the lower creatures and that God? And finally one might question whether there is not a flaw in a conceptual scheme which makes much of grades and yet provides no real standard to grade a rainbow, a butterfly, or a snake as more or less like, and therefore closer to or more distant from, a God who is the One and the Beautiful. Whatever answer one's metaphysical predilections might dictate, it surely remains that the scheme is one of the most provocative and intriguing creations in the history of Western metaphysics.[228]

NOTES

1 See Arthur O. Lovejoy, *The Great Chain of Being: A Study in the History of an Idea* (Cambridge, Mass., 1936; repr. New York, 1960). For general surveys of the topic, see Lia Formigari, "Chain of Being," in *Dictionary of the History of Ideas* (New York, 1973), I 325–35; C. A. Patrides, "Hierarchy and Order," ibid., II 434–49; and Giorgio Giannini, "Ordine," in *Enciclopedia filosofica,* 2nd ed. (Florence, 1967), IV, cols. 1203–10. None of these latter three writers studies the scheme which we shall investigate in this essay; nor, indeed, does Lovejoy himself, although he constantly alludes to the gradations of all things upward from matter to God. In like fashion, he does not appear to mention Proclus anywhere in his book, despite the fact that many of the ideas which he is analyzing came down to the Western medieval thinkers through Proclus' *Elements of Theology.* It is surely curious that Lovejoy cites Plotinus alone (pp. 62–66) when sketching the concept of hierarchy, since Proclus makes the concept much more explicit in his own thought (see following note).

Throughout his book, Lovejoy emphasizes what he calls the "principle of plenitude," according to which "no genuine potentiality of being can remain unfulfilled." That is to say, the source of being must necessarily have brought into being all possible grades of being. He appears to consider (pp. 52–66) the concept of hierarchy or gradation to be a consequence of the principle of plenitude. Lovejoy argues (pp. 67–75) that Thomas Aquinas and other medievals actually accepted the principle of plenitude, and he insists that Aquinas refused to draw the conclusion which his own premisses demanded: namely, that God necessarily wills and creates all that is outside him. Although this is not the place to discuss Lovejoy's argument regarding Thomas, it is certainly appropriate to suggest that some of his textual analyses are open to dispute. (See the last paragraph of this note for a debate on the issue.)

Recently Jaako Hintikka has taken up what he considers to be the crucial philosophical issues in the concept of the "chain of being." This he does in his essay "Gaps in the Great Chain of Being: An Exercise in the Methodology of the History of Ideas," in *Proceedings and Addresses of the American Philosophical Association, 1975–1976*, 49 (1976), 22–38. He takes Aquinas' third way to rest on the principle of plenitude, thus reading the argument in a manner which would have surprised Thomas himself. Hintikka seems unacquainted with the Avicennan metaphysical doctrines which appear to lurk in the background of the *tertia via*, and he accepts somewhat uncritically Lovejoy's analysis of Thomas' metaphysics. (For a different analysis, see Joseph Owens, "'Cause of Necessity' in Aquinas' *Tertia Via*," *Mediaeval Studies*, 33 [1971], 21–45.) Indeed, one might wonder whether both Lovejoy and Hintikka have not read Aquinas through Leibnizian eyeglasses. In any case, despite some vague allusions to the adoption of the principle of plenitude by philosophers of the Late Middle Ages in general — and the thirteenth century in particular — Hintikka never once refers to the scheme which we shall investigate in this essay, a scheme which had an extraordinary influence on the concept of hierarchy found among the Aristotelian philosophers of that period. It should be added that Hintikka himself has advised caution in reading Lovejoy's book and has argued that Lovejoy was mistaken in attributing the principle of plenitude to Aristotle. See his "Leibniz on Plenitude, Relations, and the 'Reign of Law,'" in *Leibniz: A Collection of Critical Essays*, ed. Harry G. Frankfurt (Garden City, N.Y., 1972), pp. 155–90 at 156–57. Unfortunately, another of Hintikka's papers, "A. O. Lovejoy on Plenitude in Aristotle," *Ajatus*, 29 (1967), 5–11, was unavailable to me. For a severe attack on Hintikka's essay "Gaps in the Great Chain of Being," see Moltke S. Gram and Richard M. Martin, "The Perils of Plenitude: Hintikka contra Lovejoy," *Journal of the History of Ideas*, 41 (1980), 497–511. Their article appeared after I had completed the present essay.

Lovejoy's argument that Thomas and other medievals accepted the principle of plenitude and thereby adopted a conception of a necessitated God who had to create was the basis of a rather acerbic set of interchanges some thirty-five years ago. See, first of all, Anton C. Pegis' critique of Lovejoy in his *St. Thomas and the Greeks* (Milwaukee, 1943), pp. 21–49; this was followed by a second attack, this one by Henry Veatch, "A Note on the Metaphysical Grounds for Freedom, with Special Reference to Professor Lovejoy's Thesis in 'The Great Chain of Being,'" *Philosophy and Phenomenological Research*, 7, No. 3 (March 1947), 391–412. Lovejoy replied to Veatch with his "The Duality of the Thomistic Theology: A Reply to Mr. Veatch," ibid., 413–38. For their respective replies, see "A Rejoinder to Professor Lovejoy," ibid., No. 4 (June 1947), 662–25, and "Analogy and Contradiction: A Surrejoinder," ibid., 626–34. Pegis then entered the fray a second time with his "*Principale Volitum*: Some Notes on a Supposed Thomistic Contradiction," ibid., 9, No. 2 (August 1948), 51–70; Lovejoy's "Necessity and Self-Sufficiency in the Thomistic Theology: A Reply to President Pegis," *ibid.*, 71–88. Pegis replied with "Autonomy and Necessity: A Rejoinder to Professor Lovejoy," ibid., 89–97, and Lovejoy replied with "Comment on Mr. Pegis's Rejoinder," ibid., No. 2 (December 1948), 284–90. Pegis was allowed the final word in his "Postscript," ibid., 291–93.

For an excellent introduction to the background of the concept of the "chain of being" and its role in early-medieval philosophy, see Bernard McGinn, *The Golden Chain: A Study in the Theological Anthropology of Isaac of Stella* (Washington, D.C., 1972). McGinn rightly points to the Neoplatonic background of the "Great Return" doctrine and to the way in which it was adopted by Christian theology, which teaches creation from nothing by a free God (pp. 53–54). Also of note are his allusions to Philo and Middle Platonism, Plotinus, Proclus, and Dionysius (pp. 66–69), as well as his thoughtful and just critique of Lovejoy's presentation of medievals (pp. 75–80). I regret that McGinn's book escaped my notice while I was writing this essay, and I should like to thank John H. Newell, Jr., for bringing it to my attention. See also Edouard Jeauneau, "Macrobe, source du platonisme chartrain," *Studi medievali*, 3rd ser., 1 (1960), 3–24, esp. 9–15. Macrobius appears to be the immediate source of the application of Homer's "golden chain" to the hierarchy of being. See McGinn, *Golden Chain*, pp. 67–68. For the passage in Macrobius, see *Commentarii in Somnium Scipionis* 1.14.15, ed. J. Willis (Leipzig, 1970), p. 58. The influence which Macrobius had on the medieval "perception" of the world, especially the hierarchical conception in the "golden chain of Homer," has been underscored by Carolly Erickson, *The Medieval Vision: Essays in History and Perception* (New York, 1976), pp. 10–12. Possible sources for Macrobius' identification of Homer's golden chain with the descending hierarchy of being have been suggested by Ludwig Edelstein, "The Golden Chain of Homer," in the Lovejoy Festschrift, *Studies in Intellectual History* (Baltimore, 1953), pp. 48–66. He cites Plato's identification of the golden rope with the sun in *Theatetus* 153C–D and recalls that the sun is called the offspring of the Good, the strongest of bonds, in *Republic* 508B–C. It is in Middle Platonism that Edelstein appears to find the first development of the use of Homer's golden chain to symbolize the hierarchy of being. He argues that the metaphor passed into Neoplatonism through Iamblichus and then through Iamblichus or one of his followers into Macrobius. Its use by Proclus, who independently influenced the medieval philosophers, is also pointed out. Edelstein is arguing here against the thesis of an earlier scholar who had presented the development of Macrobius' hierarchical thought as derivative from Plotinus through Porphyry. See M. Schedler, *Die Philosophie des Macrobius und ihr Einfluss auf die Wissenschaft des christlichen Mittelalters*, Beiträge zur Geschichte der Philosophie des Mittelalters 13.1 (Münster, 1916), pp. 10–19. There is also discussion regarding Proclus, Homer, and the golden chain in Albert Wifstrand, "Den Gyllene Kedjan," *Lychnos* (1957–1958), 1–13 (English summary, pp. 12–13). The only philosophers analyzed in this essay who use the phrase "golden chain" (*catena aurea*) appear to be Albert the Great, Duns Scotus, and Marsilio Ficino. See nn. 25, 105, and 128. The phrase is also used by Meister Eckhart. See n. 105. For a good presentation of the role of the terms "nearness" and "distance" in twelfth-century discussions regarding metaphysical hierarchy and the destiny of the human soul, see Robert Javelet, *Image et ressemblance au douzième siècle de saint Anselme à Alain de Lille* I (Paris, 1967), pp. 129–34, 139–57. In this essay, I shall deliberately exclude these discussions from consideration, though I hope to examine them on another occasion.

2 William of Moerbeke translated the *Elementatio theologica* (*Elements of Theology*) and other writings of Proclus. See Martin Grabmann, *Mittelalterliches Geistesleben* II (Munich, 1936), pp. 413–23; idem, *Guglielmo di Moerbeke O.P., il traduttore delle opere di Aristotele* (Rome, 1946), pp. 147–60; Gérard Verbeke, "Guillaume de Moerbeke, traducteur de Proclus," *Revue Philosophique de Louvain*, 51 (1953), 349–73. Moerbeke's translation of the *Elementatio theologica* has been edited by C. Vansteenkiste in *Tijdschrift voor Philosophie*, 13 (1951), 263–302, 491–531.

The themes of the conceptual scheme of God as measure and of everything else gaining its grade by approaching him and receding from matter are to be found scattered throughout Proclus' *Elements of Theology*. I shall base myself here on Proclus, *The Elements of Theology*, ed. E. R. Dodds, 2nd ed. (Oxford, 1963), and shall abstract from Proclus' complicated triadic schemes and the various intermediaries in his hierarchy in order to concentrate on the essential themes of the scheme. The Good and the One are the First, the measure of all things (Prop. 92; see Prop. 117), the principle and cause of all things (Prop. 12; see Prop. 133). The One is simple and above all composition; the more divided and plural a thing is, the more remote it is from the One (Props. 59, 61; see Props. 5, 154, 203, 204). To participate is to fall short; consequently, what participates more in what is above it is higher in the hierarchy (Props. 9, 12, 25; see Prop. 89). The capacity of the participant determines the measure of its participation (Props. 142, 173). Being is not the same as the One but below it, just as Life and Intelligence are below Being (Props. 115, 138, 163) — this view would be altered by the *Liber de causis* and Dionysius. Everything which exists "primarily" in each order possesses the characteristic which it gives to all that exists "secondarily" in that order; it is also unique in that order (Props. 18, 22, 160; see Prop. 110). The originative cause of each series provides the entire series with its characteristic in such fashion that each member of the series has the characteristic by derivation and with a certain remission (Prop. 97). The nearer something is to the One or the Good, the more like it it will be. That is to say, it will be more powerful and more unitary and universal (Props. 60, 62, 126, 130; see Prop. 86). Every series or order begins from a monad and proceeds into a manifold (Prop. 21; see Props. 125, 145, 181). Proclus appears to assume a principle of continuity according to which there are no jumps or gaps in a series but intermediate principles which link the extreme terms (Props. 112, 132, 147, 175); this doctrine will reappear in the Pseudo-Dionysius. Another doctrine which reappears both in the *Liber de causis* and in Dionysius is Proclus' view that the Intelligences must know in different ways if they are to differ among themselves. The higher Intelligences possess the intelligible forms in a more universal way since they themselves are more united and like the One (Props. 170, 177; see also Props. 130, 167, 171, 176). Dodds makes important comments touching on the scheme. See his "Commentary," pp. 208, 215–16, 232–33, 248, 256, 261–62, 269–70, 277. The Great Return theme of *πρόοδος* and *ἐπιστροφή* is, of course, found throughout the *Elements*. See, for example, Prop. 32.

On the Great Return doctrine in Proclus, see Werner Beierwaltes, *Proklos: Gründzuge seiner Metaphysik* (Frankfurt, 1965), pp. 118–64; Paul Bastid, *Proclus et le crépuscule de la pensée grecque* (Paris, 1969), pp. 212–53, esp. pp. 221, 224–27, 235–37, 245–50; and A. C. Lloyd in *The Cambridge History of Later Greek and Early Medieval Philosophy*, ed. A. H. Armstrong (Cambridge, 1967), pp. 307–12. The doctrine is also discussed in Eduard Zeller and Rodolfo Mondolfo, *La filosofia dei greci nel suo sviluppo storico. III. La filosofia post-aristotelica* VI, ed. Giuseppe Martano (Florence, 1961), pp. 134–40, where differences between Plotinus and Proclus are pointed out (pp. 138–39). See also R. T. Wallis, *Neo-Platonism* (New York, 1972), pp. 130–34, 142–58. The more general scheme of ascent to and descent from the One, who measures the grade which a thing has, and of the mathematical-like series of things is alluded to by various scholars who have written on Proclus. See E. Vacherot, *Histoire critique de l'école d'Alexandrie* II (Paris, 1846; repr. Amsterdam, 1965), pp. 227–34, 242, 247–52, 270–80, 307–308; Laurence Jay Rosán, *The Philosophy of Proclus: The Final Phase of Ancient Thought* (New York, 1949), pp. 66–80, 101–105, 127, 134–35, 190–92; Giuseppe Martano, *Proclo di Atene: L'ultima voce speculativa del genio ellenico* (Naples, 1974), pp. 128–29, 155–58, which is a reprint of his *L'uomo e Dio in Proclo* (Naples,

1952); Jean Trouillard, "La Monadologie de Proclus," *Revue Philosophique de Louvain*, 57 (1959), 310–15; L. H. Grondijs, "L'Ame, le nous et les hénades dans la théologie de Proclus," *Mededelingen der Koninklijke Nederlandse Akademie van Wetenschappen*, Afd. Letterkunde, 23, No. 2 (Amsterdam, 1960), 29–42, esp. 30–32; Annick Charles, "Analogie et pensée sérielle chez Proclus," *Revue Internationale de Philosophie*, 23 (1969), 69–88, esp. 69–77; Nelly Tsouyopoulos, "Die Entdeckung der Struktur komparativer Begriffe in der Antike: Zur Begriffsbildung bei Aristoteles und Proklos," *Archiv für Begriffsgeschichte*, 14 (1970), 152–71. Oddly enough, there is nothing at all about the Great Return or the conceptual scheme of ascent–descent and resulting grades in H. F. Müller, *Dionysios, Proklos, Plotinos: Ein historischer Beitrag zur neoplatonischen Philosophie*, Beiträge zur Geschichte der Philosophie des Mittelalters, 20.3–4 (Münster, 1926). Indeed, the *Elements of Theology* is nowhere discussed in the work. However, the basic themes in Proclus which we have emphasized do receive some attention in Hampus Lyttkens, *The Analogy Between God and the World: An Investigation of Its Background and Interpretation of Its Use by Thomas of Aquino* (Uppsala, 1952), pp. 66–77. See also Klaus Kremer, *Die neuplatonische Seinsphilosophie und ihre Wirkung auf Thomas von Aquin* (Leiden, 1966), pp. 199–281 (Part II: "Plotins Seinsbegriff in der Philosophie des Proklos"), esp. pp. 208–33 ("Die logisch-ontologische Struktur des proklischen Weltbildes").

It would be impossible to discuss the concept of hierarchy in Proclus without some allusions to Plotinus. Jean Trouillard sees Proclus as transfiguring Plotinus by adding vertical series to horizontal levels and thereby attaching all directly to the One so that all things are to be considered modes of unity. See the introduction to his edition, *Proclos: Eléments de théologie* (Paris, 1965), p. 24; see also pp. 50–54. And in his "Commentary" on the *Elements of Theology*, Dodds notes how Proclus hardens into a "law" what is expressed more tentatively by Plotinus. (See his remarks in *The Elements*, p. xxi; see also pp. 193–94, 213–16 for discussion on emanation, procession, and continuity.) For a general contrast of Proclus and Plotinus on key doctrines, see Vacherot, *Histoire critique* II, pp. 380–83. For a fine presentation and analysis of Plotinus' doctrine on hierarchy, see the recent monograph of Dominic J. O'Meara, *Structures hiérarchiques dans la pensée de Plotin: Étude historique et interprétative*, Philosophia antiqua 27 (Leiden, 1975), esp. pp. 4–6, 44–47, 79–85, 89–90, 97–98, 101–108, 111, 114, 120–23, where reference is made to the concepts of series, "horizontal" levels and "vertical" series of levels, the "up" and the "down," and the notion of hierarchy in general. See Émile Bréhier, *The Philosophy of Plotinus*, trans. Joseph Thomas (Chicago, 1958), pp. 148–50, 160–61, 164–65; René Arnou, *Le Désir de Dieu dans la philosophie de Plotin*, 2nd ed. (Rome, 1967), pp. 117–19, 121–22, 168, 289–91; John N. Deck, *Nature, Contemplation, and the One: A Study in the Philosophy of Plotinus* (Toronto, 1967), pp. 35–36, 40–44, 62–63, 65, 82–92, 114–16. Dr. Salvatore R. C. Lilla has pointed out to me that the conceptual scheme of the "up" and the "down" with its respective measures of God and matter is only suggested in Plotinus but becomes stabilized in Syrianus, Iamblichus, Proclus, and Damascius. For some references to the scheme in Augustine and scholarly literature on the topic, see n. 185 below.

On possible intimations of certain aspects of the scheme in Plato and Aristotle, see Friedrich Solmsen, "Antecedents of Aristotle's Psychology and Scale of Being," *American Journal of Philology*, 76 (1955), 148–64 (repr. in his *Kleine Schriften* I [Hildesheim, 1968], pp. 588–604); Hans Wagner, "Die Schichtentheoreme bei Platon, Aristoteles und Plotin," *Studium Generale*, 9 (1956), 283–91; Nicolai Hartmann, *Kleinere Schriften* II (Berlin, 1957), pp. 164–91; Gonsalv Mainberger, *Die Seinsstufung als Methode und Metaphysik: Unterschungen über "mehr und weniger" als Grundlage zu einem möglichen Gottesbeweis bei Platon und Aristoteles* (Fribourg, 1959); Walter Bröcker, "Platons ontologischer Komparativ," *Hermes*, 97 (1959), 415–25; Heinz Happ, "Die *Scala naturae* und die Schichtung des Seelischen bei Aristoteles," in *Beiträge zur alten Geschichte und deren Nachleben: Festschrift für Franz Altheim* I, edd. Ruth Stiehl and Hans E. Stier (Berlin, 1969), pp. 220–44; Tsouyopoulos, "Die Entdeckung der Struktur komparativer Begriffe," cited above. Lovejoy (*Great Chain*, pp. 39–45) sees in Plato's doctrine of the Good in the *Republic* an intimation of the hierarchical scheme which became a tenet of later philosophy; he also speaks of a "vague tendency" in Plato to view the Ideas as hierarchically ordered (p. 58). Of special note regarding participation and degrees of reality in Plato is the important study of R. E. Allen, "Participation and Predication in Plato's Middle Dialogues," in *Studies in Plato's Metaphysics*, ed. R. E. Allen (New York, 1965), pp. 43–60, esp. 47–52, 56–58. See also Gregory Vlastos, "Degrees of Reality in Plato," in *New Essays on Plato and Aristotle*, ed. Renford Bambrough (New York, 1965), pp. 1–19. For some interesting and helpful remarks regarding Plato on the hierarchy of living things, see Leonardo Taran, *Academica: Plato, Philip of Opus, and the Pseudo-Platonic "Epinomis,"* Memoirs of the American Philosophical Society 107 (Philadelphia, 1975), pp. 42–47. Plato's and Aristotle's contributions to the notion of hierarchy have also been noted by W. K. C. Guthrie in "Man's Role in the Cosmos. Man the Microcosm: The Idea in Greek Thought and its Legacy to Europe," in *The Living Heritage of Greek Antiquity* (The Hague & Paris, 1967), pp. 62–65.

There can be no doubt, of course, that Aristotle did maintain a scale or hierarchy among living things. This is brought out in such standard accounts of his philosophy as those of W. David Ross, *Aristotle* (London & New York, 1964), pp. 114–17; D. J. Allan, *The Philosophy of Aristotle* (London, 1963), pp. 86–88; Ingemar Düring, *Aristoteles* (Heidelberg, 1966), pp. 522–32; and G. E. R. Lloyd, *Aristotle: The Growth and Structure of His Thought* (Cambridge, 1968), pp. 90–93, 105–106; as well as in Solmsen's classic study ("Antecedents") just cited. For an analysis of Aristotle's conception of hierarchy among living things, which emphasizes the differences in physical structure and functions of organisms, see Anthony Preus, *Science and Philosophy in Aristotle's Biological Works* (Hildesheim & New York, 1975), pp. 95–96, 133–43, 213–18. Friedrich Solmsen has presented an excellent account of the hierarchical structure of the heavens in terms of distance from the outermost sphere, and made some probing remarks about the manner in which God is related to that hierarchy. See his *Aristotle's System of the Physical World: A Comparison with His Predecessors* (Ithaca, N.Y., 1960), pp. 227, 237–40, 304–15, 396–98, 449–51, 454. Some like Ross (*Aristotle*, p. 153) have no difficulty in discerning in Aristotle a conception of a hierarchy extending from the lowest non-living beings up through the living things, the heavenly bodies, the Intelligences, and, finally, to God. Even if Aristotle did hold such a position, it is doubtful that he would have recognized the metaphysical schemes proposed by some of the medieval and Renaissance philosophers to provide what they believed was the necessary conceptual underpinning for that hierarchy.

Professor Solmsen has emphasized to me that Aristotle does not need a metaphysical scheme in order to rank the Intelligences, since the distance of their related spheres determines their ranking among themselves. Such an explanation will also be found among those medieval and Renaissance philosophers who refused to apply to the Intelligences any conceptual scheme based on a metaphysics of participation. This group would include among others John of Jandun, John Buridan, and Elia del Medigo. Solmsen has taken up Aristotle's hierarchical views once again in his essay "Platonic Values in Aristotle's Science," *Journal of the History of Ideas*, 39 (1978), 3–23. He underscores the solemnity of Aristotle's language about the cosmos itself: namely, that it is eternal, divine, immutable, and beautiful — language which Plato would use of the Form of the

Beautiful (pp. 12–13). While he shows that both Plato and Aristotle are concerned about order in the universe (pp. 13–16), he also insists that the ordering and correlation in the plant and animal realms which Aristotle presents as an unbroken chain of continuity among species and genera is barely to be found in the *Timaeus*, the outlook of which is essentially anthropocentric (pp. 16–17). He also points out that bodily structure and function orient Aristotle's ranking of living things (pp. 18–20). Finally, he shows how God is the highest of all beings, though necessarily finite according to Aristotle (pp. 22–23).

3 James A. Weisheipl, *Friar Thomas d'Aquino: His Life, Thought, and Work* (Garden City, N.Y., 1974), p. 44.

4 René Roques, *L'Univers dionysien: Structure hiérarchique du monde selon le Pseudo-Denys* (Paris, 1954), pp. 53–54.

5 Ibid., pp. 72–81. Roques's warning (p. 73*n*1) about the term "distance" deserves attention: "Il va sans dire que le terme d'*éloignement* doit être dépouillé de toute qualification spatiale. Il désigne seulement la dignité ontologique et le rang hiérarchique propres à chaque terme de la procession." There is a discussion of Dionysius' metaphysics of hierarchy in Ronald F. Hathaway, *Hierarchy and the Definition of Order in the "Letters" of Pseudo-Dionysius* (The Hague, 1969), pp. 37–60, but nothing regarding the scheme of ascent to – descent from the One as causing grades. Some attention is paid to the scheme by V. Lossky, "La Notion des 'Analogies' chez Denys le Pseudo-Aréopagite," *Archives d'Histoire Doctrinale et Littéraire du Moyen Age*, 5 (1930), 292–93, 298–300; Otto Semmelroth, "Gottes geeinte Vielheit: Zur Gotteslehre des Ps.-Dionysius Aréopagita," *Scholastik*, 25 (1950), 399–401; idem, "Die Lehre des Ps.-Dionysius Areopagita vom Aufstieg der Kreatur zum göttlichen Licht," ibid., 29 (1954), 24–52; Endre von Ivánka, "Zum Problem des christlichen Neuplatonismus. II. Inwieweit ist Pseudo-Dionysius Areopagita Neuplatoniker?" ibid., 31 (1956), 387–93. For some comparison and contrast of Dionysius with Proclus, see idem, "Der Aufbau der Schrift 'De divinis nominibus' des Ps.-Dionysius," ibid., 15 (1940), 390–91; idem, "'Teilhaben,' 'Hervorgang' und 'Hierarchie' bei Pseudo-Dionysius und bei Proklos (Der 'Neuplatonismus' des Pseudo-Dionysius)," in *Actes du XIe Congrès International de Philosophie* XII (Brussels, Amsterdam, & Louvain, 1953), pp. 153–58. In his "La Signification du Corpus Areopagiticum," *Recherches de Science Religieuse*, 36 (1949), 5–24, esp. 15–18, von Ivánka emphasizes the contrast between the Neoplatonic gradual procession by emanation and Dionysius' Christian view that, despite all the distinctions of rank and value of being, each existing thing is equal before God, the unique and direct creator of all things. He argues that although the external Neoplatonic scheme has been preserved in the Pseudo-Dionysius, its basic motifs have been changed: there is no emanation of one sphere of being from another; nor is a lower sphere illuminated by a higher one. On the contrary, there is a direct causal relation to God by each thing and immediate participation in him. See also the remarks regarding the Pseudo-Dionysius by F. Edward Cranz, "The Transmutation of Platonism in the Development of Nicolaus Cusanus and of Martin Luther," in *Nicolò Cusano agli inizi del mondo moderno* (Florence, 1970), pp. 76–77; and those by John M. Rist, "In Search of the Divine Denis," in *The Seed of Wisdom: Essays in Honour of T. J. Meek*, ed. W. S. McCullough (Toronto, 1964), pp. 137–38. There is a good, general outline of the Pseudo-Dionysius' hierarchic thought in Joseph Mazzeo, *Medieval Cultural Tradition in Dante's "Comedy"* (Ithaca, N.Y., 1960), pp. 13–31, but very little about the precise scheme which is being investigated here. The relation of hierarchy and human knowledge is studied by Alfredo Brontesi, *L'Incontro misterioso con Dio: Saggio sulla theologia affermativa e negativa nello Pseudo-Dionigi* (Brescia, 1970), pp. 61–115.

The question of the Pseudo-Dionysius' dependence on Neoplatonism, especially on Proclus, and on various Church Fathers has interested many scholars. For good summaries and evaluations of the literature on the subject, see Salvatore R. C. Lilla, "Alcune corrispondenze tra il 'De divinis nominibus' dello pseudo-Dionigi l'Areopagita e la tradizione platonica e patristica," in *Studi in memoria di Carlo Ascheri*, Differenze 9 (Urbino, 1970), 149–77, and Michele Schiavone, *Neoplatonismo e cristianismo nello Pseudo-Dionigi* (Milan, 1963), pp. 17–43. In an essay which was published after Lilla's study, I. P. Sheldon-Williams has argued that rather than being a student of Proclus, the Pseudo-Dionysius was his fellow-student under Syrianus. See Sheldon-Williams' "Henads and Angels: Proclus and the ps.-Dionysius," in *Studia Patristica* XI, ed. F. L. Cross, Texte und Untersuchungen zur Geschichte der Altchristlichen Literatur 108 (Berlin, 1972), pp. 65–71. The scheme which we are investigating in this study is nowhere alluded to by Sheldon-Williams. There is also no discussion of the scheme in the account of the Pseudo-Dionysius to be found in Pierre Duhem, *Le Système du monde* IV (Paris, 1916), pp. 347–64, but there are many allusions to it in Schiavone. See his *Neoplatonismo e cristianesimo*, pp. 76–90, 106, 115–20, 124–25, 128–33 (most important), 198–202, 215–20. The classic study on the Pseudo-Dionysius' dependence on Proclus and Neoplatonism is Hugo Koch, *Pseudo-Dionysius Areopagita in seinen Beziehungen zum Neuplatonismus und Mysterienwesen* (Mainz, 1900), Part I: "Pseudo-Dionysius und der Neuplatonismus" (pp. 9–91). See esp. pp. 27–34, 82–84 for discussion of the Great Return theme. Of special interest for the theme of this essay are the remarks of Anders Nygren, *Agape and Eros*, trans. Phllip S. Watson (New York, 1969), 576–93, regarding the Pseudo-Dionysius. Scattered through Nygren's book are many discussions touching on the scheme.

6 *De divinis nominibus* 2.10, 4.4 (PG 3:648c, 697c, 700A). On the Divine Ideas or Wishes, according to which the different orders are created and their limits assigned, see ibid. 5.8 (PG 3:824c). Cf. Roques, *L'Univers dionysien*, pp. 59–62, 86–87. On the availability of the Pseudo-Dionysius' writings, see H.-F. Dondaine, *Le Corpus dionysien de l'Université de Paris au XIII*[e] *siècle* (Rome, 1953).

7 *De divinis nominibus* 5.6 (PG 3:821A), and *De coelesti hierarchia* 8.2 (PG 3:240B–c), 10.1 (PG 3:272D–273B). Cf. Roques, *L'Univers dionysien*, pp. 96-98, 101–104; J. Durantel, *Saint Thomas et le Pseudo-Denis* (Paris, 1919), pp. 239–40, 246–47, 249–52. For a comparison of the use of the "nearness" and "distance" language by the Pseudo-Dionysius and Proclus, see Roques, *L'Univers dionysien*, p. 106*n*3. The spatial language is noticeably strong in the first text cited (PG 3:820–821A), where the division of a thing is in proportion to its distance from Unity itself. Intelligences are also held to differ in metaphysical rank according to the nature of their intelligible objects and intellectual operations (Roques, *L'Univers dionysien*, p. 87). We shall see various philosophers simultaneously put forth both explanations for the metaphysical hierarchy of the Intelligences: namely, distance from Unity itself and mode of cognition.

8 See Julien Peghaire, "*Intellectus*" *et* "*Ratio*" *selon s. Thomas d'Aquin* (Paris & Ottawa, 1936), pp. 179–80; Bernard Montagnes, "L'Axiome de continuité chez saint Thomas," *Revue des Sciences Philosophiques et Théologiques*, 52 (1968), 201–21, esp. 212–13; Jean Pépin, "Univers dionysien et univers augustinien," in *Aspects de la dialectique*, Recherches de Philosophie 2 (Paris, 1956), p. 206.

9 On the authorship of the *Liber* and the problem of who composed the Latin version, see Otto Bardenhewer, *Die pseudo-aristotelische Schrift Ueber das reine Gute bekannt unter dem Namen Liber de causis* (Freiburg, 1882), pp. 121–51; H. Bédoret, "L'Auteur et le traducteur du *Liber de causis*," *Revue Néoscolastique de Philosophie*, 41 (1938), 519–33; Manuel Alonso Alonso, "Notas sobre los traductores Toledanos Domingo Gundisalvo y

Juan Hispano," *Al-Andalus*, 8 (1943), 155–88; idem, "El 'Liber de causis,'" ibid., 9 (1944), 43–69; idem, "El 'Liber de causis primis et secundis et de fluxu qui consequitur eas,'" ibid., 419–40; idem, "Las fuentes literarias del 'Liber de causis,'" ibid., 10 (1945), 345–82; J. Doresse, "Les Sources du *Liber de causis,*" *Revue de l'Histoire des Religions*, 131 (1946), 234–38; Adriaan Pattin, "Over de schrijver en de vertaler van het *Liber de Causis,*" *Tijdschrift voor Philosophie*, 23 (1961), 323–33, 503–26.

For useful discussions regarding the doctrine of the work and related issues, see G. C. Anawati, "Prolégomènes à une nouvelle édition du *De causis* arabe," in *Mélanges Louis Massignon* I (Damascus, 1956), pp. 73–110, esp. pp. 85–92; Duhem, *Le Système du monde* IV, pp. 329–47; Leo Sweeney, "Research Difficulties in *Liber de causis,*" *The Modern Schoolman*, 36 (1959), 109–16; idem, "Doctrine of Creation in *Liber de causis,*" in *An Etienne Gilson Tribute*, ed. Charles J. O'Neil (Milwaukee, 1959), pp. 274–89; Henri-Dominique Saffrey, "L'État actuel des recherches sur le *Liber de causis* comme source de la métaphysique au Moyen Age," in *Die Metaphysik im Mittelalter: Ihr Ursprung und ihre Bedeutung*, ed. Paul Wilpert, Miscellanea Mediaevalia 2 (Berlin, 1963), pp. 267–81; William E. Carlo, *The Ultimate Reducibility of Essence to Existence in Existential Metaphysics* (The Hague, 1966), pp. 67–83; Cornelia J. De Vogel, "Some Reflections on the *Liber de causis,*" *Vivarium*, 4 (1966), 67–82.

Besides Bardenhewer's edition of the Latin *Liber*, there are two more recent editions. One is to be found in Robert Steele's edition of Roger Bacon's *Quaestiones supra Librum de causis.* See *Opera hactenus inedita Rogerii Baconis* XII (Oxford, 1935), pp. 161–87. For the other, see Adriaan Pattin, "*Le Liber de causis*: Edition établie à l'aide de 90 manuscrits avec introduction et notes," *Tijdschrift voor Filosofie*, 28 (1966), 90–203, which was published separately as a book with its own pagination: *Le Liber de causis*, ed. A. Pattin (Louvain, 1966). I shall cite both the Steele and Pattin editions, but shall use only the book form for the latter.

10 See the remarks of H. D. Saffrey in his edition of *Sancti Thomae de Aquino Super Librum de causis expositio* (Fribourg & Louvain, 1954), pp. xxix–xxxii.

11 *Liber de causis*, Prop. 9, pp. 169–70 ed. Steele, pp. 66–70 ed. Pattin; Prop. 16, p. 174 ed. Steele, pp. 80–83 ed. Pattin; Prop. 17, p. 175 ed. Steele, pp. 83–85 ed. Pattin; Prop. 20, p. 177 ed. Steele, pp. 89–90 ed. Pattin; Prop. 21, p. 178 ed. Steele, pp. 92–93 ed. Pattin; Prop. 32, p. 187 ed. Steele, p. 114 ed. Pattin. Cf. Carlo, *Ultimate Reducibility*, pp. 75–80.

12 *Liber de causis*, Prop. 17, p. 175 ed. Steele, pp. 83–85 ed. Pattin.

13 Ibid., Prop. 24, p. 180 ed. Steele, pp. 97–99 ed. Pattin. God (*ens primum*) is called the "measure" of all things, intelligible and sensible, in Prop. 16 (p. 174 ed. Steele, p. 82 ed. Pattin): "Ens ergo primum est mensura entium primorum intelligibilium et entium secundorum sensibilium, scilicet quia ipsum est quod creavit entia et mensuravit ea mensura convenienti omni enti." Cf. Sweeney, "Doctrine of Creation," esp. pp. 278–79.

14 *Liber de causis*, Prop. 20, p. 177 ed. Steele, pp. 89–90 ed. Pattin.

15 Ibid. Prop. 10, pp. 170–71 ed. Steele, pp. 70–72 ed. Pattin. For discussion of the isomorphism between the metaphysical scale of the Intelligences and their respective intelligible forms, see Duhem, *Le Système du monde* IV, pp. 335–36.

16 *Super Dionysii De divinis nominibus*, ed. Paul Simon, *Opera omnia* XXXVII.1 (Aschendorff, 1972), ch. 1, pp. 32^2–33^1. See also ch. 1, pp. 14^1–15^2; ch. 4, pp. 183^2–194^1; ch. 5, p. 321^1; ch. 9, p. 387^2. There is almost no reference to the scheme in Albert's commentary on the Pseudo-Dionysius' *Mystical Theology*, probably written before 1248 while Albert was still teaching at Paris. But see *Super Dionysii Mysticam theologiam et epistulas*, ed. P. Simon, *Opera omnia*, XXXVII.2 (Aschendorff, 1978), ch. 2, p. 467, lines 77–83, and ch. 3, p. 471, lines 28–36.

17 *Super Dionysii De divinis nominibus*, ch. 4, pp. 130^2, 131^2. See also pp. 118^2, 120^2; ch. 5, p. 172^1; ch. 6, p. 331^1; ch. 7, p. 339^1.

18 Ibid., ch. 7, p. 356^2; ch. 10, p. 448^1; ch. 5, p. 315^2. Participating things exist only as they have existence (*habent esse*). Their being is a certain mode of existing (*aliquis modus essendi*). See p. 316^2.

19 Ibid., ch. 5, pp. 307^1–309^1. See also ch. 2, p. 98^1. On *gradus*, see ch. 4, p. 172^1. See p. 308, line 80: *gradus analogiae*. Simon gives *intentionem* in his edition (p. 308, line 8).

20 Ibid., ch. 5, p. 322^1.

21 Ibid., ch. 5, p. 312^1.

22 Ibid., ch. 4, pp. 170$^{1-2}$, 180^2; ch. 7, pp. 339^1, 354^2. Albert makes use of the *Liber de causis* in these passages.

23 *De causis et processu universitatis*, ed. A. Borgnet, in *Opera omnia* X (Paris, 1891), II, tr. 3, chs. 4–5, pp. 553^1–554^1. See also II, tr. 1, ch. 8, p. 447^2. On the composition of *esse* and *quod est* in everything outside God, see II, tr. 1, ch. 15, p. 459^2; tr. 4, ch. 5, p. 577^1. On Albert's use of Proclus and the *Liber de causis*, see Maria Feigl, "Albert der Grosse und die arabische Philosophie: Eine Studie zu den Quellen seines Kommentars zum *Liber de causis*," *Philosophisches Jahrbuch*, 63 (1955), 131–50; Rudolf Kaiser, "Die Benutzung proklischer Schriften durch Albert den Grossen," *Archiv für Geschichte der Philosophie*, 45 (1963), 1–22; idem, "Versuch einer Datierung der Schrift Alberts des Grossen *De causis et processu universitatis*," ibid., 125–36. See also Clemens Baeumker, *Witelo*, Beiträge zur Geschichte der Philosophie des Mittelalters, 3.2 (Münster, 1908), pp. 407–13. There are some uses of the scheme in the *Liber de intelligentiis*, ed. C. Baeumker, ibid., pp. 2, 8, 10, 15, 64–65, 70. Cf. Baeumker's remarks, pp. 351–52, 527–29, 597–98. Baeumker later accepted that the *Liber de intelligentiis* had been composed before the time of Witelo, and he demonstrated that it had been authored by an "Adam pulchra mulier." See his "Zur Frage nach Abfassungszeit und Verfasser des irrtümlich Witelo zugeschriebenen *Liber de intelligentiis*," in *Miscellanea Ehrle* I, Studi e Testi 37 (Vatican City, 1924), pp. 87–102. The author was in fact a secular master at Paris who composed the work sometime between 1210 and 1240, and relied heavily on the Pseudo-Dionysius. See Palemon Glorieux, "Adam Pulchrae Mulieris," *New Catholic Encyclopedia* (New York, 1967) I 118.

The fourteenth-century German Dominican Berthold of Moosburg wrote a commentary on Proclus' *Elements of Theology* which shows the continued interest in Neoplatonic thought among German Dominicans. See *Expositio elementationis theologicae*, Cod. Vat. Lat. 2192. This work shows the influence of the Pseudo-Dionysius, whose views Berthold attempts to reconcile with Augustine's, of Albert, and of Dietrich of Freiberg, who was his teacher. For a discussion of Berthold's use of these sources and a comparison of his thought with Eckhart's and Cusanus', see Willehad Eckert, "Berthold von Moosburg O.P., Ein Vertreter der Einheitsmetaphysik im Spätmittelalter," *Philosophisches Jahrbuch*, 65 (1957), 120–33, esp. 127–33. For general remarks on the structure, method, and purpose of Berthold's commentary, see Barbara De Mottoni Faes, "Il commento di Bertoldo di Moosburg all'*Elementatio theologica* di Proclo: Edizione delle proposizioni riguardanti il tempo e l'eternità," *Studi medievali*, 12 (1971), 417–61 at 423–26. Also of note is the same author's "Il problema della luce nel commento di Bertoldo di Moosburg all'*Elementatio theologica* di Proclo," ibid., 16 (1975), 325–52, in which she compares Berthold and Ulrich of Strasburg (pp. 349–52). My own study of the Vatican manuscript has revealed the not surprising fact that in his discussions of the text of Proclus' *Elements* Berthold frequently uses the conceptual scheme which we have been tracing. See, for example, Prop. 22, fols. 55rb–56ra; Prop. 57, fol. 108rb; Prop. 58, fols. 110rb–111ra; Prop. 59, fol. 112^{ra-b}; Prop. 61, fols. 113vb–114ra; Prop. 117, fol. 178^{ra-b}; Prop. 126, fol. 195^{ra-b}.

But on occasion, where the discussion would seem to call for a precise statement of the scheme, either it is not given, or, if given, not clearly set forth. See, for example, Prop. 39, fol. 85va, and Prop. 132, fols. 202vb–203va. It should perhaps be recalled that the work is a commentary, and it is thus doubly unfortunate that Berthold's now lost *Summa theologiae* is not available for study and comparison regarding the use of the scheme. For Albert's influence on German medieval thought, see Grabmann, *Mittelalterliches Geistesleben* II, pp. 324–412. Grabmann should also be consulted for his long study on Ulrich of Strasburg and the Albertist school. See *Mittelalterliches Geistesleben* I (Munich, 1926), pp. 147–221. Grabmann also authored a brief but highly informative essay on the influence of Moerbeke's translations of Proclus on medieval thought. See ibid. II, pp. 413–23. There are references to Albert, Ulrich, and Berthold (pp. 419–21), among others. Etienne Gilson presents a succinct and helpful survey regarding the Albertist and Neoplatonic strand in medieval German philosophy. See his *History of Christian Philosophy in the Middle Ages*, pp. 431–46. Limitations of space prevent me from discussing it further in this study. For a detailed summary of the scholarly literature on the German Dominicans and their Neoplatonic leanings, see Ruedi Imbach, "Le (Néo-)platonisme médiéval, Proclus latin, et l'école dominicaine allemande," *Revue de Théologie et de Philosophie*, 110 (1978), 427–48.

24 *De causis et processu universitatis*, II, tr. 2, ch. 6, p. 488^1.

25 Ibid., II, tr. 2, ch. 15, pp. 500^2–501^1; ch. 22, p. 512^{1-2}; ch. 24, pp. 514^2–515^1. For specific allusion to the concept of "distance" in Dionysius and the "Aristotelians," see I, tr. 1, ch. 10, p. 382^2. Cf. Bernhard Geyer, "Albertus Magnus und die Entwicklung der scholastischen Metaphysik," in *Die Metaphysik im Mittelalter*, ed. Wilpert, pp. 9–10. See also Albert's *Commentarium in primum Sententiarum*, ed. A. Borgnet, in *Opera omnia* XV (Paris, 1893), d. 8, A, a. 7–8, pp. 228–30 for references to God as the measure and to the doctrine of *accessus* and *recessus*. Appeal is made to Aristotle, Dionysius, and the *Liber de causis*. In the *Metaphysica: Libri VI–XIII*, ed. Bernhard Geyer, in *Opera omnia* XIV.2 (Aschendorff, 1964), X, tr. 1, ch. 3, Albert explains how one (*unum*) is the measure in discrete quantity as it is an indivisible and a minimum; and he goes on to say that the measure of each genus of being is a one (pp. 434–35). In chapter 5 (pp. 437–38), he takes up three different accounts regarding the "first" (*primum*) which measures everything else in the genus of substance: (1) that it is the First Mover; (2) that it is the nature of the most general (*natura generalissimi*); and (3) that it is prime matter. Position (1) is identified with Averroës and his followers, who say that the First Cause is the measure of being. This position maintains that all secondary beings are in their respective grade of being through their approach to the First Being (*in gradu entitatis per aliquem accessum ad primum*). After examining all three accounts, Albert opts for that of Averroës. He is careful to point out that each thing can be said to have a "quantity" (*quantitas*), at least by a similitude (*similitudo*), according to its approach (*accessus*) to or receding (*recessus*) from the First and True Being (*ens primum et verum*), that is, the First Intellect from which each being proceeds (*procedit*). All these measured beings (*mensurata entia*) have more distant or closer being (*entitas longinquior vel propinquior*) in regard to that First Intellect, and they all are measured by that First and wholly Simple Being (*mensuratur a primo penitus simplici*). It should be added here that Albert actually uses the phrase "golden chain" (*catena aurea*) on at least two occasions in his writings. He attributes the term to Pythagoras. See *De causis et processu universitatis*, II, tr. 5, ch. 19, p. 612; *De anima*, ed. Clemens Stroick, *Opera omnia* VII.1 (Aschendorff, 1968), II, tr. 2, ch. 8, p. 158.

26 *Commentum in primum librum Sententiarum*, Prol., q. 1, a. 2, ad 2, and d. 8, q. 4, a. 1, in *Opera omnia* VII (Paris, 1873), pp. 6, 115–16. On the dating of the works of St. Thomas,

see I. T. Eschmann, "A Catalogue of St. Thomas's Works," in Etienne Gilson, *The Christian Philosophy of St. Thomas Aquinas*, trans. L. K. Shook (New York, 1956), pp. 381–439; Weisheipl, *Friar Thomas d'Aquino*, pp. 355–405.

27 *Commentum in primum librum Sententiarum*, d. 8, q. 4, a. 2, ad 3, p. 118. The fundamental work on God as "measure" according to Aquinas remains Gaston Isaye, *La Théorie de la mesure et l'existence*, Archives de Philosophie 16.1 (Paris, 1940). See esp. pp. 8–16 ("La mesure et le magis et minus") and 49–71 ("Dieu, mesure de toutes choses"). Also important are the studies of Vincent de Couesnongle, "La Causalité du maximum: L'Utilisation par saint Thomas d'un passage d'Aristote," *Revue des Sciences Philosophiques et Théologiques*, 38 (1954), 433–44; "La Causalité du maximum: Pourquoi saint Thomas a-t-il mal cité Aristote?" ibid., 658–80; "Mesure et causalité dans la '*quarta via*,'" *Revue Thomiste*, 58 (1958), 55–75, 244–84. St. Thomas frequently insists that God is not really a member of any genus. Yet even so committed a Thomist as Ralph M. McInerny observes: "Despite the unequivocal nature of such statements, St. Thomas sometimes speaks as if God were in the same genus as the creature. The most striking instance of this is found in the *quarta via*, a proof of God's existence drawn from the hierarchy in reality. . . . God is here spoken of as the maximum in the genus of being, something which seemingly involves two things elsewhere emphatically rejected by St. Thomas: that God is in a genus and that being is a genus." McInerny's way out of this impasse is to argue that "genus" is to be understood here *largo modo*, that is, in an extended or analogous sense. See his *The Logic of Analogy: An Interpretation of St. Thomas* (The Hague, 1971), pp. 134–35. It is surprising that McInerny does not mention the doctrine of participation at this point in his book. As we shall see below, Marsilio Ficino at times appears to consider God as within a genus since he measures all within that genus.

28 *Commentum in primum librum Sententiarum*, d. 8, q. 5, a. 1, p. 120. Cf. Louis B. Geiger, *La Participation dans la philosophie de s. Thomas d'Aquin*, 2nd ed. (Paris, 1953), p. 210.

29 *Commentum in primum librum Sententiarum*, d. 24, q. 1, a. 1, p. 300. Thomas cites Boethius and *Metaphysics* II, 1 (993B24–32) to argue that the highest and simplest in each genus is the principle and measure of all else in the genus. The general line of argument suggests that he has also been influenced by Averroës, *Commentaria in Aristotelis Metaphysicorum libros*, II, comm. 4, in *Aristotelis opera cum Averrois commentariis* VIII (Venice, 1562), fol. 30rb. Thomas goes on to explain that the unity involved is the unity convertible with being and not the unity which is the principle of number (ad 1). He also speaks of a community of analogy between God and the creature inasmuch as creatures imitate him as much as possible (ad 4).

30 *Commentum in secundum librum Sententiarum*, d. 3, q. 1, a. 3, in *Opera omnia* VIII (Paris, 1873), p. 50. Cf. Geiger, *La Participation*, p. 246*n*3. Battista Mondin also cites this passage in his *St. Thomas Aquinas' Philosophy in the Commentary to the Sentences* (The Hague, 1975), pp. 64–65; it is regrettable that he pays no more attention than this to the scheme which we are studying here. In II, d. 3, q. 1, a. 5, pp. 53–54, Thomas discerns a specific variation in angels' likeness to God, since they can approach more and less to participating in the divine being. They are different species of the same genus, just as there are different species of numbers all related to number. And in II, d. 3, q. 3, a. 2, pp. 61–62, where he cites both Dionysius and the *Liber de causis*, Thomas puts angels in a scale according to the number and universality of their intelligible species.

31 *De ente et essentia* 4, in *Le "De ente et essentia" de s. Thomas d'Aquin*, ed. M.-D. Roland-Gosselin (Paris, 1948), pp. 33, 36–37.

32 Ibid., 5, p. 41.

33 Ibid., 6, p. 44. See the studies of de Couesnongle cited in n. 27 and the Averroës text cited in n. 29. The latter can also be found in Averroës, *In Aristotelis librum II (α) Metaphysicorum commentarius*, ed. Gion Darms (Fribourg, 1966), pp. 58–59. For Thomas' commentary on the passage, see his *In duodecim libros Metaphysicorum Aristotelis expositio*, II, lect. 2, nos. 292–98, edd. M.-R. Cathala and R. M. Spiazzi (Turin & Rome, 1971), pp. 84–85.

34 *Quaestiones disputatae De veritate*, q. 2, a. 3, ad 16, and a. 11, ad 4; q. 23, a. 7, c. and ad 9, in *Quaestiones disputatae* I, ed. R. Spiazzi (Turin, 1953), pp. 34, 51, 427–29. In the second and third of these texts, Thomas speaks of the likeness (*similitudo*) between God and a creature as a *similitudo proportionalitatis* according to which there is no proportion in the strict sense as there is between two quantities which are compared to one another. The finite and infinite are thus not proportionate (*proportionata*) to one another but proportionable (*proportionabilia*), just as four is proportionate to two, since it is twice two, but four and six are proportionable since six is to three as four is to two. Thomas remarks in q. 23, a. 7, ad 11 that the word "proportion" (*proportio*) has been transferred (*translatum*) from its strict sense to signify any relationship of one thing to another. Earlier, in q. 4, a. 6, p. 86, he cited Dionysius' remark that caused things fall short (*deficiunt*) of their causes, and refers to this as the distance (*distantia*) of cause to the caused.

On the transfer of *proportio* from quantitative relationships to any relationship of one thing to another and on the whole question of analogy, see George P. Klubertanz, *St. Thomas on Analogy* (Chicago, 1960), pp. 27, 31–32, 46–49, 83–84, 88–92; Bernard Montagnes, *La Doctrine de l'analogie de l'être d'après saint Thomas d'Aquin*, Philosophes médiévaux 6 (Louvain & Paris, 1963), pp. 75–89; James F. Anderson, *The Bond of Being* (Saint Louis, Mo., 1944), pp. 16, 168, 295. For some interesting and perceptive remarks on such transfers and whether they are to be classified as analogical or metaphorical, see Ralph McInerny, *Studies in Analogy* (The Hague, 1968), pp. 39–44, 78–84, esp. pp. 82, 84. That such a transfer had occurred in regard to distance was recognized by Goclenius (Rudolph Goeckel) in his article on "Distantia," in *Lexicon philosophicum* I (Frankfurt, 1613; repr. Hildesheim, 1964), p. 549: "Distantia proprie accipitur pro intercapedine spatii, ut cum dico longe distare coelum a terra. Deinde pro differentia vel dissimilitudine, ut cum dico asinum longius distare a Deo, id est minus ad Deum appropinquare gradu perfectionis. . . ." In saying this, Goclenius may very well have had Aquinas, among others, in mind. Thomas de Vio (Cardinal Cajetan) distinguishes types of "distance" in his *Commentaria in primam partem Summae theologiae*, in Thomas Aquinas, *Opera omnia* IV (Rome, 1888), p. 85, no. 16, where he is commenting on I, q. 8, a. 1, ad 3 (cited below in n. 44). However, he in no way brings out the significance of the metaphorical usage. At best he distinguishes "distance of nature" (*distantia naturalis*), which involves dissimilarity of nature (*dissimilitudo naturae*), from "distance of position" (*distantia situalis*).

35 *Quaestiones disputatae De veritate*, I, q. 21, a. 1, c., p. 376.

36 *Quaestiones disputatae De potentia Dei*, q. 3, a. 5, in *Quaestiones disputatae* II, edd. P. Bazzi et al. (Turin, 1953), p. 49.

37 Ibid., q. 7, a. 3, c. and ad 7, pp. 193–94.

38 *Quaestio disputata De spiritualibus creaturis*, q. 1, a. 1, c. and ad 8, in ibid, pp. 370–71. See also a. 8, c. and ad 8–10 and 18, pp. 398–99, where he again invokes the comparison of the order among species of things to that among the species of numbers.

39 *Quaestiones De anima*, q. 7, c. and ad 5, ed. James H. Robb (Toronto, 1968), pp. 119–25. It should be emphasized, however, that although Thomas states that earth is the lowest and fire the highest among the elements, he names no highest or lowest among the plants, and he makes no attempt to rank the animals other than to say that man is the

highest (pp. 122–23). For a discussion of all grades of being below God, see Hans Meyer, *Thomas von Aquin: Sein System und seine geistesgeschichtliche Stellung*, 2nd ed. (Paderborn, 1961), pp. 186–290. Meyer makes helpful remarks about the order of the universe and God its creator (pp. 368–92) and about order in the world as a whole (pp. 381–92). In his *Commentaria in Aristotelis libros De coelo et mundo*, II, lect. 18, in *Opera omnia* XXIII (Paris, 1875), p. 166, Thomas discerns five grades (*gradus*) in the order of things (*in ordine rerum*) which clearly do not match species or genera. Basing his division on the number of motions which a thing needs to attain its end, he sees God as in the first grade, since he needs no action to attain his end, and man in the third grade. The animals and plants as a group make up the fourth grade, while lifeless things, lacking their own motion, constitute the fifth grade. In like fashion, he distinguishes the orders of the heavenly bodies according to the number of their motions (p. 167). He also observes that the permanence of the separate substances is approximated most closely by the first heaven and to a lesser degree by the lower heavenly bodies (pp. 167–68). See also II, lect. 15, p. 157, where the scale of dignity of the heavenly bodies is explained in terms of the receding (*recedere*) and approaching (*appropinquare*) language. It should be noted that Thomas also alludes to the scheme of the *platonici* according to which the orders (*ordines*) of higher and lower intellects are distinguished by the former's likeness and closeness to God (*similitudo et propinquitas ad deum*) and the latter's distance from him (*distantia ad deum*). See II, lect. 4, p. 116. On the various meanings of *ordo* for Thomas, especially that of rank, see Brian Coffey, "The Notion of Order According to St. Thomas Aquinas," *The Modern Schoolman*, 27 (1949), 16–18. The connection of order, grades, and measure in Thomas, Albert, Bonaventure, and Augustine is discussed by Hermann Krings, *Ordo: Philosophisch-historische Grundlegung einer abendländischen Idee* (Halle, 1941), pp. 71–77, 88–92. On Thomas' doctrine regarding the heavenly bodies, see the comprehensive study of Thomas Litt, *Les Corps célestes dans l'univers de saint Thomas d'Aquin*, Philosophes médiévaux 7 (Louvain & Paris, 1963).

40 *Commentum in primum librum Sententiarum*, d. 2, divisio textus, p. 31. See Geiger, *La Participation*, pp. 224–27. On the influence of the Great Return theme (*exitus–reditus*) and other key Neoplatonic doctrines on St. Thomas and the structure of his works, especially the *Summa theologiae*, see Durantel, *Saint Thomas et le Pseudo-Denis*, esp. pp. 235–37; Gilson, *Christian Philosophy of St. Thomas Aquinas*, pp. 136–41, 153–63, 168–73; M.-D. Chenu, "Le Plan de la Somme théologique de saint Thomas," *Revue Thomiste*, 45 (1939), 93–107, esp. 97–100, 102–105; idem, *Introduction to the Study of Saint Thomas Aquinas*, trans. A.-M. Landry and D. Hughes (Chicago, 1964), pp. 186–87, 273–75, 304–307, 309–13; Cornelio Fabro, *La nozione metafisica di partecipazione secondo s. Tommaso d'Aquino*, 2nd ed. (Turin, 1950), pp. 70–74, 86–98, 107–13, 142–44, 164–68, 192–98; idem, *Participation et causalité* (Louvain & Paris, 1961), pp. 179–244; George Lindbeck, "Participation and Existence in the Interpretation of St. Thomas Aquinas," *Franciscan Studies*, 17 (1957), 111, 115; Nygren, *Agape and Eros*, 189*n*1. For a presentation and rejection of Chenu's thesis that the Neoplatonic doctrine of the Great Return (*exitus–reditus*) inspired the structure of Thomas' *Summa*, see Ghislain Lafont, *Structures et methode dans la Somme théologique de saint Thomas d'Aquin* (Bruges & Paris, 1961), pp. 18–22, 28–29. There appears to be no mention of Neoplatonism in Richard Heinzmann's study "Der Plan der 'Summa Theologiae' des Thomas von Aquin in der Tradition der frühscholastischen Systembildung," in *Thomas von Aquino*, ed. W. P. Eckert (Mainz, 1974), pp. 455–69. However, see 455*n*1 for a lengthy bibliography on the topic of the *Summa*'s structure.

The question of the relation of Thomas' doctrine of *esse* to the concept of being in Neoplatonism has received special attention from Kremer, *Die neuplatonische Seinsphi-*

losophie und ihre Wirkung auf Thomas von Aquin; A. Solignac, "La Doctrine de l'*esse* chez saint Thomas: est-elle d'origine neoplatonicienne? A propos d'un livre recent," *Archives de Philosophie*, 30 (1967), 439–52; Cornelio Fabro, *Tomismo e pensiero moderno* (Rome, 1969), pp. 435–60; idem, "Platonism, Neo-Platonism, and Thomism: Convergencies and Divergencies," *The New Scholasticism*, 44 (1970), 69–100.

Besides the books of Geiger and Fabro on participation, other fundamental monographs are those of Arthur Little, *The Platonic Heritage of Thomism* (Dublin, 1949) and Kurt Krenn, *Vermittlung und Differenz? Vom Sinn des Seins in der Befindlichkeit der Partizipation beim hl. Thomas von Aquin* (Rome, 1962). The bibliography on Thomas' doctrine of participation also includes many articles. See, for example, the important studies of W. Norris Clarke, S.J.: "The Limitation of Act by Potency: Aristotelianism or Neoplatonism," *The New Scholasticism*, 26 (1952), 167–94; "The Meaning of Participation in St. Thomas," *Proceedings of the American Catholic Philosophical Association*, 26 (1952), 147–57; "The Platonic Heritage of Thomism," *The Review of Metaphysics*, 8 (1954), 105–24. It is to be regretted that Father Clarke pays so little attention to the scheme which we are studying here. Among the more interesting recent articles on participation are H. H. Berger, "Participations-gedanke im Metaphysik-Kommentar des Thomas von Aquin," *Vivarium*, 1 (1965), 115–40, and Pierre-Ceslas Courtès, "Participation et contingence selon saint Thomas d'Aquin," *Revue Thomiste*, 69 (1969), 201–35, esp. 210–15, which contains many references to Plato. For further bibliography on Thomas' doctrine of participation, see Kremer, *Die neuplatonische Seinsphilosophie*, pp. 478–87; Paul O. Kristeller, *Medieval Aspects of Renaissance Learning*, trans. and ed. Edward P. Mahoney (Durham, N.C., 1974), p. 36*n*12.

Unfortunately, I was able to consult Pierre Faucon's ambitious recent study, *Aspects néoplatoniciens de la doctrine de saint Thomas d'Aquin* (Lille & Paris, 1975) only after this essay was close to completion. Although there is no mention of the conceptual scheme in a section entitled "Contributions néoplatoniciennes à la formation de l'ontologie thomiste" (pp. 427–38), there are allusions to the scheme throughout the book. See, for example, pp. 125–28, 142–43, 146–49, 187–93, 469–70, 473–74, 488–89 (and n. 275), 540, 543–46, 602*n*15, 606*n*30, and 619–21. It is regrettable that Faucon did not present a specific and separate analysis of the conceptual scheme and of Thomas' adoption of it in the context of his own metaphysics, for it is certainly one of the most important influences on his concept of order and hierarchy. Nonetheless, Faucon's book remains a useful addition to the literature on St. Thomas and will no doubt be discussed for some time to come by scholars concerned with Thomist metaphysics.

In his thoughtful and provocative book *The Five Ways: St. Thomas Aquinas's Proofs for God's Existence* (London, 1969), Anthony Kenny attempts to establish what Aquinas meant by the steps in each of the five ways, adding that he will seek illumination in parallel passages of Thomas' writings (p. 1). Kenny's basic tactic in the chapter on the fourth way (pp. 70–95) is to see the proof in terms of Plato's theory of Forms. Though he mentions the concepts of gradation and measure, which are central to the fourth way, he seems unaware of the conceptual scheme which we have been studying, yet it surely is in the background of the texts cited (pp. 80–81). Kenny is open to some criticism in regard to his unqualified assimilation of Thomas' doctrine of participation to Plato's (see esp. pp. 79–82, 94–95). Moreover, when explicating the fourth way, he makes no reference to Proclus, the Pseudo-Dionysius, Anselm, or others; nor does he set forth in sufficient detail Thomas' own doctrine of participation. On the other hand, Kenny should certainly be praised for having pointed out the serious problems engendered by the concept of paradigms or standards (p. 74) and the attempt to grade things according to a scale (pp. 80–81).

Inasmuch as the conceptual scheme itself rests on a concept of paradigm and does grade things in a scale, it obviously is open to the difficulties which Kenny underlines. See nn. 117, 208 below.

41 *Summa contra gentiles* I (Paris, 1959), ch. 28, pp. 224–26. Cf. I, ch. 42, p. 262. In II, ch. 12, Aquinas takes God to be the measure of our knowledge. See *Summa contra gentiles* II (Paris, 1954), ch. 12, p. 36. See also II, ch. 15, pp. 40–44.

42 Ibid., I, ch. 29, pp. 228–30. Thomas still insists that God is not in a genus. See I, ch. 25, pp. 212–14, and ch. 43, p. 266.

43 The classic work on the influence of Dionysius remains Durantel's *Saint Thomas et le Pseudo-Denis.* Some indications of Dionysius' influence on Thomas' views on man as in the middle of the hierarchy of being, which itself involves a pyramid and the concept of *magis–minus,* can be found in Amédée de Silva Tarouca, "L'Idée d'ordre dans la philosophie de saint Thomas d'Aquin," *Revue Néoscolastique de Philosophie,* 40 (1937), 369, 372–73. The concept of *magis–minus* in St. Thomas has received special attention in two articles by Hadrianus Borak, "De relatione inter intensionem et esse," *Laurentianum,* 3 (1962) 476–98, and "Conditiones metaphysicae et limites intensionis," ibid., 4 (1963), 309–35. But one important contemporary philosopher appears to be of the opinion that Dionysius did not in fact affect Thomas' philosophy: "It appears quite wrong to suppose that because Aquinas accepted the authenticity of pseudo-Dionysius, he was specially influenced by his doctrine." This statement of Peter Geach's, in *Three Philosophers* (Oxford, 1963), p. 79, needs some qualification.

44 *Summa theologiae,* I, q. 3, a. 5, c. and ad 2; q. 8, a. 1, c. and ad 3; q. 9, a. 1, ad 3; q. 67, a. 2, ad 3, ed. P. Caramello (Turin, 1952), pp. 18, 36, 40, 328. See also q. 13, a. 5, ad 3, p. 68. According to Isaye (*La Théorie de la mesure,* p. 49), the term *mensura* is used less frequently in the *Summa theologiae.* Montagnes (*La Doctrine de l'analogie de l'être,* pp. 88–89) rightly emphasizes Thomas' metaphorical manner of speaking when he refers to "distance" between God and creatures. Goclenius' remarks on distance cited in n. 34 above should be recalled. See also M. T.-L. Penido, *Le Rôle de l'analogie en théologie dogmatique,* Bibliothèque thomiste 15 (Paris, 1931), p. 103, who correctly lists among metaphors our speaking of God's drawing closer to (*appropinquare*) or departing from (*recedere*) us, even though he is never really "moving." One striking use of the word "metaphor" occurs in Thomas' commentary on the Apostles' Creed, which was originally a series of sermons preached in the vernacular at Naples in 1273. See *Opusculum VII: In Symbolum Apostolorum scilicet "Credo in Deum" expositio* 9, in *Opera omnia* XXVII (Paris, 1885), p. 218. Commenting on the phrase "Ascendit ad caelos, sedet ad dexteram Dei Patris omnipotentis," he explains that this is not to be taken in a material sense (*materialiter*) but in a metaphorical sense (*metaphorice*), meaning that Christ is equal to the Father as divine and next to him in the greatest goods as man. Despite the very title and subject matter of his comprehensive study *The Rule of Metaphor,* trans. Robert Czerny (Toronto, 1977), Paul Ricœur does not focus clearly on these passages in Thomas. When discussing Thomas' doctrine of analogy (pp. 272–80, 358–62), he indicates that he believes analogy to be closest to metaphor when it is defined as proportionality according to symbolic attribution, as when God is called "lion," "sun," etc. And when he comments on *Summa theologiae,* I, q. 13, a. 6, he emphasizes the technique of transposition (pp. 278–79). But what is puzzling is that while he cites *Summa theologiae,* I, q. 8, a. 3 from Montagnes he omits the latter's statement that to speak of a distance between creator and creature is to speak metaphorically. There has been a transferral from the physical order to the metaphysical order. Montagnes is following Thomas himself (*Summa theologiae,* I, q. 67, a. 2, ad 3). I shall return to the issue of metaphor in the conclusion of this study.

One possible source for Thomas' concern regarding the use of spatial language in regard to God may have been Moses Maimonides (1135–1204). In his *Guide for the Perplexed* (trans. Shlomo Pines [Chicago, 1969]), Maimonides states explicitly that language has extended the meaning of the term "place" and "made it a term denoting an individual's rank and situation." He thus takes all Scriptural references to God's "place" to signify God's rank of existence, that is, "the greatness of His portion in existence." Place in regard to God has to do with rank as known by the intellect and not the local place seen by the human eye (I.8, pp. 33–34). In like fashion, the terms "ascending" and "decending" when taken properly refer to a body moving to a higher or lower place, but when used figuratively denote sublimity and greatness — that is, one's rank is raised or lowered. Descent and ascent in regard to God Maimonides takes to mean the alighting of prophetic inspiration and the removal of that prophetic state or God's Indwelling. By reason of his existence and sublimity, God is in "the very highest position — an elevation that is not a spatial one." Consequently, when Scripture (Ex 19:3) says Moses ascended to God, it does not mean God is in a place to which one may ascend and then descend (I.10, pp. 35–37). Maimonides gives a similar analysis for "approaching" or "coming near." Besides the meaning of drawing near in space, he also discerns the meaning of union in cognition with what is known. All Scriptural references to approaching and coming near must be taken in the latter signification. Since there can be no corporeality about God, there can be nothing spatial. Accordingly, he does not draw near to anything and nothing draws near to him. Maimonides emphasizes his point by saying that whether someone is at the center of the earth or on the highest part of the ninth heavenly sphere he would be no nearer to or farther away from God (I.18, pp. 43–45; see also I.27, pp. 56–57). He exhorts his reader to endeavor to achieve "nearness" to God by prayer — that is, intellectual, not imaginative, prayer. Moses and the Patriarchs achieved this "rank" of nearness to God since their intellects were always turned toward him (III.51, pp. 620–24). Jacob's Ladder (Gn 28:12–13) thus has to do with the ascent of men to God and not with a hierarchy of being (I.15, pp. 40–41; II.10, pp. 272–73). This does not mean, however, that God does not create things in some ranking. The earth — that is, the elements — is created "low" while man is "raised" so as to have a higher "rank of existence" among things generable and corruptible (II.30, pp. 349–57). Moreover, there are grades among human beings (III.8, pp. 432–35; III.18, p. 475; III.51, pp. 618–20; see also II.37, pp. 373–74). For a succinct statement of Maimonides' hierarchical theory of things below God, see his *Livre de la connaissance* 1.2–4, trans V. Nikiprowetzky and A. Zaoui (Paris, 1961), pp. 35–67. I owe this reference to Kalman Bland. It should be noted that there is no mention of any metaphysical scheme according to which God and non-being serve as two termini measuring the grades of things by nearness to or distance from them. On Maimonides' interpretation of Jacob's Ladder, see the important study of Alexander Altmann. "The Ladder of Ascension," in his *Studies in Religious Philosophy and Mysticism* (Ithaca, N.Y., 1969), pp. 41–72, at pp. 57–59. One of the most extraordinary developments in medieval Jewish philosophy was the anthropomorphic conception of God as a gigantic body pervading and measuring the universe. For its connection with mystical and hierarchical thinking, see Gershom G. Scholem, *Major Trends in Jewish Mysticism*, 3rd ed. (New York, 1961), pp. 40–79, esp. pp. 63–65. Maimonides appears to have been influenced by this conception in his youth but to have changed his position later. See Altmann's comprehensive study of this tradition in medieval Jewish thought, "Moses Narboni's 'Epistle on *Shiʿur Qoomā'*," which appeared in *Jewish Medieval and Renaissance Studies*, ed. A. Altmann (Cambridge, Mass., 1967), pp. 225–88, at pp. 231–32. Narboni himself uses passages from Averroës and Maimonides to develop the conception of a metaphysical hierarchy in which God is the cause of the hierarchy of being and serves as the "measure" of all existing things. Narboni takes the image of God as a gigantic body and Jacob's Ladder to be symbols for this metaphysical hierarchy. See also Charles Touati, "Dieu et le monde selon Moise Narboni," *Archives d'Histoire Doctrinale et Littéraire du Moyen Age*, 21 (1954), 193–205.

45 *Summa theologiae*, I., q. 4, a. 2–3, pp. 21–23. See also I, q. 13, a. 2 and a. 5–6.

46 Ibid., I, q. 10, a. 6, p. 47. The higher angel illuminates the lower. See I, q. 45, a. 5, ad 1, p. 231.

47 Ibid., I, q. 50, a. 2, ad 1, p. 254. Thomas here suggests, borrowing once again from Aristotle, *Metaphysics* VIII, 3 (1043B36–1044A2), that species can be compared to numbers in that they involve an addition or subtraction of unity. See also I, q. 5, a. 5, pp. 27–28; q. 25, a. 6, p. 143; q. 50, a. 2, ad 1, p. 254; and q. 76, a. 3, p. 363. It should be noted that Thomas does not rank in serial order species in the natural world. He apparently intended only a general comparison between species and numbers. See n. 39 above.

48 Ibid., I, q. 75, a. 5, ad 1 and 4, pp. 354–55. See also I, q. 44, a. 1, p. 293. Cf. Anton Pegis, "A Note on St. Thomas, *Summa Theologica*, I, 44, 1–2," *Mediaeval Studies*, 8 (1946), 159–68.

49 *Summa theologiae*, I, q. 50, a. 3, ad 2, p. 255. See a. 2, ad 3, p. 254, for the terminology *quod est* and *quo est*. Cf. James Collins, *The Thomistic Philosophy of the Angels* (Washington, D.C., 1947), pp. 31–34, 77–93, 107–14, 141–55, 167–86, 219–21.

50 *Summa theologiae*, I, q. 54, a. 2–3; q. 55, a. 1 and a. 3. The Dionysian origins of Thomas' distinction between essence and power in creatures and his doctrine on intelligible species have recently been underscored by Édouard-Henri Wéber, *La Controverse de 1270 à l'Université de Paris et son retentissement sur la pensée de s. Thomas d'Aquin* (Paris, 1970). But see also Bernardo Carlos Bazan, "Le Dialogue philosophique entre Siger de Brabant et Thomas d'Aquin," *Revue Philosophique de Louvain*, 72 (1974), 53–155, esp. 98–99, 132–35. The Dionysian background of the doctrine of *species* in the angels is brought out by Collins (see previous note).

51 See *Commentaria in librum Dionysii De divinis nominibus*, ch. 2, lect. 5; ch. 4, lect. 3; ch. 5, lect. 1; ch. 13, lect. 3, in *Opera omnia* XXIX (Paris, 1876), pp. 414, 434, 496–99, 576. Cf. Durantel, *Saint Thomas et le Pseudo-Denis*, pp. 208–34.

52 *Super Librum de causis expositio*, Prop. 4a, pp. 29–32. See C. Vansteenkiste, "Notes sur le commentaire de saint Thomas du *Liber de causis*," *Études et Récherches*, 8 (1952), 171–91; idem, "Il *Liber de causis* negli scritti di san Tommaso," *Angelicum*, 35 (1958), 325–74; Lafont, *Structures et méthode*, pp. 104–23. Also of note are Daniel A. Callus, "Les sources de saint Thomas," in *Aristote et saint Thomas d'Aquin* (Louvain & Paris, 1957), pp. 149–53; Klaus Kremer, "Die Creatio nach Thomas von Aquin und dem Liber de causis," in *Ekklesia: Festschrift für Bischof Dr. Matthias Wehr* (Trier, 1962), pp. 321–44, esp. pp. 330–32; Werner Beierwaltes, "Der Kommentar zum 'Liber de causis' als neuplatonisches Element in der Philosophie des Thomas von Aquin," *Philosophische Rundschau*, 11 (1963), 192–215; Joseph chiu yuen Ho, "La Doctrine de la participation dans le commentaire de saint Thomas d'Aquin sur le *Liber de causis*," *Revue Philosophique de Louvain*, 70 (1972), 360–83, esp. 381–82; Richard C. Taylor, "St. Thomas and the *Liber de causis* on the Hylemorphic Composition of Separate Substances," *Mediaeval Studies*, 41 (1979), 506–13.

53 On the evolution, see my "Saint Thomas and Siger of Brabant Revisited," *The Review of Metaphysics*, 27 (1974), 531–53, and the bibliography given in nn. 1, 5. I also discuss this topic in my essay "Sense, Imagination, and Intellect in Albert, Thomas, and Siger," in *The Cambridge History of Later Medieval Philosophy* (forthcoming). For examples of other influences of Thomas on Siger, see William Dunphy and Armand Maurer, "A Promising New Discovery for Sigerian Studies," *Mediaeval Studies*, 29 (1967), 364–

69; R.-A. Gauthier, *Magnanimité* (Paris, 1951), pp. 475–77. The present analysis of Siger was written before the appearance of Fernand Van Steenberghen's new monograph *Maître Siger de Brabant*, Philosophes médiévaux 21 (Louvain, 1977). Although Van Steenberghen does set forth Siger's adoption of the scheme (pp. 289–302), and indicates its Neoplatonic inspiration (p. 291; cf. p. 275), he does not point out that it is also to be found in Thomas and other late–thirteenth-century thinkers.

54 *Questions sur la Métaphysique*, ed. C. A. Graiff, Philosophes médiévaux 1 (Louvain, 1948), I, q. 7, pp. 11–20. See also Fernand Van Steenberghen, "La Composition constitutive de l'être fini," *Revue Néoscolastique de Philosophie*, 41 (1938), 489–518, esp. 510–18; Armand Maurer, "*Esse* and *Essentia* in the Metaphysics of Siger of Brabant," *Mediaeval Studies*, 8 (1946), 68–86.

55 *Questions sur la Métaphysique*, I, q. 7, pp. 21–22. See also Joachim Vennebusch, "Die *Questiones metaphysice tres* des Siger von Brabant," *Archiv für Geschichte der Philosophie*, 48 (1966), 182–83.

56 *Questions sur la Métaphysique*, III, q. 17, p. 151.

57 Ibid., III, q. 7, pp. 95–96.

58 Ibid., III, q. 12, pp. 109–10; q. 8, p. 99, and p. 103.

59 See the remarks of Antonio Marlasca in his edition of *Les Quaestiones super Librum de causis de Siger de Brabant*, Philosophes médiévaux 12 (Louvain & Paris, 1972), 22, 25–29. See also A. Dondaine and L. J. Bataillon, "Le Manuscrit Vindob. lat. 2330 et Siger de Brabant," *Archivum Fratrum Praedicatorum*, 36 (1966), 209–12.

60 *Quaestiones super Librum de causis*, q. 13, p. 69.

61 Ibid., q. 24, pp. 98–99. Cf. q. 27, p. 114; q. 36, p. 143.

62 Ibid., qq. 37–43, pp. 145–58. Cf. q. 27, pp. 116–17; q. 47, pp. 167–69.

63 Ibid., q. 46, pp. 163–64.

64 Ibid., q. 45, p. 162. See q. 46, p. 164: "Quanto enim aliqua remotiora sunt a causa prima, tanto magis divisa sunt et minus unita." In q. 48, pp. 170–71, Siger contrasts the *esse purum per se subsistens* with the contracted (*contractum*), determined (*determinatum*), and participated (*participatum*) *esse* of the Intelligences. Cf. q. 9bis, pp. 59–60.

65 Ibid., q. 53, pp. 183–84.

66 See Edgar Hocedez, "La Condamnation de Gilles de Rome," *Recherches de Théologie Ancienne et Médiévale*, 4 (1932), 34–58, esp. 55–56; Norbert G. Gaughan, "Godfrey of Fontaines — An Independent Thinker," *The American Ecclesiastical Review*, 157 (1967), 43–54; M.-H. Laurent, "Godefroid de Fontaines et la condemnation de 1277," *Revue Thomiste*, 35 (1930), 273–81. For general discussion of the condemnation itself, see Pierre Mandonnet, *Siger de Brabant et l'averroïsme latin au XIIIme siècle* I (Louvain, 1911), pp. 214–77, 290–94, 303, 306; Gilson, *History of Christian Philosophy*, pp. 385–427; Fernand Van Steenberghen, *La Philosophie au XIIIe siècle* (Louvain & Paris, 1966), 472–93; John F. Wippel, "The Condemnations of 1270 and 1277 at Paris," *Journal of Medieval and Renaissance Studies*, 7 (1977), 169–201; Roland Hissette, *Enquête sur les 219 articles condamnés à Paris le 7 mars 1277*, Philosophes médiévaux 22 (Louvain & Paris, 1977); Vicente Muñoz Delgado, "La lógica en las condenaciones de 1277," *Cuadernos Salmantinos de Filosofía*, 4 (1977), 17–39; Edward Grant, "The Condemnation of 1277, God's Absolute Power and Physical Thought in the Late Middle Ages," *Viator*, 10 (1979), 211–44.

67 *Summae questionum ordinarianum*, I (Paris, 1520; repr. St. Bonaventure, N.Y., 1953), a. 26, q. 2, fol. 159v. The scheme which we have been tracing does not receive explicit attention in Jean Paulus, *Henri de Gand: Essai sur les tendances de sa métaphysique* (Paris, 1938). But see pp. 302*n*2, 308–309*n*2.

68 *Summae quaestionum ordinariarum*, I, a. 1, q. 6, fol. 27^{r}. The *Metaphysics* II, 1 is also cited in a. 25, q. 2, fol. 148^{v} for the axiom: "in quolibet ordine et genere causarum est ponere aliquod primum." See the studies of de Couesnongle cited in n. 27 and the Averroës reference in n. 29.

69 *Summae quaestionum ordinariarum*, I, a. 25, q. 2, fols. 150^{r}, 149^{r}.

70 *Summae quaestionum ordinariarum*, II (Paris, 1520; repr. St. Bonaventure, N.Y., 1953), a. 42, q. 2, fols. 6^{r}–8^{r}. See also q. 1, fols. 4^{r}, 5^{r}. Cf. José Gomez Caffarena, *Ser participado y ser subsistente en la metafisica de Enrique de Gante* (Rome, 1958), pp. 153–56. For some discussion of the relation of Henry's metaphysics to the *Liber de causis*, see pp. 117–26. The scheme of greater composition as things recede from the simplicity of the First Being, God, who is taken to be the measure of all things, is likewise found in questions on the *Liber de causis* attributed to Henry. See *Les Quaestiones in Librum de causis attribuées à Henri de Gand*, ed. John P. Zwaenepoel, Philosophes médiévaux 15 (Louvain & Paris, 1974), q. 26, pp. 64–66; q. 34, p. 83; q. 60, p. 146. Zwaenepoel had earlier presented his findings in an article in *Unitas*, 32 (1959), 799–809.

The scheme is also to be found in Henry's *Quodlibeta* (Paris, 1518; repr. Louvain, 1961); Quodl. III, q. 5, fol. 53^{r}; Quodl. IV, q. 15, fol. 124^{r-v}, 129^{r}, 130^{r}; Quodl. V, q. 1, fols. 152^{r}, 153^{r}; q. 3, fols. 155^{v}, 157^{r}; q. 11, fol. 169^{v}; q. 12, fol. 171^{r}; Quodl. VI, q. 1, fol. 215^{r-v}; q. 2, fol. 220^{r}; q. 3, fol. 221^{v}; Quodl. XI, q. 11, fols. 465^{v}, 466^{v}, 477. Special emphasis is put on the doctrine of participation in relation to the doctrine of receding in Quodl. X, q. 7, fols. 417^{v}, 418^{v}, 420^{v}; q. 8, fol. 423^{v}; Quodl. XI, q. 3, fols. 440^{v}–441^{r}, 442^{v}; q. 3, fol. 449^{v}. For the doctrine of God as "measure" and the use of the term "quantity" to refer to the *gradus* of something, see Quodl. IX, q. 1, fol. 393^{v}; q. 2, fols. 346^{r}–347^{r}. Henry relies heavily on the works of Dionysius. He also cites on occasion such sources as Albert's *De causis* (fol. 420^{v}) and the *Liber de causis* itself (fol. 442^{v}). Henry refers his readers to his *Quaestiones de Dei simplicitate* for a discussion of the many modes of composition to be found in creatures. See Quodl. V, q. 12, fol. 171. Henry may have in mind not just a. 25 (*De unitate Dei simpliciter et absolute*) of the *Summae quaestionum ordinariarum*, but other articles as well.

71 On the dispute, see Pierre Mandonnet, "Les premières disputes sur la distinction réelle entre l'essence et l'existence: 1276–1287," *Revue thomiste*, 18 (1910), 741–65; Edgar Hocedez, "Gilles de Rome et Henri de Gand sur la distinction réelle (1276–1287)," *Gregorianum*, 8 (1927), 358–84; Jean Paulus, "Les disputes d'Henri de Gand et de Gilles de Rome sur la distinction de l'essence et de l'existence," *Archives d'Histoire Doctrinale et Littéraire du Moyen Age*, 13 (1942), 323–58. See the study of John F. Wippel, "The Relationship Between Essence and Existence in Late–Thirteenth-Century Thought: Giles of Rome, Henry of Ghent, Godfrey of Fontaines, and James of Viterbo," in this volume, pp. 131–64. For the literature on Giles's own real distinction, see Wippel's article, esp. pp. 152–58. Wippel also discusses the views of Giles, Henry, and Godfrey on essence and existence in *The Metaphysical Thought of Godfrey of Fontaines: A Study in Late Thirteenth-Century Philosophy* (Washington, D.C., 1981), chap. 2, and in his "Potentiality and Actuality (Essence and Existence)," in *The Cambridge History of Later Medieval Philosophy* (forthcoming).

Giles's views on participation have been the subject of a series of important articles by Girolamo Trapé. See his "Caratteristiche dell' 'esse' partecipato in Egidio Romano," *Lateranum*, 34 (1968), 351–68; "Causalità e partecipazione ih Egidio Romano," *Augustinianum*, 9 (1969), 91–117; "Esistenza di Dio dall'esistenza partecipata secondo Egidio Romano," ibid., 515–30; "Il platonismo di Egidio Romano," *Aquinas*, 7 (1964), 309–44, which brings out the influence of Dionysius and the *Liber de causis*; "La dottrina della partecipazione in Egidio Romano," ibid., 10 (1967), 170–93; and "L' 'esse' partecipato e distinzione reale in Egidio Romano (Ipsum esse simplex, esse participatum compositum)," ibid., 12 (1969), 443–68. See also Gregorio Suarez, "La metaphysica de Egidio Romano a la luz de las 24 tesis tomistas," *La Ciudad de Dios*, 161 (1949), 93–130, 269–309, esp. 126–30, 269–73. The Neoplatonic background of Giles's metaphysical thought has been emphasized by Carlo, *Ultimate Reducibility*, esp. pp. 57–86. Although Carlo does present texts containing the scheme of receding from God, grades resulting from approach–receding, and the concept of more–less, he does not dwell on the scheme or point out that it is also present in Aquinas. In like fashion, Trapé nowhere discusses the scheme in his articles cited above.

72 *Quaestiones metaphysicales super libros Metaphysicae Aristotelis* (Venice, 1501; repr. Frankfurt, 1966), X, q. 1, fols. 35va–36ra. See q. 3, fols. 36vb–37ra.

In his *De mensura angelorum*, q. 1, Giles follows Aristotle's *Metaphysics* VIII, to explain that measure is that through which the quantity of a thing is measured and that "measure" has been transferred to all genera of things. In each genus the most perfect form serves as the measure of all others by an approach (*accessus*) and a receding (*recessus*). God is the First Being in which all separate beings participate and he thus measures all of them. Giles cites Proclus and the Pseudo-Dionysius' *De divinis nominibus*. See Giles of Rome, *De esse et essentia, de mensura angelorum, et de cognitione angelorum* (Venice, 1503), fols. 36^{r}–38^{v}.

73 Ibid., q. 6, fol. 38rb–38vb. Giles argues that although from the point of view of our knowledge *mensura* is transferred from discrete quantity, it is in fact God who properly and principally has the *ratio* of measure: namely, uniformity, simplicity, and invisibility.

74 Ibid., q. 4, fol. 37^{va-b}.

75 Ibid., XI, q. 1, fol. 39rb.

76 *Primus Sententiarum* (Venice, 1521), d. 8, pars 1, prin. 2, q. 1, a. 2, fols. 47vb–48ra. See Trapé, "Il platonismo di Egidio Romano," 330–37, for a discussion of the notion of *esse* in *Primus Sententiarum*, d. 8, esp. pp. 333, 335, where the doctrines of *magis–minus*, God as *summe simplex*, and all things outside God as composed are mentioned. The scheme itself is not analyzed or put into historical perspective.

77 *Primus Sententiarum*, a. 3, fol. 48va.

78 *In secundum librum Sententiarum quaestiones* I (Venice, 1581; repr. Frankfurt, 1968), d. 1, q. 3, a. 3, pp. 40^{1}–41^{1}. I did not find the scheme in his *Theoremata de esse et essentia*, ed. Edgar Hocedez (Louvain, 1930). Hocedez discusses the Neoplatonic influences on Giles. See introductory essay, pp. [67–74]. On the other hand, the scheme is present in Giles's *De materia caeli quaestio* (Padua, 1493), sig. A_6^{ra-b}, where he makes much of Augustine, *Confessions* 12.7. He is careful to emphasize that nearness (*propinquitas*) and distance (*distantia*) in this context have to do with perfection of a thing's nature and not with any measurable distance in physical space (*longitudo spatii*). It is noteworthy that Giles makes frequent reference to the hierarchical nature of reality when arguing for the supremacy of papal authority over civil rule in his *De ecclesiastica potestate*, ed. Richard Scholz (Weimar, 1929), I.4, pp. 12–13; I.5, pp. 16–17; I.9, pp. 32–33; II.6, pp. 62–63; II.13, pp. 122–27; III.2, pp. 150–52. These passages contain references to the Pseudo-Dionysius and the *Liber de causis*.

79 *In secundum librum Sententiarum quaestiones*, I, d. 2, q. 1, a. 2, pp. 109^{2}–110^{1}.

80 Ibid., I, d. 3, pars 1, q. 2, a. 2, a. 3, a. 5, pp. 195^{2}–197^{2}, 200^{1-2}, 206^{1}.

81 Ibid., I, d. 3, pars 2, q. 2, a. 2, p. 245^{1-2}.

82 Ibid., I, a. 4, pp. 256[1]–257[2]. There are some references to the scheme in the writings of Giles's student James of Viterbo (ca. 1255–1308). See his *Disputatio secunda de quolibet*, ed. Eelcko Ypma (Würzburg, 1969), q. 3, pp. 33, 40–42, 44–46. For further information on James's metaphysics, see Wippel's article in this volume, esp. pp. 132–34, 146–48.

83 See John F. Wippel, "Godfrey of Fontaines and the Real Distinction between Essence and Existence," *Traditio*, 20 (1964), 385–410, esp. 408–10; idem, "Godfrey of Fontaines and Henry of Ghent's Theory of Intentional Distinction between Essence and Existence," in *Sapientiae procerum amore: Mélanges médiévistes offerts à Dom Jean-Pierre Müller O.S.B.*, ed. Theodor Wolfram Köhler, Studia Anselmiana 63 (Rome, 1974), pp. 289–321. For a clear statement of the distinction *secundum rationem et modum intelligendi et significandi*, see Quodl. IV, q. 2, in Godfrey of Fontaines, *Les Quatre Premiers Quodlibets*, edd. M. De Wulf and A. Pelzer, Les Philosophes Belges 2 (Louvain, 1904), p. 235, where Godfrey rejects both the real and the intentional distinction. The definitive study of Godfrey's metaphysics is Wippel's *Metaphysical Thought of Godfrey of Fontaines*, cited in n. 71.

84 Quodl. IV, q. 3, pp. 242–47. Both Proclus and Pseudo-Dionysius are cited. See also q. 3 (brevis), 325–27. Cf. Quodl. II, q. 10, pp. 140–43. See also Quodl. VII, q. 12, in *Les Quodlibets, cinq, six et sept*, edd. M. De Wulf and J. Hoffmans, Les Philosophes Belges 3 (Louvain, 1914), pp. 388–89, where Godfrey makes use of the scheme but is careful to note that he is not determining the matter at hand. Godfrey applies the concept of receding according to more and less to the concept of friendship in Quodl. I, q. 10, p. 25. On God's unity and simplicity as the bases for his serving as the universal measure of all things, see Quodl. VII, q. 8, p. 364. There are no grades according to more and less in God, though there are such grades in everything else. See Quodl. X, q. 1, in *Le Dixième Quodlibet*, ed. J. Hoffmans, Les Philosophes Belges 4.3 (Louvain, 1931), pp. 298–99. On creatures imitating God and divine "ideas" according to grades in the creatures, see Quodl. IV, q. 2, p. 239 and also Quodl. IX, q. 7, in *Le Neuvième Quodlibet*, ed. J. Hoffmans, Les Philosophes Belges 4.2 (Louvain, 1928), pp. 231–33. Godfrey appears to see a scale of more or less freedom according as things approach God and recede from matter. See Quodl. VIII, q. 16, pp. 145–46.

85 Quodl. VII, q. 1, pp. 265–66.

86 Ibid., q. 7, pp. 359–60. See Wippel, "Godfrey of Fontaines and the Real Distinction," 405–406, esp. n. 56, for an insightful analysis of this text. He rightly points out (p. 410) the influence of Averroës here. For an interesting, though hardly fair, argument against the real distinction which is based on the doctrine of composition by "receding," see Quodl. III, q. 3, p. 186. For further discussion of Godfrey's Quodl. VII, q. 7 and of how angels are "measured," see John F. Wippel, "The Dating of James of Viterbo's Quodlibet I and Godfrey of Fontaines' Quodlibet VIII," *Augustiniana*, 24 (1974), 348–86, esp. 350–62. See also Maurice de Wulf, *Un Théologien-Philosophe du XIIIe siècle: Étude sur la vie, les œuvres et l'influence de Godefroid de Fontaines* (Brussels, 1904), pp. 116–18, 122–23.

87 Given Scotus' close knowledge of Henry and Thomas and Jandun's frequent references to Albert and Thomas, it is surely safe to assume that each was aware of the scheme. My aim in the following paragraphs is to sketch out what is necessary to show how Scotus and Jandun reject the scheme. Although I shall give a good deal of their "hierarchic" thought, I do not claim to have presented exhaustive accounts.

88 *Ordinatio*, I, d. 2, p. 1, q. 3, nn. 159 and 187, in *Opera omnia* II (Vatican City, 1950), pp. 222–23, 240–42; ibid., I, d. 8, p. 1, q. 2, nn. 1–3, in *Opera omnia* IV (Vatican City, 1956), pp. 164–68; *Lectura*, I, d. 8, 1, qq. 1–2, nn. 28–31, 37–43, in *Opera omnia* XVII (Vatican City, 1966), pp. 9–10, 12–14; *Quaestiones quodlibetales*, q. 5, n. 26, in *Opera omnia* XII (Lyons,

1639), p. 136. See Mariano Traina, "La nozione di partecipazione e le sue implicazioni metafisiche," in *Deus et homo ad mentem I. Duns Scoti*, Studia Scholastico-Scotistica 5 (Rome, 1972), pp. 429–44, esp. pp. 433–37; Eberhard Wölfel, *Seinsstruktur und Trinitätsproblem: Untersuchungen zur Grundlegung der natürlichen Theologie bei Johannes Duns Skotus*, Beiträge zur Geschichte der Philosophie und Theologie des Mittelalters, 40.5 (Münster, 1965), p. 141*n*176; Walter Hoeres, *Der Wille als reine Vollkommenheit nach Duns Scotus* (Munich, 1962), p. 34; idem, *La volontà come perfezione pura in Duns Scoto*, trans. A. Bizzotto and A. Poppi (Padua, 1966), p. 29.

89 Etienne Gilson, "Sur la composition fondamentale de l'être fini," in *De doctrina Ioannis Duns Scoti* II, Studia Scholastico-Scotistica 2 (Rome, 1968), pp. 183–98, esp. pp. 190–94. See also idem, *Jean Duns Scot* (Paris, 1952), pp. 234–35.

90 *Ordinatio*, I, d. 8, p. 1, q. 3, nn. 83, 90, 95–99, pp. 191, 196–99; *Lectura*, I, d. 8, p. 1, qq. 1–2, nn. 99–105, pp. 33–36. On the univocal concept of being, see Cyril L. Shircel, *The Univocity of the Concept of Being in the Philosophy of John Duns Scotus* (Washington, D.C., 1942); Efrem Bettoni, *Duns Scoto filosofo* (Milan, 1966), pp. 63–84. For other studies on Scotus' doctrine of univocity, see S. Belmond, "Analogie et univocité d'après J. Duns Scot," *Études Franciscaines*, 4 (1951), 173–86; T. A. Barth, "Being, Univocity, and Analogy According to Duns Scotus," in *John Duns Scotus, 1265–1965*, Studies in Philosophy and the History of Philosophy 3 (Washington, D.C., 1965), pp. 210–62; David Burrell, *Analogy and Philosophical Language* (New Haven & London, 1973), pp. 95–118, 171–93.

91 *Reportata Parisiensia*, I, d. 2, q. 2, n. 11, in *Opera omnia* XI.1 (Lyons, 1639), p. 30; ibid., IV, d. 49, q. 9, nn. 1, 19 in *Opera omnia* XI.2 (Lyons, 1639), pp. 911, 915.

92 *Ordinatio*, I, d. 8, p. 1, q. 3, nn. 92, 132–33, 197, pp. 219–20; *Reportata Parisiensia*, I, d. 8, q. 5, nn. 2, 17, pp. 77, 80.

93 *Lectura*, I, d. 8, p. 1, qq. 1–2, nn. 115–16, pp. 40–41.

94 *Quaestiones quodlibetales*, q. 5, nn. 4, 10, 25–26, pp. 118–19, 126, 136. See also q. 6, n. 9, p. 146. For discussion, see Paul Vignaux, "Etre et infini selon Duns Scot et Jean de Ripa," in *De doctrina Ioannis Duns Scoti* IV, Studia Scholastico-Scotistica 4 (Rome, 1968), pp. 43–56, esp. pp. 44–45, 56; John Duns Scotus, *God and Creatures: The Quodlibetal Questions*, trans. Felix Alluntis and Allan B. Wolter (Princeton, N.J., 1975), pp. 110–11*n*4.

95 *Reportata Parisiensia*, IV, d. 24, q. 1, n. 5, p. 775.

96 *Lectura*, I, d. 30, qq. 1–2, n. 34, p. 406; *Quaestiones quodlibetales*, q. 19, nn. 2, 5, pp. 492, 495; *Tractatus de primo principio* I, ed. Evan Roche (St. Bonaventure, N.Y., 1949), p. 4.

97 *Quaestiones quodlibetales*, q. 19, n. 5, p. 495; *Ordinatio*, I, d. 2, 1, qq. 1–2, n. 64, p. 167; ibid., I, d. 8, 1, q. 3, 191, where Scotus cites *Metaphysics* X, 1 (1052B18); *De primo principio* I, pp. 4–10. On the conception of "essential order" according to Scotus, see Robert P. Prentice, *The Basic Quidditative Metaphysics of Duns Scotus as Seen in His "De primo principio"* (Rome, 1970), esp. pp. 66–96; Allan B. Wolter, *The Transcendentals and Their Function in the Metaphysics of Duns Scotus* (St. Bonaventure, N.Y., 1946), pp. 140–61; Gilson, *Jean Duns Scot*, pp. 178–83.

98 *Quaestiones quodlibetales*, q. 5, nn. 4, 10, 26, pp. 118–19, 126, 136–37; *Reportata Parisiensia*, IV, d. 24, q. 1, n. 5, p. 775; *De primo principio* II, III, IV, pp. 24, 48, 54, 64, 68, 120. See also *Lectura*, I, d. 8, p. 2, q. 1, pp. 76–77, 84–85; *Quaestiones quodlibetales*, q. 19, n. 6, p. 497; *Ordinatio*, I, d. 19, q. 1, nn. 26–27, in *Opera omnia* V (Vatican City, 1959), p. 278; *Reportata Parisiensia*, I, d. 2, q. 2, n. 11, p. 30. See Prentice, *Basic Quidditative Metaphysics*, pp. 68–71, 74–76, 80–83, 188–89, 191–93; Giuseppe Cacciatore, "L'unità dell'individuo come interiorità del concreto secondo Duns Scoto," in *De doctrina Ioannis Duns Scoti* II, pp. 119–228, esp. pp. 200, 222–24; Gilson, "Sur la composition," 186–89;

idem, *Jean Duns Scot*, pp. 181–83; Pietro Scapin, introduction to *Duns Scoto: Il primo principio degli esseri* (Padua, 1973), pp. 41–55.

On the manner in which all "emanates in an orderly fashion" (*emanant omnia ordinate*) from the divine essence, which is both intensively and virtually infinite, and the way in which that essence measures creatures by *accessus* and *recessus*, see *Quaestiones quodlibetales*, q. 5, n. 25, p. 136. For discussion touching on this passage, see Martin Anton Schmidt, "Göttliche und geschöpfliche Wirklichkeit im Quodlibet des Johannes Duns Scotus," in *Deus et homo ad mentem I. Duns Scoti*, pp. 487–93 at pp. 491–93. Scotus also uses the scheme of *accessus* and *recessus* to determine the varying dignity and eminence of the orders in the hierarchy of the Church. He takes the priesthood as his point of reference. See *Reportata Parisiensia*, IV, d. 24, q. 1, n. 8, pp. 776–77. There seems no basis for the claim of one recent writer that Scotus wholly denied a hierarchy of being. See James C. Doig, "Denial of Hierarchy: Consequences for Scotus and Descartes," *Studies in Medieval Culture*, 11 (1977), 109–13.

99 *Ordinatio*, I, d. 8, p. 1, q. 3, nn. 108, 113, 136, pp. 202–203, 205–206, 221; *Reportata Parisiensia*, I, d. 8, q. 5, nn. 5, 13, 18, pp. 78–80. On the "transfer" of the meaning of quantity, see *Ordinatio*, I, d. 19, q. 1, nn. 18–22, pp. 273–76; *Quaestiones quodlibetales*, q. 5, n. 26, p. 137, and q. 6, n. 9, p. 146; *Quaestiones subtilissimae in Metaphysicam Aristotelis*, II, q. 6, nn. 2–3, in *Opera omnia* IV (Lyons, 1639), p. 563. For a perceptive analysis of the extending of the meaning of "quantity" and its importance in the metaphysics of Scotus, see Jan Peter Beckmann, *Die Relationen der Identität und Gleichheit nach Johannes Duns Scotus: Untersuchungen zur Ontologie der Beziehungen* (Bonn, 1967), pp. 156–66. For discussion of the disjunctive transcendentals of the finite and the infinite and of the distinction between grades or modes, on the one hand, and generic and specific structure, on the other, see Wolter, *Transcendentals*, pp. 153–54; Gilson, "Sur la composition," 183–86; Shircel, *Univocity of the Concept of Being*, pp. 142–44; Wölfel, *Seinsstruktur und Trinitätsproblem*, pp. 47–48. The most helpful accounts I have found regarding the relationship of the grade or mode with the essential or formal aspects of a thing are Beckmann, *Die Relationen*, pp. 216–26, and Hoeres, *Der Wille*, pp. 40–45 and *La volontà*, pp. 36–43.

100 *Reportata Parisiensia*, I, d. 2, q. 3, n. 3, p. 31; *Lectura*, I, d. 31, q. 1, nn. 10–11, p. 426.

101 Scotus will also use the terms "grade" and "contract" in regard to the individuating of things. The quiddity does not determine the *gradus individualis* since the individual difference adds something to the nature of quiddity. See *Lectura*, I, d. 17, p. 2, q. 2, n. 178, p. 237. The *realitas* of the individual determines the *realitas* of the species and appears to cause the contraction to a *quidditas contracta*. See *Ordinatio*, d. 3, p. 1, qq. 5–6, nn. 170–89, pp. 475–84. For Scotus' doctrine of individuation and the concept of "individual grade," see Gilson, *Jean Duns Scot*, pp. 446–77; Thomas P. McTighe, "Scotus, Plato, and the Ontology of the Bare *X*," *The Monist*, 49 (1965), 588–616, esp. 597–608; Wolter, *Transcendentals*, pp. 100–11; Bettoni, *Duns Scoto filosofo*, pp. 99–105. There are also some scattered, relevant remarks in Prospero T. Stella, "La teoria ilemorfica nel sistema scotista," in *De doctrina Ioannis Duns Scoti* II, pp. 240–95, esp. pp. 250–51, 258*n*9, 291–92.

102 Gilson, *Jean Duns Scot*, pp. 400–401; A. Vacant, "Angelologie," *Dictionnaire de Théologie Catholique* (Paris, 1930), I, col. 1243. For a convenient summary of Scotus' views on the angels, see Karl Werner, *Die Scholastik des späteren Mittelalters. I. Johannes Duns Scotus* (Vienna, 1881), pp. 311–31.

103 *Ordinatio*, IV, d. 1, q. 1, nn. 6, 7, 11, 13, in *Opera omnia* VIII (Lyons, 1639), pp. 9–11, 20–23; *Reportata Parisiensia*, I, d. 2, q. 3, n. 4, p. 32. In *Quaestiones . . . in Metaphysicam*, II, q. 6, n. 12, p. 566, Scotus distinguishes distance properly speaking, which belongs to

quantity, from the distance of perfection (*distantia perfectionis*) found between contraries. Cf. Gilson, *Jean Duns Scot*, pp. 346, 349.

104 Schmidt, "Göttliche und geschöpfliche Wirklichkeit," pp. 491–93; Heribert Mühlen, *Sein und Person nach Johannes Duns Scotus* (Werl, 1954), pp. 32–33.

105 On Scotus and the Pseudo-Dionysius, see Fidel Chauvet, "La posición del escotismo en la escolástica medieval," in *De doctrina Ioannis Duns Scoti* I, Studia Scholastico-Scotistica 1 (Rome, 1968), pp. 75–99, esp. p. 90*n*27. Scotus actually uses the phrase "golden chain" (*catena aurea*) regarding hierarchy (*hierarchia*) at one point in his writings. See *Ordinatio*, IV, d. 12, q. 2, n. 12, p. 732. For comment, see Hoeres, *Der Wille*, p. 52, and *La volontà*, pp. 51–52. One of Scotus' contemporaries — namely, Meister Eckhart — uses the phrase "golden chain" (*die goldene Kette*) in one of his sermons. See Meister Eckhart, *Deutsche Predigten und Traktate*, ed. Josef Quint (Munich, 1955), Sermon 14, p. 218. His source appears to be Macrobius.

106 On Jandun's general thought, see Pierre Duhem, *Le Système du monde* VI (Paris, 1954), pp. 543–75; Stuart MacClintock, *Perversity and Error: Studies on the "Averroist" John of Jandun* (Bloomington, Ind., 1956); Armand Maurer, "John of Jandun and the Divine Causality," *Mediaeval Studies*, 17 (1955), 185–207; Ludwig Schmugge, *Johannes von Jandun 1285/89–1328* (Stuttgart, 1966); Zdzisław Kuksewicz, *De Siger de Brabant à Jacques de Plaisance* (Warsaw, 1968), pp. 202–43.

107 *Quaestiones in duodecim libros Metaphysicae* (Venice, 1553), I, q. 3, fol. 3rb; IX, q. 10, fol. 117rb. Jandun cites *Metaphysics* II, 1 (993B24–32). Cf. n. 29 above.

108 *Quaestiones in duodecim libros Metaphysicae*, X, q. 1, fols. 119vb–120ra. Jandun explains that measure is present in the unity of numbering, that is, the number one, and in the other genera by way of analogy (*analogice*), since it belongs to them respectively according to a priority and a posteriority (*ratio mensurae debetur uni et aliis generibus analogice, quia per prius uni et posterius aliis*).

109 Ibid., X, q. 3, fol. 120va. On this reduction, see also X, q. 5, fol. 121rb.

110 Ibid., X, q. 5, fol. 121^{ra-b}. For discussion of how for Jandun God is a cause in regard to the Intelligences and the heavenly bodies, see Antonino Poppi, *Causalità e infinità nella scuola padovana dal 1480 al 1513* (Padua, 1966), pp. 112–23; Bruno Nardi, *Saggi sull'aristotelismo padovano dal secolo XIV al XVI* (Padua, 1958), pp. 188, 200–201, 293–94; Duhem, *Le Système du monde* VI, pp. 680–81; Maurer, "John of Jandun," esp. 187–94. I found Maurer's study to be particularly helpful.

111 *Quaestiones in duocedim libros Metaphysicae*, II, q. 5, fols. 26vb–28ra. Cf. V, q. 10, fol. 62ra. In his questions on the *De coelo*, Jandun again sets aside creation on the grounds that it cannot be known by philosophers, just as he again takes the perpetuity of the heavens to result from their immutable mover, God. He assumes once more that eternal substances can have true efficient causes since such causes involve a motion from potency to act, and he maintains anew that in depending on God as their final cause the heavens depend on him for their existence. See *In libros Aristotelis De coelo et mundo quaestiones subtilissimae* (Venice, 1552), I, q. 14, fol. 10vb, and q. 15, fol. 11^{ra-vb}. And in his *Expositio super sermonem Averrois De substantia orbis* IV, in ibid., fols. 48ra, 48vb–49rb, he again points out that the creation of the heavens from nothing is not held by philosophers. The first mover, God, is the final cause of the heavens and thereby gives continuity to their motion and existence to them. God for Aristotle and Averroës is not an efficient cause which gives his effect existence after non-existence; rather, he gives existence to all other eternal and necessary beings as their conserving and perfecting cause, that is, as their end. For further discussion regarding Averroës' doctrine on the Intelligences and their relation to God, see Harry A. Wolfson, "Averroës' Lost Treatise on the Prime

Mover," *Hebrew Union College Annual*, 23, No. 1 (1950–1951), 683–710, esp. 702–705; idem, "The Plurality of Immovable Movers in Aristotle, Averroës, and St. Thomas," *Harvard Studies in Classical Philology*, 63 (1958), 233–53, esp. 240–51. Wolfson makes a comparison between Averroës and Aquinas on grades and nearness to God (pp. 249–50). Of related interest is Wolfson's "The Problem of the Souls of the Spheres from the Byzantine Commentaries on Aristotle through the Arabs and St. Thomas to Kepler," *Dumbarton Oaks Papers*, 16 (1962), 65–93, esp. 81–85. All three essays have been reprinted in Wolfson's *Studies in the History of Philosophy and Religion* I, edd. Isadore Twersky and George H. Williams (Cambridge, Mass., 1973), pp. 1–59, 402–29. For further background, see Francis Carmody, "The Planetary Theory of Ibn Rushd," *Osiris*, 10 (1952), 556–86. Averroës' teachings on the Intelligences, their hierarchy, and relation to the heavenly bodies are also presented by Miguel Cruz Hernandez, *Historia de la filosofía española: Filosofía hispano-musulmana* II (Madrid, 1957), pp. 147–57. See also the classic study of Léon Gauthier, *Ibn Rochd* (*Averroès*) (Paris, 1948) esp. pp. 113–27, 160–82. For a good review of the scholarly literature on Aristotle's doctrine of the Intelligences, see Joseph Owens, "The Reality of the Aristotelian Separate Movers," *The Review of Metaphysics*, 3 (1949–1950), 319–37.

112 *Quaestiones . . . De substantia orbis*, q. 10, in his *In libros Aristotelis De caelo*, fol. 56^{va-b}. Cf. Maurer, "John of Jandun," 191; Duhem, *Le Système du monde* VI, pp. 680–81.

113 *Utrum aeternis repugnet habere causam efficientem*, ed. Maurer in "John of Jandun," 199, 202–204. See Maurer's comments on pp. 193–94.

114 Fabro, *La nozione metafisica*, p. 250. There is no interconnection between participation and the metaphysical composition of the Intelligences for Jandun. In this, of course, he is in disagreement with Siger of Brabant.

115 For use of the axiom, see *Quaestiones in duodecim libros Metaphysicae*, III, q. 7, fol. 39vb; V, q. 10, fol. 62ra; XII, q. 10, fol. 132^{ra-va}. In his *Super octo libros Aristotelis De physico auditu subtilissimae quaestiones* (Venice, 1551) I, q. 8, fol. 8vb, Jandun does refer to participating in some mode of being according to a more and a less, but he is discussing the views of others. It is perhaps revealing that the *Liber de causis* is only rarely cited by Jandun. See for example the questions on the *Physics*, VI, q. 11, fol. 90rb.

116 *Quaestiones in duodecim libros Metaphysicae*, X, q. 3, fol. 120ra; III, q. 1, fol. 41rb. See also *Quaestiones . . . De substantia orbis*, q. 10, fol. 57ra.

117 *Quaestiones in duodecim libros Metaphysicae*, XII, q. 19, fols. 140vb–141ra. In an earlier discussion regarding whether the heaven is to be considered more noble than animate things after one has abstracted from its mover — namely, the Intelligence — Jandun had emphasized the importance of the perspective assumed when making the comparison. He proposes that even the heaven can be considered to be more noble than animate things such as a fly or a worm since the eternal is more noble than the generable and corruptible. Ibid., XII, q. 12, fol. 134^{ra-b}. This same discussion appears almost to the word in Jandun's *In libros Aristotelis De coelo et mundo quaestiones*, II, q. 4, fol. 25^{va-b}. But see also Duns Scotus, *Ordinatio*, IV, d. 12, q. 2, nn. 11–12, pp. 731–32, who sees a fly and the heavens each as closer to God according as the ordering or hierarchy is based on knowledge or necessity. See n. 105 above. Later in the fourteenth century, Nicholas of Autrecourt (ca. 1300–post 1350) completely ruled out the possibility of presenting evidence for the ranking of one thing as more noble than another. That is to say, no degrees of perfection could be established. This also meant that God could not be demonstrated to be the noblest being. See the *Discussio et reprobatio errorum magistri Nicolai de Ultricuria*, ed. Joseph Lappe, in *Nicolaus von Autrecourt*, Beiträge zur Geschichte der

Philosophie des Mittelalters, 6.2 (Münster, 1908), p. 33*. See also Nicholas' *Tractatus universalis* (also called the *Exigit*), ed. J. Reginald O'Donnell, *Mediaeval Studies*, 1 (1939), 190–91. For discussion, see Julius R. Weinberg, "The Fifth Letter of Nicholas of Autrecourt to Bernard of Arezzo," *Journal of the History of Ideas*, 3 (1942), 220–27, esp. 226–27; idem, *Nicolaus of Autrecourt: A Study in Fourteenth-Century Thought* (Princeton, N.J., 1948), pp. 71–74. In similar fashion, a contemporary philosopher rules out the possibility of establishing a single scale of goodness for all things. See Kenny, *Five Ways*, 80. Needless to say, the lines of reasoning of Nicholas and Kenny are somewhat different. See also David Sanford, "Degrees of Perfection . . .," *Encyclopedia of Philosophy* (New York, 1967), II 324–26.

118 On Ockham and Buridan and the new attitude toward metaphysics, see Ernest A. Moody, *Studies in Medieval Philosophy, Science, and Logic* (Berkeley & Los Angeles, 1975), pp. 287–305, 409–51. Ockham's anti-hierarchic stand is stressed by Eugenio Garin, *Medioevo e Rinascimento*, 2nd ed. (Bari, 1961), pp. 33–37. For discussion regarding the bases of the order of the universe for Ockham, see Paul Vignaux, "Nominalisme," *Dictionnaire de Théologie Catholique* XI (Paris, 1931), cols. 764–65; idem, *Le Nominalisme au XIVᵉ siècle* (Montreal, 1948), pp. 26–28, 74–78, 91–96; Georges de Lagarde, *La Naissance de l'esprit laïque au déclin du Moyen Age. V. L'Individualisme ockhamiste: Bases de départ* (Paris, 1946), pp. 101–24 (esp. 102–103), 143–63, 212–32. For Buridan's coordination of the ranking of the spheres with the ranking of their movers, from the First Mover, God, down to the lowest Intelligence, see his *In Metaphysicen Aristotelis quaestiones argutissimae* (Paris, 1588), X, q. 1, fol. 60^{va-b}; XII, q. 12, fol. 74^{rb-vb}. The three factors which Buridan takes into account are the greater perfection of the mobile, its greater magnitude, and the greater velocity of the motion. He also discusses Aristotle's conception of the order of the world and the celestial spheres in his *Quaestiones super libris quattuor De caelo et mundo*, ed. Ernest A. Moody (Cambridge, Mass., 1942). The criterion here is the number of actions required in regard to one ultimate end. Intelligences and humans attain the contemplation of God, the former through their essences and without any action, but man, being more distant (*remotior*), needs more operations to achieve this goal. The brute animals achieve not this end but only sensitive knowledge, and the plants do not achieve even this; thus neither needs the level of activities of the beings above them (II, q. 21, pp. 223–25). In these discussions there is no mention whatever of a metaphysical scheme based on approaching toward and receding from God or non-being. In like fashion, there is no hint of a metaphysics of participation. For similar discussions, see Albert of Saxony, *Quaestiones subtilissimae Alberti de Saxonia in libros De caelo et mundo* (Venice, 1492), II, q. 17, sig. F_5^{va}; q. 18, sigs. F_5^{vb}–F_6^{ra}; q. 21, sigs. G_1^{vb}–G_2^{rb}. In his *Acutissimae quaestiones super libros De physica auscultatione* (Venice, 1516), VII, q. 5, fols. 72vb–73rb, Albert takes up the question of whether something belonging to one species can be compared to something belonging to another. After explaining that to say a thing is perfect is to say that it is in some order of beings, he turns to consider the scheme with its two extremes: namely, God (*gradus summus*), and prime matter or the zero grade (*non gradus*). He rules out *accessus* to God as a valid approach (*non valet*), arguing that all things would be of the same perfection since all are infinitely distant from the highest grade and one infinite is no greater than another. It is not clear whether he rules the zero grade (*non gradus*) out as a measure, though he would seem to do so. He maintains that if we reduce the perfection of something more perfect, such as man, to the zero grade, we can do so and yet not attain the perfection of the less perfect thing, for example, the ass. In any case, the scheme as we have traced it is clearly rejected.

119 See Edith D. Sylla, "Medieval Concepts of the Latitude of Forms: The Oxford Calculators," *Archives d'Histoire Doctrinale et Litteraire du Moyen Age*, 40 (1973–1974), 223–83, esp. 252–56; eadem, "Medieval Quantifications of Qualities: The 'Merton School,'" *Archive for History of Exact Sciences*, 8 (1971), 24–27. For general background on the doctrine of intension and remission of form in medieval philosophy, see Anneliese Maier, *Das Problem der intensiven Grösse in der Scholastik* (*De intensione et remissione formarum*) (Leipzig, 1939); eadem, *Zwei Grundprobleme der scholastischen Naturphilosophie*, 2nd ed. (Rome, 1951), pp. 1–109; Marshall Clagett, "Richard Swineshead and Late Medieval Physics," *Osiris*, 9 (1950), 131–61. For a good, comprehensive treatment of fourteenth-century developments regarding latitude of forms and the notion of grades, see John E. Murdoch, "*Mathesis in philosophiam scholasticam introducta*: The Rise and Development of Mathematics in Fourteenth Century Philosophy and Theology," in *Arts libéraux et philosophie au Moyen Age*, Actes du Quatrième Congrès International de Philosophie Médiévale (Montreal & Paris, 1969), pp. 215–54, esp. 238–49. Murdoch refers to the great chain of being in his concluding remarks (p. 248). On the use of the concept of *gradus* in another context of medieval thought, see Michael R. McVaugh, "The Development of Medieval Pharmaceutical Theory," in *Arnaldi de Villanova: Opera medica omnia*. II. *Aphorismi de gradibus*, ed. M. R. McVaugh (Granada & Barcelona, 1975), pp. 1–136. In this important study, McVaugh carefully relates Arnald's theories to contemporary philosophical discussions. See also his earlier article, "Quantified Medical Theory and Practice at Fourteenth-Century Montpellier," *Bulletin of the History of Medicine*, 43 (1969), 397–413, esp. 400–402.

120 See Sylla, "Medieval Concepts," 223–83, esp. 252–56, For discussion touching on Ripa and the scheme, see Paul Vignaux, "Note sur le concept de forme intensive dans l'œuvre de Jean de Ripa," in *Mélanges Alexandre Koyré*. II. *L'Aventure de l'esprit* (Paris, 1964), pp. 517–26, esp. pp. 520–23; idem, "Etre et infini selon Duns Scot et Jean de Ripa," pp. 43–56; André Combes, "La Métaphysique de Jean de Ripa," in *Die Metaphysik im Mittelalter*, ed. Wilpert, pp. 543–57, esp. pp. 550–54; idem, "L'Intensité des formes d'après Jean de Ripa," *Archives d'Histoire Doctrinale et Littéraire du Moyen Age*, 37 (1970), 17–147; Murdoch, "*Mathesis*," pp. 238–41; Jean Jolivet, "Schèmes néoplatoniciens chez Jean de Ripa," in *Le Néoplatonisme* (Paris, 1971), pp. 425–33; Janet Coleman, "Jean de Ripa O.F.M. and the Oxford Calculators," *Mediaeval Studies*, 37 (1975), 130–89, esp. 156ff. There are also aspects of the scheme to be found in Ugolino of Orvieto. See Francesco Corvino, "Ugolini de Orbe Veteri: *Tractatus de perfectione specierum*," *Acme*, 8 (1955), 119–204, esp. 157–58 and 174–75. See also the comments of Corvino in his article, "Il 'De perfectione specierum' di Ugolino d'Orvieto," ibid., 7 (1954), 73–105, esp. 83–88 (on *latitudo* — based on A. Maier), 93–98 (quantity of perfection), and 98–101 (zero grade of perfection). I am indebted to John E. Murdoch for bringing these two articles to my attention. For further information on this somewhat obscure figure, see Konstanty Michalski, *La Philosophie au XIVe siècle: Six études*, ed. Kurt Flasch (Frankfurt, 1969), 170–74; William J. Courtenay, "John of Mirecourt and Gregory of Rimini on Whether God Can Undo the Past," *Recherches de Théologie Ancienne et Médiévale*, 40 (1973), 170–71; Francesco Corvino, "La polemica antiaristotelica di Ugolino da Orvieto nella cultura filosofica del sec. XIV," in *Filosofia e cultura in Umbria tra Medioevo e Rinascimento*, Atti del IV Convegno di Studi Umbri–Gubbio, May 22–26, 1966 (Perugia, 1967), pp. 407–58.

In his study "From Social into Intellectual Factors: An Aspect of the Unitary Character of Late Medieval Learning," in *The Cultural Context of Medieval Learning*, edd. John E. Murdoch and Edith D. Sylla (Dordrecht & Boston, 1975), pp. 271–348, John E. Murdoch sees new "measure" languages introduced in the fourteenth century and typifying that century (pp. 280–89) and its "near frenzy to measure everything imaginable" (p. 287). These languages were applied not only in natural philosophy but also in theology, especially by Ripa (pp. 290–94). Murdoch confesses that he has been "looking for the origin of this 'measure mania,'" and seems to suggest Scotus as someone whose thought "would lead in this direction" (p. 341). In comments on Murdoch's paper, Heiko Oberman proposes that "the near frenzy" and the use of "measure languages" reflect an attack on the metaphysics of the earlier medievals, which was based on abstractions and removed from reality. No longer is the individual thing described "as placed in an ontological hierarchy"; now it is described in terms of itself and as it is distinguished from the other individual things which exist. Oberman then claims: "This at least relates these new measure languages to the whole climate of the time" (p. 340). What is surprising, of course, is that neither Murdoch nor Oberman mentions the presence of the scheme which we have been tracing in philosophers of the late-thirteenth and early-fourteenth centuries. Granted: fourteenth-century thinkers developed "measure" languages in various and unusual ways; nonetheless their more metaphysically and theologically inclined predecessors had already made use of "measure language" and incorporated the concept of measure into their hierarchical schemes. That being the case, I find the remarks of Oberman just cited to be somewhat implausible.

121 Paul of Venice, Ficino, Gaetano da Thiene, Vernia, Nifo, Pomponazzi, Zimara, Achillini, Zerbo, Grimani, and others were acquainted with the tradition of measuring the intension and remission of forms. It clearly influenced their metaphysical discussions. For surveys of the influence of Richard Swineshead's *Liber calculationum* in Italy during the fifteenth and sixteenth centuries, see Marshall Clagett, *The Science of Mechanics in the Middle Ages* (Madison, 1961), pp. 644–52, 659–71; John E. Murdoch and Edith Dudley Sylla, "Swineshead, Richard," in *Dictionary of Scientific Biography* (New York, 1976), XIII 184–213 at 209–10, 212. See also Carlo Dionisotti, "Ermolao Barbaro e la fortuna di Suiseth," in *Medioevo e Rinascimento: Studi in onore di Bruno Nardi* I (Florence, 1955), pp. 217–53; Eugenio Garin, *Storia della filosofia italiana* (Turin, 1966), pp. 444–49, 456–57; idem, *L'età nuova: Ricerche di storia della cultura dal XII al XVI secolo* (Naples, 1969), pp. 139–66; Curtis Wilson, *William Heytesbury: Medieval Logic and the Rise of Mathematical Physics* (Madison, 1956), pp. 69–93, 106–12; William A. Wallace, "Mechanics from Bradwardine to Galileo," *Journal of the History of Ideas*, 32 (1971), 15–28, esp. 22–24.

122 *Comparationes philosophorum Aristotelis et Platonis* 2.2 (Venice, 1523; repr. Frankfurt, 1965), sigs. D_4^v–D_5^r, E_7^v. On the composition and dating of the *Comparatio*, see the comprehensive study by John Monfasani, *George of Trebizond: A Biography and a Study of His Rhetoric and Logic* (Leiden, 1976), pp. 156–66, 170. George may have derived the notion that all creatures are equally distant from God, since he is infinitely distant from all of them, from Paul of Venice, whom he knew. On their connection, see Monfasani (pp. 14–16), who also argues persuasively (pp. 307–11) that on some points George's *Isagoge dialectica* shows a dependence on Paul.

123 On the composition and dating, see ibid., pp. 166, 212, 219–22. On the controversy, see Paul O. Kristeller, *Renaissance Concepts of Man and Other Essays* (New York, 1972), pp. 96–103; idem, *Renaissance Thought and Its Sources*, ed. Michael Mooney (New York, 1979), pp. 157–59. I am indebted to Professor Monfasani for answering several questions regarding George of Trebizond and Bessarion.

124 *In calumniatorem Platonis libri IV*, 3.6, in Ludwig Mohler, *Kardinal Bessarion als Theologe, Humanist und Staatsmann* II (Paderborn, 1927; repr. Aalen, 1967), pp. 238–39. I have followed the Greek text. My colleague Peter Burian was kind enough to verify my translation of the chapter.

125 Ibid., pp. 240–43. For the passage in Thomas, see *Commentum in quartum librum Sententiarum*, in *Opera omnia* X (Paris, 1873), d. 5, q. 1, a. 3, sol. 3, ad 5, pp. 122–23.

126 For Ficino's high evaluation of the *In calumniatorem Platonis*, see his letter in reply to Bessarion's. Both are presented by Mohler, *Kardinal Bessarion als Theologe, Humanist und Staatsmann*. III. *Aus Bessarions Gelehrtenkreis* (Paderborn, 1942; repr. Aalen, 1967), pp. 543–45. For comment see Arnaldo Della Torre, *Storia dell'Accademia platonica di Firenze* (Florence, 1902), pp. 584–85. In no way do I mean to suggest that Bessarion's work determined Ficino's adoption of the metaphysical scheme or served as a major influence on Ficino's philosophical development, since, as Kristeller points out, Ficino had already worked out his own philosophy. See Paul O. Kristeller, *The Philosophy of Marsilio Ficino*, trans. Virginia Conant (New York, 1943), p. 15; idem, *Studies in Renaissance Thought and Letters* (Rome, 1956), pp. 36, 170. What might be suggested is that Bessarion's work may have made Ficino more conscious of the problem of relating God's infinity to the scheme.

127 See Kristeller, *Philosophy of . . . Ficino*, chap. 6 ("Hierarchy of Being"), pp. 74–84, and chap. 7 ("Unity of the World"), pp. 98–109; idem, *Il pensiero filosofico di Marsilio Ficino* (Florence, 1953), pp. 66–77, 93–105. The latter chapter takes up the principle of "mediation," which itself is based on the concept of continuity. Since Proclus, Dionysius, and Thomas adopt "continuity" in their respective metaphysics, we may perhaps be able to discern their joint influence here on Ficino. But cf. Kristeller, *Medieval Aspects*, pp. 76–77, who wisely cautions against singling out one or two authors as the sole influences on Ficino's metaphysics of participation. The general outline of the scheme was already adopted by Ficino in an early *Tractatus de Deo, natura, et arte* written in 1454 or 1455. See Kristeller, *Studies in Renaissance Thought and Letters*, pp. 44–46, 64–65. I have been unable to find a discussion of the scheme in the important monograph of Michele Schiavone, *Problemi filosofici in Marsilio Ficino* (Milan, 1957). In the light of Schiavone's intimate knowledge of Plotinus, Proclus, and Dionysius, his omission seems all the more regrettable. It should be added, however, that Schiavone brings out clearly (pp. 30–31, 200–201) the centrality of unity and simplicity in Ficino's conception of God. See n. 5 above for reference to Schiavone's book on the Pseudo-Dionysius. In that work, the scheme is alluded to on several occasions. On Ficino's acquaintance with Swineshead (Suiseth) and the *calculatores* tradition, see Kristeller, *Philosophy of . . . Ficino*, pp. 14, 160.

128 *Commentaria in Philebum* 1.27, in *Opera omnia* (Basel, 1576; repr. Turin, 1962), pp. 1233–34. On the problem of whether God is transcendent to or included in the ascending hierarchy of things, see Walter Dress, *Die Mystik des Marsilio Ficino* (Berlin & Leipzig, 1929), pp. 34–35, 55; and Giuseppe Anichini, *L'umanesimo e il problema della salvezza in Marsilio Ficino* (Milan, 1937), pp. 34–37. Two observations about the *Commentaria in Philebum* seem in order: first of all, Ficino reveals (1.18) acquaintance with Albert's commentary on the Pseudo-Dionysius' *De divinis nominibus* (p. 1224; cf. Kristeller, *Studies*, p. 39); and, secondly, he alludes (1.27) specifically to Homer and the "golden chain" (*catena aurea*) when discussing the scheme (p. 1234). Presumably he is here dependent directly on Macrobius' *Commentarii in Somnium Scipionis*, cited in n. 1 above.

129 *Commentaria in Philebum* 1.36, pp. 1249–50. Cf. Kristeller, *Philosophy of . . . Ficino*, pp. 82–83; idem, *Il pensiero filosofico di . . . Ficino*, pp. 75–77. See also the helpful remarks in Ardis Collins, *The Secular Is Sacred: Platonism and Thomism in Marsilio Ficino's "Platonic Theology"* (The Hague, 1974), pp. 18–19, 44–45, 55–56.

130 *Theologia platonica* 2.2., in *Opera omnia*, p. 93. See *Marsile Ficin: Théologie platonicienne de l'immortalité des âmes*, ed. Raymond Marcel, 3 vols. (Paris, 1964–1970).

131 *Theologia platonica* 2.3, p. 95.

132 Ibid., 2.4, p. 96. On God's infinite perfection, the human mind's comparable power to multiply species of numbers to infinity, and God's knowledge at a glance of an infinite number of things, see 2.10, p. 105.

133 Kristeller, *Philosophy of . . . Ficino*, p. 59; idem, *Il pensiero filosofico di . . . Ficino*, p. 51.

134 *Theologia platonica* 10.3, p. 226; 11.6, pp. 259–60.

135 Ibid., 12.7, p. 281. See also Ficino, *Oratio de laudibus philosophiae*, in *Opera omnia*, pp. 767–77. Cf. Kristeller, *Philosophy of . . . Ficino*, pp. 76–78, 164–66; idem, *Il pensiero filosofico di . . . Ficino*, pp. 69–73, 173–75. Kristeller is one of the very few scholars who have touched on the scheme and also recognized the heavy use of spatial language which it involves.

136 *Theologia platonica* 15.11, p. 349.

137 Ibid., 8.4, p. 192. On the presence in Ficino's philosophy of both the Plotinian and medieval conceptions of hierarchy, the one emphasizing a few general spheres and the other accepting only grades or species, see Kristeller, *Philosophy of . . . Ficino*, pp. 75–76, 80–82; idem, *Il pensiero filosofico di . . . Ficino*, pp. 67–68, 72–75; Michael J. B. Allen, "The Absent Angel in Ficino's Philosophy," *Journal of the History of Ideas*, 36 (1975), 219–40. See also the discussion of Ficino's doctrine of grades and hierarchy in Heinrich Bornkamm, "Renaissancemystik, Luther und Boehme," *Luther-Jahrbuch*, 9 (1927), 156–97 at 158–66. There are comparisons made both to Bruno (pp. 166–71) and to Boehme (pp. 171–77). For a five-tiered hierarchic scheme in Aquinas, see n. 39 above. Although Ficino has five spheres in his hierarchy, his source is not Thomas but Plotinus. See Kristeller, *Philosophy of . . . Ficino*, pp. 106–108; idem, *Il pensiero filosofico di . . . Ficino*, pp. 102–105.

138 For a discussion of the themes of continuity, affinity, and mediation in Ficino's hierarchic doctrine, see chap. 7 ("Unity of the World") in Kristeller, *Philosophy of . . . Ficino*, pp. 92–120 (see idem, *Il pensiero filosofico di . . . Ficino*, pp. 86–123); see also chap. 9 ("Primum in aliquo genere"), esp. pp. 147, 150–53, 159–66 (*Il pensiero*, pp. 154–55, 157–61, 167–75) which brings out clearly Ficino's adoption of the scheme in his philosophy. It has recently been argued by A. K. Lloyd, "Primum in genere: The Philosophical Background," *Diotima*, 4 (1976), 32–36, that Ficino's concept of the *primum in aliquo genere* is really not "a novel construction" but a restatement of Proclus without some of the latter's important nuances. Lloyd himself makes almost no reference to medieval developments.

139 *Theologia platonica* 10.4, pp. 247–49, 252–53. Documentation has recently been published which shows that Ficino studied the *Logica* of Paul of Venice when he was about eighteen years of age. See Samuel Jones Hough, "An Early Record of Marsilio Ficino," *Renaissance Quarterly*, 30 (1977), 301–304. This document verifies Kristeller's thesis regarding the early Aristotelian background of Ficino's philosophical development. It is also possible that Ficino read Albert of Saxony during the same period. See ibid., 302*n*4. I have discussed the significance of this document with Paul O. Kristeller and John Monfasani.

140 *Scriptum super librum De anima* (Venice, 1481), I, Prol., t. c. 6, sigs. a_7^{va}–a_8^{va}. Cf. *Pauli Veneti in libros De anima explanatio* (Venice, 1504), fols. 5vb–6rb. Just previously in t. c. 2, sig. a_4^{ra} (fol. 3rb), Paul stated that the human intellect holds the lowest grade in the whole latitude of Intelligences (*tenens gradum infimum in tota latitudine intelligentiarum*). On the terminology of *gradus, non gradus,* and *latitudo*, see Murdoch and Sylla, "Swineshead, Richard," p. 190, col. 1. The application of the *calculatores* terminology to Averroës' doctrine on the unity of the intellect and the Intelligences would be adopted

by other Renaissance Aristotelians. It should be noted that while Paul here appears to relate composition to distance from God, he is commenting on Averroës. Elsewhere, as we shall see, he uniformly rejects the view that distance from God determines the grade of a thing.

On Paul's biography, see Felice Momigliano, *Paolo Veneto e le correnti del pensiero religioso e filosofico nel suo tempo* (Turin, 1907), especially pp. 9–66; Alan R. Perreiah, "A Biographical Introduction to Paul of Venice," *Augustiniana*, 17 (1967), 450–61. There has been some scholarly debate regarding the respective dating of Paul's works, especially his *Summa naturalium* and his commentary on the *Physics*. Pierre Duhem proposed that the *Summa naturalium* must be later than the commentary on the *Physics*, which was finished in 1409. See Duhem, *Études sur Léonard de Vinci* III (Paris, 1955), pp. 104–105, 482; idem, *Le Système du monde* X (Paris, 1959), pp. 392–96. However, Bruno Nardi proved from a manuscript in the Biblioteca Nazionale Marciana (Venice) that the *Summa* was composed in 1408, and he argued that the differences which Duhem discerned between Paul's *Physics* and *Summa* could also be found to exist between the *De anima* and the *Summa*. See Nardi, *Saggi*, pp. 76–77. Both Duhem and Nardi agree that the *De anima* commentary is a late work. I shall abstract from the respective datings in my brief treatment of Paul here. It might perhaps be argued that Paul has changed his position in the later commentary on the *De anima*.

141 *Scriptum super librum De anima*, II, tr. 1, ch. 3, t. c. 2, sig. E_7^{rb}. Cf. *In libros De anima explanatio*, fol. 51vb.

142 *Expositio super octo libros Physicorum Aristotelis necnon super commento Averrois cum dubiis eiusdem* (Venice, 1499), V, tr. 1, ch. 3, t. c. 19, sig. B_5^{rb}. Cf. Albert the Great, *Physicorum libri VIII*, ed. A. Borgnet, *Opera omnia* III (Paris, 1890), V, tr. 1, ch. 8, p. 374^2. However, Paul does accept that God is the first in the genera of final and efficient causality, since there is an essential order in these genera of causes. See *Expositio*, VI, tr. 1, ch. 4, sig. G_3^{ra}. For a critique of Paul's argument in V, tr. 1, ch. 3, see Agostino Nifo, *Aristotelis physicarum acroasum hoc est naturalium auscultationum liber* (Venice, 1508), V, fol. 135^{ra-b}. One of the philosophers who may have inspired Paul's discussion and criticism of God as a measure of the hierarchy of being is Albert of Saxony (1316–1390). See his *Acutissimae quaestiones super libros De physica auscultatione*, VII, q. 5, fols. 72vb–73rb, cited above in n. 118. Pierre Duhem has argued for Paul's heavy dependence on Albert. See *Études sur Léonard de Vinci* II (Paris, 1955), pp. 32, 91, 347–51, and also *Le Système du monde* IV, pp. 283–84.

143 *Summa naturalium* (Venice, 1476), sig. f_1^{va-b}, f_4^{rb}. I omit reference to Paul's remarks on infinity and the plurality of worlds. See also sig. f_2^{ra-b}.

144 Ibid., sig. y_2^{va}–y_7^{vb}, esp. y_6^{va-b}.

145 *Recollectae super octo libros Physicorum Aristotelis* (Vicenza, 1487), I, q. 19, sig. e_8^{va-b}. For the dating of his commentaries, see Silvestro Da Valsanzibio, *Vita e dottrina di Gaetano di Thiene* (Padua, 1949), pp. 23ff.

146 *Super libros De anima* (Venice, 1493), III, comm. 5, fol. 59^{ra-b}.

147 *Quaestio an dentur universalia realia*, in Urbanus Averroista, *Super librum Aristotelis De physico* (Venice, 1492), unnumbered folio 4vb. Both Vernia and Thiene were much interested in the discussions regarding intension and remission of forms which had developed in the fourteenth century. See n. 121 above. Thiene wrote a treatise on the subject (Da Valsanzibio, *Vita . . . di Gaetano di Thiene*, pp. 23–24), and he alludes to it in his *Recollectae* on the *Physics* (see for example III, q. 1, sig. g_5^{rb}).

148 *Quaestiones metaphysicales* (Bologna, 1482), I, q. 1, sig. a_3^{vb}–a_4^{ra}; XII, q. 10, sig. ee_5^{ra}–ee_6^{rb}. For a discussion regarding the relationship between the order of

separate substances and the order of the heavenly bodies, see XII, q. 19, sig. gg_1^{rb}–gg_3^{ra}. Authors mentioned include Albert, Averroës, and John of Jandun. On Zerbo, see José Riesco, "Gabriel de Zerbis, medico y filosofo humanista," *Giornale di metafisica,* 19 (1964), 90–97; Poppi, *Causalità e infinità,* pp. 151–69.

149 *Quaestiones metaphysicales,* X, q. 3, sig. aa_3^{rb}–aa_4^{rb}. For the remark regarding Swineshead, see sig. aa_4^{rb}: "quicquid dixit Calculator in suo de intensione et remissione, cuius rationes non demonstrant."

150 *Calculationes noviter emendatae atque revisae* (Venice, 1520), fols. 2ra–5ra. For discussion, see especially Clagett, "Richard Swineshead and Late Medieval Physics," 131–61; Sylla, "Medieval Concepts," 271–75; Murdoch & Sylla, "Swineshead," pp. 188–90.

151 See Pearl Kibre, "Cardinal Domenic Grimani, 'Questio de intensione et remissione qualitatis': A Commentary on the Tractate of that Title by Richard Suiseth (Calculator)," in *Didascaliae: Studies in Honor of Anselm M. Albareda,* ed. Sesto Prete (New York, 1961), pp. 187–89. See nn. 27, 29, 33 above. On Grimani's connections with Padua and philosophers like Vernia, Elia del Medigo, Pico della Mirandola, and Nifo, see Pio Paschini, *Domenico Grimani, Cardinale di San Marco († 1523)* (Rome, 1943), pp. 3–15, 125, 127–32. On his philosophical orientation, see also Mario Dal Pra, "Metafisica e scienza in una *quaestio* inedita di Domenico Grimani," in *Aristotelismo padovano e filosofia,* Atti del XII Congresso Internazionale di Filosofia IX (Florence, 1960), pp. 61–69.

152 Kibre, "Grimani," pp. 189–94.

153 Ibid., pp. 199–202.

154 *Corsi inediti dell'insegnamento padovano.* I. "*Super libello de substantia orbis expositio et quaestiones quattuor*" (*1507*), ed. Antonino Poppi (Padua, 1966), chap. 2, pp. 110–11. See also q. 1, pp. 195, 210. On Pomponazzi's opposition to the thought of the *calculatores,* see Bruno Nardi, *Studi su Pietro Pomponazzi* (Florence, 1965), p. 63. Pomponazzi further developed his critique of Swineshead and of the view that the grades in the hierarchy of being should be determined only by reference to the zero grade in his *Tractatus de intensione et remissione,* which was finished at Bologna in 1514 and published in his *Tractatus acutissimi, utilissimi et mere peripatetici* (Venice, 1525), fols. 2ra–20rb. He offers (fol. 2^{ra-b}) in behalf of the first position — namely, that intension and remission are measured by approach to and receding from the highest grade of a latitude — such authorities as Aristotle, Averroës, Plato's *Philebus,* Ficino's *Platonic Theology,* Dionysius' *De coelesti hierarchia,* and Augustine's *Confessions* 12.7. He presents (fol. 2^{va-b}) as the second opinion, whose author he claims to be unknown, that intension and remission are determined by distance from the zero grade and the highest grade of a latitude respectively. Pomponazzi shows (fol. 15vb) special concern with the objection to God as the measure that since God is of infinite perfection everything outside him will be infinitely imperfect and thus no creature will be more perfect than another. The Intelligence, the man, and the ass will all be equal, a result which is ridiculous (*derisibile*). I shall discuss Pomponazzi's somewhat abstruse reply on another occasion. What surely must be noted, however, is his careful attention to the language involved in such discussions — the entire "Sectio secunda" of the treatise is devoted to the problem (*de nominibus*), and remarks about language are scattered throughout the work. He tells us apropos of *distare* and *appropinquare,* and *distantia* and *propinquitas,* that we move from what is said properly (*indictis secundum proprietatem*) to what is said metaphorically or by transferral (*secundum transumptionem*), and he points out that the near and the distant are spoken in the proper and true sense only of place (*locus*). He goes on to suggest as one possible account that *distantia* is taken by transferral (*transumptive*) for *differentia,* just as *propinquitas* is taken for *convenientia,* that is, likeness or similarity, though he does not seem wholly satisfied with it (fol. 4rb–

4va; cf. fol. 10va). Especially perceptive are his awareness that a process of imagining is involved in the doctrine of measuring the more and the less from the zero grade (fol. 4^{va-b}) and his remark that "to be distant" (*distare*) often means "to be more distant" (*magis distare*), as when we say that Ferrara is distant from Venice but approaches another city located closer to it (fol. 5va). Swineshead's misuse of language is pointed out (fol. 13ra). For a discussion of this treatise which concentrates mostly on Pomponazzi's presentation and attack on Swineshead, see Curtis Wilson, "Pomponazzi's Criticism of Calculator," *Isis*, 44 (1953), 355–63.

155 *Opus in Metaphysicam Aristotelis Padue in thomistas discussam cum quaestionibus perutilissimis antiquioribus adiectis* (Venice, 1502), fol. 84rb. See also fols. 77vb, 94rb. For a good introduction to Trombetta, see Antonino Poppi, "Lo scotista patavino Antonio Trombetta (1436–1517)," *Il Santo*, 2 (1962), 349–67. On Trombetta's metaphysical thought and its Scotist orientation, see Pietro Scapin, "La metafisica scotista a Padova dal xv al xvii secolo," in *Storia e cultura al Santo di Padova fra il XIII e il XX secolo*, ed. A. Poppi (Vicenza, 1976), pp. 501–509. For a survey of Scotus' influence during this period, see my "Duns Scotus and the School of Padua around 1500," in *Regnum hominis et regnum Dei* II, ed. Camille Bérubé, Studia Scholastico-Scotistica 7 (Rome, 1978), pp. 215–27.

156 *In De ente et essentia D. Thomae Aquinatis commentaria*, ed. M.-H. Laurent (Turin, 1934), ch. 5, no. 103, pp. 162–63, and ch. 6, no. 131, pp. 210, 212–13. On the dating and place of composition, see M.-J. Congar, "Bio-bibliographie de Cajetan," *Revue Thomiste*, 39 (1934–1935), Special number, p. 5. For further remarks regarding Cajetan's metaphysical views during his early Paduan period, see Armand Maurer, "Cajetan's Notion of Being in His Commentary on the Sentences," *Mediaeval Studies*, 28 (1966), 268–78. Maurer shows his dependence on Capreolus. In a question finished at Pavia in 1499 entitled "Utrum Deus gloriosus sit infinitae virtutis," Cajetan raises a standard objection to measuring the perfection of things according to their approach (*accessus*) to the highest being: if God is infinite, then no being will be more perfect than any other. His reply is to say that while the nature (*ratio*) of the distance from God to creatures is infinite, on the part of the creatures that distance is limited (*finitur*), and therefore one creature is closer than another to the First Being. He distinguishes between infinite distance *simpliciter* and *secundum quid*. See the edition of his *Opuscula omnia* (Venice, 1588), pp. 193^1, 205^2. This reply may be inspired by Thomas' remarks in the commentary on *Sentences*, IV, d. 5, q. 1, a. 3, sol. 3, ad 5, cited in n. 125 above. For discussion of both these works of Cajetan, see Poppi, *Causalità e infinità*, pp. 170–85.

157 *Corona aurea* (Venice, 1496), sig. i_7^r–i_8^v. See sig. i_4^v for citation of the *De ente*. On Brutus, see Leonard Kennedy, "A Fifteenth-Century Authentic Thomist," *The Modern Schoolman*, 42 (1965), 193–97, who says the work reveals "a detailed and profound knowledge of Aquinas's writings" (p. 194).

158 *Quaestio de mundi efficientia* (1480), in John of Jandun, *Super octo libros Aristotelis De physico auditu* (Venice, 1551), fol. 140ra, 140va. Cf. Elia's *Quaestio de esse et essentia et uno* (ca. 1486), fol. 143ra and his *Quaestio de primo motore* (1480), fols. 136vb–138ra. On Elia's thought in these questions, see Poppi, *Causalità e infinità*, pp. 135–50. For his scholarly activities and relations to Pico, Grimani, and others, see Umberto Cassuto, *Gli ebrei a Firenze nell'età del Rinascimento* (Florence, 1918), pp. 282–99; Bohdan Kieszkowski, "Les rapports entre Elie del Medigo et Pic de la Mirandole," *Rinascimento*, 4 (1964), 41–91.

159 *Quaestio de primo motore*, fol. 139rb. See also fol. 130rb. In the *Quaestio de mundi efficientia*, fols. 141va–142rb, Elia speaks of the more and less noble and even of man's

being closer according to nobility to the heavenly bodies. Nonetheless, although he here discusses the ordering according to nobility of the lower forms in relation to the intellective soul and of man's relation to that soul and to the heavenly bodies, and speaks of an *ordo* of the Intelligences or separate movers of the heavenly bodies among themselves, he never introduces a metaphysical scheme involving participation, grades, and a measuring by an approaching toward or a receding from the two termini of God and prime matter. One would have expected such a commitment at fol. 138rb, where Elia says that the being of each thing comes from the unity of God and all things ascend (*ascendunt*) to the first unity, just as in the case of fire. In a word, Elia uses Averroës' *Destructio destructionum* and *Metaphysics*, XII, comm. 44 but does not attribute to Averroës participation and the scheme. On the other hand, Nifo uses these texts for precisely such an interpretation of the Commentator.

160 See *Destructiones destructionum Averroys cum Augustini Niphi de Suessa expositione* (Venice, 1497). See fol. 1^v for the dedicatory letter to Cardinal Grimani. I believe that Nifo's influence can be detected in Geronimo Taiapetra, *Summa divinarum ac naturalium quaestionum* (Venice, 1506), I, tr. 2, ch. 14, sig. $f_1{}^r$–$f_2{}^r$, and ch. 16, sig. $f_4{}^v$–$f_5{}^r$. There were obvious reactions in the thought of Marcantonio Zimara, as will be clear from the analysis below.

161 See my "Agostino Nifo and Saint Thomas Aquinas," *Memorie domenicane*, 7 (1976), 195–225, esp. 196–98. I shall discuss on another occasion the varying views on whether Averroës taught a metaphysics of participation — for example, the views of Siger, Jandun, and Nifo, and those of modern scholars. There are passages in the *Incoherence of the Incoherence* which might lead one to believe that he did. See, for example, M. Chossat, "Dieu (sa nature selon les scolastiques)," *Dictionnaire de Théologie Catholique* (Paris, 1939), IV, cols. 1228–32, 1241. But see A. Gardeil's critical review of this article, "'Destruction des destructions' du R. P. Chossat," *Revue Thomiste*, 18 (1910), 361–91. For discussion regarding Averroës' views on God, creation, and hierarchy, especially in the *Tahāfut* (*Destructio*), see Cruz Hernandez, *Historia* II, pp. 139–44; Roger Arnaldez, "La Pensée religieuse d'Averroès. I. La Doctrine de la création dans le Tahāfut," *Studia Islamica*, 7 (1957), 99–114; and "II. La Théorie de Dieu dans le Tahāfut," ibid., 8 (1958), 15–28. Nifo's constant references to participation and to the passage in *Metaphysics* II, 1 would seem to suggest that he is borrowing from Thomas and Albert. His approach should be contrasted to that of Elia, who cited the *Destructio* years earlier but rarely referred to either Thomas or Albert.

162 For references to the *Liber de causis*, see *Destructiones*, III, dub. 12, fol. 35vb; VII, dub. 3, fol. 84^{va-b}; VII, dub. 5, fol. 89ra; XIV, dub. 1, fol. 122rb. There is a reference to Albert's commentary in XIV, dub. 1, fol. 119ra.

163 Ibid., III, dub. 12, fols. 35rb–36vb. There is heavy use of *Metaphysics* II, 1. See also III, dub. 2, fol. 30ra; V, dub. 30, fol. 70ra; VIII, dub. 1, fol. 92rb.

164 Ibid., III, dub. 16, fols. 42vb–43ra. See also V, dub. 3, fol. 70rb.

165 Ibid., VIII, dub. 1, fol. 92ra. See also III, dub. 14, fol. 14vb; dub. 19, fol. 52ra.

166 Ibid., VII, dub. 3, fol. 84rb. See also VIII, dub. 1, fol. 92rb.

167 Ibid., IV, dub. 2, fol. 74vb; VIII, dub. 1, fol. 92^{ra-b}. This distinction is also found in Nifo's later works. See my "Pier Nicola Castellani and Agostino Nifo on Averroës' Doctrine of the Agent Intellect," *Rivista critica di storia della filosofia*, 25 (1970), 398–405.

168 *Destructiones*, VII, dub. 5, fol. 89ra.

169 Ibid., III, dub. 28, fol. 57^{rb-va}. See also III, dub. 16, fol. 43ra.

170 Ibid., VIII, dub. 1, fol. 92ra. See also III, dub. 19, fol. 52ra. The scheme reappears in other early works of Nifo's: namely, the *De anima* (1503), the *De intellectu* (1503), and

the *De beatitudine animae* (1508). On these works, see my article cited in n. 155. The scheme is also presented in his *De primi motoris infinitate liber*, which was dedicated to Grimani. But see the somewhat reserved comments relating to the scheme in Nifo's *Metaphysicarum disputationum dilucidarium* (Naples, 1511), X, disp. 1, ch. 3, fols. 343^{v}–344^{r}; ch. 4, fol. 345^{r}; XII, disp. 6, ch. 4, fol. 398^{v}. Indeed in the last text he appears to include Averroës' doctrine of the two grades in each Intelligence among views for which there exist only dialectical arguments and no demonstrations.

171 *Annotationes in Joannem Gandavensem super quaestionibus Metaphysicae*, in John of Jandun, *Quaestiones in duodecim libros Metaphysicae* (Venice, 1505), fols. 174^{rb-va}, 175va. Among the texts which Zimara uses for his position is Averroës' long commentary on *Metaphysics* II, comm. 4, and XII, comm. 44. Cf. Maurer, "John of Jandun," 195–97. For a good review of Zimara's works and career, see Nardi, *Saggi*, 321–55. His thought in the early works is discussed in depth by Poppi, *Causalità e infinità*, pp. 237–56.

172 *Annotationes*, fol. 170^{rb-va}. Cf. fols. 178ra, 174va. See also *Solutiones contradictionum in dictis Averroys*, in *Quaestio de primo cognito* (Venice, 1508), fol. 33ra.

173 *Theoremata seu memorabilium propositionum limitationes* (Venice, 1539), Prop. 10, fol. 6ra.

174 Ibid., Prop. 12, fol. 9ra.

175 Ibid., Prop. 13, fols. 9rb–10ra. Dionysius is also cited in the *Annotationes*, fol. 174rb. Augustine too is used as an authority. See, for example, *Theoremata*, Prop. 13, fol. 10ra.

176 *Theoremata*, Prop. 40, fols. 25vb–26rb; Prop. 62, fols. 46vb–47ra. The citation given in Scotus is to *Sentences*, I, dist. 8, q. 2. See n. 88 above. Zimara's sympathies for Scotus are well underlined by Antonio Antonaci, *Ricerche sull' aristotelismo del Rinascimento: Marcantonio Zimara* I (Lecce–Galatina, 1971), pp. 109, 304; idem, "Il pensiero di Duns Scoto negli scritti di Marcantonio Zimara," in *Regnum hominis et regnum dei*, pp. 249–56. See also my article cited in n. 155.

177 *Theoremata*, Prop. 83, fol. 61^{ra-b}.

178 *De intelligentiis quodlibeta* (Bologna, 1494), Quodl. I, q. 1, sig. A_2^{ra}. On Achillini, see Herbert Matsen, *Alessandro Achillini (1463–1512) and His Doctrine of "Universals" and "Transcendentals"* (Lewisburg, Pa., 1974); Nardi, *Saggi*, pp. 179–279, esp. pp. 182–84; Poppi, *Causalità e infinità*, pp. 186–93; Garin, *Storia della filosofia italiana*, pp. 502–504, 563–64.

179 *De intelligentiis*, Quodl. II, q. 1, sig. B_6^{ra}. See Nardi, *Saggi*, pp. 193–94.

180 *De intelligentiis*, Quodl. II, q. 4, sig. C_4^{vb}. Achillini states that at this point he is at the doors of theology: "Et hic in ianuis theologiae secundum quodlibetum complemus."

181 Ibid., Quodl. V, qq. 1–2, sigs. F_3^{ra-va}, F_4^{ra}–F_5^{ra}. For discussion of how, granted God is finite, things will vary in dignity according to their distance, that is closeness or remoteness, from God and also according to their composition, see sig. F_3^{v}. For a consideration of an ordering downward by grades (*gradatim descendendo*) from God to the lowest Intelligence according to the mode of cognition and of a ranking by orbs which are informed, see Quodl. II, q. 3, sig. C_2^{rb}–C_3^{vb}, and Quodl. V, q. 3, sig. E_6^{rb-va}. See Nardi, *Saggi*, pp. 200–201, 220–21, esp. p. 221, who alludes to the *Liber de causis* and Proclus' *Elements of Theology*. He also refers (p. 227) to Achillini's use of the schemata of the *calculatores* tradition.

182 For example, the Dominican Giovanni Crisostomo Javelli (ca. 1470–ca. 1538) presents the scheme in his *Epitome super propositionibus Libri de causis* (Venice, 1567), Prop. IV, fols. 28^{r}–30^{r}. See also Prop. IX, fol. 41^{r-v} for reference to participation. One of Pomponazzi's students, Gaspare Contarini (1483–1542), follows his teacher in making

God the measure of the latitude of being and in rejecting the zero grade as a possible measure. In the *Primae philosophiae compendium*, in his *Opera* (Paris, 1571), Contarini points out that very learned men say that all beings besides the First Being are composed of a perfection by which they approach (*accedit*) to that which is truly being and an imperfection by which they recede (*recedit*) from that being (II, pp. 106–107; cf. p. 117; III, p. 123; VI, pp. 161–62, 167). Intension and remission must take place by approach (*accessus*) to and receding (*recessus*) from the highest grade (*summus gradus*), and not by receding from the zero grade (*non gradus*). Since non-being is by nature infinite, uncertain, and fluctuating, it cannot serve as a measure (*mensura*), whereas that which is the most perfect in a genus is most finite (*maxime finitum*), certain, and one, like the target at which an archer shoots (II, p. 110). Contarini shows special concern to explain that God is absolutely infinite, since there is neither contraction or limitation within him to any definite nature nor any localization; and yet he is also finite, since he more than anything else is free of the infinity of matter and multitude. Just as the closer we approach in numbers to unity the closer we are brought to finiteness (*finitudo*), so as we approach to God, who is the very essence of unity (*ipsa essentia unitatis*), do we approach that which is the most finite of all (*maxime omnium finitum*). Both Plato and the Pseudo-Dionysius are used to argue that at the end of this approach to God only silence is appropriate (IV, pp. 141–43). I shall refrain from giving other examples here of sixteenth-century discussions of hierarchical schemes, but shall present them later in a book on the subject.

183 Galileo is critical of the attempt to measure the hierarchy of created things by taking God as a standard or measure, while Cremonini opposes all composition in the Intelligences, such as that postulated by Zimara, to account for their ordering in a hierarchy. I state their views and those of Buonamici and Mazzoni at the conclusion of my article "Neoplatonism, the Greek Commentators, and Renaissance Aristotelianism," in *Neoplatonism and Christian Thought*, ed. Dominic O'Meara (Albany, N.Y., 1981). I plan to analyze all four in greater detail on another occasion.

184 The two most famous attacks on the "chain of being" doctrine in the modern period were those of Samuel Johnson and Voltaire. See Johnson's critique of Soame Jenyns in his "Review of a Free Enquiry into the Nature and Origin of Evil," in *The Works of Samuel Johnson* IX (London, 1825), pp. 47–76; Voltaire, *Dictionnaire philosophique* I, ed. Raymond Naves (Paris, 1936), pp. 141–44. Johnson appears to believe that the "system of subordination" which he is attacking had its origins among "the Arabian metaphysicians" (p. 49), and he ends his essay by referring to "the Arabian scale of existence" (p. 75). On the other hand, Voltaire blames the "phantom" or "fable" of the ladder or chain of being wholly on Plato. Neither speaks of God and/or non-being as the "measures" of the grades of the chain. This concept was lost, it would appear, in modern thought. See n. 186 below. As I shall point out, Leibniz, Locke, and Berkeley also lack this concept of God and/or non-being as *measures* of all else in the scale of being.

185 For discussion see John Burnaby, *Amor Dei: A Study of the Religion of St. Augustine* (London, 1938, 1947), pp. 36–41, 90*n*5, 149–50, 162, 174, 193–94; Olivier Du Roy, *L'Intelligence de la foi dans la Trinité selon saint Augustin* (Paris, 1966), pp. 185–90, 324, 334–37, 477–78; Christopher J. O'Toole, *The Philosophy of Creation in the Writings of St. Augustine* (Washington, D.C., 1944), pp. 29–30; Robert J. O'Connell, *St. Augustine's Early Theory of Man, A.D. 386–391* (Cambridge, Mass., 1968), pp. 41, 45–49, 114, 117–20, 143–44; idem, *St. Augustine's Confessions: The Odyssey of Soul* (Cambridge, Mass., 1969), pp. 80–88, 146–49, 178–81; Nygren, *Agape and Eros*, pp. 488–90, 506–507, 512–32; Émilie Zum Brunn, *Le Dilemme de l'être et du néant chez saint Augustin. Des premiers dialogues aux "Confessions"* (Paris, 1969); eadem, "La Dialectique du 'magis esse' et du 'minus

esse' chez saint Augustin," in *Le Néoplatonisme*, pp. 373–80; Willy Theiler, "Porphyrios und Augustin," in *Forschungen zum Neuplatonismus* (Berlin, 1966), pp. 160–251, esp. pp. 172–74, 180–82, 186–88; Ragnar Holte, *Beatitude et sagesse: Saint Augustin et le problème de la fin de l'homme dans la philosophie ancienne* (Paris, 1962), pp. 233–38, 248–49, 287–88; F. Joachim von Rintelen, "Augustine: The Ascent in Value Towards God," *Augustinian Studies*, 2 (1971), 155–78; Frederick E. Van Fleteren, "Augustine's Ascent of the Soul in Book VII of the *Confessions*," ibid., 5 (1974), 29–72.

186 Various figures mentioned by Lovejoy in his *The Great Chain of Being* speak of a chain or series of grades extended between two termini, God and nothingness. However, in none of these figures (at least according to the texts given) is there the notion that the grade or species of a thing is *measured* by approaching toward and receding from the termini. Some of those mentioned by Lovejoy who adopt some of the elements of the scheme are Alexander Pope (pp. 60–61), John Milton (p. 164), Joseph Addison (pp. 184–85, 190–91), Edmund Law (pp. 185, 213, 216, 248–49), Soame Jenyns (p. 197), William King (p. 213), and Thomas Sprat (p. 232). See also Emil Wolff, *Die goldene Kette: Die Aurea Catena Homeri in der englischen Literatur von Chaucer bis Wordsworth* (Hamburg, 1947) for Dryden (pp. 15–16), Spenser (p. 25), Pope (pp. 57–60), Thomson (p. 65), and Young (pp. 69–70). There is also a good survey of the impact of the concept of the chain of being in E. M. W. Tillyard, *The Elizabethan World Picture* (London, 1943), pp. 23–76. For a good treatment of Milton's hierarchic views, together with background material and reference to others of his period, see C. A. Patrides, *Milton and the Christian Tradition* (Oxford, 1966), pp. 59–68. Spencer's position has been studied by James Hutton in his essay "Spenser's 'Adamantine Chains': A Cosmological Metaphor," in *Essays on Renaissance Poetry*, ed. Rita Guerlac (Ithaca N.Y., 1980), pp. 169–91, esp. pp. 173–75. Benjamin Franklin speaks of a "scale of beings" which goes down from the elephant to the oyster and up from the elephant to "the infinitely Great, Good and Wise." He assumes a gradation without gap both below and above. See his "An Arabian Tale," in *The Writings of Benjamin Franklin* X, ed. A. H. Smith (New York, 1907), pp. 123–24. For a survey of the concept of the hierarchy of being in early American thought, see Herbert Leventhal, *In the Shadow of the Enlightenment: Occultism and Renaissance Science in Eighteenth-Century America* (New York, 1976), chap. 8, "The Chain of Being," pp. 219–59.

187 Emile Lasbax, *La Hiérarchie dans l'univers chez Spinoza*, 2nd ed. (Paris, 1926), pp. 51–59; Edwin A. Burtt, *The Metaphysical Foundations of Modern Science* (New York, 1954), pp. 105–24; E. J. Dijksterhuis, *The Mechanization of the World Picture*, trans. C. Dikshoorn (Oxford, 1961), pp. 403–18; A. Rupert Hall, *The Scientific Revolution, 1500–1800*, 2nd ed. (London, 1962), pp. 94–98, 178–84; S. V. Keeling, *Descartes*, 2nd ed. (London, 1968), pp. 131–46, 282–90; Richard S. Westfall, *The Construction of Modern Science: Mechanisms and Mechanics* (New York, 1971), pp. 30–39, 92–94, 120–22; James Collins, *Descartes' Philosophy of Nature* (Oxford, 1971), pp. 23–24, 71–79, 87–93. For helpful studies on the impact of the new science and of Descartes' mechanism, see Marjorie Hope Nicolson, *The Breaking of the Circle*, rev. ed. (New York, 1960), and Leonora Cohen Rosenfield, *From Beast-Machine to Man-Machine* (New York, 1941). Though Descartes appears to reject a hierarchy of being, he does presume a gradation in the clarity and distinctness of our knowledge. He also speaks of ideas as having more and less "objective being." See in particular *Meditation* III in *Meditationes de prima philosophia* (Paris, 1970), pp. 34–52. For relevant discussion, see Keeling, *Descartes*, pp. 115–18, and Margaret D. Wilson, *Descartes* (London, 1978), pp. 111–12, 127, 132–33, 137. I have profited from conversation with Norman Wells on these points.

188 "Iis autem, qui quaerunt, cur Deus omnes homines non ita creavit, ut solo rationis ductu gubernarentur? nihil aliud respondeo, quam quia ei non defuit materia ad omnia, ex summo nimirum ad infimum perfectionis gradum, creanda . . ." *Ethica ordine geometrico demonstrata* I, Appendix, in *Opera*, ed. Carl Gebhardt (Heidelberg, 1925), p. 83. See Lovejoy, *Great Chain*, p. 223; Patrides, "Hierarchy and Order," 445. For a general study, see the Lasbax book cited in the previous note. Spinoza's views on the gradation among living things have been examined by Hans Jonas, "Spinoza and the Theory of Organism," in *Spinoza: A Collection of Critical Essays*, ed. Marjorie Grene (Garden City, N.Y., 1973), pp. 259–78, esp. pp. 269–70, 273–78.

189 *De rerum originatione radicali*, ed. C. I. Gerhardt, in *Die philosophischen Schriften* VII (Leipzig, 1931), pp. 303–304; *Nouveaux Essais sur l'entendement humain* 3.6.12, 4.16.12, in ibid. V (Berlin, 1882), pp. 285–86, 453–56; "Brief von Leibniz an Varignon über das Kontinuitätsprinzip," in *Hauptschriften zur Grundlegung der Philosophie* II, edd. A. Buchenau and E. Cassirer (Hamburg, 1966), pp. 556–59. Leibniz also uses a spatial image to represent the variety of possible worlds: namely, a pyramid which becomes more beautiful as one ascends toward the apex. See *Essai de théodicée sur la bonté de Dieu, la liberté de l'homme et l'origine du mal*, 2nd ed. (Amsterdam, 1712), nos. 413–17, pp. 613–20. On Leibniz's hierarchical thought, see Lovejoy, *Great Chain*, esp. pp. 144, 178–80, 233, 255–62; Bentley Glass, "The Germination of the Idea of Biological Species," in *Forerunners of Darwin: 1745–1859*, edd. B. Glass, O. Temkin, and W. L. Strauss, Jr. (Baltimore, 1959), pp. 37–39; Leroy E. Loemker, *Struggle for Synthesis: The Seventeenth-Century Background of Leibniz's Synthesis of Order and Freedom* (Cambridge, Mass., 1972), esp. pp. 171–75; Formigari, "Chain of Being," 327–28; Patrides, "Hierarchy of Order," 445–46.

190 *The Laws of Ecclesiastical Polity* 1.4.1, 1.6.2–3, ed. R. W. Church, 2nd ed. (Oxford, 1876), pp. 19–20, 24–25. I am indebted to Mr. James Hankins for bringing these passages in Hooker to my attention.

191 *An Essay Concerning Human Understanding* 3.6.9–12, ed. Peter H. Nidditch (Oxford, 1975), pp. 444–47. Cf. Lovejoy, *Great Chain*, p. 184. On the concept of infinity, see *Essay* 2.17, pp. 209–23. The role of the chain of being in Locke's political philosophy is brought out by John Dunn, *The Political Thought of John Locke* (Cambridge, 1969), 87–95.

192 *Essay* 4.16.12, 665–67. Cf. Gerd Buchdahl, *Metaphysics and the Philosophy of Science, The Classical Origins: Descartes to Kant* (Cambridge, Mass. 1969), p. 214.

193 *Siris* 274, 284, ed. T. E. Jessop, in *The Works of George Berkeley* V (London & Edinburgh, 1953), pp. 129, 133. Cf. John Wild, *George Berkeley* (Cambridge, Mass., 1936), pp. 422–79; A. D. Ritchie, "George Berkeley's *Siris*: The Philosophy of the Great Chain of Being and the Alchemical Theory," *Proceedings of the British Academy*, 40 (1954), 41–55; Maguib Baladi, "Le Témoignage de la *Siris*," *Revue Internationale de Philosophie*, 24, No. 92 (1970), 338–47.

194 *Siris* 294, 296, 301–303, 313, 333, 340, pp. 136–37, 139–40, 144–45, 152, 154–55.

195 For references to the *Celestial Hierarchy* and the *Divine Names*, see *Alciphron*, ed. T. E. Jessop, in *The Works of George Berkeley* III (London & Edinburgh, 1950), pp. 166–68. Berkeley speaks of God as "infinitely above" man (p. 170), and he argues by analogy from the visible things that "there are innumerable orders of intelligent beings more happy and more perfect than man" (p. 172). He makes no attempt to rank the orders of angels, however, nor does he invoke a scheme of their ascending in perfection as they approach God. There is no reference to the question of hierarchy in Peter S. Wenz, "Berkeley's Christian Neo-Platonism," *Journal of the History of Ideas*, 37 (1976), 537–46.

196 C. A. Patrides, "Renaissance Thought on the Celestial Hierarchy: The Decline of a Tradition," *Journal of the History of Ideas*, 20 (1959), 155–66; idem, "Renaissance Views on the 'Unconfused Orders Angellick,'" ibid., 23 (1962), 265–67.

197 Cranz, "Transmutation of Platonism," 97–102; Nygren, *Agape and Eros*, pp. 701–709; Erwin Metzke, *Coincidentia oppositorum: Gesammelte Studien zur Philosophiegeschichte*, ed. K. Gründer (Witten, 1961), pp. 211–13. However, Luther was much taken with the language of "ascent" and "descent," which he applied both to Christ and to the human soul. See, for example, his *First Lectures on the Psalms. I. Psalms 1–75*, ed. H. C. Oswald, Luther's Works X (Saint Louis, Mo., 1974), Psalm 18, esp. pp. 118–21, where Dionysius and Jacob's ladder are mentioned.

198 Paul Henri Michel, *The Cosmology of Giordano Bruno*, trans. R. E. W. Maddison (Paris, London, & Ithaca, N.Y., 1973), pp. 77–79, 87–88, 108–12, 178–79; Patrides, "Hierarchy and Order," 442–43. It should be noted, however, that hierarchical language is to be found in various of Bruno's works. See Hélène Védrine, *La Conception de la nature chez Giordano Bruno* (Paris, 1967), pp. 105, 108–11.

199 Nicholas of Cusa, *De concordantia catholica* I, ch. 2, ed. G. Kallen, Opera omnia XIV (Hamburg, 1963), pp. 33–36; III, ch. 7, p. 359; *De docta ignorantia*, I, ch. 4, Opera I (Paris, 1514; repr. Frankfurt, 1962), fol. 2^{r-v}; chs. 16–17, fols. 6^{v}–7^{v}; II, chs. 1–3, fols. 13–15; ch. 10, fol. 20^{r}–^{v}; III, ch. 1, fol. 24^{r-v}; ch. 3, fol. 25^{v}. There is scholarly disagreement as to whether or not Cusa did abandon the hierarchical conception of reality. For a good introduction, see Cranz, "Transformation of Platonism," pp. 82–97. But see also Ernst Cassirer, *The Individual and the Cosmos in Renaissance Philosophy*, trans. Mario Domandi (New York, 1963), esp. pp. 8–29, 176–82. I shall discuss the problem and the extensive literature on Cusa on another occasion.

200 See n. 186.

201 See, for example, J. B. Robinet, *Vue philosophique de la gradation naturelle des formes de l'être ou les essais de la nature qui apprend à faire l'homme* (Amsterdam, 1768), esp. pp. 1–37. For discussion, see Lovejoy, *Great Chain*, pp. 269–83.

202 For discussion of this topic, see Lois Whitney, *Primitivism and the Idea of Progress* (Baltimore, 1934), pp. 137–67; Emile Guyénot, *Les Sciences de la vie aux XVIIe et XVIIIe siècles: L'Idée d'évolution* (Paris, 1941), pp. 337–445, esp. pp. 380–82; Loren Eiseley, *Darwin's Century: Evolution and the Men Who Discovered It* (Garden City, N.Y., 1958), pp. 5–10, 259–64, 282–85, 337–40; Patrides, "Hierarchy and Order," 447–48. On the other hand, various scholars have underlined the sharp difference between the static chain of unalterable species and a world in which evolution occurs. See John C. Greene, *The Death of Adam: Evolution and Its Impact on Western Thought* (Ames, Iowa, 1959); Glass, "Germination of the Idea of Biological Species," pp. 30–48; J. Walter Wilson, "Biology Attains Maturity in the Nineteenth Century," in *Critical Problems in the History of Science*, ed. Marshall Clagett (Madison, Wis., 1959), pp. 405–406. I do not intend to enter this debate, but I should like to single out two articles which I have found to be very helpful. They are: Ernst Mayr, "Agassiz, Darwin, and Evolution," *Harvard Library Bulletin*, 13 (1959), 165–94; and David L. Hull, "The Metaphysics of Evolution," *The British Journal for the History of Science*, 3 (1967), 309–37. Hull argues (pp. 312–18) that Aristotle did not maintain fixity of species in the seventeenth- and eighteenth-century sense. Mayr's article has been reprinted in his *Evolution and the Diversity of Life: Selected Essays* (Cambridge, Mass., & London, 1976), pp. 251–76. On the problem of demarcating species concepts for animals, see Mayr's essays in *The Species Problem* (Washington, D.C., 1957) and his own *Animal Species and Evolution* (Cambridge, Mass., 1965), esp. pp. 12–30. On the nominalist and the realist conceptions of defining species in medieval and early modern thought,

see A. C. Crombie, "The Notion of Species in Medieval Philosophy and Science," in *Actes du VIe Congrès International d'Histoire des Sciences* I (Paris, 1950), pp. 261–69.

203 On Bonaventure's apparent adoption of the scheme, see Antonio Zigrossi, *Saggio sul neoplatonismo di S. Bonaventura: Il concetto di unità e la struttura del reale come problema teologico*, Biblioteca di Studi Francescani IV (Florence, 1954), pp. 21–22, 30–32, 55–66, 84–87; Romano Guardini, *Systembildende Elemente in der Theologie Bonaventuras*, ed. Werner Dettloff (Leiden, 1964), pp. 93–103, 115–24; J. A. Wayne Hellmann, *Ordo: Untersuchung eines Grundgedankens in der Theologie Bonaventuras* (Munich, 1974), pp. 27–28, 34–45, 95–104. In his preface to Guardini (p. XIII), Dettloff stresses how Guardini shows Neoplatonism to be secondary and instrumental in Bonaventure's thought. For excellent studies on Bonaventure's relation to the Pseudo-Dionysius, see Jacques G. Bougerol, "Saint Bonaventure et le Pseudo-Denys Aréopagite" in *Actes du Colloque Saint Bonaventure 9–12 September, 1968, Orsay, Études Franciscaines*, Annual Supplement 18 (1968), pp. 33–123, esp. pp. 41–57, 62, 69, 114–15, and "Saint Bonaventure et la hiérarchie dionysienne," *Archives d'Histoire Doctrinale et Littéraire du Moyen Age*, 44 (1969), 131–67, esp. 132–36, 161–67. On the centrality of Christ and his relation to Bonaventure's concept of metaphysical hierarchy, see the valuable studies of Ewert H. Cousins: "The Coincidence of Opposites in the Christology of Saint Bonaventure," *Franciscan Studies*, 28 (1968), 27–45; "Bonaventure, the Coincidence of Opposites, and Nicholas of Cusa" in *Studies Honoring Ignatius Charles Brady, Friar Minor* (Saint Bonaventure, N.Y., 1976), pp. 177–91; and *Bonaventure and the Coincidence of Opposites* (Chicago, 1978). Another aspect of Bonaventure's concern to readjust the concept of hierarchy so that Christ is central and the human being is directly related to God is brought out by James McEvoy, "Microcosm and Macrocosm in the Writings of St. Bonaventure" in *S. Bonaventura 1274–1974* II (Grottaferrata, 1973), pp. 308–43. For a clear analysis of the process of "hierarchization" of the soul, see Etienne Gilson, *The Philosophy of St. Bonaventure*, trans. Illtyd Trethowan and Frank J. Sheed (Paterson, N.J., 1965), pp. 391–425. Although there appears not to be an explicit discussion of the scheme of metaphysical hierarchy in John F. Quinn's comprehensive and important work, *The Historical Constitution of St. Bonaventure's Philosophy* (Toronto, 1973), there are valuable scattered remarks on the question (e.g. p. 688).

204 This is brought out by various of the historians cited in n. 185 above. See, for example, Burnaby, *Amor Dei*, pp. 81, 149–50; Nygren, *Agape and Eros*, pp. 466–75, 483–90, 512–37; O'Connell, *Augustine's Early Theory*, pp. 48–49, 83, 114, 119–20, 143–44, 154–82, 213–14, 248; idem, *Augustine's Confessions*, pp. 23–27, 78-88, 98–102, 118–19, 122–23, 131–32, 151–53, 161; Zum Brunn, *Le dilemme*, passim. For the same ambiguity of language in Plotinus, see William R. Inge, *The Philosophy of Plotinus* I, 3rd ed. (London, 1948), pp. 131–33, 202–203, 221, 254–56, 261–63; Bréhier, *Philosophy of Plotinus*, pp. 32–57, 148–53; Arnou, *Le Désir de Dieu dans la philosophie de Plotin*, pp. 114–19, 289–91; Nygren, *Agape and Eros*, pp. 186–99; Deck, *Nature, Contemplation, and the One*, pp. 34–42, 62–63, 65, 114–16; Pierre M. Schuhl, "Descente métaphysique et ascension de l'âme dans la philosophie de Plotin," *Studi internazionali di filosofia* 5 (1973), 71–84; Robert J. O'Connell, "The Plotinian Fall of the Soul in St. Augustine," *Traditio*, 19 (1963), 1–35, esp. 6–8, 21–24, 30–32.

205 The notion of "falling" had a venerable tradition in ancient philosophy. Empedocles tells us that when some of the daemons sinned, they had to wander far from the blessed and could work their way back only by traversing a scale of higher and higher degrees of living things. See G. S. Kirk and J. E. Raven, *The Presocratic Philosophers* (Cambridge, 1964), pp. 348–55. There is also the celebrated passage in Plato's *Phaedrus* 247C–248C which describes how the soul falls from "the place beyond the heavens," that is, the realm of true Being, by reason of its wrongdoing. See also *Laws* X (903D–

905c), where we learn that the soul's own choices cause it to sink to the depths of Hades or become god-like and move by a holy road to a better place (904c–d). Professor Friedrich Solmsen pointed out the relevance of these passages to the theme of this study. The important role which Empedocles played in developing the concept of metaphysical hierarchy has been studied by W. K. C. Guthrie in his thoughtful essay "Man's Role in the Cosmos," pp. 56–73, cited in n. 2.

206 The tension in Plotinus and Augustine regarding speaking of approaching toward and receding from a God who is omnipresent has been noted by some of their historians. See in particular O'Meara, *Structures hierarchiques*, pp. 54–61; O'Connell, *Augustine's Early Theory*, pp. 117–20, 152–55, 284–85; idem, *Augustine's Confessions*, pp. 81–88, 131–32, 149, and 177–78. O'Connell appears to make the tension a major theme of his two studies, and he is rather critical of Augustine on this score.

207 See n. 27 above for the reference to McInerny.

208 I do not mean to say that these six points exhaust all remaining problems. Some issues obviously needing attention are the role of God's Will in deciding the hierarchical scheme, the way the Divine Ideas also "measure" the grades or species of things, and whether the distance from God causes the grade or species which a being has or whether the grade or species determine the distance from God. In regard to the last point, some authors appeared to want it both ways. Another thorny problem, one pointed out by Anthony Kenny (n. 40), is that regarding the nature of a paradigm and the activity of grading things in a scale. The only recent philosopher who has presented an extended analysis of the concept of a scale with grades appears to be R. G. Collingwood, *An Essay on Philosophical Method* (Oxford, 1933), chap. 3 ("The Scale of Forms"), pp. 54–91. Also of interest is the important paper of J. O. Urmson, "On Grading," in *Logic and Language* (Second Series), ed. A. G. N. Flew (Oxford, 1953), pp. 159–86. See pp. 163 and 185, where Urmson speaks of "the hierarchy of grades" having a "top" and a position "low down" and recognizes that "higher" and "lower" are grading labels.

209 For this reason, I do not believe that Voltaire's objection (*Dictionnaire* I, p. 142) that the chain fails, since some species of plants and animals have been destroyed and others, such as the lions and the elephants, are beginning to become rare, has much force against the scheme as we found it in medieval and Renaissance philosophy. The criticisms of Johnson are far more telling. However, his stress on infinity and "infinite distance" was already anticipated by critics of the scheme in the fourteenth, fifteenth, and sixteenth centuries.

210 See the remarks of Lovejoy, *Great Chain*, pp. 231–36. See also Daniel J. Boorstin, *The Lost World of Thomas Jefferson* (New York, 1948), pp. 30–40. Thomas' position (n. 39) should perhaps be recalled.

211 *Summa theologiae*, I. q. 14, a. 9, p. 83; and *Quaestiones disputatae De veritate*, q. 3, a. 6, p. 72. See also Ficino, *Theologia platonica* 2.12, p. 110.

212 For general statements on the nature of metaphor, see, among others, Gustaf Stern, *Meaning and Change of Meaning* (London, 1932; Bloomington, Ind., 1964), pp. 167–68, 299–308; William B. Stanford, *Greek Metaphor* (Oxford, 1936), pp. 5–7, 35–46, 100–105; Paul Henle, "Metaphor," in *Language, Thought and Culture*, ed. P. Henle (Ann Arbor, 1958), pp. 173–95; Hedwig Konrad, *Etude sur la métaphore* (Paris, 1958), esp. pp. 33–37, 389; McInerny, *Studies in Analogy*, pp. 39–44, 66–94; David Burrell, *Analogy and Philosophical Language* (New Haven, Conn. & London, 1973), pp. 71–75, 166–78, 220–22 and 253–62; Paul Ricœur, *Interpretation Theory* (Fort Worth, 1976), pp. 52, 66–69; idem, *The Rule of Metaphor*. The literature on the subject is enormous, and the preceding is meant only as a sampling. For good reviews of the competing theories, see Max Black, *Models and*

Metaphors: Studies in Language and Philosophy (Ithaca, N.Y., & London, 1962), pp. 25–47; Monroe Beardsley, *Aesthetics* (New York, 1958), pp. 139–44, 159–63; idem, "Metaphor," *Encyclopedia of Philosophy* (New York, 1967), v 284–88. The definition which I have adopted is no doubt open to criticism, but it does allow me to work with the concept of "transferral" found in the philosophers whom we have surveyed, a "transferral" which is not analogy in the traditional sense. It is especially noteworthy that McInerny, *Studies in Analogy*, p. 82, believes that analogy can be viewed as a kind of metaphor if one goes to the etymology of "to transfer."

213 For Plato, see Pierre Louis, *Les Métaphores de Platon* (Paris, 1945); Paul Grenet, *Les Origines de l'analogie philosophique dans les Dialogues de Platon* (Paris, 1948); Victor Goldschmidt, *Le Paradigme dans la dialectique platonicienne* (Paris, 1948); Aloys De Marignac, *Imagination et dialectique: Essai sur l'expression du spirituel par l'image dans les dialogues de Platon* (Paris, 1951). For Plotinus, see first of all the basic essay of Emile Bréhier, "Images plotiniennes, images bergsoniennes," in *Les Etudes bergsoniennes* II (Paris, 1949), pp. 105–28, esp. pp. 117–22. There are also good discussions in Inge, *Philosophy of Plotinus* I, pp. 218, 260–61; Rein Ferwerda, *La Signification des images et des métaphores dans la pensée de Plotin* (Groningen, 1965), esp. pp. 5–7, 58–59, 162; O'Meara, *Structures hiérarchiques*, pp. 5–6, 55–56, 89–90; Bréhier, *Philosophy of Plotinus*, pp. 30–31, 68, 100–101, 114–15, 156–58; Joseph Moreau, "L'un et les êtres selon Plotin," *Giornale di metafisica*, 11 (1956), 204–24, esp. 216–22. The key passages in Plotinus himself are *Enneads* VI, treatises 4, 5, 8. I am grateful to Paul O. Kristeller and Kenneth Guilmart for bringing these passages to my attention and discussing them with me. Plotinus' constant use of the qualification "as if" (*οἷον*) when presenting images and comparisons should be carefully noted.

214 This danger has been pointed out by many writers. See, for example, Philip Ballard, *Thought and Language* (London, 1934), pp. 31–32; C. B. Daly, "Metaphysics and the Limits of Language," in *New Essays on Religious Language*, ed. Dallas M. High (New York, 1969), pp. 118–19; Colin M. Turbayne, *The Myth of Metaphor*, 2nd ed. (Columbia, S.C., 1970), pp. 3–6, 212.

215 D. Berggren, "The Use and Abuse of Metaphor," *Review of Metaphysics*, 16 (1962–1963), 456. Ian T. Ramsey takes "up there" language to be a sort of qualifier indicating transcendence in his *Christian Discourse: Some Logical Explorations* (London, 1965), pp. 63–74, 79–80. However, he does admit the risk of such language. See also John A. T. Robinson's celebrated book *Honest to God* (Philadelphia, 1963). Note the sober comments about spatial language in the New Testament given in the "Dutch Catechism": *A New Catechism*, trans. Kevin Smyth (New York, 1969), pp. 190–91. See n. 44 above. For discussion of the spatial references in the Bible, I have found particularly helpful W. D. Davies, *The Gospel and the Land: Early Christianity and Jewish Territorial Doctrine* (Berkeley, 1974), and Raymond F. Brown, *The Gospel According to John*, 2 vols. (Garden City, N.Y., 1966, 1970), esp. pp. 132–33, 144–46, 299–300, 308–309, 347–48, 625, 1011–17.

216 Edwyn Bevan, *Symbolism and Belief* (New York, 1938), pp. 28-29, 59–72; Dorothy M. Emmet, *The Nature of Metaphysical Thinking* (London, 1946), p. 110; Aurel Kolnai, "Dignity," *Philosophy*, 51 (1976), 251–71; idem, *Ethics, Value, and Reality*, edd. Francis Dunlop and Brian Klug (London, 1977), esp. chap. 8, "The Concept of Hierarchy," pp. 165–86. Kolnai's two essays are the most detailed and sustained philosophical discussions which I have found on the connection between spatial location and the concept of hierarchy.

217 Among those who appear to take the connection of the experience of spatial location and evaluation as common to all human cultures is Edwyn Bevan, who claims all

languages identify height and supreme worth, giving to God the "supreme degree," that is, the highest step we can take up in space (*Symbolism*, pp. 28–29, 58–59). He also maintains that the belief in a sky god is common to all religions in their primitive stage (p. 48). The causes he gives for the value attributed to height are that taller men had more power while the weak prostrated themselves before the strong, that man feels awe before mountains and the heavens, and that gravity makes ascent a conquest (pp. 59–63). Primitive man could conceive of God as transcendent only by thinking of him as in the heavens (pp. 72, 81). The up and the down were primitive evaluative concepts for both Greek religious ideas and philosophy. See G. E. R. Lloyd, "Right and Left in Greek Philosophy," *Journal of Hellenic Studies*, 82 (1962), 58–59, 61, 64–66; idem, *Polarity and Analogy* (Cambridge, 1966), esp. pp. 46, 49, 52, 225–30, 263–64. Lloyd pays special attention to Plato and Aristotle. For others who identify height and value and see this as common to human outlook, see Robert Hertz, *Death and the Right Hand of God* (Glencoe, Ill., 1960), pp. 94–96; Philip Wheelwright, *Metaphor and Reality* (Bloomington, Ind., 1962), pp. 111–13; Ricœur, *Interpretation Theory*, pp. 64–65. On the other hand, Leonard Bloomfield warns in his *Language* (New York, 1933), pp. 149–50, that although we may agree on what is the normal and what is the transferred meaning in metaphors, it is a mistake to believe that the transferred meanings in our own language are natural and inevitable in human speech. Agreement among European languages simply reflects a common cultural tradition. We might then wonder just how natural is the identification of height and value. Indeed, Benjamin L. Whorf has underscored that the use of spatial metaphors for the nonspatial is more frequent in European languages and Latin than in certain other languages. See his *Language, Thought, and Reality*, ed. John B. Carroll (Cambridge, Mass., 1956), pp. 145–47, 156–59. In reply, Kolnai (*Ethics*, p. 167) would admit that all European languages use expressions of "higher" and "lower" in fundamentally the same way, but he insists that there is more than similarity of language involved. He claims: "A reference to verticality is firmly, stably and ineliminably built into our very thought." See n. 223 below. For an ambitious philosophical investigation of the manner in which humans form the concept of space, how they structure the world according to near–far and up–down, and the significance of spatial metaphor, see Ernst Cassirer, *The Philosophy of Symbolic Forms*, trans. Ralph Mannheim, 3 vols. (New Haven, Conn., 1955, 1957), I 198–203; II 29–32, 75–104, 254–61; III 36, 150–53, 243. For more recent discussion of "up" and "down" as "orientational metaphors," see George Lakoff and Mark Johnson, *Metaphors We Live By* (Chicago & London, 1980), pp. 14–21, and "Conceptual Metaphor in Everyday Language," *The Journal of Philosophy*, 77 (1980), 461–67, 475–76. These authors provide a useful survey of examples of spatial metaphors but appear to ignore almost completely previous literature on the subject. Their two publications appeared after the present study had been completed.

218 Nelson Goodman believes that metaphor is so pervasive in our language that it would be hard to find a purely literal paragraph anywhere. See his *Languages of Art: An Approach to a Theory of Symbols* (Indianapolis, Ind., 1968), pp. 80, 90. Although most other philosophers would not make as extreme a claim, some have commented on how much of our language is indeed metaphorical. See, for example, E. H. Hutten, "The Role of Models in Physics," *British Journal for the Philosophy of Science*, 4 (1953), 289, 293; Burrell, *Analogy and Philosophical Language*, pp. 176–78, 185, 215, 220–22, 242, 253–59; I. A. Richards, *The Philosophy of Rhetoric* (New York, 1936), pp. 92–94, 120.

219 Frederick Ferré, "Mapping the Logic of Models in Science and Theology," in *New Essays on Religious Language*, ed. High, pp. 61–62, 79–86; Stephen J. M. Brown, *The World of Imagery, Metaphor, and Kindred Imagery* (London, 1927), pp. 75, 86–87, 125–27, 241–42.

220 See nn. 44, 103, 154 above. Kristeller is one of the very few to recognize clearly the spatial aspects of the language used in the scheme. See his *Philosophy of ... Ficino*, pp. 36, 164–67, 220. Roques's comments (see n. 5) should be recalled. Objections of a serious nature have been raised to using spatial metaphors based on "above," "far," or "near" to indicate God's transcendence by Karl Heim, *God Transcendent: Foundation for a Christian Metaphysics*, trans. E. P. Dickie (New York, 1936), pp. 33, 44–45, 77–78, 186.

221 Emmet, *Nature of Metaphysical Thinking*, pp. 193, 197, 215; Frederick Ferré, *Basic Modern Philosophy of Religion* (New York, 1967), pp. 374–78, 381; idem, "Mapping," pp. 55–58, 71–95; Ian T. Ramsey, *Models and Mystery* (New York, 1964), pp. 4–9, 14–15.

222 Ferré, *Basic Modern Philosophy of Religion*, pp. 373, 380–83; idem, "Mapping," pp. 66–71, 75–76, 91–93; Ramsey, *Christian Discourse*, pp. 80–82; idem, *Models*, pp. 15, 48–49, 53–54, 58–61; James Richmond, *Theology and Metaphysics* (London, 1970), pp. 49–62, 66–68, 128–29, 132–33. Ramsey and others whom we have cited are much indebted to the important work on metaphor of Black, *Models and Metaphors*, esp. chap. 3 ("Metaphor"), pp. 25–47, and chap. 13 ("Models and Archetypes"), pp. 219–43. Black argues for the philosophical respectability, so to speak, of metaphor.

223 For a well-known example, see Margaret Macdonald, "The Philosopher's Use of Analogy," in *Logic and Language* (First Series), ed. A. G. N. Flew (Oxford, 1951), pp. 80–100, esp. pp. 82, 87, 99. For a gentle demurrer to Macdonald, see Raphael Demos, "Are Religious Dogmas Cognitive and Meaningful?" in *Religious Language and the Problem of Religious Knowledge*, ed. Ronald E. Santoni (Bloomington, Ind., 1968), pp. 279–80, 282.

224 Discussion with George W. Roberts helped me to make clearer the third point. Professor Roberts also proposed a benign reading of the scheme, especially as found in Augustine and Aquinas: namely, that it is precisely God's omnipresence which makes him radically unlike, that is, "infinitely distant from," his creatures.

225 Emmet alludes to the awe and solemnity which is transferred from the experience of looking up at a height to the language of height used to express feeling for the transcendent. See her *Nature of Metaphysical Thinking*, p. 110. Similar explanations are provided by Bevan, *Symbolism*, p. 217. In his *Ethics, Value, and Reality*, p. 168, Kolnai suggests that high objects bar our way, aggressors strike us *down*, and all ascending involves effort; and he makes much of the effect of seeing things from a height, arguing that it gives us a more articulated or graded vision of things (p. 175). George W. Roberts and Gregory Lockhead have both pointed out to me the presumably universal awe which children have of the "heights" they experience around them: namely, adults.

226 Stephen C. Pepper, *World Hypotheses* (Berkeley, 1942), chap. 4 ("Root Metaphors"), pp. 84–114.

227 For a critique of Descartes' use of the metaphor of mechanism, see Turbayne, *Myth of Metaphor*. For a more tolerant reading of Descartes' mechanism, see Collins, *Descartes' Philosophy of Nature*, who does allude to the role of models (pp. 71–75).

228 The reader's attention should be drawn to two works regarding medieval views on space which I was not able to work into the discussion of the essay. They are Robert Grinnell, "The Theoretical Attitude Towards Space in the Middle Ages," *Speculum*, 21 (1946), 141–57, which studies space in sculpture and architecture; and Edward Grant, "Place and Space in Medieval Physical Thought," in *Motion and Time, Space and Matter: Interrelations in the History of Philosophy and Science*, edd. Peter K. Machamer and Robert G. Turnbull (Columbus, Ohio, 1976), pp. 137–67, esp. pp. 144–52, where Grant discusses divine omnipresence and an infinite void space as well as hierarchy and measuring distances in such a void space. Both articles further establish the importance of the concept of space in medieval intellectual outlooks.

* This study is part of a larger project which will be published as a book. I have omitted much material regarding the use of spatial metaphors in metaphysics, a topic which I expect to develop in a separate article.

I am indebted to various friends and colleagues who were kind enough to read the original version or patient enough to discuss certain problems in it which related to their own field of research. John F. Wippel read the earlier version and offered useful criticisms of the added section on Godfrey of Fontaines. F. Edward Cranz and Frederick Purnell, Jr., offered long critiques of a section on Nicholas of Cusa which has been omitted from the final version and which I shall publish separately. Edith D. Sylla examined my brief remarks on developments among such fourteenth-century thinkers as Jean de Ripa and John Dumbleton and also shared with me on more than one occasion her rich knowledge of Swineshead and medieval physics. My colleague George W. Roberts offered criticisms of the original version, frequently debated with me over the course of two years many of the philosophical and historical issues which it raised, and put to close scrutiny the philosophical analysis of the conclusion of the final version. Bernard Peach carefully studied the original version, encouraged me to set out my own thoughts on the philosophical problems raised by the scheme, and discussed with me my remarks regarding hierarchy in early modern philosophy.

Paul O. Kristeller once again shared with me his wide knowledge of Neoplatonism, and he helped me to focus my thoughts regarding that tradition and Ficino's use of the scheme. He was also kind enough to read the final version of this paper and to suggest several improvements. In like fashion, I have learned much from conversations with Salvatore R. C. Lilla concerning the Pseudo-Dionysius, Proclus, and the Neoplatonic tradition in general. Dominic O'Meara answered a variety of questions regarding Plotinus' views on hierarchy and pointed out how he differs from the medieval and Renaissance philosophers whom I study here. James A. Weisheipl was kind enough to discuss with me St. Thomas' use of the scheme. His critical comments forced me to study some texts anew and encouraged me to emphasize even more the theme of metaphor. William A. Wallace read the original version, generously shared with me his close knowledge of Galileo, and gave me leads to Buonamici and Mazzoni. Frederick Purnell, Jr., also brought to my attention and discussed at great length with me various passages in Mazzoni. Stephen F. Brown, Allan B. Wolter, Pietro Scapin, and Jan P. Beckmann will probably not agree fully with my presentation of Duns Scotus, but I am indebted to them for discussing with me difficult points in his thought. Ewert H. Cousins kindly answered questions about Bonaventure. In like fashion, John Monfasani shared with me his command of George of Trebizond and Cardinal Bessarion. Finally, I should like to thank Ernst M. Manasse and Friedrich Solmsen for their careful and critical reading of my study in its penultimate, expanded form. I regret that I could not carry out all their suggestions.

Whatever be the reaction to this study on the part of my fellow-students of medieval and Renaissance philosophy, I trust that they will admit the importance of my having focused attention on a fascinating and influential conceptual scheme which has been insufficiently studied up to now. I shall develop my ideas regarding it in a book on which I am now engaged. In that work, I shall present analyses of other medieval and Renaissance figures and shall trace in greater detail than was possible here the effects of the scheme on early modern thought. The present study would not have been possible without fellowships provided by the National Endowment for the Humanities and the Duke University Research Council. I am also indebted to the latter body for grants for microfilms and travel to Europe.

10

Attribute, Attribution, and Being: Three Islamic Views

Richard M. Frank
The Catholic University of America

The time is not yet come when one can give a succinct and accurate account or analysis of the more subtle problems involved in the questions of being and existence as they were construed by the speculative traditions which are native to Islam and are grouped under the title *al-kalâm* ("the discourse," i.e., on the foundational theses of religion: *'uṣûl ad-dîn*). In their basic structure and even in their vocabulary, the various systems of *kalâm* are not that well understood. What I propose to do, therefore, is to present in a kind of schematic outline the structure of the ontology of three theologians whose teaching gave definitive form to the thought of the two schools of *kalâm* which came to be predominant for sunnî Islam in the tenth and eleventh centuries, viz., abû ʿAlî al-Ǧubbâ'î and his son, abû Hâšim, for the Basrian Muʿtazila, and al-Ašʿarî (who like abû Hâšim had been a disciple of al-Ǧubbâ'î but who broke with him and his school), for the tradition which bears his name. Both schools are Basrian in origin, and despite their profound differences and their hostility to one another show a marked kinship when contrasted with the *kalâm* of other traditions.

In order to present their understanding of the being of things — of beings and their attributes — to re-present, that is, across a considerable chasm of time and language, the specific sense of the thought of the earlier *kalâm* (or anyhow something of the apparent and coherent sense of what they said they thought) — we must begin by examining briefly the formal expression and structure of their analysis of the problems, since it is within this framework that the issues are stated and their elements discovered, conceived, and defined and the difficulties manifested and their solutions given plausibility and coherence. The outline which I shall present here is highly schematic. Many of the specific problems — most of them, in fact — are omitted.[1] The perspective, however, is somewhat new, I think, and will serve both to shed light on the basic framework of the common Basrian tradition and to bring into clear relief the fundamentally speculative (as opposed to dogmatic) difference which, within that tradition, characterizes and divides the thought of the Muʿtazila from that of the Ašʿarites.

The beginnings of the Basrian *kalâm*, i.e., of the systematic use of the kind of analysis characteristic of the dominant theological schools which had their origin in Basra, appears first in the latter part of the eighth Christian century. The science of exegesis (*tafsîr*) was already well established, and, before the close of the century, in the work of Sîbawayh, grammatical theory had achieved virtually what was to be its definitive form. The influence of the grammarians on the Basrian *kalâm* is considerable. The reasons for this — the elements at work in the religious and intellectual context which significantly contributed to the success of the Basrian system or, if you will, which directly fostered the formation of the Basrians' speculation and its subsequent development in terms of the peculiar bias, focus, and structure which are characteristic of it — are many. Among the most fundamental are the Arabs' fascination with language and the pre-eminent place of the Koran in Islam as a verbally articulated revelation of the divine. The *kalâm*'s treatment of the questions we are here concerned with arose within the context of a discussion of "God's Beautiful Names" (*'asmâ'u llâhi l-ḥusnà*); it formed itself, in large part, around and in terms of an inquiry into the sense and significance of "the nouns and qualifiers" (*al-'asmâ'u waṣ-ṣifât*) which are used to describe Him or, to render the words in another way, into "His names and attributes." In the broader context, then, the problem of the nature of being and of beings, both the material and created and the immaterial and uncreated, is posed, and the various issues are defined and treated explicitly in terms of the *waṣf* (the act of describing or predication), the *mawṣûf* (the object described: that denoted by the subject term), and the *ṣifa* (the descriptive term or predicate or, taking the word in another acception, the "attribute" whose being is implied by the predicate).[2] The history of the *kalâm* — in its Basrian branches anyhow — is in some sense the history of these terms; it may be viewed, that is to say, in terms of how these elements were understood: what kind of being was assigned to each and how they were understood to be related to one another.

If the systems be viewed in their broader outlines, the predominant Basrian tradition — that of abû l-Hudhayl, al-Ǧubbâ'î, and abû Hâšim, on the one side, and that of Ibn Kullâb and al-Ašʿarî, on the other, taken together, as opposed, for example, to that of an-Naẓẓâm and the Baghdad Muʿtazila together with al-Mâturîdî, on the other — one sees in the latter (in the Baghdad tradition generally speaking) a greater interest in the speculation of antiquity and a kindlier view toward it, manifest, for example, in al-Mâturîdi's citation of the *ṣaḥib al-manṭiq* (the author of the *Logic*) even in his commentary on the Koran. The Baghdad tradition has a characteristically different kind of focus on the nature of physical reality, and its difference from that of Basra is, as it were, paradigmatically stated in the inclusion of the former among the *aṣḥâb aṭ-ṭabâ'iʿ* and of the latter among the *aṣḥâb al-'aʿrâḍ*.[3] The center of the Basrian speculation (and this, as we shall see, is implicit in their position as *aṣḥâb al-'aʿrâḍ*), in its origin as it is opposed to that of the *aṣḥâb aṭ-ṭabâ'iʿ*, originates and remains concentrated in the examination and analysis of the predicates of being as these are expressed in Arabic and as they are explicated and interpretated within a framework which is closely associated with grammatical theory.

The most important principles of the Basrian *mutakallimîn* which are to be attributed to the influence of the philologists and the grammarians — to the influence of these sciences: their mature presence at the time of the *kalâm*'s formation and their already established role in law and exegesis — may be seen as two. First, the words used to describe God — since the revelation, by its own testimony, is in plain, clear Arabic (*bi-lisânin ʿarabiyyin mubîn*) — must be understood as used in their proper and strict sense (*al-ḥaqîqa*) or at least according to normal Arabic usage.[4] The strict meanings of terms (and what we mean when we employ them in their strict and proper sense) do not differ when referring to creatures and to God: *al-ḥaqâ'iqu lâ taḫtalifu fî š-šâhidi wal-ġâ'ib.* Those predicates, that is, which are shared by the eternal and the temporal are in some sense univocal. The Basrians will divide on how rigidly they apply this principle, but none of them will take a position like that of an-Nâšî' (d. 906), who holds that with a single exception (sc. *ġayr*: other) any term which is predicated of both God and a creature must be understood "metaphorically" in one instance and strictly (*fî l-ḥaqîqa*) in the other. The second principle is that the inflected forms of the verb and the verbal adjectives — whatever terms are used as qualifiers and predicates of nouns — are derived from nouns, viz., from the *maṣâdir*, which, as nouns, are or may be understood to name or designate entities of some kind.[5] Thus, for example, when one says "Zayd stands," the predicate or descriptive term may be analyzed as *waqaʿa minhû qiyâmun* (an act of standing has occurred on his part); or when one says "Zayd knows," the predicate term may be analyzed as *lahû ʿilmun* (an act of knowing belongs to him).[6] The predicates or descriptive elements (*al-'awṣâf*), when taken in their strict sense (*fî l-ḥaqîqa*), may thus be conceived (the *mutakallimûn*, as we shall see, divide on the individual terms) to be derived (*muštaqqa*) from the nouns which name, designate, or in some particular way describe the thing or act, as *ʿâlim* (knowing) is derived from *ʿilm* (an act of knowing), and *'âmir* (commanding) from *'amr* (a command, an act of commanding).[7] This form of analysis furnishes — initially, at least — the formal framework of the Basrians' analysis of the predicates which are said of beings, and the divisions of the principal schools is founded in the divergence of their use of the form and of their interpretation of the terms explicitated in it.

Albeit less radical than in the authors whose teaching we shall review here, the basic division of the Basrian tradition is already apparent in the thought of abû l-Hudhayl al-ʿAllâf (d. ca. 840) and ʿAbdallâh ibn Saʿîd, commonly known as ibn Kullâb (d. 845). Though a clear view of their teaching is important to an understanding of the evolution of the doctrines of the two schools, I shall omit them here for the sake of space. Let me note simply that abû l-Hudhayl distinguished the act of creation from the thing created, identifying the former with God's creative utterance, "Be" (*kun*). He distinguished thus the thing created from the act which effects it, making the thing created an object of God's power and of the act which effects its existence. Following this, his disciple abû Yaʿqûb aš-Šaḥḥâm explicitly states that the possible (*al-maʿdûm*) is "a thing" (*šay'*): an entity which is, strictly speaking, an individual object of God's knowing and power and of which, as such, predications can be made which are, properly speaking, true or false. The individual entity or essence has reality in its possibility as an object of God's knowing and power. What predicates are validly said of the possible as such come to be a subject of considerable discussion in the later development of the school.

Now, al-Ǧubbâ'î (d. 913), who was a disciple of aš-Šaḥḥâm's, refined the system in many respects. For the purposes of our present discussion, he classified the predicates of beings — the names (*'asmâ'*): the nouns and adjectives by which things are described — in the following categories:[8]

(1) That which a thing is called by virtue of its Self (*li-nafsihî*), i.e., that which names or describes the thing essentially and specifically as that which it is. This is expressed when we say that "the atom is an atom," that "black (sc., the individual unit or quantum of the accident black) is black" (*as-sawâdu sawâdun*), or that "God is eternal" (*Allâhu qadîmun*). (God's essence, thus, is His eternity: that He exists without beginning or end and that His non-being is impossible.) In the case of contingent beings, these predicates are true and valid even though the thing does not exist in actuality since each individual has being as a real object of God's knowing and power: the individual essence is real in its possibility (*ṯâbitu l-ǧawâz*). Here also as descriptive of the thing's Self and as said of it (*li-nafsihî*) he included negative predicates, since when the predicate is denied only the subject is asserted to have being, whether as a possible or an existent entity.

(2) That which a thing is called by virtue of some other entity whose actuality in being is the cause (*ʿilla*) or referential basis (*maʿnà*) of the judgment (*ḥukm*) which affirms the predicate. These he divides into two classes: (*a*) predicates which are true by virtue of a "cause" which exists within the thing (*li-ʿillatin fîhî*), as when we say "Zayd knows," asserting thus *ʾanna lahû ʿilman* (that an act of knowing belongs to him: an entitative "accident" which exists in him); and (*b*) those which are true by virtue of "a cause which is not in him" (*li-ʿillatin lâ fîhî*), as, e.g., when we say "Zayd is mentioned" (*Zaydun madkûrun*), asserting thus the existence of a statement or other kind of utterance, whose existence is in another and in which there is a mention of or reference to Zayd (*dikrun lahû*). Some predicates of action may also fall under this category; that someone is termed *ẓâlim* (wronging) implicitly affirms the proposition *waqaʿa minhû ẓulmun* (an act of wrongdoing has occurred on his part), i.e., that there exists, through his agency, an act which is properly described as *ẓulm*.

(3) That which a thing is called "by way of stating that it has reality in being" (*ʾiḫbâran ʿan ʾiṯbâtihî*), as when it is termed *kâʾin* (being), *mawǧûd* (existent), and the like.

(4) That which a thing is called by virtue of its coming to be after not having been (*li-ḥudûṯihî*), e.g., *ḥâdiṯ*, *muḥdaṯ* (temporally contingent), etc., or because in its being existent it is the act (*fiʿl*) of an agent, as when it is termed *mafʿûl* (made) or *maḫlûq* (created).

(5) That which it is called simply "by way of distinguishing classes of beings" (*lit-tafriqati bayna l-ʾaǧnâs*), as when we say that a particular motion is an accident (*ʿaraḍ*) or that black (the unitary instance of the accident black) is a color (*lawn*). And, finally,

(6) That which it is called simply because it can be spoken of and a true statement made concerning it (*liʾannahû mumkinun ʾan yudkara wa-yuḫbara ʿanhû*), sc., that it is a being (*šayʾ*: thing). This is the ultimate and most universal category, embracing all being, the real and the possible (*al-mawǧûd wal-maʿdûm*).[9]

It is important to note the phrasing of his definitions of these categories, for it indicates a difference of conception which divides the thought of al-Ǧubbâʾî and his school from that of al-Ašʿarî which becomes particularly significant in the disputes of the eleventh century and in the Ašʿarites' attempts to adapt certain elements of the Muʿtazilite system to their own use.

The first four categories (with the exception of 2*b*: that which is *li-ʿillatin lâ fîhî*) represent assertions about or descriptions of the particular subject or essence as it is in itself or as it is particularly qualified and distinguished from another being of like essence: (*a*) that which designates a particular entity as a member of a class (e.g., "an atom") or a specific kind of composite entity (e.g., "a man") and therefore describes it as having its characteristic or essential properties, or which explicitly describes it as having one or more of them (e.g., "occupies space," said of an atom); (*b*) that which describes the particular corporeal being as qualified and therefore distinguished from a like essence or composite by the inherence of an entitative accident; or (*c*) that which describes the essence or composite as existent. These are, properly speaking, *ṣifât*$_1$: descriptions of a particular entity as it is specifically and particularly characterized or qualified in its being. The last two categories, however, do not name or describe in particular any essence or composite as such but represent, as al-Ǧubbâ'î construes it, only classes or categories by which we group and divide diverse essences or composite entities; insofar as they are not strictly descriptive of the specific and particular entities as such but may be used of a plurality of essentially different beings, they, strictly speaking, are not *ṣifât*$_1$, but rather share something of the character of *'alqâb* (sg. *laqab*), i.e., arbitrary denominations.

The primary concern of the *mutakallimîn* is most often with the ontological assertion (*al-'iṯbât*) made in the predicate. Examining al-Ǧubbâ'î's categories from this standpoint, we may note briefly the following: predicates (*ṣifât*$_1$) of the first category assert only the reality of the entity denoted by the subject (sc., *al-mawṣûf*) as in its reality it belongs to the class (*al-ǧins*) which is defined by its essence and named by the noun which properly names it as that which essentially it is. There is, however, no implication of existence or non-existence, i.e., that the entity actually exists or is merely possible. Finally, it would seem that al-Ǧubbâ'î included negative predicates within this category, since the only entity asserted to exist in such a predication is that denoted by the subject term. Predicates of this category, accordingly are termed *ṣifât*$_1$ *al-'anfus* (or *ṣifât*$_1$ *nafsiyya*), "essential predicates," and sometimes *ṣifât*$_1$ *al-'aǧnâs*, "class predicates" (i.e., of the lowest common class). Predicates belonging to the second category assert the reality of an *'illà* (= *ma'nà*), either intrinsic to the subject (*fîhî*, i.e., inherent in it: *ḥallun fîhî*) or extrinsic to it (*lâ fîhî*), by virtue of which the subject is validly described by the given expression. Since the latter relationships do not obtain between possibles ("knows" cannot be said of Zayd by virtue of a possible but non-existent act of knowing), the predicate implies the existence of the *ma'nà*, wherefore such predicates are commonly termed *ṣifât*$_1$ *al-ma'ânî* (or, later, *ṣifât*$_1$ *ma'nawiyya*). Predicates of the third and fourth categories indicate the ontological status and modality of the being of the entity denoted by the subject term; those of the third category expressly state the status of the subject, e.g., it "exists." Probably to be included here, but omitted by al-Aš'arî in the passages cited because of the context, is *ma'dûm* (non-existent, possible). Those of the fourth category indicate the mode of its existence. There is some evidence that at least in some stage of his work al-Ğubbâ'î included predicates such as *muḥdâṯ* (contingent, temporal) alongside predicates such as *ḥâll* (inherent) in a category which he termed *lâ lin-nafsi wa-lâ li-'illa* (or *wa-lâ li-ma'nà*). Predicates of the fifth category do not imply an ontological assertion as such (i.e., they are not taken, it seems from the present evidence, by al-Ğubbâ'î to imply any such assertion), but merely assign the given entity to one or another class in which it is joined with one or more essentially dissimilar beings. The sixth category is distinguished as designating the most universal of classes: entity.

Beings al-Ğubbâ'î divided into two classes: (1) God, the eternal and necessary; and (2) the contingent, which is either possible in the power of God (and so real insofar as it is known to Him and is a real object of His power: *ma'dûmun maqdûrun 'alayhî*) or real and existent through the temporal act of the agent who caused it to come to be, either God or a human agent. The conception and discussion of the being of beings, however, is formally restricted in the teaching of al-Ğubbâ'î. It is clear that he held that only nouns referring to entities, properly speaking, can be made the subject of a proposition. An entity (*šay'*) is that of which something is said (*al-muḫbaru 'anhû*) and so is *mawṣûf* (described, qualified) and is not, itself, said of something else. As we have seen, the Basrians, in order to explicitate and explicate what is asserted as true (as truly having being) in a simple proposition, analyze the predicate term into a separate sentence whose subject denotes the ontological referent of the original predicate term. But subject of this sentence (in the grammarians' terminology "the second subject" of a complex proposition) must, according to the fundamental presuppositions of the system, name, designate, or refer to (*yusammî, yadullu 'alà*) an entity (*šay', nafs, ḏât*), either the same as that referred to in the first subject or another. In paraphrasing the proposition *Zaydun 'âlimum* (Zayd is knowing), one says *Zaydun lahû 'ilmun* (Zayd, an act of knowing belongs to him), affirming the reality of two entities, viz., Zayd and the act of knowing which exists in him (which exists materially as a discrete accident in the substrate of his heart); the existence of this accident, that is, is implicitly referred to and asserted in the predicate *'âlim* when used of a material being. When he comes to analyze the proposition *Allâhu 'âlimun*, however — since God is not in any sense a composite, material being and no entity other than His Self or essence is implied or asserted — al-Ğubbâ'î is constrained to paraphrase the predicate simply by explicitating the pronoun which, according to the grammarians, is implicit (*muḍamman*) in the verbal adjective so used: *Allâhu huwa ʿâlimun* (God, He is knowing). Thus, he says that the proposition *Allâhu ʿâlîmun* implies simply "the assertion of His reality" (*'iṯbâtuhû*). It is thus that he terms *ʿâlim*, when used of God, "an essential predicate" (*ṣifatu$_1$ nafsin*), since there is no reference, explicit or implicit, to, and so no assertion of, any being save that God's Self or essence (*nafsuhû*). His treatment of the other "essential attributes," *ḥayy* (living), *qâdir* (κατεξούσιος), etc., is analogous. The different "essential" predicates, he says, are employed "because of the difference of the significant information conveyed" (*li-ḫtilâf al-fawâ'id*), distinguishing thus the information conveyed (the meaning, if you will) — *al-fâ'ida* — from the implicit reference and assertion (*al-'iṯbât*), sc., that of the existence of an entity. The various terms used to describe God's essence (*ḥayy, qâdir, ʿâlim,* etc.) are not, thus, simply equivalent to *qadîm* (eternal), which he understands as a singular term which describes God uniquely and essentially as such. What they mean and imply can be explained. *ʿÂlim*, for example, implies "that He is contrary to what cannot know, that he who holds that He is ignorant affirms a false proposition, and it indicates that there are things known to Him": *'annahû bi-ḫilâfi mâ lâ yaǧûzu 'an yaʿlama, wa-'ikḏâbu man zaʿama 'annahû ǧâhilun, wa-dalalâtun ʿalà 'anna lahû maʿlûmâtin.* About God's being knowing or Zayd's being knowing, however, the principles of al-Ǧubbâ'î's analysis allow him to say nothing, for the perfection or attribute of being knowing which is indicated by the term *ʿâlîm* is not an entity and so cannot be made the subject of a proposition. Being, in short, is taken in a strictly univocal sense. Ontologically al-Ǧubbâ'î can talk only about concrete entities (actual or possible) and their classes: about "essences" (*ḏawât*) — God's and those of atoms and accidents and about the composites of the latter. Even in the case of Zayd he cannot talk of his "being knowing" as a qualification of his being but only of Zayd as a corporeal composite in which there exists a particular act of knowing, an act which itself is a distinct entity, not a perfection of the being of Zayd save as it is one of the plurality of entities which make up the composite, living unit which is he. Only entities — *'ašyâ'*, in the strict sense — are said to be *mawǧûd* (existent) or *maʿdûm* (non-existent), *kâ'in* (being) *ḥâdiṯ* (temporally contingent), or the like. Only entities can be the subject of predication. The attribute, then, has being — can be considered an entity and be an object which can be spoken of and described (*mawṣûf*) — only as it is represented and reified in speech, as a linguistic entity the meaning of which can be discussed. Thus he can talk neither about existence as such nor about being in any sense, but only about *'iṯbâtu š-šay'* (the assertion of the reality of the thing), *'iṯbâtu 'anna š-šay'a mawǧûdun* (the assertion that the thing is existent) or *al-'iḫbâru ʿan* *'itbâtihî* (the assertion of the proposition affirming its reality in being). The fragments of his writings which have been preserved are, in fact, very interesting in their careful avoidance of any turn of phrase which would tend to imply the violation of this principle.[10]

Now, there is no doubt that al-Ğubbâ'î's treatment of these matters is quite sophisticated (the present outline gives little indication, I fear, of the richness of its detail) and that it is fully Islamic in its inspiration. His semantic analysis, i.e., his explication of the *fawâ'id* of the various predicates used of God, in fact, remained normative for the Muʿtazila and, in part, for the Ašʿarites as well. Yet there were serious problems which he was unable to solve. Of these, plainly, the central one lay in the way in which he had, following the Basrian tradition as a whole, construed being in so strictly univocal a sense that he simply could not talk about being as such or about its qualities and perfections. That the main focus of the *kalâm* — at least in its Basrian branches which were to become predominant — was on the attributes of things and on God's attributes in particular necessarily had to make his position a little uncomfortable. Within the historical context, however — that is, looking at the situation from within the context of the Basrian *kalâm* and the notions and principles to which it felt itself committed at the most basic level — the difficulty most likely was apparent chiefly in the inconsistency which al-Ğubbâ'î's analysis and his interpretation of it had introduced into the *ḥaqâ'iq* (the strict meanings of words and the reality we refer to when we use them in their strict and proper sense). As we have noted several times now, the general tendency of the Basrian schools was to explicate the *ḥaqîqa* of a term through a paraphrase which makes explicit what being is referred to, explicitly or implicitly, and so is asserted to have reality *fî l-ḥaqîqa* (in the strict sense of the term: in truth). In al-Ğubbâ'î's analysis, however, the *ḥaqâ'iq* differ *fî š-šâhidi wa-fî l-ġâ'ib*: the strict sense of the terms, what we really mean and refer to differs when one speaks of the material and created and when one speaks of the immaterial and eternal. This is plain in the paraphrase: *ʿâlim*, used of a corporeal being, asserts "truly and strictly" *'anna lahû ʿilman* (that an act of knowing belongs to him, that there exists, inherent in a part of the material composite which is he, an entity which is an act of knowing); but used of God, the same expression ontologically asserts only that God exists: His essence. In the former case, it is *ṣifatu*$_1$ *maʿnan*; in the latter, it is *ṣifatu*$_1$ *nafsin*. Al-Ğubbâ'î's attempt to keep the common meaning of the term in giving account of its *fâ'ida* (i.e., by insisting on the consistency of the meaning as distinct from the reference and the ontological assertion implicit in it) does not solve the problem within the framework to which the school was committed, seemingly from its earliest beginnings, and within which it continued to develop.

To solve this problem al-Ǧubbâ'î's son abû Hâšim (d. 933), adapting a term and notion from grammatical theory, formulated the concept of the attribute as a state (*ḥâl*, pl. *'aḥwâl*), i.e., as an ontologically real state, perfection, or quality of the being of the thing. The attribute (*ṣifa*$_3$), thus understood (and note here the shift in the meaning of the word *ṣifa*), is, he says, "the state by which the object described is specifically qualified so that one says it is *ʿalà ṣifatin*,[11] meaning that by virtue of which it is distinguished from something else": *mâ yuḫtaṣṣu bihi l-mawṣûfu mina l-'aḥwâli fa-yuqâlu 'innahû ʿalà ṣifatin wa-yurâdu bihî mâ yufâriqu ġayrahû fîhî*. Terms such as *ʿalà ḥâlin* or *ʿalà ṣifatin* simply could not be handled by al-Ǧubbâ'î; he could not explicate the ontological significance of the *bi-* in his formula *'innahû bi-ḫilâfi mâ lâ yaǧûzu 'an yaʿlama*, cited above. The state, for abû Hâšim, is not an entity (*šay'*) and so cannot be said to be *mawǧûda* (existent); nor can one say of it that it has come to be (*ḥadaṯat*). It has actuality (*ḥuṣûl*), however, and so can be said to have come to actuality (*ḥaṣalat*) or to have arisen (*taǧaddadat*) as an ontologically real perfection of the being of the *mawṣûf*. The unity of the *ḥaqâ'iq* is thus restored as the proposition *'innahû ʿâlimun* (he is knowing) is understood, in all cases, to refer to the attribute (*ṣifa*$_3$) and to assert its actuality. In the examples which we have been using, *yadullu ʿalà kawnihî ʿâliman* (it signifies or refers to his being knowing). As a formal expression, *kawnuhû ʿâliman* occurs, together with other analogous expressions, for the first time in the work of abû Hâšim with the sense of "his *being knowing*" and not merely as a grammatically convenient equivalent for *'annahû ʿâlim* (that he [is] knowing). Similarly, one can talk of *kawnuhû mawǧûdan* (his being existent) and use *wuǧûduhû* (his existence) as its equivalent and not as a substitute for *'annahû mawǧûdun*. The predicates classed by al-Ǧubbâ'î as *li-ʿillatin lâ fîhî* (2*b* in the list above) are not taken to assert the reality of *'aḥwâl* or "attributes" in the strict sense, for obvious reasons. Likewise those predicates which al-Ǧubbâ'î had placed in his categories 5 and 6 are considered, not to refer to attributes, but as mere names which we use to designate more or less arbitrarily assigned categories of things; they are quasi *'alqâb*, not truly descriptive or qualifying terms (*ṣifât*$_1$).

The true attributes (*ṣifât*$_3$ in abû Hâšim's formal sense), whose actuality the mind grasps (*ʿaqala*) through their various characteristics (their *'aḥkâm*; note the shift in the meaning of this term too) which are manifest in the thing (*al-mawṣûf*), abû Hâšim classifies under five basic headings. (1) The attribute of the essence is the thing's being itself: the way it is in itself (*mâ huwa ʿalayhî fî ḏâtihî*); this is expressed in our saying, e.g., "the atom is an atom" or "God is eternal." (2) The essential attribute is the attribute which belongs to a thing "by virtue of the way it is in itself" (*li-mâ huwa ʿalayhî fî nafsihî*), that whose actuality is entailed (*muqtaḍan*) by the attribute of the essence when it exists, as, for example, the atom's occupying space or God's being living and knowing, etc. (3) Those attributes whose actuality is caused (*maʿlûl*) by an entitative cause (*li-ʿilla, li-maʿnà*), as, for example, Zayd's being knowing or a body's being in motion. (4) Those attributes whose actuality (or whose qualifying the *mawṣûf* — a distinction is made here) is or results directly from the action of an agent or from one of his states which qualifies the performance of his act. These include, besides the meaningfulness of speech and the ethical qualities of actions, the existence of contingent entities. (5) These are those which are termed *lâ lin-nafsi wa-lâ li-ʿilla*.[12]

Existence (*al-wuǧûd*) then — a thing's being existent (*kawnuhû mawǧûdan*) — is in all beings an attribute or perfection or state which is the ground (*'aṣl*) of the actuality of its essential attributes and is the immediate ground of the possibility of whatever other attributes it may have (*al-muṣaḥḥiḥu lahâ*). It entails, thus, the manifestation of the essence itself (*yaqtaḍî ẓuhûrahâ*). Any being is intelligible — is available to our knowledge and understanding — only through its essential attributes and their characteristics. The characteristic of existence (*ḥukmu l-wuǧûd*) — i.e., of being existent — is thus the actuality of the manifestation of whatever attributes it has; e.g., that the atom occupies space (*taḥayyaza*) and that "pressure" (*al-iʿtimâd*, e.g., the weight of a body or its momentum which is manifest in its resistance to our effort to lift it or to move it in a contrary direction) pushes (*dâfaʿa*) in a particular direction. Existence, then, he says, has two modalities (*kayfiyya*): that the entity be necessary and eternal (*wâǧib, lâ 'awwala lahû*) or contingent and temporal (*ǧâ'iz, muḥdaṯ*). The actuality of the existence of the possible is effected (*'aṯṯara*) through the action of an agent since the reality of its possibility resides in the agent's autonomous power to produce its being. The actuality of the existence of the eternal, on the other hand, is entailed by the way it is in itself (*muqtaḍan li-mâ huwa ʿalayhî fî nafsihî*). Being, thus, abû Hâšim conceives in a number of senses: in the existence of entities, in the possibility of the contingent, and in various ways for different attributes and for their characteristics.[13]

The tradition to which al-Ašʿarî (d. 935) belongs and which comes to bear his name evolves much differently from that of the Muʿtazila and, until the end of the tenth century, at a much slower pace. Insofar as the questions we are examining here are concerned, the teaching of al-Ašʿarî, in fact, appears to differ in no major respect from that of ibn Kullâb, who died almost a century before him.

The system employs the same basic formulas — the same paraphrasing of predicates — in order to explicitate the *dalâla* (the reference) and the *'iṯbat* (the ontological assertion). (In his extant writings al-Aš'arî speaks most often in terms of *ad-dalâla*.) The treatment and interpretation of these basic common elements, however, differ in a number of significant respects from what is found in the Mu'tazilite tradition. The predicates of beings are classed in only three categories according as what is understood as the implicit referent of the particular term is distinguished, in relation to the subject, under three headings:

First, there are those expressions (*'awṣâf, 'asmâ'*) which name or implicitly refer simply to the thing itself — the thing's Self (*nafsuhû*, conceived, it would seem, in contrast to the Mu'tazila, more as object than as essence): *tadullu 'alà nafsi l-mawṣûf*. Besides those predicates which name or describe the particular entity as such, i.e., those of al-Ǧubbâ'î's first category, included here are also such predicates as *mawǧûd* (existent) and those which al-Ǧubbâ'î classes in his fifth category as well as *šay'* (al-Ǧubbâ'i's sixth category) which al-Aš'arî takes to be coextensive with *mawǧûd*. Thus, with *Allâhu mawǧûdun* (God exists) or *al-ḥarakatu 'araḏun* (the [particular] motion [or, every motion] is an "accident") al-Aš'arî takes simply as *'iṯbâtu nafsi l-mawṣûf* (the assertion of the existence of the entity denoted by the subject term); they refer to the Self of the *mawṣûf*.

Secondly, there are those predicates which refer to a *ma'nà* (pl. *ma'ânî*; he seems to prefer this term to *'illa*, though the two are synonymous in the context), viz., al-Ǧubbâ'î's category 2: e.g., an inherent accident in *Zaydun 'âlimun* or an extrinsic entity in *Zaydun maḏkûrun*, as was explained above. Included here too are ethical terms; an action is said to be *wâǧib* (obligatory), for example, because it is commanded (*ma'mûr*), implying the reality of and referring to the command (*'amr*), which is a form of speech (*kalâm*, viz., God's in this instance). These entities whose being is implied by predicates of this class (sc., the *ma'ânî* or *'ilal*) are frequently, and in some contexts normally, referred to as *sifât* (*ṣifa*$_4$ = *ma'nà* = *'illa*), "attributes."

Thirdly, then, there are those predicates which refer to and therefore assert the reality of an action performed by the subject, e.g., *Zaydun ẓâlimun* = *Zaydun waqa'a minhû ẓulmun*, as I explained above. Actions also, since they are the referents of predicates of action, are also sometimes referred to by the As'arites as *ṣifat*$_4$. One must, therefore, mind the terminology carefully, for when one speaks of *ṣifatu*$_1$ *fi'lin* (a predicate of action), one refers to an expression, e.g., "*ḍâribun*" ("strikes"), but when one speaks of *ṣifatu*$_4$ *fi'lin* (an "attribute" of action), one refers to the act itself, e.g., *aḍ-ḍarb* (the blow which is actually struck).

Against al-Ǧubbâ'î, al-Aš'arî insists that, for any given expression, the *ḥaqîqa* is invariant; no term, used in its strict sense (*fî l-ḥaqîqa*), can belong to more than one category. That is to say, *'alim* cannot be *ṣifatu*$_1$ *nafsin* (an essential predicate) when used of God and *ṣifatu*$_1$ *ma'nan* (a predicate which asserts the being of a *ma'nà*) when used of Zayd. The paraphrase of any given term is, thus, always the same and so its referent: the *'iṯbât* is, in all cases, either of the *mawṣûf* as such, of a *ma'nà*, or of an action (*fi'l*). Thus *'âlim* is always equivalent to *lahû 'ilmun* (an act of knowing belongs to him). *Takâfa'a l-qawlân* (the two expressions are equivalent to one another). The ontological assertion is always the same for any given expression, and the *waṣf* (the descriptive term) is "derived from the most particular of its names" (*muštaqqun min 'aḫaṣṣi 'asmâ'ihî*), i.e., is derived in all such cases from a noun which specifically names the entity to which the adjective implicitly refers or which describes it in some particular way. *'Âlim*, for example, is derived from *'ilm*. Thus, to predicate the term *'âlim*, employing it in it strict sense (*fî l-ḥaqîqa* and not as *maǧâz* nor *talqîban*), of any being, whether of God or of Zayd, implies and asserts (*'awǧaba*; the term is taken from the grammarians) the actuality of existence of an act of knowing which is the "attribute" (*sifa*$_4$, *ma'nà*); reciprocally the reality of the *ṣifa*$_4$ — in our example, *al-'ilm*: the act of knowing — in the *mawṣûf* "requires that the *mawṣûf* so be described" (*'awǧaba waṣfahû bihâ*). It belongs to the thing — the thing deserves — to be so described (*yastaḥiqqu l-waṣfa*) by virtue of the *ṣifa*$_4$ (the attribute) which, al-Aš'arî says, is "its deserving to be so described" (*istiḥqâqu l-waṣf*). Analgously, the same is true of the "predicates of action" (*ṣifâtu*$_1$ *l-'af'âl*). On the other hand, motion, for example, deserves to be called "motion" or "existent" or "contingent" or "an accident" because it is and, being, is what it is. That is, these terms, the essential predicates (*ṣifâtu*$_1$ *l-'anfus*), refer to and assert the ontological reality of the *mawṣûf* as such.

In Zayd the *ṣifa*$_4$ or "attribute" — the act of knowing, for example — is a contingent entity, an accident (*'araḍ*), contingent both in itself and in its relation to the body which is Zayd. It is, thus, a being distinct from Him and so, strictly speaking, "other than He" (*ġayruhû*). God's "attributes," however, are eternal, neither contingent as such nor in respect to His being; therefore, according to al-Aš'arî's definition of the terms, since they are not in any way separable from God's Self, they are not said to be "other than He." As eternal and inalienable from God's Self (*nafsuhû*), thus, they are termed *ṣifâtu*$_4$ *n-nafs*. Neither can God's attributes be said to be His Self. The implicit referent (*al-madlûlu 'alayhî*), e.g., of *'âlim* is not *nafsu š-šay'* (the thing's Self) — *nafsu l-mawṣûf* (the Self of the described) — but must be rather the *ṣifa*$_4$ or "attribute," for the *ḥaqîqa of 'âlim* is *lahû 'ilmun*.

Accordingly, therefore, he says of God's attributes that "they are neither said to be He (sc., His Self) nor are they said to be other than He." Again one is in a framework in which being is conceived univocally and one talks only in terms of what are taken to be entities. Against al-Ǧubbâ'î, however, al-Aš'arî, holding rigidly to the univocity of the *ḥaqâ'iq*, can argue that what is grasped when one understands, for example, that the sense and truth of the statement *huwa 'âlimun* is not and cannot be correlated to the subject as entity or essence (i.e., to the Self which is said to know: *nafsu l-'âlim*, *ḏâtu l-'âlim*) simply and as such, but in all instances must be taken as correlated to the act of knowing, i.e., to the *ṣifa*$_4$ or *ma'nà*: the entitative "attribute." On the other hand, he does not say — and seemingly refused to discuss — what kind of being belongs to God's "attributes"; rather, he insists that they affirmed *bi-lâ takyîf* (without explanation as to how). Of God's "attributes" he uses the term *qadîma* (eternal) but nowhere that I have noted does he say of them that they are *mawǧûda* (existent), a term which is employed by his later followers. Ibn Kullâb is reported to have held that God's attributes are not denumerable (*ma'dûda*), but even though this question is much discussed by later Aš'arites I have found no report of an opinion expressed by al-Aš'arî himself.

At the risk of redundancy and of belaboring the obvious, I would again point out that though the Basrians share a common vocabulary — and this is particularly clear if one but compare that of the Baghdad Mu'tazila or of al-Mâturîdî — and though their formulas are, thus, often parallel in wording, the two systems present significantly different contexts, and the formulas, similar though often they may be, are not equivalent.

Now, al-Aš'arî and his followers in the classical period simply deny the distinction which is made by the Mu'tazila between essence and existence. The possible (*al-ma'dûm*) simply is not. God's essence, thus, is His existence, whose non-being is impossible (*yastaḥîlu 'adamuhû*). Ibn Kullâb says that He is existent "not through an act of existence" (*mawǧûdun lâ bi-wuǧûdin*) and is a being (*šay'*) "not by a *ma'nà* by virtue of which He is a being" (*lâ li-ma'nan lahû kâna šay'an*); though no explicit statement is made to this effect in the extant writings of al-Aš'arî, it is quite clear from his discussion of the predicates used of God that he did hold such a position. Any being which is contingent and temporal (*muḥdaṯ*)—i.e., bodies and accidents—*is* simply the act of its being created; *al-ḫalq* = *al-maḫlûq* (the act of creating / being created is the thing created). The act of creation is the Self or essence which is the existence of the creature, and the totality of the being of any contingent being is its being created. The act is the thing done (*al-fi'l* = *al-maf'ûl*). The totality of the being of any contingent being, thus, is the action of God, and accordingly al-Aš'arî, dividing being into two categories, says that "the existent, when it is not an action, is eternal" (*al-mawǧûdu' iḏâ lam yakun fiʿlan huwa qadîmun*).[14] All existence, thus, is divided between God, on the one, side, and His acts, on the other. All predication ultimately refers to God: to His Self or to His attributes, or to His actions.

Being and existence are not discussed explicitly as such in the writings of al-Ašʿarî — no more than in that of al-Ǧubbâ'î and for much the same reasons. *Al-wuǧûd* (existence) occurs only as a grammatically convenient paraphrase of *'annahû mawǧûdun* (and this in contexts where it is clear that the sense of the phrase as *being* existent is not in question); phrases such as *kawnuhû ʿâliman* occur but rarely, and again as equivalents of *'annahû ʿâlimun* and the like. Indeed, it is not unlikely that the rarity of such phrases is due to a desire to avoid the overtones of abû Hâšim's usage. As is also true in the teaching of the master, al-Ǧubbâ'î, the vocabulary and concepts of abû Hâšim have no place in al-Ašʿarî's thought, and when, at a later stage of the school's development, they are introduced, it is only with considerable awkwardness (though the influence of abû Hâšim is, in certain other questions, not insignificant in later Ašʿarite thinking).

Now, as we have seen, al-Ašʿarî has taken the term *ṣifa* (i.e., *ṣifâ*$_4$), distinguishing it from the *waṣf* (description, act of describing, predication, predicate), to denote the attribute, conceived as an ontologically real entity (a *maʿnà*), distinct and separate in the creature and prudently unexplained in God. Using a more general term to express a broader concept, he made an analogous distinction between the *ism* (name, noun) and the *tasmiya* (naming, describing by a noun or adjective). In a notorious and oft-quoted formula, it is said that "the name is the named" (*al-ismu huwa l-musammà*) or, to render it another way, "the name [noun] is that which is referred to by name," i.e., referred to in the act of predication or description; it is that whose being is implicitly referred to and asserted to be in the act of calling (*at-tasmiya*) something by a word which describes it in some way. It is that whose reality is asserted by a given predicate when the particular predicate is affirmed of some object. For convenience we may use for "name"/"noun" in the usual sense *ism*$_1$ and for "name"/"noun" in this peculiar sense *ism*$_2$. Al-Ašʿarî, it will be recalled, classed the predicates of being under three headings according to the reference (*ad-dalâla*) and the ontological assertion (*'iṯbat*) implicit in the *waṣf* (= *at-tasmiya*). The *ism*$_2$ ("name"/"noun"), thus, need not be identified with the subject of the *tasmiya* (the subject of which the predication is made), just as the *waṣf*, in the analysis we have examined, need not refer to and assert the *mawṣûf* as such. From az-Zaǧǧâǧî (a grammarian, d. 949) we learn that those who hold that the *ism* (sc., *ism*$_2$) is the *musammà* consider the *ism*$_2$ to be the *istiḥqâqu t-tasmiya*: the thing's deserving to be called by the given noun or adjective. It is the entitative reality, thus, which constitutes the ontological basis of the truth and validity of a thing's being called (*'an yusammà = at-tasmiya*) whatever it is called: that which requires the descriptive predication (*mâ 'awǧaba i-waṣfa*), in the phrase of al-Aš'arî cited earlier. The *ism*, then, for any being, is "its deserving to be called" whatever it is called when the word by which it is validly called or described is used in its strict sense (*fî l-ḥâqîqa*), e.g., *ǧawharun* (atom), *'araḍun* (accident), *'ilmun* (act of knowing), *mawǧûdun* (existent), *muḥdaṯun* (temporally contingent), *'âlimun* (knowing), *ḫâliqun* (creating), *'âmirun* (commanding), *ẓâlimun* (wronging), *ma'mûrun* (commanded), *maḏkûrun* (mentioned), etc. The thing's deserving to be so called or described (*istiḥqâquhû lit-tasmiya = istiḥqâquhû lil-waṣf*) is the entity the predicate term refers to (*dalla 'alà*) as such and whose existence, therefore, is the basis of the truth of the predication. It is named and described by the noun (the nominal expression: *ism*$_1$, i.e., the participle or verbal adjective) which is predicated of the subject. The predicate or descriptive term which is the "act of calling by a name" (*at-tasmiya*) is a nominal expression (*ism*$_1$) which particularly "names" the thing referred to by it (*al-musummà*); it is either "one of its most particular names" (*min 'aḫaṣṣi 'asmâ'ihî*$_1$) or an adjectival form derived from such a noun (*muštaqqun min 'aḫaṣṣi 'asmâ'ihî*$_1$). The "names" (*al-'asmâ*$_2$), then, in this formal sense, are divided and categorized according to the categories of the *'awṣâf* which assert them: if an entity is called, for example, *ǧawharun* (an atom), the *ism*$_2$, viz., its deserving to be called by this name, is its being itself what it is: its Self. The same is true if motion be called an "accident" (*'araḍ*). If Zayd is called by the *tasmiya* "knowing" (= "knows," "who knows"), the "noun" (*ism*$_2$), "his deserving to be so called," is the concrete act of knowing (*al-'ilm*) which exists in him. As in the grammarians' analysis "*al-'ilm*" is the noun of "*'âlim*" (*ismu*$_1$ "*l-'âlim*") and is the linguistic base (*al-maṣdar*) of which the descriptive forms, verbal and adjectival, are semiotically derivative and which is sometimes called the (semiotic) referent (*ma'nà*) or significate (*madlûl*) of such forms, so here the concrete act of knowing which exists materially in Zayd is said to be the "noun" of "knowing" (*ismu*$_2$ "*l-'âlim*") and "his deserving the predication" (*istiḥqâquhû lit-tasmiya*). Similarly, if *ḍâribun* (strikes, striking) is said of Zayd, the *ism*$_2$ (his deserving the predicate), i.e., the referent which is the ontological basis of the truth of the predication, is the blow (*aḍ-ḍarb*) which he strikes; the blow struck is the "noun" of "strikes" (*ismu*$_2$ "*ḍ-ḍârib*") and that which it "names" (*al-musammà*).

Now, from one standpoint this is a game of words (and not a dull one either, though the rules may be perplexing at the outset). Its importance for al-Aš'arî, however, is plain enough. On the one hand, it gives him a common term for what is referred to (*al-madlûlu ʿalayhî*) and asserted to exist (*al-muṯbat*) for all predicates of any given being, including those of God (*'asmâ'u*$_1$ *llâhi l-ḥusnà*). But more than this, all being is thus reduced to God's names (*'asmâ'u*$_2$ *llâhi*), even while retaining its own names and identity, for all being is divided into two classes: the Eternal and the created, which is to say God's Self and His attributes (*nafsuhû wa-ṣifâtuhû*$_4$) on the one hand, and His acts (*'afʿâluhû*), on the other. In Zayd, for example, the totality of his being — each element of the material composite of atoms and accidents which is he — is the existence which is its being created (*al-maḫlûq* = *al-ḫalq*); it is (Zayd is) the act of creation (*al-ḫalq*), thus, which is "the named" (*al-musammà*) when God is called *ḫâliq* (creating, creator). Furthermore, this will include Zayd's unbelief (*kufr*) if he is an unbeliever (*kâfir*). That is, if Zayd is an unbeliever, then the *kufr* which is "the named" when Zayd is called *kâfir* (and which belongs to him as *muktasib*) is, as a created entity (*maḫlûq*), an action of God's (*fiʿlun lahû*) and as a created entity belongs to the named when God is called *ḫâliq*. As the created entity is, insofar as it exists as a created entity, one of God's "names" (i.e., *ismu*$_2$ *fiʿlin lahû*), so also it is one of his "attributes," not an essential "attribute" (*ṣifatu*$_4$ *nafsin*) but an "attribute" of action (*ṣifatu*$_4$ *fiʿlin lahû*): an "attribute," thus, or "name" which is not eternal and inalienable from His essential being, but one which is contingent and extrinsic. To put it another way: as *kufr*, it is "the named" and the "noun" (*ism*$_2$) of *kâfir*, which is said of Zayd, while as a temporally contingent entity (*šay'un muḥdaṯ*), it is "the named" and the "noun" of *ḫâliq*, which is said of God. Furthermore, God has forbidden unbelief (*nahâ ʿanhû*) and for this reason (and for this reason alone, according to al-Ašʿarî) it is evil (*qabîḥ*). If his unbelief (the *ism*$_2$ of *kâfir*), then, is called *qabîḥ*, "the named" (viz., the *ism*$_2$ of *qabîḥ*), which is to say the being whose reality is referred to in the predicate "evil" and whose being is the basis of the truth of the predicate, is God's prohibition of it (*an-nahyu ʿanhû*) which is His eternal speech (*kalâmuhu l-qadîm*): one of His eternal "attributes" (*ṣifâtuhû*$_4$). The fact is that this use of *ism* can be (and is), to say the least, a trifle confusing in almost any context. It is, however, employed or alluded to quite infrequently save in the few places where the thesis that the *ism*$_2$ is the *musammà* is set forth (not always clearly either). Otherwise al-Ašʿarî and his followers use the term *ism* in its normal senses. The contextual resonance of the word, however, is established: all predication refers ultimately to God and all naming (*tasmiya*, not *talqîb*) ultimately to His names.

The outline which I have given here is too brief and schematic to give any indication of the complexity and richness of the thought of the three authors whose teaching we have discussed. I hope, however, that it will be found sufficient to clarify something of the basic principles on which the ontologies of the Basrian systems were built and of their general character.[15]

The systems we have examined are essentially Islamic in their origin and conception. It is worth noting, however, that though characteristically Islamic, the central importance of the term *ḥaqîqa* in its various senses (viz., truth and reality: the true and strict sense of a term and that which we really and truly mean and signify when we use the term in its strict sense and the being which is referred to when the term is so used: its true nature as it is, is known, and is referred to by the term) are not restricted to the *mutakallimîn* among Muslim thinkers. The term *ḥaqîqa* is of central importance also in the work of al-Kindî (d. ca. 870), the first major proponent of Greek philosophy in Islam. It not merely is a conspicuous term in his *On First Philosophy* but serves to supply and express the overall order of the extant first part of the work.[16] Thus, within the general Neoplatonic framework within which the book is conceived, he begins by defining philosophy as "the knowing of things in their *ḥaqâ'iq*" and stating that "the cause of every being and of its reality is the truth (*al-ḥaqq*), since every thing which has entity has a trueness (*ḥaqîqa*); the truth (*al-ḥaqq*) necessarily exists, therefore, for existent entities" (i.e., they participate in it and exist insofar as they participate in it). Accordingly, the first part of the work is devoted primarily to an examination of the "trueness" (*ḥaqîqa*) of the categories and the predicables: what we mean really and truly (*fî l-ḥaqîqa*) when we use the terms strictly and in their true sense and the reality or true nature of things as they are in themselves which is thereby revealed for understanding. The grasp, then, of the "trueness" of things and of their degrees of oneness and being (their participation in being one, strictly speaking), revealed in the analysis of the categories and the predicables, leads him to assert the existence of that which alone is one in the strict sense (*al-wâḥidu fî l-ḥaqîqa*): The True One, the One which is Truth (*al-wâḥidu l-ḥaqq*).

NOTES

1 Nor is this the place to draw out the tedious philological apparatus required to document and justify the schema presented here. Most of the terminology cited and most of the formulas are common enough in the sources and will readily be recognized by those familiar with them. Concerning the thought of abû Hâšim, a detailed outline is to be found in my *Beings and Their Attributes* (Albany, N.Y., 1978). What is sketched here concerning

the doctrines of al-Ǧubbâ'î and al-Aš῾arî I hope to elaborate within the context of a full analysis of the texts in a subsequent study. The present remarks concerning al-Aš῾arî are based chiefly on his *Risala ilà ahl aṯ-ṯaǧr*, printed in *Ilahiyat Fakültesi Mecmuasi*, 8 (1928), 93–96 and *K. al-Luma῾*, §§ 13ff. (see n. 14).

2 The word *ṣifa* is used in the texts in several plainly distinct (though not always and everywhere unambiguously distinguishable) senses, which may be defined briefly as follows. *Ṣifa*$_1$: a descriptive expression or predicate; *ṣifa*$_2$: a set of such expressions which are taken to be equivalent; *ṣifa*$_3$: an attribute, perfection, property, or quality of a being (= *ḥâl*, in abû Hâšim's usage); *ṣifa*$_4$: an entitative property or "attribute" according to the Aš῾arite usage (= *ma῾nà* = *῾illa* and, in speaking of corporeal entities, = *῾araḍ*: an entitative "accident"); *ṣifa*$_5$ is used by al-Bâqillânî and al-Ǧuwaynî in their adaptation of abû Hâšim's conception of the *ḥâl* (= *ṣifa*$_3$) and need not concern us in the present context. "*Ṣifa*$_1$" and "*ṣifa*$_2$" are employed by both schools (though al-Aš῾arî himself seems to avoid it and some of his followers tend to, favoring "*waṣf*," which is contextually equivalent); "*ṣifa*$_3$" is used only by the Mu῾tazilite school of Basra following abû Hâšim; "*ṣifa*$_4$" is used by the Aš῾arite school from ibn Kullâb on; it is the equivalent of "*῾illa*" and "ma῾nà" in the common terminology, but is sometimes used also for acts (*ṣifâtu*$_4$ *fi῾lin* = an attribute" of action) where it designates the act (the concrete entity which is the act) — e.g., where the Aš῾arites distinguish God's eternal "attributes," which belong to His Self or essential being (*ṣifâtu*$_4$ *nafsihî*) and those which are contingent and extrinsic to His essence (*ṣifâtu*$_4$ *'af῾âlihî*). In the passages in which one school is arguing polemically against the doctrines of the other, the ambivalence of the word, which is often exploited for the sake of the polemic, can be somewhat confusing if one does not keep the several senses distinctly in mind. It should be noted that indefinite nouns — e.g., *ḥarakatun* (= "a motion," in English, not "motion") or *sawâdun* (= "a black," i.e., a discrete quantum of the entitative "accident" black) — are understood to designate concrete individual entities and the definite forms — e.g., *al-ḥarakatu* or *as-sawâdu*, to designate either a given, concrete instance or the class (*al-ǧins*) as distributed to its members. Abstract or intentional entities are not recognized by either school in the period with which we are currently concerned.

3 That is, the Baghdad school characteristically seeks to understand and explain certain properties, qualities, and operations of bodies in terms of the four "natures" (*aṭ-ṭaba'i'*, sc., the hot, the dry, the cold, and the damp) and so are reckoned among "the proponents of the natures" (*'aṣḥâb aṭ-taba'i῾*). The Basrians, on the other hand, deny the reality of the natures as such and of those characteristics and operations of bodies which the Baghdadis ascribe to the interaction of the natures which they describe and account for in terms of entitative "accidents" (*'a῾râḍ*, sg., *῾araḍ*, most often referred to by the terms *῾illa* and *ma῾nà*) inherent in the corporeal subject (*al-maḥall*). The reality of the accidents, they argue, is directly implied in certain predicates which are said of corporeal beings. The conception of the *'a῾râd*, in fact, originates within the Basrian system; i.e., it is the Basrian's analysis of the predicates of being which discovers, so to speak, the "accidents" as *ma῾ânî*, *῾ilal*.

4 The matter is more complex than may seem to be suggested here. The words used to describe God in the Koran (paraphrased where necessary into a nominal, i.e., participial or adjectival, form) are taken to follow the normal use of literary Arabic (*al-luġa*) and to be understood in their basic and proper sense whenever the context does not require that they be interpreted in an extended or metaphorical sense. In a number of cases, however, the theologians do distinguish in the *ḥaqîqa* (the basic, fundamental, or strict sense) of a word that which it may have as a specialized or technical term (*iṣṭilâḥ*) within

the formal context of theological speculation (*iṣṭilâḥu l-mutakallimîn, taʿârufu l-mutakallimîn*) and prefer the latter. In their analysis of the predicates used of God, individual theologians and the separate schools may thus locate the "fundamental sense" (*al-ḥaqîqa*) of a given word as they use it either in the common usage or in the specialized usage of the individual or school, but whichever is chosen the *ḥaqiqa* is taken to be constant and univocal.

5 Two things should be noted in this connection: first, that in Arabic the "noun of action" (*ism al-fiʿl*) or "noun of the event" (*ism al-ḥadaṯ*) is absolute. It simply names the action or event; as such it is without reference to time or to the completion or incompletion of the action or event and is neither active nor passive, being determined in these respects only as the semantics of the stem, the particular use, and the context may determine, require, or suggest. Secondly, the notion that this verbal noun is the base or "source" (*al-maṣdar*) from which the inflected forms of the verb as well as all the various adjectives of the stem are derived is understood as a purely grammatical concept by the Basrian grammarians, to whose school tradition the thesis is native. That is to say, the grammarians of the Basrian tradition, in setting forth their position and in arguing it against those of the Kufan tradition, are quite explicit in their insistence that the notion of derivation (*ištiqâq*) is entirely formal and grammatical here and has nothing whatsoever to do with the relationships which may obtain between the things and events (real things: actions, agents, patients, and states of affairs) to which nouns, verbs, and their derivatives may be understood to refer.

6 The form of the sentence *lahû ʿilmun* is important: i.e., though it may quite correctly be translated "he has an act of knowing," the term *ʿilmun* is grammatically the subject and to render it otherwise is to distort the structure of the formula, the analysis of which is of fundamental significance to the Basrian *kalâm*, Muʿtazilite and Ašʿarite alike.

7 Here the derivation (*ištiqâq*) is not purely formal, as it is when one speaks of the relationship between the maṣdar and the forms (*al-'amṯila*) derived from it (n. 5 above), but has to do with the implicit semantic relationships of words and forms as they are used in their strict sense in speaking of real beings. Though both kinds of derivation are recognized and dealt with by the grammarians and the lexicographers, it is the latter alone which is discussed by the *mutakallimîn*. But in doing so, they strictly follow, not the analyses of the grammarians and lexicographers (though, to be sure, there are some mutual influences), but their own theoretical preoccupations and presuppositions. It should be remarked that of the predicates with which we are primarily concerned in the pages which follow none save those of "action" is taken to be "derived" by al-Ğubbâ'î and abû Hâšim. One has to go back to abû l-Hudhayl, i.e., to the earliest stage of the Basrian Muʿtazilite tradition, in order to see this common link in the tradition.

8 The list is taken from al-Ašʿari's *Maqâlât al-Islâmiyyîn*, ed. H. Ritter (Istanbul, 1929–1930), pp. 161f. and 522. Further study of al-Ğubbâ'i will no doubt require some expansion and perhaps some revision of what is proposed here. I am confident, however, that the present analysis is correct within its own, rather limited, scope. The absence of a category of predicates of action is conspicuous. It is possible that it is omitted from al-Ašʿarî's report because of the context; on the other hand, it may be that such predicates are to be located, as is fitting in each case, under those which are "*li-ʿillatin fîhî*" or those which are "*li-ʿillatin lâ fîhî*," as is suggested below. In the absence of any direct evidence, however, one cannot be certain.

9 Only the real and the possible, i.e., that which is or can be a true object of knowing, is termed *šay'*. The impossible (*al-mustaḥîlu wuğûduhû*: that whose existence is impossible) is thus not a *šay'*, and in reference to a true proposition whose subject is something

whose being is impossible, one speaks of "a knowing which has no object" (*'ilmun lâ ma'lûma lahû*). In defining his sixth category of predication al-Ğubbâ'î here follows Sîbawayh's definition of *šay'*; the more common definition employed by the Basrian Mu'tazila, however (and one also found in the writings of the grammarians), is that it is *al-ma'lûmu l'muḫbaru 'anhû*: that which is (or may be) known and of which something can be said. Concerning the possibles, see my "*Al-Ma'dûm wal-Mawjûd*," MIDEO, 14 (1980), 185–210.

10 Unfortunately, as was mentioned above, al-Ğubbâ'î's semantic analysis of the terms *kâ'in* and *mawğûd* is not reported (not at least insofar as I have been able to discover).

11 This phrase with *'alà* ("upon," "according to," etc.) is difficult to render adequately into English without distorting its structure and meaning. Basically, it is adverbial (meaning, thus, "[qualified] by an attribute"), so that *'innahû 'alà ṣifatin* is "it [is qualified] by an attribute," the adverbial expression qualifying the implicit notion of being. Explicating this, then, and explicitating what is implied, one may say that *'alà ṣifatin* indicates *kawnuhû 'alà ṣifatin* (his being [qualified] by an attribute) and so, simply, *kawnuhû kaḏâ* (his being thus-and-so).

12 The designation *lâ lin-nafsi wa-lâ li-'illa* abû Hâsim has taken from al-Ğubbâ'î, though he conceives the category in an altogether different manner and therefore as embracing a totally different set of predications. An account of the way he construes it and of what predicates he includes in it (all negatives among them) and why would be too lengthy an undertaking for the present outline. On this as well as the other categories distinguished by abû Hâšim, see my *Beings and Their Attributes*.

13 The vocabulary of these distinctions is highly nuanced and too complex to be detailed here.

14 *K. al-Luma'*, § 37, ed. R. McCarthy (Beirut, 1953), p. 19, 8. The editor's emendation (ibid., n. 17) is incorrect; one should read with the manuscript.

15 It should be noted that the position of al-Aš'arî in the development of the As'arite tradition is, apart from his having gathered into one "system" of theology a number of originally scattered theses or elements, really quite hard to assess, as is, for this reason and others, the evolution of the system as a whole to the point of its maturity. As I indicated somewhat obliquely above, there is an entire set of questions having to do with being and existence — God's attributes and those of creatures — which he simply dodges, burying them quite explicitly in his *Risâla ilà ahl aṯ-ṯaġr* with the phrase *bi-lâ takyîf*. This failure to pursue the implications of his basic formulas and theses is paralleled in other questions too (e.g., that of the *kasb*). Some of these issues — e.g., the denumerability of God's attributes and whether they are termed *'ašyâ'* — had been treated by ibn Kullâb before him. The problem plainly is not merely one of the paucity of his writings which are available to us, for his successors in his own school did not know his position in many instances either. In explicating his basic theses and formulations and in elaborating their sense and their implications, the great Aš'arite masters of the eleventh century, e.g., al-Bâqillânî, ibn Fûrak, and abû Isḥâq al-Isfarâ'înî, formulate in a number of questions conceptions which are altogether opposed to one another and in some cases attribute them to al-Aš'arî himself.

16 This work has been translated into English, with a commentary, by Alfred L. Ivry: *al-Kindî's Metaphysics* (Albany, N.Y., 1974).

11

Al-Suhrawardī's Critique of the Muslim Peripatetics (*al-Mashshā'ūn*)

MAJID FAKHRY
American University of Beirut

THE DISAFFECTION WITH PERIPATETISM which marked the later stages of ibn Sīnā's thought finds its full expression in al-Suhrawardī's writings. Like ibn Sīnā, al-Suhrawardī does not reject the Peripatetic method entirely out of hand but regards it as adequate for purposes of discourse only. It is inadequate, however, for the more lofty purposes of the "divine sage," who should go beyond this method to combine the discursive and the experiential, ensuring thereby the unity and perenniality of that "ancient wisdom" which has its origins in the writings of Aristotle, Plato, Hermes, and other pillars of Western (Greek), and Jamasp, Farashauster, Buzurjimhr, Zoroaster, and other pillars of Eastern (Persian), wisdom.[1]

Our principal aim in the present essay is to set out al-Suhrawardī's major criticisms of the Peripatetic or discursive method the advocates of which claim, erroneously according to him, to have derived it from Aristotle himself, but of which the First Master was entirely innocent, as he personally assured al-Suhrawardī in a memorable apparition at Jabarse. In this apparition, "the succour of souls and paragon of wisdom," upon being questioned by al-Suhrawardī about genuine knowledge, conjunction, and union, informed him that only the Sufi sages, by combining the discursive and experiential methods or modes of knowledge, are the genuine inheritors of that ancient and universal wisdom.[2]

These two general criticisms of Arabic Peripatetism may be summarized as follows: (*a*) the "discursive" method used by its adherents is not the genuine method of Aristotle (by whom we should understand the Aristotle of the pseudo-*Theology*, i.e., Plotinus) or of the ancient sages of Greece and the Orient; and (*b*) this method is not adequate for the attainment of the higher aims of wisdom unless it is coupled with the experiential method of the mystics. Other, more specific, criticisms are also levelled against the Peripatetics.

Their theory of the categories, for example, is shot through with difficulties. The traditional number of ten cannot be justified, nor its exhaustiveness proved. It contains some derivative concepts, such as when, where, possession, and posture, which are all modes of relation; and action and passion, which are modes of motion. The table is derived, not from Aristotle, but from a certain Pythagorean called Archytas.[3] Ibn Sīnā himself, having reviewed some conflicting opinions about their number, reaffirmed the traditional number.

Another logical criticism may be levelled at the Peripatetic concept of definition. It is well known that in the Peripatetic tradition generally the definition is made up of two components: the genus, which al-Suhrawardī calls the "general essential," and the *differentia,* which he calls the "particular essential." But in so far as the second component is not intuitively known, al-Suhrawardī argues, invoking in it the process of definition contradicts the Aristotelian maxim that the truth of the unknown is arrived at only through what is already known. Should the logician happen to light upon the *differentia* accidentally, he obviously cannot be certain that it is the only *differentia* or that other *differentiae,* equally essential to the definition in question, do not actually exist.

These difficulties in Peripatetic doctrine arise with respect not only to accidents, but to substances as well, including the soul and the separate substances. According to the Peripatetics, the *differentiae* of these substances are unknowable; it follows on these premisses that their definitions are not possible. The accidents, on the other hand, are known through the senses, and consequently cannot be defined either. The whole Peripatetic theory of definition is therefore entirely futile.

These difficulties notwithstanding, the Peripatetic philosophers define substance as that which exists in no subject, thereby contradicting "the ancients,"[4] who defined substance as that which exists in no substratum. The first definition, according to al-Suhrawardī, is not a sound one since it applies equally to substances and to their forms, whereas the second applies to substances only. The form cannot in fact be said to be present in a subject, in so far as the substratum, al-Suhrawardī writes somewhat cryptically, requires it as a determinant thereof.[5]

The Peripatetics sometimes define substance as something which "exists in a thing, without being a part thereof." But this variation on the original theme is useless since it leaves out of account the intellect, on the one hand, and the world at large, on the other. For the intellect and the world, which are regarded as substances, do not exist in something of which they form a part. Accidents, on the other hand, do exist in something of which they do not form a part and are accordingly substances, which is absurd.[6]

A related criticism bears on the Peripatetic division of substances into three parts: individuals, species, and genera. It is part of Peripatetic doctrine that only individuals exist in act; therefore, on this view, neither species nor genera would actually exist, i.e., would belong to the general class of substance, as the Peripatetics assert. Moreover, if they should add that the essential characteristic of substance is that it is an object of "sensible or intellectual demonstration," they would involve themselves in contradiction; for "separate substances" and "universal entities" are not objects of "sensible demonstration," whereas corporal substances, on the other hand, are not objects of "intellectual demonstration."[7]

Al-Suhrawardī dwells at considerable length on other defects of the Peripatetic doctrine of substance, as equated with existence, with the express purpose of showing that it is hopelessly confused and even self-contradictory. His own doctrine, as outlined in *Ḥikmat al-Ishrāq* in particular, appears to be that substance is distinguishable from and more general than existence. It is, he writes, "the perfection [*kamāl*] of the essence of an entity, in so far as it can dispense with the substratum in its mode of self-subsistence."[8] In that respect, it may be regarded as one of the "transcendentals" of Peripatetic logic, which included being, non-being, essence, relation, etc., without being determined existentially.[9]

Al-Suhrawardī is equally critical of another fundamental aspect of the Peripatetic doctrine of substance, i.e., the duality of matter and form. His criticisms here can best be understood in the light of his own concept of the emanation of all things from the primary source of all reality (or the Light of Lights), through a process of irradiation, or gradual devolution from the highest plane of luminosity to the lowest — a process in which, so he claims, duality does not enter at all. Yet this duality is central to Peripatetic doctrine, in which matter was introduced to serve as the bearer of the continuous and discontinuous, or of magnitude and number. Nonetheless, the Peripatetics deny that magnitude (*miqdār*) is part of the essence of body, this essence being materiality, which is characterized by continuity. But continuity, according to al-Suhrawardī, is purely a function of the relation of one body to the other, unlike magnitude, which is an inseparable aspect of body. Hence, for him the essence of body "is nothing other than pure magnitude, which is susceptible of the three modes of extension. . . ."[10] Absolute body is thus synonymous with absolute magnitude, so that a piece of wax which changes from one perceptible condition to another when it is exposed to heat remains unchanged in one essential respect in the process, i.e., its magnitude. If we apply this result to body in general, we shall be forced to conclude that magnitude, rather than materiality, is the essential characteristic of body.[11]

Form, on the other hand, is asserted by the Peripatetic philosophers to be the cause of matter, in so far as it determines and individuates it. But, from the fact that form and matter exist in conjunction, it does not follow that form is the cause of its correlate, or that it is the determinant thereof, as they maintain. In fact, argues al-Suhrawardī, it is the accidents which should be regarded as the actual determinants of substance, in so far as they enter into the conception thereof causally or conditionally.

A group of criticisms are next levelled at the Peripatetic theory of knowledge. Al-Suhrawardī rejects in the first instance the Peripatetic contention that immateriality is the essential condition of knowledge, arguing instead for luminosity as that condition. Things are knowable to the extent that light enters into their composition. Thus the most luminous of entities, i.e., God, is the most knowable; things emanating from him, in so far as they are made up of light and darkness, are known in proportion as light or darkness predominates in them.[12]

In the second instance, he rejects the Peripatetic thesis that, in the act of knowledge, the knower becomes identical with the form of the object known, on the ground that it is impossible for any entity to become identical with any other entity. His own view is that the knowing self "is a single and constant entity, before and after the [acquisition of] form . . . and you are always fully yourself, with or without the act of knowledge."[13]

He likewise rejects the Peripatetic view, advanced by both al-Fārābī and ibn Sīnā, that knowledge is the act of conjunction (*ittiṣāl*) or union (*ittiḥād*) with the active intellect, on the ground that in this act the soul is conjoined either to one part of the active intellect or to the whole thereof. In the former case, (*a*) the active intellect will be composite, and (*b*) the soul will know only that part to which it is conjoined. In the latter, it will apprehend all things, of which the active intellect is said to be cognizant, whenever it apprehends any individual object, which is absurd.[14]

As to the soul's knowledge of itself, al-Suhrawardī's view is analogous to that of Plotinus and ibn Sīnā. The soul, he argues, apprehends itself directly and intuitively. For, he writes,

> you are never oblivious of your self or of your apprehension of it. . . . It follows that your apprehension of the self is for itself and as it is *per se*, and that it will not be absent to the [whole of] yourself or the part thereof — so that if you were to look closely, you will find that what constitutes your essence [*mā anta bihi anta*] is nothing but a self-knowing entity which is your very selfhood [*anāniyah*].[15]

This selfhood is in fact a pure and self-apprehending light.

The Peripatetic view of divine knowledge calls for the same strictures. This knowledge is bound up, according to the Peripatetics, with the immateriality of the Necessary Being, who through the act of self-apprehension causes the whole series of emanations beneath him. This view, however, is open to two objections: (*a*) were divine self-apprehension the cause of created objects, it would be dependent on these objects; and (*b*) since its effect (i.e., the world) is other than itself, God's knowledge of himself and of the world would be different, and this would introduce composition into his nature.

Al-Suhrawardī's view of divine knowledge is bound up, as one would expect, with his theory of light. "God's knowledge of himself is that act of being a light unto himself and therefore manifest to himself." His knowledge of other objects, on the other hand, is the act of recognizing their "manifestness" (*zuhūr*) unto him, either through themselves or through the agency of the higher entities which minister to them.[16] In short, things are known to him ultimately by virtue of that luminosity which they derive from him.

In conclusion, a careful appraisal of these strictures against the Arab Peripatetics in general and ibn Sīnā in particular would reveal that many of them are purely verbal. For, with the exception of al-Suhrawardī's vindication of the experiential or mystical element as an essential ingredient of wisdom (which is perhaps the genuinely distinguishing mark of *Ishrāq*, as opposed to *Ittiṣāl*), almost all the key concepts in his system have their own counterparts in ibn Sīnā's metaphysics and cosmology. Thus where ibn Sīnā speaks of emanation (*Ṣudūr*), al-Suhrawardī speaks of irradiation (*Ishrāq*); where he speaks of compound entities, his successor speaks of isthmuses (*al-barza khiyāt*), which separate the two realms of light and darkness. The duality of form and matter which he rejects, as we have seen, reemerges as the duality of light and darkness. Immateriality, which for the Peripatetics is the precondition of knowledge, is replaced by luminosity, or the fact that the knowledge of an object is commensurate with the degree of light inherent in it.

A final remark might be made about the place of Aristotle in all this litigation. Al-Suhrawardī claims that his attack on the Muslim Peripatetics is launched in the name of Aristotle, whose doctrine they either distorted or misunderstood. But close examination of his arguments would reveal that it is not the historical Aristotle whom he has in view, but rather the Aristotle of the pseudo-*Theology* — in other words, Plotinus. This will partly explain his adulation for Plato, "the paragon of wisdom and its chief," as he calls him, and whom he casts again in the role of Plotinus as the philosopher who has combined the two methods of discourse and experience, unlike the Muslim Peripatetics who, according to him, fell short of this ideal.

NOTES

1 The complete list of ancient sages given in *Ḥikmat al-Ishrāq* (see *Œuvres philosophiques et mystiques* [Tehran & Paris, 1952], pp. 10f.), *al-Mashāriʿ* (see *Opera metaphysica et mystica* [Istanbul, 1945], pp. 493, 503), and *al-Talwiḥāt* (*ibid.*, p. 111) also includes Agathadaimon, Asclepius, Pythagoras, Empedocles, and "other ancient Babylonian, Khosroan, Indian, Egyptian, and Greek sages."

2 *Al-Talwiḥāt*, p. 74, and *al-Mashāriʿ*, pp. 503–504. The chain of transmission of this mystical tradition is said to have come down, in one line, from the Pythagoreans, through Duu'l-Nūn al-Misri, to al-Tustari, and, in another line, from the Khosroans, through al-Hallāj and al-Basṭāmi, to Abu'l-Ḥasan al-Kharqāni and al-Suhrawardī himself.

3 Cf. al-Fārābī, *Al-Alfāz al-Mustaʿmalah* (Beirut, 1968), p. 109. The Pythagorean Archytas was a Sicilian philosopher and mathematician whom Plato met during his first visit to Sicily in 388 B.C. See Diogenes Laertius 8.2.4.

4 By the ancients, al-Suhrawardī appears to mean Aristotle and his immediate followers. But in *Categories* 5 Aristotle defines substance as that which is neither predicable of nor present in a subject. Ibn Sīnā and others understood "not predicable of a subject" to refer to the essential attributes, and "that which is present in a subject" to refer to the accidents which inhere in a substance. See *al-Maqulāt* (*al-Shifā'*) (Cairo, 1959), p. 23.

5 *Al-Muqāwamāt*, p. 129. By substratum, al-Suhrawardī appears to mean, like other Peripatetics, the matter which, when joined to the compound, gives rise to substance (*al-jauhar*).

6 In *al-Maqūlāt*, p. 28, ibn Sīnā "describes" the accident as an "existent in something of which it forms no part," but does not confuse accident and substance at all.

7 *Al-Mashāriʿ*, p. 232.

8 *Ḥikmat*, p. 70.

9 Ibid., pp. 64f.

10 Ibid., p. 75.

11 Ibid. Compare here Descartes' identification of body with extension, in *Meditation* II, as well as the example of the wax which he gives.

12 *Ḥikmat*, p. 115.

13 *Al-Mashāriʿ*, p. 475.

14 See ibid., p. 476.

15 *Ḥikmat*, p. 112. Cf. *al-Mashāriʿ*, p. 484, and *al-Talwiḥāt*, pp. 70f. In the pseudo-*Theology*, Plotinus' view is given as follows: "That is why nothing corporeal can contemplate that form [i.e., that of the intelligible world] properly for the reason we mentioned above. If you wish to contemplate that form, return to yourself, and regard yourself as a soul without body, and then contemplate that form as if it were a single entity without other-ness." See ʿA. Badawi, *Plotinus apud Arabes* (Cairo, 1955), p. 116. Ibn Sīnā writes: "Return to yourself, and consider, if you are sound [of body and mind] . . . so as to be able to grasp things properly, whether you are ever oblivious of the existence of yourself. . . . with what will you apprehend yourself then or before and after? And what is the apprehending part of yourself? And do you apprehend through an intermediary or without an intermediary? For I do not believe that you require then an intermediary, seeing that there is no intermediary. There remains the alternative that you apprehend yourself without any need for any other power or an intermediary." See *Al-Ishārāt wa'l-Tanbihāt* (Cairo, 1960), Part 2, pp. 319f.

16 *Ḥikmat*, p. 152.

12

Greek Sources of Some Near Eastern Philosophies of Being and Existence

PARVIZ MOREWEDGE
Baruch College
The City University of New York

INTRODUCTION

THIS ESSAY ATTEMPTS TO ANSWER the following two interrelated questions: How are being and existence viewed in Near Eastern philosophies?[1] And what can we learn about ontology from the Near Eastern philosophies of being and existence?[2] In the course of examining these questions we shall develop theses which are in part historical and in part systematic. The historical findings are: (*a*) that three problems embedded in the Neoplatonized versions of Aristotelian texts, which enlarged Aristotle's notion of being and existence, played a decisive role in the Near Eastern perspectives on being and existence; and (*b*) that three distinct philosophies of being and existence can be found in Persian and Arabic texts, many of which have hitherto been unavailable in English. Our systematic findings are: (*c*) that an important issue of ontology is or should be the depiction of a satisfactory relation between what might be designated as "the ultimate being" and "persons"; (*d*) that no Aristotelian categorial language in which the notion of "substance" is considered primitive (in the Carnapian[3] sense of "primitive") can adequately explain the ontological problem formulated in (*c*); and finally (*e*) that, instead of limiting its analysis to those issues which can be easily expressed in a clear language or in the exact languages of the physical sciences or mathematics, ontology should use the best available language to depict significant problems. In the case of being and existence, we wish to show how the Arabic and Persian equivalents are used to clarify the relationship between two perennial questions of both Western and Near Eastern philosophies: What is the nature of an individual existent? How can we talk about the ultimate being and depict a satisfactory relation between the ultimate being and persons?

In any historical reconstruction of the philosophical issues in the Aristotelian and the Neoplatonic traditions transmitted to the Near Easterners, there are a number of difficulties. For example, the basic primary text devoted to the analysis of being and existence is Aristotle's *Metaphysics*; yet in the early period of Near Eastern philosophy there is no clear counterpart to this text, merely a work called *The Theology of Aristotle*, which was a combination of Aristotle's own writings and two other works — a *Theologia*,[4] derived from Proclus' (411–485)[5] *Elements of Theology*, and a celebrated *Liber de causis* (*Fi'l Khair al-Mahd*; literally, "On the Absolute Good"),[6] a paraphrase of the last three books of Plotinus' *Enneads*. Moreover, Near Easterners read all the works of Aristotle, as well as the marginal commentaries of the Neoplatonists and of other, later Greek philosophers such as Alexander Aphrodisias (ca. 250) and Themistius (d. 390).[7] Consequently, a Near Eastern philosopher would not only have to attempt to make sense of his Aristotelian source containing *οὐσία* before constructing his own philosophy of being and existence, but also have to come to terms with Plotinus' and Proclus' doctrine of "the One" and Plato's "Form of the Good." Difficulties of analyzing the transmission of vocabulary and the extent of the Near Eastern philosopher's involvement with the various theological and ontological aspects of the matter at hand have forced us to be selective in this essay and have dictated our choice of the following three problems, which not only are of importance for contemporary ontology but display aspects of being and existence philosophically significant for Near Eastern thinkers.

The first problem involves the legitimate scope of "ontology." In what sense can ontology investigate entities other than "first substances" and "their accidents"? Can it investigate, for example, possible unactualized or impossible entities? Should the entire realm of "reality," which may or may not extend beyond Aristotle's nature (*φύσις*) be regarded as an individual or a closed "entity"? In passing, we note that Neoplatonic treatments of Aristotle's texts and Neoplatonic doctrines provided the Near Easterners such as ibn Sīnā with a concept of an "ultimate being" type of entity which went beyond the Aristotelian concept of the prime mover and the entire Aristotelian *φύσις*.

The second question concerns the ontological implications of the predication of species. The historical roots of this problem lie in Porphyry's (232–270) addition of species (*εἶδος*) to Aristotle's account of the four predicables (genus, property, definition, and accident) in the *Topics*. Now, if one predicates over "species," then its designatum *species* is named as the subject of a sentence. Because first substances or "individuals" were usually named by subjects of sentences, predication over species led some philosophers to regard the *Topics* of Aristotle (in spite of its anti-Platonic features, e.g., 113A24–32, 148A14–22) as a source of a Platonic theory of universals.[8] The predication over species brings us to the issue of determining the ontological implications of using a certain kind of language. The modern version of this issue is well known and deals with the controversy over the possible implications of certain conditions governing the quantification of signs of levels higher than zero.[9] Older historical scholarship concerned itself with such problems as how Porphyry's *Isagoge*[10] reflected a misunderstanding of Aristotle and gave birth to the world of universals, the nominalists' rejection of this realm of entities notwithstanding. Porphyry's formulation had two specific features: (*a*) the statement of the problem of universals in terms of "thing-universals" and (*b*) the inclusion of species as a predicable. It will become clear, in the course of this essay, how in Near Eastern philosophy Ṭūsī's[11] reaction was a representative clarification of the problem, recently reformulated by M. K. Munitz,[12] who draws a distinction between "syntactic" and "ontologic" senses of predication. As is to be expected, Ṭūsī does not treat the crucial problem of "semantic" predication in a satisfactory manner.

The third problem inquires into the role of syntactical analysis in dealing with ontological problems. If one can develop an ontology with a notion of "ultimate predicates," should one do so? A general problem which arises out of this peculiar formulation is the specification of the role of the primitive schema of logic, e.g., "the subject–predicate form," in shaping our metaphysics of being and existence. The historical counterpart of this problem deals with the question: "What did Aristotle mean by his categories?" It is obvious that the Neoplatonists could not have accepted the metaphysical implication of the categories, which did not make a distinction between the sensible and the intelligible realms; but many Neoplatonists were teachers of logic and had to rely on the entire organon for the texts on logic. A. C. Lloyd[13] has argued that some aspects of Neoplatonic logic freed the categories from their metaphysical implications. If this hypothesis is true, then one is led to ask: "What did the Near Easterners do with the Neoplatonic versions of the categories?" It seems that many of them, including ibn Sīnā,[14] had two notions of the categories: one for logic and one as a tool for the analysis of being and existence. As is to be expected, ibn Sīnā and others did not believe that a categorial analysis of existent entities was the initial task of metaphysics; they began with a wider notion of being *qua* being (*hastī*) which permitted them to discuss non-existent types of entities prior to proffering a discussion of the categorial types of entities.

The interdependence of the problems raised in the above questions precludes answering each in isolation and suggests that a better approach would be to focus on the positions taken by three schools of Near Eastern philosophy; such an approach would allow us to highlight their differences as well as their agreements on two issues: (*a*) the impossibility of defining an "existent" and (*b*) the rejection of the categories as a suitable framework for the depiction of the ultimate being.

(*a*) The first school holds the view that there are two distinct domains in which the problem of being and existence may be discussed; in the realm of actual existents by means of an empirical inquiry, and in the realm of conceptual essences (*mahiyyāt*) by means of logical and linguistic distinctions (*farq-i lafḍī*). This position anticipates to some extent certain aspects of Carnap's philosophy[15] touching on "abstract entities" when it attempts to consider the use of abstract entities as legitimate without admitting a realistic ontology. The major figure in this school is ibn Sīnā (980–1037). Doctrines similar to his may be found in the works of the earlier philosopher al-Fārābī (870–950),[16] whose logical works have been studied by N. Rescher and D. M. Dunlop.[17] Moreover, some of the works of a later Iranian philosopher, N. Ṭūsī (1201–1274), contain similar doctrines. Apart from making mention of a few studies in English, we shall present the first English translation of passages taken from the works of writers of this school, including Ṭūsī's *Foundations of Derivations* (*Asās al-Iqtibās*[18]), and ibn Sīnā's *Indications and Remarks* (*al-Ishārāt wa-l-Tanbīhāt*[19]). We shall also provide a modified translation of al-Fārābī's remarks on the *Categories* of Aristotle[20] and shall consider his recently edited book, which devotes a section to existence.

(*b*) For a representative of the school which emphasized the Platonic approach to the metaphysics of essence (*māhiyya*), we turn to another Iranian philosopher, ʿA. Nasafī (ca. 1250),[21] and a section of his recital "Analysis of the Primary Foundations [of the World] and an Account of the Worlds of Necessity, of the Heavenly, and of the Terrestrial [Realms]" ("*Mabdāʿ-i Awwal wa Baiān-i ʿAlam-i Jabburāt wa ʿĀlam-i Malakūt wa ʿAlami Mulk*"[22]). Nasafī's mystical account of the existence of persons and the ultimate being is taken from other sources, such as his *Perfect Man* (*Al-Insān al-Kāmil*[23]) and *Revelations of Truths-Realities* (*Kashf al-Haqāʿiq*).[24]

(*c*) As representative of "the philosophers of existents," we shall examine selected passages from *The Peripatetics* (*Al-Mashaʿir*[25]) written by still another Iranian philosopher, Mullā Ṣadrā (1572–1640),[26] and note Fazlur Rahman's observations on his major work, *The Spiritual Journey* (*Al-Asfār al-Arbaʿa*).[27] Mullā Ṣadrā leads a major school of philosophers who maintain that "existents" are the only significant concern of philosophy and consider "existence" an abstract term which, in fact, is an essence which cannot capture the features of that which is "an existent." God is considered "an existent" which cannot be discussed in essence-types of terms such as "being a substance."

Two Preliminary Problems: The Transmission of Philosophical Vocabulary and the Extent of the Concern with Being and Existence in the Near East

In the first phase of our investigation, we should briefly take cognizance of two minor problems: the transmission of Greek philosophical vocabulary, itself a representative illustration of the transmission of ideas, and the extent to which Near Eastern philosophers concerned themselves with being and existence in their relevant metaphysical and logical works.

Let us acquaint ourselves, on the one hand, with the transmission of *ὕλη* and *οὐσία* to become familiar with various modes of transmission and, on the other, with *ḥaqq* to learn about Persian and Arabic terms lacking Greek equivalents. *Ὕλη*, meaning "primary matter," is a concept pointing to the nature of the ultimate material constituent of a corporeal individual existent in *Physics* 192A22–34[28] and *Metaphysics* 1029A20–26 and 1042A27–28. Where a correspondence between the Greek concept and the Persian–Arabic concept can be detected, four renditions into the Persian–Arabic concept can be observed: (1) *hayūlā*, a blind transliteration of the Greek word, probably copied from a Syriac version of a Greek text; (2) *jins-i basīt*, the formation of a composite of two terms meaning "a simple body," coined to signify the fundamental meaning of the Greek term; (3) *mādda*, a slight modification of the Greek term used sometimes for *ὕλη* and sometimes for *ὑποκείμενον* ("subject"); (4) *māya*, a thematic extension to a Persian word, probably derived from the Middle Persian *māta*, which has two meanings: one corresponds to matter–substratum, as does *ὕλη*; the other is used like the Indic-Zoroastrian concept *māyā*.[29] These four different modes illustrate that the correlation of a term in Greek with any one Arabic–Persian term is an inadmissible reduction which fails to recognize the impossibility of simply converting a Greek philosophical problem into an Arabic-Persian counterpart.

In the case of being and existence, not only is a more consistent set of *termini technici* employed in the translation, but the Near Eastern terms used for *οὐσία* (usually translated as "substance") and *τὸ ὂν ᾗ ὄν* (usually translated as "being *qua* being") are invariably more refined in meaning than their Greek counterparts.

There is, to be sure, no sharp specification of *οὐσία* observable in Aristotle, and several translators have attempted to find alternative terms for "substance." R. Hope,[30] for instance, translates it as "primary being," while J. Owens[31] prefers a neutral term — "entity." It is our conjecture that the constant refinements in the Arabic–Persian translations and analyses of Aristotelian texts, beginning with topics such as *οὐσία*, led to the eventual emergence of divergent Near Eastern philosophies on being and existence. For example, some consider *maujūd* ("an existent") to be the primary concern of ontology, while others take *hastī* ("being *qua* being") as the fundamental term from which an ontology of possible essence is derived. But most philosophers agree on relatively standard usages of the basic terms significant for debates on philosophies of being and existence. Among these, in addition to *maujūd* and *hastī*, are the following terms and the meaning corresponding to them: *wujūd*: "existence"; the Persian *gauhar-i awwalī* and the Arabic–Persian *jauhar awwal*: "a first substance"; the Persian *gauhar-i duwwumī* and the Arabic–Persian *jauhar thānī*: "a second substance"; the Arabic–Persian *huwiyya* and *dhāt*: "essence." Some philosophers match some of the above-mentioned words specifically with an Aristotelian concept and use it uniformly in their own writings. For instance, Aristotle heads the list of the categories with *οὐσία* in *Categories* (1B26) and with *τί ἐστι* in *Topics* (103B22) — both are usually translated as "substance," the former as a general notion of substance, the latter as a concept related to essence (a secondary sense of a substance). Ibn Sīnā, in his account of the categories in the *Book of Definitions* (*Kitāb al-Hudūd*[32]), refers specifically to Aristotle as the prime source of the categories and heads the list with *jauhar*. Moreover, in all his works on metaphysics and logic, ibn Sīnā uses *jauhar* (and its Persian version, *gauhar*) consistently as "substance," while using *wujūd* (or *anniyya*) for "existence." Al-Fārābī, in his commentary on Aristotle's *Metaphysics* entitled *Book of Letters* (*Kitāb al-Ḥurūf*),[33] explains how "is" is used in Persian, Greek, and Sodgian, and how Arabs, in spite of the fact that they have no proper copula, can use various other words to distinguish "existence" from "existent" or "existence" from "being." In sum, much of Greek philosophical vocabulary was refined through the conscious efforts of Near Eastern philosophers who not only possessed an intimate knowledge of the Greek texts but used this knowledge to draw subtle distinctions in meaning in the philosophical vocabulary received and transmitted, including the terms related to being and existence.

Yet a noteworthy exception should be mentioned at this point. Certain key terms which lacked Greek counterparts were used in the Near East with multiple meanings, all related to being and existence. For example, a term transliterated as *ḥaqq* or *ḥaqiqat* is sometimes used as "truth" (in the sense of Heidegger's interpretation of the Greek *ἀλήθεια*), "reality" (in the sense of "that which ultimately exists"), "essence" (in the sense of "that feature of an existent necessary for its persistence as an actual entity"), "God," and "a person's most intimate existential features" (not in the sense of his essence — e.g., humanity — but what some existentialists may call one's authentic experiences or the memory of such events which is considered crucial for one's own identity). When the mystic Ḥallāj[34] utters "*Anā al-Ḥaqq*," for which he was killed by the Muslim orthodoxy, one cannot go back to Greek works to find the meaning for the peculiar medieval mystical doctrine of "I am reality–truth–God." A meaningful inquiry into the Near Eastern philosophical usage of being and existence should, therefore, take into account, but not limit itself to, Greek philosophical vocabulary; for from the perspective of Near Eastern philosophers this vocabulary is not adequate for the discussion of such topics as ultimate being and its relation to the self. It is in these latter designations of terms such as "being" and "existence" that new and pregnant doctrines in Near Eastern philosophy are most manifest.

Although the mere listing of the texts concerned with being and existence is no substitute for an analysis of the problem, it can serve as an index to the magnitude of the contributions of the Near Easterners to logic and ontology, fields which are related to being and existence. The 166 authors writing on logic in Arabic and Persian from 728 to 1545, mentioned by Rescher, is matched by the number of metaphysical texts in this and later periods.[35] As anyone working in related problems will realize, the problem is complicated by questions of actual and attributed authorship. For instance, 134 works[36] are attributed to Ṭūsī; and 244 titles to ibn Sīnā, in one count, but 276 titles in another.[37] A conservative estimate would conjecture a minimum of 300 treatises and commentaries dealing with being and existence. It goes without saying that the texts in question are not simply copies of Greek doctrines. Ibn Sīnā's attitude to Aristotle's writings exemplifies how he and other philosophers investigating the Greek texts preserved their philosophical independence in spite of their interest in Aristotle's doctrines. As ibn Sīnā notes in his autobiography, "I read the *Metaphysics* [of Aristotle] forty times . . . to the extent where I had memorized it."[38] Although it was only after he had read al-Fārābī's commentary on the text that he grasped its meaning, ibn Sīnā nonetheless affirms that "one should clarify the confusion in his [Aristotle's] discourse and correct any mistake in his [system]; [one should moreover] expand the foundations of his [philosophy]."[39] And this is precisely what ibn Sīnā did when he rejected Aristotle's notion of the ultimate being as a substance. In another instance ibn Sīnā ridicules Greek philosophers, especially Porphyry:

> There is a story about a man who is called Porphyry, and he wrote a text on intelligence and intelligibles. The Peripatetics praised him for the book, for they do not know that this book is totally worthless and

> absurd, as Porphyry who [obviously] did not know [the worthlessness of this book] and thus wrote it. One of his contemporaries wrote a book criticizing Porphyry's book; Porphyry wrote a book criticizing the critique [of his first book] and his [Porphyry's] new book was more ridiculous and valueless than his first.[40]

Avicenna's basic critique of Porphyry's work is based on the assumption that Porphyry attempted to identify the known with a knower in the act of knowledge. Ibn Sīnā's example demonstrates that each text must be examined separately for its particular philosophy of being and existence.

Three Major Problems: Ontology (the Scope of Being), Porphyry's Five Predicables (Species [εἶδος] as a "Thing"?), and the Categories (the Role of Logic in a Metaphysical Explanation of Being)

Let us proceed with these three topics to demonstrate how Near Eastern philosophers received and responded to problematic formulations of issues crucial to the question of being and existence.

Ontology, or What is the scope of being?

That Aristotle's notion of ontology as a study of being *qua* being (*τὸ ὂν ᾗ ὄν*) and his view on substance (*οὐσία*) are confusing is corroborated by his own remarks as well as by the criticism of many of his interpreters, such as W. D. Ross, J. Owens, and others.[41]

In addressing themselves to these problems, some of these interpreters have given serious consideration to passages such as the following: "Therefore that which is primary, i.e., not in a qualified sense but without qualification, must be substance" (*Metaphysics* 1028A29–30). From it they have concluded that Aristotle focuses on what actually exists in the sense of the first substance and on whatever might be related to such an existent. C. Kirwan notes, for example, that for Aristotle "metaphysics is concerned only with a restricted 'genus' of things that are."[42] M. K. Munitz asserts, in a similar vein, that "Aristotle's theory of existence (the other dimension of his general theory of being) is best seen as taking the form of a theory of substances, the primary constituents of the world of nature."[43] E. A. Moody follows an Ockhamian line of Aristotelianism in reporting that metaphysics "is a speculative science and not an art, because it is concerned with that which is. . . ."[44] He goes on to note that for the Ockhamian version of Aristotle

> The distinction between *ens per se* and *ens per aliud,* or between substance and accident, is not a metaphysical [ontological] distinction — not a distinction between two ultimate kinds of entities. It is rather a distinction between two ways in which individual things (which are what they are *per se* or by their individual nature) are apprehended or signified in discursive thought.[45]

Any examination of Greek Platonic ontology and of its Neoplatonic counterpart, together with a few Near Eastern ontologies, will reveal that Aristotle's attempt to restrict the subject of ontology to individual substances and their accidents proved unacceptable to Near Eastern thinkers in at least three areas. (1) The first stumbling block was his concept of the prime mover as a substance which is essentially separate from the material world. As will be explained later, Etienne Gilson considers this particular feature of Aristotle's ultimate being extremely important since it prevented the Aristotelian model from serving as a unitary type of metaphysics. (2) Two specific passages in his work suggesting the opposite notwithstanding,[46] individual persons, according to Aristotle, are limited substances composed of a soul and a body.[47] Since substances in the Aristotelian scheme cannot "blend" or be united with each other in the manner which mystical literature indicates when it describes such events as processes through analogies such as "the ocean waves," some Near Eastern philosophers rejected the Aristotelian substance theory of the self and resorted to other media of expression and to the use of concepts such as the active intelligence (already present in Aristotle) to depict the mystical union. For ontology, this resulted in the invention and application of a new ontological category of process as well as a heavy reliance on similes and allegories to depict the union of two initially separate entities — a non-substance concept of a person and an ultimate being — in the last stage of mystical self-realization. Finally (3) in several passages Aristotle interprets the Platonic forms as abstractions of "natural entities."[48] Moreover, his obviously naïve comparison of Plato's "participation" and Pythagorean "imitation," his view of "participation" as but a replacement of this "imitation," and many other interpretations which could be cited demonstrate that there is no room for unactualizable universals (i.e., in medieval terminology, "essences" with no "existents") in his ontology. As will become obvious Near Easterners rejected Aristotle's ontology for this reason as well. Before turning to these Near Eastern theories, let us take note of a few representative passages from Plato and Plotinus which present an ontology with an ultimate being extending beyond the Aristotelian notion of *οὐσία.*

The problem of being and existence in Plato's philosophy unfolds in the "generator" relation between the Form of the Good and other entities in Plato's universe. In the following passage, Socrates uses the typical analogy of the Sun–World relation to clarify his ontology of being. Socrates states: "The Sun, I presume you will say, not only furnishes to visibles the powers of visibility but it also provides for their generation and growth and nurture though it is not itself generation."[49] This passage suggests that the Form of the Good itself is an independent type of being upon which other entities depend. Socrates subsequently focuses explicitly on the ontological dimensions of this issue, asserting:

> In like manner, then, you are to say that the objects of knowledge [i.e., forms] not only receive from the presence of the good [τοῦ ἀγαθοῦ] their being known, but their very existence [το εἶναι] and essence (substantiality) [τὴν οὐσίαν] is derived to them from it, though the good itself is not an essence (substantiality) [οὐσίας] but still transcends [ἐπέκεινα] essence (substantiality) [τῆς οὐσίας] in dignity and surpassing power.[50]

The above formulation of the basis of ontology is ambiguous and contains prima facie paradoxes. We note that the Form of the Good is beyond and distinct from other forms. But in what sense, we may ask, is an entity a reality but not an existence (being-substantiality) (τὴν οὐσίαν)? However we choose to translate the Greek expressions τὸ εἶναι and τὴν οὐσίαν, it follows that the Form of the Good is neither a particular nor a specific unique universal. Obviously, Plato's Form of the Good here is a prototype of the ultimate being of Plotinus' ontology, i.e., the One. Let us now turn to an examination of this concept in Plotinus' ontology.

Plotinus begins the *Enneads* VI[51] by giving reasons for his rejection of the categories and for the introduction of his own doctrines of the authentic existence of numbers, of the generation of the Ideal Forms, of the Good, the One, the will of the One, and the identification of the One with the Good. Plotinus' basic objection to Aristotle's categorial explanation is evident in his question: "Are the ten [categories] found alike in the Intellectual and in the Sensible realms?" (VI [1]). Plotinus' presupposition about the distinction which can be made between intellectual entities and what one can consider sensible entities precludes any common bond between them. For example, the intellectual aspect of the secondary substantial being cannot intimately be related to the material aspects of the first substantial being. But apart from this distinction between the two realms, another reason made it impossible for Plotinus to accept the categories: his One exists prior to Forms, and is not a being to which intellectual discourse can make any type of categorial application, e.g., by calling it a being of a non-sensible "substance" (VI [9] 2).

A similar theme appears in another passage in which the One is viewed as the generator of entities which transcends οὐσία or being.

> The One [τὸ ἕν] is all things but not one of them; the source [ἀρχή] of all things is not all things; and yet it is all things in a transcendental sense — all things, so to speak, having run back to it; or, more correctly, not all as yet are within it, they will be. [But why does the universe form] an unbroken unity, in which there appears no diversity, not even duality? It is precisely because there is nothing within the One [i.e., the One is "simple"] that all entities are from it. In order that an entity may be brought about, the source must be no entity [οὐκ ὄν] but the entity's generator [γεννετής] in what is to be thought of as the prime act of generation.[52]

Other Neoplatonists followed the same view. Proclus, for example, depicts the ultimate being as separate from the world: "Now, that the One is God follows from its identity with the Good: for the Good is identical with God." He goes on to state that "every God is above being [πᾶς θεὸς ὑπερούσιός ἐστι], above life, and above intelligence";[53] yet the One is more significant than all other gods, for "Every God is 'participable,' except the One."[54] In addition to naming individual actual existent entities and whatever else might be "a being" (e.g., round squares and unicornness), the Neoplatonic concepts mentioned above name the One which in a sense is the generator of being, and is not a being in the world. It follows from this analysis that in the Greek texts Plato and some Neoplatonists presented a non-Aristotelian notion of the ultimate being.

Another notion of a non-categorial type of entity found in Near Eastern as well as in some Western philosophies is the concept of "persons." In his account of al-Ghazālī's doctrine which is embedded in *The Alchemy of Happiness*, R. C. Zaehner cites a paradigm case illustrating this point. Zaehner concentrates on two features of al-Ghazālī's doctrines: "the indwelling of God in creatures" and "the denying not only to God but to the human soul as it is in its essence of any attribute whatever." According to al-Ghazālī, the human soul-self has neither *chun* ("property") nor *chigūnagī* ("a kind" or "a classification"). In this aspect it is said to be like God, a secret which one should not reveal explicitly.[55] It will become clear that an important feature of Near Eastern philosophies of being is the oft-expressed doctrine that the ultimate being, as in the Greek cases studied, is the model or the last stage of the perfection of the experiencing subject. Lacking a limit in the world, the ultimate being cannot be designated as the substance of a category. One way of approaching the issue is to consider an ontology in which "persons" become in a Carnapian sense a "primitive term" in one's ontology. The approach differs from that taken by Aristotle in formulating his concept of the self, in which a physical body is connected to a formal soul — Aristotle's remarks on the active intelligence notwithstanding. The approach is illustrated in part by P. F. Strawson, who has concluded that one can explain the mental and the physical constituents of experience only if one takes the concept of persons as a primitive notion.[56] A variant of the aforementioned approach is found in Wittgenstein, where the self is depicted as the metaphysical subject which is not in the world but is a limit of the world and as such cannot be experienced or referred to as an individual object.[57]

In sum, ample illustrations substantiate that not all Greek philosophical systems depict persons and the ultimate being as *οὐσία*. Moreover, in some systems it is impossible to conceive of these two entities as ultimate existents. Gilson made a similar point:

> Since being is thinkable apart from actual existence, whereas actual existence is not thinkable apart from being, philosophers will simply yield to one of the fundamental facilities of the human mind by positing *being* minus actual existence as the first principle of metaphysics.
>
> Let us go farther still. It is not enough to say that *being* is conceivable apart from existence; in a certain sense it must be said that *being* is always *conceived* by us apart from existence, for the very simple reason that existence itself cannot possibly be *conceived*.[58]

We shall show that any conception of the self and the ultimate existent as substances implies an unbridgeable separation between them. Cherniss points out that "hav[ing] a separate existence in the manner of particular entities"[59] is the essential feature of the Aristotelian concept of substance. For this and related reasons Aristotle's limited ontology could not serve as a satisfactory framework for the Near Eastern thinker who wished to depict a union between the ultimate being and persons. What may be called "an open" or "non-substantial" view of the ultimate being — more in line with Platonic and Neoplatonic traditions than with others — proved better suited to their purposes than the Aristotelian ontology.

The Problem of "Species" (εἶδος) in the Light of Porphyry's Fifth Predicable

Aristotle introduces the predicables in the *Topics* by making distinctions among four kinds of reasoning, three uses of his own treatises, and methods of inquiry which include propositions and problems. He thereafter notes that every proposition and problem indicates four specific elements: property, genus, definition, and accident.[60] It is clear, on the one hand, that he introduced the so-called "four predicables" to single out those elements of propositions which are used in arguments of demonstrative sciences; in this respect there is no mention of species (εἶδος) or secondary substances which may be taken as references to Platonic forms. On the other hand, some argue that by including the concept of the genus and by making assertions about it in other passages, Aristotle indicated his wish to include "species" among the predicables. But when Porphyry wrote his *Introduction* (*Isagoge*) to Aristotle's logical works, his inclusion of species as a predicable, and of species and genus, which are "things-universals," made it possible for some medieval philosophers to take "thing-universals" as individuals, on the basis of passages such as

> For the present I shall not discuss the question whether genera and species really exist or are in bare notions only; and if they exist, whether they are corporeal things or incorporeal; and whether they are separated or exist in things perceived by the senses and in relation to them. For these questions are profound and demand other and more acute examination.[61]

The *Isagoge* was translated into Latin by Marius Victorinus (ca. 370), and subsequently retranslated by Boethius (ca. 510) when he found the earlier rendering unsatisfactory. It was Boethius' translation and commentary on this work which led to the popularization of the classical positions of realism, conceptualism, and nominalism on the status of such universals as "species" and "genera." Conceptualism presents us with non-existent kinds of entities — mind-dependent concepts which may or may not, depending on the philosopher's position, have supra-mental status. Contemporary commentators have reached different evaluations of Porphyry's role in the development of medieval ontology.

Moody takes an Ockhamist position on Aristotle and criticizes Porphyry for changing what some commentators call a syntactic or a logical problem in Aristotle into an ontological or a metaphysical problem. On this point Moody states: "In the *Categories* Aristotle is concerned with terms as incomplex modes of signification, considered in abstraction from questions of existence or fact, and from truth or falsity of any propositions such as can by voluntary act of judgement be formed through the synthesis of such terms."[62] Moody harshly judges Prophyry for his "idea of using the predicables as an introduction to the *Categories* of Aristotle [which] stands as a master stroke, though probably an unconscious one, in the struggle to restore to dialectic the primacy that Plato had claimed for it, and that Aristotle had denied."[63]

W. and M. Kneale join Moody in his criticism of Porphyry, but place some of the blame on Aristotle and Boethius. While acknowledging his "share in the transmission of ancient learning," Kneale and Kneale consider Porphyry to be "the source of a misinterpretation of Aristotle's doctrine of the predicables which produced some confusion in later times"; and claim that the doctrine of predicables for Aristotle was to "set out the different relations in which a predicate might stand to a subject in a general statement. . . ."[64] Moreover, the Kneales maintain that a reading of Aristotle's and Porphyry's writings "suggests that [Aristotle] thinks there is a species named 'man' and a genus named 'animal.' . . ."[65] The Kneales blame Aristotle for this confusion since he uses "substance" to name such universals. Furthermore, according to the Kneales, the damage done by Boethius was that he perpetuated "the puzzle about universals which exercised the minds of medieval philosophers."[66] The importance of Boethius is that he presented Aristotle's views in such a way that, according to Kneale and Kneale, it established a position "without presuming to decide definitely against Plato's view that universals are not only thinkable apart from bodies but capable also of existing in separation."[67] In contrast to the Kneales, who assume an Aristotelian position and criticize Porphyry for keeping to his own Neoplatonic doctrine, Aaron holds that the basis of a non-logical theory of predicables lies in Aristotle's own writings. Aaron's interpretation rests on two key points: the first, which resembles the Near Eastern theories on existents, points out that, for Aristotle, though "real individuals elude our thought, we do nonetheless think real qualities are shared in common by a number of individuals. It is because real individuals have such common qualities that we can group and classify them and speak of them as members of species and genera."[68] Two special issues are raised here (*a*) Aaron's statement that "individuals elude our thought" may be taken to mean that no "individual existent per se as an individual existent without any consideration of concepts" can be thought about, and (*b*) Aaron's mention of "real qualities" may already presuppose a non-nominalist position on universals. We shall demonstrate that (*a*) was adopted as the basis of a philosophy of universals in the Near East. Concerning the problem of existence of species in (*b*), Aaron presents an interesting quotation from Aristotle's *De partibus animalium* 644A23–27, where Aristotle states,

> The individuals comprised within a species, such as Socrates and Coriscus, are the real existences; but inasmuch as these individuals possess one common specific form, it will suffice to state the universal attributes of the species, that is, the attributes common to all its individuals, once and for all, as otherwise there will be endless reiteration.

On the basis of this passage and related sources, Aaron concludes that

> the Aristotelian doctrine of the "common specific form" which gives the universal and genus a real reference, in spite of the remoteness from thought of the real individual, is thus rooted upon the apprehension of "the universal attributes of the species" possessed by individuals, and the sciences which deal with universals are possible only because of this apprehension.[69]

In defense of Porphyry, Lloyd mentions that we should not forget that "the categories are predicates and the predicables manners of predicating."[70] Moreover, the *Isagoge* is an introduction, not to the *Topics*, but to the *Cate-*

gories, which are logically prior to the *Topics*, and the *quinque voces* are terms considered necessary to the understanding of the *Categories*.

In sum, no common agreement has been reached by several key interpreters of Aristotle on the following issues: (*a*) What was Aristotle's position on the significance of predication over species? (*b*) Did Porphyry in fact, as Moody and others claim, misunderstand Aristotle's logic? (*c*) Was it really a tragedy to bring to the attention of the medieval philosophers the ontological problem of universals? (*d*) Did the Neoplatonists' logic assist or retard the development of logic? But there is no doubt that Porphyry's modification of Aristotelian texts had an influence on the medieval concepts of being and existence, as Moody, Kneale and Kneale, and Aaron all agree.

The *Isagoge* also affected Near Eastern philosophy. Originally, it was translated into at least three Syriac versions, which included commentaries by Hibba (d. 457), Probha (d. 480), and Athanasius of Baladh (d. 696). Arabic and Persian translations or commentaries soon multiplied and have continued to the present.[71] With regard to the concepts of being and essence, the reaction of the Near East can be divided into three classes:

(1) First, there were the philosophers who wanted to be as faithful as possible to Aristotle's own texts and disliked Porphyry as some "bastard" offspring of Neoplatonism and Aristotelianism. This school is represented by Averroës, who wrote a short commentary on the *Isagoge* but expressed misgivings about the work and was reluctant, for two reasons, to translate it. Believing that whatever can be demonstrated about the predicables is found in the *Posterior Analytics*, and whatever is generally accepted is found in the *Topics*, he asserted that "I do not consider the *Isagoge* necessary for beginning the art of logic, since its contents cannot belong to what is common to the entire art, as some imagine";[72] and concludes that the "*Isagoge* is not a part of logic, though al-Farabi implies that it is." Averroës also cites the simple nature of the text, but admits that "at some point [in the book] there is room for speculation."[73] Nonetheless, he was indirectly affected by Porphyry insofar as he devoted much argumentation to the topic of universals, challenging the ibn Sīnian "essence–existence" version of the problem. The latter was to a degree supported in ibn Sīnā's own lengthy version of the *Isagoge*.

(2) A second school of philosophy basically followed the arguments contained in Porphyry's work and those of later commentators on it. These philosophers themselves wrote long detailed commentaries on every point of philosophical import in the *Isagoge* and developed in turn an interpretative viewpoint of their own. Ibn Ṭayyib (980–1043), for example, in writing his commentary on the work, interjected his own notes into the Arabic

translation; the commentary below, including the parenthetical remarks, belongs to him:

> Porphyry: Are they separate or perceptible in objects? (He means: if genera and species are incorporeal, are they absolutely separable from matter, or are they in some way dependent upon sensible and concrete existence?) Since an inquiry into that is difficult, it requires another investigation loftier than this. (He means: since the inquiry into genera and species in terms of these questions is a complicated one, it requires another [branch of] knowledge which is loftier than logic.)
>
> Commentator: The translation of this passage is confused. The passage should be translated in this way: If they (i.e., genera and species) are incorporeal, are they separable or are they dependent upon sensible things? The interpretation of this statement is this: If they are incorporeal, are they absolutely separable from matter like God and the Platonic Forms?[74]

We note here ibn Ṭayyib's immediate attempt to connect the Porphyrian question to Plato's theory of the ultimate being. In objecting to Porphyry's texts, ibn Ṭayyib often introduces a new point of view. For example, following Porphyry's statement as it is rendered in Arabic, ibn Ṭayyib writes: "Porphyry [states]: As the genus is predicated triply, the discussion of philosophers concerns only the third." In clarifying the meaning of this passage, ibn Ṭayyib objects:

> how did you begin, Porphyry, by defining the genus at the time of your opening a discussion of it, while you know from logical laws that every thing investigated is investigated only under the following inquiries: Firstly, does it exist? Secondly, what is it? You should have prefaced your investigation of the genus by discussing whether it exists, and then, discuss what it is.[75]

It is evident from these quotations that for some Near Eastern philosophers Porphyry's text was not taken as an authority on questions dealing with being and essence, especially when some of the commentators' remarks on Porphyry were read along with the translation of the *Isagoge.*

(3) The third approach to the *Isagoge* is illustrated by the philosophical school represented by ibn Sīnā and Ṭūsī. Both philosophers wrote their own versions of the text without attempting to furnish a paraphrase of Porphyry's actual work. Indeed, they expound on the *Isagoge* (*al-Madkhal*) as if it were a standard topic in logic about which each logician wrote his own book. In his version of this text, ibn Sīnā does not refer to Porphyry by name but alludes to "the author of the book." At one place, ibn Sīnā states that he has taken into account what previous philosophers have said on the subject of the *Isagoge,* adding to it whatever resulted from his own thinking (*fikr*) and from solving problems by his own speculative (*naẓar*)

faculty, especially in the sciences of physics, metaphysics, and logic.[76] Analogously, Ṭusī demonstrated his independence from Porphyry by introducing his own *Isagoge* as follows:

> In the *Introduction* [*Madkhal*] on logic which is called [by the Greeks] "Isaghugi," four techniques are found: first, expressions; second, universality and particularity; third, essentiality and accidentality; and, fourth, the universal five [predicables].[77]

Ṭūsī proceeds to furnish Persian philosophical terminology for the readers of the *Isagoge* and to discuss different schools of thought on the philosophical issues in this book. Later in our discussion we shall illustrate how these Near Eastern philosophers used only the logical aspects of Porphyry's *Isagoge* in their own works of logic, whereas in their works on metaphysics they distinguished between two senses of a species: one sense applicable to the actual domain; one, to syntactical analyses.

In sum, Porphyry's *Isagoge* was instrumental both in focusing philosophical discussions on the problem of universals, and on those issues which were ambiguous in Aristotle's philosophy — the realm of being, predication over species, and the categories — and in bringing about the distinction between the logical and the metaphysical senses.

The Problem of Categories

Another important source for analyzing being and essence, and one which in itself has generated much confusion among Near Eastern philosophers, is the doctrine of the categories. Aristotle introduces the list of categories with the statement that "Expressions which are in no way composite signify . . . " (*Categories* 1B25–26). The only other place where he renders the entire list is in *Topics* 103B20–23 where he writes: "we must distinguish between the classes of predicates in which the four orders in question [i.e., where one finds the four predicables of an entity: namely, accident, genus, property, and definition] are ten in number. . . ." Although "substance," called *οὐσία* (presumably "primary" or "first" substance, meaning an individual particular existent), begins the first list, the second list starts with *τί ἐστι* or "essence." In some of the more difficult passages of the *Metaphysics*, Aristotle is busy with the specification of "universals" and "individuals" and does not use his categories, except in a few places not directly related to "first substance." Nonetheless, some of these passages demonstrate the significance of Aristotle's analysis of "being" as it relates to the subject of the categories: he states in *Metaphysics* 1017A23–25 that "The kinds of essential being [*αὑτὰ δὲ εἶναι*] are precisely those that are indicated by the figures of predication [*τῆς κατηγορίας*]; for the senses of 'being' [τὸ εἶναι] are just as many as there are these figures." Hence, any language analysis or ontological investigation which claims to clarify the nature of being must focus on the categories, for whatever does not belong to a category cannot be a "being."

In short, what did Aristotle attempt to accomplish by means of the categories? It seems that there is a confusion among modern Aristotelian commentators concerning this topic. The confusion may be clarified by delineating two alternative views of the categories, both of which were adopted as the basis for the Near Eastern analyses of being and existence. There are many who follow our account of Moody's position, outlined in the previous section, that categories as tools of linguistic and logical analyses are relevant, not directly to the world, but only indirectly to the ways in which language is used to talk about the world. Anscombe's account of the categories points to them as a "crude sketch" for correct usage.

> The doctrine of the *Categories* is indeed a relatively crude sketch upon which Aristotle never improved, . . . while he nevertheless continued to allude to it . . ., in developing his account of *per se* existence in the *Metaphysics*. . . . we must consider what Aristotle is getting at in propounding his ten categories. These obviously correspond in some way to a set of things which it would make sense to say of e.g. a human being. . . . Aristotle's intention was to find a complete list of fairly simple kinds of things, with significant logical differences between them, that might be said about a subject.[78]

In a manner similar to Moody's, I. M. Bochenski notes that this theory of the categories[79] "constitutes an attempt at classifying objects according to the ways in which they are predicable. . . ." Following the same line of interpretation, G. Ryle asserts that "Aristotle's list [of categories] is intended to be a list of the ultimate types of predicates."[80] To establish such a list, for Ryle, means to "collect a range of simple, singular propositions, all similar in being about the same particular or particulars; then the respects in which these propositions differ from one another will be their predicates."

Insistent on preserving his own method in the analysis of Aristotelian texts, Ryle also claims that "In the main Aristotle seems to content himself with taking ordinary language as his clue to the list of heads of questions, and so of types of predicates."[81] Both Ryle and Anscombe attempt to criticize Aristotle because, in their opinion, he did not develop his "ordinary language ability" to a sufficient degree of perfection.

J. L. Ackrill has observed further complications in the Aristotelian analysis of being. He expresses the view, for instance, that Aristotle developed his theory of the categories in two ways: (*a*) in the classification of the different kinds of questions asked about substances; and (*b*) in the various answers appropriate to "one particular question which can be asked about anything whatsoever — the question 'what is it?'"[82] Still other interpreters provide us with a broader approach to Aristotle's categories. J. M. E. Moravcsik, for example, holds:

> The theory of categories is partly a theory about language and partly a theory about reality. . . . elements of a language have key-designating roles, the full understanding of which requires that we understand the designata as falling within those classes which jointly form the set definitive of that to which a sensible particular must be related. . . . [Aristotle] did believe that there are specific items of language and reality the correlation of which forms the crucial link between the two.[83]

Kneale and Kneale provide us with the most comprehensive and illuminating perspective in noting the troubles which confronted the Near Eastern philosophers who attempted to develop a theory of being and existence which was based upon a metaphysical analysis of the categories: they point out that it was not Aristotle's decision to include the *Categories* in the *Organon* but that of compilers who, during their time, were unable to draw sharp distinctions between logic and non-logical studies.[84] Accordingly, the Kneales assert that "much of the doctrine of the *Categories* must be regarded as metaphysical rather than logical."[85] The two ambiguities which they pinpoint in the categories are: (*a*) "whether Aristotle is classifying symbols or what they symbolize, words or, in a very wide sense, things, . . . a question which has exercised commentators since ancient times";[86] and (*b*) "whether Aristotle is concerned with predicates only or with terms in general, including subjects."[87] The ambiguities specified by Kneale and Kneale had far-reaching logical consequences for philosophers attempting to use the categories in their analyses of being and existence. Kneale and Kneale list three major consequences: (*a*) "Aristotle's emphasis on primary substance as the ultimate subject of predication led to an over-emphasis on the subject–predicate form of proposition which still restricted logical development at the time of Leibniz";[88] (*b*) "Aristotle's use of the term *οὐσία* to signify both primary and secondary substance blurs the all-important distinction between singular and general propositions";[89] and (*c*) "the *Categories* seems to be the first attempt at what has recently been called a theory of type-distinctions, that is to say a theory in which entities are classified according to what can be said about them significantly. Plato had already remarked that to be capable of expressing a truth a linguistic formula must be complex, containing at least both noun and verb [*Sophist* 262A]. This is a necessary, but not a sufficient, condition of meaningfulness."[90] When we transfer the logical queries of Kneale and Kneale to their ontological counterparts, we discover the emergence of three questions on being and existence which led to the formation and development of different schools dealing with these concepts.

Several factors are apparently responsible for the confusion noted in the doctrine of the categories. To begin with, it is unclear what Aristotle himself meant by the categories and why he did not make a more extensive use of categorical analysis in his account of being in his metaphysics. Another ambiquity stems from the fact that Neoplatonists who used Aristotle's texts to teach logic could not have accepted their metaphysical premisses; this difficulty resulted in the Neoplatonic attempt — noticeable especially in the case of Porphyry — to restrict the metaphysical implications of the categories. Lloyd, for instance, points out that "After Porphyry, Aristotle is credited with having consciously restricted the scope of the Categories. The ten Categories themselves are decided to be neither terms nor things, but terms *qua* signifying; each is γένη τῶν ὄντων, 'a genus of being,' but indirectly for they classify terms with respect to the things they designate."[91] A third difficulty stems from the Near Eastern interpretation of the categories. In the Near Eastern Aristotelian tradition, the doctrine of the categories was treated in two distinct ways: as a branch of logic, the *Categories* (*Maqūlāt*) usually preceded seven other "logical texts" of Aristotle, the last of which was the *Poetics*; and as a part of metaphysics, as was customarily done by the school of ibn Sīnā, who began his discussion of metaphysics by giving an account of the categories. We shall illustrate the interrelationship between the two treatments in the next section.

Three Near Eastern Philosophies of Being and Existence

Three problematic issues of Greek philosophy, specifically the problem of being and existence, predication over species, and the role of logic in the discussion of metaphysical issues, were extensively debated by Near Eastern philosophers. Here we shall present the views of three different schools which treated these topics.

The "Analytical" School of ibn Sīnā

The first school is characterized by a method of "analysis," and the basic tools which its philosophers used are (*a*) syntactical (*lafḍī*) inquiry, which deals only with words and belongs to the domain of logic yet allows for purely conceptual (*wahmī*) activity independent of actual existents; and (*b*) empirical (*ḥissī*) inquiry referring to existents, an inquiry essentially conducted by the empirical sciences about the actual world. The philosophers of the analytical school used these preliminary distinctions to satisfy what we may call an Ockhamized Aristotelian position on being and existence in a syntactical context. Most of our discussion will be devoted to ibn Sīnā's approach; nonetheless, in order to illustrate the continuity of the approach, we shall select a few passages from al-Fārābī (d. 950), who preceded ibn Sīnā, and from Ṭūsī (d. 1274), who succeeded ibn Sīnā.

In an interesting passage, al-Fārābī draws a distinction between two domains within which one may ask the question "Is existence a predicate?" The account of his views is given by Rescher as:

> He was asked about the following problem: Does the proposition "Man exists" have a predicate or not?
>
> He answered: This is a question on which both the ancients and the moderns have disagreed: some have said it does not have a predicate, others that it has. My position is that both assertions are true in different senses. When this proposition is studied by a scientist who investigates the world it does not have a predicate, because the existence of a thing is nothing but the thing [itself], and the predicate ought to be a concept whose existence or non-existence is judged *about* the thing. So from this angle it is not a proposition that has a predicate. But when it is studied by a logician, since it is composed of two expressions, which are its two parts, and is capable of truth and falsehood, from this angle it has a predicate. So the two assertions are both true, each one in a certain sense.[92]

Note the two domains which are postulated here: "the domain for an empirical scientist" in which basic elements are actual existents, and the domain of expressions, a syntactical domain, which is investigated by the logician. Now, if we wish to formulate a language which is applicable to the actual world of empirical sciences, then we choose terms of our predicate constants which name properties corresponding to non-empty classes. "Unicorn" is not a useful term for the science of zoology, whereas "cat" is.

Another passage, in this case from al-Fārābī's Categories, makes a distinction between the interrelationship of a second substance (a universal) and a first substance (an individual existent).

> Individual substances [*ashkhās al-jauhar*] are what are called "primary substances" while their universals are [called] secondary [substances] because individuals are [in a sense] more appropriately substances, as their beings are more determined [*'akmal*] than [the being of] their universals. . . . A thing is understood intellectually when its essence [*māhiyya*; literally, "what it is"; similar to τί ἐστι] is known. Individual substances thus became intellectually known [to us] as their universals were [understood] intellectually. Intelligibles [such as universals] are realized only due to their individual existents [cases or instances of them]; with respect to being intelligible [and understandable, nameable], individual substances need their universals. Their universals need their

specific cases in order to be considered as [concepts, the cases of which are] existents. For if their individual instances would not exist, then whatever we thought of them in our minds would be due to our own imagination and lies [and would not correspond to the actual world], and whatever is a lie [and does not correspond to the actual world] is other than existents. Consequently, universals are realized as existents only with respect to their individual [instances], while individuals are intellectualized only due to their universals. Thus universals are also [may be regarded as] substances because they are intelligible features of substances; their realization however is secondary as their existence depends on the existence of individuals.[93]

In this passage a preliminary distinction is specified by means of a universal, such as species (*εἶδος*); we can have intelligibility or discourse about existents, though any actual existent has to be examined in reference to a particular substance. Now, did al-Fārābī describe "this particular" substance? In another text he states that we can refer to this substance only ostensibly by gestures and that an "existent" cannot be defined by itself:

> It has become customary to state that this to which one points is sensible [*al-imahsus*] and that it is not used to describe [*wasf*] anything unless in an accidental or unnatural way. What is known by what it is — when one indicates it — is the simple (first substance).[94]

Al-Fārābī's ontology contains existents which can be only experienced not totally described. Any partial description of an existent needs to be expressed by the mediacy of a universal. Hence, "What is being?" is answered in terms of two features — existents which can be only experienced not totally described, and intelligible concepts which, as universals, are used to speak about existents.

Before acquainting ourselves with the system of ibn Sīnā, let us examine two hitherto untranslated texts of Ṭūsī's which argue in favor of the position that only individual existents can be actual and that logical analysis is not in need of information about existents. The following is a close paraphrase of Ṭūsī's *Principles* (*Fuṣūl*):

> Whoever learns anything about an entity must without doubt assume that the entity in question exists, for whatever is received [as known] must necessarily exist, as one cannot know [anything] about an entity which does not exist. Consequently, that aspect of a being which is its "existential status" must be recognized. Moreover, since this "existential status" is an aspect of being, whoever knows the universal feature [of an existing entity] must also be acquainted with its specific feature [namely, that it is an existent]. [Thus our argument is valid.] Since the meaning of this issue is manifest, it becomes clear that before knowing anything about an entity, one must inquire whether or not the entity in question exists, and before receiving any information about the entity, the knower must be informed about the reality of the entity in question.

> Whoever wishes to describe the meaning [of a fact] in terms of other facts needs to know that an entity exists [or at least needs to be able to assume] that the entity exists.[95]

Although he is not defining what existence is within the domain of actual existents, Ṭūsī proceeds to show that any factual description of such an entity can be given only within the particular (*juz'*) context of the reality of its existents.

The passage reproduced below is a translation of the first chapter of Ṭūṣī's text on the *Categories*, which is Book Two of his logical collection *Al-Asās al-Iqtibās.* From our perspective the major points of interest in this passage are: (*a*) that Ṭūsī's treatment of categories is no copy of the Aristotelian doctrine (Persian and Arabic texts on logic bearing the same title as an Aristotelian text were not necessarily copies of the Greek work in question); (*b*) that Ṭūsī draws a sharp distinction between, on the one hand, a logical inquiry about concepts, derivation, and related analytical activities, and, on the other, empirical analyses dealing with questions about the existence of actual entities; and (*c*) that logical analysis of categories and the use of logic in general be recommended for various inquiries, since there is a distinction between justifications of principles in analytical contexts and their workability for practical purposes.

The Categories (al-Maqulāt)

> It is obvious that the first phase of logic analyzes the highest kinds [*ajnās*; literally, "genera"] which are called the ten categories. Contemporary [thinkers] are of the opinion both that [(i)] a determination of [the status] of the universals of any [level] of generality or determinateness and [(ii) our act of pointing] to what is substantial or accidental in an ostensive manner are outside the province of logic; and that the method using the techniques of logic is not applicable [to such factual matters]. [Moreover, contemporary thinkers are also of the opinion that] the preoccupation of logicians with the aforementioned subjects is wrong and [should be considered] unfortunate. [In spite of such strong opposition to the concern which logicians have demonstrated for the highest [kinds (genera)], we should observe that without the consideration of the categories and without our ability to distinguish between them, it is impossible to make progress in the art [of logic] in such matters as stating definitions, making descriptions, and abstracting premisses from various syllogisms. Knowledge of this science [i.e., logic] is useful for evaluating every problem or deducing cases [from general theorems or axioms], due to the fact that logic can clarify that line of reasonings [different analytical moves] in all the [problems which attempt to prove a point]. Even in stories we notice [informal] accounts of the points and laws of this science; for such an account is necessary in order to grasp the proper way of deriving the basic

[argument embedded in the story in question]. And [all] investigators of truth have written [in one way or another about] this [science] — may God grant them success.

Prior to beginning our inquiry, we say that all the wise men agree that ordering the essential features of whatever is conceivable or intelligible to us falls into one of these ten categories. [Indeed] there are more general [determinable] concepts than these ten categories, such as existence, necessity, contingency, establishing, the extrema in domains of certain kinds — e.g., "unity," "point," and the reality of such notions. [We admit] that these notions do not belong to the domain of logic proper. However, whatever can be analyzed by means of language in the domain of actual existents does not fall outside these categories. Even though much has been said about the nature of these categories, we hope to say more about them [in our subsequent discussions].

When we say that "existence" is not a genus common to these categories, we mean that we can conceive the meaning [of each category] without necessarily assuming that the [category] in question has [an instance in the actual world] and [that] we can conceive an essence although it has not been realized [by the mediacy of its instance]. Had "existence" been a feature of these categories, we could not have thought of essences without knowing whether their instances were realized [in the actual world]. It is true that we do not necessarily inquire whether [the concept] of "color" is also a [more determinate entity such as a] "black" [patch] or whether [the concept of] a figure is a[n actual triangle]; when a black entity or a triangle has been realized, we wonder about the cause which realized it. Consequently, if existence were a genus or a predicate, its [realization] would be due to conditions of other genera or predicates [e.g., if there is "blackness," then there is also "being" a color]. It is possible to predicate a genus to a lower kind [e.g., a species] and individuals which exist under it [i.e., the sign "genus" can be predicated of a sign of a lower level — e.g., "species" or "an individual"] but one cannot attribute "existence" to "existence" since an existent exists only due to itself and persists only with respect to itself [i.e., we need no other "essence" to know that "an existent" is in fact "an existent"]. The distinction between what is an existent and what is not an existent is due to the First Existent [to God, who is the Principle of Sufficient Reason determining why certain contingent propositions about existents are true]. Consequently "existence" is not a genus of these categories but is added to them [in the sense that some of their instances are realized] due to [other] conditions.[96]

Let us consider how Ṭūsī treats the predication of species simply as a problem of logic rather than as one of metaphysics in the context of a theory of types.[97] His implicit notion of predication found in the above quotation is followed in a later section by his explanation of what he means by the expressions "a species" and "a genus." In order to clarify his analysis without using unnecessary expressions, let us consider a simple language governed by the "level" aspects of the theory of types.

There are certain individuals of level zero — e.g., "s" (which according to our rule of designation names Socrates); there are one-place predicates of various levels, among them the following: "H" (standing for "humanity") of level "1," "A" (standing for "animality") of level "2," "L" (for "living") of level "3," and "B" (for "having a bodily feature") of level "4"; let us assume that there are indefinitely many levels in our language and that each predicate on a given level is a one-place constant the designation of which is specified in such a way that "well-formed sentences" of our language correspond to ordinary English following the standard rules of formulation such that if we predicate X to Y, then the level of X is greater than the level of Y. According to this rule, "H(s)" (Socrates is a human), "A(s)" (To be a human is to be an animal), "B(s)" (Socrates has a body) are legitimate sentences (well formed), while "s(H)" (humanity has Socratesness) or "A(B)" (to be a body is to be an animal) is illegitimate. According to the theory of types in a legitimate predication, the level of the sign naming the predicate must be greater than the level of the sign naming the subject. Now, let us note how Munitz' scheme applies to Ṭūsī's concept of predication. For Munitz "predication" has three senses: the syntactic, the semantic, and the ontologic. Munitz notes that "Syntactic predication is to be understood as the tie that holds between two sets of linguistic expressions designated respectively as the subject and predicate of some sentence or proposition."[98] In Ṭūsī's system this sense of predication is easily implemented by the rule that any sign can predicate a sign of a lower level. Munitz notes that "By a semantic predication we shall understand a relation or a tie between an extralinguistic subject and the predicate taken as a linguistic item." A similar theme is expressed in the works of Ṭūsī; here he provides us with one specific rule: namely, that the only kinds of existent statements are those the subject of predication of which is of the lowest level. Accordingly, "A(H)" or "L(H)" is a legitimate statement about "essences" but not about existents, which are named by the signs of level zero. Consequently, the only language-thing implication which a sentence would have is determined by the number of the level of its signs. Obviously, this method is incomplete, for cases like "H(s)v–H(s)" contain a sign of level zero. But it asserts nothing significant for the actual world and does not imply an existential fact. This and many other obvious difficulties notwithstanding, we observe that Ṭūsī's semantical sense of predication does not even permit the question of treating "humanity" (a Porphyrian "species") as an individual; since "humanity" can meaningfully be predicated of "Socrates," "humanity" is not a name of an individual, for its level must be higher than zero. This condition explains clearly what it means to say that "a first substance is not predicated of any subject." Now, let us turn to Munitz' third distinction.[99] "By ontologic predication is meant a relation or a tie between subject and predicate where both are extra linguistic." In this context, Ṭūsī would say that logic has nothing to do with the ontologic sense of predication. Accordingly, in Ṭūsī's *Isagoge* the problem of universals, which Porphyry himself excluded from his logical work, is not even raised. Ṭūsī's position may be summed up as follows: if we apply logic to the actual world, then sentences in which individuals of the lowest levels function as subjects are existent-type of sentences. The contingent truth value of a sentence belongs, not to logic, but to semantical considerations when we interpret the language. In the first sense, the notion of species as "predicables" is irrelevant to existence; in the second sense, we could say that "species" are not individuals; and, in the third sense, "predication" is an alogical problem.

When we turn to the most prominent Near Eastern philosopher, ibn Sīnā, we observe a series of philosophical analyses which deal specifically with being and existence. First, a few observations concerning his methodology. Ibn Sīnā differentiates between two kinds of justifications: a theoretical justification by means of which we can decide, for instance, whether or not the concept of a "bodily substance" can have an instance; and a sensible justification which is the only kind which can enable us to decide whether or not a particular body (a first substance) exists in the actual world. For example, when Strawson claims that he can explain "the close connexion between the idea of an individual in a logical sense, and the idea of existence, of what exists," he does so in order "to have . . . some reason in the idea that persons and material bodies are what primarily exist."[100] Strawson needs only a "theoretical justification" for his analysis, for he is only talking about "kinds of existents" and not pointing to an actual specific existent. When we come to the problem of explaining how categorial analysis is relevant to the questions of being and existence, we note that for ibn Sīnā there are two senses of categories. Asserting that categories belong to logic,[101] he wrote what may be the most extensive book on the logic of categories ever to have appeared in Greek, Arabic, or Persian. Like Aristotle, ibn Sīnā gave to the categories a logical sense; unlike Aristotle, he also endowed them with a metaphysical sense, a sense which he integrated into his metaphysical texts as *the second* most primitive tool for a conceptual analysis of terms related to being and existence. His Persian text begins with the assertion that being *qua* being (*hastī*)[102] is the most general concept of metaphysical analysis.

> Being is recognized by reason itself without the aid of definition or description. Since it has no definition, it has neither genus nor differentia because nothing is more general than it. Being does not have a description since nothing is better known than it. It is possible that one recognizes its name in one language by means of another language.

He mentions, moreover, two kinds of being: the impossible essences, which cannot be realized, and the Necessary Existent, which is neither an individual existent nor part of the categories of substance and accident. Consequently, his first argument focuses, not on categorial analysis, but on the conceptual analysis of modalities. Accordingly he assumes that being can legitimately be concatenated with the three modalities: necessity (*wājibī*), contingency (*mumkinī*), and impossibility (*mumtaniʿī*). The combination of "being" with the last two modal terms leads to a specification of an "essence" but not of an "existent." Ibn Sīnā asserts that the "essence of a Necessary Being" is none other than "existence." Only in the case of "the Necessary Being," which is identified with "that which is none other than 'existence' [*wujū*d]," can we use a metaphysical analysis of being to speak about an actual existent. As we shall note later, this entity is not an "individual" existent. Impossible essences — e.g., "being a round square" — have no instances. In ibn Sīnian metaphysics contingency can be applied to both essences and existents. All existents, except the Necessary Existent (*al-Wājib al-Wujūd*), are contingent existents because their realization is due to an external cause. Ibn Sīnā distinguishes between two kinds of "contingent essences": (*a*) those which can be predicated of actual existents, as "humanity" can be predicated of Socrates; and (*b*) those which have no instances in the actual world, as illustrated by the case of "being a unicorn." Ibn Sīnā points out that, in the case of humanity, understanding the meaning of "humanity" (*mardumī*) is not an empirical inquiry but an inquiry into "essences." By contrast, an inquiry into the essence of a particular entity which exists — e.g., that Socrates' essence is "humanity" — must presuppose the existence of the entity in question. We should note here that even though a contingent existent such as Socrates is not a Necessary Existent, he is nevertheless hypothetically a Necessary entity in the context of the entire world. Literally speaking, an existent exists if it is realized due to a cause which goes back ultimately to the Necessary Existent because the actual world conforms to the best of all possible designs; this he calls "the Good Universal Order" (*niẓām-i khair-i kullī*). In legitimate philosophizing we should be careful, ibn Sīnā warns us, to distinguish between two distinct kinds of entities: essential beings and actual existents. The following text, hitherto unavailable in English, illustrates this point:

From al-Ishārāt wa-l-Tanbihāt

> Know that anything [*shai'i*] which has an essence may be realized among existents and may be conceived intentionally when all its elements are present. But [the concept in question] has a meaning other than that [its instance is an] existent, [this meaning] which is a feature of what neither exists [in the realm of actual entities] nor is conceived [by us along with other accidents in the context of its instance]. Thus it follows that for [any entity] "existence" [i.e., the realization of an entity] has a meaning which is different from its "essence." That which determines its existence [i.e., its realization in this world, as a "thing"] differs from factors determining its essence [i.e., the conceptual element in the specification of an essence]. [The latter is] irrespective of its realization among sensibles or its [psychological considerations] in our intention. Consideration of neither of these factors [its realization among actual existents or our mental attention to the concept in question] is needed for [establishing the meaning of a concept such as humanity: these factors — i.e., the realization of an instance of an essence and our conception of it —] are additional [features] of it. Should existence be the basis of the [meaningfulness] of an essence, then it would be impossible for us to establish the meaning of that reality [essence, universal] by ourselves independently of instances [which would have been the basis of the essence in question]. Moreover, it would have been impossible for us to understand the meaning of "being a human" only on the basis of our thoughts alone [if the meaning of an essence would depend on its existent instances]. We would have to know whether or not there is an instance [of the essence in question among the sensibles before being able to know about the essence].[103]

Let us now turn our attention to the entire realm of being in the ibn Sīnian system.

There are:

(1) one Necessary Existent
(2) an indefinite number of intentional concepts of impossible essences, e.g., a round square
(3) an indefinite number of contingent essences which are divided into two groups
    (a) unactualizable contingent essences which could be realized but are not actualized in this world, the best of all possible worlds, and
    (b) contingent essences which are realized by their actual instances due to causes which ultimately relate to the Necessary Existent
(4) individual first substances, along with their realized accidental features, e.g., "a white patch" of snow on a mountain would be an accidental concrete aspect of a substance (the mountain).

The last-mentioned — i.e., individual substances — include the heavens and bodies in the sublunary realm. The status of the soul of a person is a controversial topic in ibn Sīnian philosophy. We have expressed our view on this topic elsewhere, and recommended the adoption of a process (instead of a substance-event) language for clarification of ibn Sīnā's concept of the self and its relation to his "intelligences" (the forms of the heavenly bodies).[104] To answer questions posed in this paper, let us note how the existence of the soul-person (*nafs*) can be discussed in terms of the Necessary Existent.

Without any question the most important feature of ibn Sīnā's philosophy is his concept of the Necessary Existent, which is neither Neoplatonic nor Aristotelian. As we have noted, for Plotinus and Proclus the One is above being, but for ibn Sīnā the Necessary Existent is a being — specifically, that being which is a necessity. Numerous other distinctions between the Necessary Existent of ibn Sīnā and the Neoplatonic One can be documented.[105]

A comparison between Aristotle's and ibn Sīnā's doctrines of the ultimate being establishes that there are three major distinctions between them. The first is that Aristotle's prime mover, being co-eternal with the world, does not generate matter. Gilson uses this feature of the Aristotelian system to distinguish it from the Thomistic:

> In short, because the God of Aristotle is one of the causes and one of the principles of all things, but not *the* cause nor *the* principle of all things, there remains in the Aristotelian domain of being something which the God of Aristotle does not account for, which is matter, and for this reason the metaphysics of Aristotle cannot be reduced to unqualified unity.[106]

In contrast to Aristotle's view of the ultimate being, in the ibn Sīnian depiction of this principle, the Necessary Existent emanates bodies. Secondly, there is no "mystical union" between the prime mover and the ψυχή of Aristotle, while, as we shall demonstrate, ibn Sīnā advocates a mystical union between persons and the ultimate being. But, thirdly, the most significant feature of the ibn Sīnian doctrine of the ultimate being is that it is neither a substance nor an accident, and thus posits a being outside the Aristotelian categories.

In his argument on the ultimate being, ibn Sīnā presupposes the significance of such terms as "dependence," "essence," and "cause," terms which are part of Scholastic vocabulary, which he was instrumental in developing. Though it is beyond the scope of this essay to analyze each of these terms, we can offer some examples from ordinary language which may be helpful in understanding ibn Sīnā's use of them. Ibn Sīnā's argument to prove that the Necessary Existent is not a first substance may be outlined as follows.

To begin with, every first substance is a composite of an essence and a substratum of which the essence in question is predicated. For example, in the case of the individual substance Socrates, the essence humanity is attributed to the substratum, the body of Socrates. In addition to these elements, there must be some laws which keep the elements together. He uses the term *dāranda* (which may be translated as "the beholder of") to express his view that the persistence of a composite actual existent is dependent upon several factors. For example, in the case of a house, the persistence of the house depends not only on the elements constituting the house or the shape (the formal cause) of the house in question, but on gravity and other laws governing the chemical reactions between elements constituting the house, e.g., the cement which connects the glass window and the brick wall. According to ibn Sīnā, all these various factors — namely, the elements, the form, and the laws necessary for the persistence of an entity X — are "causes of X." But since ibn Sīnā assumes that no necessary entity can have a cause, the Necessary Existent cannot be a composite, and thus it cannot be a substance. In the same manner, since accidents depend on substances for their realization, the Necessary Existent cannot be an accident. Therefore, since ibn Sīnā rejects outright the *οὐσία* (*jauhar*, "substance") theory of the ultimate being, what is his ultimate being? One interesting clue, which does not describe the ontological status of the Necessary Existent but may "point to" its relation with the realm of existent individuals, is found in the *Dānish Nāma*:

> Thus it became evident that there is for the world a primary [entity] which is unlike the world; moreover, the existence of the world is due to it and its existence is a necessity. Its existence is due to itself. In fact it is absolute Existence [or existence per se; *wujūd-i maḥḍ*].[107]

The ultimate being for ibn Sīnā, then, is that which is the source of the existence of individual existents; to be an existent is to have been caused by the ultimate being. Is it possible to explain and analyze this basis of all existents? Ibn Sīnā answers this question firmly in the negative; in the metaphysics of *al-Shifa'*, he points out that we cannot reason (*burhān*) or argue about the nature of the Necessary Existent.[108] But, we may ask, what other means can we find to point to the Necessary Existent in order to distinguish it from other existents? The answer leads us to the notion of "self."

Man, according to ibn Sīnā, can be depicted not as a fixed substance but in terms of a process of a revelation, a spiritual journey described in different languages, e.g., by means of a series of philosophical insights which make us aware of our own "modal" dependence on a Spinozaic type of an ultimate being. The last stage on this way of salvation, according to ibn

Sīnā, lies in the "highest happiness" and in "the ultimate success" of persons: namely, to be united (*paivand*)[109] with the Necessary Existent. This relation of "union" is not a metaphor used to relate man to the ultimate being. In his *Treatises on Love*,[110] ibn Sīnā envisions an eschatological scale of degrees of "love" which is based on two factors: (*a*) the notion of man as that entity which was originated from the Divine Source retaining within him a theophany, the existent aspect of the Necessary Existent; and (*b*) a concept of *ittihād* or union the aim of which is our own perfection (*kamāl*, *ἀρετή*). The Necessary Existent is also called "the Absolute Good" (*al-Khair al-Mutlaq*) in Platonic terminology but in a non-monotheistic mode;[111] the emanation of the contingent realm from the Necessary Existent is determined in the following sense of "determination." In monotheistic cosmologies it is logically possible for God, an absolutely transcendent entity, to exist while there is no other entity in the world. By contrast, in the ibn Sīnian cosmology, it is logically impossible for God to exist while the contingent world does not exist. The differences between "rational" and "mystical" perspectives of the ultimate being lessen when the normative dimension of man's salvation is discussed. For example, in the *Dānish Nāma*[112] the mystical union is treated as an abstract metaphysical topic related to the notion of different degrees of pleasures. In the *Najāt*, ibn Sīnā develops a similar theme in relating that it is the aim of the rational soul to become united with the Absolute Good, and describing this vision as the "perfection" or "the virtue" of the rational soul.[113] In the *Ishārāt* (III.53) he states specifically that there is exactly one way of indicating (or pointing to, *Ishāra*) the Necessary Existent: namely, by means of the mystical intelligence (*al-ʿirfān al-ʿaqli*).

Thus, it is clear that in ibn Sīnā's philosophical system the ultimate entity, which is identified with the first cause (*ʿilat-i awwal*), is that entity in terms of which we can claim our own existence. To be an existent is to have been derived from the ultimate entity. Moreover, we can relate to the Necessary Existent only by our most perfect insight in a mystical vision of the ultimate entity and existence per se. This vision is achieved by our love for the ultimate being, not when we are constituted in terms of an Aristotelian Body–Soul composite, but when our personal ego perspective of the self is transformed by what our highest philosophical intuition can achieve: a reflection upon the Necessary Existent. This vision leads man from a contemplation of his own existence to a contemplation of the ultimate being.

In sum, ibn Sīnā's realm of being (which contains entities other than existents), and existence (which interrelates existents of persons and other existents to a vision of Existence per se) is a radical modification of the Aristotelian *οὐσία* theory of ontology.

A Philosophy of "Essence"

In the medieval world the problem of universals divided the philosophers into realist, nominalist, and conceptualist camps; in the Near East similar debates also served as rallying points for philosophical positions. The "essence–existence" distinction initiated by ibn Sīnā became the *point d'appui* for different ontological positions. Some philosophers, numbering in their forefront the followers of al-Suhrawardī, who created a school of illuminationistic monism, held the view that philosophy proper should consider the ontological status of entities which have no relationship to existents. There were other philosophers who considered those signs which in some sense point to, but never "capture," the realm of existent entities as the only signs which have meaning. Let us focus on the views of Nasafī, a philosopher belonging to the former camp whose writings have hitherto not been discussed in English.[114]

Nasafī (ca. thirteenth century) postulates two different perspectives according to which the structure of the world may be schematized. In the first perspective there are three realms, which for simplicity's sake we shall designate as R^1, R^2, and R^3. R^1 contains only God, whose role in Nasafī's system is analogous to the Principle of Sufficient Reason. According to him, all statements about the existence of every actual entity are based on God's existence, God's nature, and the structure of the best of all possible worlds. R^2 contains two sets of universals: a set of impossible entities — e.g., "a round square," which only can be named but cannot be conceived by God or by creatures; and a set of universals, which may or may not have instances in the actual world, e.g., "humanity" or "being a unicorn." Nasafī refers to the latter as *quwwa* or "contingent" kind of entities. His peculiar use of "contingency" as applied to universals may be explained by the following reasons: (*a*) unlike their instances universals in their totality are not objects of sense experience and are not "actual" (*fā*ʿ*il*) determinate particulars in the sensible world — e.g., by means of our senses we can never experience "humanity"; and (*b*) universals not expressing contradictory properties may or may not have instances in the actual world. Among the members of this latter realm, God's will decides which of the contingent entities will be instantiated. Instantiated actual cases of contingent potential entities in R^2 constitute particular existents which endure only for a limited time in R^3. Members of R^3 are actual entities which, according to Nasafī's position, are inferior and posterior to potential beings. We recall from Aristotle's *Metaphysics* (Book *O*, chap. 8) that "actuality" (ἐνέϱγεια) is prior to "potentiality" (δύναμις) in definition, time, and substance. It follows from this that no "suspended form" or universal without an instance is a legitimate subject matter of metaphysics. Nasafī presents arguments showing that potentiality (*quwwa*) is applicable to *abstracta* and is prior to actuality (which is also true of *concreta*). Let us paraphrase some of Nasafī's arguments.

To begin with, for Nasafī, potentiality need not be instantiated, nor, for that matter, can it "begin" or be "created." For example, it is nonsense to talk about "the origin of the concept of circularity in time $t(o)$" such that prior to $t(o)$ no instance of circles could have existed; moreover, literally speaking, potential entities, like non-material concepts, are not events which can be initiated or terminated; nor are they composite terms which can be assembled. It is true that one may say that at time $t(o)$ someone began talking about a concept, e.g., about the "smallest infinite number larger than the size of natural integers"; but it would be difficult to understand what saying that a number began at a particular time would mean. Conversely, every composite entity and all bodies which are composites can be assembled at a time or can be conceived of as a composite in their present form at a given time. Thus Nasafī regards potentiality prior in time to actuality.

Now, let us move to the subject matter of definitions. A definition takes a few determinable features through a potential essence which can define them — e.g., "humanity" is "being a 'rational' animal." However, "being an individual of every particular bodily existent" in R^3 has an indefinite number of determinable features, e.g., shades of color, physical size, a relationship to other entities, a rate of decay or growth, and the like. Since there is no definition of individual existents and since potential senses are relatively simple and can be specified by means of a few universals, we should note that if "individuals" are the only actual entities, then "potentiality" is prior by definition to actuality.

The final point in Nasafī's system, priority in substance, may be discussed in the following way. There are two senses of "substantiality": one with regard to being the "first substance," as in not being a predicate of a subject; and one with regard to being the "second substance," as in "being an essence." Nasafī takes the "persistence" of an entity to mean a relationship to its substantiality and assumes that "being an essence," going back to the time argument, is a more "persistent" feature than being a temporally limited existent. In this second sense of substantiality, actualities are prior to potentialities.

Nasafī's second ontological perspective opens on two domains: the realm of the annihilated entity, which Nasafī mistakenly calls *maʿdūm* but which in Arabic–Persian philosophical vocabulary is the traditional equivalent of "privation," and the realm of essences the "existential reality" of which is determined as follows. All particular existents: (*a*) have been realized, (*b*) are realized, (*c*) will be realized, or (*d*) may be realized in another possible world which can be conceived by God, who, due to his own nature, did not choose to realize it. Now, an essence is "existentially real" if and only if a member of classes of entities belonging to groups (*a*), (*b*), or (*c*) possesses the property of the essence in question. An essence is "totally God-dependent" if and only if it is neither an impossible essence nor "existentially real" (which means that its ontological status depends on God's knowledge). Even though Nasafī emphasized "essences" over "existents," in the context of "existential reality," his essences turn out to be dependent either on actual cases or on God, who is an existent. Let us examine some passages from Nasafī which delineate his system. (The following is an original translation.)

On the Analysis of Essences (Māhiyyāt)

Know that essences are the being-reality [*haqa'iqi*] of existents. Any entity which is an existent in an actual mode has a being-reality such that the entity in question is an existent because of that being-reality. Had the being-entity not existed, then the entity in question would not have been realized as an actual existent. Such a being-reality is called "an essence" [*māhiyyāt*], but it is also called a "possibility" [*mumkinī*]. The reality in question is other than "existence" (*wujūd*) and "privation — not-being" [*ʿadam*].

External existence [meaning that an essence has a instance in R^3] as well as external non-existence [meaning that an instance of an essence in R^3 is lacking] are two of the features of essences. Such a being-reality [essence] can be described by its predicate which is "existence" [meaning that an instance of it exists] or by its predicate which is "privation–non-existence" [meaning that it lacks an instance in R^3].

Concerning the existence of God the exalted, the first generator, there are arguments which support and arguments which deny the position that he has an essence. Some hold that there is no essence for the existence of God the exalted, since there cannot be a multiplicity in the essence of God in any way whatsoever; God the exalted is an independent existent as an absolute unity. Others have asserted that the existence of God is identical with his being-reality [essence]. Still others have claimed that the existence of God the exalted is other than his essence because, although God's existence is known to man, God's essence is not so known. Consequently, his being-reality [essence] is other than his existence. Concerning the possible existents we note that they all have essences, since essences are the being-reality of existents and since having an essence is not the same as simply existing. Names of entities are the names of such essences as correspond to the names given to the world, the heaven, the earth, humanity; in sum, there is a name for each of the essences

> [i.e., for each existent in question]. One may be able to describe [a] world with respect to its property of being an existent [i.e., with respect to its correspondence to the actual world] or not-being an existent [with respect to its difference from the actual world]. Consequently, "being a world" must be the name of an entity other than "existence" or "non-existence"; that [entity] is [none other than] an essence.[115]

In the foregoing text Nasafī's use of at least two different languages is striking. In analyzing different types of entities which can be conceived, he stipulates distinct realms of being which are isolated by the manner in which they exist. But when he attempts to discuss "existence of persons" and relationships of persons with a divine-like "ultimate being," he discards the theoretical distinctions, thus allowing the person-self to become once again, in a way familiar to us through ibn Sīnā, related with the divine. Nafasī relates, for example, the following incident. "Someone asked ibn Sīnā 'What exists?' a question to which ibn Sīnā is said to have replied, 'That to which one can [physically] point [*ishāra*].'" But Nasafī continues, "Someone asked ʿAlī (who represents the mystics) 'What is an existent?' and ʿAlī answered with a question, 'What is that (or what can be that) which *is not* an existent?'"[116] Comparing[117] "absolute existence" (of God) to a(n infinite, unlimited) light "without beginning or end," Nasafī observes that this sense of "existence" as a totality cannot be the subject matter of analytical discourse. With regard to the subject of the mystical return, Nasafi holds, with Proclus, that all entities return to their source (*ἀρχή*, *aṣl*);[118] for the depiction of the mystical return, he uses the familiar drowning analogy[119] in which an individual existent finds his perfection as a mode blending with existence or God. He concludes that "There is no existence but God's existence,"[120] and reiterates the principle that "Pure life which comes from God goes back to God."[121] By "pure life" he means the eternal aspect of persons which is embodied for a limited duration and then returns to its source.

In Nafasī's writings the development of two languages can be observed: one for the analysis of entities about which we can speak, and another to facilitate discourse about topics such as the ultimate being, "existents," and the self. Whereas the first language is totally non-Aristotelian, the second approaches in certain ways the ibn Sīnian process language depicting a mystical union. In spite of his anti-Aristotelianism, Nasafī follows ibn Sīnā in admitting that "an existent" cannot be defined; moreover, his classification of different kinds of essences depends in fact on existents.

Mullā Ṣadrā — A Philosopher of "Existents"

In the philosophy of Mullā Ṣadrā (1572–1640), which championed the position that "existence" and not "essence" is the primary term by which "being" (*haqīqat*) can be analyzed, "existent" itself can be only experienced, not analyzed.

Mullā Ṣadrā advanced the notion that we cannot talk legitimately about the relationship between "existence" and "essence" since, when we use "existence," we are actually abstracting it into a mental essence the reality of which is distinct from any existent. He claims, moreover, that there are only existents and that other terms, including "existence" and "to be 'an existent,'" are essences rather than facts which should be assigned to a realm which one cannot discuss in language. What exists is uniquely particular and incapable of being known. In talking about it, we mistakenly talk about a conceptualized abstraction of existence as if it were an individual reality. In his *Kitāb al-Māshāʿir* (*Peripatetic Philosophy*),[122] Mullā Ṣadrā notes that there are two kinds of analyses of terms: either (*a*) "one expressing a linguistic usage," a method which we can clarify by citing examples of the position of the term in question and by comparing its syntactical features with other concepts; or (*b*) an ontological analysis (*haqīqī*), which in itself is carried out either by a method of "real definition" (*ḥadd*) or by description (*rasm*).[123] For philosophies of "existents," he holds that the latter procedure is impossible, while the former is useful in presenting us with examples of linguistic analyses of terms which point to, but do not explain, existents.

To show that the ontological analysis of "existence" is impossible, Mullā Ṣadrā points out that a real definition is derived from the specification of an entity in terms of its genus and differentia. Moreover, the genus of an entity X must be common, well known, and more determinable than X; for example, in the definition of "man" as a rational animal, animality, the genus of man, is more determinable than humanity. However, nothing can be more determinable and common than "existence"; it follows that "existence" cannot be defined.

When we turn to the problem of describing a class, the description in question singles out a property which belongs, in a unique manner, to every member of that class: e.g., "man is that entity which has a straight backbone and is a biped." Now, since *wujūd*, or existence, is the most evident constituent of actual entities, we cannot single out any particular existent per se, since there is nothing which does not exist; whatever is is an existent.

Having shown the limitation of analyses of "existence," Mullā Ṣadrā proceeds to clarify *wujūd* by its uses in ordinary Arabic discourse. He starts by inquiring into the problem of whether or not "existence exists" or whether there is existence, and observes that whatever exists prior to its realization is incomprehensible unless it is possible to account for it by privation. For example, in the sentence "You do not have a kind uncle who will take care of you," "a kind uncle" is supposed to be a kind of entity which could be mentioned by privation, whereas the actual "kind uncle" cannot be described since the description implies listing an indefinite number of facts.

In considering existence as a predicate of an entity along with other predicates, such as "being happy," we note that the most "evident" feature of any entity is the fact that it exists, that it is an existent. Thus, the question "Are there existents?" is restated to mean "Is that which is the most evident feature of any entity evident?" To this we may reply "Yes." If so answered, this question utters only a vacuous truth like "Is *p p*?" Mullā Ṣadrā also notes that existence is that aspect of an entity which becomes evident as a potentially existing entity is realized. This feature of his use of "existence" is obviously modeled on a definition of the "soul" (ψυχή) given by Aristotle. One may object to both these "definitions" because of their circularity; we recall that Aristotle depicts the soul in terms of "being potentially alive" or "being potentially organic," in spite of the fact that "soul" carries in a sense the vacuous implication "to be alive" or "to be organic." It is questionable whether one can understand "a potentially existing entity" without understanding something about "existence." By confronting this difficulty explicitly, Ṣadrā, in his use of existence in terms of "potentiality," "actuality," "realization," and "privation," shows that a description of "existence" ends at best in circularity.

Let us now focus on Mullā Ṣadrā's philosophical views concerning "essence." He mentions that the notion of "essence" (*māhiyya*) is either useless or vacuous. To prove his point, he distinguishes between two senses of *māhiyya*, which we can designate as "essence 1" and "essence 2." His concept of "essence 1" corresponds to Aristotle's use of τί ἐστι and ibn Sīnā's *māhiyya*, illustrated by the case of "humanity" which can be considered as the essence of Socrates. Mullā Ṣadrā points out that this notion of an essence does not further our understanding of the peculiar nature of the entity in question, for it fails to distinguish it from other entities, an essence being common to many individuals; "humanity," for example, can be attributed to Plato, Aristotle, and others. To explain his use of "essence 2," he mentions the phrase *mā bi al-shi'a huwa huwa*, which expresses the question "What is the thing [which it is]?" According to Mullā Ṣadrā one can answer this question, not by the statement "It is a human," but by a vacuous tautology "This which is is this which is." Since Mullā Ṣadrā's examples are not clearly translatable into ordinary English, let us try to clarify his views by the following explanation. Syntactically all predicates can be attributed to more than one entity, but an individual existent, represented by an individual constant, is not predicated of any entity and belongs to the level zero in the context of the theory of type. Supposedly, one may argue that this syntactical distinction between the predicate and individual signs implies an ontological distinction between what is designated by these signs — namely, individual existents and universals. It follows from such a position that no combination of universals can be substituted in fact for an actual existing individual, even though a combination of predicate terms may be used in a language to distinguish individual constants. Mullā Ṣadrā affirms that when we experience an individual existent, the entity in question exists as a unique entity; the predicates which we use to describe this entity merely point to some of its features which may also be applicable to other entities. According to Mullā Ṣadrā, essences, which are expressed by predicates, are at best useful guideposts which point to kinds of existents; no conceptualization of essences can be a sufficient substitute for the experience of actual existents.

Since ibn Sīnā's well-known "essence–existence" distinction was based on his differentiation between being (*hastī*) and existence (*wujūd*), the followers of Mullā Ṣadrā[124] attempted to equate *hastī* with *wujūd* for the following reason: although the ibn Sīnian study of metaphysics admitted some non-existent beings — e.g., "being a round square" — the followers of Mullā Ṣadrā considered only particular existents to be the legitimate objects to metaphysical inquiry and related all discussions of universals to actual existents. Consequently, for Mullā Ṣadrā and his followers there are no "impossible essences" or "essences which apply to no actual existents." For Mullā Ṣadrā, a universal (*kullī*) is a "general term" which has meaning only when the condition is met which requires the "universal" to be attributed to an actual individual existent. He holds, moreover, that there are no "ideal universals" — circularity, for example; rather, our universals are generalizations of different kinds of actual entities, e.g., the round ball, the round moon, etc. Our understanding of particulars is strengthened when we notice that the terms used for particulars could not ordinarily behave as predicates in language; there is, for example, no correct usage for "Socrates-ness." Now, since "existence" cannot serve as the subject or the clarification, "existence" is neither a universal nor a particular, for it cannot be properly defined. The only "existents" are particulars. As an abstraction, "existence" is an essence which is different from actual existents.

Mullā Ṣadrā's criteria of "universality" are so constructed that higher level universals — e.g., "being a figure" — are universals because they can be attributed to a lower order universal — e.g., "'triangularity' is a figure" and "triangularity" is significant because we can say "this tower is triangular."

Let us now direct our attention to Mullā Ṣadrā's views on the relationship between the world and the ultimate being. Rahman summarizes Ṣadrā's views as follows:

> For Ṣadrā, the world is real when related to God; when not related, it has no being whatever. Indeed, the world is not even *related*; it is a *pure relation* or manifestation. . . . He therefore describes the relationship of the world to God, not as a building is related to the builder or even a writing is related to its writer, but as speech is related to the speaker; the moment the speaker ceases to speak, speech vanishes.[125]

With the assistance of Rahman's analysis of Ṣadrā's arguments, we may construct his views on the relationship between persons and the ultimate being in terms of the following steps: (*a*) "God is nothing but existence"; (*b*) we are also existents, but, unlike God, we are determinate and finite; (*c*) the wonder that there is existence — or Munitz' "the Mystery of Existence" — for a follower of Mullā Ṣadrā is not a question but an attitude about the world which reaffirms Ḥallāj's statement "*Anā al-Ḥaqq*" ("I am reality–truth–God"). The analysis of this aspect of Mullā Ṣadrā's philosophy brings us to the topic of normative ethics which is outside the scope of ontology proper.

This last aspect of Mullā Ṣadrā's views presents us with a problem demanding analysis since it appears to contain philosophically significant theses embedded in a highly ambiguous language. Within Mullā Ṣadrā's philosophical and mystical framework, the individual reflects on two modes of his existence: on himself as a particular existent who is distinct from other particulars in the actual world, and on the sense that he too, among others, is an existent who can wonder about the meaning of Ḥallāj's statement "I am reality–truth–God." Even though it may not be totally clear to him what Ḥallāj meant by his statement, Ḥallāj's thesis undoubtedly asserts some kind of affinity between the existence of the individual and the existence of God (who for Mullā Ṣadrā is "nothing but pure existence"). Mullā Ṣadrā ponders over the degree of affinity between the existence of man and God's existence, which he sees reaffirmed in the Qur'ānic symbolical remarks that God is nearer to man than man's jugular vein and that if man were thrown to the very bottom of the earth, he would fall upon God. Our problem now is to determine whether these ambiguous remarks express a significant philosophical position. To begin with, we may interpret Mullā Ṣadrā's views in line with the traditional mystical doctrines which affirm the existence of a divine aspect in man. This aspect is said to persist after the mind–body combination, customarily designated as "person," has been destroyed, i.e., when man's active intelligence returns to God. But a more sophisticated interpretation of his views suggests that when Mullā Ṣadrā asserts that God is nothing but existence, it follows that in his philosophy reflection about the question "Why is there existence?" or the feeling of astonishment "that there is existence!" is equivalent to "Why is there God?" and to the feeling of astonishment "that there is God!" Yet the God in question is, not the transcendent deity of monotheism, but what ibn Sīnā calls *wājib al-Wujūd.* (We take this concept to be "the ground of existence" or "the Necessary Existent" in terms of which our own actualization can be explained, in the same sense as the actualization of particular existents is explained by an appeal to the so-called Principle of Sufficient Reason.) These questions may result either in a verbal answer or in an attitude which leads to the awareness that probing into the mystery of existence is a primary problem of philosophical inquiry. We note that in Mullā Ṣadrā's philosophy one cannot offer a verbal analysis of "existence" (*wujūd*); consequently, we may look for another answer in the so-called mystical states in which the mystic is supposedly confronted with the divine in his last stage of self-realization. At this point it is appropriate to recall that Aristotle's heavens react to the immobility of the immaterial prime mover by imitating that immobility in a circular movement. In mystical literature this motion is often represented by a circular dance, a salient feature of *samāʿ* — the last stage of mystical self-realization. A circular dance, an ecstatic trance, is the mystic's reaction to the wonder which he experiences when he is confronted with the problem of the mystery of existence in its specific element of "the feelings of astonishment" in the last stage of mystical self-realization. We are now able to see that mystic's astonishments expressed by the equivalent statements "that there is existence!" and "that there is God" (in Mullā Ṣadrā's sense of "God") are merely linguistic expressions of the underlying philosophical attitude which a person achieves who has contemplated various aspects of the universe, including what may be eternal in him. These questions are not uttered in ordinary discourse; consequently a philosopher who focuses on the ordinary usage of language would not be concerned with them. But for a mystic or a philosopher who is interested in an inquiry into the nature of the universe these expressions embody serious problems which cannot be "answered" in simple sentences. We should note that the simplicity with which a version of the mystery of existence is formulated is misleading if it gives us the illusion that either there must be a single simple answer to the question of the astonishment about "existence" or else the entire inquiry is meaningless. The reaction of mystics to this philosophical astonishment or to the confronting of the various problems of existence in what they consider to be the last stage of self-realization is symbolized by the dance which is analogous to an eternal circular motion — the best way in which the creature can imitate the divine or can give expression to the divine aspect in himself.

Mystical literature often distinguishes two aspects of this last stage of self-realization, calling them, respectively, *fanā'* and *baqā*. *Fanā'* — literally, "annihilation" — indicates that we no longer view our own existence as distinct from that of other existents; and *baqā* — literally, "eternity" or "persistence" — indicates that only in the context of our relationship with the divine, with God, or with the world can we view ourselves as being eternal. The mystical dance is that gesture which leads us supposedly from the *fanā'* aspect of the last stage of self-realization to an awareness of ourselves as a mode of the eternal divine substance or of the world in which our ultimate persistence (*baqā*) lies.

To avoid any misunderstanding we should make clear that the numerous questions concerning the legitimacy of such a position, which may be attributed to the so-called "existence" and "monist" (*waḥdat al-wujūd*) school of mystics, have not yet been answered satisfactorily. One objection to the solution which we have outlined may be raised by anyone who is committed to a rationalist position holding that no human situation should be beyond clarification by means of language. Obviously, followers of Mullā Ṣadrā would deny the capability of language to describe existents. Similarly, mystics who consider the result of their philosophy an activity rather than an intellectual understanding would refuse to commit themselves to the position of the rationalists. It is beyond the scope of this essay to discuss further normative aspects of Mullā Ṣadrā's philosophy since we have limited the scope of our inquiry to the ontological dimensions of the problems of being and existence in Near Eastern philosophy.

Conclusion: Some Methodological Limitations of the Philosophies of Being and Existence

We have surveyed the development of a few representative Near Eastern ontologies of being and existence and have noticed both their marked differences from the Aristotelian models, and the perseverance of the salient features peculiar to them in spite of Neoplatonic tendencies embedded in the Arabic and Persian Aristotelian texts. In concluding, we should like to point out that these Near Eastern philosophers attempted to solve an important philosophical problem which has also found a place in the works of philosophers of many different traditions: e.g., Augustine, Descartes, Wittgenstein, M. K. Munitz, and H. D. Lewis. Let us briefly cite those attempts which in some significant aspect parallel the Near Eastern solutions discussed in this essay.

A number of ways have been mentioned in the course of this essay by which to approach the problem of being and existence. One approach is to provide a single philosophical framework, analogous to a Carnapian "axiomatization" of a theory, in which the entire "realm of being" is explained by an analytical method, thus providing clear and distinct names for constants of the theory and a set of rules which shows how these terms can be combined, how we can deduce truths from the basic assumptions of the theory in question, and how our system is to be interpreted for the actual world. The metaphysics in Whitehead's early writings[126] offers a perfect example of such an approach. The Aristotelian notion of categories or what one may call a "thing-event" language may be viewed as another manifestation of this approach. According to this view, the domain of being consists basically of individual existents — first substances which include the prime mover as an individual agent. Apparently such a scheme was not accepted in practice by Platonists, Neoplatonists, or the Near Eastern philosophers, who, instead of following this "substance" approach, followed what Gilson calls a "unitary approach" in which material entities and the ultimate being are essentially related.

It is beyond the scope of this essay to explain causally "why" some philosophers rejected the Aristotelian delineation of being and existence. All we can do is to argue hypothetically on the basis of the logical implications arising out of the various positions examined. We claim accordingly that there is a certain number of "philosophical problems" or "implicit relationships" sought between "individual existents such as persons" and "the ultimate being" which cannot be explained within the closed system of the Aristotelian categories. Let us take note of several cases in which philosophers agree that the problem of relating the finite "person" or "particular" to the ultimate being is one of the most important problems of philosophy.

Wittgenstein assigns to "God" and "the self" similar status in the following passage: "There are two Godheads; the world and my independent I" (N. 8.7.16). Wittgenstein's notion of God is related to the world as follows, "How things stand, is God. God is how things stand" (N. 1.8.16). According to Max Black and E. Zemach, in Wittgenstein's system God can or should be identified with or related intimately to the philosophical self which cannot be experienced. Black expresses the point thusly:

> That which experiences is not itself an experience, is not *part* of the world (5.641*c*). The metaphysical subject must be looked for in the boundary or "limit" of the world (5.632, 5.641*c*): it is, as it were, that *outside* the

> world on which the existence of everything depends — it might as plausibly be identified with God as with my very self.[127]

Black's notion of "that *outside* the world on which the existence of everything depends" is identical to a phrase which ibn Sīnā uses to describe the Necessary Existent, which in his system cannot be defined. Zemach adds a normative dimension to the God–self relation in Wittgenstein by stating that in the German philosopher the definition of "happiness" in the sense of "be[ing] in agreement with the world" "provides us with a unique solution to a baffling problem: how can the independence of the 'second Godhead' [the self] be reconciled with the absoluteness of the 'first Godhead'?"[128] To acquire happiness, according to Wittgenstein, one must establish a harmony between "the world of the willing I" and "the world of God." On the basis of Wittgenstein's own text and the interpretations given to his writings by Black and Zemach two observations may be made: (*a*) the self and the ultimate being cannot be specified as individuals in the world; and (*b*) the highest happiness of man lies in a close relationship with the ultimate being. In his account of what constitutes the content of religious awareness, H. D. Lewis observes that "the question of the feeling or the content of religious awareness . . . begins to be formed from the first apprehension of finite being as having a supreme infinite source."[129] Other philosophers also relate the religious feeling which Lewis mentions to the ontological problem. Using such an approach, M. K. Munitz declares:

> The chief problem of ontology, as I have argued, is to give a satisfactory account of existence, and this amounts to giving an analysis of the relation of the domain of plural existents to the transcendent One that is Existence. In traditional "religious" terms it is to give an account of the relation of the finite to the infinite.[130]

For Descartes, the "finite" was his self-person; the infinite — which he claimed to know as the basis of the finite — was God.[131] Augustine began with the quest for the same two entities in his celebrated statement "God and the soul are all I desire to know."[132] He came to love the two in his quest, proclaiming "now I love nothing else than God and the soul, neither of which I know." In his *Confessions*, Augustine points to the goal of his quest — namely, the longing for a close affinity between the soul and God: "And when Thou art poured forth on us, Thou art not cast down, but we are uplifted."[133] In sum, the problem of the self and God and their interrelationship has been a prime concern for philosophers of different traditions at vastly different times.

The silence which the Aristotelian system maintains on this crucial topic may be attributed not only to a possible lack of interest in this problem on Aristotle's part but also to his inability to proffer a descriptive account of the relationship and its constituents using his substance language. For this language reduces individual existent persons and the ultimate being to the same category of substance, and such a classification precludes any affinity between the two. As has been pointed out, Near Eastern philosopher-mystics, such as Nasafī and ibn Sīnā, attempt to portray this relationship between the finite and the infinite as a process of self-realization in a language which contains what the earlier Wittgenstein calls "similes." Such relationships emerge in the depiction of the stages of love in the *Risāla fi-l-ʿishq*, in the stages of the mystical way in *al-Ishārāt*,[134] and in the process which reveals the interdependence between a person's origin from the divine and his role in the world, described, for example, in the *Ḥayy ibn Yaqzān*.[135] It should be noted that the philosophical perspective revealed in the ibn Sīnian vision is not what Munitz calls "creationism,"[136] for in the mysticism of Ḥallāj and ibn Sīnā God does not "create" the world; in their systems, God is not an alien conscious entity to which one can point as an entity distinct from our own existence. Near Eastern mystics seem to assume that such differences as may exist for a person between the "philosophical I" and the "ultimate being" are diminished through an acquaintance with the various ways of mystical experiences, even though existents and the ultimate being are not clearly defined in these systems. The objection may be raised that a methodologically correct treatment of ontology should specify the nature of being and the nature of existence. This approach presupposes that it is the task of an ontology to formulate a coherent language rather than to concern itself primarily with problems which remain invariant with respect to language. There are two suitable answers to this objection. The first points to the uses of such ontological terms as "Existence!" or "God!" in contexts such as the sayings of the Rūmī-mystics in their ṣūfic dances. In these contexts, when we take account of the "pragmatics" of the words, we note that no clarification of concepts is intended; rather, the mystics use these terms as a response to the problem that, in their system of philosophy, existence cannot be defined and God cannot be known. Consequently, the question "What is existence?" leads not to an answer but to an activity — a dance. This dance corresponds to the circular motion of the heavens which in the Aristotelian system *imitates* the prime mover. It follows that in one system at least the result of an ontological search is an activity rather than a clarification of words. Another response was the invention of non-Aristotelian terms (for "God"), which indicates that the problem later discussed by Wittgenstein, Munitz, Lewis, and others cannot be handled satisfactorily by using Aristotelian terminology. Consequently, Near Easterners, confronted with this problem, adopted a notion of an ultimate entity not unlike the Neoplatonic model, one which was essentially connected with a process-like concept of the self. And when the topic of union arose in philosophical texts, these philosophers used either similes[137] or an allegorical language replete with such images as illumination and drowning to depict a closer affinity between the ultimate being and persons. In the actual philosophizing about being and essence in Near Eastern philosophy, the question of the specification of being and existence is not meaningful outside of specific contexts. Just as Plato's theory of the soul in the *Republic* was introduced as a means of depicting a just society, so being, existence, and related concepts were introduced in Near Eastern philosophy to solve the problems we have mentioned. Besides supporting our claims about the philosophical methodology which shaped Near Eastern ideas of being and essence, we have shown that Greek sources to some extent affected the formulation of the Aristotelian question to which Near Eastern philosophers in turn gave new answers. We have shown elsewhere how some of these answers affected the course of later Western philosophies.[138] An account of Near Eastern ontology has yet to be written. It is our hope that this essay constitutes an introduction to both Greek influences and later Near Eastern formulations of ontological positions on the topics discussed.

NOTES

1 By "Near Eastern philosophy" we mean philosophical issues embedded in Persian and Greek philosophical texts written from the middle of the eighth century to the present era. For an account of some of these issues, see M. Fakhry, *A History of Islamic Philosophy* (New York, 1970) and P. Morewedge, "Contemporary Scholarship in Near Eastern Philosophy," *The Philosophical Forum*, 2, No. 1 (Fall 1970), 22–140.

2 By "philosophies of being and existence" we mean philosophical problems in which mention is usually made of the terms "being" and "existence" and related words such as "substance," "essence," and the like.

3 See R. Carnap, *Introduction to Symbolic Logic and Its Application*, trans. W. H. Meyer and J. Wilkinson (New York, 1958), pp. 171–73. In Carnap's formulation of an axiomatic system for an Aristotelian theory, "substance" would be one of the axiomatic primitive constants of the system. Such terms can be presented without a definition, and their uses can be specified by the so-called rules of formation of the language in question.

4 See ʿA. Badawi, *Arisṭū ʿina-l-ʿArab* I (Cairo, 1947), pp. 12–21, 329–33; and R. Walzer's "New Light on the Arabic Translations of Aristotle" and "On the Arabic Versions of Books *A*, *α* and *Λ* of Aristotle's *Metaphysics*," in his *Greek into Arabic: Essays on Islamic Philosophy*, Oriental Studies 1 (Cambridge, Mass., 1962), pp. 60–113, 114–28, respectively.

5 *Proclus: The Elements of Theology*, ed. E. R. Dodds (London, 1963), pp. xxix–xxxiii.

6 Fakhry, *History of Islamic Philosophy*, p. 33.

7 *The Fihrist of al-Nadīm : A Tenth-Century Survey of Muslim Culture*, ed. and trans. B. Dodge, 2 vols. (New York, 1970), II 606.

8 For an analysis of Aristotle's criticism of Plato's position see C. J. De Vogel, "Aristotle's Attitude to Plato and the Theory of Ideas According to the *Topics*," in *Aristotle on Dialectic: The Topics*, ed. G. E. L. Owen (London, 1968), pp. 91–102. De Vogel argues (102) that although Aristotle's spirit is alien to authentic Platonism and in spite of the tendency to favor Platonism which appears in this book, there definitely are arguments against Platonic ideas in this work.

9 See W. V. O. Quine, *From a Logical Point of View* (Cambridge, Mass., 1953). For a discussion of this topic in the context of Quine's entire ontology, see Guido Küng, *Ontology and the Logistic Analysis of Language* (Dordrecht, 1967), pp. 127–60; and J. Kaminsky, *Language and Ontology* (Carbondale, Ill., 1969), pp. 47–64.

10 *Commentaria in Aristotelem graeca* IV, ed. A. Busse (Berlin, 1874), I.II.1–22.

11 Khāwja Naṣīr al-Dīn Ṭūsī is best known for his works on logic, mathematics, and ethics. See *Encyclopedia of Islam*, 4 vols. (Leiden, 1913–1942), IV 980–82. For a list of his works, see Carl Brockelmann, *Geschichte der arabischen Literatur*, 5 vols., 2nd ed. (Leiden, 1937–1949), 1.2.673.

12 *Existence and Logic* (New York, 1974), pp. 48–50.

13 "Neo-platonic Logic and Aristotelian Logic, Part I," *Phronesis*, 1 (1955–1956), 58–72; "Part II," ibid., 2 (1957), 146–60, esp. 155–56.

14 See S. H. Afnan, *Avicenna: His Life and Works* (London, 1958).

15 "Empiricism, Semantics, and Ontology," in *Semantics and the Philosophy of Language*, ed. Leonard Linsky (Urbana, Ill., 1952), pp. 208–28.

16 See I. Madkour, *La Place d'al-Fārābi dans l'école philosophique musulmane* (Paris, 1934).

17 See Rescher's *Al-Fārābī: An Annotated Bibliography* (Pittsburgh, Penn., 1962), pp. 42–43.

18 Ed. M. Mudaras Razawi (Tehran, 1948).

19 Ed. S. Dunya, 4 vols. (Cairo, 1960); hereafter referred to as *al-Ishārāt*.

20 D. M. Dunlop, "Al-Fārābī's Paraphrase of the *Categories* of Aristotle, Part I," *Islamic Quarterly*, 4 (1957), 168–97; "Part II," ibid., 5 (1959), 21–54.

21 ʿAziz ibn Muhammad Nasafī was a follower of al-Suhrawardī's school of illuminationism, which developed the mystical elements of ibn Sīnian philosophy. Six philosophical texts and numerous treatises are attributed to him. See the introductory remarks of A. M. Damghānī in his edition of Nasafī's *Kashf al-Ḥaqāʾiq* (Tehran, 1965), pp. 1–36.

22 *Kitāb al-Insān al-Kāmil*, ed. M. Mole (Tehran, 1962), pp. 344–61; hereafter referred to as *al Insān al-Kāmil*.

23 Ibid., pp. 1–309.

24 See n. 21.

25 Ed. H. Corbin (Tehran, 1964).

26 Ṣadr al-Dīn Muḥammad Shīrāzī, known as Mullā Ṣadrā, is the most important Near Eastern philosopher of the sixteenth and seventeenth centuries. See H. S. Nasr, *Ṣadr al-din Shīrāzī and His Transcendent Theosophy* (Tehran, 1978).

27 *The Philosophy of Mullā Ṣadrā* (Albany, N.Y., 1976).

28 All references to the works of Aristotle are taken from *The Works of Aristotle*, ed. W. D. Ross, 12 vols. (Oxford, 1908–1952), unless otherwise indicated.

29 In ordinary Persian the primary use of a phrase such as "the *māya* of so and so" means "the active ingredient of so and so." When one refers to an entity without a "*māya*," one usually means, not that the entity in question has no bodily constitutent, but that the entity is weak or has no power. R. C. Zaehner explains the role of *māyā* in the *Rig-Veda* as follows: "Varuna and Mitra are distinguished from other Gods by their possession of māyā, '*mysterious power.*' . . . This '*māyā*' in the *Rig-Veda* may be used for either good or evil ends, but in case of Varuna it is always regarded as being beneficent" (*The Dawn and Twilight of Zoroastrianism* [New York, 1961], p. 68). In Aristotle there is at least one normative of *ὕλη* in which it is the opposite of *māyā*. Aristotle notes that "matter [*ὕλη*]" desires form and adds that "the truth is that what desires the form is matter [*ὕλη*], as the female desires the male and the ugly the beautiful — only the ugly or the female not per se but per accidens" (*Physics* 192A22–25). The Persian use of *māyā* never is negative but follows more what Zaehner describes as the Indic use of *māyā*. In the development of philosophy in Iran, some of the Zoroastrian themes which were originally developed from Indic thought persisted and were not modified by Greek theories; see E. Panoussi, "La Théosophie iranienne, Source d'Avicenne?" *Revue Philosophique de Louvain*, 66 (1968), 239–66. Consequently, a complete analysis of being and existence should in fact take into account the Avestan and Pahlavi Zoroastrian texts as well as those written in other Near Eastern languages (some of Mani's writings, for example, were written in eastern Aramaic).

30 *Aristotle: Metaphysics* (Ann Arbor, Mich., 1966).

31 Owens notes four conditions for finding a suitable translation for *οὐσία* and concludes that a neutral term such as "entity" is "entirely non-committal" while both "substance" and "essence" are unsatisfactory (*The Doctrine of Being in the Aristotelian Metaphysics* [Toronto, 1936], pp. 137–54).

32 Ed. A. M. Goichon (Cairo, 1963), pp. 23–24.

33 *Alfārābī's Book of Letters (Kitāb al-Ḥurūf) : Commentary on Aristotle's Metaphysics*, ed. M. Mahdi (Beirut, 1969), pp. 110–28.

34 Abū'l Manṣūr Hallāj (857–922), the celebrated Iranian theologian–mystic, is the author of several texts on mysticism including twenty-seven recitals, eleven shorter works, and several poems. His famous assertion "I am *Ḥaqq*" has been a stimulus to the development of monistic mysticism symbolizing the view that persons have a close affinity with God or in a sense, as some say, are God.

35 *The Development of Arabic Logic* (Pittsburgh, Penn., 1964), pp. 87–91.

36 *Asās al-Iqtibās*, pp. yaj-yah. Of these, 113 are definitely his texts.

37 Y. Mahdawi lists 244 titles in his *Bibliographie d'Ibn Sīnā* (Tehran, 1954); G. C. Anawati gives 276 in his *Essai de bibliographie avicennienne* (Cairo, 1950).

38 *The Life of Ibn Sīnā : A Critical Edition and Annotated Translation*, ed. and trans. W. E. Gohlman (Albany, N.Y., 1974), p. 33.

39 *Manṭiq al-Mashriqiyyīn* (Cairo, 1949), pp. 2–4.

40 *Al-Ishārāt*, III 271.

41 Ross observes distinctions in Aristotle's concept of what ontology is supposed to be: "Aristotle has in the main two ways of stating the subject matter of metaphysics. In one set of passages it is stated as *τὸ ὂν ᾗ ὄν*, the whole of being, as such." To support this view Ross refers to Book *Γ*, 1025B3, 1060B31, 1061B4, 26, 31, and to instances of *σοφία* in 981B28, 982B9. About the second meaning Ross notes: "But more frequently metaphysics is described as studying a certain part of reality *viz.* that which is *χωριστόν* (exists independently) and *ἀκίνητον* (is independent of motion)"; to support this, he cites 1064B4, 1069B1, and *Physics* 192A34, 194B14, and *De anima* 403B15 (*Metaphysics* [London,

1958], I 252–53). Owens, in pointing out that variations of the legitimate subject matter of ontology as listed by Aristotle range from those which we have listed to "causes of the visible divine things" (*Met.* 1026A16–18), "the science of truth" (*Met.* 983B2–3), and "the science of Form" (*Physics* 192A34–36), asks "Can all these different modes of expression denote the same doctrine of Being?" while noting that "Aristotle himself appears conscious of no inconsistency or contradiction in these various designations" (*Doctrine of Being in the Aristotelian Metaphysics*, p. 43).

42 *Aristotle's Metaphysics: Books, Γ, Δ, and E* (London, 1971), p. 77.

43 *Existence and Logic*, p. 69.

44 *The Logic of William of Ockham* (New York, 1965), p. 119.

45 Ibid., p. 122.

46 The first is the celebrated passage about the active intelligence in *De anima* 430A 10–25; the second, in *De generatione animalium* 736B15–25, states that *νοῦς* enters man as an additional factor from the outside. In spite of these two minor remarks, no trace of what might be called the "mystical" can be found in the Aristotelian corpus.

47 For a support of this view, see J. L. Ackrill, "Aristotle's Definition of *Psuche*," in *Proceedings of the Aristotelian Society*, 73 (1972–1973), 119–32. Ackrill holds that Aristotle's concept of a person is one of the primary substance, which is a combination of matter and form (*ψυχή*). No one takes into account Aristotle's remarks on the active intelligence; but in most Near Eastern philosophies, a "person" is immortal, after the death of the body, because of his active intelligence. Though this formulation often is conceptually unsatisfactory, we can think of no case in which the Aristotelian concept of a person, as Ackrill states it, was adopted in Near Eastern philosophies.

48 In *Met.* 1070A18–21, Aristotle asserts, "Plato was not far wrong when he said that there are as many Forms as there are kinds of natural objects (if there *are* Forms distinct from the things, of this earth)." Earlier, at 990B1–8, Aristotle had affirmed the notion that what others mean by Forms must be abstract entities which must correspond numerically to natural entities. It follows that there is no single Aristotelian interpretation of Plato's ontology of forms. This ambiguity in Aristotle's interpretation of Plato's metaphysics was a source of confusion for early Muslim thinkers who tried to find the development of a single ontology from the master Plato to the student Aristotle. Among the post-Averroës Muslim thinkers there was a tendency to take sides in the Plato–Aristotle controversy.

49 *Plato: The Republic*, trans. P. Shorey (London & Cambridge, Mass., 1935), 509B, p. 107.

50 Ibid.

51 *Plotinus: The Enneads*, trans. S. MacKenna (London, 1930). All references are given with the number of the *Enneads* followed by the section number.

52 *Plotini opera* II, edd. P. Henry and H.-R. Schwyzer (Paris & Brussels, 1959), p. 291. We have introduced a slight modification in our translation of this passage from MacKenna's text in order to preserve uniformity with the vocabulary used in this essay.

53 *Elements of Theology*, p. 101.

54 Ibid., p. 103. The Greek reads *πᾶς θεὸς μεθεκτός ἐστι, πλὴν ἑνός*, which means that every particular can partake of every transcendent (divine) entity except the One.

55 *Hindu and Muslim Mysticism* (London, 1960), p. 163.

56 In *Individuals : An Essay in Descriptive Metaphysics* (New York, 1963), Strawson clarifies his position in several ways. He asserts, for example, that "What we have to acknowledge, in order to begin to free ourselves from these difficulties, is the primitiveness of the concept of a person. What I mean by the concept of a person is the concept of a

type of entity such that *both* predicates ascribing states of consciousness *and* predicates ascribing corporeal characteristics, a physical situation etc. are equally applicable to a single individual of that single type" (p. 98). Even though Strawson argues that "material bodies, in a broad sense of the expression, were basic particulars" (p. 81), he nevertheless designates "persons" as a peculiar kind of primitive term in his metaphysical language, and does so, moreover, in such a way that no logical construction of "bodies" or "physical events" can give us an indication as to what is meant by "persons." According to Strawson's scheme, both "material bodies" and "persons" must be primary particulars (p. 256).

57 Wittgenstein's positions are outlined in the *Tractatus Logico-Philosophicus* (edd. D. F. Pears and B. F. McGinnes [London, 1961]) and *Notebooks, 1914–1916* (edd. G. H. von Wright and G. E. M. Anscombe, trans. G. E. M. Anscombe [Oxford, 1961]). Our references to these texts will cite the section number in the *Tractatus* and the date in the *Notebooks*. Wittgenstein notes that "the I" or "the metaphysical subject" signifies an indefinable constituent of "experiencing" rather than something in the world which can be named. He notes, accordingly, that "the philosophical self is not the human being, nor the human body, nor the human soul, with which psychology deals, but rather the metaphysical subject, the limit of the world — not part of it" (5.641). Elsewhere he observes that "The I, the I, is what is deeply mysterious! The I is not an object. I objectively confront every object. But not the I" (N 7.8.16–11.8.16). By means of analogy Wittgenstein attempts to explain the indefinability of "persons" in another passage, "Where in the world is a metaphysical subject to be found? You say that it is just as it is for the eye and the visual field. But you do *not* actually see the eye. And I think that nothing in the visual field would enable one to infer that it is seen from an eye" (N 4.8.16). Even though in the above passage Wittgenstein calls "the thinking subject a mere illusion," the analogy between the connection of the eye and the visual field, on the one hand, and that of the metaphysical subject and the world, on the other, indicates that no "limited" or "substantial" definition of the metaphysical subject is permitted in the Wittgensteinian system.

58 *Being and Some Philosophers* (Toronto, 1952), p. 3.

59 *Aristotle's Criticism of Plato and the Academy* (New York, 1962), p. 318.

60 In *Topics* 100A–102B27, the predicables are described as follows: *property* — "a predicate which does not indicate the essence of a thing, but yet belongs to that thing alone and is predicated convertibly of it"; *genus* — "what is predicated in the category of essence of a number of things exhibiting differences in kind"; *definition* — "a phrase signifying a thing's essence"; and *accident* — "(1) something which, though it is none of the foregoing — i.e. neither a definition nor a property nor a genus — yet belongs to the thing; (2) something which may possibly either belong or not belong to any one and the self-same thing. . . ."

61 We have adopted the translation of R. I. Aaron in *The Theory of Universals* (London, 1967), p. 1.

62 *Logic of William of Ockham*, p. 68.

63 Ibid., p. 67.

64 *The Development of Logic* (Oxford, 1962), p. 187.

66 Ibid., p. 196.

67 Ibid., pp. 196–97.

68 *Theory of Universals*, p. 9.

68 Ibid., pp. 9–10.

70 "Neo-platonic Logic and Aristotelian Logic, Part II," 154.

71 See Kwame Gyekye, *Arabic Logic: Ibn al-Ṭayyib's Commentary on Porphyry's* EISAGOGE (Albany, N.Y., 1979).

72 *Averroës' Middle Commentary on Porphyry's Isagoge and Aristotle's Categoria*, trans. H. A. Davidson (Berkeley & Los Angeles, 1969), p. 27.

73 Ibid.

74 Gyekye, *Arabic Logic*, pp. 41–42.

75 Ibid., p. 56.

76 *Al-Shifā', Al-Manṭiq (Al-Madkhal)*, edd. M. El-Khodeiri, A. F. El Ehwani, G. Anawati, and I. Madkour (Cairo, 1952), p. 10.

77 *Asās al-Iqtibās*, p. 6.

78 G. E. M. Anscombe and P. T. Geach, *Three Philosophers* (Oxford, 1963), pp. 16, 14, 15.

79 *A History of Formal Logic*, trans. I. Thomas (Notre Dame, Ind., 1961), p. 54.

80 *Collected Papers* II (New York, 1971), p. 171.

81 Ibid.

82 *Aristotle's Categories and De Interpretatione* (London, 1963), p. 79.

83 "Aristotle's Theory of Categories," in *Aristotle*, ed. J. M. E. Moravscik (New York, 1967), p. 145.

84 *Development of Logic*, p. 25.

85 Ibid.

86 Ibid.

87 Ibid.

88 Ibid., p. 31.

89 Ibid.

90 Ibid., p. 32.

91 "Neo-platonic Logic and Aristotelian Logic, Part II," 151.

92 *Studies in Arabic Logic* (Pittsburgh, Penn. 1963), p. 40.

93 "Al-Fārābī's Paraphrase of the *Categories* of Aristotle, Part I," 170; we have modified Dunlop's translation of section 4 of this text.

94 *Alfārābī's Book of Letters*, p. 36.

95 Ed. M. Danish Pashuh (Tehran, 1956), p. 10.

96 *Asās al-Iqtibas*, pp. 34–35.

97 Ṭūsī explicitly places the relative positions of "being a species" or "being a genus" in a definite order. He calls the species which can be predicated only of the individual *nauʿ-i sāfil*, and states that this species "because it is predicated of individuals [*ashkhās*] is also called the 'real' species" (ibid., p. 29). For a clear exposition of a version of the theory of type see Carnap, *Introduction to Symbolic Logic*, pp. 112–13.

98 *Existence and Logic*, p. 48.

99 Ibid., pp. 49–50.

100 *Individuals*, p. 256.

101 *Al-Shifa', al-Mantiq (al-Maqulāt)*, edd. M. El-Khodeiri, A. F. El Ehwani, G. C. Anawati, and S. Zayed (Cairo, 1959), p. 4.

102 *Dānish Nāma*, ed. M. Mʿīn (Tehran, 1952), p. 102; see also our translation of and commentary on this text: *The Metaphysica of Avicenna (ibn Sīnā)* (New York, 1973). In his Arabic texts on *Metaphysics* (p. 29), ibn Sīnā presents another version of the primitives of metaphysics: an existent (*maujūd*), a thing (*shai'ī*), and necessity (*darrūrī*). From the context of the following discussion it becomes clear that he is using the concepts of necessity, contingency, and impossibility (p. 35) in subsequent passages in such a way that no meaning differing from that found in the Persian version is rendered. See *al-Shifā'*,

Illahiyyat, edd. G. C. Anawati, S. Zaid, M. Y. Moussa, and S. Dunya, 2 vols. (Cairo, 1960; hereafter referred to as *al-Shifā'*.

103 I 202–203.

104 See "Ibn Sīnā's Concept of the Self," *The Philosophical Forum*, 6, No. 1 (Fall 1972), 49–73.

105 For example, ibn Sīnā rejects the separation of the sensible world from the intelligible world by means of universals; Plotinus affirms this separation. Ibn Sīnā's Necessary Existent is a kind of being; Plotinus' One is beyond being. Plotinus regards numbers as substantial and associates them with the soul (*Enneads* VI [9] 5); for ibn Sīnā numbers are accidents (*Dānish Nāma* 10).

106 *Being and Some Philosophers*, p. 135.

107 P. 38.

108 P. 354.

109 *Dānish Nāma*, p. 37.

110 *Risāla fi l-ʿishq*, ed. M. A. F. von Mehren in *Traités mystiques d'Abou Ali al-Hosain b. Abdallāh Sinā ou d'Avicenne: Texte arabe avec l'explication en français*, 3 vols. (Leiden, 1894).

111 Ibid., II 21.

112 Chap. 37.

113 P. 293.

114 *Kashf*, p. 35.

115 *Al-Insān al-Kāmil*, pp. 365–66.

116 *Kashf*, p. 31.

117 *Al-Insān al-Kāmil*, p. 289.

118 *Kashf*, pp. 132–33.

119 *Al-Insān al-Kāmil*, p. 113. The reference is made in the context of the lover (the philosopher–mystic who is aware of the significance of the Necessary Existence) who is drowning in his love for the beloved. This kind of love symbolizes the loss of the separated ego (*fanā'*) for the sake of the eternal state (*baqā*) of union with the Necessary Existent.

120 *Ahl-i wahdat mīgūyand ki wujūd yikī bīsh nīst wa an wujūd khudāist* ("The followers of unity assert that there is only one Existence and that is God"), *Kashf*, p. 22.

121 *Al-Insān al-Kāmil*, p. 144.

122 Our analysis covers the first eleven steps, which deal with the foundations of Mullā Ṣadrā's basic metaphysical language; for example, the first section or "step" deals with "the reality of existence," the question of talking about "the essence of existence," understanding existence by using words, and the problem of the peculiarity of existent entities.

123 Pp. 6, 82–83.

124 Ibid., p. 79. ʿUmad al-Daulata, in his Persian commentary on this work, adds that *hastī* is *wujūd*, which is not found in the corresponding section of the Arabic text. Al-Fārābī, however, mentions the ordinary uses of the Persian *hastī* and the Arabic *maujūd* (an existent), and discusses the use of similar terms in Arabic, Persian, and Sodgian; see *Kitāb al-Ḥurūf*, pp. 111–13.

125 *Philosophy of Mullā Ṣadrā*, p. 77.

126 See his *An Inquiry Concerning the Principles of Natural Knowledge* (London, 1955). See Carnap's remarks (in *Introduction to Symbolic Logic*, pp. 171–76) that the Whiteheadian system in this text, especially Part III (on the method of extensive abstraction), may be axiomatized as physics. An example of an extended vision of the world in terms of value-bearing actual entities in the language of process is found in Whitehead's later system

in *Process and Reality* (New York, 1955). It is beyond the scope of this paper to discuss Whitehead's later system and its relevance to our analysis, but we might point out a remark in the later text (p. 28): "The notion of 'substance' [in his *Process and Reality* system] is transformed into that of 'actual entity.'" See Morewedge, "Ibn Sīnā's Concept of the Self" for a notion of "processes" as a substitute for "substance" in the context of "mystical union."

127 *A Companion to Wittgenstein's 'Tractatus'* (Ithaca, N.Y., 1964), pp. 308–309.

128 "Wittgenstein's Philosophy of the Mystical," in *Essays on Wittgenstein's 'Tractatus'*, edd. I. M. Copi and R. W. Beard (New York, 1966), p. 370.

129 *Our Experience of God* (London, 1959), p. 112.

130 *Existence and Logic*, p. 204.

131 In his third meditation, Descartes notes, "I clearly understand that there is more reality in an infinite, than of the finite — rather of God, than of myself. How could I understand my doubting and desiring — that is, my lacking something and not being altogether perfect — if I had no idea of a perfect being as a standard by which to recognise my own defects" (*Descartes' Philosophical Writings*, trans. E. Anscombe and P. T. Geach [New York, 1963], p. 85).

132 *Soliloquies* 2.7.1, in *Basic Writings of Saint Augustine* I ed. W. J. Oates (New York, 1948), p. 262.

133 *The Confessions* 1.2 (ibid., p. 4).

134 The last section of this text is devoted to mystical stations (*maqāmāt*).

135 Ed. and trans. H. Corbin as *Avicenne et le récit visionnaire* (Tehran, 1952).

136 *Existence and Logic*, pp. 204–205. Here Munitz shows why his so-called "creationism" and "illuminationism" are unsatisfactory attempts to solve the ontological question at hand. His use of "illuminationism" should not be confused with Suhrawardī's illuminationistic (*ishrāqi*) doctrine, which became the source of Nasafī's philosophical ontology of light rays emanating from the sun-like God. In Islamic illuminationism there is no distinction between "appearance" and "reality." It is a monism in which Munitz' "ontological question" cannot be formulated.

137 See L. Wittgenstein, "A Lecture on Ethics," *The Philosophical Review*, 74 (1965), 3–12. Wittgenstein notes here (9) that "I want to impress on you that a certain characteristic misuse of our language runs through *all* ethical and religious expressions. All these expressions *seem*, prima facie, to be just *similes*." Wittgenstein goes on to say (11) that, "For all I wanted to do with them [the ethical and religious expressions which are prima facie similes] was just *to go beyond* the world and that is to say beyond significant language [statements about facts *in the world*, e.g., statements in physics]." Among the normative experiences, he mentions (8) one dealing with the fact that "the world exists" and another with the "experience of feeling absolutely safe."

138 For the development of the essence–existence distinction, see P. Morewedge, "Philosophical Analysis of Ibn Sīnā's 'Essence–Existence' Distinction," *Journal of the American Oriental Society*, 92, No. 3 (1972), 425–35.

13

Post-Avicennan Islamic Philosophy and the Study of Being

SEYYED HOSSEIN NASR
Temple University

THE HISTORY OF THE QUEST of post-Avicennan Islamic philosophers for the understanding of being differs markedly from that of Western philosophers following St. Thomas and other masters of Scholasticism. While gradually in the West the possibility of the experience of Being nearly disappeared and the vision of Being gave way to the discussion of the concept of being and finally to the disintegration of this very concept in certain schools, in the Islamic world philosophy drew even closer to the ocean of Being Itself until finally it became the complement of gnosis and its extension in the direction of systematic exposition and analysis. If the final chapter of the history of Western philosophy, at least in several of its major schools, wed philosophy to external experience and experiment with the forces and substances of the material world, resulting in various forms of empiricism, in the Islamic world as well philosophy became inseparable from experience. But in this case the experience in question was of a spiritual and inward character, including ultimately the vision of Pure Being, the tasting of a reality which is the origin of this sapiential wisdom or *ḥikmah*, a wisdom which for this reason is called *ḥikmah dhawqiyyah, dhawq* having the same meaning in Arabic as the root of sapiential (*sapere*) in Latin.

The early Islamic philosophers such as al-Fārābī and Avicenna,[1] who are called masters of discursive philosophy (*ḥikmah baḥthiyyah*) rather than of sapiential wisdom, nevertheless established the conceptual framework within which later discussions of being occurred, although new meaning was often given to the terms and concepts which they had established. Al-Fārābī in his *Kitāb al-ḥurūf*[2] and Avicenna in numerous works, especially the *Shifā'*, *Najāt*, and *Dānishnāma-yi ʿalā'ī*,[3] already established the major distinctions between existence (*wujūd*) and quiddity (*māhiyyah*), on the one hand, and necessity (*wujūb*), contingency (*imkān*), and impossibility (*imtināʿ*), on the other, as well as many of the other basic concepts which colored the study of being in both the later Islamic world and the Occident.

The period immediately following in the wake of Avicenna's magisterial exposition of Peripatetic philosophy — namely, the 5th/11th and 6th/12th centuries — was the era of the dominance of Ashʿarite *Kalām* in the eastern lands of Islam and therefore of an eclipse of interest in the study of that discipline which with Wolf and Suarez came to be called ontology in the West. *Kalām* was based on a voluntarism[4] which concentrated exclusively upon the Will of God and disregarded His Being and Nature, of which the Will is but one Quality. Hence, the champions of *Kalām*, in contrast to Latin theologians, were not particularly interested in the study of being, even if they often used the terminology of the Peripatetics as far as the distinction between *wājib al-wujūd* and *mumkināt* was concerned.

The founder of the school of illumination, Shaykh al-ishrāq Shihāb al-Dīn Suhrawardī, revived the interest in ontology, but approached the entire problem of existence from a new angle of vision.[5] He considered existence to be only an accident added to the quiddities, which possess reality. He thereby created an "essentialistic" metaphysics which attracted many followers over the centuries. Yet he made of light the very substance of reality, and attributed to light what all the other philosophers had considered as belonging to *wujūd*. To study the question of being in al-Suhrawardī and his school, it would not be sufficient to seek pages on which the word *wujūd* appears. It would be necessary to study his doctrine of light in its totality.

Almost contemporary with al-Suhrawardī, another major intellectual figure and the foremost expositor of Sufi metaphysics, Muḥyī al-Dīn ibn ʿArabī, expounded the most profound doctrine possible of Being and its manifestations in a manner which is, properly speaking, gnostic and metaphysical rather than simply philosophical in the usual sense of the word. Ibn ʿArabī spoke of the Divine Essence (*al-dhāt*), Names and Qualities, theophany (*tajallī*), and the like, and did not use the language of the Islamic philosophers who dealt with *wujūd*. He expounded a metaphysics which transcends ontology, which begins with the Principle, standing above Being, of which Being is the first determination (*taʿayyun*). Yet his doctrine of necessity included the most penetrating exposition of the meaning of *wujūd* as both Being and existence, even if he viewed the problem from quite another angle than did the philosophers. It is in fact of interest to note that he usually treated the question of existence when dealing with the theme of Divine Mercy.[6] In any case, ibn ʿArabī had the profoundest effect upon both later Sufism and later Islamic philosophy, especially as far as the study of *wujūd* was concerned. It was he who first formulated the doctrine of the "transcendent unity of being" (*waḥdat al-wujūd*) which crowns nearly all later studies of *wujūd* and represents in a certain sense the summit of Islamic metaphysical doctrines.[7]

The revival of Peripatetic philosophy by Naṣīr al-Dīn Ṭūsī in the 7th/13th century brought the teachings of Avicenna back to life, but this time Avicenna was often interpreted in the light of the doctrines of al-Suhrawardī and ibn ʿArabī and not solely in the more rationalistic vein in which he came to be known in the West. Moreover, such later masters of gnosis as Ṣadr al-Dīn al-Qunyawī, Kāshānī, and Sayyid Ḥaydar Āmulī gave a more systematic exposition of the study of being than is to be found in ibn ʿArabī. Such texts as the *Naqd al-nuqūd fī maʿrifat al-wujūd* of Āmulī had a profound effect upon later Islamic philosophy itself.[8]

The school of Isfahan, founded by Mīr Dāmād in Safavid Persia, marks a sudden rise of interest in the study of *wujūd*. In fact, during this period a new chapter was added to the exposition of traditional philosophy under the name of "general matters" (*al-umūr al-ʿammah*), with which most later texts of philosophy start and which deals more than anything else with *wujūd*. It was also at this time that the distinction between the principiality of existence (*aṣālat al-wujūd*) and the principiality of quiddity (*aṣālat al-māhiyyah*) was discussed for the first time and the entire history of philosophy viewed accordingly.[9]

It is usually thought that the Safavid period was dominated by the teachings of Mullā Ṣadrā. But such is far from the case. This period was marked by a rather varied philosophical life, and at least three distinct trends are discernible: that of Mīr Dāmād and his students, who followed Avicenna with a Suhrawardian color; that of Mullā Rajab ʿAlī Tabrīzī whose views are somewhat similar to Proclus' interpretation of the teaching of Plato and who considered the Divine Principle to be above both Being and non-Being and totally discontinuous with the chain of existence; and finally Mullā Ṣadrā and his followers, who, like Mullā Muḥsin Fayḍ Kāshānī, transformed the "essentialistic" metaphysics of al-Suhrawardī into an "existential" one.[10] In his *Asfār*, *al-Shawāhid al-rubūbiyyah*, and *al-Mashāʾir*,[11] Mullā Ṣadrā has given the most extensive and systematic exposition of the "philosophy of being" to be found anywhere in Islam, combining the vision of the gnostics and the logical acumen of the Peripatetics. His metaphysics is based on the three principles of the unity, gradation, and principiality of being and marks the opening of a new chapter in the development of Islamic philosophy.[12]

The doctrines of Mullā Ṣadrā concerning being were so profound and all-embracing that they found their echo among most of the leading Persian philosophers of the centuries which followed and were also influential among many thinkers of Muslim India. As far as Persia is concerned, such 13th/19th century figures as Mullā ʿAlī Nūrī, Ḥājjī Mullā Hādī Sabziwārī, and Mullā ʿAlī Zunūzī added important commentaries to Mullā Ṣadrā. And during this century such traditional masters as Mīrzā Mahdī Āshtiyānī and Sayyid Muḥammad Kāẓim ʿAṣṣār have continued this particular tradition of philosophy in which the study of being is carried out through a highly developed dialectic but is ultimately based upon the experience of Being and its epiphanies, this experience having been made possible through the aid of Being Itself in the form of that objective theophany of the Universal Intellect which is tradition.

It is hardly possible to do justice in such a short space to the depth and richness of this late Islamic philosophical school insofar as the study of being is concerned. Men of great intelligence and perspicacity have spent lifetimes in the study and contemplation of these doctrines. But it is possible to summarize at least some of the salient features of the mainstream of this school, which culminated with Mullā Ṣadrā and his disciples.

Perhaps the most striking feature of the discussion of being in this school is that it is concerned with the act of being and not with the existent, with *esse*, the *actus essendi*, rather than with *ens*. Western Scholasticism was gradually led to the study, not of being itself, but of that which exists and, therefore, of things. The gradual forgetting of the reality of Being in favor of the concept of being and then the disintegration of even this concept in the mainstream of Western philosophy was directly connected to the dissociation of *ens* from the act and reality of being itself. If it took several centuries before certain philosophers of existence in the modern West realized the importance of distinguishing between *das Sein* and *das Seiende*, the later Islamic philosophers had already based ontology on the act of being centuries earlier when within the confines of Islamic philosophy the experience of the reality of Being became the source for the intellectual discussion of its concept.[13]

The doctrine of the unity, gradation, and principiality of being, which is the foundation of the transcendent theosophy (*al-ḥikmat al-mutaʿāliyah*) of Mullā Ṣadrā, sees the whole of reality as nothing but the stages and grades of existence, and the quiddity of each object which has been brought into existence as nothing but the abstraction by the mind of a particular determination of existence.[14] The essences of things are not realities to which existence is added, but abstractions made by the mind of a particular state of being which is called existent merely because the untrained mind perceives only the external and apparent aspect of things. Outwardly, existents seem to be quiddities which have gained existence. But true awareness created through the disciplining of the intellect and through spiritual vision allows the perceiver to see everything for what it really is: namely, the very act of existence, each of whose instances appears as a quiddity to which existence is added; whereas in reality it is only a particular act of existence from the limitations of which the quiddity is abstracted. The ordinary man is usually aware of the container, whereas the sage sees content which is at once being (*wujūd*), presence (*ḥuḍūr*), and witness (*shuhūd*).

The later Islamic philosophers often insist on the identity of *wujūd*, *ḥuḍūr*, and *shuhūd* because their vision has penetrated into the depth of reality which *is* at once being and knowledge, awareness and presence. In fact, the degree of awareness of being is itself dependent upon the degree of awareness of the knower, the degree and mode according to which he *is*. The more man *is*, the more he is able to perceive being. The Universe itself is a series of presences (*ḥaḍrah*, pl. *ḥaḍarāt*) which man is able to comprehend and penetrate, to the extent that he himself is *present*.

Islamic metaphysics envisages Reality as the Principle (*al-mabdaʿ*) which is also the giver of existence (*al-mubdiʿ*) and which stands above even Being. It is the Non-Being which comprehends Pure Being. The first determination of this Principial Reality is Being, which itself is the source of creation. The first effusion of Pure Being is at once the Intellect and Universal Existence, what the Sufis call the Breath of the Compassionate (*nafas al-raḥmān*) and which is ultimately the very substance of the created order. Particular modes of existence are themselves the rays of Universal Existence (often called *al-wujūd al-munbasiṭ* or *al-fayḍ al-muqaddas*). Inasmuch as *wujūd* is also *ḥuḍūr*, these grades have also been enumerated by the gnostics such as ibn ʿArabī as the "Five Divine Presences" (*al-ḥaḍarāt al-ilāhiyyat al-khams*) extending from the Divine Essence through the various stages of existence to the world of spatio-temporal existence.[15] Yet, despite the multiplicity of the levels of existence, there is but one Being, and all the presences are ultimately the Presence of the One who alone is.

The philosophy of being of the later Islamic philosophers has a direct bearing for man and his entelechy. Modern existentialism limits itself to the existence of individual man, and for many of the philosophers of this school this existence comes to an end with the death of the individual. But in the Islamic perspective, existence is not an accidental and faltering flame to be extinguished by the wind of death. Death is the gate to a more intense degree of existence, whether this be natural death or initiatic death accomplished through spiritual practice. Annihilation (*fanā'*), which is the goal of the spiritual life, ends, not in extinction in the ordinary sense of the word, but in subsistence in the Divine and, therefore, in the most intense mode of being possible. Through spiritual death man becomes never less than what he was but more.[16]

The study of being in later Islamic philosophy is related profoundly to the practical import of its teachings for human life, for it is inseparable from the practice of an inner discipline which is the sole guarantee of a true understanding of the meaning of existence. Ordinary man is too deeply immersed in things, in existents, to become aware of the great mystery of existence itself. It is easy to perform this or that act, but it is very difficult simply to exist. It is much easier to play with concepts than to still the mind and to create an awareness to enable man to perceive the mystery of existence itself, to realize that "all things are plunged in God."

The study of existence in later Islamic philosophy is therefore only outwardly concerned with the analysis of the concepts of existence, quiddity, necessity, contingency, and the like. Beneath this rigorous logical analysis there stands the invisible presence of the profound spiritual experience of pure existence and ultimately of Being Itself. Therein lies the great message of this school for the modern world, which suffers profoundly from the divorce between conceptual knowledge and the mode and manner of one's being. Man is not what he thinks, and his being does not follow from his thinking; rather, man's thought is the function of what he is. The *cogito ergo sum* of Descartes, which turned ontology in the West away from the study of Being to the analysis of its mental reflection, would be corrected by the sages of this sapiential tradition as *sum ergo est Esse*, to quote a formulation of Frithjof Schuon's.[17] I am; therefore God is; Pure Being is. Being is inferred from human existence itself, provided one turn toward the Center of oneself to experience Being, rather than fleeing from the Center into the bosom of congealed forms, whether they be external objects and acts or concepts running through an agitated mind.

The more one *is*, the more one is able to understand being. And the best way to study Being is to live in conformity with Its demands. The central message of the later tradition of Islamic philosophy and theosophy seems to be that the study of being might begin with the concept of being, but it must end with its reality. Man might study the concept of being without ever transcending the confines of his own limitations and the prison of his own accidental nature. This would be, not *ḥikmah*, but mental acrobatics. In contrast, the veritable study of the reality of being, which is the goal of *ḥikmah*, brings with it freedom and deliverance from all confinement, for it opens the limited existence of man to the revivifying rays of a Reality which is at once being, consciousness, and joy or bliss, *wujūd*, *wujdān*, and *wajd*. The correct study of being leads to that state of wonder which is the origin of all wisdom, as well as to participation in that joy or bliss the attainment of which is the goal of all knowledge and the end of human life itself, and which is woven into the very texture of the substance of human nature.

NOTES

1 Ibn Sīnā or Avicenna has in fact been called first and foremost a philosopher of being. See A. M. Goichon, "L'Unité de la pensée avicennienne," *Archives Internationales d'Histoire des Sciences*, 20–21 (1952), 290ff.

2 This major work, edited for the first time by M. Mahdi (Beirut, 1969), has caused contemporary scholars to revise completely their views concerning the study of ontology among the earlier Islamic philosophers.

3 See P. Morewedge, *The Metaphysics of Avicenna* (*Ibn Sīnā*) (New York, 1973); for the ontology of Avicenna, see also A. M. Goichon, *La Distinction de l'essence et de l'existence d'après Ibn Sina* (*Avicenna*) (Paris, 1937); S. H. Nasr, *An Introduction to Islamic Cosmological Doctrines* (Cambridge, Mass., 1964), chap. 12.

4 See F. Schuon's *Logic and Transcendence*, trans. P. Townsend (New York, 1975), chaps. 7, 13; as well as his *Islam and the Perennial Philosophy*, trans. P. Hobson (London, 1976).

5 On al-Suhrawardī, see S. H. Nasr, *Three Muslim Sages* (New York, 1976), chap. 2; and H. Corbin, *En Islam iranien* II (Paris, 1971). On al-Suhrawardī's views on existence, see his *Ḥikmat al-ishrāq*, ed. H. Corbin in *Oeuvres philosophiques et mystiques* II (Tehran, 1976), pp. 125ff. See also chap. 11 of the present volume.

6 On ibn ʿArabī in general, see Nasr, *Three Muslim Sages*, chap. 3. As for his doctrine of Divine Mercy, see T. Izutsu, *A Comparative Study of the Key Philosophical Concepts in Sufism and Taoism* I (Tokyo, 1966), pp. 109ff. Izutsu quotes the famous commentator of ibn ʿArabī, ʿAbd al-Razzāq Kāshānī, as saying, "Existence [*wujūd*] is the first overflowing of the Mercy which is said to extend to everything" (p. 109).

7 On this basic doctrine, which has often been mistaken for philosophical pantheism, existential monism, and the like, see T. Burckhardt, *An Introduction to Sufi Doctrine*, trans. D. M. Matheson (Lahore, 1959), chap. 3; and M. Lings, *A Sufi Saint of the Twentieth Century* (London, 1971), chap. 5.

8 *La Philosophie Shiʿite*, edd. H. Corbin and O. Yahya (Tehran & Paris, 1969), pp. 620ff. of the Arabic text.

9 On the meaning of these terms, see T. Izutsu. *The Concept and Reality of Existence* (Tokyo, 1971), pp. 99ff. On the School of Isfahan itself, see H. Corbin, *En Islam iranien* IV (Paris, 1972), Book 5; and S. H. Nasr, "The School of Isfahan," in *A History of Muslim Philosophy* II, ed. M. M. Sharif (Wiesbaden, 1966), pp. 904–32.

10 All these three schools are represented in the second volume of the anthology of the philosophers of Persia since Mīr Dāmād being prepared by S. J. Ashtiyani and H. Corbin. See *Anthologie des philosophes iraniens* II (Tehran & Paris, 1975). The discussion of the three schools, as described by Corbin on p. 5, occupies nearly the entire volume. See also Corbin's "Présence de quelques philosophes iraniens," in his *Philosophie iranienne et philosophie comparée* (Paris & Tehran, 1977), Part II, pp. 55–81.

11 The *Mashāʿir* is in fact devoted to ontology. See the analysis of its content by H. Corbin in his edition and translation of the work: *Le Livre des pénétrations métaphysiques* (Tehran & Paris, 1964).

12 On Mullā Ṣadrā's doctrine of the unity of being, see my "Mullā Ṣadrā and the Doctrine of Unity of Being," *Philosophical Forum*, 4, No. 1 (Fall 1972), 153–61.

13 See Corbin's introduction to the introduction of Mullā Ṣadrā's *Mashaʿir*, in *Le livre des pénétrations métaphysiques*, pp. 62ff.

14 See my "Ṣadr al-Dīn Shīrāzī," in *History of Muslim Philosophy* II, ed. Sharif, pp. 942ff.; see also Izutzu, *Concept and Reality of Existence*, Part IV.

15 See F. Schuon, *Dimensions of Islam*, trans. P. Townsend (London, 1970), chap. 2.

16 The following famous verses of Rumi attest this truth:

I died as mineral and became a plant,
I died as plant and rose to animal,
I died as animal and I was Man.
Why should I fear? When was I less by dying?
Yet once more I shall die as Man, to soar
With angels blest; but even from angelhood
I must pass on: *all except God doth perish.*
When I have sacrificed my angel-soul,
I shall become what no mind e'er conceived.
O, let me not exist! for Non-existence
Proclaims in organ tones: "To Him we shall return."

R. A. Nicholson, *Rumi: Poet and Mystic* (London, 1950), p. 103.

17 *Logic and Transcendence*, p. 44. Shuon also quotes (ibid.) Franz von Baader's formulation to the same effect, the German theosopher having said in answer to Descartes *cogitor, ergo cogito et sum* ("I am thought [by God], therefore I think and I am").